European Private International Law

Usable both as a student textbook and as a general introduction for legal professionals, *European Private International Law* is designed to reflect the reality of legal practice throughout the EU. The private international law of the Member States is increasingly regulated by the EU, making private international law ever less 'national' and ever more EU based. Consequently, EU law in this area has penetrated national law to a very high degree, making it an essential area of study and an area of increasing importance to practising lawyers throughout the EU. This book provides a thorough overview of core European PIL, including the Brussels I, Rome I and Rome II Regulations (jurisdiction, applicable law for contracts and tort), while additional chapters deal with PIL and insolvency, freedom of establishment and corporate social responsibility.

European Private
International Law

Geert Van Calster

·H A R T·
PUBLISHING

OXFORD AND PORTLAND, OREGON
2013

Published in the UK by Hart Publishing
16C Worcester Place, OX1 2JW
Telephone: +44 (0)1865 517530
Fax: +44 (0)1865 510710
E-mail: mail@hartpub.co.uk
Website: http://www.hartpub.co.uk

Published in North America (US and Canada) by
Hart Publishing
c/o International Specialized Book Services
920 NE 58th Avenue, Suite 300
Portland, OR 97213-3786
USA
Tel: +1 503 287 3093 or toll-free: (1) 800 944 6190
Fax: +1 503 280 8832
E-mail: orders@isbs.com
Website: http://www.isbs.com

British Library Cataloguing in Publication Data

Data Available

ISBN: 978-1-84946-241-9

Typeset by Forewords, Oxford
Printed and bound in Great Britain by
TJ International Ltd, Padstow, Cornwall

To all VGCs

To Green, sleeping tight on His lap.

To Belle: Grand bonheur, grand chagrin.

Preface

This volume introduces the reader to the most important parts of European private international law. It focuses on what a practitioner, student and policy-maker will be most confronted with. In doing so, it covers the legislative history of the relevant instruments only insofar as this is required to help understand, and apply, the current provisions. It prioritises the areas which are of most relevance to commercial practice in the EU, leaving out, in this volume in particular, family law.

European private international law, as this book shows, is evolving fast. It is hoped that this overview both assists daily practice, and enables further study where needed.

Thanks are due to my fellow faculty members at KU Leuven, in particular former Dean Paul Van Orshoven, for the opportunity to teach the Conflicts chair at Leuven; to my colleagues at DLA Piper, for continuously involving me in facts greater than fiction; to my hosts at King's College, London, and Monash University, Melbourne, for showing me the common law angle to many of the issues discussed here; and to my in-laws, Roger and Angelika Garnett Krabbe, for providing me with the room in the Montaut attic where I was able to make the first real progress in writing this book.

Recent developments are posted on my blog, www.gavclaw.com.

Geert Van Calster
Leuven
14 November 2012

Contents

Preface		vii
Table of Cases		xv
Table of Legislation		xxv
Table of Conventions, Treaties, etc		xxxix

1   Introduction   **1**

1.1   The Concept, Nature and Development of Private International Law   1

1.2   Sources of Private International Law   3

1.3   The 3 Processes of PIL, and Standard 'Connecting Factors'   3

    1.3.1   Procedural issues   3

    1.3.2   Application of the law   4

        1.3.2.1   Characterisation [*qualification* |FR] of the legal question   5

        1.3.2.2   Connecting Factor   5

        1.3.2.3   *Lex Causae*   5

1.4   Characterisation, *Renvoi* and the 'incidental' issue or *Vorfrage*   5

1.5   Forum shopping and forum non conveniens   8

1.6   The Impact of European Law on the Private International Law of the Member States   9

    1.6.1   Legal basis   9

    1.6.2   The Development of European Private International Law Policy   13

2   The Core of European Private International Law: Jurisdiction   **19**

2.1   Summary   19

    2.1.1   The Brussels I Regulation   19

    2.1.2   Scope of Application: Subject-Matter   21

    2.1.3   Scope of Application – Ratione Personae   22

    2.1.4   The Jurisdictional Rules of the Regulation   23

2.2   Detailed Review of the Regulation   24

    2.2.1   Trust is Good, Control is Better   24

    2.2.2   Scope of application: subject-matter.   25

        2.2.2.1   The existence of an international element   25

        2.2.2.2   Civil and commercial matters   27

        2.2.2.3   Case 29/76 *Eurocontrol*   28

        2.2.2.4   Case 814/79 *Ruffer*   29

        2.2.2.5   Case C-271/00 *Gemeente Steenbergen*   29

        2.2.2.6   Case C-292/05 *Lechouritou*   31

2.2.2.7 Exclusions, inter alia arbitration   32
2.2.3 Scope of application – Ratione Personae   41
       2.2.3.1 Domicile   41
2.2.4 The International Impact of the Regulation   44
2.2.5 The Jurisdictional Rules of the Regulation   51
       2.2.5.1 A jurisdictional matrix   51
2.2.6 Exclusive Jurisdiction, Regardless of Domicile: Article 22   51
2.2.7 Jurisdiction by appearance: Article 24   60
2.2.8 Insurance, consumer and employment contracts: Articles 8–21   61
       2.2.8.1 Protected categories – Generally   61
       2.2.8.2 Consumer contracts   62
       2.2.8.3 Contract   63
       2.2.8.4 Consumer contract   64
       2.2.8.5 Concluded with a consumer   64
       2.2.8.6 Type of contract – and application in an internet context 65
       2.2.8.7 Extended notion of 'domicile' for jurisdiction over
                consumer contracts   72
       2.2.8.8 Alternative fora introduced by agreement   72
       2.2.8.9 Contracts for individual employment   74
       2.2.8.10 Insurance Contracts   76
2.2.9 Agreements on Jurisdiction ('choice of forum' or 'prorogation of
       jurisdiction'): Article 23   77
       2.2.9.1 'In writing or evidenced in writing'   81
       2.2.9.2 In a form which accords with practices which the parties
                have established between themselves   82
       2.2.9.3 In international trade or commerce, in a form which accords
                with a usage of which the parties are or ought to have been
                aware and which in such trade or commerce is widely
                known to, and regularly observed by, parties to contracts
                of the type involved in the particular trade or commerce
                concerned   82
2.2.10 General Jurisdiction: Defendants Domiciled in a Member State
       Where a Court is Seized: Article 2   85
2.2.11 'Special' Jurisdiction: Defendants Domiciled in Another Member
       State: Articles 5–7   86
       2.2.11.1 Article 5(1): Actions Relating to a Contract – Forum
                Contractus   86
       2.2.11.2 The Special Jurisdictional Rule for Tort: Article 5(3) JR –
                Forum delicti commissi   92
2.2.12 Multipartite Litigation and Consolidated Claims: Articles 6 (and 7) 99
       2.2.12.1 Multiple Defendants: Article 6(1)   100

2.2.12.2 Warranties, Guarantees and any other Third Party
Proceedings: Article 6(2) 103

2.2.12.3 Counterclaims: Article 6(3) 103

2.2.12.4 Matters Relating to Rights in Rem in Immovable Property:
Article 6(4) 104

2.2.13 'Residual' Jurisdiction: Defendants not Domiciled in any Member
State: Article 4 104

2.2.14 Loss of Jurisdiction: *lis alibi pendens*; and Related Actions:
Articles 27–30 105

2.2.14.1 *Lis alibi pendens* 106

2.2.14.2 Identity of Parties 106

2.2.14.3 Identity of Object or 'Subject-Matter' 107

2.2.14.4 Identity of Cause of Action 107

2.2.14.5 Lis alibi pendens and the Forum Non Conveniens doctrine 107

2.2.14.6 Related Actions 111

2.2.15 Applications for Provisional or Protective Measures: Article 31 112

2.2.16 Recognition and Enforcement 115

2.2.16.1 Recognition 116

2.2.16.2 Enforcement 122

**3 The Core of European Private International Law: Applicable Law –
Contracts** **125**

3.1 Summary 125

3.1.1 Principles 125

3.1.2 Scope of application 126

3.1.3 Basic principle: Freedom of choice 126

3.1.4 Applicable law in the absence of choice 126

3.2 Detailed review of the Regulation 127

3.2.1 Scope of application 127

3.2.2 Exclusions 129

3.2.3 Universal Application 131

3.2.4 Freedom of Choice 131

3.2.5 Protected Categories 134

3.2.6 Applicable Law in the Absence of Choice 135

3.2.7 Formal Validity, Consent and Capacity 139

3.2.8 Mandatory Law, and Public Order 142

3.2.9 The Relationship with Other Conventions 149

4 The Core of European Private International Law: Applicable Law – Tort **151**

4.1 Introduction 151

4.2 General Principles 153

4.3	Scope of Application	154
	4.3.1 'Situations Involving a Conflict of Laws'	154
	4.3.2 Only Courts and Tribunals? Application to Arbitration Tribunals	155
	4.3.3 'Non-Contractual Obligations'	155
	4.3.4 Excluded Matters	157
	4.3.5 Civil and Commercial Matters	163
4.4	Applicable Law – General Rule: *Lex loci damni*	163
4.5	One General Exception to the General Rule and one Escape Clause	165
	4.5.1 General Exception: Parties Habitually Resident in the Same Country	165
	4.5.2 Escape Clause: Case Manifestly More Closely Connected with Other Country	165
4.6	Specific Choice of Law Rules for Specific Torts – No Specific Rules for 'Protected Categories'	166
	4.6.1 Product Liability	166
	4.6.2 Unfair Competition and Acts Restricting Free Competition	170
	4.6.3 Environmental Damage	172
	4.6.4 Damage Caused by Infringement of Intellectual Property Rights	174
	4.6.5 Damage Caused by Industrial Action	175
4.7	Freedom to Choose Applicable Law	177
4.8	Scope of the Law Applicable	178
4.9	Contract-Related Tort Claims	181
4.10	'Overriding' Mandatory Law and Public Order	181
5	**The Insolvency Regulation**	**183**
5.1	The overall nature of and core approaches to insolvency and private international law	183
5.2	Genesis of the Insolvency Regulation	184
5.3	Scope of application and overall aim	185
	5.3.1 Link with the 'bankruptcy' exception under the Jurisdiction Regulation	185
	5.3.2 Four cumulative conditions	188
	5.3.2.1 Collective proceedings	188
	5.3.2.2 Based on the debtor's insolvency	188
	5.3.2.3 Which entail the *partial or total divestment* of a debtor	189
	5.3.2.4 Which entail the appointment of a '*liquidator*'	189
	5.3.3 Opening by a 'court' or judicial authority?	189
	5.3.4 Core aim of the Regulation	190
5.4	The international impact of the Regulation	191
5.5	The jurisdictional model: Universal jurisdiction based on COMI, alongside limited territorial procedures	192

5.5.1	Main insolvency proceeding: Centre of Main Interest – COMI	193
	5.5.1.1 'COMI' as (un)defined by the Regulation	193
	5.5.1.2 European and national case-law on COMI	194
	5.5.1.3 Universality of the proceedings opened in the COMI Member State	197
	5.5.1.4 When is an insolvency procedure 'opened' within the meaning of the Regulation?	198
5.5.2	Secondary and territorial insolvency proceedings	199
	5.5.2.1 Territorial insolvency proceedings	200
	5.5.2.2 Secondary insolvency proceedings	201
5.6	Applicable law	201
	5.6.1 Exceptions	202
5.7	Recognition and enforcement of insolvency proceedings	204
	5.7.1 Judgments concerning the opening of insolvency proceedings	205
	5.7.2 Other judgments in the course of insolvency proceedings	206
	5.7.3 Defences against recognition and enforcement	206
5.8	Powers of the liquidator	207
5.9	Future amendment of the Regulation	207
6	**Free Movement of Establishment, *Lex Societatis* and Private International Law**	**211**
6.1	*Daily Mail*	215
6.2	*Centros*	217
6.3	*Überseering*	218
6.4	*Inspire Art*	219
6.5	*Cartesio* – and its mirror image: *Vale*	221
6.6	*Grid Indus*	223
7	**Private International Law, Corporate Social Responsibility and Extraterritoriality**	**227**
7.1	The role of Private International Law in operationalizing Corporate Social Responsibility	227
7.2	The United States: Litigation Based on The Alien Tort Statute	228
	7.2.1 Corporate Liability under ATS	230
	7.2.2 Standard Operating Procedure or a Lack Thereof	232
	7.2.3 International or Domestic Law	232
	7.2.4 Obstacles to Justice	234
	7.2.4.1 Procedural Dismissal	234
	7.2.4.2 Political Dismissal	235
	7.2.5 Conclusion on the United States	237
7.3	The European Union	237

7.3.1 Jurisdiction   237

      7.3.1.1 General jurisdictional rule: Article 2 JR   237

      7.3.1.2 Special jurisdictional rule: Article 5(5) JR: operations
                arising out of a branch   238

      7.3.1.3 Special jurisdictional rule: Article 5(3) JR: Tort   239

      7.3.1.4 Special jurisdictional rule: Article 5(4) JR   239

      7.3.1.5 Review of the JR – The 'international dimension' of the
                Regulation   239

7.3.2 Applicable law   239

Annexes   **241**

  Brussels I   241

  Regulation 1015/2012   264

  Rome I   296

  Rome II   307

  Insolvency Regulation   317

Index   **335**

Table of Cases

Belgium

Commercial Court, Mons (*Tribunal de Commerce de Mons*), 2 November 2000, RDC
    2001, 617 146

Canada

Schwebel v Ungar [1964] 48 DLR (2d) 644 5

European Court of Justice/Court of Justice of the European Union

Alphabetical

A (Case C-523/07) [2009] ECR I-2805 138
Allianz v West Tankers (Case C-185/07) [2009] ECR I-663 . . . . .35, 37–38
Arblade and *Leloup* (Joined Cases C-369/96 and C-376/96) [1999] ECR I-8453 . . .145
AS-Autoteile Service (Case 220/84) [1985] ECR 2267 59
ASML (Case C-283/05) [2006] ECR I-12041 122
Benincasa (Case C-269/95) [1997] ECR I-3767 65
Besix (Case C-256/00) [2002] ECR I-1699 108
Bier v Mines de Potasse d'Alsace (Case 21/76) [1976] ECR 1735 . . . . . . 92–94, 96, 99,
    160, 239
Blanckaert (Case 139/80) [1981] ECR 819 86
BVG (Case C-144/10), not yet reported 56
C (Case C-435/06) [2007] ECR I-10141 32
Cartesio (Case C-210/06) [2008] ECR I-9641 . . . . .208, 221–25
Centros (Case C-212/97) [1999] ECR I-1459 . . . . .197, 214, 217–21
ČEZLand Oberosterreich (Case C-343/04) [2006] ECR I-4557 . . . . 31 53
Color Drack (Case C-386/05) [2007] ECR I-3699 . . . . .86, 90–91
Colzani (Case 24/76) [1976] ECR 1831 . . . . .78, 81–82
Coreck Maritime (Case C-387/98) [2000] ECR I-9337 78
Daily Mail and General Trust (Case 81/87) [1988] ECR 5483 . . . . . . 213, 215–16, 218,
    220–21, 223–25
Dansommer (Case C-8/98) [2000] ECR I-393 54
De Bloos v Bouyer (Case 14/76) [1976] ECR 1497 . . . . .86, 89
de Lasteyrie du Saillant (Case C-9/02) [2004] ECR I-2409 .214
Denilauler (Case 125/79) [1980] ECR 1553 . . . . .113–114, 117–118
Deutsche Genossenschaftsbank (Case 148/84) [1985] ECR 1981 122
DFDS Torline (Case C-18/02) [2004] ECR I-1417 . . . . .98–99, 175–76

Draka NK Cables (Case C-167/08) [2009] ECR I-3477 122
Duffryn (Case C-214/89) [1992] ECR I-1745. 82
Dumez France and Tracoba (Case C-220/88) [1990] ECR I-49 93
Eco Swiss (Case C-126/07) [1999] ECR I-3055. 121
eDate Advertising GmbH v X and *Olivier Martinez and Robert Martinez v MGN*
    Limited (the *Kylie Minogue* case) (Joined Cases C-509/09 and C-161/10),
    not yet published in ECR 94–97, 162–63
Effer (Case 38/81) [1982] ECR 825 89
Elefanten Schuh (Case 150/80) [1981] ECR 1671 60
Engler (Case C-27/02) [2005] ECR I-481 . . . . .63–64, 87–88, 156
Eurofood IFSC (Case C-341/04) [2006] ECR I-3813. . . . . .25, 194–95, 199
FBTO Schadeverzekeringen (Case C-463/06) [2007] ECR I-11321 60
Folien Fischer (Case C-133/11), not yet published in ECR. 21, 99
Football Dataco (Case C-173/11), not yet published in ECR 67
Frahuil (Case C-265/02) [2004] ECR I-1543. . . . . .22, 31
Freeport (Case C-98/06) [2007] ECR I-8319. 101
G v Cornelius de Visser (Case C-292/10), not yet published in ECR. 97
Gabriel (Case C-96/00) [2002] ECR I-6367. 64
Gambazzi (Case C-394/07) [2009] ECR I-2563. 117–18
Gantner Electronic (Case C-111/01) [2003] ECR I-4207. .107
Gasser (Case C-116/02) [2003] ECR I-14693 . . . . 20, 24–25, 34–35, 198
Gaz de France – Berliner Investissement (Case C-247/08) [2009] ECR I-9225 214
Gemeente Steenbergen v Baten (Case C-271/00) [2002] ECR I-10489. 7, 22, 27, 29–32
Gerling (Case 201/82) [1983] ECR 2503 73
German Graphics (Case C-292/08) [2009] ECR I-8421 . . . . .185, 206
Gesellschaft fur Antriebstechnik (GAT) (Case C-4/03) [2006] ECR I-6509 56–58
GIE Groupe Concorde and Others (Case C-440/97) [1999] ECR I-6307. 108
Glaxosmithkline (Case C-462/06) [2008] ECR I-3965. 100
Gothaer Allgemeine Versichering et al (Case C-456/11), not yet published in
    ECR 79, 118
Gourdain (Case 133/78) [1979] ECR 733. . . . . .33, 185–86
Gruber (Case C-464/01) [2005] ECR I-439 64–65
Gubisch Maschinenfabrik (Case 144/86) [1987] ECR 4861 . . . . .106, 111
Hacker v Euro-Relais (Case C-280/90) [1992] ECR I-1111 53–54
Handte (Jakob) (Case C-26/91) [1992] ECR I-3967 . . . . .87–88, 128, 156
Hassett (Case C-372/07) [2008] ECR I-7403 56
Hendrikman (Case C-78/95) [1996] ECR I-4943. 120
Hoffmann (Case 145/86) [1988] ECR 645 120
Homawoo v GMF Assurances (Case C-412/10), not yet published in ECR 153
Ilsinger (Renate) v Martin Dreschers (Case C-180/06) [2009] ECR I-3961. . .63, 70, 88
Ingmar GB (Case C-381/98) [2000] ECR I-9305. 143–44
Inspire Art (Case C-167/01) [2003] ECR I-10155 219
Intercontainer (Case C-133/08) [2009] ECR I-9687 136
Interedil (Case C-396/09), not yet published in ECR. 12, 194–96, 200, 208
International Transport Workers' Federation and Finnish Seamen's Union v Viking
    Line ABP and OU Viking Line Eesti (Case C-438/05) [2007] ECR I-10779 177
Kalfelis (Case 189/87) [1988] ECR 5565 . . . . .92, 101, 156

Kefalas (Case C-367/96) [1998] ECR I-2843 217

Klein v Rhodos Management (Case C-73/04) [2005] ECR I-8667 . . . . .52, 54

Koelzsch (Case C-29/10), not yet published in ECR 134

Krombach v Bamberski (Case C-7/98) [2000] ECR I-1935 121

L'Oreal (Case C-324/09), not yet published in ECR 67, 97

Laval un Partneri Ltd v Svenska Byggnadsarbetareforbundet, Svenska
   Byggnadsarbetareforbundets avdelning 1, Byggettan and Svenska
   Elektrikerforbundet (Case C-341/05) [2007] ECR I-11767 177

Lechouritou (Case C-292/05) [2007] ECR I-1519 . . . . 7, 22, 31–32, 163

Leclerc (Edouard) (Case 229/83) [1985] ECR 1 216

Lieber (Case C-292/93) [1994] ECR I-2535 53

Lindner (Case C-327/10), not yet published in ECR 26, 42

LTU v Eurocontrol (Case 29/76) [1976] ECR 1541 . . . . .22, 27–32

Lugano I (Opinion 1/03) [2006] ECR I-1145 . . . . .27, 37

Marc Rich v Impianti (Case C-190/89) [1991] ECR I-3855 . . . . .33–34, 36, 38

Marinari (Antonio) v Lloyds Bank et al (Case C-364/93) [1995] ECR I-2719 . . .93, 164

MG Probud Gdynia (Case C-444/07) [2010] ECR I-417 . . . . .25, 198

MSG (Case C-106/95) [1997] ECR I-911 . . . . .82, 90

Muhlleitner (Daniela) v Ahmad Yusufi and Wadat Yusufi (Case C-190/11), not yet
   published in ECR 69–70

Mulox v Geels (Case C-125/92) [1993] ECR I-4075 75

National Grid Indus VB (Case C-371/10), not yet published in ECR 223–25

Netherlands v Ruffer (Case 814/79) [1980] ECR 3807 . . . . .22, 27, 29–31

Opinion 1/09 of 8 March 2011, not yet published in ECR .101

Opinion 1/03 *Lugano I* [2006] ECR I-1145 . . . . .27, 37

Owusu v Jackson (Case C-281/02) [2005] ECR I-1383 . . . . 26, 52, 79, 107, 237

Pammer and *Alpenhof* (Joined Cases C-585/08 and C-144/09) [2010]
   ECR I-12527 67–71

Papillon (Case C-418/07) [2008] ECR I-8947 214

Peters (Martin) (Case 34/82) [1983] ECR 987 87

Pinckney (Case C-170/12) 96, 97

Porta-Leasing (Case 784/79) [1980] ECR 1517 81

Preservatrice fonciere TIARD (Case C-266/01) [2003] ECR I-4867 31

Prism Investments (Case C-139/10) [2011] ECR I-0000 123

Rastelli v Hidoux (Case C-191/10), not yet published in ECR 194, 196

Reichert v Dresdner Bank (Case C-261/90) [1992] ECR 2149 . . . . .52, 59, 113

Reisch Montage (Case C-103/05) [2006] ECR I-6827 101

Renault (Case C-38/98) [2000] ECR I-2973 121

Réunion européenne (Case C-51/97) [1998] ECR I-6511 . . . . .93, 100

Roche Nederland and Others (Case C-539/03) [2006] ECR I-6535 101–103

Rohr (Case 27/81) [1981] ECR 2431 61

Rosler v Rottwinkel (Case 241/83) [1985] ECR 99 53–54

Rutten (Case C-383/95) [1997] ECR I-57 21

Sanders v Van der Putte (Case 73/77) [1977] ECR 2383 . . . . .52, 55

Sar Schotte (Case 218/86) [1987] ECR 4905 86

SCT Industri v Alpenblume (Case C-111/08) [2009] ECR I-5655 186

Seagon (Case C-339/07) [2009] ECR I-767 196

Segoura (Case 25/76) [1976] ECR 1851..81–82
SGI (Case C-311/08) [2010] ECR I-487..214
Shevill v Presse Alliance (Case C-68/93) [1995] ECR I-415..............94–96, 160
Slot (Case C-98/12), pending...70
Solo Kleinmotoren (Case C-414/92) [1994] ECR I-237........................117
Solvay (Case C-616/10), not yet published in ECR 58, 96, 102, 112
Somafar (Case 33/78) [1979] ECR 2183 ....72, 86, 238
Sonntag (Volker) v Hans Waidmann et al (Case C-172/91) [1993] ECR I-1963 ...7, 27
Staubitz-Schreiber (Case C-1/04) [2006] ECR I-701 ....196, 209
Swaddling v Adjudication Officer (Case C-90/97) [1999] ECR I-1075...........138
Tacconi (Case C-334/00) [2002] ECR I-7357.............................89
Tessili v Dunlop (Case 12/76) [1976] ECR 1473 90–91
The Tatry (Case C-406/92) [1994] ECR I-5439 106
Tilly Russ (Case 71/83) [1984] ECR 2417 81
Trade Agency (Case C-619/10), not yet published in ECR 123
Turner (Case C-159/02) [2004] ECR I-3565 .... 20, 24, 35, 38, 199
Uberseering (Case C-208/00) [2002] ECR I-9919.................212, 214, 218–19
Unamar v Navigation Maritime Bulgare (Case C-184/12), pending...........147–48
Vale (Case C-378/10), not yet published in ECR 222–223
Van Uden v Deco Line (Case C-391/95) [1998] ECR I-7091 ....33–34, 38, 112–13
Vienna Insurance Group (Case C-111/09) [2010] ECR I-4545 60
Voogsgeerd (Case C-384/10), not yet published in ECR 134–35
Webb v Webb (Case C-294/92) [1994] ECR I-1717......................53, 56
Weryński (Case C-283/09) [2011] ECR I-601.............................12
Wintersteiger AG v Products 4U Sondermaschinenbau GmbH (Case C-523/10),
  not yet published in ECR 95, 97
Wood Floor Solutions (Case C-19/09) [2010] ECR I-2121 ....21, 23
Zaza Retail (Case C-112/10), not yet published in ECR 200–201
Zuid Chemie (Case C-189/08) [2009] ECR I-6917............................93

Chronological

12/76 *Tessili v Dunlop* [1976] ECR 1473.................................90–91
14/76 *De Bloos v Bouyer* [1976] ECR 1497...............................86, 89
21/76 *Bier v Mines de Potasse d'Alsace* [1976] ECR 1735.... 92–94, 96, 99, 160, 239
24/76 *Colzani* [1976] ECR 1831 ....78, 81–82
25/76 *Segoura* [1976] ECR 1851 81–82
29/76 *LTU v Eurocontrol* [1976] ECR 1541..............................22, 27–32
73/77 *Sanders v Van der Putte* [1977] ECR 2383 ....52, 55
33/78 *Somafar* [1979] ECR 2183 ....72, 86, 238
133/78 *Gourdain* [1979] ECR 733 ....33, 185–186
125/79 *Denilauler* [1980] ECR 1553 ....113–14, 117–18
784/79 *Porta-Leasing* [1980] ECR 1517.....................................81
814/79 *Netherlands v Ruffer* [1980] ECR 3807 ....22, 27, 29–31
139/80 *Blanckaert* [1981] ECR 819 86
150/80 *Elefanten Schuh* [1981] ECR 1671..................................60
27/81 *Rohr* [1981] ECR 2431 61

38/81 *Effer* [1982] ECR 825 89
34/82 *Martin Peters* [1983] ECR 987......................................87
201/82 *Gerling* [1983] ECR 2503 73
71/83 *Tilly Russ* [1984] ECR 2417 81
229/83 *Edouard Leclerc* [1985] ECR 1......................................216
241/83 *Rosler v Rottwinkel* [1985] ECR 99 53–54
148/84 *Deutsche Genossenschaftsbank* [1985] ECR 1981....................122
220/84 *AS-Autoteile Service* [1985] ECR 2267.............................59
144/86 *Gubisch Maschinenfabrik* [1987] ECR 4861 ....106, 111
145/86 *Hoffmann* [1988] ECR 645 120
218/86 *Sar Schotte* [1987] ECR 4905.....................................86
81/87 *Daily Mail and General Trust* [1988] ECR 5483.....213, 215–16, 218, 220–21,
                                                                       223–25
189/87 *Kalfelis* [1988] ECR 5565................................92, 101, 156
C-220/88 *Dumez France and Tracoba* [1990] ECR I-49......................93
C-190/89 *Marc Rich v Impianti* [1991] ECR I-3855 ....33–34, 36, 38
C-214/89 *Duffryn* [1992] ECR I-1745......................................82
C-261/90 *Reichert v Dresdner Bank* [1992] ECR 2149.................52, 59, 113
C-280/90 *Hacker v Euro-Relais* [1992] ECR I-1111 53–54
C-26/91 *Jakob Handte* [1992] ECR I-3967 ....87–88, 128, 156
C-172/91 *Volker Sonntag v Hans Waidmann et al* [1993] ECR I-1963...........7, 27
C-125/92 *Mulox v Geels* [1993] ECR I-4075...............................75
C-294/92 *Webb v Webb* [1994] ECR I-1717................................53, 56
C-406/92 *The Tatry* [1994] ECR I-5439 106
C-414/92 *Solo Kleinmotoren* [1994] ECR I-237............................117
C-68/93 *Shevill v Presse Alliance* [1995] ECR I-415...................94–96, 160
C-292/93 *Lieber* [1994] ECR I-2535.......................................53
C-364/93 *Antonio Marinari v Lloyds Bank et al* [1995] ECR I-2719.........93, 164
C-78/95 *Hendrikman* [1996] ECR I-4943..................................120
C-106/95 *MSG* [1997] ECR I-911..82, 90
C-269/95 *Benincasa* [1997] ECR I-3767 65
C-383/95 *Rutten* [1997] ECR I-57...21
C-391/95 *Van Uden v Deco Line* [1998] ECR I-7091 ....33–34, 38, 112–13
C-367/96 *Kefalas* [1998] ECR I-2843.....................................217
C-369/96 and C-376/96 *Arblade* and *Leloup* [1999] ECR I-8453...............145
C-51/97 *Réunion européenne* [1998] ECR I-6511 ....93, 100
C-90/97 *Swaddling v Adjudication Officer* [1999] ECR I-1075...............138
C-212/97 *Centros* [1999] ECR I-1459.........................197, 214, 217–21
C-440/97 *GIE Groupe Concorde and Others* [1999] ECR I-6307...............108
C-7/98 *Krombach v Bamberski* [2000] ECR I-1935..........................121
C-8/98 *Dansommer* [2000] ECR I-393 54
C-38/98 *Renault* [2000] ECR I-2973......................................121
C-381/98 *Ingmar GB* [2000] ECR I-9305...................................143–44
C-387/98 *Coreck Maritime* [2000] ECR I-9337 78
C-96/00 *Gabriel* [2002] ECR I-6367......................................64
C-208/00 *Uberseering* [2002] ECR I-9919....................212, 214, 218–19
C-256/00 *Besix* [2002] ECR I-1699 108

C-271/00 *Gemeente Steenbergen v Baten* [2002] ECR I-10489 . . . . . . 7, 22, 27, 29–32

C-334/00 *Tacconi* [2002] ECR I-7357 89

C-111/01 *Gantner Electronic* [2003] ECR I-4207 107

C-167/01 *Inspire Art* [2003] ECR I-10155 219

C-266/01 *Preservatrice fonciere TIARD* [2003] ECR I-4867 31

C-464/01 *Gruber* [2005] ECR I-439 64–65

C-9/02 *de Lasteyrie du Saillant* [2004] ECR I-2409 214

C-18/02 *DFDS Torline* [2004] ECR I-1417 . . . . 98–99, 175–76

C-27/02 *Engler* [2005] ECR I-481 . . . . 63–64, 87–88, 156

C-116/02 *Gasser* [2003] ECR I-14693 . . . . 20, 24–25, 34–35, 198

C-159/02 *Turner* [2004] ECR I-3565 . . . . 20, 24, 35, 38, 199

C-265/02 *Frahuil* [2004] ECR I-1543 . . . . 22, 31

C-281/02 *Owusu v Jackson* [2005] ECR I-1383 . . . . 26, 52, 79, 107, 237

C-4/03 *Gesellschaft fur Antriebstechnik (GAT)* [2006] ECR I-6509 56–58

C-539/03 *Roche Nederland and Others* [2006] ECR I-6535 101–103

C-1/04 *Staubitz-Schreiber* [2006] ECR I-701 . . . . 197, 209

C-73/04 *Klein v Rhodos Management* [2005] ECR I-8667 . . . . 52, 54

C-341/04 *Eurofood IFSC* [2006] ECR I-3813 . . . . 25, 194–95, 199

C-343/04 *ČEZLand Oberosterreich* [2006] ECR I-4557 . . . . 31, 53

C-103/05 *Reisch Montage* [2006] ECR I-6827 101

C-283/05 *ASML* [2006] ECR I-12041 122

C-292/05 *Lechouritou* [2007] ECR I-1519 . . . . 7, 22, 31–32, 163

C-341/05 *Laval un Partneri Ltd v Svenska Byggnadsarbetareforbundet, Svenska Byggnadsarbetareforbundets avdelning 1, Byggettan and Svenska Elektrikerforbundet* [2007] ECR I-11767 177

C-386/05 *Color Drack* [2007] *ECR* I-3699 . . . . 86, 90–91

C-438/05 *International Transport Workers' Federation and Finnish Seamen's Union v Viking Line ABP and OU Viking Line Eesti* [2007] ECR I-10779 177

C-98/06 *Freeport* [2007] ECR I-8319 101

C-180/06 *Renate Ilsinger v Martin Dreschers* [2009] ECR I-3961 . . . . 63, 70, 88

C-210/06 *Cartesio* [2008] ECR I-9641 . . . . 208, 221–25

C-435/06 *C* [2007] ECR I-10141 32

C-462/06 *Glaxosmithkline* [2008] ECR I-3965 100

C-463/06 *FBTO Schadeverzekeringen* [2007] ECR I-11321 60

C-126/07 *Eco Swiss* [1999] ECR I-3055 121

C-185/07 *Allianz v West Tankers* [2009] ECR I-663 . . . . 35, 37–38

C-339/07 *Seagon* [2009] ECR I-767 196

C-372/07 *Hassett* [2008] ECR I-7403 56

C-394/07 *Gambazzi* [2009] ECR I-2563 117–18

C-418/07 *Papillon* [2008] ECR I-8947 214

C-444/07 *MG Probud Gdynia* [2010] ECR I-417 . . . . 25, 198

C-523/07 *A* [2009] ECR I-2805 138

C-111/08 *SCT Industri v Alpenblume* [2009] ECR I-5655 186

C-133/08 *Intercontainer* [2009] ECR I-9687 136

C-167/08 *Draka NK Cables* [2009] ECR I-3477 122

C-189/08 *Zuid Chemie* [2009] ECR I-6917 93

C-247/08 *Gaz de France – Berliner Investissement* [2009] ECR I-9225 214

C-292/08 *German Graphics* [2009] ECR I-8421 . . . . 185, 206
C-311/08 *SGI* [2010] ECR I-487 214
C-585/08 and C-144/09 *Pammer* and *Alpenhof* 2010] ECR I-12527 67–71
C-19/09 *Wood Floor Solutions* [2010] ECR I-2121 . . . . 21, 23
C-111/09 *Vienna Insurance Group* [2010] ECR I-4545 60
C-283/09 *Weryński* [2011] ECR I-601 12
C-324/09 *L'Oreal*, not yet published in ECR 67, 97
C-396/09 *Interedil*, not yet published in ECR 12, 194–96, 200, 208
C-509/09 and C-161/10 *eDate Advertising GmbH v X* and *Olivier Martinez and Robert Martinez v MGN Limited* (the *Kylie Minogue*), not yet published in ECR 94–97, 162–63
C-29/10 *Koelzsch*, not yet published in ECR 134
C-112/10 *Zaza Retail*, not yet published in ECR 200–201
C-139/10 *Prism Investments* [2011] ECR I-0000 123
C-144/10 *BVG*, not yet published 56
C-191/10 *Rastelli v Hidoux*, not yet published in ECR 194, 196
C-292/10 *G v Cornelius de Visser*, not yet published in ECR 97
C-327/10 *Lindner*, not yet published in ECR 26, 42
C-371/10 *National Grid Indus VB*, not yet published in ECR 223–25
C-378/10 *Vale*, not yet published in ECR 222–23
C-384/10 *Voogsgeerd*, not yet published in ECR 134–35
C-412/10 *Homawoo v GMF Assurances*, not yet published in ECR 153
C-523/10 *Wintersteiger AG v Products 4U Sondermaschinenbau GmbH*, not yet published in ECR 95, 97
C-616/10 *Solvay*, not yet published in ECR 58, 96, 102, 112
C-619/10 *Trade Agency*, not yet published in ECR 123
C-133/11 *Folien Fischer*, not yet published in ECR 21, 99
C-154/11 *Mahamdia*, not yet published in ECR 27, 75
C-173/11 *Football Dataco*, not yet published in ECR 67
C-190/11 *Daniela Muhlleitner v Ahmad Yusufi and Wadat Yusufi*, not yet published in ECR 69–70
C-456/11 *Gothaer Allgemeine Versicherung et al*, not yet published in ECR 79, 118
C-98/12 *Slot*, pending 70
C-170/12 *Pinckney* 96, 97
C-184/12 *Unamar v Navigation Maritime Bulgare*, pending 147–48
Opinion 1/03 *Lugano I* [2006] ECR I-1145 . . . . 27, 37
Opinion 1/09 of 8 March 2011, not yet published in ECR 101

France

CA Paris, *Club Mediterranee v Caisse des conges spectacles* (1976) 54 RCDIP 485 . . 145
TGI Paris (Case C-278/09), Order of the Court of 20 November 2009 23–24
Crim, 3 March 2011, *Ministere public v Joseph Weiler* 45
Cass (Case C-170/12) *Pinckney* 96–97
Cass No 11–40101, 29 February 2012 45
Cass No 11–26.022, 26 September 2012, *La societe Banque privee Edmond de Rothschild Europe v X* 84

Netherlands

Milieudefensie et al v Shell, BK8616, Rechtbanks-Gravenhage, HA ZA 330891
   09-579 237–38

United Kingdom

Brac rent-a-car international Inc (2003) EWHC (Ch) 128 191
British Airways BD v Laker Airways [1985] AC 85. 35
CALYON v Wytwornia Sprzetu Komunikacynego PZL Swidnik SA [2009] EWHC
   1914 (Comm). 56
Catalyst v Lewinsohn [2009] EWHC 1964 (Ch). 109
Cherney v Deripaska [2008] EWHC 1530 (Comm). 109
Collins & Aikman Corp Group, In re [2005] EWHC 1754 (Ch). 195
Cox v Ergo Versicherung [2011] EWHC 2806 (QB); [2012] EWCA Civ 1001 181
*Dallah Real Estate and Tourism Holding Company v The Ministry of Religious
   Affairs, Government of Pakistan* [2010] UKSC 46 8
Erich Gasser GmbH v MISAT Srl [2004] 1 Lloyd's Rep 445 25
Foster v Driscoll 1929] 1 KB 470. 147
Haji-Ioannou & Ors v Frangos & Ors [1999] EWCA Civ 1148. 42
Harding v Wealands [2007] 2 AC 1 (HL). 179
Iran v Berend [2007] EWHC 132 (QB) 8
Joint Stock Asset Management Company Ingosstrakh Investments v BNP Paribas SA
   [2012] EWCA Civ 644 35
JP Morgan Europe Ltd v Primacom AG [2005] EWHC 508 (Comm) 112
King v Crown Energy Trading AG & Anor [2003] EWHC 163 (Comm) 44
KME Yorkshire et al v Toshiba Carrier UK et al [2012] EWCA Civ 1190 100
KN v JCN [2010] EWHC 843 109
Konkola Copper Mines Plc v Coromin Ltd [2005] EWHC 898 (Comm); [2006]
   APP.L.R. 01/17 . . . . .25, 109
M v M [2007] EWHC 2047 (HL) 138
Ogden v Ogden [1908] P 46 (CA). 5
Owusu v Jackson (Case C-281/02) [2005] QB 801 . . . . .25, 52
Regazzoni v KC Sethia (1944) Ltd [1956] 3 WLR 79 147
Rubin v Eurofinance SA [2012] UKSC 46 . . . . .183, 186
Shashoua v Sharma [2009] EWHC 957 (Comm). 35
Simpson v Intralinks (EAT), UKEAT/0593/11/RN 137, 146
Spiliada Maritime Corporation v Cansulex Ltd [1987] AC 460 . . . . .9, 107, 109
Turner v Grovit [2001] UKHL 65 . . . . .34–35, 37–38
West Tankers Inc v Allianz Spa & Arno [2011] EWHC 829 (Comm) (QBD);
   [2012] EWHC 854 (Comm) 37–38

United States of America

Aguinda v Texaco Inc 303 F 3d 470 (2d Cir 2002) 235
Bowota v Chevron 621 F 3d 1116 (9th Cir 2010) 233
Chevron corporation v Hugo Gerardo Camacho Naranjo, et al (US Supreme
   Court, October 2012). 229

Doe v Unocal (1997) 227

Doe I v Unocal Corporation 395 F 3d 932 (9th Cir 2002), *rehearing en banc
    granted* 395 F 3d 978 (9th Cir 2003), *vacated and appeal dismissed following
    settlement* 403 F 3d 708 (9th Cir 2005) 231, 233

Ecuador v Chevron 228

Filartiga v Pena-Irala 630 F 2d 876 (2d Cir 1980) 229

J McIntyre Mach Ltd v Nicastro 131 S Ct 2780 (2011) .169

Khulamani v Barclay National Bank Limited 504 F 3d 254 (2d Cir 2007) 231

Kiobel v Royal Dutch Petroleum 621 F 3d 111 (2d Cir 2010), *cert filed* (6 June
    2011) 228, 230–33, 236

Kiobel et al v Shell 06–4800-cv & 064876-cv (2nd cir 2011) 236

Laker Airways Ltd v Sabena Belgian World Airlines 235 US App DC 207, 731 F
    2d 909 (DC Cir 1984) 34–35

Marbury v Madison 5 US (1 Cranch) 137 (1803) 235

Sarei v Rio Tinto PLC 221 F Supp 2d 1116 (CD Cal 2002) 235–236

Sosa v Alvarez-Machain 124 S Ct 2739 (2004) 229–30, 232, 234

Table of Legislation

Belgium

Judicial Code 103
Law of 13 April 1995 relating to commercial agency contracts
    Art 18. 147
    Arts 20–21 147
Law of 16 July 2004 on private international law
    Art 98. 84
Lois de police 145

European Union

EC Treaty. *See* Treaty establishing the European Community
EEC Treaty. *See* Treaty establishing the European Economic Community
Treaty on European Union (TEU) 15
    Art 6. 16
    Art 19. 19
Lisbon Treaty 12, 19
Maastricht Treaty 10, 151
    Art K 10
    Art K.1 10
    Art K.1(1)–(3) 10
    Art K.1(3)(a)–(c) 10
    Art K.1(4)–(5) 10
    Art K.1(6). 10, 151
    Art K.1(7)–(9) 10
    Title VI. 10
Treaty of Amsterdam 10–11, 15, 151–152
    184
    Art 62(1) 11
    Art 62(2)(b)(i)–(iv) 11
    Art 63(1) 11
    Art 63(2)(a) 11
    Art 65. 10–11
    Art 65(a)–(c) 10
    Art 67. 10
    Art 67(1)–(5) 11
    Art 68. 11
    Art 68(1)–(3) 11

Art 69 11
Treaty establishing the European Community (EC Treaty) 151, 222
    Title IV 12
    Art 48(2) 9, 214
    Art 52 216
    Art 58 216
    Art 65 . . . . 152–153, 184
    Art 67 174
    Art 67(1) 184, 241
    Art 68 12
    Art 234 11
    Art 251 11
    Art 293 (formerly Art 220 EEC, now repealed) 9, 151, 214
    Art 300 3
    Protocol on the position of Denmark 11
    Protocol on the position of the United Kingdom and Ireland 11
    Protocol on the application of certain aspects of Art 14 11
Treaty establishing the European Economic Community (EEC Treaty) 19–20
    Art 85 (now Art 81 EC) 121
    Art 220 EEC (subsequently Art 293 EC, now repealed) 9, 13, 20–21, 33
Treaty on the Functioning of the European Union (TFEU) 12, 153
    Art 39(2) 213
    Art 49 (ex Art 43 TEC) 209, 213, 218, 222–224
    Art 50 (ex Art 44 TEC) 213
    Art 50(1)–(2) 213
    Art 50(2)(a)–(e) 213
    Art 50(2)(f)213–214
    Art 50(2)(g)–(h) 214
    Art 54 . . . . 43, 213–214
    Art 67 (ex Art 61 TEC and ex Art 29 TEU) 3, 12, 47
    Art 67(1)–(4) 12
    Art 81 (ex Art 65 TEC) 12
    Art 81(1)–(2) 12–13
    Art 81(2)(a)–(h) 13
    Art 81(3) 13
    Art 101 . . . . 100, 171
    Art 102 171
    Art 267 12
    Art 297(1) 154

Decisions

Council Decision 2006/719 on the accession of the Community to the Hague
    Conference on Private International law, [2006] OJ L297/1 3

Directives

Council Directive 73/239/EEC of 24 July 1973 on the coordination of laws,
  regulations and administrative provisions relating to the taking–up and pursuit
  of the business of direct insurance other than life assurance (as amended by
  Council Directives 88/357/EEC(8) and 90/618/EEC(9)) 77
Directive 85/374 on the approximation of laws, regulations and administrative
  provisions of the Member States concerning liability for defective products
  (Product Liability Directive), [1985] OJ L210/29 .156, 169
  Art 2 169
  Art 6 169
Council Directive 86/653/EEC of 18 December 1986 on the coordination of the
  laws of the Member States relating to self–employed commercial agents
  (Commercial Agents Directive). 143, 147–148
Council Directive 93/7/EEC on the return of cultural objects unlawfully removed
  from the territory of a Member State 49
  Art 34 50
Directive 93/13, Unfair Contract Terms Directive, [1993] OJ L95/29. 73
Directive 95/46/EC of the European Parliament and of the Council of 24 October
  1995 on the protection of individuals with regard to the processing of personal
  data and on the free movement of such data 161
Directive 96/9, Database Directive 67
  Art 7 67
Directive 96/71/EC of the European Parliament and of the Council of 16 December
  1996 concerning the posting of workers in the framework of the provision of
  services 176
  Art 3(1) 176
Directive 2001/17 on insurance undertakings, [2001] OJ L110/28 187
Directive 2001/24 on credit institutions, [2001] OJ L125/15. 187
Directive 2001/86 supplementing the Statute for a European company with regard
  to the involvement of employees, [2001] OJ L294/22 (Societas Europaea
  Directive) 214
Directive 2002/83/EC of the European Parliament and of the Council of 5
  November 2002 concerning life assurance
  Art 2 128
Directive 2004/35, Environmental Liability Directive, [2004] OJ L143/56 172–174
  Recital 14 173
  Recitals 172
  Art 2(6) 174
  Art 3(2) 172
  Art 6 174
  Art 8 174
  Art 8(4)(a) 174
  Annex III 174
Directive 2004/39/EC of the European Parliament and of the Council of 21 April
  2004 on markets in financial instruments
  Art 4(1) 136
Directive 2004/48, IP Enforcement Directive, [2004] OJ L195/16 58–59

Directive 2005/32 on ecodesign requirements for energy–using products,
   [2005] OJ L191/29
   Art 2(4) 170
Directive 2005/56 on cross–border mergers of limited liability companies,
   [2005] OJ L310/1(Cross–border Merger Directive). .214
Directive on the approximation of the laws of the Member States and the
   safeguarding of employees' rights in the event of transfers of undertakings,
   businesses or parts of businesses 208
Directive on consumer rights. 135, 143–144
   Recital 10. 135
   Recital 58. 143
   Art 4. 144
   Art 25. 135
Directive on the protection of employees in case of insolvency of the employer. . . .209

Regulations

Regulation 1346/2000 Insolvency Regulation, [2000] OJ L160/1 IReg 7, 25, 32,
                                                                          183–210
   Preamble. 194
      Recital 2 202
      Recital 4 190
      Recital 6 . . . . .185, 195
      Recital 9 187–188
      Recital 11 192
      Recital 12 200
      Recital 13 193
      Recital 14 191
      Recital 17 200
      Recital 22 198
      Recitals 193
   Ch I
      Art 1 . . . . .186–187, 190, 208
      Art 1(1) 186–187, 190, 199
      Art 1(2) 186–187, 190, 208
      Art 2 . . . . .186, 208
      Art 2(a) 186
      Art 2(b) 186–187, 189
      Art 2(c) 186, 188
      Art 2(h) 199
      Art 3 . . . . 190, 205, 207, 209
      Art 3(1) 193, 195–196, 204–205
      Art 3(2) 200, 205
      Art 3(4) 200
      Art 3(4)(a) 200
      Art 3(4)(b) 200
      Art 4 201–203

Art 4(1)–(2)...201
Art 4(2)(a)–(d)...201
Art 4(2)(e)–(l)..201
Art 4(2)(m)..7, 202
Art 5...202–204, 206
Art 6..202
Art 7...185, 202, 204
Arts 8–9..203–204
Art 10...203–204, 209
Art 11...203–204
Art 12..204
Art 13..7, 203–204
Art 14...203–204
Art 15...203–204, 209
Ch II
Art 16...198, 205
Art 16(1)..198–199, 205
Art 16(2)..205
Art 17..205
Art 17(1)..205
Art 17(2)..205–206
Art 18...198, 205, 207
Art 19..205
Art 20..204
Art 20(1)–(2)..204
Arts 21–24..205
Art 25..206
Art 25(1)–(3)..206
Art 26...205, 207
Ch III...200, 205
Art 28..202
Art 29...201, 207
Arts 31–37..206–207
Ch V
Art 45...187
Annex A...186–190, 199, 208–209
Annex B...186–188, 208
Annex C...186–187, 189, 199
Council Regulation (EC) No 1348/2000 of 29 May 2000 on the service in the
    Member States of judicial and extrajudicial documents in civil or commercial
    matters...122
Council Regulation (EC) No 44/2001 of 22 December 2000 on jurisdiction and the
    recognition and enforcement of judgments in civil and commercial matters
    (Brussels I Regulation/Jurisdiction Regulation (JR)/EEX Regulation), OJ [2001]
    L12/1...7–8, 19–22, 24–28, 30, 33–51,

3–54, 58, 60–66, 68, 70–73, 75, 78–81, 83–87, 90, 92–93, 96, 100, 104,106–107, 109, 111–123, 125, 128–130, 137–138, 140, 144, 152, 155–156, 160, 162–164, 170, 172, 176, 178, 184–186, 191, 198, 206, 208, 229, 237–239

Recital 11 43
Recital 11(f) 49
Recital 25 114
Ch I
  Art 1 . . . . .21, 46, 117
  Art 1(1) 27
  Art 1(2)(b) 185
  Art 1(2)(d) 36
Ch II
  Section 1
    Art 2 . . . . 23, 30, 42, 44, 47, 51, 61, 85, 92, 96, 107, 164, 237
    Art 2(a) 114
    Art 2(1)–(2) 44
    Art 3 . . . . .44–45, 47–48
    Art 3(1) 44
    Art 4 . . . . 23, 42, 44–48, 49–51, 60, 62, 74, 76, 86, 104, 119, 238
    Art 4(1) 44, 46, 104
    Art 4(2) 44–46, 104
    Art 4a 49–50
  Section 2 44
    Art 5 . . . . .23, 47–48, 51, 64, 74–76, 86, 89–90, 92, 238
    Art 5(a) 63, 129
    Art 5(1) 21, 71, 75, 86–92
    Art 5(1)(a) 86–87, 90–91
    Art 5(1)(b) 21, 86–87, 90–91
    Art 5(1)(c) 87, 91
    Art 5(3) 21, 23, 36–37, 57, 75, 92–93, 96–99, 163, 239
    Art 5(4) 239
    Art 5(5) 72, 86, 238
    Art 6 . . . . 23, 47–48, 51, 86, 99–100
    Art 6(1) 100–103
    Art 6(2) 100–101, 103, 245–246
    Art 6(3) 100, 103
    Art 6(4) 55, 100, 104
    Art 7 . . . . 23, 47–48, 51, 86, 99
  Section 3 . . . . 39, 44, 60, 76, 84, 119
    Arts 8–9 . . . . 23, 47, 51, 61, 76
    Art 9(1) 76
    Art 9(1)(a)–(c) 76
    Art 9(2) 76
    Art 10 . . . . 23, 47, 51, 61, 76
    Art 11 . . . . 23, 47, 51, 61, 76
    Art 11(1)–(2) 76
    Art 12 . . . . 23, 47, 51, 61, 76

Art 12(1)–(2) 76
Art 13 . . . . 23, 47, 51, 61, 77–78
Art 13(1)–(2) 77
Art 13(3) 73, 77
Art 13(4) 77
Art 13(5) 62, 77
Art 14 . . . . 23, 47, 51, 61–62, 77
Art 14(1) 77
Art 14(1)(a)–(b) 77
Art 14(2) 77
Art 14(2)(a)–(b) 77
Art 14(3)–(5) 77
Section 4 . . . . 39, 44, 60, 62–63, 73, 84, 119
Art 15 . . . . 23, 47, 50–51, 54, 61–63, 65–67, 70–72, 88–89
Art 15(1) 62–63, 66
Art 15(1)(a)–(b) 62
Art 15(1)(c) 62, 68–70, 89
Art 15(2) 62, 71–72
Art 15(3) 62
Art 16 . . . . 23, 47, 51, 61–62, 66, 72
Art 16(1) 49, 62
Art 16(2) 43, 62
Art 16(3) 63
Art 17 . . . . 23, 47, 51, 61, 63–64, 72–73, 78, 81–82, 90
Art 17(1) 63
Art 17(2) 63, 72
Art 17(3) 63
Section 5 . . . . 39, 44, 60, 74, 84
Art 18 . . . . 23, 47, 51, 60–61, 74, 87
Art 18(1) 50, 74
Art 18(2) 74, 76
Art 19 . . . . 23, 47, 51, 61, 74
Art 19(1) 74
Art 19(2) 50, 74
Art 19(2)(a)–(b) 74
Art 20 . . . . 23, 47, 51, 61, 74
Art 20(1)–(2) 74
Art 21 . . . . 23, 47, 51, 61, 74, 78, 106
Art 21(1)–(2) 74
Section 6 . . . . 44, 119
Art 22 . . . . . .22–23, 41–42, 44–47, 51–55, 57–61, 73, 78–79, 96, 104, 106, 109
Art 22(1) 51–55
Art 22(2) 44, 55–56
Art 22(3) 57
Art 22(4) 56–58, 112, 119
Art 22(5) 59
Section 7 44

Art 23 . . . . 22–23, 41–42, 44, 46–47, 51, 54, 56, 60, 73, 75, 77–85, 90, 103–104, 119, 178

Art 23(1). 77, 81–82

Art 23(1)(a) 77, 81

Art 23(1)(b)–(c) 78, 81

Art 23(2). 78

Art 23(3). 78–79

Art 23(4). 78

Art 23(5). 52, 78, 84

Art 24 . . . . 23, 47, 51–52, 60, 71, 75, 84, 121

Section 8

Art 25 . . . . .47, 50

Art 26 . . . . .48, 50

Art 26(2). 122

Section 9 105

Art 27 . . . . 20, 23, 34, 51, 104–107, 111–112

Art 27(1)–(2) 105

Art 27(3). 106

Art 28 . . . . .23, 51, 103, 105–106, 111–112

Art 28(1). 105

Art 28(2). 105

Art 28(3). 105, 111–112

Art 29 . . . . 23, 51, 55, 105

Art 29(4). 40

Art 30 . . . . .23, 51, 105, 112

Art 30(1)–(2) 105, 112

Section 10 112

Art 31 . . . . 23, 33–34, 51, 58, 96, 112–113

Ch III 79, 104, 114–115, 117–119

Art 32 . . . . .80, 84–85, 117–118

Art 32(1)–(2). 84

Art 32(2a)–(2b). 84

Section 1 115

Art 33 . . . . .80, 116

Art 33(1). 116

Art 33(2). 116

Art 33(3). 40, 116

Art 34 . . . . 46, 48, 50, 111, 119–121, 123

Art 34(1). 48, 120, 123

Art 34(1)(a)–(c) 48

Art 34(2). 48, 120, 123

Art 34(3). 37, 48, 111, 120, 122

Art 34(3)(a)–(c) 49

Art 34(4). 49, 120

Art 35 . . . . 46, 62, 79, 119, 123

Art 35(1). 52, 119

Art 35(2)–(3) 119

Art 36 119
Section 2 115–116
Art 42 123
Art 45 46
Section 3 115–116
Art 53 123
Art 54 123
Ch IV
Art 57 117
Ch V
Art 59 . . . . .22, 41, 43
Art 59(1) 41
Art 59(2) 41
Art 60 . . . . .22, 41–44, 55
Art 60(1) 41
Art 60(1)(a)–(c). 41
Art 60(2) 22, 41, 43
Art 60(3) 41
Art 65 103
Ch VI
Art 66 119
Ch VII
Art 71 38
Art 72 . . . . .46, 119, 122
Ch VIII
Art 84 40
Annex I 44–46, 104, 121, 123
Regulation 2157/2001 on the Statute for a European company (SE), [2001] OJ
L294/1 214
Regulation 2201/2003 on jurisdiction and the recognition and enforcement of
judgments in matrimonial matters and in matters of parental responsibility,
OJ [2003] L338/1 (Brussels IIa or Brussels II bis Regulation). 32, 109, 138
Art 1(2) 32
Art 1(2)(a)–(d). 32
Art 5(2) 32
Arts 8–14 110
Art 15. 109–110
Art 15(1) 110
Art 15(1)(a)–(b). 110
Art 15(2) 110
Art 15(2)(a)–(c) 110
Art 15(3) 110
Art 15(3)(a)–(e) 110
Art 15(4)–(6) 110
Art 53. 110
Regulation 861/2007, European Small Claims Procedure Regulation, [2007] OJ
L199/1 115

Regulation 1393/2007 on service of documents in civil or commercial matters,
    [2007] OJ L324/79
    Art 19(1) 122
Regulation 4/2009 on jurisdiction, applicable law, recognition and decisions and
    cooperation in matters relating to maintenance obligations, [2009] OJ L7/1 . .32, 129
Regulation 1259/2010 implementing enhanced cooperation in the area of the law
    applicable to divorce and legal separation, [2010] OJ L343/10 (Rome III) 129,
                                                                        138, 158
Council Implementing Regulation 583/2011, [2011] OJ L160/52 187
Regulation 650/2012 on jurisdiction, applicable law, recognition and enforcement
    of decisions and acceptance and enforcement of authentic instruments in matters
    of succession and on the creation of a European certificate of succession,
    [2012] OJ L201/107 111
    Arts 4–6 111
    Art 6(a)–(b) 111
    Art 10 111
    Art 22 111
Regulation (EC) No 593/2008 of the European Parliament and of the Council of
    17 June 2008 on the law applicable to contractual obligations (Rome I
    Regulation), [2008] OJ L177/6 . . . . 7, 14, 59, 61, 71, 73, 84, 87, 104, 125–141,
    143–146, 148–149, 151–152, 155–157, 159–160, 165–166, 170, 172, 178, 180–181,
                                                                               184
    Recital 7 128
    Recital 12 . . . . .126, 132
    Recitals 13–14 133
    Recital 15 143
    Recital 19 139
    Ch I
        Art 1 . . . . .125, 127
        Art 1(1) 126–127
        Art 1(2) 126–127
        Art 1(2)(a)–(e) 127
        Art 1(2)(f) 127
        Art 1(2)(g)–(j) 128
        Art 1(2)(i) 129
        Art 1(4) 144
        Art 2 . . . . .125–126, 131
    Ch II
        Art 3 . . . . 131–133, 135, 142–143, 148
        Art 3(1) 126, 131, 134, 165
        Art 3(2) 131
        Art 3(3) 132, 142–144, 158
        Art 3(4) 128, 132, 142–144, 147
        Art 3(5) 132
        Art 4 134–135
        Art 4(1) 127, 135–137, 139
        Art 4(1)(a) 127, 135–137

Art 4(1)(b). 136–137
Art 4(1)(c)–(d). 136
Art 4(1)(e)–(f) 136–137
Art 4(1)(g). 136
Art 4(1)(h). 136
Art 4(2) 127, 136–137, 139
Art 4(3)–(4). 127, 136–137, 139
Art 5 . . . . .132, 134–135
Art 5(2) 126
Art 6 . . . . 127, 134–135, 140, 143
Art 6(1) 143
Art 6(2) 143
Art 7 . . . . 128, 132, 134–135, 144
Art 7(3) 126
Art 8 134–135
Art 9 . . . . .142, 144–148
Art 9(1) 144–145
Art 9(2) 145
Art 9(3) 145, 148
Art 10 . . . . 132, 139–141, 275, 278
Art 10(1) 7, 14, 139
Art 10(2) 139, 141
Art 11 . . . . .132, 139, 142
Art 11(1) 139–140
Art 11(2)–(5). 140
Art 11(5)(a)–(b). 140
Art 13 . . . . 127, 129, 132, 140–142
Art 18 128
Ch III
Art 19 137
Art 19(1) 137
Art 19(2) 138–139
Art 19(3) 138
Art 21 . . . . 142, 148
Art 22(1) 132
Art 22(2) 131
Art 23 135
Art 25 . . . . 149, 167
Art 26 149
Art 28 . . . . 126, 128
Regulation 864/2007 on the law applicable to non–contractual obligations
  (Rome II Regulation), [2007] OJ L199/40. . . . 14, 59, 61, 87, 92, 99, 104, 125–126,
            128–129, 138, 144, 151–166, 169–170, 172, 174–182, 184, 239
Preamble. 151
  Recital 6 . . . . .152, 155
  Recital 7 . . . . .155, 163
  Recital 10 158

Recital 11 156
Recital 12 180
Recital 15 163
Recital 16 164
Recital 19 166
Recital 20 167
Recitals 24–25. 172
Recital 26 174
Recitals 27–28. 176–177
Recital 31 177
Recital 32 181
Recitals 155, 169, 180
Ch I
Art 1 163
Art 1(1) 154, 157
Art 1(2) 157–158, 289
Art 1(2)(a)–(g). 157
Art 1(3) 157, 179, 181
Art 2(1) 156, 164
Art 2(2) 155
Art 3 . . . . .154, 160, 176
Ch II
Art 4 . . . . .167–168, 170
Art 4(1) 163–165, 172, 239–240
Art 4(2) 162, 164–167, 175, 239
Art 4(3) 162, 164–165, 239
Art 5 . . . . .166, 169, 171
Art 5(1) 156, 166, 171
Art 5(1)(a)–(b). 166–167
Art 5(1)(c) 167
Art 5(2) 167, 171
Art 5a. 162
Art 5a(1)–(4). 162
Art 6 . . . . .166, 169–171
Art 6(1)–(2). 170
Art 6(3) 170
Art 6(3)(a)–(b). 170
Art 6(4) 171
Art 7 . . . . .172, 240
Art 8 174
Art 8(1)–(3). 174
Art 8a. 176
Art 9 . . . . .175, 177
Ch III
Art 10(1) 181
Art 11(1) 181
Art 12(1) 181

Ch IV
   Art 14 . . . . 155, 162, 171, 174, 177–178
   Art 14(1) 177
   Art 14(1)(a)–(b). 177
   Art 14(2) 177
   Art 14(3) 144, 177–178
Ch V
   Art 15 . . . . 14, 178–179
   Art 15(a)–(d) 178
   Art 15(c) 180
   Art 15(e)–(h) 178
   Art 16 181
   Art 17 . . . . 164, 173–174, 240
   Art 21 . . . . 157, 179
   Art 22 . . . . 157, 179
Ch VI
   Art 23 165
   Art 23(1)–(2) 165
   Art 26 181
   Art 28 167–168
   Art 28(1)–(2) 167
Ch VII
   Art 30(2) 161
   Arts 31–32. 153
Regulation 4/2009 on jurisdiction, applicable law, recognition and decisions and
   cooperation in matters relating to maintenance obligations, [2009] OJ L7/1 158

Resolutions

Resolution of 14 October 1996 laying down the priorities for cooperation in the
   field of
justice and home affairs for the period from 1 July 1996 to 30 June 1998 151

France

Civil Code (*Code civil*) 45

Germany

Code of Civil Procedure (*Zivilprozessordnung*)
   Art 23. 104

Greece

Code of Civil Procedure (*Κώδικας Πολιτικής Δικονομίας*)
   Art 40. 66

Netherlands

Civil code 29
Wet op de formeel buitenlandse vennootschappen (Law on formally foreign companies)
219–220

United Kingdom

Civil Jurisdiction and Judgments Act 1982
  s 42(3) 44
Income and Corporation Taxes Act 1970 215

United States of America

Alien Torts Statute 1789. 230
Alien Torts Statute, 28 USC §1350 (2000). 227–237, 239

Table of Conventions, Treaties, etc

Berne Convention for the Protection of Literary and Artistic Works of 1886. 175
Brussels Convention on Jurisdiction and the Enforcement of Judgments in Civil
   and Commercial Matters 1968 (Brussels I Convention) 13, 19–22, 24–31,
   33–34, 36–37, 43–44, 46, 60–63, 65, 68, 70, 72–75, 78, 81–82, 85, 87, 89, 91–93,
   100–101, 103–104, 108–109, 112–113, 115–117, 119, 125, 130, 151–152, 156, 184–185
   Preamble. 25
     Recital 326
     Recital 3(4) 25
   Title II
     Section 1
       Art 2 . . . . .26, 75, 108, 112
       Art 2(2). 26
       Art 3 46
       Art 4 . . . . 46, 63
     Section 2
       Art 5 112
       Art 5(1). 90
       Art 5(3). 176
       Art 5(5). 63
       Art 6 112
     Section 3
       Arts 7–12 112
     Section 4
       Art 13 . . . . .63–64, 66, 112
       Art 13(1). 63–64, 89
       Art 13(2). 63–64
       Art 13(3). 63–64, 66
       Art 13(3)(a) 63–64
       Art 13(3)(b) 63–64, 66
       Art 14 112
       Art 14(1). 64
       Art 15 112
     Section 5
       Art 16 . . . . 26, 112
       Art 16(2). 56
     Section 6
       Art 17 112
       Art 17(1). 81
       Art 18 112
     Section 8 106

      Arts 21–23 26
    Section 9
      Art 24 33–34
  Title III 28
    Section 1
      Art 28 111
  Title V
    Art 53 43
  Title VII
    Art 59 46
  1971 Protocol 19
Convention on the Grant of European Patents 1973 (Patent Convention) . . . 57, 101–102
  Art 64(3) 101
Convention on Insolvency Proceedings 1995 . . . . 184–185, 187–188, 192, 195
  Art 49(3) 184
Convention on the Recognition and Enforcement of Foreign Arbitral Awards
  1958 (New York Convention) 21, 33, 35, 38, 40, 130
Council of Europe Convention on Certain International Aspects of Bankruptcy
  1990 (Istanbul Convention) 187
Double Taxation Convention between the UK and The Netherlands
  Art 4(3) 223
EU Charter of Fundamental Rights 239
EU Convention on extradition 1995 16
EU Convention on extradition 1996 16
European Convention for the Protection of Human Rights and Fundamental
  Freedoms 121–122, 212, 239
Geneva Conventions 159
Hague Convention on the jurisdiction of the contractual forum in matters relating
  to the international sale of goods 1958 78
Hague Convention on the Service Abroad of Judicial and Extrajudicial Documents
  in Civil or Commercial Matters 1965 251
  Art 15 251
Hague Convention on the choice of court 1965 . . . . 78, 85
Hague Convention on choice of court agreements 2005 . . . . 3, 119
Hague Convention on the Law Applicable to Products Liability 1972 (Products
  Liability Convention) 167
Hague Convention on Traffic Accidents 167
Istanbul Convention. *See* Council of Europe Convention on Certain International
  Aspects of Bankruptcy 1990
Lugano Convention on Jurisdiction and the Enforcement of Judgments in
  Civil and Commercial Matters 1988 . . . . 20, 52, 74–75, 80, 119
Lugano Convention on Jurisdiction and the Enforcement of Judgments in
  Civil and Commercial Matters 2007 20
New York Convention. *See* Convention on the Recognition and Enforcement of
  Foreign Arbitral Awards 1958
Paris Convention for the Protection of Industrial Property 1883 174
Patent Convention. *See* Convention on the Grant of European Patents 1973

Principles of European Contract Law 133
Products Liability Convention. *See* Hague Convention on the Law Applicable
  to Products Liability 1972
Rome Convention on the law applicable to contractual obligations 1980 125–126,
                               128–129, 132–134, 136–143, 146–148, 151, 159, 166
  Art 1(1) 133
  Arts 3 147
  Art 6(2) 135
  Art 6(2)(a)–(b) 135
  Art 7 146
  Art 7(1) 146
  Art 7(2) 146–147
  Art 10 179
  Art 11 141
  Art 18 137
Schengen Implementing Agreement 16
Uncitral Model Law 208
UNIDROIT Principles 133
Vienna Convention on contracts for the international sale of goods 3
Vienna Convention on Diplomatic Relations 75

1

Introduction

1.1 THE CONCEPT, NATURE AND DEVELOPMENT OF PRIVATE INTERNATIONAL LAW

Sometimes viewed as a rather musty set of doctrinal principles rooted in nineteenth century European jurisprudence, it is in fact a dynamic and rapidly evolving field of direct relevance to sophisticated lawyers working in a broad spectrum of international and transnational contexts.[1]

This quote of course to some degree may be self-serving, as one likes to think that one's area of expertise is exciting, relevant. Etc. However even for the practicing lawyer not generally interested in the conceptual analysis of law, private international law is an increasingly relevant part of practice in a globalised world, with globalised clients, and with a level of sophistication of those clients even if they are of the SME type (Small and medium sized enterprises).

The terminology employed to denote the subject-matter of this volume, varies. The two most commonly used terms are 'conflict of laws' and 'private international law'. The former conjures up *clash of civilisation* type scenarios: *Economic exchange brings people into contact; it does not bring them into agreement.*[2] This is not a true reflection of the overall nature of the subject: very often private international law involves calm determination rather than strive, and often (especially in EU private international law) legal certainty takes precedence over suitability.

Private International Law or 'International private law' by contrast would seem to suggest a more mundane view on the 'international' conflicts which we shall study in this volume. I have opted to employ the term 'private international law' for this volume, especially because the among common lawyers more prevalent use of 'conflict of laws' refers more specifically to the second of the three steps in private international law only.

There are three distinct processes in PIL (more on this below), which have led to varying degrees of convergence or harmonisation: Jurisdiction: what court has jurisdiction to hear the case – Applicable law: what law will that court apply – and Recognition and enforcement of foreign judgments. The classic, narrow view of PIL equates with

---

[1] Stewart, D., Private international law: A dynamic and developing field, *University of Pennsylvania Journal of International* law, 2009, 1121–1131.

[2] Samuel P. Huntington, *The Clash of civilisations and the remaking of world order*, New York, Simon & Schuster, 1996, 218.

Conflict of laws proper:' the rules applied by *domestic* courts to determine which laws apply to cases that involve people in different countries or different nationalities, or transactions which cross international boundaries.'[3] The broader approach includes jurisdiction and enforcement: what are the rules and needs – if any – for restricting the authority of domestic courts to hear disputes involving foreigners and foreign transactions, and is there /should there be a binding obligation to recognise and enforce judgments resulting from adjudication in foreign courts.[4]

In all three areas of Private international law, there has been increasing international convergence or even harmonisation, with the European example being the most advanced (as well as residually disputed), however it is important to keep in mind that private international law conceptually neither seeks nor requires regulatory convergence: private international law is and remains *national* law, with the potential and evolving exception of a growing number of subject-matter in European law. Lack of convergence in national private international law approaches may be an externality of the nature of these laws but not necessarily one which has traditionally been seen as triggering a requirement for regulatory convergence or harmonisation. Rather, conversely, private international law divergence has acted as a means for regulatory competition[5] (or even an instrument to attract foreign direct investment) and e.g. the English courts have always been quite happy under common law to entertain claims with a foreign element. Recently, other jurisdictions, too, such as France and The Netherlands, have appreciated the 'commercial' interest in attracting cases through the use of private international law.

Notwithstanding convergence and harmonisation, private international al law remains dramatically different from public international law in 2 main aspects:[6] it aims to regulate relationships between private parties, not States; it is designed to function primarily at the domestic level, in domestic courts.

There is limited overlap, in particular in sovereign and diplomatic immunity; and government seizure of property,[7] however these will not be addressed in this volume. More recently, the rekindling of the discussions with respect to extraterritoriality of 'public' law (CSR or corporate social responsibility, which is discussed further in this book; and jurisdiction of criminal courts to try crimes committed abroad). With the exception of the latter point, however, private international law does not traditionally relate to 'public' law: criminal law; extradition; immigration or deportation.

---

[3] Stewart, D., note above, 1121.

[4] Ibid, 1122.

[5] Alex Mills refers to other benefits attributed to not pursuing harmonisation of substantive law: accountability, legitimacy., cultural diversity. See Mills, A., *The Confluence of Public and Private International Law*, Cambridge, CUP, 2009, p.186 (with reference to a range of authors).

[6] Ibid, 1123; Stewart adds a third: private international law functions 'to harmonize and unify diverse national laws and practices in order to facilitate the movement of goods, services, and peoples around the globe.' – something however which increasing parts of public international law strive to achieve, too.

[7] See also Briggs, A, *The Conflict of Laws*, Oxford, OUP, 2008, 2.

1.2 SOURCES OF PRIVATE INTERNATIONAL LAW

Over and above EU law and national law, the Hague Conference on private international law, established in 1893, is an important source of private international law. It is active in largely 3 areas: protection of children, family and property relations; international legal co-operation and litigation (including the 2005 Convention on choice of court agreements); and international commerce and finance law (including a potential future Convention on choice of law for contracts). It has adopted 39 Conventions, and has 72 Members (States), including the EU separately.[8] As the Conference works with Conventions, there is unequal ratification practice.

UNCITRAL works mostly through 'model laws', e.g. on international commercial arbitration, and the 1980 Vienna Convention on contracts for the international sale of goods (application of which may be excluded by the contracting parties). However one could argue that UNCITRAL is concerned with harmonisation of substantive law, thus falling outside the traditional scope of private international law. Other organisations, such as the Council of Europe, have issued the occasional Conventions, for instance on foreign money liabilities.

1.3 THE 3 PROCESSES OF PIL, AND STANDARD 'CONNECTING FACTORS'

As noted, private international law involves the determination of jurisdiction (forum), applicable law (*lex causae*) – often also denoted as choice of law or conflict of laws proper – and recognition and enforcement. Focus in the classic area of academic development, i.e. the 19th /early 20th century was on applicable law, especially though the works of Friedrich Carl von Savigny (see further). Practice has recently re-emphasised the relevance of jurisdiction, so much so that once jurisdiction is established parties may be tempted to settle out of court, as the jurisdiction may fairly predictably determine the outcome of the case. Jurisdiction is relevant for a variety of reasons:[9]

1.3.1 Procedural issues

Choice of law never applies to these issues: they always depend on the law of the country where the proceedings are successfully brought: the *lex fori*.[10] Needless to say, what is and what is not part of 'procedure' in itself may be the subject of discussion. Recovery of cost[11] and the possibility of legal aid are fairly undisputed examples of procedural issues. Whether conditional fees are allowed and under what format, another, as is whether the

---

[8] Council Decision 2006/719 on the accession of the Community to the Hague Conference on Private International law, OJ [2006] L297/1. The legal base was what is now Article 67 TFEU (see further), in combination with Article 300 EC: the Treaty Article on the conclusion of international agreements.

[9] See also Hartley, T.C., *International Commercial Litigation*, Cambridge, CUP, 2009, 6 ff.

[10] See generally Panagopoulos, G., 'Substance and procedure in private international law', *Journal of Private International Law*, 2005, 69–92.

[11] 'Justice is what you can afford to be done' in practice often turns out to be rather true.

losing party pays the fees of winning party?[12] Obtaining evidence[13] (such as extensive depositions in the US in pre-trial discovery); whether there is trial by jury or not (e.g. the presence of jury trial in civil cases in the US cf. elsewhere); whether parties need to furnish the bench with their own proof of the foreign law which may apply, or whether the bench is supposed to know this itself (*ius novit curia*): these, too, are definitely part of procedural aspects. Whether statutes of limitation are, is more disputed.

1.3.2 Application of the law

Even when applicable law has been determined, not all judges will apply it in the same way. This is quite obviously the case where provisions of these laws are fairly open-ended (e.g. 'general wellbeing of the child' in custody cases) and whence the cultural context of the court. Differences in competence and know-how of the bench play a role here, too. Not all judges in all States will be *au fait* with securitisation contracts, or patent-licensing agreements. More simply: *Gleichlauf*, the circumstance in which the court with jurisdiction (the forum) applies 'his own' laws (i.e. the laws of that State) to the dispute, may often seem attractive.[14] Bias (e.g. against foreign corporations), incompetence and corruption, finally, are evidently strong reasons why one might not (or conversely, prefer to) wish to end up in one court or another.

Carl Friedrich von Savigny (1779–1861)'s *A Treatise on the Conflict of Laws and the limits of their operation in respect of place and time*,[15] the eighth and final volume of his standard work on Roman private law, advocates a 'blindfold' approach to private international law. The rules of private international law identify applicable law without taking account of the contents of that law or of any other.

Von Savigny rejects both the personal focus of tribal law after the fall of the Roman empire (nowadays still present in nationality and personal capacity issues), and the territorial focus of the early Middle-Ages (custom applies to a given territory), as well as the predominant attention in the late Middle Ages to what the scope of application of the statute ought to be. Von Savigny's focus is on the *Sitz* or 'seat' of a relationship in law: which legal order has the closest connection to the specific facts at issue, where lies the nexus of the case, which legal order *connects* predominantly to the case. In the von Savigny approach, conflict of laws ought to become neutral. As one might expect, however, there are plenty of opportunities for the court seized, to 'massage' the result of this objective analysis: *inter alia* by the very classification (see below), the approach to the 'incidental issue' (see further), and the application of public policy exceptions.

Despite discussion and criticism of the impact of von Savigny's work, his working method continues to determine the private international law process especially in the choice of law stage. Determination of applicable law involves 3 steps:

---

[12] Although in that case recovery of such costs may not always be straightforward at the enforcement stage.

[13] Evidence may play a role though in the substantial part of the trial, e.g. in assessing damages in tort cases.

[14] In fact, sometimes the very opposite is true: especially in cases of express choice of law by commercial parties, one or other of the parties may wish to have say English law applied by a non-English court. For one risks having the truly initiated apply the law in a way which differs from the general understanding of that law.

[15] It is generally available in English in the 1869 translation by William Guthrie, and published in Edinburgh by T & T Clark.

1.3.2.1 Characterisation [qualification |FR] of the legal question

This requires the facts to be accommodated within one –perhaps more- legal categories to which a choice of law rule may be applied. Further details on characterisation are included below. Characterisation is obviously a crucial step. Whether it is harmonised or not, i.e. whether national courts have full discretion to characterise the issue or not, determines in large degree the applicable law outcome. Briggs employs the rather useful reference to a mail room sorter: the judge needs to put the facts into a particular pigeon hole which in turn will lead to the parcel being delivered on one or other doorstep.[16]

1.3.2.2 Connecting Factor

Each legal category then has a connecting factor (European law tends to call this the 'linking factor'): which legal system connects most closely with this category of legal questions.

1.3.2.3 Lex Causae

Finally, one applies the substantive law of the legal system identified by step 2: that is, the *lex causae*.

To give a simple example: capacity to marry (qualification) of a Belgian (nationality: connecting factor) is determined by Belgian law (applicable law).

The standard connecting factors may be divided into two categories: personal, and causal.[17] *Personal connecting factors* are:

domicile; residence, which can be either habitual = ordinary = usual residence or simple residence; and nationality.

Causal connecting factors are in the main:

Lex domicilii; Lex fori; Lex contractus (which may or may not be determined by *lex voluntatis*); *Lex loci contractus; Lex loci actus; Lex delicti* (tort), including the *lex loci delicti commissi*, or the *lex damni; Lex situs* (typically but not exclusively re real estate); *Lex loci celebrationis* (marriage); *Lex incorporationis; Lex protectionis*.

1.4 CHARACTERISATION, *RENVOI* AND THE 'INCIDENTAL' ISSUE OR *VORFRAGE*

Characterisation (French: qualification) of the legal question, '*requires the facts to be accommodated within one – perhaps more – legal categories to which a choice of law rule may be applied.*'[18] These legal categories essentially are branches of private law: capacity to marry; marriage; marital property law; dependence; hereditary succession;

---

[16] Briggs, A., n 7 above, 9.
[17] Briggs, A., n 7 above, 21 ff.
[18] *Ibid*, 9. See also Fawcett, JJ and Carruthers, JM, *Cheshire, North & Fawcett's Private International Law*, 14th ed. Oxford, OUP, 2008, 42 ff.

contracts; torts, etc. Characterisation is a direct result of von Savigny's influence: one employs an objective approach in search of the *Sitz* of the facts. It is not without its faults: in particular, it pays no regard to whether the rule of law chosen to apply in the case was intended to be applied to the facts (whence the US theory of governmental interest analysis, which holds that the State with the greatest interest in having its law applied to a given case, should see it applied). Neither is it without correction: as we shall see in detail below, European private international law often allows for correction of the objective 'Sitz' so as to have the law apply with the 'closest and most real' connection to the case.

Continuing Briggs' mailroom analogy above, it is the manager of the mailroom where the parcel has ended up who will determine what pigeon hole the parcel goes into: is it tort? Is it contract? This is of course a very relevant determination, because not all national private international law uses the same categories. For instance, statutes of limitation are procedural law in some (hence *lex fori*), substantive law in others e.g. linked to the contract, in which case the *lex contractus* will apply which often will be *lex voluntatis*. It is for this reason that harmonisation by the EU attempts as much as possible to harmonise characterisation, too.

A subcategory of characterisation is the so-called 'incidental' issue or *Vorfrage:* it may very well be that national (or EU, as the case may be) law has determined which applicable law is connected to a given legal category, however before one may apply it, one needs to decide on the actual existence of the category in the facts at issue. It is somewhat telling that only two examples always re-surface when the *Vorfrage* is discussed in scholarship.

In *Ogden v Ogden*,[19] The Court of Appeal for England and Wales had to determine whether the marriage, celebrated in England, between an English and a French national, was valid, even though no parental consent was given. The Court of Appeal held that this is a matter of formal validity of the marriage, a characterisation which leads to the *lex locus celebrationis* and hence the application of English law. This made consent not relevant. Had it been considered part of one's capacity to marry, applicable law would have been the law of the nationality of the person alleged to lack marital capacity (hence French law), and hence the marriage would have been invalid.

In *Schwebel v Ungar*,[20] the Canadian Supreme Court had to decide the case of a Jewish husband and wife, married and domiciled in Hungary. En route to relocate to Israel, they stay in Italy, where the husband divorces the wife by *get*. Neither Hungary nor Italy recognise *get*; however Israel, their subsequent domicile of choice, does. The wife subsequently moved to Canada but remains domiciled in Israel, and went through a second ceremony of marriage. The husband subsequently files for nullity of marriage, on the basis of bigamy. The main question therefore relates to the wife's capacity to marry, a characterisation which under Canadian law calls for the application of *lex domicilii*, meaning Israel. The incidental question, however, relates to the validity of the divorce, which under Canadian law leads to either the *lex domicilii* at the relevant time (Hungary), or Italian law, as *lex loci actus*. The Supreme Court nevertheless applies Israeli law, the law applicable to the main question.

Given the relatively few cases in which the *Vorfrage* is dealt with specifically, many argue that notwithstanding the scholarly relevance of the issue of which law decides

[19] [1908] P 46 (CA).
[20] [1964] 48 DLR (2d) 644.

characterisation, and also which one decides the incidental question, in practice they are most often and most probably dealt with in passing. This led to Ehrenzweig famously referring to the *Vorfrage* as *another miscreant of a conceptualism gone rampant*.[21] However, whether characterisation is carried out in accordance with the *lex fori*, not the *lex causae*, even if it may not be subject to great debate in the courts, in practice has a considerable impact.

European law, which is the subject-matter of this volume, has some good examples of the relevance of the issue. For instance, the Regulations which we discuss apply to civil and commercial matters only, not to those resulting from the exercise of public law powers. Whether a particular dispute concerns civil and commercial matters or not, and hence whether it falls within the scope of application of either of these Regulations, may[22] sometimes be adjudicated by the court seized by simple reference to the facts on which the applicant bases his claims.[23] [24] On other occasions the adjudicating court will have to assume jurisdiction temporarily and then apply its conflicts rules to determine which law would apply to the relationship, subsequently to assess under that law whether or not the matter truly is 'civil and commercial'.[25]

European Regulations have also quietly harmonised the approach to the *Vorfrage* in contract law and in torts. For instance, the Rome I Regulation on applicable law in contracts, provides in Article 10(1)[26] that

> The existence and validity of a contract, or of any term of a contract, shall be determined by the law which would govern it under this Regulation if the contract or term were valid.

This cancels out *lex fori* to decide the *Vorfrage*.

Within the context of the insolvency Regulation,[27] the *Vorfrage* takes on a specific form in its Article 13 on 'detrimental' acts, in conjunction with its Article 4(2)(m) on 'the rules relating to the voidness, voidability or unenforceability of legal acts detrimental to all creditors' (see further review of this Article in the relevant Chapter, below).

Renvoi essentially relates to the question whether a reference, by application of conflict of laws rules, to the laws of State X, includes a reference to all laws of that State, including in other words State X' own private international law rules. There are essentially two types of *renvoi*:

a. *Renvoi* = remission |*Rückverweisung* |*Terugverwijzing, herverwijzing* : referral to the *lex fori*
b. *Renvoi au second degré* = transmission |*Weiterverweisung* |*Verderverwijzing*

---

[21] Ehrenzweig, A., *A Treatise on the Conflict of Laws*, St. Paul, 1962, p340. See also Schmidt, T.S., 'The Incidental Question in Private International Law', in *Recueil des Cours: Collected Courses of the Hague Academy of International Law*, 1992, II, 305 ff.

[22] Dickinson, A., *The Rome II Regulation*, Oxford, OUP, 2008, 150.

[23] Case C-292/05 *Lechouritou*, [2007] ECR I-1519: operations conducted by armed forces are one of the characteristic emanations of State sovereignty and as a result, actions based upon them by their very nature do not fall within the scope of the 'Brussels I' Regulation on jurisdiction in civil and commercial matters.

[24] But see Case C-172/91 *Volker Sonntag v Hans Waidmann et al*, [1993] ECR I-1963, where the ECJ found civil and commercial matters even if that was not clear from the legal tradition of the Member State concerned (and where other Member States, too, may have held differently).

[25] In C-271/00, *Gemeente Steenbergen v Baten*, [2002] ECR I-10489, whether the Dutch town acted in a civil and commercial matter or not, had to be determined with reference to Dutch procedural and administrative law.

[26] Further detail in the relevant chapter, below.

[27] Regulation 1346/2000, OJ [2000] L160/1. See the discussion of the Regulation in relevant chapter below.

Advocates of *renvoi* argue that akin to governmental interest analysis, foreign law should only be applied where it is interested in being applied; should foreign law point away from itself, that should be respected. *Renvoi* also plays a role in preventing forum shopping: the case ought to be as closely as possible decided according to what a court would decide which is in all likelihood closest connected to the case. Although one of course wonders why one does not decline jurisdiction altogether (which of course is what English courts regularly do under *forum non conveniens* rules).

Arguments against *renvoi* generally win the day, and certainly have done so principally in EU law. In the case of *renvoi*, the *lex fori* may re-refer to the other law, and a carousel starts which has to stop at some point. Simple *renvoi* halts this however there would not seem to be any particular reason why *lex fori* ought to apply, other than to stop the carrousel, i.e. for reasons of convenience: one wonders why one has *renvoi* at all then.

This argument against *renvoi* holds even more strongly in the case of *Renvoi au second degré*: the carrousel has to be stopped arbitrarily hence why does one have it at all? In this case, moreover, the burden of proof becomes quite heavy.

Consequently many[28] treaties and indeed national laws simply exclude *renvoi*: EU law does too as a more or less general rule,[29] as do, for reasons of legal certainty, most commercial contracts.[30]

1.5 FORUM SHOPPING AND FORUM NON CONVENIENS

Given the relevance of jurisdiction, outlined above, forum shopping is of high importance even to the unsophisticated litigant. Forum shopping is the technique whereby a litigant selects his forum to sue, on the basis of suitability. Suitability lies in any of the reasons outlined above.

Forum shopping is by no means a negative or suspect phenomenon. It arguably only takes on an abusive nature, in those instances where a litigant selects a forum purely on the basis of 'qualities' of the forum which do not serve the rule of law. This would include fora selected for the time they take to decide a case, the technique of the so-called 'torpedo'. In combination with the impossibility of the other party to sue elsewhere,[31] torpedo action literally torpedoes the possibility for the bona fide party to seek timely settlement of his action (justice delayed is justice denied).

According to the doctrine of *forum non conveniens*, as understood in English law, a national court may decline to exercise jurisdiction[32] on the ground that a court in another State, which also has jurisdiction, would objectively be a more appropriate forum for the

---

[28] But see perhaps recent developments in Australia: Gray, A., 'The rise of *renvoi* in Australia: Creating the theoretical framework', *UNSWLJ*, 2007, 103–126.

[29] Recent examples of the discussion include in particular *Iran v Berend*: [2007] EWHC 132 (QB); and Dallah Real Estate: [2010] UKSC 46.

[30] A typical clause would read 'This Agreement shall be governed by and construed and enforced in accordance with the laws of the State of [ ] , excluding its choice of law rules.

[31] In particular, in the case of the Brussels I Regulation, the strict application of the *lis alibi pendens* rule: see below in relevant chapter.

[32] Although the doctrine may also play a role in the enforcement stage: see Whytock, C., and Robertson, C., 'Forum non conveniens and the enforcement of foreign judgments', *Columbia Law Review*, 2011, 1444–1521.

trial of the action, that is to say, a forum in which the case may be tried more suitably for the interests of all the parties and the ends of justice.[33] *Forum non conveniens* is discussed at length further in this volume.

Finally, forum shopping is sometimes also used in a different sense, referring to choice of law: parties opting for one law to apply to their legal relationships rather than another, for reasons of the chosen law giving the parties possibilities which the other law does not have. The most often used (or at least pondered) use of choice of law in this respect lies with parties, both domiciled in one jurisdiction, nevertheless using the laws of a different State because it offers legal instruments which the other does not possess (trusts, for instance, unknown in civil law jurisdictions). I shall clarify further that although European private international law has a certain amount of sympathy for commercially mature parties employing the law in such a way, it does put a certain amount of obstacles in their way, so as to avoid simple avoidance of the law in cases where the State concerned considers a given law to be particularly sensitive to its legal order.

1.6 THE IMPACT OF EUROPEAN LAW ON THE PRIVATE INTERNATIONAL LAW OF THE MEMBER STATES

1.6.1 Legal basis

The legal basis for European private international law has evolved as follows.[34]

---

a. Treaty establishing the European (Economic) Community: Article 220 EEC, subsequently Article 293 EC, now repealed

Member States shall, so far as is necessary, enter into negotiations with each other with a view to securing for the benefit of their nationals:

— the protection of persons and the enjoyment and protection of rights under the same conditions as those accorded by each State to its own nationals,
— the abolition of double taxation within the Community,
— the mutual recognition of companies or firms within the meaning of the second paragraph of Article 48, the retention of legal personality in the event of transfer of their seat from one country to another, and the possibility of mergers between companies or firms governed by the laws of different countries,
— the simplification of formalities governing the reciprocal recognition and enforcement of judgments of courts or tribunals and of arbitration awards.

---

[33] The House of Lords, in *Spiliada Maritime Corporation v Cansulex Ltd* [1987], AC 460, particularly at p 476.
[34] For a good overview of the consecutive changes and their implications, see Dickinson, A., 'European Private International Law: Embracing new horizons or mourning the past?', *Journal of private international law*, 2005, 197–236; Fiorini, A., 'The evolution of European Private International Law', *International and Comparative Law Quarterly*, 2008, 969–984.

b. Maastricht Treaty

TITLE VI – PROVISIONS ON COOPERATION IN THE FIELDS OF JUSTICE AND HOME AFFAIRS

ARTICLE K

Cooperation in the fields of justice and home affairs shall be governed by the following provisions.

ARTICLE K.1

For the purposes of achieving the objectives of the Union, in particular the free movement of persons, and without prejudice to the powers of the European Community, Member States shall regard the following areas as matters of common interest:

1. asylum policy;
2. rules governing the crossing by persons of the external borders of the Member States and the exercise of controls thereon;
3. immigration policy and policy regarding nationals of third countries;
    (a) conditions of entry and movement by nationals of third countries on the territory of Member States;
    (b) conditions of residence by nationals of third countries on the territory of Member States, including family reunion and access to employment;
    (c) combatting unauthorized immigration, residence and work by nationals of third countries on the territory of Member States;
4. combating drug addiction in so far as this is not covered by 7 to 9;
5. combating fraud on an international scale in so far as this is not covered by 7 to 9;
6. judicial cooperation in civil matters;
7. judicial cooperation in criminal matters;
8. customs cooperation;
9. police cooperation for the purposes of preventing and combating terrorism, unlawful drug trafficking and other serious forms of international crime, including if necessary certain aspects of customs cooperation, in connection with the organization of a Union-wide system for exchanging information within a European Police Office (Europol).

---

c. Treaty of Amsterdam

Article 65

Measures in the field of judicial cooperation in civil matters having cross-border implications, to be taken in accordance with Article 67 and in so far as necessary for the proper functioning of the internal market, shall include:

(a) improving and simplifying:
— the system for cross-border service of judicial and extrajudicial documents,
— cooperation in the taking of evidence,
— the recognition and enforcement of decisions in civil and commercial cases, including decisions in extrajudicial cases;
(b) promoting the compatibility of the rules applicable in the Member States concerning the conflict of laws and of jurisdiction;
(c) eliminating obstacles to the good functioning of civil proceedings, if necessary by promoting the compatibility of the rules on civil procedure applicable in the Member States.

Article 67

1. During a transitional period of five years following the entry into force of the Treaty of Amsterdam, the Council shall act unanimously on a proposal from the Commission or on the initiative of a Member State and after consulting the European Parliament.

2. After this period of five years:

— the Council shall act on proposals from the Commission; the Commission shall examine any request made by a Member State that it submit a proposal to the Council,
— the Council, acting unanimously after consulting the European Parliament, shall take a decision with a view to providing for all or parts of the areas covered by this title to be governed by the procedure referred to in Article 251 and adapting the provisions relating to the powers of the Court of Justice.

3. By derogation from paragraphs 1 and 2, measures referred to in Article 62(2)(b) (i) and (iii) shall, from the entry into force of the Treaty of Amsterdam, be adopted by the Council acting by a qualified majority on a proposal from the Commission and after consulting the European Parliament.

4. By derogation from paragraph 2, measures referred to in Article 62(2)(b) (ii) and (iv) shall, after a period of five years following the entry into force of the Treaty of Amsterdam, be adopted by the Council acting in accordance with the procedure referred to in Article 251.

5. By derogation from paragraph 1, the Council shall adopt, in accordance with the procedure referred to in Article 251:

— the measures provided for in Article 63(1) and (2)(a) provided that the Council has previously adopted, in accordance with paragraph 1 of this article, Community legislation defining the common rules and basic principles governing these issues,
— the measures provided for in Article 65 with the exception of aspects relating to family law.

Article 68

1. Article 234 shall apply to this title under the following circumstances and conditions: where a question on the interpretation of this title or on the validity or interpretation of acts of the institutions of the Community based on this title is raised in a case pending before a court or a tribunal of a Member State against whose decisions there is no judicial remedy under national law, that court or tribunal shall, if it considers that a decision on the question is necessary to enable it to give judgment, request the Court of Justice to give a ruling thereon.

2. In any event, the Court of Justice shall not have jurisdiction to rule on any measure or decision taken pursuant to Article 62(1) relating to the maintenance of law and order and the safeguarding of internal security.

3. The Council, the Commission or a Member State may request the Court of Justice to give a ruling on a question of interpretation of this title or of acts of the institutions of the Community based on this title. The ruling given by the Court of Justice in response to such a request shall not apply to judgments of courts or tribunals of the Member States which have become *res judicata*.

Article 69

The application of this title shall be subject to the provisions of the Protocol on the position of the United Kingdom and Ireland and to the Protocol on the position of Denmark and without prejudice to the Protocol on the application of certain aspects of Article 14 of the Treaty establishing the

European Community to the United Kingdom and to Ireland.

Article 68 EC's provision, post Amsterdam, that only courts or tribunals against whose decisions there is no judicial remedy under national law, could petition the Court of Justice for a preliminary ruling, disappeared with the entry into force of the Lisbon Treaty (see below). Pursuant to Article 267 TFEU, the courts and tribunals against whose decisions there is a judicial remedy under domestic law have enjoyed, since that date, the right to refer questions to the Court where acts adopted formerly on the basis of Title IV of the EC Treaty are concerned.[35]

---

d. Treaty on the functioning of the EU – TFEU

Article 67

(ex Article 61 TEC and ex Article 29 TEU)

1. The Union shall constitute an area of freedom, security and justice with respect for fundamental rights and the different legal systems and traditions of the Member States.

2. It shall ensure the absence of internal border controls for persons and shall frame a common policy on asylum, immigration and external border control, based on solidarity between Member States, which is fair towards third-country nationals. For the purpose of this Title, stateless persons shall be treated as third-country nationals.

3. The Union shall endeavour to ensure a high level of security through measures to prevent and combat crime, racism and xenophobia, and through measures for coordination and cooperation between police and judicial authorities and other competent authorities, as well as through the mutual recognition of judgments in criminal matters and, if necessary, through the approximation of criminal laws.

4. The Union shall facilitate access to justice, in particular through the principle of mutual recognition of judicial and extrajudicial decisions in civil matters.

Article 81

(ex Article 65 TEC)

1. The Union shall develop judicial cooperation in civil matters having cross-border implications, based on the principle of mutual recognition of judgments and of decisions in extrajudicial cases. Such cooperation may include the adoption of measures for the approximation of the laws and regulations of the Member States.

2. For the purposes of paragraph 1, the European Parliament and the Council, acting in accordance with the ordinary legislative procedure, shall adopt measures, particularly when necessary for the proper functioning of the internal market, aimed at ensuring:

(a) the mutual recognition and enforcement between Member States of judgments and of decisions in extrajudicial cases;
(b) the cross-border service of judicial and extrajudicial documents;

---

[35] Case C-283/09 *Weryński* [2011] ECR I-601, paras 28 and 29 (Judgment of 17 February 2011); Case C-396/09 *Interedil*, not yet published in ECR, paras 18 ff (Judgment of 20 October 2011).

(c) the compatibility of the rules applicable in the Member States concerning conflict of laws and of jurisdiction;

(d) cooperation in the taking of evidence;

(e) effective access to justice;

(f) the elimination of obstacles to the proper functioning of civil proceedings, if necessary by promoting the compatibility of the rules on civil procedure applicable in the Member States;

(g) the development of alternative methods of dispute settlement;

(h) support for the training of the judiciary and judicial staff.

3. Notwithstanding paragraph 2, measures concerning family law with cross-border implications shall be established by the Council, acting in accordance with a special legislative procedure. The Council shall act unanimously after consulting the European Parliament.

The Council, on a proposal from the Commission, may adopt a decision determining those aspects of family law with cross-border implications which may be the subject of acts adopted by the ordinary legislative procedure. The Council shall act unanimously after consulting the European Parliament.

The proposal referred to in the second subparagraph shall be notified to the national Parliaments. If a national Parliament makes known its opposition within six months of the date of such notification, the decision shall not be adopted. In the absence of opposition, the Council may adopt the decision.

1.6.2 The Development of European Private International Law Policy

As the successive Treaty texts above show, European Union policy on private international law has changed quite dramatically. From a mere and superfluous reference to the possibility for the Member States to conclude Treaties in the private international law area, EU competence has now grown to a more or less standard competence, subject only to the general limits to EU heads of power, including subsidiarity and proportionality.

It was not always thus. The finely tuned legal basis in successive EU Treaties has in the past required some creativity from the European Commission. For instance, Article 220 EEC as it then stood (it has now been repealed, as the copy above shows), did not list choice of law/applicable law as one of the elements of private international law for which, at least with formal Commission involvement, harmonisation through Treaty could be sought.[36] The special jurisdictional rules for contracts led to an increased possibility of forum shopping, as for jurisdiction for contracts, the (then un-harmonised) determination of applicable law also determined the outcome of characteristic performance, upon which the jurisdictional rule hinges. Similarly, for torts, the 'place giving rise to the damage' and the 'place where the damage occurs' are each in themselves determined differently, depending on the applicable law of the contract. This led the Commission to contemplate

---

[36] As noted, neither did 'jurisdiction' per se, which of course did not stop the Brussels Convention, with Commission input, from including it.

the use of the impact, on jurisdiction, of non-harmonised choice of law rules, as a justification or indeed legal basis for harmonisation of choice of law.[37]

Predictability of forum is, as shall be explained at length below, a cornerstone of the jurisdictional regime of the EU. This is apparent both in the relevant statutory instruments themselves, and, perhaps even more so, in their interpretation by the Court of Justice. However, notwithstanding predictability, there are quite a number of instances in the jurisdictional regulations, which lead to a multitude of fora. The preferred European Commission method to ensure predictability, may therefore lie less in promoting singularity of jurisdiction, and ever more in unification of applicable law, both by harmonising substantive law through positive harmonisation (especially in consumer protection law and in other areas where the EU legislator perceives 'weaker' parties in legal relationships), and on harmonising conflicts rules on choice of law.[38]

The European 'conflicts resolution' lies in an ever expanding harmonisation of the rules on all three steps of private international law.[39] The original Treaty foundations for EU intervention in this sector are but a distant memory. As noted, the origins of European private international law lie in Internal Market law. Currently, the emphasis is on the European judicial area, with undeniably a much stronger emphasis on the citizen.

The further harmonisation of substantive EU law may be, some advocate, the next logical step in the European conflicts resolution. Over and above the debate on, inter alia, the draft common frame of reference,[40] a quiet harmonisation revolution has already taken place in those instances where European Regulations have harmonised the approach to the *Vorfrage* in contract law and in torts. The Rome I Regulation on applicable law in contracts, provides in Article 10(1)[41] that

> The existence and validity of a contract, or of any term of a contract, shall be determined by the law which would govern it under this Regulation if the contract or term were valid.

This cancels out *lex fori* to decide the *Vorfrage*. A more advanced degree of harmonisation in a similar context is reached by the Rome II Regulation on the law applicable to non-contractual obligations, which defines in Article 15 what shall be the scope of the applicable law; among the list of issues, there are definitely some (e.g. 'assessment of damages') which some of the Member States would have otherwise classified as being of a procedural nature, hence subject to *lex fori*.

One obvious disadvantage of the current Commission focus, lies in its disregard for the benefits of regulatory competition. As the very existence of debate especially on applicable law shows, Member States have a different approach to a wide variety of issues in private law. Far from merely serving as an obstacle to the Internal Market, this competition is essential in shaping, through commercial trial and error, attractive

---

[37] See also Pocar, F. 'Some remarks on the relationship between the Rome I and the Brussels I Regulations', in Ferrari and Leible (eds.), *Rome I Regulation – The Law applicable to contractual obligations in Europe*, Munich, Sellier, 2009, (343–348) 343.

[38] See also Pocar, n 37 above, 344. Incidentally, Prof Pocar would seem to favour parallelism between forum and applicable law as 'the best way to ensure the coherence of the system and the predictability of its solutions' (344). It might. However it would also deny the very nature of private international law.

[39] See also Symeonides, S., 'Rome II and tort conflicts: A missed opportunity', *American Journal of Comparative Law*, 2008, 174.

[40] Further discussed in the chapter on the Rome I Regulation, below.

[41] Further detail in the relevant chapter, below.

contractual and other provisions which assist in the creation of an internal market and moreover help European business that act on a global scale.[42]

The *Tampere European Council* is often signalled out as a turning point in the Commission (and Council) approach to private international law. The European Council held a special meeting on 15 and 16 October 1999 in Tampere on the creation of an area of freedom, security and justice in the European Union. The boost which had been given to this part of the EU Treaty in the Treaty of Amsterdam, gave the Commission especially a mandate to put forward proposals in areas of national law which until then had been the exclusive domain of the Member States. The Presidency Conclusions after the meeting, read in relevant part

---

B. A GENUINE EUROPEAN AREA OF JUSTICE

28. In a genuine European Area of Justice individuals and businesses should not be prevented or discouraged from exercising their rights by the incompatibility or complexity of legal and administrative systems in the Member States.

V. Better access to justice in Europe

29. In order to facilitate access to justice the European Council invites the Commission, in co-operation with other relevant fora, such as the Council of Europe, to launch an information campaign and to publish appropriate "user guides" on judicial co-operation within the Union and on the legal systems of the Member States. It also calls for the establishment of an easily accessible information system to be maintained and up-dated by a network of competent national authorities.

30. The European Council invites the Council, on the basis of proposals by the Commission, to establish minimum standards ensuring an adequate level of legal aid in cross-border cases throughout the Union as well as special common procedural rules for simplified and accelerated cross-border litigation on small consumer and commercial claims, as well as maintenance claims, and on uncontested claims. Alternative, extra-judicial procedures should also be created by Member States.

31. Common minimum standards should be set for multilingual forms or documents to be used in cross-border court cases throughout the Union. Such documents or forms should then be accepted mutually as valid documents in all legal proceedings in the Union.

32. Having regard to the Commission's communication, minimum standards should be drawn up on the protection of the victims of crime, in particular on crime victims' access to justice and on their rights to compensation for damages, including legal costs. In addition, national programmes should be set up to finance measures, public and non-governmental, for assistance to and protection of victims.

VI. Mutual recognition of judicial decisions

33. Enhanced mutual recognition of judicial decisions and judgements and the necessary approximation of legislation would facilitate co-operation between authorities and the judicial protection of individual rights. The European Council therefore endorses the principle of mutual

---

[42] See also my contribution 'To unity and beyond? The boundaries of European Private International Law and the European Ius Commune', in A. Verbeke et al (eds.), *Liber Amicorum Walter Pintens*, Cambridge, Intersentia, 2012, 1459–1485.

recognition which, in its view, should become the cornerstone of judicial co-operation in both civil and criminal matters within the Union. The principle should apply both to judgements and to other decisions of judicial authorities.

34. In civil matters the European Council calls upon the Commission to make a proposal for further reduction of the intermediate measures which are still required to enable the recognition and enforcement of a decision or judgement in the requested State. As a first step these intermediate procedures should be abolished for titles in respect of small consumer or commercial claims and for certain judgements in the field of family litigation (e.g. on maintenance claims and visiting rights). Such decisions would be automatically recognised throughout the Union without any intermediate proceedings or grounds for refusal of enforcement. This could be accompanied by the setting of minimum standards on specific aspects of civil procedural law.

35. With respect to criminal matters, the European Council urges Member States to speedily ratify the 1995 and 1996 EU Conventions on extradition. It considers that the formal extradition procedure should be abolished among the Member States as far as persons are concerned who are fleeing from justice after having been finally sentenced, and replaced by a simple transfer of such persons, in compliance with Article 6 TEU. Consideration should also be given to fast track extradition procedures, without prejudice to the principle of fair trial. The European Council invites the Commission to make proposals on this matter in the light of the Schengen Implementing Agreement.

36. The principle of mutual recognition should also apply to pre-trial orders, in particular to those which would enable competent authorities quickly to secure evidence and to seize assets which are easily movable; evidence lawfully gathered by one Member State's authorities should be admissible before the courts of other Member States, taking into account the standards that apply there.

37. The European Council asks the Council and the Commission to adopt, by December 2000, a programme of measures to implement the principle of mutual recognition. In this programme, work should also be launched on a European Enforcement Order and on those aspects of procedural law on which common minimum standards are considered necessary in order to facilitate the application of the principle of mutual recognition, respecting the fundamental legal principles of Member States.

VII. Greater convergence in civil law

38. The European Council invites the Council and the Commission to prepare new procedural legislation in cross-border cases, in particular on those elements which are instrumental to smooth judicial co-operation and to enhanced access to law, e.g. provisional measures, taking of evidence, orders for money payment and time limits.

39. As regards substantive law, an overall study is requested on the need to approximate Member States' legislation in civil matters in order to eliminate obstacles to the good functioning of civil proceedings. The Council should report back by 2001.

The 2005 the Hague programme[43] illustrates the ambitions of the European Commission in this respect:

---

[43] COM(2005) 184

(9) Civil and criminal justice: guaranteeing an effective European area of justice for all

A European area of justice is more than an area where judgements obtained in one Member State are recognised and enforced in other Member States, but rather an area where effective access to justice is guaranteed in order to obtain and enforce judicial decisions. To this end, the Union must envisage not only rules on jurisdiction, recognition and conflict of laws, but also measures which build confidence and mutual trust among Member States, creating minimum procedural standards and ensuring high standards of quality of justice systems, in particular as regards fairness and respect for the rights of defence. Mutual understanding can be further pursued through the progressive creation of a "European judicial culture" that the Hague Programme calls for, based on training and networking. A coherent strategy in the EU's relations with third countries and international organisations is also needed.

In the field of civil justice, completion of the Programme on mutual recognition of decisions in civil and commercial matters is of the utmost importance. It will involve the adoption of legislative proposals already presented by the Commission, or in the process of being put forward, and launching consultations in order to prepare new legislation not yet subject to mutual recognition (such as family property issues, successions and wills). Another fundamental aspect to be addressed is the enforcement of judicial decisions and mutual recognition of public and private documents. Regarding the EU substantive contract law, a Common Frame of Reference (CFR), to be used as a toolbox to improve coherence and quality of EU legislation, will be adopted in 2009 at the latest.

Regarding criminal justice, approximation and the establishment of minimum standards of several aspects of procedural law (such as ne bis in idem, handling evidence or judgements in absentia) are instrumental in building mutual confidence and pursuing mutual recognition. Concerning the latter, several actions must be carried forward in order to ensure efficient and timely action by law enforcement authorities (such as mutual recognition of non-custodial pre-trial supervision measures, or recognition and execution of prison sentences) and, more generally, to replace traditional mutual assistance with new instruments based on mutual recognition. Eurojust should be considered as the key actor for developing European judicial cooperation in criminal matters. Its role should be supported and its potentialities fully exploited in the light of the experience acquired and in view of future developments. In this context, the Commission will also follow up its previous work and the possibilities afforded by the Constitution, as regards improving the protection of the Union's financial interests.

The 2010 European Council's *Stockholm Programme*[44] continues on this path:

As regards civil matters, the European Council considers that the process of abolishing all intermediate measures (the exequatur), should be continued during the period covered by the Stockholm Programme. At the same time the abolition of the exequatur will also be accompanied by a series of safeguards, which may be measures in respect of procedural law as well as of conflict-of-law rules.

Mutual recognition should, moreover, be extended to fields that are not yet covered but are essential to everyday life, for example succession and wills, matrimonial property rights and the property

[44] OJ [2010] C115/1.

consequences of the separation of couples, while taking into consideration Member States' legal systems, including public policy, and national traditions in this area.

The European Council considers that the process of harmonising conflict-of-law rules at Union level should also continue in areas where it is necessary, like separation and divorces. It could also include the area of company law, insurance contracts and security interests.

The European Council also highlights the importance of starting work on consolidation of the instruments adopted so far in the area of judicial cooperation in civil matters. First and foremost the consistency of Union legislation should be enhanced by streamlining the existing instruments. The aim should be to ensure the coherence and user-friendliness of the instruments, thus ensuring a more efficient and uniform application thereof.

The European Council invites the Commission to:

— assess which safeguards are needed to accompany the abolition of exequatur and how these could be streamlined,
— assess whether there are grounds for consolidation and simplification in order to improve the consistency of existing Union legislation,
— follow up on the recent study on the possible problems encountered with regard to civil status documents and access to registers of such documents.

In light of the findings, the Commission could submit appropriate proposals taking into account the different legal systems and legal traditions in the Member States. In the short term a system allowing citizens to obtain their own civil status documents easily could be envisaged. In the long term, it might be considered whether mutual recognition of the effects of civil status documents could be appropriate, at least in certain areas. Work developed by the International Commission on Civil Status should be taken into account in this particular field.

Throughout this volume, references are made to specific examples of the ambitious program of both Council and Commission in the development of a harmonised European private international law. The pace and depth of this harmonisation process is such as to have triggered calls for codification of European private international law.[45]

---

[45] See for an accurate perception of the challenges involved, Fallon, M., Lagarde, P., Poillot-Peruzzetto (eds.), *Quelle architecture pour un code européen de droit international privé*, Brussels, Peter Lang, 2012, 388p.

2

The Core of European Private International Law: Jurisdiction

2.1 SUMMARY

2.1.1 The Brussels I Regulation

Jurisdiction for civil and commercial matters in courts of the EU Member States is subject to the 'Brussels I' Regulation, *Regulation 44/2001 on jurisdiction and the recognition and enforcement of judgments in civil and commercial matters*. The Regulation is alternatingly referred to as 'Brussels I', or 'JR' ('Jurisdiction Regulation') or the 'EEX' Regulation.[46] Precursor to this Regulation was the Brussels Convention with the same name, of 27 September 1968, generally known as the 'EEX' Convention. This was a classic instrument of international law, a Treaty, sanctioned by but otherwise outside of the EEC Treaty,[47] and had entered into force on 1 February 1973. With successive Member States joining up as they entered the Community, the EEX Convention became a re-re-re-amended text.

Interestingly, as this was a Convention, rather than EEC law, there are no EEC *travaux préparatoires*. Hence these Conventions work with 'reports', prepared by officials (Council, Commission and/or Parliament), with a little help from academics. Somewhat bizarrely therefore, these non-Union instruments often have an interpretative source which is easier to handle than those of Union law, and which continue to this day to inform the application of the Regulations. This is not without controversy. Relying heavily and fairly inflexibly on now sometimes very old reports to assist with the application of current EU private international law instruments effectively deprives those instruments of the moulding and reshaping in practice which they arguably require. Of course should one hold — such as is the view of the ECJ[48] – that the first and foremost aim of EU law in

---

[46] OJ [2001] L12/1.

[47] Indeed until the 1971 Protocol, the Court of Justice did not have jurisdiction to interpret the Convention.

[48] Since the Treaty of Lisbon, some confusion has crept in on the exact acronym for the European Courts. The 'Court of Justice of the European Union' – CJEU is the collective term for the EU's judicial arm (see Article 19 of the Treaty on European Union), consisting of three separate courts. The predominant court of relevance to questions of EU private international law, is the Court of Justice (CJ), formerly known as the European Court of Justice (ECJ), for most if not all of the relevant cases reach the CJEU via the preliminary review procedure (leading national courts to ask 'Luxemburg' for its authoritative view on a matter of interpretation). It would seem that while 'CJ' would be the most correct form of reference [see also Francis Jacobs in

this area is harmonisation, then adaptation to current requirements may not necessarily be the most important consideration. It makes reliance on pre-EU preparatory documents, perfectly acceptable.

The Lugano Conventions (a 1988 and a 2007 version) have been developed in parallel first with the EEX convention and subsequently with Brussels I. They apply between the EU and most Member States of the European Free Trade Association. Denmark, and the United Kingdom and Ireland, take up a specific position, the former having negotiated a fairly inflexible opt-out of the EU's PIL laws, the latter two a more flexible opt-in regime.

The overriding principle of the JR is that of mutual trust: in *Gasser*,[49] the ECJ noted

> "it must be borne in mind that the Brussels Convention is necessarily based on the trust which the Contracting States accord to each other's legal systems and judicial institutions. It is that mutual trust which has enabled a compulsory system of jurisdiction to be established, which all the courts within the purview of the Convention are required to respect, and as a corollary the waiver by those States of the right to apply their internal rules on recognition and enforcement of foreign judgments in favour of a simplified mechanism for the recognition and enforcement of judgments."

This extract also clearly shows the 'mission creep' which European PIL displayed from its very origin. The initial Treaty basis for European PIL, Article 220 EEC, required the Member States to negotiate conventions i.a. for the purpose of recognition of judgments.[50] In the ensuing Lugano Convention it was quickly determined that mutual recognition of judgments would be easier to stomach if these judgments were based on the same grounds for jurisdiction. From an institutional point of view, this extension of the mandate was probably acceptable, because the Lugano Convention, much as it was the result of an EEC Treaty instruction, took the form of a classic international Treaty.

The 'mutual trust' which the Court emphasised has not in fact led to a high degree of independent application by the Courts of the Member States. Rather the opposite: the strict *lis alibi pendens* rule of Article 27 JR (obliging courts seized last to give way to those seized first – we shall look at the principle in detail below) has made courts keep a rather beady eye on how their counterparts in the other Member States interpret the Regulation. It often results in lack of confidence of those courts. This helps explain the increasing amount of preliminary reviews to the Court of Justice, spurred on by

---

the House of Lords' Select Committee on the EU, http://www.publications.parliament.uk/pa/ld201011/ldselect/ldeucom/128/12805.htm#n8 (para 9)], common form is to continue using 'ECJ'. Which is that I decided to do in current volume, too.

[49] Case C-116/02, [2003] ECR I-14693, para 72. *Idem* in Case C-159/02 *Turner*, [2004] ECR I-3565, para 24.

[50] See also Vandekerckhove, K., in Van Houtte, H., and Pertegas Sender, M. (eds.), *Het nieuwe Europese IPR: Van Verdrag naar Verordening*, Antwerp, Intersentia, 2001, 11 (in particular n 4).

the insistence of the Court that terminology in the regulation be given an 'autonomous' interpretation,[51] and by its tendency to micro-manage the application of the Regulation.[52]

By its nature, the Brussels I Regulation takes precedence over national law, including procedural law on locus standi and interest to bring a case. A national court therefore must first decide whether it has jurisdiction to hear the case under the JR, prior to subsequently (should it find it does have such jurisdiction) reviewing whether the party concerned has an interest in bringing the proceedings.[53]

2.1.2 Scope of Application: Subject-Matter

As determined by Article 1 of the JR, the Regulation applies to 'civil and commercial matters whatever the nature of the court or tribunal' – 'en matière civile et commerciale et quelle que soit la nature de la juridiction'. The Regulation exempts matters from its scope of application, including for 'arbitration',[54] a much discussed exemption which is more likely to apply in a business to business (B2B) context than in business to consumer (B2C).[55]

What is meant by 'civil and commercial', and who decides what it is? In the light of the aforementioned Court of Justice insistence on concepts in the Regulation requiring an autonomous 'European' meaning, there has to be one approach rather than reliance on national law. Common perception has it that the qualification 'civil and commercial' implicitly harbours a distinction between 'civil and commercial' law on the one hand, and 'public law', on the other, and that for lawyers of the original Member States (all of them continental, with a civil law system) the distinction is (or at least was) fairly

---

[51] See e.g. Case C-383/95 *Rutten*, [1997] ECR I-57, para 12–13: 'It is settled law (…) that, in principle, the Court of Justice will interpret the terms of the [Brussels Convention] autonomously so as to ensure that it is fully effective, having regard to the objectives of Article 220 of the EEC Treaty, for the implementation of which it was adopted. That autonomous interpretation alone is capable of ensuring uniform application of the Convention, the objectives of which include unification of the rules on jurisdiction of the Contracting States, so as to avoid as far as possible the multiplication of the bases of jurisdiction in relation to one and the same legal relationship and to reinforce the legal protection available to persons established in the Community by, at the same time, allowing the plaintiff easily to identify the court before which he may bring an action and the defendant reasonably to foresee the Court before which he may be sued.' Note that the Convention having been replaced by the Regulation, the interpretation of the Convention, *mutatis mutandis* (especially of course where material changes to the text have been made), applies to the Regulation.

[52] E.g. recently in Case C-19/09 *Wood Floor Solutions*, [2010] ECR I-2121. The Court interpreted Article 5(1) (b) of the Regulation. Article 5(1) provides for 'special' jurisdiction (jurisdiction over and above the standard rule of the domicile of the defendant) in the case of contracts, and 5(1)(b) in particular adds a presumption for the determination of the 'place of performance of the obligation'. The Court in *Wood Floor Solutions* not only held that the presumption also holds in the case of services provided in several Member States (as opposed to just one), but went on to instruct the national court in detail where the "place of performance of the obligation' lies in the case of commercial agency contracts.

[53] See e.g. Case C-133/11 *Folien Fischer*, not yet reported in ECR, in particular Jaaskinen AG's Opinion. In this case, the defendant argued that plaintiff had no interest in seeking a negative declaration for liability in tort for alleged breach of competition law, because the defendant arguably was not a competitor of plaintiff in that market nor had sought to be for some time. *Folien Fischer* is reviewed further below, under the special jurisdictional rule of Article 5(3) JR.

[54] Arbitration is exempt on the basis of it already being covered by the 1958 New York Convention. See further details below and see generally on the sometimes difficult relationship between EU law and arbitration (including using public policy arguments to deny an arbitration clause), Bermann, G., 'Reconciling European Union law demands with the demands of international arbitration', *Fordham International Law Journal*, 2011, 1192–1216.

[55] See Wolff, S. 'Tanking arbitration or Breaking the System to fix it?', *Columbia Journal of European Law*, 2009, 65.

straightforward,[56] no doubt helped by the presence of 'civil' and 'public' or 'administrative' courts in those Member States. However things were never quite as easy as suggesting that all matters dealt with by 'public' law or 'administrative' courts were excluded from the Brussels Convention cq Regulation. Indeed the Convention already ruled that the decisive element was the 'civil/commercial' v 'public' law nature of the subject-matter, rather than of the court adjudicating on it,[57] and in the 'administrative' law of the original Member States, the correct distinction between these two sets of law has never really been fully settled[58] and continues to lead to complications, e.g. in public procurement law, education etc.

In *LTU/Eurocontrol*, the ECJ held that the Convention (and now by extension, the Regulation), applies to disputes between a public authority and a private individual, where the former has not acted in the exercise of its public powers.[59]-[60] *Frahuil* added that the specific legal obligation which lies at the foundation of the claim, determines applicability.[61] Litigation in environmental matters is a current example of how things can get a bit muddled, private enforcement of 'public' law such as competition law undoubtedly a future complication.[62]

2.1.3 Scope of Application – Ratione Personae

The Brussels I Regulation is applicable in three cases:

1. The defendant in the legal proceedings is domiciled in a Member State. Its nationality is irrelevant – as is the nationality and domicile of the plaintiff; or
2. A court in a Member State has exclusive jurisdiction on the basis of one of the grounds listed in Article 22, whatever the domicile of the parties; or
3. At least one of the parties (which could be the plaintiff) is domiciled in one of the Member States and a valid choice of forum clause has been made in accordance with Article 23.

A core jurisdictional claim of the Regulation is the domicile of the defendant. For natural persons, Article 59 holds that the laws of the Member States determine whether a person is domiciled in that State. For a company, legal person or association of natural persons, Article 60 aims to make the rules more transparent and perhaps encourages harmonisation by listing three possible locations only: statutory seat (a term not known in English

---

[56] See e.g. the *Schlosser* report, [1979] OJ C59/71, para 23 ff.

[57] Occasionally, both criminal and administrative courts give judgment in a civil or commercial matter: see *ibid*, 23.

[58] See e.g. the *service public v puissance publique* discussion in Schwarze, J., *European Administrative Law*, London, Sweet & Maxwell, 1992, 14.

[59] Case 29/76, [1976] ECR 1541, as recalled by Colomer AG in his opinion in Case C-292/05 *Lechouritou*, [2007] ECR I-1519, 25. See also Case 814/79 *Ruffer*, [1980] ECR 3807, and C-271/00 *Gemeente Steenbergen v Baten*, [2002] ECR I-10489.

[60] See also the Evrigenis/Kerameus Report which speaks of the exercise of 'sovereign power' as the distinctive element: [1986] OJ C298/1, para 28.

[61] Case C-265/02, [2004] ECR I-1543.

[62] See also Hess, Pfeiffer, Schlosser, *The Brussels I Regulation 44/2001 – Application and Enforcement in the EU*, Oxford, Hart, 2008, 22 ff (generally referred to as the *Heidelberg* report).

or Irish law: hence Article 60(2) refers to registered office or place of incorporation[63]); central administration; principal place of business. These three concepts occurring in the Regulation, they have to be given an autonomous meaning. 'Registered office', central administration and principal place of business are however also concepts used within the context of the Treaty Articles on free movement of establishment. Hence inspiration may probably be sought there.

2.1.4 The Jurisdictional Rules of the Regulation

The most logical way of studying the Regulation, is by reviewing jurisdiction in descending order of exclusivity and specificity: the most specific and exclusive first.[64] This leads to the following matrix:

1. Exclusive jurisdiction, regardless of domicile: Article 22;
2. Jurisdiction by appearance: Article 24;
3. Insurance, consumer and employment contracts: Articles 8–21;
4. Agreements on Jurisdiction ('choice of forum'): Article 23;
5. General jurisdiction: defendants domiciled in the Member State where a court is seized: Article 2[65]
6. 'Special' jurisdiction: defendants domiciled in another Member State: Articles 5–7;
7. 'Residual' jurisdiction: defendants not domiciled in any Member State: Article 4;
8. Loss of jurisdiction: *lis alibi pendens* and related actions: Articles 27–30;
9. Applications for provisional or protective measures: Article 31.

Many ifs and buts apply to each of the entries in the matrix and these will be further studied below. Suffice to say here that, encouraged by the ECJ's hands-on approach to the interpretation of the Regulation,[66] some courts are less inclined than others to rule with confidence on the application of the Regulation. For instance, in an e-commerce context (which will be further reviewed in detail elsewhere), in Case C-278/09, the *Tribunal de Grande Instance* of Paris wanted to hear:

Must Article 2 and Article 5(3) of Council Regulation (EC) No 44/2001 of 22 December 2000 on jurisdiction and the recognition and enforcement of judgments in civil and commercial matters be interpreted to mean that a court or tribunal of a Member State has jurisdiction to hear an action brought in respect on an infringement of personal rights allegedly committed by the placing on-line of information and/or photographs on an Internet site published in another Member State by a company domiciled in that second State – or in a third Member State, but in any event in a State other than the first Member State – :

On the sole condition that that Internet site can be accessed from the first Member State,

---

[63] The special consideration for the UK and Ireland is not just relevant for UK and Irish courts; the courts of other Member States will equally have to apply them where they are called upon to consider whether a company is 'domiciled' in the UK or Ireland.

[64] Similarly: Briggs, A., *The Conflict of Laws*, Oxford, OUP, 2008, 65.

[65] Consequently while 'domicile of the defendant' is generally quoted of the overall rule of the Regulation, its actual place in the hierarchy is not altogether very high.

[66] See e.g. the jurisdictional angle for commercial agency contracts: Case C-19/09 *Wood Floor Solutions*, n 52 above.

On the sole condition that there is between the harmful act and the territory of the first Member State a link which is sufficient, substantial or significant and, in that case, whether that link can be created by:

— the number of hits on the page at issue made from the first Member State, as an absolute figure or as a proportion of all hits on that page,
— the residence, or nationality, of the person who complains of the infringement of his personal rights or more generally of the persons concerned,
— the language in which the information at issue is broadcast or any other factor which may demonstrate the site publisher's intention to address specifically the public of the first Member State,
— the place where the events described occurred and/or where the photographic images put on-line were taken,
— other criteria?

That case was held inadmissible,[67] however the reader will get the gist: these are not questions asked by a court happy with its jurisdiction adjudication – or indeed conscious of the ECJ deciding jurisdiction cases in quite a detailed manner.

2.2 DETAILED REVIEW OF THE REGULATION

Throughout the text below, reference will be made to mooted amendments which at the time of writing[68] were finding their way through the Institutions. Of particular relevance are the December 2010 European Commission Proposal;[69] the draft European Parliament Committee Report of June 2011,[70] and a June 2012 'General Approach' document by the Council.[71] All changes were eventually adopted as Regulation 1215/2012.

2.2.1 Trust is Good, Control is Better

The overriding principle of Brussels I is that of mutual trust: In *Gasser*,[72] the ECJ noted

> "it must be borne in mind that the Brussels Convention is necessarily based on the trust which the Contracting States accord to each other's legal systems and judicial institutions. It is that mutual trust which has enabled a compulsory system of jurisdiction to be established, which all the courts within the purview of the Convention are required to respect, and as a corollary the waiver by those States of the right to apply their internal rules on recognition and enforcement of foreign judgments in favour of a simplified mechanism for the recognition and enforcement of judgments."

---

[67] Order of the Court of 20 November 2009.
[68] Work on the contents of this volume was finalised on 11 November 2012.
[69] Commission Proposal COM(2010) 748 of 14 December 2010 for a recast of the Brussels I Regulation.
[70] Tadeusz Zwiefka MEP, PE 467.046v01-00.
[71] Document 10609/12, in particular addendum 1, both available via http://www.consilium.europa.eu/council/open-sessions/related-documents?debateid=1675&lang=en .
[72] Case C-116/02, [2003] ECR I-14693, para 72. *Idem* in Case C-159/02 *Turner*, [2004] ECR I-3565, para 24.

The theme of mutual trust runs through European PIL, extending from the JR into e.g. the Insolvency Regulation[73] (the ECJ in *Eurofood*[74]).

The overall themes running through the ECJ's application of the JR, are: recognition and enforcement facilitated by common adjudication of jurisdiction; this adjudication by courts in one Member State not to be second-guessed by courts of other States, and subject to an autonomous 'European' interpretation. The combination of all these elements is firmly promoted by the Court as the only road to legal certainty. In doing so it arguably equates legal certainty with predictability, an equation which may be debatable. Indeed among practitioners generally and especially those of common law Member States, there is growing dissatisfaction with the Court's principled disregard for commercial arguments in interpreting the JR, and for the aforementioned notion of legal certainty.[75] In *Gasser*, the United Kingdom specifically put forward the argument that the Convention had to be interpreted taking into account the needs of international trade[76] — a suggestion not much entertained by the ECJ.

Perhaps, though, the common law and civil law/JR do not diverge all that much on the issue of substance: as Rix LJ said in *Konkola Copper Mines*:

> The Brussels Convention on Jurisdiction and the Enforcement of Judgments in Civil and Commercial Matters 1968 (and now Council Regulation No. 44/2001 ('the Regulation')) also approaches the risk of inconsistent decisions with the same dislike. However, the techniques of the English common law and of the Regulation are different. The common law ultimately relies on an exercise of discretion to reach what in each case seems to the court to be the right result. The Convention and Regulation state rules designed to avoid inconsistent decisions, but if those rules fail in a particular case to avoid that danger, there can be no fall-back on discretionary powers: see Erich Gasser GmbH v MISAT Srl [2004] 1 Lloyd's Rep 445, Owusu v Jackson (Case C-281/02) [2005] QB 801.[77]

2.2.2 Scope of application: subject-matter.

2.2.2.1 The existence of an international element

Application of the Regulation, and of the Convention before it, requires the existence of an international element. The Brussels Convention included language in its preambles, which referred specifically to the Convention determining the international jurisdiction of the courts of the Member States. It is to this preamble which the Report Jenard refers where it notes

> As is stressed in the fourth paragraph of the preamble, the Convention determines the international jurisdiction of the courts of the Contracting States. It alters the rules of jurisdiction in force in each Contracting State only where an international element is involved. It does not define this concept, since the international element in a legal relationship may depend on the particular facts of the proceedings of which the court is seised. Proceedings instituted in the courts of

---

[73] Regulation 1346/2000, OJ [2000] L 160/1, as amended.
[74] Case C-341/04 *Eurofood IFSC*, [2006] ECR I-3813, para 39; see also C-444/07, *MG Probud Gdynia*, [2010] ECR I-417.
[75] See e.g. Andrew Dickinson on Conflict of Laws.net, 8 June 2009 (http://conflictoflaws.net/2009/brussels-i-review-online-focus-group/).
[76] *Gasser*, n 72 above, para 31.
[77] *Konkola Copper Mines Plc v Coromin Ltd* [2006] APP.L.R. 01/17, at para 27.

a Contracting State which involves only persons domiciled in that State will not normally be affected by the Convention; Article 2 simply refers matters back to the rules of jurisdiction in force in that State. It is possible, however, that an international element may be involved in proceedings of this type. This would be the case, for example, where the defendant was a foreign national, a situation in which the principle of equality of treatment laid down in the second paragraph of Article 2 would apply, or where the proceedings related to a matter over which the courts of another State had exclusive jurisdiction (Article 16), or where identical or related proceedings had been brought in the courts of another State (Article 21 to 23).

It is clear that at the recognition and enforcement stage the Convention governs only international legal relationships since ex hypothesi it concerns the recognition and enforcement in one Contracting State of judgments given in another Contracting State.[78]

In *Owusu*, the ECJ clarified

the international nature of the legal relationship at issue need not necessarily derive, for the purposes of the application of Article 2 of the Brussels Convention, from the involvement, either because of the subject-matter of the proceedings or the respective domiciles of the parties, of a number of Contracting States. The involvement of a Contracting State and a non-Contracting State, for example because the claimant and one defendant are domiciled in the first State and the events at issue occurred in the second, would also make the legal relationship at issue international in nature. That situation is such as to raise questions in the Contracting State, as it does in the main proceedings, relating to the determination of international jurisdiction, which is precisely one of the objectives of the Brussels Convention, according to the third recital in its preamble.[79]

It expressly confirmed the flexible interpretation of the presence of an 'international' element, in *Lindner*:[80]

the foreign nationality of one of the parties to the proceedings is not taken into account by the rules of jurisdiction laid down by the Regulation, however (...) a distinction must be made between, on the one hand, the conditions under which the rules of jurisdiction pursuant to that regulation must apply and, on the other, the criteria by which international jurisdiction is determined under those rules. (...) the foreign nationality of the defendant may raise questions relating to the determination of the international jurisdiction of the court seised. In a situation such as that in the main proceedings, the courts of the Member State of which the defendant is a national may also consider themselves to have jurisdiction even though the place in that Member State where the defendant is domiciled is unknown. In those circumstances, application of the uniform rules of jurisdiction laid down by Regulation No 44/2001 to replace those in force in the various Member States would be in accordance with the requirement of legal certainty and with the purpose of that regulation, which is to guarantee, to the greatest extent possible, the protection of defendants who are domiciled in the European Union.

In the case at issue, the fact that the defendant was a foreign national whose domicile was unknown at the time of the proceedings means the courts of the Member State of which the defendant is a national may also consider themselves to have jurisdiction even though the place in that Member State where the defendant is domiciled is unknown.

---

[78] Report Jenard, [1979] OJ C59/8.
[79] Case C-281/02 *Owusu*, [2005] ECR I-1383, para 26.
[80] Case C-327/10 *Lindner*, not yet reported in ECR (judgment of 17 November 2011), para 31 ff.

The Brussels I Regulation unifies the rules on jurisdiction of the Member States, not only for disputes within the EU but also for those with an external element. The obstacles to the functioning of the Internal Market which the Regulation seeks to eliminate, follow from disparities between national legislations on jurisdiction, whether the elements external to that jurisdiction have a European, or a non-European element.[81]

2.2.2.2 Civil and commercial matters

Article 1(1) JR provides that the Regulation applies to 'civil and commercial matters whatever the nature of the court or tribunal'. The French text reads 'en matière civile et commerciale et quelle que soit la nature de la juridition'. The Article adds by way of illustration that the Regulation shall in particular not extend to 'revenue, customs or administrative matters'.

Common perception has it that the qualification 'civil and commercial' implicitly harbours a distinction between 'civil and commercial' law on the one hand, and 'public law', on the other, and that for lawyers of the original Member States (all of them continental, with a civil law system) the distinction is (or at least was) fairly straightforward,[82] no doubt helped by the presence of 'civil' and 'public' or 'administrative' courts in those Member States. However things were never quite as easy as suggesting that all matters dealt with by 'public' law or 'administrative' courts were excluded from the Brussels Convention cq Regulation. Indeed the Convention already ruled that the decisive element was the 'civil/commercial' v 'public' law nature of the subject-matter, rather than of the court adjudicating on it,[83] and in the 'administrative' law of the original Member States, the correct distinction between these two sets of law has never really been fully settled[84] and continues to lead to complications, e.g. in public procurement law, education etc. A good illustration of the latter, incidentally, is Case C-172/91, *Sonntag*, in which the parents of a pupil sought the enforcement in Germany of the civil-law provisions of a judgment given by an Italian criminal court.[85]

Standard references for what exactly has to be understood by 'civil and commercial', are Cases 29/76 *Eurocontrol*, 814/79 *Ruffer*, and C-271/00 *Gemeente Steenbergen*.

---

[81] See ECJ Opinion 1/03 *Lugano I*, [2006] ECR I-1145, para 144, referred to most recently in Case C-154/11 *Mahamdia*, not yet published in ECR, para 40.

[82] See e.g. the *Schlosser* report, [1979] OJ C59/71, para 23 ff.

[83] Occasionally, both criminal and administrative courts give judgment in a civil or commercial matter: see *Ibid*, 23.

[84] See e.g. the *service public v puissance publique* discussion in Schwarze, J., *European Administrative Law*, London, Sweet & Maxwell, 1992, 14.

[85] Case C-172/91 *Volker Sonntag v Hans Waidmann et al*, [1993] ECR I-1963. Herr Sonntag and the regional state authorities argued that the criminal judgment of the Bolzano court related to a claim under public law, since the supervision of pupils by Herr Sonntag in his capacity as a civil servant was a matter that fell within the province of administrative law. The Court held that even though it is joined to criminal proceedings, a civil action for compensation for injury to an individual resulting from a criminal offence is civil in nature; that such an action falls outside the scope of the Convention only where the author of the damage against whom it is brought must be regarded as a public authority which acted in the exercise of public powers; and that in the majority of the legal systems of the Member States the conduct of a teacher in a State school, in his function as a person in charge of pupils during a school trip, does not constitute an exercise of public powers, since such conduct does not entail the exercise of any powers going beyond those existing under the rules applicable to relations between private individuals – that finding of the ECJ would certainly not undisputedly be the position in quite a few Member States.

2.2.2.3 Case 29/76 Eurocontrol

In *LTU/Eurocontrol*, Eurocontrol sought enforcement in Germany of an order by the Belgian courts that LTU pay it a sum by way of charges imposed by Eurocontrol for the use of its equipment and services. Eurocontrol is a public body and the use of its services by airlines is compulsory and exclusive. The Court referred unsurprisingly to the only specification in the Convention (all arguments below apply equally to the Regulation): that its provisions apply 'whatever the nature of the court or tribunal to which the matter is referred'. The Court added,

> Therefore, the concept in question must be regarded as independent and must be interpreted by reference, first, to the objectives and scheme of the Convention, and, secondly, to the general principles which stem from the corpus of the national legal systems. (at para 3, in fine).

Germany in particular[86] had referred to the (then) future membership to the Convention of common law countries, where the distinction between 'private' and 'public' law is even less straightforward than in civil law countries. The understanding of the concept of 'civil and commercial' therefore becomes a mix of on the one hand, independent interpretation guided by the objectives and scheme of the Convention, and on the other hand the 'ius commune' of national legal systems. The latter in fact may very much be the junior partner in this coalition, precisely because of the lack of common approach in the Member States. The Court continues however with an often overlooked reference, namely that:

> if the interpretation of the concept is approached in this way, in particular for the purpose of applying the provisions of Title III of the Convention, certain types of judicial decision must be regarded as excluded from the area of application of the Convention, either by reason of the legal relationships between the parties to the action or of the subject-matter of the Convention. (at 4) (emphasis added)

'In particular for the purpose of applying the provisions of Title III of the Convention': this is the Title of the Convention (the Regulation has a similar structure) which sees to recognition and enforcement. Recognition and enforcement were as noted the only parts of private international law which the Member States had specifically been instructed to harmonise via the instrument of Treaties. In my view the specific reference by the Court goes beyond a mere wink at the specific facts of the case: the Court arguably, purposely links Title III to the overall scope of application of the Regulation, because it reasoned that it would not serve any purpose to bring matters within the scope of application of the Convention which would run into trouble at the enforcement stage. The vast majority of the Convention's Parties did not allow for enforcement against public authorities, indeed for quite a few of them this remains a recent development. Given the relevance of Title III to the Court's finding in *Eurocontrol*, I would submit that the Court's core reasoning in that judgment may need revisiting in view of the developments in redress against public authorities.

The Court further held that

---

[86] See the summary of its arguments in the ECR.

Although certain judgments given in actions between a public authority and a person governed by private law may fall within the area of application of the Convention, this is not so where the public authority acts in the exercise of its powers.

Other language versions of the judgment read *inter alia* 'Où l'autorité publique a agi dans l'exercise de la puissance publique'; *'Eine Entscheidung en die Behörde im Zusammenhang met der Ausübung hoheitlicher Befugnisse geführt hat'*; 'wanneer de overheidsinstantie krachtens overheidsbevoegdheid handelt'.

'Where the public authority acts in the exercise of its powers' hence would seem to be the overall criterion which the Court suggests in *Eurocontrol*. This amounts to a negative approach to the scope of application in the context of public authorities: using the wording of the Evrigenis/Kerameus Report, the exercise of 'sovereign power' is the distinctive element.[87]

2.2.2.4 *Case 814/79* Ruffer

An action for the recovery of the costs involved in the removal of a wreck in a public waterway, administered by the State responsible in performance of an international obligation and on the basis of provisions of national law which, in the administration of that waterway, confer on it the status of public authority in regard to private persons, was held by the Court as being outside the ambit of the Convention. The fact that in this case the action pending before the national court did not concern the actual removal of the wreck but rather the costs involved in that removal and that the Netherlands State was seeking to recover those costs by means of a claim for redress and not by administrative process as provided for by the national law of other Member States was not found to be sufficient to bring the matter in dispute within the ambit of the Brussels Convention (at 13). The Court reiterated the Eurocontrol double foundation:

the area of application of the Convention is essentially determined either by reason of the legal relationships between the parties to the action or of the subject-matter of the action. (at 14)

2.2.2.5 *Case C-271/00* Gemeente Steenbergen

In *Gemeente Steenbergen v Luc Baten*, the municipality of Steenbergen in The Netherlands had paid subsistence grants to the former spouse of Mr Steenbergen. The spouse had relocated to The Netherlands. Mr Steenbergen continued to live in Belgium. Gemeente Steenbergen subsequently sought to have the payments reimbursed by Mr Baten. The couple had however agreed a divorce settlement, certified by public notary, in which Mr Baten agreed to pay maintenance for the couple's child, but not for his former wife. The subsistence payment covered both the ex-wife and the child. A Dutch court ordered Mr Baten to pay the full claim, on the basis of a provision in the Dutch civil code, which allows the authorities to set aside any agreements between former spouses which have an impact on the mutual maintenance obligations. Upon referral by a Belgian court that was asked to enforce the Dutch judgment, the Court of Justice held that:

[87] [1986] OJ C298/1, para 28.

the concept of 'civil matters' encompasses an action under a right of recourse whereby a public body seeks from a person governed by private law recovery of sums paid by it by way of social assistance to the divorced spouse and the child of that person, provided that the basis and the detailed rules relating to the bringing of that action are governed by the rules of the ordinary law in regard to maintenance obligations. Where the action under a right of recourse is founded on provisions by which the legislature conferred on the public body a prerogative of its own, that action cannot be regarded as being brought (at para 37)

The Court stuck to the *Eurocontrol* formula ['exclusion of certain judicial decisions from the scope of the Brussels Convention, owing either to the legal relationships between the parties to the action or to its subject matter': at para 29 in *Gemeente Steenbergen*], and subsequently would seem to view both *Eurocontrol* and *Rüffer* as examples of just one application: namely *where the public authority is acting in the exercise of its public powers*. Subsequently however it reformulates the *Eurocontrol* formula as requiring an examination of

the basis and the detailed rules governing the bringing of that action (Gemeente Steenbergen, at para 31).

Applied in the particular case at issue, the civil code determines the redress which may be sought; and specifies that these proceedings may be brought before a civil court (i.e. the court in ordinary) — do note of course Article 2 JR: the very nature of the court before which the claim is brought cannot be sufficient indication — and that the rules of civil procedure apply. Hence prima facie the case would be one which is governed by the JR. However to the degree that the same rules of civil procedure subsequently as it were revive public powers by granting public authorities the right unilaterally to trump the contractual arrangements between former spouses, the claim at issue nevertheless is excluded from the scope of application of the JR.

The ECJ however would not seem to clarify whether *the mere possibility* for the authorities to trump these arrangements, in itself suffices to take the case outside of the ambit of the JR, or whether, conversely, these authorities need to actually deploy these powers. One would imagine that the former would be the most plausible. It is fairly inconceivable for the ECJ to have created a mechanism whereby the procedural behaviour of a public authority would decide the (in)applicability of the Regulation.

Incidentally, the Court in *Gemeente Steenbergen* also reviewed the application of the social security exception. The referring court asked whether if indeed the case does have to be seen as principally falling within the field of application of the Directive, perhaps the exception for social security would apply. The Court applied a strict interpretation, with reference to the *Jenard* and *Schlosser* reports: the exception only relates to litigation arising out of relations between the authorities on the one hand, employers and/or employees on the other.

The Brussels Convention is applicable where the administration exercises a direct right of action against a third party liable for injury or is subrogated as regards that third party to the rights of a victim insured by it, because it is then acting under the rules of the ordinary law. (at para 48)

In reaching this conclusion, the Court referred to (then) secondary EC law in support. That was not all that obvious at the time of the judgment, given that the EEX Convention obviously did not qualify as 'EC' law.

Frahuil added that the specific legal obligation which lies at the foundation of the claim, determines applicability.[88]

2.2.2.6 Case C-292/05 Lechouritou

In *Lechouritou*,[89]-[90] the Court summarised the current position as follows:[91]

> It is to be remembered that, in order to ensure, as far as possible, that the rights and obligations which derive from the Brussels Convention for the Contracting States and the persons to whom it applies are equal and uniform, the terms of that provision should not be interpreted as a mere reference to the internal law of one or other of the States concerned. It is thus clear from the Court's settled case-law that "civil and commercial matters" must be regarded as an independent concept to be interpreted by referring, first, to the objectives and scheme of the Brussels Convention and, second, to the general principles which stem from the corpus of the national legal systems (...)

> According to the Court, that interpretation results in the exclusion of certain legal actions and judicial decisions from the scope of the Brussels Convention, by reason either of the legal relationships between the parties to the action or of the subject-matter of the action (...)

> Thus, the Court has held that, although certain actions between a public authority and a person governed by private law may come within the scope of the Brussels Convention, it is otherwise where the public authority is acting in the exercise of its public powers (...).

The Court essentially reiterates the specific cases of *Eurocontrol* and *Ruffer* as one expression of the overall *Eurocontrol* formula: 'the exclusion of certain legal actions and judicial decisions from the scope of the Brussels Convention, by reason either of the legal relationships between the parties to the action or of the subject-matter' (at para 30). It subsequently yet again zooms in on public authority as an application, this time formulating it positively:

> Disputes (that) result from the exercise of public powers by one of the parties to the case, as it exercises powers falling outside the scope of the ordinary legal rules applicable to relationships. (at para 34).

The applicants in the case argued in vain that illegal or illegitimate acts can never qualify as *acta iure imperii*.

In summary, the *Eurocontrol* formula which was put forward so succinctly, still rules happily: litigation may be excluded *by reason either of the legal relationships between the parties to the action or of the subject-matter of the action*. Yet, the Court[92] has hitherto

---

[88] Case C-265/02 *Frahuil* [2004] ECR I-1543.

[89] Case C-292/05 *Lechouritou* [2007] ECR I-1519, paras 29 to 31.

[90] The main proceedings had their origins in the massacre of civilians by soldiers in the German armed forces which was perpetrated on 13 December 1943 and of which 676 inhabitants of the municipality of Kalavrita (Greece) were victims. Plaintiffs sued in Greece for compensation from the German State in respect of the financial loss, non-material damage and mental anguish caused to them by the acts perpetrated by the German armed forces.

[91] With reference to *Eurocontrol* and to Case 814/79 *Netherlands v Rüffer* [1980] ECR 3807, para 7; Case C-271/00 *Baten* [2002] ECR I-10489, para 28; Case C-266/01 *Préservatrice foncière TIARD* [2003] ECR I-4867, para 20; and Case C-343/04 *ČEZ* [2006] ECR I-4557, para 22.

[92] See by contrast the Opinion of AG Leger in Case C-266/01 *Préservatrice*, who does distinguish conceptually between both.

only ever applied the first criterion, never the last — indeed it is very difficult to conceive an example of what the second application would look like.[93] As such this is not a big problem. In *Eurocontrol*, the formula was set as alternative conditions, not cumulative: either one, or the other. Consequently if the Court found the conditions of one fulfilled, it need not review the other.[94] However it would seem a bit redundant to formulate the exception as presenting two different options when the second option is never seriously entertained – for at the very least, the presence of a second leg in an exception does affect the overall balance of the construction. Moreover, the alternative *Gemeente Steenbergen* formula (*'the basis and the detailed rules governing the bringing of that action'*) has in my view only had its first leg applied, too.

It is noteworthy that the term 'civil matters' also features in Regulation 2201/2003,[95] which, too, has left it undefined. However in *C*, the Court's Grand Chamber held that the two concepts have to be given a meaning fit for the specific purposes of the respective Regulations,[96] hence excluding mutual interchangeability of meaning between the same words used in the two Regulations.

2.2.2.7 Exclusions, inter alia arbitration

The Regulation excludes (Article 1(2)):

(a) the status or legal capacity of natural persons, rights in property arising out of a matrimonial relationship, wills and succession;
(b) bankruptcy, proceedings relating to the winding-up of insolvent companies or other legal persons, judicial arrangements, compositions and analogous proceedings;
(c) social security;
(d) arbitration.

The issues sub(a)[97] were excluded because they were not considered as having much relevance for international business. The intention was gradually to cover these with different instruments, a process which is still on-going.[98] Litera b of course does have direct relevance for business however this, too, was the subject of separate discussions. The eventual 'Insolvency' Regulation, Regulation 1346/2000,[99] reviewed elsewhere in this volume, was 30 years in the making. Social security issues are clearly not 'civil or commercial' and hence are excluded. An action is related to bankruptcy if it derives

---

[93] See also Gärtner, V., 'The Brussels Convention and Reparations – Remarks on the Judgment of the European Court of Justice in *Lechouritou and others v the State of the Federal Republic of Germany*', *German Law Journal*, 2007, (417) n 29.

[94] See for instance in *Lechouritou*: the fact that the applicants claimed damages in tort – without doubt an action of a civil nature – was of no relevance once the Court had established *acta iure imperii*.

[95] On jurisdiction and the recognition and enforcement of judgments in matrimonial matters and in matters of parental responsibility, OJ [2003] L338/1 – commonly referred to as the Brussels IIa or Brussels II bis Regulation ('bis' or 'a' on account of it repealing a previous Regulation, 1347/2000).

[96] Case C-435/06 *C*, [2007] ECR I-10141.

[97] Do note however the special jurisdictional rule for maintenance payments in Article 5(2), which has now been superseded by Regulation 4/2009 on jurisdiction, applicable law, recognition and decisions and cooperation in matters relating to maintenance obligations, OJ [2009] L7/1.

[98] See the various references throughout this volume. The Commission's pace is such as to now propose for these matters one Regulation on all three steps of the PIL cycle.

[99] OJ [2000] L160/1.

directly from the bankruptcy and is closely linked to proceedings for realising the assets or judicial supervision.[100]

The exclusion for arbitration would seem straightforward enough at first sight, even if hesitation about the precise scope of the exception was clear in the Schlosser report already.[101] In a perhaps unusual mood of deference,[102] Member States at the time considered that the 1958 New York Convention appropriately regulates international arbitration.[103] What was then Article 220 EEC, which as noted above provided the legal basis for the Member States to adopt International Conventions in the area of private international law, referred not just to judicial decisions but also to arbitral awards: it mentioned 'the simplification of formalities governing the reciprocal recognition and enforcement of judgments of courts or tribunals and of arbitration awards.'

The Brussels Convention, by including judgments of courts and tribunals only, specifically determined to exclude arbitration. 'The Contracting Parties intended to exclude arbitration in its entirety, including [arbitration] proceedings brought before national courts'[104] such as in the case of *Rich*, the appointment of an arbitrator by a national court, in accordance with national law, as a default option where one of the parties to the agreement refuses to appoint an arbitrator. In *Rich*, the ECJ noted that the New York Convention includes a number of obligations for the courts of the Member States, hence the simple involvement of a court is not enough for the issue not to be excluded from the JC/JR, under the 'arbitration' exemption. *Rich* of course did leave open a number of questions. The ECJ held that:

> In order to determine whether a dispute falls within the scope of the Convention, reference must be made solely to the subject-matter of the dispute. If, by virtue of its subject-matter, such as the appointment of an arbitrator, a dispute falls outside the scope of the Convention, the existence of a preliminary issue which the court must resolve in order to determine the dispute cannot, whatever that issue may be, justify application of the Convention.[105]

Hence the English courts were within their rights to have *Rich* serve notice on his Italian adversary not to continue proceedings in Italy, however what ought to be understood by the 'subject-matter' really is unclear.

With respect to provisional measures, in *Van Uden* the Court emphasised the standalone nature of Article 31 JR (then Article 24 JC):

> provisional measures are not in principle ancillary to arbitration proceedings but are ordered in parallel to such proceedings and are intended as measures of support. They concern not arbitration as such but the protection of a wide variety of rights. Their place in the scope of the Convention is thus determined not by their own nature but by the nature of the rights which they serve to protect.[106]

---

[100] Case 133/78 *Gourdain* [1979] ECR 733, para 4.

[101] Harris, J., and Lein, E., 'A Neverending story? Arbitration and Brussels I: The recast', in *The Brussels I Review Proposal Uncovered*, Lein, E. (ed.), London, British Institute of International and Comparative Law, 2012, (31) 32.

[102] Explained too by the nature of the 1968 Convention, a classic instrument of public international law rather than 'European' law proper.

[103] See also Report *Jenard*, OJ [1979] C59/13.

[104] Case C-190/89 *Marc Rich v Impianti*, [1991] ECR I-3855, para 18.

[105] *Ibid*, para 26.

[106] Case C-391/95 *Van Uden v Deco Line*, [1998] ECR I-7091, para 33.

In other words where the Court can make recourse to Article 31, in support of arbitration proceedings, these measures are not ancillary to arbitration but rather stand-alone, parallel to such arbitration. They are therefore not excluded from the JR.

The difference between ancillary and other proceedings in itself is challenging enough. However the difficulty to see consistency in the Court's *Rich* and *Van Uden* case-law, was confounded when the arbitration exclusion subsequently and gradually became embroiled in the ECJ's refusal to have case-specific considerations of procedural justice stand in the way of the overall aim of predictability.[107] The ins and outs of *lis alibi pendens* ('LAP') are not our main concern here (see further in this volume) however a brief introduction is now required. Indeed some of the seminal judgments on LAP led directly to the ECJ's quagmire on the arbitration exclusion.

As we review elsewhere in this volume in detail, the *lis alibi pendens* rule of Article 27 JR obliges a Court to stay proceedings if another Member State court has already been seized in the same matter, and to trust the proper application by the latter of the jurisdictional grounds of the Regulation. Article 27 JR has given malevolent parties a means to obstruct proceedings, by seizing a court in a Member State with no or desperate grounds for jurisdiction, banking on the tardiness of its judicial proceedings to gain time and 'torpedo' the case of the bona fide party.[108] The ECJ's refusal to discipline this manoeuvre has undoubtedly sparked a race to court attitude. In *Gasser*,[109] the referring court asked specifically to what extent the excessive and generalised slowness of legal proceedings in the Contracting State where the court first seized is established, is liable to affect the application of the *lis alibi pendens* rule of the Brussels Convention. In the case at issue, Gasser sought to have the Austrian court claim jurisdiction on the basis of an exclusive choice-of-court clause, despite an earlier run to an Italian court by his adversary. The ECJ declined, citing the need for mutual trust referred to above: the Italian court had to be trusted eventually to decline jurisdiction. In *Turner*, the English Courts issued an 'anti-suit' injunction[110] barring Mr Grovit and a number of his companies from pursuing court proceedings in Spain which in the view of the English Courts had been initiated purely with a view to irritate Turner's own action – initiated first – in an English employment tribunal. Mostly on the basis of the principle of mutual trust,[111] the ECJ dismissed the

---

[107] See also Hartley, T., 'The European Union and the systematic dismantling of the common law of conflict', *International & Comparative Law Quarterly*, 2005, 813–828: Prof Hartley suggests that the EU and the ECJ in particular give priority to State interests over parties' interests, and obsesses (my words, not his) with systematic interpretation of the legislation.

[108] A manoeuvre often deployed using either Italian or Belgian courts.

[109] n 72 above.

[110] Known as 'anti-suit injunctions', these are injunctions whereby a party is prohibited – and non-compliance constitutes contempt of court – from commencing or continuing proceedings before another judicial authority, even one abroad. In the proceedings before the ECJ, the United Kingdom (and indeed the referring court, the House of Lords) preferred the term 'restraining order', partially no doubt because the concept 'anti-suit injunction' more immediately implies restriction of jurisdiction of the foreign court, which the UK knew would not be met favourably by the ECJ, while the notion 'restraining order' sounds more akin to a measure of a procedural kind, which the ECJ in *Van Uden* (Case C-391/95, [1998] ECR I-7091), and in accordance with Article 24 of the Brussels Convention (now, Article 31 JR) had given the green light. The compatibility with the Brussels Convention of anti-suit injunctions directed against the deplorable conduct of the defendant (as opposed to those based upon the argument that the foreign court has no jurisdiction), was also put forward in the leading English authority, *Dicey & Morris*, and referred to by the House: Dicey & Morris: *Conflict of Laws* 13th Edn. at §12–066, 419.

[111] Leger AG briefly reviewed the application of anti-suit injunctions in common law, identifying a number of additional reasons to reject them for the JC/JR, including the potential for incompatible anti-suit injunctions issued by various jurisdictions, as famously in *Laker Airways* (which had also been quoted in the referral: *Laker*

possibility of anti-suit injunctions, effectively telling the English Courts they had to trust the Spanish courts to recognise the vexatious nature of the proceedings in Spain, and eventually to decline jurisdiction and conceding to the English employment tribunal.[112]

Gasser and *Turner* effectively meant that anti-suit injunctions are always incompatible with the Regulation, even when they are issued by the court having jurisdiction under that Regulation. They continue to be used to great effect however in proceedings which clearly fall outside the scope of the Regulation, for instance because the defendants are not based in the EU (and none of the jurisdictional grounds apply which make that irrelevant),[113] or because the matter falls outside the JR for reason of it not being a civil or commercial matter.

Turning now to the subject-matter of current heading: discussions on the extent of the arbitration exclusion met with the ECJ's restrictive agenda on anti-suit injunctions in *Allianz v West Tankers*.[114]

The *Front Comor*, a vessel owned by West Tankers and chartered by Erg collided in Syracuse (Italy) with a jetty owned by Erg, and caused damage. The charterparty was governed by English law and contained a clause providing for arbitration in London. Erg claimed compensation from its insurers Allianz and Generali up to the limit of its insurance cover and commenced arbitration proceedings in London against West Tankers for the excess. West Tankers denied liability for the damage caused by the collision. Having paid Erg compensation under the insurance policies for the loss it had suffered, Allianz and Generali brought proceedings against West Tankers before the Tribunale di Siracusa (Italy) in order to recover the sums they had paid to Erg. The action was based on their statutory right of subrogation to Erg's claims. West Tankers raised an objection of lack of jurisdiction on the basis of the existence of the arbitration agreement. In parallel, West Tankers brought proceedings before the High Court, seeking a declaration that the dispute between itself, on the one hand, and Allianz and Generali, on the other, was to be settled by arbitration pursuant to the arbitration agreement. West Tankers also sought an injunction restraining Allianz and Generali from pursuing any proceedings other than arbitration and requiring them to discontinue the proceedings commenced before the Tribunale di Siracusa: this was the anti-suit injunction, which was granted by the High Court, and appealed to the House of Lords by Allianz and Generali.

The House of Lords referred of course to *Gasser* and *Turner*, however suggested that the prohibition on anti-suit injunctions cannot be extended to arbitration, given its exclusion from the Regulation. The House of Lords specifically referred to the attraction of anti-suit injunctions in ensuring the enforcement of arbitration clauses, and suggested

---

Airways Ltd. v Sabena Belgian World Airlines, 235 U.S. App. D.C. 207, 731 F.2d 909 (D.C. Cir. 1984) – one of the seminal cases on comity. Eventually, the House of Lords lifted the English injunction: *British Airways BD v Laker Airways,* [1985] AC 85, 84 (Diplock, LJ), 95–96 (Scarman, LJ) (1984).

[112] See also Spencer Wolff, 'Tanking Arbitration or Breaking the System to fix it?', *Columbia Journal of European Law*, 2009, (65) 66.

[113] See e.g. *Joint Stock Asset Management Company Ingosstrakh Investments v BNP Paribas SA* [2012] EWCA Civ 644: anti-suit injunction even against a third party to an arbitration clause, ordering it to halt proceedings in Russia for reason of these being vexatious, and collusive with the party held by the clause; see also *Shashoua v Sharma*, [2009] EWHC 957 (Comm): anti-suit injunction preventing the party from pursuing the matter in India. Cooke J explicitly rejected the argument made that the decision of the ECJ in *West Tankers* has an impact on proceedings with third States, whether or not those are Parties to the New York Convention.

[114] Case C-185/07 *Allianz v West Tankers*, [2009] ECR I-663.

its adoption by courts of the other Member States, too, so as to add to the appeal of the EU as a seat of arbitration.

The ECJ was not open to any of these arguments: it firstly granted that the proceedings in the United Kingdom, per *Rich*, did not come within the purview of the Regulation:

22. In that regard it must be borne in mind that, in order to determine whether a dispute falls within the scope of Regulation No 44/2001, reference must be made solely to the subject-matter of the proceedings (Rich, paragraph 26). More specifically, its place in the scope of Regulation No 44/2001 is determined by the nature of the rights which the proceedings in question serve to protect (Van Uden, paragraph 33).

23. Proceedings, such as those in the main proceedings, which lead to the making of an anti-suit injunction, cannot, therefore, come within the scope of Regulation No 44/2001.

However the ECJ then turned to the impact on the proceedings in Italy, where the Court undoubtedly would have jurisdiction (on the basis of Article 5(3), the jurisdictional rule *re* tort, which I review later), were one to disregard the arbitration clause:

24. However, even though proceedings do not come within the scope of Regulation No 44/2001, they may nevertheless have consequences which undermine its effectiveness, namely preventing the attainment of the objectives of unification of the rules of conflict of jurisdiction in civil and commercial matters and the free movement of decisions in those matters. This is so, inter alia, where such proceedings prevent a court of another Member State from exercising the jurisdiction conferred on it by Regulation No 44/2001.

25. It is therefore appropriate to consider whether the proceedings brought by Allianz and Generali against West Tankers before the Tribunale di Siracusa themselves come within the scope of Regulation No 44/2001 and then to ascertain the effects of the anti-suit injunction on those proceedings.

26. In that regard, the Court finds, as noted by the Advocate General in points 53 and 54 of her Opinion, that, if, because of the subject-matter of the dispute, that is, the nature of the rights to be protected in proceedings, such as a claim for damages, those proceedings come within the scope of Regulation No 44/2001, a preliminary issue concerning the applicability of an arbitration agreement, including in particular its validity, also comes within its scope of application. This finding is supported by paragraph 35 of the Report on the accession of the Hellenic Republic to the Convention of 27 September 1968 on Jurisdiction and the Enforcement of Judgments in Civil and Commercial Matters (OJ 1978 L 304, p. 36) ('the Brussels Convention'), presented by Messrs Evrigenis and Kerameus (OJ 1986 C 298, p. 1). That paragraph states that the verification, as an incidental question, of the validity of an arbitration agreement which is cited by a litigant in order to contest the jurisdiction of the court before which he is being sued pursuant to the Brussels Convention, must be considered as falling within its scope.

27. It follows that the objection of lack of jurisdiction raised by West Tankers before the Tribunale di Siracusa on the basis of the existence of an arbitration agreement, including the question of the validity of that agreement, comes within the scope of Regulation No 44/2001 and that it is therefore exclusively for that court to rule on that objection and on its own jurisdiction, pursuant to Articles 1(2)(d) and 5(3) of that regulation.

28. Accordingly, the use of an anti-suit injunction to prevent a court of a Member State, which normally has jurisdiction to resolve a dispute under Article 5(3) of Regulation No 44/2001, from ruling, in accordance with Article 1(2)(d) of that regulation, on the very applicability of the regulation to the dispute brought before it necessarily amounts to stripping that court of the power to rule on its own jurisdiction under Regulation No 44/2001.

There are a number of striking considerations in the judgment. Chiefly among them,[115] the view of the ECJ that no less than 'unification of the rules of conflict of jurisdiction in civil and commercial matters' is the objective of the Regulation. This is a particularly expansionist view of the aims of the Regulation and one which, as I phrased it above, is testimony to the ECJ's refusal to have case-specific considerations of procedural justice stand in the way of the overall aim of uniformity and predictability. It is also strikingly different from what is (or was, pre-*West Tankers*) the general view of common law as to the nature of the Regulation, as described by Lord Hobhouse in *Turner v Grovit* (albeit vis-à-vis the Convention but with no less applicability to the Regulation): 'It is not the purpose of the Convention to require uniformity but to have clear rules governing jurisdiction.'[116]

'Even though proceedings do not come within the scope of Regulation No 44/2001, they may nevertheless have consequences which undermine its effectiveness':[117] that is how the ECJ summarily justifies the rejection of using anti-suit injunctions to safeguard clear exceptions to the Regulation's scope. This is an extensive *effet utile* approach of which I am not convinced. Exceptions of course have an impact on the effectiveness of a Regulation. However by having excepted these categories, the drafters specifically acknowledge non-application notwithstanding the consequential impact on the instrument from which they are being exempt.

West Tankers of course does not deny the validity of arbitration clauses, and therefore does not rule out that such clause (and the consequential inapplicability of the Regulation) eventually will be vindicated by the court which is not a court of the Member State where the arbitration forum is located. In the meantime, the High Court has validated the arbitral award,[118] with the decision in Italy still pending. This certainly leads to a number of interesting questions, including whether the High Court validation can be seen as a 'judgment' in the sense of Article 34(3) JR (which would lead to any eventual Italian decision not being enforceable in other Member States). The West Tankers decision continues to ripple in UK proceedings. In the latest (however undoubtedly not last) episode, the High Court has ruled that the panel was wrong in assuming that the Court of Justice's finding in *West Tankers*, circumscribed its jurisdiction to award damages for breach of an obligation to arbitrate, by virtue of the right of the Respondents to bring proceedings under Article 5(3) before the Italian courts. The tribunal essentially held (as summarised in the judgment) that like the English court, it was bound by the principle of effective judicial protection not to interfere with or deprive the Respondents of that right in European law. Flaux J, seeking support in Kokott AG's very opinion in *West Tankers* (and the Court of Justice's absence of disagreement on that point), held that the jurisdiction Regulation, as is evident from the Judgment in West Tankers, curtails the English *courts* in their power to issue anti-suit injunctions. However it does not curtail the jurisdiction of the arbitral panel. Leave to appeal was granted.[119]

---

[115] See also Wolff, n 55 above, 67.

[116] Lord Hobhouse of Woodborough in *Turner v Grovit*, [2001] UKHL 65 at 37.

[117] See a prelude in the external sphere, ECJ Opinion 1/03 *Lugano I*, [2006] ECR I-1145, and Niedzwiedz, M., and Mostowik, P, 'Implications of the ECJ 'Lugano II' Opinion for European union's external actions concerning private international law', Yearbook of Polish European Studies, 2010, 129–148.

[118] 11 March 2011, [2011] EWHC 829 (Comm).

[119] [2012] EWHC 854 (Comm) (4 April 2012).

In sum, once the Court had stretched the requirement of mutual trust in *Turner*, the Court's findings in *West Tankers* were not all that surprising. However they are a far cry from *Rich*, where the ECJ saw appointment of an arbitrator by a court as being *part of the process of setting arbitration proceedings in motion*.[120] Safeguarding the desired impact of an arbitration clause by use of an anti-suit injunction arguably ought to be part of that category, too.

The consequences of *West Tankers* do reverberate in the arbitration community and avenues have been explored to address the inevitable delay (at the least) in getting arbitration proceedings underway after the Court's findings in *West Tankers*. Many ideas were being footballed around in the build-up to the review of the JR. The matrix of desiderata has become quite complex, however. Addressing the ECJ's hostility in particular vis-à-vis anti-suit injunctions even where these are, as noted, directed towards procedures which would otherwise be exempt from the JR, would either require a formal intervention to remove the Court's overall rejection of such injunctions (unlikely) or a specific mentioning of such injunctions in a tailor-made regime for arbitration under the JR [or another means to discourage obstruction of arbitration] (more likely). Arbitration practice also increasingly would seem to recognise for instance the attraction of having the recognition and enforcement part of the JR apply to arbitral awards.[121] Currently, some Member States do (e.g. Germany) employ the JR to recognise foreign decisions which merged an arbitral award.[122] Others, e.g. England and Wales, do not.[123]

While *prima facie* arbitration practice would seem fairly unanimous in rejecting any suggestion to extend the JR to arbitration, in reality there are points of contact between the two and solving the interface between the JR and the New York Convention would seem most urgent for 4 specific issues: anti-suit injunctions for enforcing the integrity of an arbitration agreement, and the linked issue of declaratory judgments on the validity of the agreement; the appointment of arbiters and other ancillary measures, typically in interlocutory proceedings,[124] including the granting of supportive provisional relief and the taking of evidence by ordinary courts; the recognition and enforcement of arbitral awards;[125] and conflicts between awards and judgments.

The Hess, Pfeiffer, Schlosser Report (also known as the '*Heidelberg*'Report) suggested two possible ways forward.[126] Either a simple deletion of the exception, and preservation of the priority of the New York Convention using Article 71 JR. Or alternatively a more proactive embrace of arbitration by including a specific provision on supportive proceedings to arbitration, in particular (but not limited to) giving the courts of the Member State in which the arbitration takes place, exclusive jurisdiction for ancillary proceedings concerned with the support of arbitration.[127] In its Green Paper on the review of the

---

[120] *Rich*, n 104 above, para 19.

[121] Especially since bringing arbitration under the JR in some fashion, would not *ipso facto* wipe the New York Convention out of the EU: under Article 71 JR, the prevalence of the New York Convention would be safeguarded: see *inter alia*. Hess, Pfeiffer, Schlosser, n 62 above, 39 (para 130).

[122] Hess, Pfeiffer, Schlosser, n 62 above, 33 (para 111).

[123] *Ibid.*

[124] *Inter alia* signalled by the Dutch report, *ibid*, 33, at para 113, and also of course the fall-out of the *Van Uden* case.

[125] English Report for the *Hess et al* preparatory report on the review of the JR, referred to in relevant part in Hess, Pfeiffer, Schlosser, n 62 above, 32 (para 109), and summary of further reports on 34.

[126] Hess, Pfeiffer, Schlosser, n 62 above, 39 (para 130 ff).

[127] For details see *ibid.*

JR,[128] the Commission listed a variety of options however limited its intervention to asking stakeholders what they see as the best solution. These stakeholders reacted in large numbers, with differing views on the best way forward.

The absence of consensus, in particular among the Member States, then prompted the European Parliament's *rapporteur* at least (and the EP in full afterwards[129]), to suggest no movement on the issue at all,[130] other than a clearer proviso on the arbitration exclusion, specifying that

> not only arbitration proceedings, but also judicial procedures ruling on the validity or extent of arbitral competence as a principal issue or as an incidental or preliminary question, are excluded from the scope of the Regulation.[131]

Consequently the *rapporteur* called for a more robust protection of arbitration, not by employing a positive intervention of some kind (see above: i.e. a specific proviso precisely outlining the relationship between arbitration and the JR), but rather, because no consensus may be found on such fancy proposal, by ring-fencing arbitration in a more aggressive way. By making recourse to the aggressive format of total exclusion, the *rapporteur* does of course also miss out on the option to include a provision creating an exclusive head of jurisdiction for the Member State in which the arbitration is due to take place, such as suggested in the *Heidelberg* report.

In its eventual proposal on the review of the JR,[132] the European Commission proposed the specific inclusion of a jurisdictional ground for arbitration,

---

'Where the agreed or designated seat of an arbitration is in a Member State, the courts of another Member State whose jurisdiction is contested on the basis of an arbitration agreement shall stay proceedings once the courts of the Member State where the seat of the arbitration is located or the arbitral tribunal have been seized of proceedings to determine, as their main object or as an incidental question, the existence, validity or effects of that arbitration agreement.

This paragraph does not prevent the court whose jurisdiction is contested from declining jurisdiction in the situation referred to above if its national law so prescribes.

Where the existence, validity or effects of the arbitration agreement are established, the court seized shall decline jurisdiction. This paragraph does not apply in disputes concerning matters referred to in Sections 3, 4, and 5 of Chapter II.'

[the latter are the sections dealing with the protected parties: insurance contracts; consumers; employment contracts].

---

[128] COM(2009) 175.

[129] Resolution of 7 September 2010.

[130] Report of Tadeusz Zwiefka MEP of 29 June 2010 on the implementation and review of Council Regulation (EC) No 44/2001 on jurisdiction and the recognition and enforcement of judgments in civil and commercial matters (2009/2140(INI), A7-0219/2010.

[131] *Ibid*, para 10.

[132] COM(2010) 748.

Parliament continued to reject such amendment and stuck to its insistence to keep arbitration out of the Regulation altogether.[133]

The June 2012 'General Approach' document by the Council[134] in my view adopts the worst possible scenario. With respect to arbitration, the Council suggests

- *Not* to adopt the aforementioned Articles 29, paragraph 4, and 33, paragraph 3 (these suggested amendments would therefore be deleted in their entirety).
- To include the following in Article 84:

  2. This Regulation shall not affect the application of the Convention on the Recognition and Enforcement of Foreign Arbitral Awards, done at New York on 10 June 1958.

- Finally, to include a recital as follows:

  "— This Regulation should not apply to arbitration. Nothing in this Regulation should prevent the courts of a Member State, when seised of an action in a matter in respect of which the parties have made an arbitration agreement, from referring the parties to arbitration[135] of from staying or dismissing the proceedings and from examining whether the arbitration agreement is null and void, inoperative or incapable of being performed, in accordance with their national law.
  — A ruling given by a court of a Member State as to whether or not an arbitration agreement is null and void, inoperative of incapable of being performed should not be subject to the rules of recognition and enforcement of this Regulation, regardless of whether the court decided on this as a principal issue or as an incidental question. On the other hand, where a court, exercising jurisdiction under this Regulation or under national law, has determined that an arbitration agreement is null and void, inoperative or incapable of being performed, this should not prevent that the court's judgment on the substance of the matter be recognised and, as the case may be, enforced in accordance with this Regulation. This should be without prejudice to the competence of the courts of the Member States to decide on the recognition and enforcement of arbitral awards in accordance with the Convention on the Recognition and Enforcement of Foreign Arbitral Awards, done at New York on 10 June 1958, which takes precedence over this Regulation.
  — This Regulation should not apply to any action or ancillary proceedings relating to, in particular, the establishment of the arbitral tribunal, the powers of the arbitrators, the conduct of the arbitration procedure or any other aspects of such a procedure, nor to any action or judgment concerning the annulment, review, appeal, recognition and enforcement of an arbitral award."

The Council would therefore maintain the principal exclusion for arbitration, and emphasise the priority of the New York Convention. However it also maintains the confusion over the exact scope of the arbitration exclusion. Its curious use of an extended recital basically re-iterates all the points of discussion resulting from the current text and the case-law applying it. Any party wanting to stall, torpedo, or otherwise sabotage proceedings with even a hint of arbitration elements in them, will find itself well served with the

---

[133] Draft Committee report of 28 June 2011, PE 467.046, as well as draft Committee Report of 25 September 2012, PE496.504. A vote in first reading was scheduled for January 2012, was then moved to June 2012, and is now scheduled to take place in November 2012.

[134] Document 10609/12, in particular addendum 1, both available via http://www.consilium.europa.eu/council/open-sessions/related-documents?debateid=1675&lang=en .

[135] Footnote not in the original text: Eventual insertion of this recital might in my view (although probably suffering from wishful thinking) even serve as an argument that West Tankers has been overruled: 'referring the parties to arbitration' ought to cover any procedural means employed to facilitate this referral.

recital which — rather adroitly, it has to be said — manages to integrate all unsettled points of discussion in a matter-of-factly way which amounts to sheer denial of the problems that arise in practice.

Council reports that it has been in consultation with the Parliament, in the run-up to the General Approach. While I had hoped that this recital is not one that the EP would be happy to sign off on, the September 2012 draft Committee report suggests otherwise. With some minor editorial amendments, Parliament now supports the Council's view.

2.2.3 Scope of application – Ratione Personae

The Brussels I Regulation is applicable in three cases:

1. The defendant in the legal proceedings is domiciled in a Member State. Its nationality is irrelevant – as is the nationality and domicile of the plaintiff; or
2. A court in a Member State has exclusive jurisdiction on the basis of one of the grounds listed in Article 22, whatever the domicile of the parties; or
3. At least one of the parties (which could be the plaintiff) is domiciled in one of the Member States and a valid choice of forum clause has been made in accordance with Article 23.

2.2.3.1 Domicile

Article 59

1. In order to determine whether a party is domiciled in the Member State whose courts are seized of a matter, the court shall apply its internal law.

2. If a party is not domiciled in the Member State whose courts are seized of the matter, then, in order to determine whether the party is domiciled in another Member State, the court shall apply the law of that Member State.

Article 60

1. For the purposes of this Regulation, a company or other legal person or association of natural or legal persons is domiciled at the place where it has its:

(a) statutory seat, or
(b) central administration, or
(c) principal place of business.

2. For the purposes of the United Kingdom and Ireland "statutory seat" means the registered office or, where there is no such office anywhere, the place of incorporation or, where there is no such place anywhere, the place under the law of which the formation took place.

3. In order to determine whether a trust is domiciled in the Member State whose courts are seized of the matter, the court shall apply its rules of private international law.

A core jurisdictional claim of the Regulation is the domicile of the defendant.

Domicile for natural persons. For natural persons, Article 59 holds that the laws of the Member States determine whether a person is domiciled in that State. For a company, legal person or association of natural persons, Article 60 aims to make the rules more transparent and perhaps encourage harmonisation by listing three possible locations only.

Where domicile is a contributing factor in determining jurisdiction (see the heads of jurisdiction, reviewed below), the court seized of the matter shall therefore always apply its own definition of domicile, and only if no domicile can be established on the basis of these laws, will it apply the domicile rules of other Member States. However there may be a head of jurisdiction other than domicile (either through Article 22 or 23, or any of the 'special' grounds of jurisdiction reviewed below), hence domicile of the defendant obviously is not the be all and end all of jurisdiction.

Review of the domicile rules of another Member State is not as bizarre as it may seem at first sight. Firstly, it could very well be that the jurisdiction of the forum on the basis of the JR, depends on another Member State's domicile rules. A case in point is the application of Article 23 JR between one party with clearly domicile outside of the EU, and one potentially within (but not in the forum state). Further, review of another Member States' domicile rules may be required where the forum court may well have jurisdiction on the basis of its national laws, in accordance with Article 4 JR, however stays its procedure in favour of a court of another MS which may have JR-based jurisdiction (typically on the basis of Article 23 JR although also potentially on the basis of Article 2) on the basis of the latter's rules on domicile.[136]

There have been a number of calls to replace the domicile criterion with a more harmonised and factual concept, e.g. 'habitual residence' linked to a minimum time of residence in the forum. However in practice it is highly uncertain whether such attempt at harmonisation would cancel any let alone all uncertainties which it aims to remedy.

In *Lindner*[137], the courts of the Czech Republic had to decide whether and how to apply the Regulation to a case where the defendant is a foreign national and has no known place of domicile in the State of the court seised. The consumer was a German national, living in the Czech Republic, who had taken out a loan from a Czech bank, with a jurisdiction clause in favour of the 'local court' of the bank, determined according to its registered office.[138] At the time when the contract was concluded, Mr Linder was deemed to be domiciled in Mariánské Lázně (Czech Republic). The place where the consumer was domiciled was more than 150 km from Prague, where the 'local court of the bank' designated by the parties to the contract is situated. According to the bank, it brought an action before the' court with general jurisdiction over the defendant' rather than before the 'local court of the bank' since, at the date on which the proceedings were brought, it was unable, for reasons beyond its control, to submit the original contract to its local court and thereby fulfil the statutory requirement that it bring proceedings before the latter court. Under the relevant rules of procedure, the defendant was considered a person whose domicile was unknown.

The ECJ held that Article 16(2) of the Regulation (establishing jurisdiction against consumers in the case of consumer contracts, only in the courts of the domicile of the

---

[136] See e.g. *Haji-Ioannou & Ors v Frangos & Ors,* Court of Appeal – Civil Division, March 31, 1999, *[1999]* EWCA Civ 1148

[137] n 80 above.

[138] The precise wording being 'in relation to any disputes arising out of this … contract, the local court of the bank, determined according to its registered office as entered in the commercial register at the time of the lodging of the claim, shall have jurisdiction'.

consumer) should apply where the domicile of the consumer is currently unknown but where there was a last known domicile.[139,140]

Domicile of a legal person. In the words of the Regulation (at Recital 11), the domicile of a legal person 'must be defined autonomously so as to make the common rules more transparent and avoid conflicts of jurisdiction.' The mirror provision of Article 60 JR in the Brussels Convention had provided that 'For the purposes of this Convention, the seat of a company or other legal person or association of natural or legal persons shall be treated as its domicile. However, in order to determine that seat, the court shall apply its rules of private international law' (Article 53 BC).

The Commission proposal[141] flagged two reasons for changing the BC approach to corporate domicile in the JR: firstly, the preference in the JR for autonomous concepts as opposed to reliance on Member States' private international law. And secondly, the – in the view of the Commission, consequential – avoidance of negative or positive conflicts of jurisdiction. However if those were indeed the goals of this intervention, the solution chosen (domicile of companies and other legal persons is now defined by three alternative criteria – the statutory seat [or alternatives in the case of the UK and Ireland],[142] the central administration or the principal place of business) would seem to be ill-fated from the start.

Firstly, the use of 3 alternative criteria without any hierarchy or exclusion between them may of course ensure a high degree of likeliness that no negative conflict of jurisdiction will occur (i.e. that no court were to come forward claiming jurisdiction) however is less satisfactory on the positive conflicts side. Moreover, as the Commission also explicitly underlines in its proposal, the three alternative criteria correspond to the three criteria in Article 54 TFEU (right of establishment of companies within the EU) — in fact the goals of Article 54 TFEU and those of the JR do not necessarily coincide.

Having three alternative criteria leads to forum shopping which does have one positive effect on the enforcement stage: if the three connecting factors lead to different

---

[139] 'Regulation No 44/2001 must be interpreted as meaning that: [i] in a situation such as that in the main proceedings, in which a consumer who is a party to a long-term mortgage loan contract, which includes the obligation to inform the other party to the contract of any change of address, renounces his domicile before proceedings against him for breach of his contractual obligations are brought, the courts of the Member State in which the consumer had his last known domicile have jurisdiction, pursuant to Article 16(2) of that regulation, to deal with proceedings in the case where they have been unable to determine, pursuant to Article 59 of that regulation, the defendant's current domicile and also have no firm evidence allowing them to conclude that the defendant is in fact domiciled outside the European Union; [ii] that regulation does not preclude the application of a provision of national procedural law of a Member State which, with a view to avoiding situations of denial of justice, enables proceedings to be brought against, and in the absence of, a person whose domicile is unknown, if the court seised of the matter is satisfied, before giving a ruling in those proceedings, that all investigations required by the principles of diligence and good faith have been undertaken with a view to tracing the defendant.'

[140] In line with established case-law but somewhat distinct from the recent approach of the Grand Chamber to relax the micro-management of the Regulation by the ECJ, the Court (first chamber) posits its conclusion in a very case-specific way, thus leaving open the question if and how it applies in circumstances outside of those of the actual case.

[141] COM(1999) 348.

[142] The special proviso of Article 60(2) only applies 'for the purposes of the United Kingdom and Ireland', meaning where any court – not just a UK or Irish court- is called upon to review whether a corporation has its domicile in these Member States. An Irish court, say, having to decide whether a company has its domicile in France, will apply the statutory seat criterion.

jurisdictions, plaintiff is likely to opt for one where enforcement of the judgment against assets of the defendant is the easiest.

It is noteworthy that there is an exception to Article 60 JR: for the exclusive jurisdictional rule of Article 22(2) (see further below), the 'seat' of the company is determined in accordance with the private international law of the forum.

The *Heidelberg* report did not as yet signal any widespread confusion or jurisdiction conflicts as a result of the Article 60 introduction of alternative domicile rules for companies. However I would concur with those reports which raised doubt as to the necessity and clarity[143] of three different – albeit in practice often overlapping – connecting factors,[144] especially given the declared intent of autonomous application.

2.2.4 The International Impact of the Regulation

Article 2

1. Subject to this Regulation, persons domiciled in a Member State shall, whatever their nationality, be sued in the courts of that Member State.

2. Persons who are not nationals of the Member State in which they are domiciled shall be governed by the rules of jurisdiction applicable to nationals of that State.

Article 3

1. Persons domiciled in a Member State may be sued in the courts of another Member State only by virtue of the rules set out in Sections 2 to 7 of this Chapter.

2. In particular the rules of national jurisdiction set out in Annex I shall not be applicable as against them.

Article 4

1. If the defendant is not domiciled in a Member State, the jurisdiction of the courts of each Member State shall, subject to Articles 22 and 23, be determined by the law of that Member State.

2. As against such a defendant, any person domiciled in a Member State may, whatever his nationality, avail himself in that State of the rules of jurisdiction there in force, and in particular those specified in Annex I, in the same way as the nationals of that State.

The Brussels I Regulation as it stands displays 4 main weaknesses with respect to its external impact:[145,146]

---

[143] See e.g. the application of the BC rule in the UK Civil jurisdiction and judgments Act 1982, Section 42(3): A corporation or association has its seat in the United Kingdom if and only if (a) it was incorporated or formed under the law of a part of the United Kingdom and has its registered office or some other official address in the United Kingdom; or (b) its central management and control is exercised in the United Kingdom. 'Central management and control' clearly is something different than 'administration' or 'central administration', as aptly described by Chambers QC in *King v Crown Energy Trading A.G. & Anor*, Court of Appeal – Commercial Court, February 11, 2003, [2003] EWHC 163 (Comm): 'That aspect has something of the back office about it'.

[144] n 66 above, 178 (52).

[145] See also Layton, A., 'The Brussels I Regulation in the international legal order: Some reflections on reflectiveness', *The Brussels I Review Proposal Uncovered*, Lein, E. (ed.), London, British Institute of International and Comparative Law, 2012, 75 (mentioning three of these).

[146] Generally and excellently on the impact of the Brussels regimes on third States: Kruger, T., *Civil Jurisdiction rules of the EU and their impact on third States*, Oxford, OUP, 2008.

- the protection (through recognition and enforcement) of judgments given under Member States' residual jurisdiction,[147] without any account for third countries' interests;
- the lack of provisions (a lis alibi pendens rule) in the event of jurisdiction exercised under the Regulation, with parallel proceedings in a third State;
- along similar lines (for there is a strong likelihood of parallel proceedings), the exercise of jurisdiction under the Regulation where the subject-matter concerned [typically: one of the exclusive jurisdictional grounds of Article 22 however without the conditions being fulfilled (e.g. an action in rem vis-a-vis real estate in a third State)] is strongly connected to a third State; and finally
- forum clauses in favour of the courts of a third State.

Throughout the Regulation, it is the position of the defendant which is determinant, not that of the plaintiff. The Regulation aims to protect the defendant domiciled in any of the Member States — whatever his or its (in the case of legal persons) nationality — against exorbitant claims of jurisdiction: but the protection is indeed only provided for those domiciled there. Nowhere in the Regulation is this clearer than in Article 3 and 4. Article 3 firstly confirms that for defendants domiciled in one of the Member States (evidently only for matters falling within the material scope of application of the Regulation, see above), only the grounds of jurisdiction included in the JR may be invoked. Article 3(2) adds superfluously that against such defendants, the rules of jurisdiction set out in Annex I of the Regulation, cannot apply. Annex I contains a number of national jurisdictional claims which were regarded as being particularly 'exorbitant'[148] chiefly among them the parochial intuition[149] of France in jurisdictional matters, holding jurisdiction in France over almost any action[150] brought by a plaintiff of French nationality.[151] By virtue of Article 4(2), this large claim of jurisdiction has now been extended to all those domiciled in France, regardless of nationality (again though: only against those *not* domiciled in the EU). The provision, incidentally, has not been formally checked by the French Constitutional Court on its constitutionality. On 29 February 2012, the French Cour de Cassation decided not to grant leave for the constitutionality (or not) of Article 14 of the French Code Civil to be reviewed by the French Constitutional Court.[152] The alleged unconstitutionality at a French level, lies in the perceived 'unfairness' of such trials vis-a-vis the (non-French, indeed by virtue of the Brussels I Regulation the non EU) defendants. The Cour de Cassation saw no merits in the arguments, arguably mostly on the ground of the diminishing practical impact of the provision. The Cour's decision means that for the time being at least, the issue will not be sub judice in the French Constitutional Court, however that does not mean of course that it might not end up at the European Court of Human Rights before long.

---

[147] The meaning of this will become clear below.

[148] Russell, K.A.,, 'Exorbitant jurisdiction and enforcement of judgments: the Brussels system as an impetus for the United States action', *Syracuse Journal of International Law and Commerce*, 1993, 2; cited by Struyven, O., 'Exorbitant jurisdiction in private international law: An introduction', *Jura Falconis*, 1998, 521–548.

[149] K. Clermont and J. Palmer, 'French Article 14 jurisdiction, viewed from the United States', Cornell Law School research paper 04–011, 2004, 2 (available on SSRN). The authors suggest the shock value of France's jurisdictional claims needs to be taken with a pinch of salt.

[150] Issues related to real estate are the most commonly applied exception.

[151] See however Paris criminal court, 3 March 2011, *Ministère public v Joseph Weiler*, declining jurisdiction in a case initiated by an aggrieved author with no links to France other than nationality, against Prof Weiler, with no links to France at all, for the publication of a book review (not by his hand) in an online law journal.

[152] Cour de Cassation No 11–40101.

Indeed whilst Article 3(2) adds superfluously that 'parochial' national claims cannot be invoked against those domiciled in the EU, Article 4(2) provides equally superfluously that these rules can be invoked against those not domiciled in the EU, by anyone domiciled in the particular Member State concerned. In accordance with Article 4(1), national rules of jurisdiction do not apply to defendants domiciled outside of the EU only in the cases of Articles 22 (exclusive jurisdiction: see further) and 23 (choice of court: see further).

Importantly, judgments applying the national grounds of jurisdiction in accordance with Article 4 enjoy the recognition and enforcement provisions of the Regulation (as opposed to the subject-matter which escapes the Regulation completely by virtue of Article 1). This implies that other Member States called upon to recognise and enforce such judgments, have very limited room for manoeuvre to refuse.[153]

The way in which the EU, through the JR, condones[154] or, through the enforcement provisions, perhaps even sponsors exorbitant jurisdiction of some of its Member States, has attracted some international criticism. However most of the EU Member States which previously (for some of them really quite a long time ago) may have employed such wide reach, have since abandoned them. Moreover, other jurisdictions are not averse to similar claims. Consequently it would be fair to say that the theory of 'extraterritorial' EU/ Member States jurisdictional claims, far exceeds its practice.[155] Indeed in its Green Paper on the review of the JR,[156] the European Commission's attention to the workings of the JR in the international legal order focuses more on the issue of 'subsidiary jurisdiction' or 'third State defendants', in other words those national jurisdictional rules which do not concern a party domiciled in any of the EU Member States, or the exclusive grounds of jurisdiction in Article 22 JR, or finally the choice of court clauses under Article 23 JR where at least one of the parties is domiciled in the EU. The concern here is with those domiciled in the EU acting as a *plaintiff*, as opposed to the JR's focus on the defendant.

Natural or legal persons domiciled in the EU but not domiciled in the Member State with an 'interesting' and wide jurisdictional claim, cannot therefore – at least on the basis of the JR – make recourse to such rules. I do not subscribe to the view that this difference is *hardly according to the principle of establishing an area of freedom, justice and security as described by Article [67 TFEU]*[157] which now also seems to be the point of view of the European Commission. The Commissions' view is that

---

[153] See Arts 34 and 35, and Article 45. See also a very limited extra layer of protection for third State domiciliaries in Article 72 JR: This Regulation shall not affect agreements by which Member States undertook, prior to the entry into force of this Regulation pursuant to Article 59 of the Brussels Convention [sic – somewhat sloppy grammar], not to recognise judgments given, in particular in other contracting States to that Convention, against defendants domiciled or habitually resident in a third country where, in cases provided for in Article 4 of that Convention, the judgment could only be founded on a ground of jurisdiction specified in the second paragraph of Article 3 of that Convention. [NB: Article 3 of that Convention is now included in Annex I to the JR. It is not entirely clear why the JR limits the application of Article 72 to agreements concluded prior to its entry into force. There are in fact only two such agreements: one between the UK and Canada, and one between the UK and Australia. Hence only UK courts and only in limited circumstances will be able to refuse recognition and enforcement of the relevant judgment of another Member State.

[154] Certainly not 'creates': exorbitant claims are not directly put forward by the JR. See however the proposals to extend the territorial reach of the JR, below.

[155] Similarly, the *Heidelberg* report, n 62 above, at 156 (46).

[156] n 128 above, 3–4.

[157] *Heidelberg Report*, n 62 above, at 158 (46).

The good functioning of an internal market and the Community's commercial policy both on the internal and on the international level require that equal access to justice on the basis of clear and precise rules on international jurisdiction is ensured not only for defendants but also for claimants domiciled in the Community. The jurisdictional needs of persons in the Community in their relations with third States' parties are similar. The reply to these needs should not vary from one Member State to another, taking into account, in particular, that subsidiary jurisdiction rules do not exist in all the Member States. A common approach would strengthen the legal protection of Community citizens and economic operators and guarantee the application of mandatory Community legislation.[158]

Hence the Commission invited reflection (but would obviously encourage the development of) upon the necessity and appropriateness of additional jurisdictional grounds for disputes involving third State defendants (subsidiary jurisdiction), albeit with a word of caution on the 'international courtesy' implications of such extension (a reference to the international public law issue of 'comity', which I come back to in the chapter on corporate social responsibility, below).

According to the Commission in its eventual proposal for amendment, each defendant as well as plaintiff in the EU should have 'equal' (what it means in fact is 'identical') access to the courts. It suggested specific additional jurisdictional grounds:

- The proposal extends the Regulation's special jurisdiction rules to third country defendants.[159] This amendment is likely to have the most impact in the case of contracts (jurisdiction at the place of contractual performance).
- The protective jurisdiction rules available for consumers, employees and insured will also apply if the defendant is domiciled outside the EU.[160]
- The proposal further harmonises the so-called 'subsidiary' jurisdiction rules: i.e. those where the Member States so far had retained their national PIL rules. Article 4 of the Regulation would be deleted in its entirety, and two additional fora created for disputes involving defendants domiciled outside the EU.

First, the proposal provides that a non-EU defendant can be sued at the place where moveable assets belonging to him are located, provided their value is not disproportionate to the value of the claim and that the dispute has a sufficient connection with the Member State of the court seized: the presence of assets in the EU offsets the absence of the defendant in the EU:

COM(2010) 748 proposes:

Article 25

Where no court of a Member State has jurisdiction in accordance with Articles 2 to 24, jurisdiction shall lie with the courts of the Member State where property belonging to the defendant is located, provided that the value of the property is not disproportionate to the value of the claim; and the dispute has a sufficient connection with the Member State of the court seised.

---

[158] *Ibid*, 3.
[159] COM(2010) 748: deletion of '*A person domiciled in a Member State may, in another Member State, be sued*' from Article 5, introductory sentence.
[160] COM(2010) 748: deletion of '*domiciled in a Member State*' in each of the relevant sub-headings.

In addition, the courts of a Member State will be able to exercise jurisdiction if no other forum guaranteeing the right to a fair trial is available and the dispute has a sufficient connection with the Member State concerned (*"forum necessitatis"*). This provision is regarded to be of particular relevance for EU companies investing in countries with immature legal systems.

The proposed Article 26 reads:

> Where no court of a Member State has jurisdiction under this Regulation, the courts of a Member State may, on an exceptional basis, hear the case if the right to a fair trial or the right to access to justice so requires, in particular:
>
> (a) if proceedings cannot reasonably be brought or conducted or would be impossible in a third State with which the dispute is closely connected; or
> (b) if a judgment given on the claim in a third State would not be entitled to recognition and enforcement in the Member State of the court seised under the law of that State and such recognition and enforcement is necessary to ensure that the rights of the claimant are satisfied; and the dispute has a sufficient connection with the Member State of the court seised.

Given that in each of these cases, there is a likelihood of clashing jurisdictional claims by third countries, the proposal provides for a discretionary *lis pendens* rule for disputes on the same subject matter and between the same parties which are pending before the courts in the EU and in a third country. A court of a Member State can exceptionally stay proceedings if a non-EU court was seized first and it is expected to decide within a reasonable time and the decision will be capable of recognition and enforcement in that Member State. This amendment aims at avoiding parallel proceedings in- and outside the EU. There are of course important differences between such 'discretionary *lis alibi pendens*' rule, and *forum non conveniens* (see also elsewhere in this volume). Nevertheless, the introduction, within the JR, of a discretionary LAP rule is an interesting development. Once sampled, Member States' courts might well develop a taste for it outside the specific context of non-EU based defendants.

The relevant Article in the Commission proposal is Article 34, which reads

> 1. Notwithstanding the rules in Articles 3 to 7, if proceedings in relation to the same cause of action and between the same parties are pending before the courts of a third State at a time when a court in a Member State is seised, that court may stay its proceedings if:
>
> (a) the court of the third State was seised first in time;
> (b) it may be expected that the court in the third State will, within a reasonable time, render a judgment that will be capable of recognition and, where applicable, enforcement in that Member State; and
> (c) the court is satisfied that it is necessary for the proper administration of justice to do so.
>
> 2. During the period of the stay, the party who has seised the court in the Member State shall not lose the benefit of interruption of prescription or limitation periods provided for under the law of that Member State.
>
> 3. The court may discharge the stay at any time upon application by either party or of its own motion if one of the following conditions is met:
>
> (a) the proceedings in the court of the third State are themselves stayed or are discontinued;
> (b) it appears to the court that the proceedings in the court of the third State are unlikely to be concluded within a reasonable time;
> (c) discharge of the stay is required for the proper administration of justice.

4. The court shall dismiss the proceedings upon application by either party or of its own motion if the proceedings in the court of the third State are concluded and have resulted in a judgment enforceable in that State, or capable of recognition and, where applicable, enforcement in the Member State.

The Council's General Approach document of June 2012[161] displays quite a different view on the issue of domicile being the central tenet of the Regulation. Pro memoria (for indeed noted above), the Commission proposal

1. extends the Regulation's special jurisdiction rules to third country defendants;
2. makes the protective jurisdiction rules available for consumers, employees and insured also applicable if the defendant is domiciled outside the EU; and
3. further harmonises the so-called 'subsidiary' jurisdiction rules: i.e. those where the Member States so far had retained their national PIL rules. Article 4 of the Regulation would be deleted in its entirety, and two additional fora created for disputes involving defendants domiciled outside the EU.

The Council, by contrast,

1. reinstates the domicile condition for the special jurisdictional rules[162];
2. reinstates the domicile condition for the protective jurisdictional rules with respect to insurance, however then inserts a slightly confusing section for consumer contracts, and a rather mixed regime for employment contracts.

With respect to *consumer contracts*, the Council re-inserted the reference to Article 4 of the Regulation (albeit in a renumbered 4a fashion, see below), thus in principle reaffirming the domicile criterion: However it then oddly inserts in Article 16(1):

A consumer may bring proceedings against the other party to a contract either in the courts of the Member State in which that party is domiciled or, **regardless of the domicile of the other party**, in the courts for the place where the consumer is domiciled.

(the extract in bold is the Council's addition to the Commission proposal)

I had first assumed that this insertion in Article 16(1) did not trump the Council's re-insertion of Article 4, hence the counterparty would still have to be domiciled in the EU, for the consumer contracts section to apply. However Parliament's suggested recital 11(f) now suggests otherwise:

However, in order to ensure the protection of consumers and employees, to safeguard the jurisdiction of the courts of the Member States in situations where they have exclusive jurisdiction and to respect party autonomy, certain rules of jurisdiction in this Regulation should apply regardless of the defendant's domicile.

Were this amendment to go ahead, the condition of 'directing activities to' the Member State' in Article 15 JR, will gain ever more importance for the territorial scope of the Regulation.

---

[161] Note 134 above.
[162] And adds an additional rule for rights in rem vis-à-vis cultural objects: 'as regards a dispute concerning rights in rem in, or possession of, cultural objects as defined in Council Directive 93/7/EEC on the return of cultural objects unlawfully removed from the territory of a Member State, in the courts for the place where the object is situated at the time the court is seised.'

As far as *employment contracts* are concerned, here, too, the Council refers to Article 4 (4a), in Article 18(1), however then adds in Article 19(2), that an employer not domiciled in a Member State may be sued in a court of a Member State, either in the courts for the place where or from where the employee habitually carries out his work or in the courts for the last place where he did so, or if the employee does not or did not habitually carry out his work in any one country, in the courts for the place where the business which engaged the employee is or was situated.

Non-EU based employers, therefore, are now also within the reach of the JR. In carrying out the contract in the EU, these issues are assumed to have a strong territorial EU link.

3. With respect to the subsidiary jurisdiction rules, the Council re-instates Article 4 (as noted, in a renumbered Article 4a), and does not support the introduction of either an assets-based rule of forum necessitatis: the proposed Articles 25 and 26 have been deleted. However the Council does maintain the discretionary lis alibi pendens rule in Article 34 (parallel proceedings in a third State), by and large along the lines of the Commission proposal, albeit

- specifically limited to cases where jurisdiction of the court of the EU Member State is based on the general rule (domicile of the defendant) or on any of the special jurisdictional rules (for the concept, see further below), not on the basis of exclusive jurisdiction, court of choice agreements, voluntary appearance, or the protected categories. This limitation is less clear in the Commission proposal; and
- with a recital to clarify the meaning of 'proper administration of justice':

When taking into account the proper administration of justice, the court should assess all the circumstances of the particular case. This could include the connections between the facts of the case and the parties and the third State in question, the stage to which the proceedings in the third State have progressed by the time proceedings are initiated in the court of the Member State and whether or not the court of the third State can be expected to give a judgment within a reasonable time.

This assessment could also include whether the court of the third State has exclusive jurisdiction in the particular case in circumstances where a court of a Member state would have exclusive jurisdiction.[163]

The amended Regulation therefore will address only one of the four main problems[164] associated with the external (non-EU) impact of the Regulation: a lis alibi pendens rule where there are parallel proceedings in a third State. The fact that this has been maintained by Council and Parliament is interesting, for the Commission had introduced it precisely because of the new, additional grounds for jurisdiction (the assets rule and forum necessitatis) – neither of which, as noted, has been withheld by the other Institutions.

---

[163] Note 134 above, Article 34.
[164] See note 145 above and the discussion there.

2.2.5 The Jurisdictional Rules of the Regulation

2.2.5.1 A jurisdictional matrix

The most logical way of studying the Regulation, is by reviewing jurisdiction in descending order of exclusivity and specificity: the most specific and exclusive first.[165] This leads to the following matrix:

1. Exclusive jurisdiction, regardless of domicile: Article 22;
2. Jurisdiction by appearance: Article 24;
3. Insurance, consumer and employment contracts: Articles 8–21;
4. Agreements on Jurisdiction ('choice of forum'): Article 23;
5. General jurisdiction: defendants domiciled in the Member State where a court is seized: Article 2[166]
6. 'Special' jurisdiction: defendants domiciled in another Member State: Articles 5–7;
7. 'Residual' jurisdiction: defendants not domiciled in any Member State: Article 4;
8. Loss of jurisdiction: *lis alibi pendens* and related actions: Articles 27–30;
9. Applications for provisional or protective measures: Article 31.

Many ifs and buts apply to each of the entries in the matrix and these will be further studied below.

2.2.6 Exclusive Jurisdiction, Regardless of Domicile: Article 22

The Regulation foresees in five cases of exclusive jurisdiction, regardless of where the defendant is domiciled: rights *in rem* and tenancies of, immovable property; the incorporation of companies and certain other aspects of company law; the validity of entries in public registers; the registration or validity of registered intellectual property rights; and the enforcement of judgments. The adjudication made by the Regulation is at Member State level only. The Regulation does not confer jurisdiction to a particular court of that Member State: that is for the national rules to decide (in other words the internal rules of jurisdiction are not affected by the Regulation).

In the rather exceptional case where exclusive jurisdiction is given to two courts, in particular for the application of Article 22(1), second para, Article 29 prescribes that the court first seized, has exclusive jurisdiction.

The exclusive heads of jurisdiction are said to be required for the proper administration of justice[167] and are also of very practical value: a number of Member States (Germany, Italy) considered in particular the heads of jurisdiction with regard to immovable property to be a matter of public policy. Hence a judgment by another Member State disregarding this principle would not have been recognised in those Member States – which would have been a serious obstacle to the free movement of judgments.[168]

It is the subject-matter of the action which is relevant for the purpose of the proper administration of justice, not the capacity of the defendant. Hence the exclusive grounds for jurisdiction apply regardless of the domicile or nationality of the parties, meaning of

---

[165] Similarly: Briggs, A., *The Conflict of Laws*, Oxford, OUP, 2008, 65.
[166] Consequently while 'domicile of the defendant' is generally quoted of the overall rule of the Regulation, its actual place in the hierarchy is not altogether very high.
[167] Report *Jenard*, OJ [1979] C-59/29.
[168] *Ibid*, 35.

course that those domiciled outside of the EU may very well fall under a Member State jurisdiction by virtue of Article 22. Article 22 is given strict interpretation since it results in depriving the parties of the choice of forum which would otherwise be theirs and, in certain cases, results in their being brought before a court which is not that of any of them.[169]

The matters referred to in this Article will be the subject of exclusive jurisdiction only if they constitute *the principal subject-matter* of the proceedings of which the court is to be seized.[170]

The purpose of Article 22 is to protect the interests of the State which has the exclusive jurisdiction. Hence the defendant cannot grant a different court jurisdiction by virtue of Article 24 (voluntary appearance), nor can parties make a choice of court agreement to such effect (Article 23(5)), and a judgment which conflicts with Article 22 must be denied recognition (Article 35(1)).

However the only interests protected are those of the Member States (and Lugano States, through the Lugano Convention). Whether the courts are allowed to or indeed even may be required to relinquish jurisdiction in favour of non-EU (Lugano) States, was pondered in the run-up to and the aftermath of *Owusu*, reviewed below.

Rights in rem and tenancies of, immovable property

Article 22

The following courts shall have exclusive jurisdiction, regardless of domicile:

1. in proceedings which have as their object rights in rem in immovable property or tenancies of immovable property, the courts of the Member State in which the property is situated.

Over and above the general reasons for exclusivity, recalled above, in the particular case of rights *in rem*, the essential reason for conferring exclusive jurisdiction on the courts of the State in which the property is situated is that the courts of the *locus rei sitae* are the best placed, for reasons of proximity, to ascertain the facts satisfactorily and to apply the rules and practices – including customary law[171] – which are generally those of the State in which the property is situated.[172] These are of course considerations which reflect choice of law rather than jurisdiction – and indeed the *lex rei sitae* is generally the applicable law for actions *in rem*.

The more practical element of having to take into account the need to make entries in land registers located where the property is situated is also referred to[173] however would not in fact seem to have been the heaviest on the mind of the drafters.

In *Reichert*, the ECJ clarified the meaning of "proceedings which have as their object rights in rem in immovable property". Dresdner Bank, as creditor, applied by means of an action available under French national law (specifically an *actio pauliana*), to have a donation of immovable property set aside on the ground that it was made by its debtor in

---

[169] See also Case 73/77 *Sanders v Van der Putte*, [1977] ECR 2383; Case C-73/04 *Klein*, [2005] ECR I-8667, para 15 and relevant case-law cited there.
[170] Report Jenard, 34.
[171] Report *Jenard*, 35.
[172] Case 73/77 *Sanders*, n 169 above.
[173] Report *Jenard*, 35.

fraud of its rights. The Court held that rights *in rem* in immovable property as included in Article 22 are

> actions which seek to determine the extent, content, ownership or possession of immovable property or the existence of other rights in rem therein and to provide the holders of those rights with the protection of the powers which attach to their interest.[174]

In the case at issue, the *actio pauliana* is

> based on the creditor's personal claim against the debtor and seeks to protect whatever security he may have over the debtor's estate. If successful, its effect is to render the transaction whereby the debtor has effected a disposition in fraud of the creditor's rights ineffective as against the creditor alone. The hearing of such an action, moreover, does not involve the assessment of facts or the application of rules and practices of the locus rei sitae in such a way as to justify conferring jurisdiction on a court of the State in which the property is situated.[175]

Likewise, actions, including preventive action, to halt nuisance emanating from a particular use of immovable property, have as their main object the halting of the nuisance, not the rights in rem related to the property concerned.[176] 'It is not sufficient that a right in rem in immovable property be involved in the action or that the action have a link with immovable property: the action must be based on a right *in rem* and not on a right *in personam*, save in the case of the exception concerning tenancies of immovable property.'[177] Thus in the case of *Webb v Webb*, the action for a declaration that a person holds immovable property as trustee and for an order requiring that person to execute such documents as should be required to vest the legal ownership in the plaintiff, did not constitute an action in rem within the meaning of Article 22 of the Regulation.

As for all exclusive grounds of jurisdiction, the 'principal' object of the proceedings has to be rights *in rem* or tenancies. This is not a denoter present in the text of the JR but rather distilled from the *Jenard* report and emphasised in case-law.

Specifically with respect to the extension to tenancies

The *raison d'être* of the extension to tenancies is the fact that tenancies are closely bound up with the law of immovable property and with the provisions, generally of a mandatory character, governing its use, such as legislation controlling the level of rents and protecting the rights of tenants, including tenant farmers.[178] The extension to 'tenancies of immovable property' does not add the qualification 'rights in rem', hence Article 22(1) with respect to tenancies, applies to any proceedings concerning rights and obligations arising under an agreement for the letting of immovable property, irrespective of whether the action is based on a right *in rem* or on a right *in personam*.[179]

The *Jenard* report indicates specifically that the Convention draftsmen intended to cover inter alia disputes over compensation for damage caused by tenants,[180] and in *Rösler* the Court extended the reach of Article 22(1) with respect to tenancies, gener-

---

[174] Case C-115/88 *Mario Reichert et al v Dresdner Bank*, [1990] ECR I-27, para 11.
[175] *Ibid*, para 12.
[176] Case C-343/04 *Land Oberösterreich*, [2006] ECR I-4557.
[177] Case C-294/92 *Webb v Webb*, [1994] ECR I-1717.
[178] Case C-280/90 *Hacker v Euro-Relais*, [1992] ECR I-1111, para 8.
[179] Case C-292/93 *Lieber*, [1994] ECR I-2535, para 10, 13, 20).
[180] Report Jenard, 34–35.

ally to disputes concerning the respective obligations of landlord and tenant under the agreement.[181] Only disputes which are only indirectly related to the use of the property let, such as those concerning the loss of holiday enjoyment and travel expenses, do not fall within the exclusive jurisdiction.[182]

While the advantage of this wide approach is indeed to ensure that almost all potential disputes between landlord and tenant will be caught by the Article 22(1) exclusive ground of jurisdiction,[183] the Heidelberg report nevertheless suggests that it would seem too inflexible in the case of tenancy of office space, and hence suggested amending the Regulation on this point.[184] The Commission has picked this up in its final proposal, which read in relevant part

> in agreements concerning tenancies of premises for professional use, parties may agree that a court or the courts of a Member State are to have jurisdiction in accordance with Article 23;

In other words for professional use only, the Commission had intended for parties to be able to avoid the exclusive jurisdiction by choice of court. This however was not withheld by Council and Parliament.

Regardless of the extensive line taken by the Court as described above, in line with the overall requirement strictly to apply the exclusive grounds of jurisdiction, the principal aim of the agreement does have to be of a tenancy nature for it to be caught by Article 22(1). More complex agreements of the travel operator type, which include transport arrangements etc. are not covered by Article 22,[185] neither are timeshare club memberships[186] [187] where these do not provide for a clear link between the membership and one specific property actually to be used by the member. The very presence of a tour operator in the chain of parties, however, must not confuse: tour operators quite regularly, by virtue of contractual or statutory arrangements, are subrogated ['*through subrogation, one person steps into the shoes* of another in order to enable the former to exercise rights belonging to the latter',[188] so that, in such case, the tour operator is not acting in its capacity as a professional tour operator but as if it were the owner of the property in question] in the rights and duties of the landlord: in that case, the dispute takes place as if it were between the landlord and the tenant, and Article 22(1) can have full impact.

Article 22(1) has two ancillary rules:

Short-term holiday lets

Firstly, Article 22(1), 2° grants additional jurisdiction to the courts of the domicile of the defendant, in cases which effectively involve holiday lets only, subject to conditions which do not need much clarification:

---

[181] Case 241/83 *Rösler v Rottwinkel*, [1985] ECR 99,

[182] *Ibid.*

[183] Fawcett, JJ and Carruthers, JM, *Cheshire, North & Fawcett's Private International Law*, 14th ed. Oxford, OUP, 2008, 280.

[184] Heidelberg report, n 62 above, para 319.

[185] *Hacker*, n 178 above, para 11 ff.

[186] Case C-73/04 *Klein v Rhodos Management*, [2005] ECR I-8667.

[187] Such time-share contracts are covered by the Article 15 protection for consumer contracts: see the Commission proposal leading to the adoption of the JR, COM(1999) 348, 16.

[188] Case C-8/98 *Dansommer*, [2000] ECR I-393, para 37.

However, in proceedings which have as their object tenancies of immovable property concluded for temporary private use for a maximum period of six consecutive months, the courts of the Member State in which the defendant is domiciled shall also have jurisdiction, provided that the tenant is a natural person and that the landlord and the tenant are domiciled in the same Member State.

This rule is exactly the situation where Article 29 JR might come in: the landlord might well want to sue in the more natural forum of Article 22(1), while the consumer would normally be more inclined to sue in the Member State of his domicile. In such instance, Article 29 clearly rewards the party who got their first.

Contractual action in combination with actio in rem

Further, Article 6(4) JR allows for contractual action to be combined with an action *in rem* against the same defendant, which is useful in particular in mortgages actions:

A person domiciled in a Member State may also be sued (…)

in matters relating to a contract, if the action may be combined with an action against the same defendant in matters relating to rights in rem in immovable property, in the court of the Member State in which the property is situated.

The incorporation of companies and certain other aspects of company law

Article 22

The following courts shall have exclusive jurisdiction, regardless of domicile: (…)

2. in proceedings which have as their object the validity of the constitution, the nullity or the dissolution of companies or other legal persons or associations of natural or legal persons, or of the validity of the decisions of their organs, the courts of the Member State in which the company, legal person or association has its seat. In order to determine that seat, the court shall apply its rules of private international law;

This 'exclusive' ground for jurisdiction, too, may lead to a need to apply Article 29 JR, as not all Member States apply the same definition of 'seat' of a company. Hence while the cancellation in this particular case of the three-tier 'harmonised' EU definition of company domicile in Article 60 JR, is meant to safeguard exclusive jurisdiction, in practice Article 29 JR may need to settle in favour of the court first seized (provided the plaintiff can make a valid case that under the private international law rules of the forum, the company concerned has its 'seat' there).

The specific aim of the exclusive jurisdiction in the event of Article 22(2) is to avoid conflicting judgments being given as regards the existence of a company or as regards the validity of the decisions of its organs.[189] The courts of the Member State in which the company has its seat appear to be those best placed to deal with such disputes, inter alia because it is in that State that information about the company will have been notified and made public.[190]

---

[189] Report Jenard, 35.
[190] Case 73/77 *Sanders*, [1977] ECR 2383, paras 11 and 17.

By analogy with *Webb v Webb*, referred to above, Article 22(2) needs to be interpreted strictly. In the face of differences in the language versions of Article 22(2), it is not sufficient for the exclusive jurisdiction to apply that the legal action has some link with a decision adopted by an organ of the company. It follows that Article 22(2) covers only disputes in which a party is challenging the validity of a decision of an organ of a company under the company law applicable or under the provisions governing the functioning of its organs, as laid down in its Articles of Association,[191] inter alia because these are the cases where consultation of the publication formalities applicable to a company may be necessary. Disputes regarding the manner in which company organs exercise their functions,[192] are not covered by Article 22(2). If all disputes involving a decision by an organ of a company were to come within the scope of that article, that would mean that all legal actions brought against a company – whether in matters relating to a contract, or to tort or delict, or any other matter – would almost always come within the jurisdiction of the courts of the Member State in which the company has it seat,[193] and indeed it would mean that it would be sufficient for a company to plead as a preliminary issue that the decisions of its organs that led to the conclusion of a contract or to the performance of an allegedly harmful act are invalid in order for exclusive jurisdiction to be unilaterally conferred upon the courts where it has its seat, which would at the same time make the jurisdiction in such cases extremely unpredictable, as it would depend on whether such defence was or was not claimed, for the case to have to be heard exclusively in the Member State where the company has its seat.[194] Further support for this stance is found in the Report Jenard.[195] An important application lies in *not* applying Article 22(2) in cases where a defendant claims that a company representative had no authority to enter into a forum clause under Article 23 JR.[196]

The Court's case-law on this point differs from the issues under consideration in Article 22(4), reviewed below. Per *GAT*[197], the court seized must at the very least halt its proceedings until the Court (if that is different) which by application of Article 22(4) has jurisdiction on the validity of the patent, has ruled on that validity. The ECJ distinguishes between the two on the basis of a much closer link between the jurisdictional ground in Articled 22(4), and the dispute at issue: in any procedure launched because of an alleged patent etc. infringement, the validity of that patent lies at the core of the dispute. By contrast, the Court held in *BVG* that in a dispute of a contractual nature, questions relating

---

[191] Case C-372/07 *Hassett*, [2008] ECR I-7403, para 26.

[192] In the case of *Hassett*, the applicants were doctors who were members of the MDU. The MDU is a professional association, established as a company incorporated under English law and having its registered office in the United Kingdom. The MDU's mission is inter alia to provide indemnity to its members in cases involving professional negligence on their part. Accordingly, the doctors sought an indemnity and/or a contribution from the MDU in respect of any sum which either of them might be required to pay by way of indemnity to the relevant health board. The Board of Management of the MDU, relying on Articles 47 and 48 of the company's Articles of Association, under which any decision concerning a request for an indemnity comes within its absolute discretion, refused to grant their requests.

[193] *Hassett*, n 191 above.

[194] Case C-144/10 *BVG*, not yet reported, para 34.

[195] Report Jenard, 35: According to the report, 'Article 16(2) of the convention provides for exclusive jurisdiction in proceedings which are '*in substance*' concerned with the validity of the constitution, the nullity or the dissolution of the company, legal person or association, or with the validity of the decisions of its organs.' (emphasis added).

[196] See e.g. the High Court in *CALYON v Wytwornia Sprzetu Komunikacynego PZL Swidnik SA [2009] EWHC 1914 (Comm)* at 93 ff.

[197] n 200 below.

to the contract's validity, interpretation or enforceability are at the heart of the dispute and form its subject-matter. Any question concerning the validity of the decision to conclude the contract, taken previously by the organs of one of the companies party to it, must be considered ancillary. While it may form part of the analysis required to be carried out in that regard, it nevertheless does not constitute the sole, or even the principal, subject of the analysis.[198]

The validity of entries into public registers

Article 22

The following courts shall have exclusive jurisdiction, regardless of domicile: (…)

3. in proceedings which have as their object the validity of entries in public registers, the courts of the Member State in which the register is kept;

This provision does not require lengthy commentary. It covers in particular entries in land registers, land charges registers and commercial registers.[199]

Proceedings concerned with the registration or validity of patents, trade marks, designs, or other similar rights required to be deposited or registered

Article 22

The following courts shall have exclusive jurisdiction, regardless of domicile: (…)

4. in proceedings concerned with the registration or validity of patents, trade marks, designs, or other similar rights required to be deposited or registered, the courts of the Member State in which the deposit or registration has been applied for, has taken place or is under the terms of a Community instrument or an international convention deemed to have taken place.

Without prejudice to the jurisdiction of the European Patent Office under the Convention on the Grant of European Patents, signed at Munich on 5 October 1973, the courts of each Member State shall have exclusive jurisdiction, regardless of domicile, in proceedings concerned with the registration or validity of any European patent granted for that State;

As with all the other grounds for exclusive jurisdiction, the matters referred to in this sub para will be the subject of exclusive jurisdiction only if they constitute *the principal subject-matter* of the proceedings of which the court is to be seized (Report Jenard, referred to above). Simple actions for infringement do not fall within Article 22 but are covered by Article 5.3 JR. Per the judgment in *GAT*, where in the course of such action of infringement, the validity of the patents etc. is challenged (by way of defence), the court with the infringement claim must not entertain the question of validity,[200] however it is unclear whether the infringement proceedings have to be stayed until the court with exclusive jurisdiction has ruled, or perhaps even transferred to that court. In view of the exceptional nature of Article 22, one would assume that the most likely interpretation has

---

[198] n 194 above, para 37–39 and 45–46.
[199] Report Jenard, 35.
[200] Case C-4/03 *Gesellschaft fur Antriebstechnik – GAT*, [2006] ECR I-6509.

to be the former – however special jurisdictional rules themselves are an exception to the general rule of the domicile of the defendant, hence there might not be a reason for it to trump Article 22 on that point. The proposed Commission amendment to this part of Article 22 merely specifically endorses the *GAT* judgment, however does not address the uncertainty as to whether the procedure in such case needs to be stayed or rather completely transferred.

The reach of Article 22(4) is all the more apparent in interim proceedings for provisionary measures, which routinely co-incide with a procedure on the substance. This therefore raises the question of the relationship between Article 22(4) and provisionary measures, including Article 31 JR, which looks at provisionary measures (and which will be looked at in detail below). In *Solvay*,[201] the referring court asked, in essence, whether the fact that a defence of invalidity of a patent has been raised in interim proceedings for a cross-border prohibition against infringement, in parallel to main proceedings for infringement, is sufficient, and, if so, under what formal or procedural conditions, for Article 22(4) to become applicable.

Cruz Villalon AG, after a brief 'tour d'horizon' of the various procedural realities that might exists, opined that Article 22(4) is not applicable when the validity of a patent is raised only in interim proceedings, only in so far as the decision likely to be adopted at the end of those proceedings does not have any final effect. Whether the latter is the case depends on the applicable (national) law.

The ECJ itself adopted a more or less similar approach: Article 22 and Article 31 are part of different Titles of the Regulation. Hence they are very different in nature and quite unconnected. However on the other hand, the application of one part of the Regulation may of course have an impact on the remainder, hence one cannot simply apply different parts of the Regulation in splendid isolation. The ECJ notes that according to the referring court, the court before which the interim proceedings have been brought does not make a final decision on the validity of the patent invoked but makes an assessment as to how the court having jurisdiction under Article 22(4) of the Regulation would rule in that regard, and will refuse to adopt the provisional measure sought if it considers that there is a reasonable, non-negligible possibility that the patent invoked would be declared invalid by the competent court. Hence there is no risk of conflicting decisions: the interim proceedings that have been brought will not in any way prejudice the decision to be taken on the substance by the court having jurisdiction under Article 22(4).

'...does not make a final decision': this effectively means that the Court simply states that as long as the main condition of Article 31 is met [measures covered by Article 31 need to be 'provisional' see further, below], Article 22(4) does not interfere with a court's jurisdiction under Article 31. The remaining crucial consideration after *Solvay*, which was hinted at the by the referring court but not quite captured by the ECJ, is the impact of Article 22(4) on interim measures based *not* on Article 31 JR, but rather on other Articles of the Regulation (see also below, in the review of Article 31).

It is noteworthy that the IP enforcement Directive,[202] while providing for minimum harmonisation of a number of procedural standards, has no impact on either jurisdictional

---

[201] Case C-616/10, not yet reported in ECR. See further in this volume for the Article 6 aspects of this judgment.
[202] Directive 2004/48, OJ [2004] L195/16. The Commission's report on the application of the Directive identified no issues with specific relevance for either jurisdiction or applicable law: COM(2010) 779.

or indeed applicable law (the Rome I and II Regulations, see below). The Directive requires all Member States to apply effective, dissuasive and proportionate remedies and penalties against those engaged in counterfeiting and piracy, and so creates a level playing field for right holders in the EU. All Member States will have a similar set of measures, procedures and remedies available for right holders to defend their intellectual property rights (be they copyright or related rights, trademarks, patents, designs, etc.) if they are infringed.

Proceedings concerned with the enforcement of judgments

Article 22

The following courts shall have exclusive jurisdiction, regardless of domicile: (…)

5. In proceedings concerned with the enforcement of judgments, the courts of the Member State in which the judgment has been or is to be enforced.

The key word for this exclusive jurisdictional ground is 'enforcement'. 'Proceedings concerned with the enforcement of judgments' means 'those proceedings which can arise from recourse to force, constraint or distraint on movable or immovable property in order to ensure the effective implementation of judgments and authentic instruments'.[203] Difficulties arising out of such proceedings come within the exclusive jurisdiction of the courts for the place of enforcement, as was already the case in a number of bilateral Treaties concluded between a number of the original States, and also in the internal private international law of those States.

The Jenard report does not quote a specific reason for the reasoning behind this exclusivity, however one assumes that such proceedings are so intimately linked to the use of judicial authority and indeed force, that any complications in their enforcement ought to be looked at exclusively by the courts of the very State whose judicial authorities are asked to carry out the enforcement. In the words of the Court of Justice:

the essential purpose of the exclusive jurisdiction of the courts of the place in which the judgment has been or is to be enforced is that it is only for the courts of the Member State on whose territory enforcement is sought to apply the rules concerning the action on that territory of the authorities responsible for enforcement.[204]

There must have been a 'judgment': proactive steps taken to facilitate an eventual judgment, which are in other words preparatory to the enforcement of a decision, e.g. freezing injunctions, are outside the scope of the Article.[205] The strict interpretation also means that the Article 22(5) ground for jurisdiction must not thwart jurisdiction of other courts who would have jurisdiction had the case not been brought as part of an enforcement difficulty. For instance, the court which has jurisdiction on the basis of Article 22(5), cannot hear the defence against enforcement which is based on a request for compensation with a different mutual debt.[206]

---

[203] Report Jenard, 36, with reference to Braas, *Précis de procedure civile*.
[204] Case C-261/90 *Reichert v Dresdner Bank*, [1992] ECR 2149, para 26.
[205] *Ibid*, re *Actio Pauliana*.
[206] Case 220/84 *AS-Autoteile Service*, [1985] ECR 2267.

2.2.7 Jurisdiction by appearance: Article 24

> Apart from jurisdiction derived from other provisions of this Regulation, a court of a Member State before which a defendant enters an appearance shall have jurisdiction. This rule shall not apply where appearance was entered to contest the jurisdiction, or where another court has exclusive jurisdiction by virtue of Article 22.

Jurisdiction by appearance or 'submission' was thought of in particular vis-à-vis the 'exorbitant' jurisdictional claims of some of the Member States:[207] these cannot in principle be invoked against those with domicile in another Member State, however they can voluntarily be submitted to. Article 24 generally assists legal certainty by acting as an implicit choice of forum clause. Indeed submission trumps any prior explicit choice of forum between the parties: the plaintiff evidently has given its consent by initiating the procedure in the court concerned; the defendant consents by its appearance.[208] Submission however is not possible for cases included in Article 22, although it is possible for the cases included in the sections dealing with the protected categories.[209]

Whether the defendant must be domiciled in the EU, is the object of some discussion. Most of the arguments pro and contra use *a contrario* reasoning, for instance by contrasting Article 23 JR (which does refer to either or the parties having to have domicile in the EU), or refer simply to the Jenard Report.[210] However it would seem that the discussion now ought to be fairly settled, given that Article 4 JR explicitly provides that if the defendant is not domiciled in the EU and neither Article 22 nor 23 apply, national PIL of the Member States determines jurisdiction. Member States law of course typically allows for submission, too, however any such judgment will not be covered by the JR (including the enforcement title).

There will be no submission if the defendant merely appears to contest jurisdiction. Quite a few of the language versions of the Convention (e.g. in English, the Convention read '*solely to contest the jurisdiction*' – emphasis added) seemed to suggest that the protective force of the second sentence of Article 24 was lost from the moment the defendant argued on the merits of the case. In *Elefanten Schuh* however the Court held that given that civil procedure in quite a few of the Member States requires that a party proceed with a defence on the merits lest it lose the possibility to raise this defence at all, the objectives of the Convention/Regulation (legal certainty, and rights of the defence[211]) would be jeopardised were no defence on the merits at all possible so as not to lose the protection of the second sentence. The Court consequently set aside the majority of

---

[207] Report Jenard, 38 – France's rules were singled out.

[208] Case C-150/80 *Elefanten Schuh*, [1981] ECR 1671, para 11.

[209] Case C-111/09 *Vienna Insurance Group*, [2010] ECR I-4545, para 30: '(...) although in the fields concerned by Sections 3 to 5 of Chapter II of that regulation the aim of the rules on jurisdiction is to offer the weaker party stronger protection (see, in that regard, Case C-463/06 *FBTO Schadeverzekeringen* [2007] ECR I-11321, para 28), the jurisdiction determined by those sections cannot be imposed on that party. If that party deliberately decides to enter an appearance, Regulation No 44/2001 leaves him the option to defend himself as to substance before a court other than those determined on the basis of those sections.'

[210] Report Jenard, p.38: 'Article 18 governs jurisdiction implied from submission. *If a defendant domiciled in a Contracting State* is sued in a court of another Contracting State which does not have jurisdiction under the Convention...' (emphasis added). The report however mentions this in passing only – relying to such degree on every single reference in the Jenard report in the face of the text of the Convention/Regulation itself, would not necessarily seem warranted. See also above re the in my view problematic impact of the preparatory reports generally.

[211] *Elefanten Schuh*, n 208 above, para 14.

language versions and held that defence on the merits does not amount to submission, provided the rejection of jurisdiction is not entered after the very first defence on the merits.[212] This is now reflected in all language version of the JR.[213]

2.2.8 Insurance, consumer and employment contracts: Articles 8–21

2.2.8.1 Protected categories – Generally

It is a feature of both the jurisdiction Regulation and the Regulations concerning applicable law (in particular Rome I and Rome II, see below), to include a number of headings which aim to provide for protective measures to the benefit of what are seen as weaker parties. These 'protected categories' have now become 'European', or 'harmonised' protected categories, in that European policy itself consider that these weaker categories need to be protected against abuse which would result from standard clauses in contracts forced upon them by the contracting party with the upper hand. The original Brussels Convention's angle to the protected categories was more practical. With a number of original Member States having such protective clauses, the drafters of the Convention predicted complications at the recognition and enforcement stage: 'Failure to take account of the problem raised by these rules of jurisdiction might not only have caused recognition and enforcement to be refused in certain cases on grounds of public policy, which would be contrary to the principle of free movement of judgments, but also result, indirectly, in general re-examination of the jurisdiction of the court of the State of origin.'[214] In harmonising the jurisdiction stage for categories such as these described below, the Convention highlighted the immediate link between the first and the final step of private international law: one could have continued to allow Member States to refuse recognition on the basis of public policy, including consumer protection etc. However this would have simply postponed the uncertainty to the third stage. Much better with a view to legal certainty, therefore, to seek harmonisation at the very first stage.[215] A similar approach of course was adopted vis-à-vis the exclusive jurisdictional grounds of Article 22.

For the protected categories, the Convention and subsequently Regulation chose a middle way in terms of party autonomy: for insurance and consumer contracts[216] it did not opt for a single jurisdiction (cf. for the matters of exclusive jurisdiction falling under Article 22). 'A choice, albeit a limited one, exists between the courts of the different States where *the plaintiff* is a protected person.' (emphasis added)[217] The specificity for the protected categories indeed lies in their position as a plaintiff: they can insist that they be sued in their place of domicile, however that is not out of the ordinary: that is the general rule of Article 2 JR. Rather, they are protected in that they can insist to sue themselves in their Member State of domicile – the *forum actoris* – if they are consumer

---

[212] *Idem*: Case 27/81 *Rohr*, [1981] ECR 2431.

[213] See also the Commission proposal which led to the JR, COM(1999) 348, p.19: 'a defendant who enters an appearance may contest the jurisdiction of the court seised no later than the time at which he is considered by national law as presenting his defence on the merits. In other words, the fact of presenting a defence on the merits may render the argument contesting the jurisdiction nugatory only if that argument is presented no later than the defence on the merits.'

[214] Report Jenard, 28.

[215] *Ibid*, 29.

[216] Employment contracts were only included in the Regulation – neither the original BC nor the later amendments included them.

[217] Report Jenard, page 29.

or insured (insureds in fact have an even bigger choice), or their place of employment in the case of contracts for employment, added in the JR. As reported in the Jenard Report, the drafters of the BC opted not to impose these fora too restrictively, rather, to insert conditional options for choice.

It is noteworthy that the condition of inequality is assumed: actual inequality need not be proven.[218]

The provisions for the protected categories are reinforced by Article 35 JR: courts in the other Member States are bound not to recognise judgments held in breach of the insurance and consumer contract provisions. Oddly the JR did not extend this to the newly inserted category of employment contracts.

Below we review the two sections which lead to most disputes in practice: consumer contracts, and contracts for employment. Where the text of the JR speaks for itself, we let it do exactly that.

2.2.8.2 Consumer contracts

Section 4 Jurisdiction over consumer contracts

Article 15

1. In matters relating to a contract concluded by a person, the consumer, for a purpose which can be regarded as being outside his trade or profession, jurisdiction shall be determined by this Section, without prejudice to Article 4 and point 5 of Article 5, if:

(a) it is a contract for the sale of goods on instalment credit terms; or
(b) it is a contract for a loan repayable by instalments, or for any other form of credit, made to finance the sale of goods; or
(c) in all other cases, the contract has been concluded with a person who pursues commercial or professional activities in the Member State of the consumer's domicile or, by any means, directs such activities to that Member State or to several States including that Member State, and the contract falls within the scope of such activities.

2. Where a consumer enters into a contract with a party who is not domiciled in the Member State but has a branch, agency or other establishment in one of the Member States, that party shall, in disputes arising out of the operations of the branch, agency or establishment, be deemed to be domiciled in that State.

3. This Section shall not apply to a contract of transport other than a contract which, for an inclusive price, provides for a combination of travel and accommodation.

Article 16

1. A consumer may bring proceedings against the other party to a contract either in the courts of the Member State in which that party is domiciled or in the courts for the place where the consumer is domiciled.

2. Proceedings may be brought against a consumer by the other party to the contract only in the courts of the Member State in which the consumer is domiciled.

---

[218] Although in the specific case of insurance of large risks, Article 13(5) juncto Article 14 extend the possibilities of choice of forum: the insured can be assumed to act in a professional capacity for risks of this nature.

3. This Article shall not affect the right to bring a counter-claim in the court in which, in accordance with this Section, the original claim is pending.

Article 17

The provisions of this Section may be departed from only by an agreement:

1. which is entered into after the dispute has arisen; or

2. which allows the consumer to bring proceedings in courts other than those indicated in this Section; or

3. which is entered into by the consumer and the other party to the contract, both of whom are at the time of conclusion of the contract domiciled or habitually resident in the same Member State, and which confers jurisdiction on the courts of that Member State, provided that such an agreement is not contrary to the law of that Member State.

Article 15 lists the conditions for this section to apply. These are quite different from the Brussels convention, which read in relevant part (Article 13)

In proceedings concerning a contract concluded by a person for a purpose which can be regarded as being outside his trade or profession, hereinafter called the 'consumer', jurisdiction shall be determined by this Section, without prejudice to the provisions of Articles 4 and 5(5), if it is:

(1) a contract for the sale of goods on instalment credit terms, or
(2) a contract for a loan repayable by instalments, or for any other form of credit, made to finance the sale of goods, or
(3) any other contract for the supply of goods or a contract for the supply of services and
    (a) in the State of the consumer's domicile the conclusion of the contract was preceded by a specific invitation addressed to him or by advertising, and
    (b) the consumer took in that State the steps necessary for the conclusion of the contract. Where a consumer enters into a contract with a party who is not domiciled in a Contracting State but has a branch, agency or other establishment in one of the Contracting States, that party shall, in disputes arising out of the operations of the branch, agency or establishment, be deemed to be domiciled in that State.

This Section shall not apply to contracts of transport.

2.2.8.3 Contract

First of all, there has to be a 'contract'. It has been difficult for the ECJ to define 'contract' within the meaning of Article 15 without wading into national territory on what a 'contract' implies. Purely unilateral commitments do not suffice however this is not always easy to discern.[219] The Court's view on 'contract' within the meaning of Article 15 is stricter than its view on 'contract' in the broader jurisdictional rule for contracts in Article 5(1)(a) (discussed below): i.e. a relationship will be more easily accepted as

---

[219] See Case C-180/06 *Ilsinger* [2009] ECR I-3961. There was indeed some discussion as to whether the finding on this point in *Engler* (n 221, below) had to be revised given the changing in wording in the consumer title, between the Brussels Convention and the Regulation. In particular, the condition that *the consumer took in that State the steps necessary for the conclusion of the contract* no longer exists in the Regulation. The ECJ nevertheless held that in particular because of the reference to 'matters related to a contract *concluded by...*' in Article 15(1), the Regulation, too, requires an element of mutual obligations.

'contractual' under Article 5 than it is under Article 17. In *Gabriel*,[220] and *Engler*[221] the Court held that the consumer contracts heading is applicable only in so far as, first, the claimant is a private final consumer not engaged in trade or professional activities (see below), second, the legal proceedings relate to a contract between that consumer and the professional vendor for the sale of goods or services which has given rise to reciprocal and interdependent obligations between the two parties[222] and, third, in the current version of the Regulation, that the condition with respect to 'directing activities' is fulfilled (see also below).

The condition of 'reciprocal and interdependent obligations between the two parties' certainly includes a subsection of contracts, only.

2.2.8.4 Consumer contract

Further, the contract has to be a 'consumer' contract. *Gruber* is the standard reference.[223] Johann Gruber, an Austrian farmer, had purchased tiles from a store in Germany. The tiles were destined to be used partly for private and partly for business purposes. To assess the new conditions of the JR, one had best review the conditions which applied previously: Article 13 of the Brussels Convention was worded as follows:

> In proceedings concerning a contract concluded by a person for a purpose which can be regarded as being outside his trade or profession, hereinafter called "the consumer", jurisdiction shall be determined by this Section … if it is:
>
> 1. a contract for the sale of goods on instalment credit terms; or
> 2. a contract for a loan repayable by instalments, or for any other form of credit, made to finance the sale of goods; or
> 3. any other contract for the supply of goods or a contract for the supply of services, and
>   (a)   in the State of the consumer's domicile the conclusion of the contract was preceded by a specific invitation addressed to him or by advertising; and
>   (b)   the consumer took in that State the steps necessary for the conclusion of the contract.…

2.2.8.5 Concluded with a consumer

In Gruber the ECJ first of all revisited its conclusions in Benincasa, where it stated that the concept of 'consumer' for the purposes of the first paragraph of Article 13 and the first paragraph of Article 14 of the Brussels Convention must be strictly construed, reference being made to the position of the person concerned in a particular contract, having regard to the nature and aim of that contract and not to the subjective situation of the person concerned, since the same person may be regarded as a consumer in relation to certain supplies and as an economic operator in relation to others. The Court held that only contracts concluded outside and independently of any trade or professional activity or purpose, solely for the purpose of satisfying an individual's own needs in terms of private consumption, are covered by the special rules laid down by the Convention to protect the

---

[220] Case C-96/00 *Gabriel* [2002] ECR I-6367.
[221] Case C-27/02 *Engler* [2005] ECR I-481, para 29.
[222] The court did however hold that there was a contract within the meaning of Article 5 JR.
[223] Case C-464/01 *Gruber* [2005] ECR I-439.

consumer as the party deemed to be the weaker party. Such protection is unwarranted in the case of contracts for the purpose of a trade or professional activity.[224]

Given that the rule for the protected categories is an exception to the standard rule, the burden of proof has to lie with the person invoking the exception. In the case of purchase for dual use, such as in *Gruber*, it is for the person invoking the protection, to show that the business use of the purchase is only negligible. For that purpose, the national court should take into consideration not only the content, nature and purpose of the contract, but also the objective circumstances in which it was concluded.[225] The 'objective evidence' of the case ought normally to suffice, without having to review whether the seller could have been aware of the business purpose. Should the objective evidence not suffice, then the awareness of the buyer may play a role, albeit with a presumption in favour of the buyer: for even if jurisdiction for the protected categories is an exception, nevertheless consumers ought not to be casually deprived of the protection of the relevant title of the JR. Here the ECJ instructs the national courts to determine whether the other party to the contract could reasonably have been unaware of the private purpose of the supply because the supposed consumer had in fact, by his own conduct with respect to the other party, given the latter the impression that he was acting for business purposes: that would be the case, for example, where an individual orders, without giving further information, items which could in fact be used for his business, or uses business stationery to do so, or has goods delivered to his business address, or mentions the possibility of recovering value added tax.[226]

2.2.8.6 Type of contract – and application in an internet context

Article 15 JR next lists the categories of contracts which are covered by the exception. It includes two specific contracts and one generic, however the generic category only applies if the consumer has in some way been actively recruited across border. The precise wording of the relevant provision was adapted with a view to specifying its application in an e-commerce context.[227] In comparison with the BC provision, Article 15 JR has included 3 major changes: 'any other contract for the supply of goods or a contract for the supply of services' had been replaced with 'in all other cases'; the specific indication of exactly what type of activity of the seller had to precede the contract (a specific invitation, or advertising), has been replaced with two alternatives: either 'activities pursued in' the Member State of the consumer's domicile; or 'directed towards' that State. And finally the deletion of the condition that the consumer must have taken necessary steps for the conclusion of his contract in his home State.

In its proposal for the JR, the European Commission listed the application of the consumer contracts title to e-commerce as one of just 4 'chief innovations' of the jurisdictional rules of the JR as compared to the BC: 'the material scope of the provisions governing consumer contracts has been extended so as to offer consumers better protec-

---

[224] Case C-269/95 *Benincasa* [1997] ECR I-3767, para 16–18 and as summarised by the Court in *Gruber* para 36.

[225] *Gruber* para 46–47.

[226] Ibidem para 48 ff.

[227] For an overview outside the context of the Jurisdiction Regulation, too, see Tang, Z., 'Exclusive choice of forum clauses and consumer contracts in E-Commerce', *Journal of Private International Law*, 2005, 237–268.

tion, notably in the context of electronic commerce'.[228] Specifically within the context of Article 15, the proposal states

'The criteria given in Article 13(3) of the Brussels Convention have been reframed to take account of developments in marketing techniques. For one thing, the fact that the condition in old Article 13 that the consumer must have taken the necessary steps in his State has been removed means that Article 15, first paragraph, point (3), applies to contracts concluded in a State other than the consumer's domicile. This removes a proved deficiency in the text of old Article 13, namely that the consumer could not rely on this protective jurisdiction when he had been induced, at the co contractor's instigation, to leave his home State to conclude the contract. For another, the consumer can avail himself of the jurisdiction provided for by Article 16 where the contract is concluded with a person pursuing commercial or professional activities in the State of the consumer's domicile directing such activities towards that State, provided the contract in question falls within the scope of such activities.

The concept of activities pursued in or directed towards a Member State is designed to make clear that point (3) applies to consumer contracts concluded via an interactive website accessible in the State of the consumer's domicile. The fact that a consumer simply had knowledge of a service or possibility of buying goods via a passive website accessible in his country of domicile will not trigger the protective jurisdiction. The contract is thereby treated in the same way as a contract concluded by telephone, fax and the like, and activates the grounds of jurisdiction provided for by Article 16.

The removal of the condition in old Article 13(3)(b) that the consumer must have taken necessary steps for the conclusion of the contract in his home State shall also be seen in the context of contracts concluded via an interactive website. For such contracts the place where the consumer takes these steps may be difficult or impossible to determine, and they may in any event be irrelevant to creating a link between the contract and the consumer's State. The philosophy of new Article 15 is that the co contractor creates the necessary link when directing his activities towards the consumer's State.

(...)

The Commission has noted that the wording of Article 15 has given rise to certain anxieties among part of the industry looking to develop electronic commerce. These concerns relate primarily to the fact that companies engaging in electronic commerce will have to contend with potential litigation in every Member State, or will have to specify that their products or services are not intended for consumers domiciled in certain Member States. One such concern relates to the perceived problems with the notion of "directing his activities" in Article 15, first paragraph, point (3), which is considered difficult to comprehend in the Internet world.'

While the Commission proposal and indeed the eventual Regulation hence acknowledge the difficulties in applying the consumer protection provisions in an internet context, the text does not actually offer any definitive guidance in how it ought to be applied.[229] The

---

[228] COM(1999) 348, 7.

[229] The Commission itself near acknowledged as much by announcing in its explanatory memorandum that notwithstanding the application of the express provisions for the internet context, it would hold a hearing on the topic.

most specific statutory hook to which to attach internet jurisdiction became 'the direction of activities towards the Member State of the consumer.' Precisely how 'interactivity' is to be determined in the internet context, was not specified by the proposal. Consequently this proviso had led to speculative analysis as to the level of website interaction which triggers Article 15.[230] The Article itself, as noted, employs 'directed to'[231] and 'by any means'. In a joint 'Statement on Articles 15 and 73,[232] Council and Commission specifically mention that the language or currency which a website uses do not constitute a relevant factor. Likewise, as already noted, the fact that a consumer simply had knowledge of a service or possibility of buying goods via a passive website accessible in his country of domicile will not trigger the protective jurisdiction. Hence the question remains what does trigger the application of Article 15 in an internet context.

In my view, the changes to the consumer title in Article 15 JR are neither here nor there. They were announced as having been introduced with specific consideration for the internet however they seemed to provide little in the way of real guidance which would address the very uncertainty for E-tailers which they professed to address. In the Joined Cases *Pammer* and *Alpenhof*,[233] the Court of Justice hands national courts a number of criteria which helps them apply the Article in an internet context. In *Pammer*, Mr Pammer, whose domicile is in Austria, booked a crossing by freight liner, with Reederei Karl Schlüter, a company established in Germany, however through an intermediary company, whose seat was also in Germany and which operates in particular via the internet. The intermediary company had promised all kinds of facilities on board the ship which Mr Pammer found were not actually on board – whence he refused to board the ship and sought compensation. Reederei Karl Schlüter contended that it did not pursue any professional or commercial activity in Austria and raised the plea that the

---

[230] Gillies, L., 'Addressing the Cyberspace Fallacy": Targeting the Jurisdiction of an Electronic Consumer Contract', *International Journal of Law & Information Technology*, 2008, (242) 253.

[231] See in the trademark context, the *L'Oréal/Ebay* litigation and the ECJ's instruction that where goods located in a third State, which bear a trade mark registered in an EU Member State or a Community trade mark and have not previously been put on the market in the EEA or, in the case of a Community trade mark, in the EU, (i) are sold by an economic operator on an online marketplace without the consent of the trade mark proprietor to a consumer located in the territory covered by the trade mark or (ii) are offered for sale or advertised on such a marketplace targeted at consumers located in that territory, the trade mark proprietor may prevent that sale, offer for sale or advertising by virtue of the rules set out in relevant EU legislation. It is the task of the national courts to assess on a case-by-case basis whether relevant factors exist, on the basis of which it may be concluded that an offer for sale or an advertisement displayed on an online marketplace accessible from the territory covered by the trade mark is 'targeted at' consumers in that territory: When the offer for sale is accompanied by details of the geographic areas to which the seller is willing to dispatch the product, that type of detail is of particular importance in the said assessment: Case C-324/09 *L'Oréal*, not yet reported in ECR. The ECJ itself noted in para 64 of its *L'Oréal* judgment the analogy with the *Pammer and Alpenhof* litigation 'Intended target of information' as a criterion of applicability was also confirmed as the criterion for application of the Database Directive, Directive 96/9 in Case C-173/11 *Football Dataco*, not yet reported in ECR (judgment of 18 October 2012): 'Article 7 of Directive 96/9/EC of the European Parliament and of the Council of 11 March 1996 on the legal protection of databases must be interpreted as meaning that the sending by one person, by means of a web server located in Member State A, of data previously uploaded by that person from a database protected by the *sui generis* right under that directive to the computer of another person located in Member State B, at that person's request, for the purpose of storage in that computer's memory and display on its screen, constitutes an act of 're-utilisation' of the data by the person sending it. That act takes place, at least, in Member State B, where there is evidence from which it may be concluded that the act discloses an intention on the part of the person performing the act to target members of the public in Member State B, which is for the national court to assess.' In other words, mere accessibility of data does not suffice to grant jurisdiction under the Database directive.

[232] OJ [2001] L12/1.

[233] Joined Cases C-585/08 and C-144/09 [2010] ECR I-12527.

Austrian court lacked jurisdiction. In *Alpenhof*, after finding out about the hotel from its
website, Mr Heller reserved a number of rooms for a period of a week. His reservation
and the confirmation thereof were effected by email, the hotel's website referring to an
address for that purpose. Mr Heller then found fault with the hotel's services and left
without paying his bill despite Hotel Alpenhof's offer of a reduction. Hotel Alpenhof then
brought an action before an Austrian court. Mr Heller raised the plea that the court before
which the action had been brought lacked jurisdiction. He submits that, as a consumer, he
can be sued only in the courts of the Member State of his domicile, namely the German
courts, pursuant to Article 15(1)(c) JR.

The Court first of all remarks that the conditions for application which consumer
contracts must fulfil are now worded more generally than they were in the BC, in
order to ensure better protection for consumers with regard to new means of communication and the development of electronic commerce (at para 59). In particular
the use of the words 'by any means' indicates, in the view of the Court, a wider
range of activities (at para 61). However as the Court acknowledges, the wording of
the JR does not make it clear whether the words 'directs such activities to' refer to
the trader's intention to turn towards one or more other Member States or whether
they relate simply to an activity turned *de facto* towards them, irrespective of such
an intention (at para 63). The mere existence of a website is not enough proof of a
direction of one's activity towards a particular State. By their nature, websites, once
created, are accessible worldwide and a company need not, as it would have had to
do for more traditional forms of advertising, incur extra costs simply for the consumers in other States to be able to access the website (at para 66 ff). For the Court,
the trader must have manifested its intention to establish commercial relations with
consumers from one or more other Member States, including that of the consumer's
domicile (at para 75).

> It must therefore be determined, in the case of a contract between a trader and a given
> consumer, whether, before any contract with that consumer was concluded, there was evidence
> demonstrating that the trader was envisaging doing business with consumers domiciled in other
> Member States, including the Member State of that consumer's domicile, in the sense that it
> was minded to conclude a contract with those consumers. (at para 76).

> Whether it was minded to conclude a contract with those customers', or, put in different words,
> what is required are 'clear expressions of the intention to solicit the custom of that State's
> consumers (at para 80).

The Court subsequently lists a number of criteria which indicates such state of mind (at
para 81 ff): mention that it is offering its services or its goods in one or more Member
States designated by name; the disbursement of expenditure on an internet referencing
service to the operator of a search engine in order to facilitate access to the trader's
site by consumers domiciled in various Member States; the international nature of the
activity at issue, such as certain tourist activities; mention of telephone numbers with the
international code; use of a top-level domain name other than that of the Member State
in which the trader is established, for example '.de', or use of neutral top-level domain
names such as '.com' or '.eu'; the description of itineraries from one or more other
Member States to the place where the service is provided; and mention of an international
clientele composed of customers domiciled in various Member States, in particular by
presentation of accounts written by such customers.

With respect to the language or currency used, the Court states

the joint declaration of the Council and the Commission(...)states that they do not constitute relevant factors for the purpose of determining whether an activity is directed to one or more other Member States. That is indeed true where they correspond to the languages generally used in the Member State from which the trader pursues its activity and to the currency of that Member State. If, on the other hand, the website permits consumers to use a different language or a different currency, the language and/or currency can be taken into consideration and constitute evidence from which it may be concluded that the trader's activity is directed to other Member States. (at para 84)

The criteria which the Court therefore withholds in summary, are (para 93–94):

the international nature of the activity, mention of itineraries from other Member States for going to the place where the trader is established, use of a language or a currency other than the language or currency generally used in the Member State in which the trader is established with the possibility of making and confirming the reservation in that other language, mention of telephone numbers with an international code, outlay of expenditure on an internet referencing service in order to facilitate access to the trader's site or that of its intermediary by consumers domiciled in other Member States, use of a top-level domain name other than that of the Member State in which the trader is established, and mention of an international clientele composed of customers domiciled in various Member States. It is for the national courts to ascertain whether such evidence exists.

On the other hand, the mere accessibility of the trader's or the intermediary's website in the Member State in which the consumer is domiciled is insufficient. The same is true of mention of an email address and of other contact details, or of use of a language or a currency which are the language and/or currency generally used in the Member State in which the trader is established.

The judgment in *Pammer* and *Alpenhof* handed the national courts what must be a near-complete set of indications which ought to enable them to judge intention to solicit custom from customers in other Member States.

The Alpenhof judgment triggered speculation as to whether Article 15(1)(c) requires a contract between consumer and trader, concluded at a distance. In Pammer/Alpenhof, Alpenhof had argued amongst others that that its contract with the consumer is concluded on the spot and not at a distance, as the room keys are handed over and payment is made on the spot, and that accordingly Article 15(1)(c) cannot apply. The Court of Justice had answered this with the very paragraph which then tempted the Oberster Gerichtshof – Austria, into the preliminary review in *Mühlleitner*,[234] Article 87:

In that regard, the fact that the keys are handed over to the consumer and that payment is made by him in the Member State in which the trader is established does not prevent that provision from applying if the reservation was made and confirmed at a distance, so that the consumer became contractually bound at a distance.

This paragraph seemed to suggest 'at a distance' as the trigger for the application of Article 15(1)(c) which in turn led to the preliminary question:

Does the application of Article 15(1)(c) [ ] presuppose that the contract between the consumer and the undertaking has been concluded at a distance?

---

[234] Case C-190/11 *Daniela Mühlleitner v Ahmad Yusufi and Wadat Yusufi.*

Villalon AG replied making specific reference to the history of Article 15, in particular with reference to the old text, under the Brussels Convention. That old provision seemed to imply that where the consumer's contracting party had encouraged him to leave his Member State of domicile so as to conclude the contract elsewhere, the consumer could not make recourse to the protective regime. Other changes to the relevant title, too, suggested if anything that Council and Commission's intention with the new provisions was definitely not to limit their scope of application: had they intended to do so, the AG suggests, the Institutions would have limited Article 15's scope to contracts concluded at a distance. Court of Justice case-law hints at the same need for a wide approach [in particular, Ilsinger,[235] where the Court of Justice held that the scope of Article 15(1)(c) appears 'to be no longer being limited to those situations in which the parties have assumed reciprocal obligations.']

The AG concluded with the suggestion that the reference to 'distance' in para 87 of *Alpenhof* refers to a factual circumstance, rather than a condition for application. The Court of Justice agreed.[236] It stuck to both a literal (no mention of distance contracts in the relevant provision), teleological (protection of consumers) and historical (purpose of the change in the Regulation as compared with the previous text in the Convention) interpretation. The relevant Article now only requires that the trader pursue commercial or professional activities in the Member State of the consumer's ('consumer' is separately defined) domicile or, by any means, directs such activities to that Member State or to several States including that Member State and, secondly, that the contract at issue falls within the scope of such activities.

To many the conclusion may have seemed obvious, and the issue covered by acte clair (meaning the national court could have referred to the arguably obvious meaning of the provision, not to have to refer to the Court of Justice). In particular, the ECJ has repeatedly emphasised the relevance of the consumer title in the Jurisdiction Regulation. On the other hand, however, the same Court has been quite anxious to give national courts detailed and specific instructions on the application of tiny details in the Regulation, making application of the acte clair doctrine quite difficult: many things one thought were clear, have been answered by the Court in unexpected ways.

National courts therefore are caught between the proverbial rock and the hard stone. Either they refer profusely, thereby feeding the cycle of micromanagement. Or they make extended use of acte clair, thereby risking unequal application of the Regulation (and potentially European Commission irk). On the issue of Article 15(1)(c) at least, the former would seem to have prevailed: in *Slot*, Case C-98/12 (hitherto still pending),[237] the German Bundesgerichtshof has asked essentially the same question.

For E-tailers, the application of Article 15 ff is not without consequences. As plaintiffs they can principally only sue in the domicile of the defendant-consumer. If they are being sued, they can find themselves hauled in front of the courts of the consumer's domicile (the consumer may choose to sue in the Member state of the E-tailer's domicile, however they are unlikely to prefer that in lieu of the courts of their own Member State). This has procedural as well as substantive consequences. Evidently procedural issues are determined by the forum (statutes of limitation, legal fees etc.) however this would not seem

---

[235] Case C-180/06 *Renate Ilsinger v Martin Dreschers*, [2009] ECR I-3961.
[236] Judgment of 6 September 2012 in Case C-190/11 Mühlleitner, not yet published in ECR.
[237] One would imagine the case will be struck off the register.

a dramatic inconvenience to the average E-tailer: the possibility of being sued in other Member States ought not to scare a serious E-tailer. With respect to substantive law, the consumer protection laws of the forum may well, at the least partially, become applicable, in spite of a standard choice of law clause in the contract (see the analysis of the Rome I Regulation, below in this volume). However this, too, for EU-based E-tailers, need not be an obstacle of a serious kind, particularly in light of the increased ('maximum') harmonisation of consumer law across the EU. In other words, for those E-tailers who are domiciled in the EU (in the extensive sense of Article 15(2) JR), *Pammer* and *Alpenhof* has opened a clarified if not new possibility that they will be *sub judice* in a Member State outside their standard corporate domicile.

Therefore prima facie at least the impact of Article 15 in the internet context would seem to be more relevant to non-EU based E-tailers. This intuition however clashes with the territorial limitations to the JR. Lest consumer and E-tailer conclude a valid choice of forum clause in favour of a court in the EU, or lest both parties submit to the jurisdiction of an EU court[238] — neither of these scenarios being very likely in light of the position of the non-EU based E-tailer — the JR simply does not apply to conflicts between EU consumers and non-EU based E-tailers, even with the extended notion of 'domicile' (see below). An E-tailer without any physical presence in the EU escapes the application of the Regulation.

It is noteworthy that the European Commission should like to change this. In its proposal to amend the JR,[239] it inter alia extended the application of all special jurisdictional rules to defendants without domicile in the EU. In particular the special jurisdictional rule with respect to contracts (Article 5(1) as well as the jurisdictional rules with respect to the protected categories, would be brought within the purview of plaintiffs acting against non-EU based defendants. The European Parliament had — in my view justifiably — expressed serious reservations with respect to this proposal, however as I note above, after the lengthy preparation process of the review of the JR, both Parliament and Council now favour an extension indeed of the consumer title of the JR to defendants not domiciled in the EU.

A final note on the application of European private international law in the internet context may be taken from Michael Bogdan: 'it is no longer possible to claim that the existing conflict rules on contracts and torts in general stem from pre-Internet days and can be disregarded because they are not suitable for the Internet environment.'[240] While a comment made in terms of applicable law rather than jurisdiction, it applies to jurisdictional issues, too. Current private international laws have not ignored the internet. Where they have inserted specific provisions to capture e-commerce, they have in themselves not brought more clarity. It is the common sense of national courts and ultimately of the ECJ which will have to make the rule adapt to the factual circumstance.[241]

---

[238] See however the analysis of Article 24, above, re submission and non-EU based parties.

[239] COM(2010) 748.

[240] Bogan, M., 'Some reflections on contracts and torts in cyberspace in view of Regulations Rome I and Rome II', in Boele-Woelki, K., Einhorn, T., Girsberger, D., and Symeonides, S. (eds), *Convergence and Divergence in Private International Law – Liber Amicorum Kurt Siehr*, Munchen, Schulthess, 2010, (375) 387.

[241] In that sense I would support Michael Bogdan's second suggestion made ibidem, rather than the first: i.e. a reasonable and flexible interpretation of the Regulations' provisions, rather than amending the Regulations.

2.2.8.7 Extended notion of 'domicile' for jurisdiction over consumer contracts

Article 15 JR reads in relevant part

> Where a consumer enters into a contract with a party who is not domiciled in the Member State but has a branch, agency or other establishment in one of the Member States, that party shall, in disputes arising out of the operations of the branch, agency or establishment, be deemed to be domiciled in that State.

The Court of Justice has clarified both 'branch, agency or other establishment' and 'operations' within the context of Article 5(5) JR:

> The concept of branch, agency or other establishment implies a place of business which has the appearance of permanency, such as the extension of a parent body, has a management and is materially equipped to negotiate business with third parties so that the latter, although knowing that there will if necessary be a legal link with the parent body, the head office of which is abroad, do not have to deal directly with such parent body but may transact business at the place of business constituting the extension.[242]

> This concept of operations comprises on the one hand actions relating to rights and contractual or non-contractual obligations concerning the management properly so-called of the agency, branch or other establishment itself such as those concerning the situation of the building where such entity is established or the local engagement of staff to work there. Further it also comprises those relating to undertakings which have been entered into at the abovementioned place of business in the name of the parent body and which must be performed in the Contracting State where the place of business is established and also actions concerning non-contractual obligations arising from the activities in which the branch, agency or other establishment within the above defined meaning, has engaged at the place in which it is established on behalf of the parent body.[243]

The objectives of Article 5(5) are of course not those of Article 15(2). The former's aim is to facilitate proceedings.[244] The latter's aim is to protect the consumer, from a public policy point of view. Hence one may indeed have to be careful simply to apply the interpretation of one, to the other.[245]

2.2.8.8 Alternative fora introduced by agreement

Article 17 (mutually agreed alterations to the rule of Article 16) would seem fairly straight-forward at first sight. There are one or two unclear aspects which have been addressed neither by the initial BC, nor by the JR (and their respective preparatory works).

Article 17(2) allows for agreements which 'allow the consumer to bring proceedings in courts other than those indicated in this Section'. The text of the JR does not say so, however given the protective intention of the section, it would seem safe to assume that the forum or fora assigned by such agreement must not be exclusive: i.e. they must be fora where the consumer can sue over and above those identified by Article 16.[246]

---

[242] Case 33/78 *Somafar*, [1979] ECR 2183, para 12.
[243] *Ibid* para 13.
[244] *Ibid* para 7.
[245] Anoveros Terradas, B, 'Restrictions on Jurisdiction Clauses in Consumer Contracts in the European Union, Oxford U Comparative L Forum, 2003, 1, at ouclf.iuscomp.org, consulted July 2011, text after n 136.
[246] Pro: *ibid*, text after n 173.

Next, common assumption is that the conditions of Article 17 are supplementary to those of Article 23.[247] The ECJ has hinted so much with respect to the similar agreements in the insurance title of the JR.[248] This however most certainly does not follow from the text of either JR or Convention, neither is there any trace of it in the preparatory works (pre Schlosser). It would be tempting to say that the conditions of Article 23 must apply, for otherwise the seemingly flexible conditions of Article 17 stand-alone, would leave the consumer less protected under Article 17 than he would in a standard application of Article 23. However, would it? Article 17 indeed does not impose any formal conditions, which Article 23 does (see further below). The substantive conditions of Article 17 on the other hand are much stricter. As noted by the *Jenard Report*, the provisions for the protected categories are a halfway house between the exclusive jurisdictional grounds of Article 22, and the 'complete' freedom of Article 23.[249] In the specific case of consumer contracts, complete freedom to agree on a forum only rules once the dispute has arisen. Lest one assumes that consumers need absolute protection even at a stage when the consumer is likely to have sought legal advice [the JR assumes that once the dispute has arisen, both parties are on a more equal footing with respect to deciding where one ought to litigate; moreover, jurisdiction clauses at that stage tend not to be part of 'take it or leave it' general terms and conditions, where disadvantageous clauses can easily be smuggled into], there would seem no need to make such agreement subject to much conditions. Other than the absolute freedom once the dispute has arisen, Article 17 severely limits the possible fora that may be selected, all heavily in favour of the consumer. Consequently I would submit that making such clauses subject to the stricter rules of Article 23, would rather work against the consumer.

Does the defendant have to be domiciled in a Member State, for Article 17 to apply? It might be tempting to say that he does not,[250] in other words that Article 17 on this point follows Article 23, however in my view the *a contrario* argument is too strong. The JR does not include many instances where the domicile of the defendant is irrelevant (see Article 22 and 23, and to some degree Article 13(4), and a departure from that point in my view must not too freely be assumed.[251]

Finally, by virtue of positive harmonisation in the consumer protection law field, any agreements on jurisdiction in the context of contracts caught by Chapter II Section 4 of the JR, have to abide by the conditions of the Unfair Contract Terms Directive,[252] although in my view this is more relevant with respect to choice of law (and the relation with the Rome I Regulation: see below), than it is for jurisdiction clauses.[253]

---

[247] See e.g. Fawcett, JJ and Carruthers, JM, n 183 above, 271. See also the Schlosser Report, para 161: 'Although Article [17] is not expressed to be subject to Article [23] the Working Party was unanimously of the opinion that agreements on jurisdiction must, in so far as they are permitted at all, comply with the formal requirements of Article [23]. Since the form of such agreements is not governed by Section 4, it must be governed by Article [23].

[248] Case 201/82 *Gerling*, [1983] ECR 2503, para 20: "where in a contract of insurance a clause conferring jurisdiction is inserted for the benefit of the insured who is not a party to the contract but a person distinct from the policy-holder, it must be regarded as valid within the meaning of Article 17 of the Convention provided that, as between the insurer and the policy-holder, the condition as to writing laid down therein has been satisfied and provided that the consent of the insurer in that respect has been clearly and precisely manifested".

[249] Report Jenard, 29.

[250] E.g. Fawcett, JJ and Carruthers, JM, n 183 above, 272.

[251] See also ibidem.

[252] Directive 93/13, OJ [1993] L95/29, as amended.

[253] See i.a. the analysis by Anoveros Terradas, B, n 245 above.

2.2.8.9 Contracts for individual employment

Section 5 Jurisdiction over individual contracts of employment

Article 18

1. In matters relating to individual contracts of employment, jurisdiction shall be determined by this Section, without prejudice to Article 4 and point 5 of Article 5.

2. Where an employee enters into an individual contract of employment with an employer who is not domiciled in a Member State but has a branch, agency or other establishment in one of the Member States, the employer shall, in disputes arising out of the operations of the branch, agency or establishment, be deemed to be domiciled in that Member State.

Article 19

An employer domiciled in a Member State may be sued:

1. in the courts of the Member State where he is domiciled; or
2. in another Member State:
    (a) in the courts for the place where the employee habitually carries out his work or in the courts for the last place where he did so, or
    (b) if the employee does not or did not habitually carry out his work in any one country, in the courts for the place where the business which engaged the employee is or was situated.

Article 20

1. An employer may bring proceedings only in the courts of the Member State in which the employee is domiciled.

2. The provisions of this Section shall not affect the right to bring a counter-claim in the court in which, in accordance with this Section, the original claim is pending.

Article 21

The provisions of this Section may be departed from only by an agreement on jurisdiction:

1. which is entered into after the dispute has arisen; or
2. which allows the employee to bring proceedings in courts other than those indicated in this Section.

The BC contained one or two gradually introduced specific provisions on contracts for employment, however no overall title such as for consumer and insurance contracts. Such a title was contemplated at the drafting stage, however eventually abandoned.[254] Firstly the Committee drawing up the Convention, in a somewhat sloppily drafted explanation (where it mixed choice of law rules with positive harmonisation of substantive law[255]) argued that disputes over contracts of employment should as far as possible[256] be brought

---

[254] Report Jenard, 23 ff.

[255] Which may have been a prospect of some promise at the time of the original Convention however became of course ever trickier with the accession of new Member States to the EEC and of non-EEC Member States to the Lugano Convention.

[256] The Report does not elaborate however one assumes that the drafters were mindful of the interplay between collective and individual labour law, and of collective labour agreements being a very nationally driven part of the law applicable between employment relations.

before the courts of the State whose law governs the contract. With attempts already then under way by the European Commission to harmonise applicable law, the Committee therefore did not think that rules of jurisdiction should be laid down which might not coincide with those which may later be adopted for determining the applicable law.[257] In order to lay down such rules of jurisdiction, the Committee would have had to take into account not only the different ways in which work can be carried out abroad, but also the various categories of worker: wage-earning or salaried workers recruited abroad to work permanently for an undertaking, or those temporarily transferred abroad by an undertaking to work for it there; commercial agents, management, etc. The Committee feared that any attempt by it to draw such distinctions might have provided a further hindrance to the Commission s work. Further, in the view of the Committee, contractual freedom still ruled happily at the time of drafting the Convention (one assumes that this is far less the case now, as labour law has grown exponentially since the 1970s), and the Committee wanted to respect that by making contracts for individual employment generally subject to the standard rules.

The following courts consequently were given jurisdiction: the courts of the State where the defendant is domiciled (Article 2); the special jurisdictional rule for contracts of (now) Article 5 JR, if that place is in a State other than that of the domicile of the defendant – with a specific formula for employment contracts to determine the 'place of performance of the obligation in question';[258] and any court on which the parties have expressly or impliedly agreed (Articles 23[259] and 24). In the case of proceedings based on a tort committed at work Article 5 (3), which provides for the jurisdiction of the courts for the place where the harmful event occurred, could also apply.

The JR now collects all relevant provisions with respect to employment contracts in one Section. Authoritative source for much of the provisions is the *Jenard and Möller* report which accompanied the 1988 Lugano Convention, as well as extensive case-law of the Court of Justice. This book is not the place for extensive review of that body of case-law. One case however may be worth highlighting, inter alia because of its impact on other parts of the Regulation. In *Mahamdia*,[260] a former driver working for the Algerian embassy in Germany, had at the time of the start of the employment, concluded an agreement with the embassy which designated Algerian courts as the courts with exclusive jurisdiction. The Court first of all applied the Vienna Convention on Diplomatic Relations and held that an Embassy often acts iure gestionis, not iure imperii, and that under the Vienna rules, the EU is perfectly entitled to apply the JR given that it applies to 'civil

---

[257] But see Kidner, R., 'Jurisdiction in European Contracts of Employment', *Industrial Law Journal*, 1998, (103) 104, n 5: In Case C-125/92 *Mulox v Geels*, [1993] ECR I-4075, the Advocate General thought it would be a mistake to exaggerate the importance of the link between jurisdiction and the *lex causae.* I agree.

[258] 'In matters relating to a contract, in the courts for the place of performance of the obligation in question; in matters relating to individual contracts of employment, this place is that where the employee habitually carries out his work, or if the employee does not habitually carry out his work in any one country, the employer may also be sued in the courts for the place where the business which engaged the employee was or is now situated'. (this specific proviso was added in 1989).

[259] With specific provision for employment contracts: 'In matters relating to individual contracts of employment an agreement conferring jurisdiction shall have legal force only if it is entered into after the dispute has arisen or if the employee invokes it to seise courts other than those for the defendant's domicile or those specified in Article 5 (1).'

[260] Case C-154/11 *Mahamdia*, not yet published in ECR.

and commercial' matters.[261] In that vein, an embassy may very well have to be regarded as an 'establishment' within the meaning of Article 18(2).

2.2.8.10 Insurance Contracts

Section 3 Jurisdiction in matters relating to insurance

Article 8

In matters relating to insurance, jurisdiction shall be determined by this Section, without prejudice to Article 4 and point 5 of Article 5.

Article 9

1. An insurer domiciled in a Member State may be sued:

(a) in the courts of the Member State where he is domiciled, or
(b) in another Member State, in the case of actions brought by the policyholder, the insured or a beneficiary, in the courts for the place where the plaintiff is domiciled,
(c) if he is a co-insurer, in the courts of a Member State in which proceedings are brought against the leading insurer.

2. An insurer who is not domiciled in a Member State but has a branch, agency or other establishment in one of the Member States shall, in disputes arising out of the operations of the branch, agency or establishment, be deemed to be domiciled in that Member State.

Article 10

In respect of liability insurance or insurance of immovable property, the insurer may in addition be sued in the courts for the place where the harmful event occurred. The same applies if movable and immovable property are covered by the same insurance policy and both are adversely affected by the same contingency.

Article 11

1. In respect of liability insurance, the insurer may also, if the law of the court permits it, be joined in proceedings which the injured party has brought against the insured.

2. Articles 8, 9 and 10 shall apply to actions brought by the injured party directly against the insurer, where such direct actions are permitted.

3. If the law governing such direct actions provides that the policyholder or the insured may be joined as a party to the action, the same court shall have jurisdiction over them.

Article 12

1. Without prejudice to Article 11(3), an insurer may bring proceedings only in the courts of the Member State in which the defendant is domiciled, irrespective of whether he is the policyholder, the insured or a beneficiary.

2. The provisions of this Section shall not affect the right to bring a counter-claim in the court in which, in accordance with this Section, the original claim is pending.

---

[261] Whether the embassy at issue acted iure imperii or iure gestionis was held to be up to the national court to decide.

Article 13

The provisions of this Section may be departed from only by an agreement:

1. which is entered into after the dispute has arisen, or
2. which allows the policyholder, the insured or a beneficiary to bring proceedings in courts other than those indicated in this Section, or
3. which is concluded between a policyholder and an insurer, both of whom are at the time of conclusion of the contract domiciled or habitually resident in the same Member State, and which has the effect of conferring jurisdiction on the courts of that State even if the harmful event were to occur abroad, provided that such an agreement is not contrary to the law of that State, or
4. which is concluded with a policyholder who is not domiciled in a Member State, except in so far as the insurance is compulsory or relates to immovable property in a Member State, or
5. which relates to a contract of insurance in so far as it covers one or more of the risks set out in Article 14.

Article 14

The following are the risks referred to in Article 13(5):

1. any loss of or damage to:
(a) seagoing ships, installations situated offshore or on the high seas, or aircraft, arising from perils which relate to their use for commercial purposes;
(b) goods in transit other than passengers' baggage where the transit consists of or includes carriage by such ships or aircraft;
2. any liability, other than for bodily injury to passengers or loss of or damage to their baggage:
   (a) arising out of the use or operation of ships, installations or aircraft as referred to in point 1(a) in so far as, in respect of the latter, the law of the Member State in which such aircraft are registered does not prohibit agreements on jurisdiction regarding insurance of such risks;
   (b) for loss or damage caused by goods in transit as described in point 1(b);
3. any financial loss connected with the use or operation of ships, installations or aircraft as referred to in point 1(a), in particular loss of freight or charter-hire;
4. any risk or interest connected with any of those referred to in points 1 to 3;
5. notwithstanding points 1 to 4, all "large risks" as defined in Council Directive 73/239/ EEC(7), as amended by Council Directives 88/357/EEC(8) and 90/618/EEC(9), as they may be amended.

2.2.9 Agreements on Jurisdiction ('choice of forum' or 'prorogation of jurisdiction'): Article 23

Article 23

1. If the parties, one or more of whom is domiciled in a Member State, have agreed that a court or the courts of a Member State are to have jurisdiction to settle any disputes which have arisen or which may arise in connection with a particular legal relationship, that court or those courts shall have jurisdiction. Such jurisdiction shall be exclusive unless the parties have agreed otherwise. Such an agreement conferring jurisdiction shall be either:

(a) in writing or evidenced in writing; or

(b) in a form which accords with practices which the parties have established between themselves; or

(c) in international trade or commerce, in a form which accords with a usage of which the parties are or ought to have been aware and which in such trade or commerce is widely known to, and regularly observed by, parties to contracts of the type involved in the particular trade or commerce concerned.

2. Any communication by electronic means which provides a durable record of the agreement shall be equivalent to "writing".

3. Where such an agreement is concluded by parties, none of whom is domiciled in a Member State, the courts of other Member States shall have no jurisdiction over their disputes unless the court or courts chosen have declined jurisdiction.

4. The court or courts of a Member State on which a trust instrument has conferred jurisdiction shall have exclusive jurisdiction in any proceedings brought against a settlor, trustee or beneficiary, if relations between these persons or their rights or obligations under the trust are involved.

5. Agreements or provisions of a trust instrument conferring jurisdiction shall have no legal force if they are contrary to Articles 13, 17 or 21, or if the courts whose jurisdiction they purport to exclude have exclusive jurisdiction by virtue of Article 22.

The provisions on forum clauses are drafted in a way 'not to impede commercial practice, yet at the same time to cancel out the effects of clauses in contracts which might go unread',[262] or otherwise 'unnoticed'.[263] Both the overall deference which the BC and JR show for choice of court agreements as well as the conditions imposed upon them, are heavily influenced not just by the pre-existing bilateral treaties between quite a number of the initial Convention States, but also the relevant Hague instruments: the Hague Convention of 15 April 1958 on the jurisdiction of the contractual forum in matters relating to the international sale of goods, and the Hague Convention of 25 November 1965 on the choice of court – both since updated. The drafters also opined that in order to ensure legal certainty, the formal requirements applicable to agreements conferring jurisdiction should be expressly prescribed, but that ' excessive formality which is incompatible with commercial practice' should be avoided.[264] Hence for instance the words 'have agreed' in Article 23 JR do not require the court to be determined on its wording alone: it is sufficient that the clause state the objective factors on the basis of which the parties have agreed to choose a court to which they wish to submit any disputes.[265]

Their place in the hierarchy indicates, and Article 23(5) confirms, that choice of court agreements are not an option for subject-matter included in the exclusive jurisdictional grounds of Article 22. Neither must they infringe the jurisdictional rules for the protected categories (see the specific conditions attached to choice of court agreements in the various sections). The 'exclusivity' of choice of court clauses under Article 23 is weaker

---

[262] Report Jenard, 37.

[263] Case 24/76 *Colzani*, [1976] ECR (1832) 1835 – observation by the appellant in the main proceedings.

[264] Report Jenard, 37, with reference to Hague Conference on private international law, documents of the eighth session. FREDERICQ, Report on the work of the Second Committee, 303.

[265] Case C-387/98 *Coreck Maritime*, [2000] ECR I-9337. In the case at issue the choice of court and choice of law clause, read 'Any disputes arising under this Bill of Lading shall be decided in the country where the carrier has his principal place of business and the law of such country shall apply except as provided elsewhere herein' – the discussion subsequently focusing inter alia on who exactly the 'carrier' was in the complex contractual arrangement.

than that under Article 22: in accordance with Article 35, a judgment denying Article 23 and/or its conditions cannot be refused recognition.

A choice of court agreement which meets with the conditions of Article 23, cannot be ignored either by the court which has been assigned by it, or by those who have not. The court assigned may only refuse to claim jurisdiction if neither of the parties concerned is domiciled in the EU (see Article 23(3)) — the JR therefore does not oblige Member State courts to accept such forum clauses, however it does grant them gentle protection: courts of other Member States must not exercise any jurisdiction unless the court to whom jurisdiction was granted refuses to accept it (which it would have to do in accordance with its own PIL rules). Moreover should the designated court chose to accept its jurisdiction, the resulting judgment will enjoy the recognition and enforcement Title of the Regulation.

Agreements granting jurisdiction to a court outside of the EU, are not covered by Article 23.[266] Whether the courts of an EU Member State on that occasion are entitled to (perhaps indeed obliged to) decline jurisdiction in favour of the non-EU court, is unclear. Case C-281/02 *Owusu*, discussed at length elsewhere, does not answer it as the question was not asked by the High Court. Léger AG does refer to the issue once or twice in his opinion however does not really entertain it – as the question was not *sub judice*. However it would seem fair to say that under the *Owusu* approach, the ECJ almost certainly would argue that the courts of an EU Member State, where they have jurisdiction under an alternative ground in the Regulation, have to exercise that jurisdiction. The question is not properly answered by the Commission proposal for review.

The inclusion or non-inclusion of choice of court agreements in favour of non-EU courts, resurfaces in the recognition and enforcement title of the Regulation. In *Gothaer*,[267] Krones AG, a German company whose transport insurers are Gothaer and others, had sold a brewing installation to a Mexican undertaking. Krones engaged Samskip GmbH, the German subsidiary of Samskip Holding BV, a transport and logistics undertaking founded in Iceland and established in Rotterdam (Netherlands), to organise and perform the transport of that equipment from Belgium to Mexico under a bill of lading which contained a term conferring jurisdiction on the courts of Iceland. The consignee and Gothaer and Others brought proceedings against Samskip GmbH in the Belgian courts, alleging that the consignment had been damaged during transport.

The Antwerp Court of Appeal declared, in the operative part of its judgment, that it had 'no authority to hear and decide the case' after finding, in the grounds of the judgment, that the term in the bill of lading conferring jurisdiction on the courts of Iceland was valid and that, while Gothaer and Others could sue as successors in title to Krones AG, they were bound by that term. Antwerp did not, incidentally, clarify whether it found the choice of court clause (again: away from the EU) to be covered by the Jurisdiction Regulation or not. The validity of the clause was not sub judice: only the applicability to the insurers was.

Krones AG and Gothaer and Others brought a fresh action for compensation before the German courts: on what jurisdictional grounds is not mentioned in the documents before the ECJ. The Landgericht Bremen stayed the proceedings and referred to the

---

[266] See also Report Jenard, 38.
[267] Case C-456/11 *Gothaer Allgemeine Versichering et al*, Opinion Bot AG, not yet published in ECR. See also further below, n 404.

European Court of Justice, raising the question of the legal effects of the judgment given in Belgium.

Bremen's questions (reformulated by the AG) essentially were

- whether the term 'judgment' within the meaning of Article 32 of Regulation No 44/2001 covers a judgment by which a court of a Member State declines jurisdiction on the ground of an agreement on jurisdiction, even though that judgment is classified as a 'procedural judgment' by the law of the Member State addressed.
- If the answer to the first two questions is in the affirmative, it has to be determined whether Articles 32 and 33 of Regulation No 44/2001 must be interpreted as meaning that the court before which recognition is pleaded of a judgment by which a court of another Member State has declined jurisdiction on the basis of an agreement on jurisdiction is bound by the finding relating to the validity and scope of that agreement which appears in the grounds of the judgment.

The first two questions are reviewed below, under 'Recognition and enforcement'. In the AG's view, a judgment by a court in a Member State, finding that it does not have jurisdiction because of a choice of forum clause pointing away from the EU (in the case at issue: Iceland), is a 'judgment' within the meaning of Article 32 JR.

The AG then refers to the usual suspects to underline the consequences of that finding: the principle of mutual trust per Gasser and Turner; the strict lis alibi pendens rule; the high degree of predictability built into the Regulation. Consequently (at 53 of the Opinion) the Regulation in the AG's view includes among judgments that are capable of being recognised judgments by which the court first seised has ruled on its jurisdiction, whether it has declared itself to have jurisdiction or, on the contrary, has declined jurisdiction.

This is clear, the AG suggests where the court declares that it has jurisdiction. However Bot AG suggests it also ought to be the case where the court declines jurisdiction. The court asked to recognise and enforce the judgment, in doing so in cases of the first court refusing recognition, in the AG's reasoning regains its freedom to review its own jurisdiction under the Regulation. The AG in this respect refers to the need to help avoid negative conflicts: i.e. one where no court is happy to entertain the claim. As the AG writes at 58, 'A conflict of that kind could arise if the court second seised refused to acknowledge the judgment previously given and declined jurisdiction on the ground that the court first seised had jurisdiction.'

However in the case at issue, of course, the 'negativity' of the conflict is such only between EU courts: an Icelandic court may be happy to (indeed feel itself obliged to) take the case, on the basis of the choice of court clause. This is where the answer to the third question becomes relevant: is the court asked to recognise, bound by the substantive reasons of the court which issued the judgment, as to the rejection of jurisdiction? The AG acknowledges that choice of court in favour of a non-EU court is not covered by Article 23 JR – however the AG refers to a similar proviso in the Lugano Convention to justify essentially the extension of the means and motives of the JR to the facts at issue, This is where I disagree with the Opinion: Iceland may be a party to the Lugano Convention – however jurisdiction of an Icelandic court in casu was not established by virtue of the Lugano Convention. Both parties to the contract at issue were domiciled in the EU and employed the JR's room for court of choice agreements, to agree forum in favour of an Icelandic court.

As noted, the question whether choice of court agreements pointing away from the EU are included in the JR, is not properly answered by the Commission proposal for review, neither is it in my view by the AG in Gothaer. It is to be expected however that the Court given its flavour for judicial economy, will not even go as far as the AG in pondering so many issues.

Article 23 JR specifies a number of issues which were left open to interpretation in the BC. In particular, it states specifically that jurisdiction clauses are exclusive lest the parties specifically agree otherwise, and it specifies 3 possible methods of reaching agreement (see Article 23(1) a-c: the BC only listed *littera* a). Each of the 3 methods needs to be read in conjunction with ECJ case-law and neither of them is now absolutely clear. The application of each of the possibilities must be guided by one principle only: that the courts satisfy themselves that there was 'true agreement'[268] between the parties. This also means that the validity of such clauses must be strictly construed to ensure that the parties have actually consented to the clause and that their consent is clearly and precisely demonstrated.[269]

> the validity of clauses conferring jurisdiction must be strictly construed. By making such validity subject to the existence of an 'agreement' between the parties, Article 17 imposes on the court before which the matter is brought the duty of examining, first, whether the clause conferring jurisdiction upon it was in fact the subject of a consensus between the parties, which must be clearly and precisely demonstrated. The purpose of the formal requirements imposed by Article 17 is to ensure that the consensus between the parties is in fact established.[270]

2.2.9.1 *'In writing or evidenced in writing'*

There is a considerable amount of ECJ case-law on this issue, in particular on standard terms and conditions in contractual relations.

> (T)he mere fact that a clause conferring jurisdiction is printed among the general conditions of one of the parties on the reverse of a contract drawn up on the commercial paper of that party does not of itself satisfy the requirements of Article 17, since no guarantee is thereby given that the other party has really consented to the clause waiving the normal rules of jurisdiction. where a clause conferring jurisdiction is included among the general conditions of sale of one of the parties, printed on the back of a contract, the requirement of a writing under the first paragraph of Article 17 of the Convention is fulfilled only if the contract signed by both parties contains an express reference to those general conditions.[271]

Note that the express reference need not specifically refer to the presence of a choice of court clause in the standard terms and conditions.

In the case of a contract concluded by reference to earlier offers, which were themselves made with reference to the general conditions of one of the parties including a clause conferring jurisdiction, the requirement of 'in writing' is satisfied only if the reference is express and can therefore be checked by a party exercising 'reasonable care'.[272] It is noteworthy that in both written and oral submissions before the ECJ, quite a number

---

[268] Report Jenard, 37.
[269] Case 24/76 *Salotti*, [1976] ECR 1831; Case 25/76 *Segoura*, [1976] ECR 1851; Case 784/79 *Porta-Leasing*, [1980] ECR 1517; Case 71/83 *Tilly Russ*, [1984] ECR 2417.
[270] *Colzani*, n 263 above, para 7.
[271] *Ibid*, para 9 ff.
[272] *Ibid*, para 13.

of comments looked at the impact of national law on the validity of the clause, e.g. with respect to the reference to earlier offers. However the Court did not refer to national law at all,[273] preferring instead to focus solely on the European context of the question (see further below, re validity of the underlying contract).

2.2.9.2 In a form which accords with practices which the parties have established between themselves

This alternative is directly influenced by the ECJ's decision in *Segoura*[274] where the Court held that the fact that the purchaser does not raise any objections against a confirmation issued unilaterally by the other party does not amount to acceptance on his part of the clause conferring jurisdiction unless the oral agreement comes within the framework of a continuing trading relationship between the parties which is based on the general conditions of one of them, and those conditions contain a clause conferring jurisdiction. In such conditions it would be contrary to good faith for the recipient of the confirmation to deny the existence of a jurisdiction conferred by consent, even if he had given no acceptance in writing.

2.2.9.3 In international trade or commerce, in a form which accords with a usage of which the parties are or ought to have been aware and which in such trade or commerce is widely known to, and regularly observed by, parties to contracts of the type involved in the particular trade or commerce concerned

This is of course a factual question which has to be decided by the national courts.[275]

All the above conditions and in particular the three litterae under Article 23(1) prima facie mention formalities with respect to consent only.[276] However the Court of Justice in its rulings on Article 23 and its BC predecessor, keeps utterly silent on national conditions relating to the actual formation of consent. Not only does it not entertain the most important common law/English law requirement of 'consideration'; it is silent on much more than that: capacity, mistake, fraud, duress, agency, assignment…[277]. All that is said in Article 23 is the requirement of 'agreement' (*parties have* agreed') which, however one looks at it, has to imply a review of substance, rather than formality only.

In my view the strongest indication that the Court wishes to keep national law entirely out of the equation when it comes to validity of forum clauses, may be found in *Colzani*,[278] where conditions imposed by national laws were flagged in submissions but ignored by the Court. This problem is even more compounded when one distinguishes between the validity (formal and substantive) of the forum clause, and the validity of the

---

[273] See also Case C-214/89 *Duffryn*, [1992] ECR I-1745, paras 13–14, in particular that 'it is important that the concept of 'agreement conferring jurisdiction' should not be interpreted simply as referring to the national law of one or other of the States concerned. (…) the concept of 'agreement conferring jurisdiction in Article 17 must be regarded as an independent concept'.

[274] Case 25/76 *Segoura*, [1976] ECR 1851.

[275] See e.g. Case C-106/95 *MSG*, [1997] ECR I-911.

[276] See also Heidelberg Report, at para 324 ff.

[277] See Magnus, U., 'Choice of Court Agreements in the Review Proposal for the Brussels I Regulation', in *The Brussels I Review Proposal Uncovered*, Lein, E. (ed.), London, British Institute of International and Comparative Law, 2012, (83) 87.

[278] n 263 above.

actual underlying agreement. The majority of ECJ authority would seem to favour having the validity of the forum clause to be exclusively determined by the conditions of Article 23. I would however agree[279] that the material validity of the forum clause ought to be determined by the *lex contractus*.

The result of the discussion is unsatisfactory, as in practice it leaves it up to the Member States to decide how to address the substantive validity of choice of court agreements. As a result, 'the law of some Member States refers to the lex fori (since choice-of-forum agreements constitute a procedural contract) whereas others refer to the lex causae.'[280] Consequently choice of court agreements may be considered valid in one Member State and invalid in another. The Heidelberg report saw scope for remedy under the Draft Common Frame of Reference,[281] however I find that suggestion uncharacteristically feeble, as the nature of the DCFR even at the time of compilation of the Heidelberg report quite evidently did not support this.

When assessing the law which ought to apply to the validity of a forum clause, there are a variety of options:[282]
- Lex fori prorogati: the law of the State of the designated forum;
- Lex fori derogati: the law of the State which has been derogated from hearing the case (in those instances where the clause has such derogative effect – which is the case in principle in the JR, since it provides that prorogation clauses are in principle exclusive);[283]
- Lex fori aditi: the law of the state where the case is actually pending;
- A combination of any of the above.

Any of the above may of course lead to lex causae, typically the lex contractus.

This elephant in the room was addressed by the Commission in its proposal for review of the JR: the proposal introduces a harmonised conflict of law rule on the substantive validity of choice of court agreements, thus attempting to ensure a similar outcome on this matter whatever the court seized. The Commission proposal at this point firstly does away with the requirement that at least one of the parties be domiciled in the EU, and introduces a harmonised conflict of law rule on the substantive validity of choice of court agreements. The proposal on this point reads:

> If the parties have agreed that a court or the courts of a Member State are to have jurisdiction to settle any disputes which have arisen or which may arise in connection with a particular legal relationship, that court or those courts shall have jurisdiction, unless the agreement is null and void as to its substance under the law of that Member State. (…)

---

[279] See also Fawcett, JJ and Carruthers, JM, n 183 above, 287.

[280] Heidelberg Report at para 377.

[281] *Ibid* at para 378: 'In the long run, it might be helpful in this respect if the planned Common Frame of Reference for European Contract Law will be accepted; in this case a reference to that instrument, which is intended to operate as a toolbox for European legislation and which therefore could also be used for the purposes of Art. 23 JR, could be advisable'.

[282] Kuypers, P., *Forumkeuze in het Nederlandse Internationaal Privaatrecht*, Antwerpen, Kluwer, 2008, p.242.

[283] In particular in jurisdictions which do not operate a forum non conveniens rule, the difference between exclusive and non-exclusive choice of forum clauses is very relevant. See e.g. Fawcett, J., *Declining jurisdiction in private international law*, Report to the XIVth Congress of the International Academy of Comparative Law, Oxford, Clarendon, 1995, p.51. Under German law, for instance (and outside of the context of the JR), in the case of a a non-exclusive prorogation, the German court would have to exercise its principle jurisdiction, for lack of a forum non conveniens safety valve.

Preferably some degree of precision ought to be added to this proposal, as it still does not quite clearly distinguish between formal and material validity of the underlying agreement. Reading the text as it stands, it is not very clear what 'the agreement' in the final part of the sentence refers to. Grammatically it refers to the agreement to confer jurisdiction, in other words the forum clause. However one wonders whether the Commission actually means to refer to the underlying agreement, i.e. contract.

The Council, in its General Approach document to the review of the Brussels I Regulation[284] does provide for some more clarity. The Council proposes the following with respect to choice of court agreements:

> If the parties, regardless of domicile, have agreed that a court or the courts of a Member State are to have jurisdiction to settle any disputes which have arisen or which may arise in connection with a particular legal relationship, that court or those courts shall have jurisdiction, unless the agreement is null and void as to its substantive validity under the law of that Member State.

The Commission, as noted, had proposed 'substance' rather than the words 'substantive validity'. The Council also suggest inserting a recital as follows:

> The question as to whether a choice of court agreement in favour of a court or the courts of a Member State is null and void as to its substantive validity should be decided in accordance with the law of that Member State. The reference to the law of the Member State of the chosen court should include the conflict of laws rules of that State.

The Council would also add a para 5 to Article 23 JR as follows:

> 5. An agreement conferring jurisdiction which forms part of a contract shall be treated as an agreement independent of the other terms of the contract.

> The validity of the agreement conferring jurisdiction cannot be contested solely on the ground that the contract is not valid.

A lis alibi pendens rule will be introduced to support choice of forum clauses.[285]

The Council amendment aims at making the solution clearer still: the validity of the forum clause, an independent agreement, is determined by the law of the designated forum, [286] including its conflict of laws rules.[287] Of note is that the reference to 'null and

---

[284] Document 10609/12, in particular addendum 1, both available via http://www.consilium.europa.eu/council/open-sessions/related-documents?debateid=1675&lang=en .

[285] The amendment as is stands (following the Council and EP interventions referred to above, n 70 ff above), reads: Article 32: 1. Where actions come within the exclusive jurisdiction of several courts, any court other than the court first seised shall decline jurisdiction in favour of that court. 2. Without prejudice to Article 24, where a court of a Member State on which an agreement referred to in Article 23 confers exclusive jurisdiction is seised, any court of another Member State shall stay the proceedings until such time as the court seised on the basis of the agreement declares that it has no jurisdiction under the agreement. 2a. Where the court designated in the agreement has established jurisdiction in accordance with the agreement, any court of another Member State shall decline jurisdiction in favour of that court. 2b. Paragraphs 2 and 2a shall not apply to matters governed by Sections 3, 4 and 5 when the policyholder, the insured, the injured party or a beneficiary of the insurance contract, the consumer or the employee is the claimant and the agreement is not valid under those Sections.

[286] See contra, under the current version of the JR, the French Cour de Cassation, 26 September 2012 (11–26.022), *La société Banque privée Edmond de Rothschild Europe v X:* when one of the parties to the contract (a bank) can effectively ignore the agreed exclusive forum at will, the clause was held not to be binding under French law, even though the agreed forum was Luxembourg.

[287] See e.g. as far as residual jurisdiction is concerned, Article 98 of the Belgian Private International Law Act, which in general extends the scope of application of the Rome I Regulation and hence applicability of the lex contractus to its excluded areas (which means also, to forum clauses).

void' is not altogether satisfactory, as it leaves unanswered deficiency in consent which do not lead to invalidity but rather are 'voidable', i.e. where there is a deficiency which may however lead to a corrected clause.[288]

Oddly, the Council adds *renvoi* to the mix (see 'The reference to the law of the Member State of the chosen court should include the conflict of laws rules of that State.'). EU private international law, for good (mostly practical) reasons typically excludes *renvoi*, as I have noted elsewhere. I am not entirely convinced that adding it here has any merit,[289] other than of course providing for clarity (although in that case the more logical conclusion, given the aversion against *renvoi* in EU private international law, would have been to exclude *renvoi*). Importantly, it is the private international law of the *chosen court* which will have to be applied: not that of the forum (which may be different). This is relevant in cases where proceedings are not pending before the chosen court (for in that case the new lis alibi pendens rule of Article 32 JR will oblige all other courts to stay proceedings), and the existence of a forum clause is raised by the defendant.

Finally, it is of note that although the new regime under Article 23 JR on one important issue will align the EU with the Hague Convention on choice of court agreements (neither of the parties need to have domicile in the EU), it does differ from that Convention on a number of issues (e.g. the EU not requiring written agreement).[290]

2.2.10 General Jurisdiction: Defendants Domiciled in a Member State Where a Court is Seized: Article 2

The general jurisdictional rule of the JR reflects the maxim *Actor sequitur forum rei*: the plaintiff follows the forum of what is under dispute, meaning the plaintiff sues in the jurisdiction where the subject of the lawsuit or the defendant is located- rather than the *forum actoris* rule, which would give preference to the jurisdiction of the plaintiff. Originally conceived in the law of obligations (making it incumbent on the creditor to go and collect the performance due to him[291]), the drafters of the original BC opined that the maxim expresses the fact that the law leans in favour of the defendant. Arguably and without going into the legal philosophy merits of the discussion, while in criminal law indeed this certainly tends to be true, I am less aware of civil law 'in fact' leaning in favour of the defendant. The reflection in the BC is relevant, for indeed throughout the Convention there is more than passing deference to the rights and interests of the defendant. While perhaps it may be disputed whether in civil law this necessarily is or ought to be the overall rule, it certainly is a starting point which the BC had every right to opt for. However as already discussed in the first chapter, the professed bias in the BC for the position of the defendant, is less evident in the case of the transformation of the BC into the JR.

'Domicile' has already been discussed above. And I have also already emphasised both that the 'general' jurisdictional rule of the JR is not so general, given its many exceptions and its low rank in the actual hierarchy; and that despite this low rank, its 'general' nature

---

[288] See also Magus, U, note 277 above, 93.
[289] Contra: ibidem, 94, who gives four reasons as to why this ought to be welcomed.
[290] Ibidem, 91.
[291] In German civil law: *Holschuld*.

nevertheless reverberates throughout the JR, in that all exceptions to the general rule need to be applied strictly.

The 'domicile' of the defendant determines the Member State of jurisdiction only. A defendant domiciled in a Member State need not necessarily be sued in the court for the place where he is domiciled or has his seat. He may be sued in any court of the State where he is domiciled which has jurisdiction under the law of that State. The internal rules of jurisdiction of that State determine where precisely the defendant needs to be sued.

2.2.11 'Special' Jurisdiction: Defendants Domiciled in Another Member State: Articles 5–7

In US jargon this is what is called 'specific' jurisdiction: it applies only where there is an appropriate connection or 'close link'[292] between the cause of action and the state of the forum. Hence 'special jurisdiction' may arguably be regarded as an application of *forum conveniens* — although a forum non conveniens argument can certainly not annihilate jurisdiction on the basis of Articles 5–7. There are many categories of special jurisdiction in Article 5 JR; multipartite litigation is considered in Article 6; and the specific case of liability in maritime cases in Article 7. However for a volume such as the current one, Article 5's special jurisdictional rules for contracts and torts would seem the most relevant ones [Article 5(5) with respect to disputes arising out of the operation of a branch, agency or other establishment, is often applied in a consumer contract context — where it broadens the possibilities for consumers to pick a forum on the basis of practical considerations], as well as in disputes between companies and intermediaries[293]].

Special jurisdictional rules create a supplementary jurisdiction: In the case of proceedings for which a court is specifically recognized as having jurisdiction under these Articles the plaintiff may, at his option, bring the proceedings either in that court or in the competent courts of the State in which the defendant is domiciled.

2.2.11.1 Article 5(1): Actions Relating to a Contract – Forum Contractus

A person domiciled in a Member State may, in another Member State, be sued:

1. (a) in matters relating to a contract, in the courts for the place of performance of the obligation in question;
   (b) for the purpose of this provision and unless otherwise agreed, the place of performance of the obligation in question shall be:
   — in the case of the sale of goods, the place in a Member State where, under the contract, the goods were delivered or should have been delivered,
   — in the case of the provision of services, the place in a Member State where, under the contract, the services were provided or should have been provided,

---

[292] Case C-386/05 *Color Drack*, [2007] *ECR* I-3699.

[293] See for more details Fawcett, JJ and Carruthers, JM, n 183 above, 258 ff, and references to four core cases at the ECJ: Case 14/76 *De Bloos*; 33/78 *Somafer*; 139/80 *Blanckaert*; and 218/86 *Sar Schotte*. This provision concerns only defendants domiciled in a Member State (Article 5), that is, companies or firms having their seat in one Member State and having a branch, agency or other establishment in another Member State. Companies or firms which have their seat outside the Community but have a branch, etc. in a Member State, are covered by Article 4 JR: see Report Jenard, 26.

(c) if subparagraph (b) does not apply then subparagraph (a) applies;

The original provision in the BC read: 'in matters related to a contract, a person domiciled in one Member State can, in another Member State, be sued in the courts of the place of performance of the obligation in question'. Article 5(1) was twice amended: once in the BC to include more specific provisions for employment contracts (now Article 18 JR, see above); and a second time in the Regulation to include specific provision for the sale of goods and for services, the details of which we shall see below.

2.2.11.1 [a] When does a claim relate to a 'contract'?

In the overall spirit of the Regulation, the ECJ insists that this be a European concept, not one left to national law:

> Having regard to the objectives and the general scheme of the Convention, that it is important that, in order to ensure as far as possible the equality and uniformity of the rights and obligations arising out of the Convention for the Contracting States and the persons concerned, that concept should not be interpreted simply as referring to the national law of one or other of the States concerned. Therefore, (...) the concept of matters relating to a contract should be regarded as an independent concept which, for the purpose of the application of the Convention, must be interpreted by reference chiefly to the system and objectives of the Convention, in order to ensure that it is fully effective.[294]

However, once jurisdiction settled on the basis of the Regulation, national law regains discretion to requalify the 'contract' as 'tort', or indeed as anything else, for deciding upon applicable law/choice of law, albeit that there is increased harmonisation on this issue, too (see further below, the review of the Rome I and II Regulations).

The Court has not been able to give a truly 'European' positive definition of 'contract'. There is a certain level of abstract clarification in ECJ case-law,[295] however in unclear cases parties have to wait for certainty until the ECJ holds upon judicial review. In *Handte* the Court held:

> the phrase 'matters relating to a contract [ ] is not to be understood as covering a situation in which there is no obligation freely assumed by one party towards another.[296]

However this is not quite the same as saying that there has to be an 'obligation freely assumed' for Article 5(1) to apply (note the use of the double negative in the court's judgment), hence *Handte* did not settle all dust. *Engler* clarified things to some degree.

In *Engler*, Ms Engler received a letter personally addressed to her at her domicile from Janus Versand, which carries on business as a mail order company. That letter contained a 'payment notice', whose form and content led her to believe that she had won a prize of ATS 455 000 in a 'cash prize draw' organised by Janus Versand, and a catalogue of goods marketed by the latter (which apparently also called itself, in its relations with its customers, 'Handelskontor Janus GmbH') with a 'request for a trial without obligation'. In the advertising brochure sent to Ms Engler, Janus

---

[294] Case 34/82 *Martin Peters*, [1983] ECR 987, para 9–10.
[295] Sometimes quite abstract indeed: e.g. in *Martin Peters*, n 294 above, para 13, the Court simple referred to *close links of the same kind as those which are created between the parties to a contract.*
[296] Case C-26/91 *Jakob Handte*, [1992] ECR I-3967, para 15.

Versand stated that it could also be contacted on the Internet at the following address: www.janus-versand.com. On the 'payment notice' the word 'confirmation' appears in the title together with the winning number printed in bold characters. The name and address of the addressee and beneficiary of the payment notice are those of Ms Engler, and it is accompanied by the words 'personal – not transferable'. The 'payment notice' states, also in bold print, the amount of the prize in figures (ATS 455 000) and the same amount in letters underneath, together with a confirmation signed by a Mr Ulrich Mändercke, certifying that 'the amount of the prize stated is correct and in accordance with the document in our possession', the words 'chambers and office of certified and sworn experts' accompany that signature. Furthermore, Ms Engler was requested to affix to the 'payment notice', in the space provided for that purpose, the 'official stamp of the chambers' accompanying the letter and to return the request for the 'trial without obligation' to Janus Versand. A box for the date and signature, a request to 'fill it in' and a reference in small print to the terms and conditions and the award of the prize supposedly won also feature on the 'payment notice'. Ms Engler had to declare on the 'payment notice' that she had read and accepted those conditions. Finally, it also urged the addressee to return 'today' the document duly completed in order that it could be processed, and an envelope was attached for that purpose. In those circumstances Ms Engler, as Janus Versand had requested, returned the 'payment notice' to it, as she believed that that was sufficient in order to obtain the promised prize. At first Janus Versand did not react, it then refused to pay that sum to Ms Engler. Ms Engler therefore brought an action against Janus Versand before the Austrian courts, based primarily on Paragraph 5j of the Konsumentenschutzgesetz, for an order that Janus Versand pay her the sum of ATS 455 000, plus costs and ancillary amounts. Ms Engler argues that that claim is a contractual claim since Janus Versand, by promising to award a prize, had encouraged her to conclude a contract with that company for sale of goods. However, such a claim is also founded on other grounds, in particular, the breach of pre-contractual obligations. In the alternative, Ms Engler takes the view that her claim is brought in tort, delict or quasi-delict. Janus Versand contested the jurisdiction of the Austrian courts to hear the claim stating, first of all, that the letter on which that claim is founded did not come from it but from Handelskontor Janus GmbH, a company which is a separate legal entity; second, that it had not promised any prize to Ms Engler and, finally, that it did not have any contractual relationship with her. On 2 October 2001 the Landesgericht Feldkirch (Austria) dismissed Ms Engler's action for lack of jurisdiction, since it held that she had not shown the connection between Janus Versand and the sender of the prize notification, namely 'Handelskontor Janus GmbH, Postfach 1670, Abt. 3 Z 4, D-88106 Lindau': domiciled in Germany.

The ECJ firstly confirmed the subsidiary nature of the jurisdictional rule for tort, and hence the need to review the applicability of the rule for contracts, first.[297] It subsequently clarified the use of the double negative in the *Handte* formula, holding that

> the application of the rule of special jurisdiction provided for matters relating to a contract in Article 5(1) presupposes the establishment of a legal obligation freely consented to by one person towards another and on which the claimant's action is based.[298]

The facts in *Engler* and the subsequent finding by the ECJ would seem to suggest that there need not be a mutual element in the relationship for it to fall under the notion of 'contract' in Article 5(1) — which incidentally under Article 15, as noted, is required. In *Ilsinger* the Court hinted obiter that a situation without mutual legal obligations, 'would at most be liable to be classified as pre-contractual or quasi contractual and might there-

---

[297] Case C-27/02 *Engler*, [2005] ECR I-481, para 29.
[298] *Ibid* para 51.

fore, where appropriate, be covered solely by Article 5(1) of [the] regulation, a provision which must be acknowledged as having, on account of its wording and its position in the scheme of that regulation, a broader scope than that of Article 15 thereof'[299] although to be complete the Court also held in the same judgment

> It follows that, although the Court has held that the application of the first paragraph of Article 13 of the Brussels Convention is limited to contracts which give rise to reciprocal and interdependent obligations between the parties, basing itself, moreover, expressly on the wording of that provision referring to a 'contract for the supply of goods or a contract for the supply of services' (see Gabriel, paragraphs 48 to 50, and Engler, paragraphs 34 and 36), the scope of Article 15(1)(c) of Regulation No 44/2001 appears, by contrast, to be no longer being limited to those situations in which the parties have assumed reciprocal obligations.

Frankly, I am confused, perhaps due the German/Austrian specialty of litigation on tombolas/price notifications by direct mail.[300]

It is also noteworthy that jurisdiction to hear disputes concerning the existence of a contractual obligation must be determined in accordance with Article 5(1) of the JR and that that provision is therefore applicable even when the existence of the contract on which the claim is based is in dispute between the parties[301] [which is what is meant by the ECJ's statement that 'Article 5(1) does not require the conclusion of a contract'], albeit that the identification of an obligation is none the less essential for the application of that provision, since the jurisdiction of the national court is determined in matters relating to a contract by the place of performance of the obligation in question.[302]

2.2.11.1 [b] Jurisdictional consequences

In its original form, as noted, Article 5(1) gave jurisdiction to the courts 'for the place of performance of the obligation in question'; in French: *devant le tribunal du lieu où l'obligation qui sert de base à la demande a été ou doit être exécutée*; in Dutch *voor het gerecht van de plaats waar de verbintenis die aan de eis ten grondslag ligt, is uitgevoerd of moet worden uitgevoerd*. The English version in fact is far from the clearest.

'The obligation in question' was left undefined in both the Convention and the preparatory works. Indeed the Jenard Report is very brief on the special jurisdictional clause for contracts. In *De Bloos* the Court specified

> For the purpose of determining the place of performance within the meaning of Article 5 (...) the obligation to be taken into account is that which corresponds to the contractual right on which the plaintiff's action is based.[303]

This really is not a straightforward question whatsoever, as it is by no means easy or even possible for this obligation to be determined, indeed in complex (or even fairly straightforward ones, such as distribution agreements) contracts there may be quite a variety of such obligations which one has to base one's action on. In such a

---

[299] n 219 above, para 57.
[300] See also *Brussels I Regulation*, Magnus, U. and Mankowski, P. (eds). Munich, Sellier, first ed. 2007.
[301] Case 38/81 *Effer*, [1982] ECR 825, para 7 and 8.
[302] Case C-334/00 *Tacconi*, [2002] ECR I-7357, para 22.
[303] Case 14/76 *De Bloos*, [1976] ECR 1497.

case (unless of course the plaintiff chooses to consolidate the case by suing in the place of the defendant only), for each specific obligation the court(s) seized would establish 'place of performance' and hence jurisdiction on the basis of its own PIL: it applied its choice of law rules to determine which law governs the contract, and then uses that law to specify the place of performance. This ultimately means that the court seized may decide it does, does not, or does have jurisdiction but only over part of the claims.

The Court in *Tessili v Dunlop* held that it was in no position to impose a European definition:

> having regard to the differences between national laws of contract and to the absence at this stage of legal development of any unification in the substantive law applicable, it does not appear possible to give any more substantial guide to the interpretation of [ ] 'place of performance' of contractual obligations. This is all the more true since the determination of the place of performance of obligations depends on the contractual context to which these obligations belong.[304]

Tessili therefore is one of few cases where the ECJ does not insist on an autonomous 'European' IP of a harmonised PIL concept. Arguably the *Tessili* deference to national law, also applies to determining whether a particular contract is one for the sale of goods, or for the provision of services. Transport contracts, for instance, may be regarded as either one, depending on the law of the Member State concerned and in the absence of European harmonisation.

Article 5(1) has now been amended to harmonise 'the place of performance' at least for two categories of contracts (the most standard contracts): contracts for the sale of goods and the provision of services. For those contracts at least there will therefore be one place of jurisdiction: see the extract from the JR above. For these two, the 'place of performance of the obligation in question' is now settled, even if the actual claim is e.g. for the payment of the price. In other words the connecting factor which the Regulation identifies, is the connecting factor for all claims arising out of that contract: not just those attached to the connecting factor itself.[305]

Article 5(1)(b) is the exception: where the conditions are not fulfilled, the general rule of 1 (a) regains application, i.e. where the conditions are not fulfilled (e.g. where place of delivery or of provision of services lies outside any MS, or where there is no sale but rather e.g. lease), and where parties have agreed otherwise, and for all other contracts than those in the subpar. Where parties 'have agreed otherwise', such a choice must conform to Article (1). a): i.e. it has to relate to the genuine place of performance (unless of course parties have agreed a proper choice of court agreement under Article 23, respecting all whistles and bells of formality (less strict for Article 5). See in this respect also *MSG*:[306]

> An oral agreement on the place of performance which is designed not to determine the place where the person liable is actually to perform the obligations incumbent upon him, but solely to establish that the courts for a particular place have jurisdiction, is not governed by Article 5(1) of the Convention, but by Article 17, and is valid only if the requirements set out therein are complied with. Whilst the parties are free to agree on a place of performance

---

[304] Case 12/76 *Tessili*, [1976] ECR 1473, para 14.
[305] See also *Color Drack*, n 292 above, para 26.
[306] n 275 above.

for contractual obligations which differs from that which would be determined under the law applicable to the contract, without having to comply with specific conditions as to form, they are nevertheless not entitled, having regard to the system established by the Convention, to designate, with the sole aim of specifying the courts having jurisdiction, a place of performance having no real connection with the reality of the contract at which the obligations arising under the contract could not be performed in accordance with the terms of the contract.

For 'place for performance' for all other contracts, the *Tessili* formula referred to above still stands: there is no European definition and the national (now ever more harmonised) rules take over.

What if the place of the actual delivery of the goods or indeed services, differs from what had been agreed? In the Brussels Convention, the French and indeed Dutch versions of the Convention were fairly clear; in French: *devant le tribunal du lieu où l'obligation qui sert de base à la demande a été ou doit être exécutée*; in Dutch *voor het gerecht van de plaats waar de verbintenis die aan de eis ten grondslag ligt, is uitgevoerd of moet worden uitgevoerd*. These versions identified special jurisdiction as lying either with the courts of the State where delivery had actually taken place or, if no delivery at all had taken place, where it should have taken place. Actual delivery took precedence over consented delivery. This arguably does lead to the unwarranted result of the party which in spite of consented place of delivery, delivered elsewhere, being able to determine the additional forum. In my view, if the place of the actual delivery of the goods, or indeed services, differs from what had been agreed, by virtue of Article 5(1)(c), Article 5(1)(a) will regain the upper hand and the place of actual 'performance' (determined as per *Tessili* by *lex fori*) will decide the special jurisdiction.

What if there is more than once place where the goods are to be delivered? Does 5(1)(b) apply or 5(1)(a)? In *Color Drack*, which was the first case under the new Article 5(1), the ECJ first of all notes that its judgment only holds on the situation where there are various points of delivery within one Member State (at para 16): hence not if delivery takes place in two or more Member States, neither if in two States, one of which is not a Member State. The Court subsequently refers to the general idea behind special jurisdiction: a particularly close linking factor between the contract and the court called upon to hear the litigation, so as to ensure efficient organisation of the proceedings (at para 40). It then decides that consequently if there are several places of delivery, the national court needs to identify that with the closest connecting factor, which is the place of the 'principal delivery' (to be determined on the basis of economic criteria).

If there is no such place of principal delivery: the plaintiff may sue the defendant in the court of the place of delivery of its choice.

It is reasonable to assume but not certain that once sued in one place, that court will become the only court to hear all issues related to the contract: in other words the collective nature of Article 5(1)(b) then revives. It is also reasonable to assume that if there is delivery in more than one Member State, the old case-law presumably still stands: the place of principal delivery has to be determined, and if this is not possible, then there will only be special jurisdiction over a portion of the claim (presumably the court seized will want to avoid that and find a place of principal delivery or indeed of principal obligation in the event of more than one obligations relied on).

2.2.11.2 The Special Jurisdictional Rule for Tort: Article 5(3) JR – Forum delicti commissi

Article 5

A person domiciled in a Member State may, in another Member State, be sued: (…)

3. in matters relating to tort, delict or quasi-delict, in the courts for the place where the harmful event occurred or may occur;

Road accidents were a particular reason for including a special jurisdictional rule on torts in the Convention. In *Kalfelis*, the ECJ defined 'tort' as

all actions which seek to establish liability of a defendant and which are not related to a 'contract' within the meaning of Article 5(1) [307]

The scope of Article 5(3) is quite wide and includes actions for defamation, negligent misstatement, negligent and fraudulent misrepresentation, negligence, conversion, infringement of intellectual property rights, passing off, unfair competition, and actionable breaches of EU law.[308] Whether pre-contractual liability is tort or contract, is subject to debate. National and EU authority exists for both sides of the argument however with the Rome II Regulation now assigning choice of law rules for pre-contractual liability to those for tort, authority deciding for Article 5(3) is likely to become stronger.

Jurisdiction is established under Article 5(3) for the court of the place where the harmful event occurred 'or may occur' (the latter is new in the Regulation and particularly relevant for intellectual property law suits).

The Jenard Report merely reported that '(t)he Committee did not think it should specify whether that place is the place where the event which resulted in damage or injury occurred or whether it is the place where the damage or injury was sustained.[309] Consequently it fell to the Court to interpret the provision.

2.2.11.2 [a] *Bier*: **Alternative Jurisdiction**

In *Bier* or *Mines de Potasse*,[310] the Court held that the connecting factor can be both the place of the event giving rise to the damage (the '*Handlungsort*'), and the place where the damage occurred (the '*Erfolgsort*'). Both of them are component parts of any liability. Hence both of them can be very helpful, depending upon the circumstances, from the point of evidence and the conduct of the proceedings (see the '*forum conveniens*' idea underlying the special jurisdictional rules, above). Moreover, were one to only withhold the place of the event giving rise to the damage, this would almost always coincide with the domicile of the defendant. Hence that interpretation would not offer much of an extra jurisdictional rule compared to Article 2. In the converse case, where the place of the damage coincides with the domicile of the defendant, a particularly helpful connecting factor might be excluded for no apparent reason.

---

[307] Case 189/87 *Kalfelis*, [1988] ECR 5565, para 18.
[308] See the list of Fawcett, JJ and Carruthers, JM, n 183 above, 247, with specific references to ECJ case-law for each of them.
[309] 26.
[310] Case 21/76 *Mines de Potasse d'Alsace*, [1976] ECR 1735.

The place where the damage occurred is the place where the event which may give rise to liability in tort etc., resulted in damage. Hence in the case of a defective product, it is not the place of delivery of that product but rather (where this is different), the place where the defective product subsequently caused damage, e.g. because it is then employed in a production process, and even if that damage results in a purely economic loss (in the case at issue, making the product 'off-spec' or 'off-specification', hence not unusable per se but rather not in line with the technical requirements of the purchaser).[311]

2.2.11.2 [b] Post-*Bier* Management of the Consequences

There is a drawback to the *Mines de Potasse* ruling, namely that it may lead to a multitude of fora. The Court has sought to reduce that possibility and encourage plaintiffs to sue in one place only,

- *firstly* by holding in *Dumez France* that *Bier* applies to direct damage only, not to indirect damage: Article 5(3) and the subsequent rulings in *Bier* and *Marinari* cannot be interpreted as permitting a plaintiff pleading damage which he claims to be the consequence of the harm suffered by other persons who were direct victims of the harmful act to bring proceedings against the perpetrator of that act in the courts of the place in which he himself ascertained the damage to his assets.[312] *Marinari* added in the case of one person suffering damage, that damage occurs where damage or loss first materialises, not (if different from the former) where its consequence is subsequently felt.

  The term 'place where the harmful event occurred' in Article 5(3) (…) does not, on a proper interpretation, cover the place where the victim claims to have suffered financial damage following upon initial damage arising and suffered by him in another Contracting State. Although that term may cover both the place where the damage occurred and the place of the event giving rise to it, it cannot be construed so extensively as to encompass any place where the adverse consequences can be felt of an event which has already caused damage actually arising elsewhere.[313]

However this is not always easy to discern in practice and a large number of problems exist.[314] The ECJ has added

- *secondly* if the plaintiff chooses a court purely on the basis of the former, the court of that Member State may only rule on that part of the damage which has occurred

---

[311] Case C-189/08 *Zuid Chemie*, [2009] ECR I-6917.

[312] Case C-220/88 *Dumez France and Tracoba* [1990] ECR I-49. The Court argued along the following lines: in a case such as this, the damage alleged is no more than the indirect consequence of the harm initially suffered by other legal persons who were the direct victims of damage which occurred at a place different from that where the indirect victim subsequently suffered harm. It is necessary to avoid the multiplication of courts of competent jurisdiction which would heighten the risk of irreconcilable decisions. And in the spirit of the BC and JR, recognition of the jurisdiction of the courts of the plaintiff's domicile must be avoided, and would enable a plaintiff to determine the competent court by his choice of domicile.

[313] Case C-364/93 *Marinari*, [1995] ECR I-2719.

[314] See also e.g. Case C-51/97 *Réunion Européenne*, [1998] ECR I-6511, where the ECJ incidentally displayed selective forum conveniens tendencies: in international maritime transport, the place where the damage is ascertained could certainly qualify as a forum closely linked to the case, however because this more often than not coincides with the domicile of the plaintiff, the Court chose to rule it out.

in that Member State: that was the conclusion of the Court in *Shevill*,[315] [316] which extended the *Bier* rule to immaterial damage. The ruling in *Shevill* was specifically meant to discourage forum shopping on the basis of extremely weak links to the case (in the particular context of the case: libel also arising in a State where a tiny volume of the article may have been distributed). The Court specified that 'place where the harmful event occurred' in the context of media infringement of personality rights (or using the terms which the Court employs in the judgment, defamation and libel) is the place where the publisher of the defamatory publication is established: that is the place where the harmful event originated and from which the libel was issued and put into circulation.[317] The place where damaged occurred is than determined by the place of distribution, where the victim claims to have suffered injury to his reputation.

2.2.11.2 [c] Problems with *Shevill* in the internet age: eDate Advertising ('Kylie Minogue')

Shevill more or less satisfactorily addressed the issue of infringement of one's personality rights at a time (1995) when media distribution through the internet was in its infancy. Media distribution by and large was territorially organised or at the very least, its multiple territorial impact could be quantified: by circulation numbers of printed media, or subscriptions in the case of television channels. The internet, including viral marketing, live and recorded video streaming, and internationally broadly available websites of media outlets, has made *Bier* and *Shevill* less apt in the media context. As discussed by Cruz Villalón AG in his Opinion in Joined Cases *eDate Advertising* and *Martinez* (otherwise known as the *Kylie Minogue* case),[318] the internet challenges the *Shevill* rule both from the point of view of the victim, and of the publisher. From the victim's point angle, as data (in this case: alleged defamation) become available swiftly, on a global basis, and in principle forever; from the publisher's angle.

> (T)he global and immediate distribution of news content on the internet makes a publisher subject to numerous local, regional, State and international legal provisions. Moreover, the absence of a global regulatory framework for information activities on the internet, together with the range of provisions of private international law laid down by States, exposes the media to a fragmented, but also potentially contradictory, legal framework, since that which is prohibited in one State may, in turn, be permitted in another. Accordingly, the need to provide the media with legal certainty, by preventing situations which discourage the lawful exercise of freedom of information (the so-called chilling effect), acquires the character of an objective which the Court must also take into consideration.[319]

The Court (Grand Chamber) followed the AG's view. The internet reduces the usefulness of the criterion relating to distribution, in so far as the scope of the distribution of content placed online is in principle universal. Moreover, it is not always possible, on a technical level, to quantify that distribution with certainty and accuracy in relation to a particular Member State or, therefore, to assess the damage caused exclusively within

---

[315] Case C-68/93 *Shevill v Presse Alliance*, [1995] ECR I-415.

[316] Lest of course another rule gives it more all-encompassing jurisdiction: in particular: where that court is also the State of the defendant's domicile.

[317] *Shevill*, n 315 above, para para 24.

[318] Joined Cases C-509/09 and C-161/10, *eDate Advertising GmbH v X* (C-509/09) and *Olivier Martinez and Robert Martinez v MGN Limited* (C-161/10), not yet published in ECR.

[319] Opinion Cruz Villalón AG, in *eDate* Advertising, n 318 above, at 46 (footnote omitted).

that Member State.[320] (Arguably only) in the context of the internet, therefore, the Court held that the criterion of distribution no longer is fit to apply solely, and held that it must be supplemented with the following:

> a person who has suffered an infringement of a personality right by means of the internet may bring an action in one forum in respect of all of the damage caused, depending on the place in which the damage caused in the European Union by that infringement occurred. Given that the impact which material placed online is liable to have on an individual's personality rights might best be assessed by the court of the place where the alleged victim has his centre of interests, the attribution of jurisdiction to that court corresponds to the objective of the sound administration of justice (…)[321]

The Court continued

> The place where a person has the centre of his interests corresponds in general to his habitual residence. However, a person may also have the centre of his interests in a Member State in which he does not habitually reside, in so far as other factors, such as the pursuit of a professional activity, may establish the existence of a particularly close link with that State.[322]

The Court argues that both for the publisher and for the plaintiff, this forum is reasonably foreseeable. The ECJ however maintains a *Shevill*-like criterion for online access: the criterion of the place where the damage occurred, derived from *Shevill*, continues to confer jurisdiction on courts in each Member State in the territory of which content placed online is or has been accessible. Those courts will continue to have jurisdiction only in respect of the damage caused in the territory of the Member State of the court seised.[323]

In *Wintersteiger*,[324] the Court confirmed that the connecting factor 'centre of interests' in *eDate Advertising* only holds for infringement of personality rights in an internet context. The applicant here is the proprietor of an Austrian trade mark. The defendant was a competitor established in Germany, who had registered Wintersteiger's name as an AdWord on Google's German search service. Whence users of google.de entering 'Wintersteiger' (looking for that make's ski and snowboarding service tools) receive a link to Wintersteiger's website as first search result, but also as the first AdLink on the right hand side of the screen, an advert for and link to the competitor's website – which Wintersteiger considered an abuse of its trademark.

The judgment of the Court of Justice confirms that the connecting factor 'centre of interests' in *Kylie Minogue and eDate Advertising* only holds for infringement of personality rights in an internet context. Trademark violation is distinguished, on the grounds that rebus sic stantibus intellectual property rights are protected on a territorial basis. The Court confines the 'place where the damage occurred' as the Member State in which the trade mark is registered. For the 'place where the event giving rise to the damage', the Court upheld 'place of establishment of the advertiser' as the jurisdictional basis (the Advocate General's 'means necessary for producing, a priori, an actual infringement of a trade mark in another Member State' is a more generic criterion however the Court did not uphold this as such).

---

[320] Judgment of the Court of *eDate* Advertising, n 318 above, para 46.
[321] *Ibid*, para 48.
[322] *Ibid*, para 49.
[323] *Ibid*, para 51.
[324] Case C-523/10 *Wintersteiger AG v Products 4U Sondermaschinenbau GmbH*, Judgment of 19 April 2012, not yet reported in ECR.

Precedent value of the judgment may be limited due to the specific facts of the case and the questions put to the Court. In particular, the conclusion may only hold absolutely where there is only one trade mark held, in only one Member State. The referring court moreover did not flag the many issues surrounding provisionary measures and intellectual property rights (see Article 31 of the Regulation and the judgment in Solvay, below).[325]

Adding the 'centre of his interests' as an additional forum with complete jurisdiction, is arguably at odds with the natural swing of Article 5(3) since the *Bier/Mines de Potasse* case.

In *Bier*, the court as noted justified the extension of jurisdiction to the place where the damage occurred, both on 'usefulness' grounds vis-a-vis the substance of the case (establishing liability in tort) and in order to ensure a proper extension of the jurisdictional rule: the connecting factor can be both the place of the event giving rise to the damage (the '*Handlungsort*'), and the place where the damage occurred (the '*Erfolgsort*'). Both of them are component parts of any liability. Hence both of them can be very helpful, depending upon the circumstances, from the point of evidence and the conduct of the proceedings (see the '*forum conveniens*' idea underlying the special jurisdictional rules, above). Moreover, were one to only withhold the place of the event giving rise to the damage, this would almost always coincide with the domicile of the defendant. Hence that interpretation would not offer much of an extra jurisdictional rule compared to Article 2. In the converse case, where the place of the damage coincides with the domicile of the defendant, a particularly helpful connecting factor might be excluded for no apparent reason.

Following *Bier*, the Court as noted had to massage the consequences of this extension, for it threatened to open up too wide a list of potential for a. In *eDate Advertising* the Court could have actually stayed with *Shevill*. Granted, applying it in an internet context is not straightforward. However the applicant still has an attractive set of potential fora. Domicile of the defendant, per the general rule of Article 2 JR; Member State of the establishment where the publication emanates, if different from the publisher.[326]

In my view, the *eDate Advertising* judgment illustrates the inherent weakness in *Bier* itself. The suitability of a forum for reasons of applicable law is not a general modus operandi in the set-up of the Regulation. Safeguarding the defendant's interests is; predictability is, too; mutual trust as well. It is only in Article 22's exclusive jurisdictional grounds that applicable law filters through into forum selection. The approach in *Bier* leaned too much towards accommodating applicable law in deciding jurisdiction.

One question inevitably leads to another. No better illustration than Case C-170/12. In *Pinckney*, on 11 April 2012, the French Cour de Cassation referred the following question for preliminary review with the ECJ:

Is Article 5(3) of Council Regulation (EC) No 44/2001 of 22 December 2000 on jurisdiction and the recognition and enforcement of judgments in civil and commercial matters to be interpreted as meaning that, in the event of an alleged infringement of copyright committed by means of content placed online on a website,

---

[325] Case C-616/10, not yet reported in ECR. Further analysis below.
[326] See also Dickinson, A., 'By royal appointment: No closer to an EU private international law settlement?', conflictoflaws.net, 24 October 2012 (and last consulted by me on that date).

– the person who considers that his rights have been infringed has the option of bringing an action to establish liability before the courts of each Member State in the territory of which content placed online is or has been accessible, in order to obtain compensation solely in respect of the damage suffered on the territory of the Member State before which the action is brought,

or

– does that content also have to be, or to have been, directed at the public located in the territory of that Member State, or must some other clear connecting factor be present?

Is the answer to Question 1 the same if the alleged infringement of copyright results, not from the placing of dematerialised content online, but, as in the present case, from the online sale of a material carrier medium which reproduces that content?

The Cour de Cassation is assuming two ECJ precedents need to be distinguished from *Pinckney*:[327]

Case C-324/09, *L'Oréal*, which concerns the territorial scope of the EU's trademark laws and revolves around websites 'targeting' consumers as opposed to merely being accessible to them; and

eDate Advertising, in which the Court added the connecting factor 'centre of interests' for internet infringements of personality rights. As noted, in *Wintersteiger* the ECJ confirmed that the connecting factor 'centre of interests' in *eDate Advertising* only holds for infringement of personality rights in an internet context. Trademark violation is distinguished, on the grounds that rebus sic stantibus intellectual property rights are protected on a territorial basis. In *Pinckney*, which also concerns intellectual property, the Cour de Cassation moreover points out that the offending item was in fact a material carrier: a vinyl record, illegally compiling songs.

Plenty of factual elements therefore, complicating the finding of 'place of the harmful event'/damage under Article 5(3) Brussels I.

Finally, In 'G',[328] the Court was asked to provide input in the event of the defendant's domicile being unknown (but with the defendant presumed to be an EU citizen), and the precise location of the server on which the website is stored, also unknown, although most probably in EU territory. The Landgericht Regensburg asked no fewer than 11 questions of some complexity, with a degree of interdependence between them. The Court answered that Article 5(3) may certainly apply in such case, giving preference to legal certainty. However it expects due diligence on behalf of the national courts in making sure that a prima facie case of a link to the EU was established.

The ECJ failed subsequently to entertain the questions on the location of the harmful event given the uncertainty signalled above, for the relevant questions had been dropped by the referring court following the judgment in *eDate Advertising*. In my view, an answer to some of the now dropped questions on location of the harmful event (the locus delicti commissi) were certainly not nugatory, even after *eDate Advertising*. There is no Opinion of the Advocate General to assist.

---

[327] See also Vousden, S., 'Case C-170/12 Pinckney- where is the harm with an internet sales offer? EU Law Radar, 24 May 2012, last consulted 11 November 2012.
[328] Case C-292/10 *G v Cornelius de Visser*, judgment of 15 March 2012, not yet reported in ECR.

2.2.11.2 [d] *DFDS Torline*: Determining Location of Damage

DFDS Torline[329] concerned the legality of a notice of industrial action given by SEKO against DFDS, with the object of securing a collective agreement for Polish crew of the cargo ship *Tor Caledonia* owned by DFDS, serving the route between Göteberg (Sweden) and Harwich (United Kingdom). The *Tor Caledonia* was registered in the Danish international ship register and is subject to Danish law. At the time of the facts in the main proceedings, the Polish crew were employed on the basis of individual contracts, in accordance with a framework agreement between a number of Danish unions on the one hand, and three Danish associations of shipping companies on the other. Those contracts were governed by Danish law. After DFDS rejected a request by SEKO on behalf of the Polish crew for a collective agreement, on 21 March 2001, SEKO served a notice of industrial action by fax, with effect from 28 March 2001, instructing its Swedish members not to accept employment on the *Tor Caledonia*. The fax also stated that SEKO was calling for sympathy action. Following that request, the Svenska Transportarbetareförbundet (Swedish Transport Workers Union, STAF) gave notice, on 3 April 2001, of sympathy action with effect from 17 April 2001, refusing to engage in any work whatsoever relating to the *Tor Caledonia*, which would prevent the ship from being loaded or unloaded in Swedish ports. DFDS brought an action against SEKO and STAF, seeking an order that the two unions acknowledge that the principal and sympathy actions were unlawful and that they withdraw the notices of industrial action.

The day before the first day of sympathy action called by STAF, DFDS withdrew the *Tor Caledonia* from the Göteborg-Harwich route, which was served from 30 May by another ship leased for that purpose. DFDS brought an action for damages against SEKO before the Sø-og Handelsret (Denmark), claiming that the defendant was liable in tort for giving notice of unlawful industrial action and inciting another Swedish union to give notice of sympathy action, which was also unlawful. The damages sought were for the loss allegedly suffered by DFDS as a result of immobilising the *Tor Caledonia* and leasing a replacement ship. The court decided to stay its decision on the action for damages pending the decision of the Arbejdsret on the legality of the action. The Arbejdsret referred to the ECJ.

The national court asked, essentially, whether Article 5(3) must be interpreted as meaning that the damage resulting from industrial action taken by a trade union in a State to which a vessel registered in another State sails can be regarded as having occurred in the flag State, with the result that the ship-owner can bring an action for damages against that trade union in the flag State.

The Court held that the event giving rise to the damage was the notice of industrial action given and publicised by SEKO in Sweden, the State where that union has its head office. Therefore, the place where the fact likely to give rise to tortious liability of the person responsible for the act can only be Sweden, since that is the place where the harmful event originated (at para 41). Furthermore, the damage allegedly caused to DFDS by SEKO consisted in financial loss arising from the withdrawal of the *Tor Caledonia* from its normal route and the hire of another ship to serve the same route. The ECJ instructed the national court to inquire whether such financial loss may be regarded as having arisen at the place where DFDS is established. In the course of that assessment

---

[329] Case C-18/02 *DFDS Torline*, [2004] ECR I-1417.

by the national court, the flag State, that is the State in which the ship is registered, must be regarded as only one factor, among others, assisting in the identification of the place where the harmful event took place. The nationality of the ship can play a decisive role only if the national court reaches the conclusion that the damage arose on board the *Tor Caledonia*. In that case, the flag State must necessarily be regarded as the place where the harmful event caused damage.

The outcome of *DFDS Torline* resulted in a rule on industrial action in the Rome II Regulation, which we review in relevant chapter.

2.2.11.2 [e] 'Negative' declarations for tort

Does Article 5(3) cover an action for declaration as to the non-existence of liability? This was the question in *Folien Fischer* and it was answered by the ECJ in the affirmative. The question was referred for a preliminary ruling by the German Bundesgerichtshof in the course of a dispute between, on the one hand, Folien Fischer AG ('Folien Fischer') and Fofitec AG ('Fofitec'), companies established in Switzerland, and, on the other hand, Ritrama SpA, which has its registered office in Italy. Folien Fischer and Fofitec had been accused of essentially infringement of competition law in their sales practice and in Fofitec's refusal to grant a license to Ritrama for one of its patents. Ritrama had issued a shot across the bows in sending Folien Fischer a letter alleging the incompatibility with competition law of its commercial practices.

Folien Fischer subsequently took the case to court first, in Hamburg, where it was found to be inadmissible for lack of international jurisdiction. Hamburg had taken its cue from that part of German scholarship which argued that negative declarations are not covered by Article 5(3), thus leaving Folien Fischer no choice but to seek that declaration in Italy. Upon appeal the issue came before the ECJ.

Unlike Jaaskinen AG, the ECJ itself did not think that the reversal of roles in a negative declaration of liability, merits the non-application of Article 5(3) and the *Bier* formula. Jaaskinen AG had in so many words suggested that although the Court does not expressly say so in *Bier*, its holding in that case had a strong whiff about it of protecting the presumed victim, who is generally the claimant in the proceedings.[330] The Court itself laid more emphasis on negative and positive declarations of liability essentially relating to the same matters of law and fact.[331]

2.2.12 Multipartite Litigation and Consolidated Claims: Articles 6 (and 7)

Article 6 includes four cases which are all inserted because of procedural expediency and because of the need to avoid irreconcilable judgments. However they all do harbour scope for abuse hence the ECJ has interpreted each of them fairly strictly. Procedural efficiency and forum shopping often tempts plaintiffs into identifying an 'anchor defendant' in one jurisdiction, subsequently to employ Article 6 (or similar provisions in national law for

---

[330] Opinion of Jaaskinen AG in Case C-133/11 *Folien Fischer*, not yet reported in ECR, at 48.
[331] Case C-133/11 *Folien Fischer*, not yet reported in ECR, para 48.

subjects outside of the JR) to engage other parties in the same jurisdiction. As repeatedly emphasised in this volume, this technique is not wrong per se.[332]

It is also noteworthy that the hierarchical position of the protected categories means that Article 6 cannot be applied to a dispute falling under any of the protected categories.[333]

Article 6

A person domiciled in a Member State may also be sued:

1. where he is one of a number of defendants, in the courts for the place where any one of them is domiciled, provided the claims are so closely connected that it is expedient to hear and determine them together to avoid the risk of irreconcilable judgments resulting from separate proceedings;
2. as a third party in an action on a warranty or guarantee or in any other third party proceedings, in the court seized of the original proceedings, unless these were instituted solely with the object of removing him from the jurisdiction of the court which would be competent in his case;
3. on a counter-claim arising from the same contract or facts on which the original claim was based, in the court in which the original claim is pending;
4. in matters relating to a contract, if the action may be combined with an action against the same defendant in matters relating to rights in rem in immovable property, in the court of the Member State in which the property is situated.

2.2.12.1 Multiple Defendants: Article 6(1)

A group of defendants domiciled in two or more of the Member States[334] may all be sued in the courts of the MS where one of them is domiciled. Jurisdiction derived from the domicile of one of the defendants was adopted by the BC because it makes it possible to obviate the handing down in the Member States of judgments which are irreconcilable with one another.[335] That defendant need not be the principal target of the claim and indeed may even chose not to defend the jurisdiction claim (e.g. by showing he is not actually domiciled there): he would still drag all other defendants into the procedural bath with him. This evidently opens some scope of abuse however it was impossible to include

---

[332] See for an interesting example in the competition law sector, the Court of appeal in September 2012, *KME Yorkshire et al v Toshiba Carrier UK et al* [2012] EWCA Civ 1190: a connected undertaking that had implemented, but not been party to, an anti-competitive agreement, can nevertheless be in breach of Article 101 TFEU (the foundation Article for EU competition law) and therefore ground jurisdiction against all other defendants who had been originally named in the Commission decision fining the companies concerned.

[333] See Case C-462/06 *Glaxosmithkline*, [2008] ECR I-3965 with respect to the relationship between Article 6(1) and the consumer contracts title – arguably extendable to all provisions of Article 6 and to all protected categories.

[334] Article 6(1) cannot be applied to bring an action before the Court of a Member State against a defendant who could only be sued in that Member State by virtue a joinder with a suit against a party not domiciled in any of the Member States: in *Réunion européenne*, the Court held 'the objective of legal certainty pursued by the Convention would not be attained if the fact that a court in a Contracting State had accepted jurisdiction as regards one of the defendants not domiciled in a Contracting State made it possible to bring another defendant, domiciled in a Contracting State, before that same court in cases other than those envisaged by the Convention, thereby depriving him of the benefit of the protective rules laid down by it': Case C-51/97 *Réunion européenne*, [1998] ECR I-06511, para 46.

[335] Report Jenard, 27.

a criterion to offset this (e.g. requiring the defendant which brings in all the others, be the 'principal target' of the suit), as it would lead to great difficulties of interpretation.

That the application of Article 6(1) requires that 'the claims are so closely connected that it is expedient to hear and determine them together to avoid the risk of irreconcilable judgments resulting from separate proceedings' was not included as such in the original BC and was added as a condition in *Kalfelis*.[336]

The joinder still holds even if the action against the first defendant, domiciled in the forum, is inadmissible from the start, unless per *Reisch Montage* the claim is made against a number of defendants for the sole purpose of removing one of them from the jurisdiction of the courts of his MS of domicile.[337] This is a condition which is expressly provided for in Article 6(2) – see below, but extended by the ECJ to Article 6(1) in particular in *Kalfelis*.[338] However where the close connection as per the *Kalfelis* formula mentioned above is established, one need not separately review the absence of sole purpose to remove a defendant from his natural jurisdiction.[339]

It is the national court's task to consider whether the proceedings are 'so closely connected that it is expedient to hear and determine them together to avoid the risk of irreconcilable judgments resulting from separate proceedings.' In order that decisions may be regarded as contradictory, it is not sufficient that there be a divergence in the outcome of the dispute, but that divergence must also arise in the context of the same situation of law and fact.[340] The legal basis of the action brought before that court may be one indication however it is certainly not necessary for that legal basis to be identical.[341]

In particular in intellectual property cases, the Court's approach to 'same situation of law and fact' has been criticised. In *Roche*,[342] the ECJ controversially held that parallel actions for infringement in different Member States, which, in accordance with Article 64(3) of the Munich Convention,[343] must be examined in the light of the national law in force, are not in the context of the same legal situation and hence any divergences between decisions cannot be treated as contradictory – leaving no room for application of Article 6(1) to the benefit of holders of European patents vis-a-vis actions for

---

[336] Case 198/87 *Kalfelis*, [1988] ECR 5565, para 12.

[337] Case C-103/05 *Reisch Montage*, [2006] ECR I-6827, para 32.

[338] n 336 above.

[339] Case C-98/06 *Freeport*, [2007] ECR I-8319, para 51 ff.

[340] Case C-539/03 *Roche Nederland and Others* [2006] ECR I-6535, para 26.

[341] *Freeport*, n 339 above, para 41.

[342] n 340 above.

[343] The 'patent Convention' or the Convention on the Grant of European Patents, signed at Munich on 5 October 1973. It has 38 Signatory States, including all EU Member States however not the EU itself. The ECJ was critical of the introduction of a unified patent litigation system which piggybacked on the Munich Convention and which would create a European and Community Patents Court to which non-EU Member States would be party but which would issue interpretative judgments on the Community Patent: see Opinion 1/09 of 8 March 2011, not yet published in ECR, para 89: 'the envisaged agreement, by conferring on an international court which is outside the institutional and judicial framework of the European Union an exclusive jurisdiction to hear a significant number of actions brought by individuals in the field of the Community patent and to interpret and apply European Union law in that field, would deprive courts of Member States of their powers in relation to the interpretation and application of European Union law and the Court of its powers to reply, by preliminary ruling, to questions referred by those courts and, consequently, would alter the essential character of the powers which the Treaties confer on the institutions of the European Union and on the Member States and which are indispensable to the preservation of the very nature of European Union law.' See i.a. Kant, M., 'A specialised Patent Court for Europe? An analysis of Opinion 1/09 of the Court of Justice of the European Union from 8 March 2011 concerning the establishment of a European and Community Patents Court and a proposal for an alternative solution', NIPR 2012, p. 193–201.

infringement in different Member States. For intellectual property practice, this made cross-border litigation almost impossible to plan coherently.

In *Solvay*,[344] Solvay SA, a company established in Belgium and holding a European patent,[345] brought an action in the Rechtbank 's-Gravenhage in the Netherlands for infringement of several national parts of the patent, in particular against three companies originating from two different Member States, Honeywell Fluorine Products Europe BV, established in the Netherlands, and Honeywell Belgium NV and Honeywell Europe NV, established in Belgium, for marketing a product manufactured by Honeywell International Inc. that was identical to the product under the above patent. In the course of the proceedings, Solvay lodged an interim claim against the defendants in the main proceedings, seeking provisional relief in the form of a cross-border prohibition against infringement for the duration of the main proceedings.

With respect to the application of Article 6(1), Cruz Villalon AG proposed to distinguish, not to overturn, *Roche* on the ground that in the case at issue, the objectionable behaviour concerned more than one undertaking, domiciled in more than one Member State, however accused of the same behaviour in the same Member State. If Article 6(1) were not to be applicable, the suggested, the courts concerned would hence hold on the basis of the same lex loci protectionis (that of the Member State in which the alleged conduct is said to have taken place) and hence the risk of irreconcilable judgments would be great.

The ECJ agreed with its AG that Roche still holds: the same situation of law cannot be inferred where infringement proceedings are brought before a number of courts in different Member States in respect of a European patent granted in each of those States and those actions are brought against defendants domiciled in those States in respect of acts allegedly committed in their territory. A European patent continues to be governed, per the Munich Convention, by the national law of each of the Contracting States for which it has been granted. However in the specific circumstances of a case, Roche may be distinguished: whether there is a risk of irreconcilable judgments if those claims were determined separately, is for the national court to determine. The Court of Justice instructs the national court to take into account, inter alia, the dual fact that, first, the defendants in the main proceeding are each separately accused of committing the same infringements with respect to the same products and, secondly, such infringements were committed in the same Member State, so that they adversely affect the same national parts of the European patent at issue.

The ECJ therefore somewhat softens the blow in *Solvay* however as noted it has confirmed its core reasoning in *Roche*. The ECJ's approach would seem overly formalistic, albeit with the advantage of clarity. Even though formally the legal basis for these patents is different, in practice harmonisation between the Member States has gone so far as to make it artificial to speak of different legal basis.[346] This issue is addressed amongst others in the CLIP principles at Max Planck.[347]

---

[344] Case C-616/10, not yet reported in ECR, judgment of 12 July 2012.

[345] Such patent is valid in more than one Member State; European patent law is less harmonised than one might hope and even a 'European' patent does not necessarily and automatically cover all Member States.

[346] See van Eechoud, M., and Kur, A., 'Internationaal privaatrecht in intellectuele eigendomszaken – De CLIP principes, NIPR 2012, p.252–265

[347] Principles on Conflict of Laws in Intellectual Property, 31 August 2011, available via http://www.cl-ip. eu/en/pub/home.cfm (last consulted 6 November 2012).

There is generally some discussion as to the degree of 'contradiction' or not required for judgments to be 'irreconcilable' within the meaning of Article 6(1). Leger AG has opined in *Roche*[348] that there ought to be a more flexible interpretation of 'irreconcilable' within the context of Article 6(1) as opposed to related actions within Article 28, however the Court consistently uses the term 'contradictory', which is the same notion as it has applied in the context of Article 28 (see further on this notion, below).

2.2.12.2 Warranties, Guarantees and any other Third Party Proceedings: Article 6(2)[349]

An action on a warranty or guarantee is brought against a third party by the defendant in an action for the purpose of being indemnified against the consequences of that action ('*Streitverkundung*' or *litis denunciatio*). It is in the interests of the proper administration of justice that the jurisdiction over the warranty joins the original jurisdiction (unless the warrantor and the beneficiary of the warranty have agreed a forum clause in accordance with Article 23, and the clause covers warranty).

Warranties and guarantees necessarily require involving a third party. The drafters of the BC thought it useful to include general third party proceedings in Article 6(2), with reference to the Belgian judicial code which did indeed rather nicely define such proceedings:

> Third party proceedings are those in which a third party is joined as a party to the action. They are intended either to safeguard the interests of the third party or of one of the parties to the action, or to enable judgment to be entered against a party, or to allow an order to be made for the purpose of giving effect to a guarantee or warranty. The third party's intervention is voluntary where he appears in order to defend his interests. It is not voluntary where the third party is sued in the course of the proceedings by one or more of the parties.[350]

Article 6(2) adds specifically that a joinder in this event is not admissible when these proceedings 'were instituted solely with the object of removing him from the jurisdiction of the court which would be competent in his case'. Moreover, the warranties etc. need to involve exactly the same claim: the defendant in other words may use Article 6(2) to 'forward' the claim to the third party, warrantor etc. however Article 6(2) must not be used for the defendant to launch an independent claim against any of the parties listed therein.

2.2.12.3 Counterclaims: Article 6(3)

In order to establish this jurisdiction the counterclaim must be related to the original claim. Since the concept of related actions was not recognized in all the legal systems at the time, the provision in question, following the draft Belgian Judicial Code of the period, states that the counterclaim must arise from the contract or from the facts on which the original claim was based.[351]

---

[348] n 340 above.
[349] Please note the unusual territorial exception to Article 6(2) for Germany, Austria and Hungary in Article 65 JR.
[350] Report Jenard, 28.
[351] *Ibid.*

2.2.12.4 Matters Relating to Rights in Rem in Immovable Property: Article 6(4)

See above under the discussion of Article 22.

2.2.13 'Residual' Jurisdiction: Defendants not Domiciled in any Member State: Article 4

Article 4

1. If the defendant is not domiciled in a Member State, the jurisdiction of the courts of each Member State shall, subject to Articles 22 and 23, be determined by the law of that Member State.

2. As against such a defendant, any person domiciled in a Member State may, whatever his nationality, avail himself in that State of the rules of jurisdiction there in force, and in particular those specified in Annex I, in the same way as the nationals of that State.

As noted above, Article 4 *expressis verbis* allows the plaintiff to sue defendants not domiciled in the EU, whatever their nationality,[352] on the basis of the national jurisdictional rules of the Member State in which the plaintiff is domiciled. Article 4 does leave Article 22 and 23 unaffected. Moreover, and importantly, Article 27 on *lis alibi pendens* applies to these suits, as does automatic recognition under Chapter III of the Regulation.

The Report Jenard does not entertain the international sensitivities which we have already referred to. Rather like the European Commission in its follow-up proposals in particular for the original JR and the current review of the JR, the Committee that drafted the JR is more concerned about bringing the exercise of these 'exorbitant' (a term used by the report Jenard itself) jurisdictional claims within the purview of the JR. The Report justifies Article 4 on two grounds:[353]

> First, in order to ensure the free movement of judgments, this Article prevents refusal of recognition or enforcement of a judgment given on the basis of rules of internal law relating to jurisdiction. In the absence of such a provision, a judgment debtor would be able to prevent execution being levied on his property simply by transferring it to a Community country other than that in which judgment was given. Secondly, this Article may perform a function in the case of lis pendens. Thus, for example, if a French court is seized of an action between a Frenchman and a defendant domiciled in America, and a German court is seized of the same matter on the basis of Article 23 of the Code of Civil Procedure, one of the two courts must in the interests of the proper administration of justice decline jurisdiction in favour of the other. This issue cannot be settled unless the jurisdiction of these courts derives from the Convention.

I have not in this volume reviewed the sometimes complex arrangements made vis-a-vis treaties, pre-existing or otherwise, between EU Member States and third States. The Brussels I Regulation as well as the Rome I and II Regulations make (complex) provisions for such.[354]

---

[352] To make the point *ad nauseam* perhaps: for the BC and the JR, the nationality of the parties is irrelevant. Domicile is the relevant criterion. Hence just as non-EU nationals who are domiciled in an EU Member State can avail themselves of the jurisdictional rules of that Member State against non-EU domicileds, EU nationals domiciled outside of the EU will see Article 4 JR invoked against them.

[353] Report Jenard, 20–21.

[354] See e.g. De Miguel, P., and Bergé, J-S, 'The place of international agreements and European law in a European Code of Private International Law', in Fallon, M., Lagarde, P., Poillot-Peruzzetto (eds.), *Quelle architecture pour un code européen de droit international privé*, Brussels, Peter Lang, 2012, 185–211.

2.2.14 Loss of Jurisdiction: *lis alibi pendens*; and Related Actions: Articles 27–30

Section 9 *Lis pendens* – related actions

Article 27

1. Where proceedings involving the same cause of action and between the same parties are brought in the courts of different Member States, any court other than the court first seized shall of its own motion stay its proceedings until such time as the jurisdiction of the court first seized is established.

2. Where the jurisdiction of the court first seized is established, any court other than the court first seized shall decline jurisdiction in favour of that court.

Article 28

1. Where related actions are pending in the courts of different Member States, any court other than the court first seized may stay its proceedings.

2. Where these actions are pending at first instance, any court other than the court first seized may also, on the application of one of the parties, decline jurisdiction if the court first seized has jurisdiction over the actions in question and its law permits the consolidation thereof.

3. For the purposes of this Article, actions are deemed to be related where they are so closely connected that it is expedient to hear and determine them together to avoid the risk of irreconcilable judgments resulting from separate proceedings.

Article 29

Where actions come within the exclusive jurisdiction of several courts, any court other than the court first seized shall decline jurisdiction in favour of that court.

Article 30

For the purposes of this Section, a court shall be deemed to be seized:

1. at the time when the document instituting the proceedings or an equivalent document is lodged with the court, provided that the plaintiff has not subsequently failed to take the steps he was required to take to have service effected on the defendant, or
2. if the document has to be served before being lodged with the court, at the time when it is received by the authority responsible for service, provided that the plaintiff has not subsequently failed to take the steps he was required to take to have the document lodged with the court.

For the whole of section 9, Article 30 JR specifies what is meant by a court having been 'seized'.

2.2.14.1 *Lis alibi pendens*

The general gist of the *lis alibi pendens* rule has already been explored above (where I reviewed the use of anti-suit injunctions in the context of arbitration). The Report Jenard is in fact very brief on this issue. As noted, the *lis alibi pendens* rule applies to concurrent proceedings in the Member States courts, regardless of whether the jurisdiction is established on the basis of the JR, provided however the subject-matter is within the scope of application of the JR.

> Article 21, together with Article 22 on related actions, is contained in Section 8 of Title II of the Convention, a section intended, in the interests of the proper administration of justice within the Community, to prevent parallel proceedings before the courts of different Contracting States and to avoid conflicts between decisions which might result therefrom. Those rules are therefore designed to preclude, in so far as is possible and from the outset, the possibility of a situation arising such as that referred to in Article 27(3), that is to say the non-recognition of a judgment on account of its irreconcilability with a judgment given in a dispute between the same parties in the State in which recognition is sought.[355]

The rule is (fairly) simple and clear: where the *same action*, between the *same parties* is brought before the courts of two Member States, Article 27 obliges the court seized second, to at least freeze its jurisdiction.[356] At the most, it can stay proceedings until the first court has decided it has jurisdiction. The rule makes no distinction between jurisdictional rules, despite their hierarchy. That may even apply for jurisdiction under Article 22 (although there is no decisive authority on this point). The court seized second has no authority to investigate the jurisdiction of the first court.

The conditions for Article 27 to apply are that the case involves the same action, between the same parties. The ECJ has clarified in *Gubish Machinenfabrik*[357] and in *The Tatry*[358] what was already clearer in other language versions (including Dutch),[359] namely that Article 27 requires three identities: identify of parties; identify of object or 'subject-matter'; and identity of cause. The English version and the German version mention 'same parties' and 'same cause of action' only: they do not expressly distinguish between the concepts of "object" and "cause" of action.

2.2.14.2 Identity of Parties

> (W)here some of the parties are the same as the parties to an action which has already been started, Article [27] requires the second court seized to decline jurisdiction only to the extent to which the parties to the proceedings pending before it are also parties to the action previously started before the court of another Contracting State; it does not prevent the proceedings from continuing between the other parties.'[360] 'that interpretation of Article [27] involves fragmenting the proceedings. However, Article [28] mitigates that disadvantage. That article allows the second court seized to stay proceedings or to decline jurisdiction on the ground that the actions are related, if the conditions there set out are satisfied.[361]

---

[355] Case C-406/92 *The Tatry*, [1994] ECR I-5439, para 31.

[356] Instead of declining jurisdiction, the court which is subsequently seized of a matter may, however, stay its proceedings if the jurisdiction of the court first seized is contested. This rule was introduced so that the parties would not have to institute new proceedings if, for example, the court first seized of the matter were to decline jurisdiction. The risk of unnecessary disclaimers of jurisdiction is thereby avoided: see Report Jenard, at page 41.

[357] Case 144/86 *Gubisch Maschinenfabrik*, [1987] ECR 4861.

[358] n 355 above.

[359] 'Wanneer voor gerechten van verschillende verdragsluitende Staten tussen dezelfde partijen vorderingen aanhangig zijn, welke hetzelfde onderwerp betreffen en op dezelfde oorzaak berusten'; see also the French 'Lorsque des demandes ayant le même objet et la même cause sont formées entre les mêmes parties'.

[360] *The Tatry*, n 355 above, para 33.

[361] *Ibid*, para 34.

2.2.14.3 Identity of Object or 'Subject-Matter'

'The "object of the action" for the purposes of Article [27] means the end the action has in view.[362] This cannot be restricted so as to mean two claims which are entirely identical.[363] Rather, they will more often than not be the flip sides of the same coin: an action seeking declaration that a contract is invalid; and a competing action seeking enforcement of that very contract; or an action seeking liability of a party; and a competing action seeking a declaration that that party is not liable. Basically, and with a view to the enforcement issue, if the orders sought could contradict each other were they both granted, their object will be the same.

2.2.14.4 Identity of Cause of Action

> (T)he 'cause of action' comprises the facts and the rule of law relied on as the basis of the action.[364]

In this respect account should be taken only of the claims of the respective applicants, to the exclusion of the defence submissions raised by a defendant.[365]

2.2.14.5 Lis alibi pendens and the Forum Non Conveniens doctrine

The Regulation's rules on *Lis pendens* are the ultimate expression of the Regulation's search for clarity and especially predictability – therefore also inflexibility. The result of that is nowhere clearer than in *Owusu v Jackson*.[366]

According to the doctrine of *forum non conveniens*, as understood in English law, a national court may decline to exercise jurisdiction on the ground that a court in another State, which also has jurisdiction, would objectively be a more appropriate forum for the trial of the action, that is to say, a forum in which the case may be tried more suitably for the interests of all the parties and the ends of justice.[367] An English court which decides to decline jurisdiction under the doctrine of *forum non conveniens* stays proceedings so that the proceedings which are thus provisionally suspended can be resumed should it prove, in particular, that the foreign forum has no jurisdiction to hear the case or that the claimant has no access to effective justice in that forum.

Mr Owusu was a UK national who had rented a holiday home in Jamaica from one of the defendants, Mr Jackson, a Jamaican national but domiciled in the UK, and who suffered severe physical injuries in a diving accident as a result, allegedly, of a badly maintained and not properly signposted private beach that came with the holiday home. Mr Owusu also sued a number of Jamaican based companies with links to the case.

It was obvious from the start that the only procedural link to the UK under the JR was Article 2 for one of the defendants. It was also clear that had the claim been brought outside of the context of the JR, the English courts most likely would have applied forum

---

[362] *The Tatry*, n 355 above, para 40.
[363] *Gubisch Maschinenfabrik*, n 357 above, at 17.
[364] *Gubisch Maschinenfabrik*, n 357 above, para 38.
[365] Case C-111/01 *Gantner Electronic*, [2003] ECR I-4207, para 31.
[366] Case C-281/02 *Owusu v Jackson*, [2005] ECR I-553.
[367] The House of Lords, in *Spiliada Maritime Corporation v Cansulex Ltd* [1987], AC 460, particularly para 476.

non conveniens to dismiss the case. The House of Lords pointed out that, would it be forced to accept jurisdiction and hence issue a judgment on the merits of the case, this judgment would be very difficult to enforce in Jamaica. The specific questions of the case are worth repeating in full:

1. Is it inconsistent with the Brussels Convention, where a claimant contends that jurisdiction is founded on Article 2, for a court of a Contracting State to exercise a discretionary power, available under its national law, to decline to hear proceedings brought against a person domiciled in that State in favour of the courts of a non-Contracting State:

(a) if the jurisdiction of no other Contracting State under the 1968 Convention is in issue;
(b) if the proceedings have no connecting factors to any other Contracting State?

2. If the answer to question 1(a) or (b) is yes, is it inconsistent in all circumstances or only in some and if so which?

The Court held – rather concisely (the reader may wish to consult Léger AG's Opinion):

That for the jurisdiction rules of the Brussels Convention to apply at all, the existence of an international element is required.

That the international nature of the legal relationship at issue need not necessarily derive, for the purposes of the application of Article 2 of the Brussels Convention, from the involvement, either because of the subject-matter of the proceedings or the respective domiciles of the parties, of a number of Contracting States.

That moreover, the rules of the Brussels Convention on exclusive jurisdiction or express prorogation of jurisdiction are also likely to be applicable to legal relationships involving only one Contracting State and one or more non-Contracting States.

That the uniform rules of jurisdiction contained in the Brussels Convention are not intended to apply only to situations in which there is a real and sufficient link with the working of the internal market, by definition involving a number of Member States: it is not disputed that the mother instrument, i.e. the Brussels Convention, helps to ensure the smooth working of the internal market.

With respect to the compatibility with the BC of the FNC doctrine, the Court observed, first, that Article 2 of the Brussels Convention is mandatory in nature and that, according to its terms, there can be no derogation from the principle it lays down except in the cases expressly provided for by the Convention

That respect for the principle of legal certainty, which is one of the objectives of the Brussels Convention (see, inter alia, Case C-440/97 *GIE Groupe Concorde and Others* [1999] ECR I-'[sic]6307, paragraph 23, and Case C-256/00 *Besix* [2002] ECR I-'1699, paragraph 24), would not be fully guaranteed if the court having jurisdiction under the Convention had to be allowed to apply the *forum non conveniens* doctrine.

That Application of the *forum non conveniens* doctrine, which allows the court seized a wide discretion as regards the question whether a foreign court would be a more appropriate forum for the trial of an action, is liable to undermine the predictability of the rules of jurisdiction laid down by the Brussels Convention, in particular that of Article 2, and consequently to undermine the principle of legal certainty, which is the basis of the Convention.

That the legal protection of persons established in the Community would also be undermined. In particular, a defendant, who is generally better placed to conduct his defence before the courts of his domicile, would not be able, in circumstances such as those of the main proceedings, reasonably to foresee before which other court he may be sued.

That moreover, allowing *forum non conveniens* in the context of the Brussels Convention would be likely to affect the uniform application of the rules of jurisdiction contained therein in so far as that doctrine is recognised only in a limited number of Contracting States, whereas the objective of the Brussels Convention is precisely to lay down common rules to the exclusion of derogating national rules.

The Court's ruling left many issues unanswered, including with respect to court of choice agreements [what if there is an express choice of court agreement for a third State[368]]; or what the impact of the ruling is, if any, if there is already a proceeding pending in a third State;[369] or what if that third State, had it been a Member State, would have had exclusive jurisdiction under Article 22. However, the Court's general gist is clear: it emphasises the predictability and legal certainty as core issues of the BC and the JR; and it sees the application of FNC in spite of its criteria as developed by the House of Lords (now Supreme Court) in *Spiliada*, as unpredictable and as relying too much on the individual 'discretion' of the national judge (perhaps a more suited word would have been 'judgment': 'discretion' would indeed seem to suggest a completely free range for the English judge, which considering *Spiliada* is certainly not the case).

The English courts most certainly have not given up on FNC altogether. They happily continue to apply FNC outside of the JR context, not just where no European harmonisation at all is involved,[370] but also outside of the JR context but within EU law, for instance with respect to the Brussels IIa Regulation.[371]

Interestingly, the European Parliament Rapporteur for the review of the Brussels I Regulation, had early on in the proceedings suggested a forum non conveniens mechanism for the JR, along the lines of the Brussels II Regulation:[372]

Suggests, in order to avoid the type of problem which came to the fore in Owusu v. Jackson, a solution on the lines of Article 15 of Regulation No 2201/2003 so as to allow the courts of a Member State having jurisdiction as to the substance to stay proceedings if they consider that a court of another Member State or of a third country would be better placed to hear the case, or a specific part thereof, thus enabling the parties to bring an application before that court or to enable the court seised to transfer the case to that court with the agreement of the parties; welcomes the corresponding suggestion in the proposal for a regulation on jurisdiction, applicable law, recognition and enforcement of decisions and authentic instruments in matters of succession.[373]

The relevant provision in that Regulation reads:

---

[368] Pro application of FNC: See e.g. *Konkola Copper Mines plc. v Coromin* [2005] EWHC 898 (Comm): a provision of the contract conferred exclusive jurisdiction on a non-Member State.

[369] Contra application of FNC: Barling J in *Catalyst v Lewinsohn*, [2009] EWHC 1964 (Ch).

[370] See e.g. *Cherney v Deripaska*, [2008] EWHC 1530 (Comm).

[371] *KN v JCN* [2010] EWHC 843, in which the English Court retained its power to grant a stay on grounds of *forum non conveniens*: High Court, family division, 19 April 2010.

[372] Regulation 2201/2003 concerning jurisdiction and the recognition and enforcement of judgments in matrimonial matters, OJ [2003] L338/1.

[373] Report Tadeusz Zwiefka MEP of 29 June 2010 on the implementation of the Brussels I Regulation, PE 439.997v02-00, at 14.

Article 15

Transfer to a court better placed to hear the case

1. By way of exception, the courts of a Member State having jurisdiction as to the substance of the matter may, if they consider that a court of another Member State, with which the child has a particular connection, would be better placed to hear the case, or a specific part thereof, and where this is in the best interests of the child:

(a) stay the case or the part thereof in question and invite the parties to introduce a request before the court of that other Member State in accordance with paragraph 4; or
(b) request a court of another Member State to assume jurisdiction in accordance with paragraph 5.

2. Paragraph 1 shall apply:

(a) upon application from a party; or
(b) of the court's own motion; or
(c) upon application from a court of another Member State with which the child has a particular connection, in accordance with paragraph 3.

A transfer made of the court's own motion or by application of a court of another Member State must be accepted by at least one of the parties.

3. The child shall be considered to have a particular connection to a Member State as mentioned in paragraph 1, if that Member State:

(a) has become the habitual residence of the child after the court referred to in paragraph 1 was seised; or
(b) is the former habitual residence of the child; or
(c) is the place of the child's nationality; or
(d) is the habitual residence of a holder of parental responsibility; or
(e) is the place where property of the child is located and the case concerns measures for the protection of the child relating to the administration, conservation or disposal of this property.

4. The court of the Member State having jurisdiction as to the substance of the matter shall set a time limit by which the courts of that other Member State shall be seised in accordance with paragraph 1.

If the courts are not seised by that time, the court which has been seised shall continue to exercise jurisdiction in accordance with Articles 8 to 14.

5. The courts of that other Member State may, where due to the specific circumstances of the case, this is in the best interests of the child, accept jurisdiction within six weeks of their seisure in accordance with paragraph 1(a) or 1(b). In this case, the court first seised shall decline jurisdiction. Otherwise, the court first seised shall continue to exercise jurisdiction in accordance with Articles 8 to 14.

6. The courts shall cooperate for the purposes of this Article, either directly or through the central authorities designated pursuant to Article 53.

This forum non conveniens provision clearly leaves a lot less room for manoeuvre for the courts seized, or at the least it aims to impose substantial conditions upon that room for manoeuvre.

Likewise, in the new succession Regulation,[374] Article 6 provides

Article 6

Declining of jurisdiction in the event of a choice of law

Where the law chosen by the deceased to govern his succession pursuant to Article 22 is the law of a Member State, the court seised pursuant to Article 4 or Article 10:

(a) may, at the request of one of the parties to the proceedings, decline jurisdiction if it considers that the courts of the Member State of the chosen law are better placed to rule on the succession, taking into account the practical circumstances of the succession, such as the habitual residence of the parties and the location of the assets; or

(b) shall decline jurisdiction if the parties to the proceedings have agreed, in accordance with Article 5, to confer jurisdiction on a court or the courts of the Member State of the chosen law.

In conclusion, even if the Parliament Rapporteur eventually dropped his idea for an overall forum non conveniens rule, clearly the new generation European private international law instruments are not as hostile to forum non conveniens as the ECJ had perceived the previous generation to be. This in my view may at some point have to lead to a review of the overall negative approach of the ECJ towards forum non conveniens in the Jurisdiction Regulation.

2.2.14.6 *Related Actions*

Article 28 applies for actions which do not conform to the Article 27 conditions, e.g. for actions between different parties, however where the actions are so related that separate proceedings would risk irreconcilable judgments. The purpose of that provision is to avoid the risk of conflicting judgments and thus to facilitate the proper administration of justice in the Union.[375] To achieve proper administration of justice, the interpretation of 'related actions' must be broad and cover all cases where there is a risk of conflicting decisions, even if the judgments can be separately enforced and their legal consequences are not mutually exclusive.[376] 'Irreconcilable' is at least in the English version, used in Article 34(3), too (refusal of recognition of judgment: see below), other language versions (German, Italian) use different terms. Moreover the goals of Article 28 and Article 34 are radically different. Article 34(3) JR enables a court, by way of derogation from the principles and objectives of the Regulation, to refuse to recognize a foreign judgment. Consequently the term "irreconcilable ... judgment" there referred to must be interpreted by reference to that objective. The objective of the third paragraph of Article 28 of the Convention, however, is to improve coordination of the exercise of judicial functions within the Community and to avoid conflicting and contradictory decisions, even where the separate enforcement of each of them is not precluded.[377] Thus the risk of conflicting

---

[374] Regulation 650/2012 on jurisdiction, applicable law, recognition and enforcement of decisions and acceptance and enforcement of authentic instruments in matters of succession and on the creation of a European certificate of succession, OJ [2012] L201/107. The United Kingdom is as yet not covered by this Regulation. The Regulation will be reviewed in a future edition of this handbook.

[375] *Gubisch Maschinenfabrik*, n 357 above, para 51, with reference to the Jenard Report.

[376] *Ibid*, para 52.

[377] *Ibid* para 54.

decisions is enough to trigger Article 28(3), without necessarily involving the risk of giving rise to mutually exclusive legal consequences.[378]

Article 28 gives the court much more leeway than Article 27: it can stay its proceedings; reject its jurisdiction in favour of the other court; or simply go ahead.

Article 30 clarifies what is meant by court 'seized':

Article 30

For the purposes of this Section, a court shall be deemed to be seised:

1. at the time when the document instituting the proceedings or an equivalent document is lodged with the court, provided that the plaintiff has not subsequently failed to take the steps he was required to take to have service effected on the defendant, or
2. if the document has to be served before being lodged with the court, at the time when it is received by the authority responsible for service, provided that the plaintiff has not subsequently failed to take the steps he was required to take to have the document lodged with the court.

2.2.15 Applications for Provisional or Protective Measures: Article 31

Section 10 Provisional, including protective, measures

Article 31

Application may be made to the courts of a Member State for such provisional, including protective, measures as may be available under the law of that State, even if, under this Regulation, the courts of another Member State have jurisdiction as to the substance of the matter.

A court which has jurisdiction under any of the provisions of the JR, will be able to order any provisional or protective measures it deems necessary, even if it has stayed its jurisdiction by application of the *lis alibi pendens* rule.[379] This was confirmed in *Van Uden*:[380]

a court having jurisdiction as to the substance of a case in accordance with Articles 2 and 5 to 18 of the Convention also has jurisdiction to order any provisional or protective measures which may prove necessary.

This is not in itself surprising[381] and it is not what is meant by Article 31. Article 31 basically amounts to the JR (and the BC before it) specifying its field of application: it does not regulate 'provisional, including protective, measures' and hence in each State, application may therefore be made to the competent courts for provisional or protective measures to be imposed or suspended, or for rulings on the validity of such measures,

---

[378] *Ibid*, para 57.

[379] See e.g. *JP Morgan Europe Ltd v Primacom AG*, [2005] EWHC 508 (Comm) at 70–73; see Fawcett, JJ and Carruthers, JM, n 183 above, 315 n 956.

[380] Case C-391/95 *Van Uden*, [1998] ECR I-7122, para 19.

[381] Although as noted above, neither is it free of difficulty: in particular, for interim measures in intellectual property disputes, the application of the exclusive jurisdictional ground of Article 22(4) sits uneasily with other courts' jurisdiction for provisionary measures. The ECJ answered some of the issues concerning the delineation with Article 31 JR in Solvay (Case C-616/10, n 201 above and further analysis there) however it did not entertain the relationship between Article 22(4) and provisional measures based on the core jurisdictional rules of the JR, rather than on Article 31.

without regard to the rules of jurisdiction laid down in the Regulation.[382] Article 31 is therefore an additional, subsidiary rule of jurisdiction with reference to national law.

As regards the measures which may be taken

- reference should largely be made to the internal law of the country concerned.[383] However the core issue of whether the measure is 'provisional', is determined by European law: it is not the lex fori which decides whether the measure is provisional, but rather the JR. The measures must be provisional measures only: not measures taken in expedient procedures:

(T)he expression "provisional, including protective, measures" within the meaning of Article [31] must therefore be understood as referring to measures which, in matters within the scope of the Convention, are intended to preserve a factual or legal situation so as to safeguard rights the recognition of which is sought elsewhere from the court having jurisdiction as to the substance of the matter.[384]

This is interpreted strictly: in the case at issue, the *Actio Pauliana* was held as not preserving a legal situation but rather seeking to vary it, by ordering the revocation as against the creditor of the disposition effected by the debtor in fraud of the creditor's rights.[385]

- moreover, the granting of provisional or protective measures on the basis of Article 31 is conditional on the existence of 'a real connecting link' between the subject-matter of the measures sought and the territorial jurisdiction of the Member State of the court before which those measures are sought (a typical link evidently is the presence of assets in the Member State concerned).[386] A measure ordering interim payment of a contractual consideration does not constitute a provisional measure within the meaning of that article unless, first, repayment to the defendant of the sum awarded is guaranteed if the plaintiff is unsuccessful as regards the substance of his claim and, second, the measure sought relates only to specific assets of the defendant located or to be located within the confines of the territorial jurisdiction of the court to which application is made.[387]

The *Denilauler* criteria (see more on this below) for a ruling to be considered a 'judgment' within the context of the Regulation, are a challenge within the context of provisional measures. In *Denilauler* the ECJ clarified that for a ruling to be a 'judgment' it has to follow an 'inquiry in adversarial proceedings'.[388] Quite a few provisional measures however (indeed often the most efficient ones) are/have to be taken *ex parte* and hence arguably fall outside the Regulation. The main consequence of such issue not being covered is of course not that the measure concerned is in any way illegal: that is not for the Regulation to consider. Rather, those measures that fall outside the Regulation will not enjoy its recognition and enforcement title, which especially in the case of provisional

---

[382] Report Jenard, 42.

[383] *Ibid.* Lex fori therefore applies to the types of available measures and conditions imposed upon them. See also Bogdan, M., 'The proposed recast of rules on provisional measures under the Brussels I Regulation', in *The Brussels I Review Proposal Uncovered*, Lein, E. (ed.), London, British Institute of International and Comparative Law, 2012, (125) 130.

[384] Case C-261/90 *Reichert v Dresdner Bank*, [1992] ECR 2149, para 34.

[385] *Ibid*, para 35.

[386] Bogdan, M. n 383 above.

[387] Case C-391/95 *Van Uden*, [1998] ECR I-7091.

[388] n 401 above.

measures may be rather crucial (especially in cases where assets need to be recovered from abroad or evidence preserved).

The Commission proposal on the review of the JR,[389] and indeed the Council and Parliament discussion of same, reveal the intention largely of clarifying the article on provisional measures. There are one or two issues of note, however.

Firstly, the new regime in all likelihood will restrict the current regime, in that it will exclude all provisional measures taken by the court of a Member State which does not have jurisdiction over the matter by virtue of the Regulation, from its enforcement title. Only provisional measures ordered by the court with substantive jurisdiction under the Regulation will continue to be principally enforced across the EU by virtue of the Regulation.[390] It is of course not excluded that they might be enforced following subsidiary national law, which on the whole however will be much more cumbersome.

While one may sympathise with the Commission view expressed in its Green Paper preceding the review, that the scope of provisional measures is so wide and diverse across the EU that mutual recognition is particularly difficult,[391] such mutual recognition is also particularly useful. It fits entirely with the Internal Market credentials of the Regulation however as we have noted once or twice already, those are no longer the driving force behind the JR.

The (EP and Council approved) text as it stands on this point would read:
In recital 25 in relevant part:

> Where provisional, including protective, measures are ordered by a court of a Member State not having jurisdiction as to the substance of the matter, the effect of such measures should be confined, under this Regulation, to the territory of that Member State.

Article 2(a), second para: with respect to the definition of 'judgment':

> For the purposes of Chapter III, the term 'judgment' includes provisional, including protective, measures ordered by a court or tribunal which by virtue of this Regulation has jurisdiction as to the substance of the matter. It does not include a provisional, including protective, measure which is ordered without the defendant being summoned to appear, unless that judgment has been served on the defendant prior to enforcement;

However on another point the new regime is also likely to overrule *Denilauler* and bring ex parte measures within the remit of the Regulation, however not in an altogether satisfactory manner:
Again, Recital 25 in relevant part:

> However, provisional, including protective, measures which were ordered by such a court without the defendant being summoned to appear should not be recognised and enforced under this Regulation unless the judgment containing the measure is served on the defendant prior to enforcement. This should not preclude recognition and enforcement of such measures under national law.

Having to serve the judgment prior to enforcement of course largely takes away the ex parte effect. While one cannot rule out abuse, nevertheless I cannot see why ex post

---

[389] See n 69 ff above.
[390] See Kiesselbach, P., 'The Brussels I Review Proposal – An overview', in Lein, E. (ed.), London, British Institute of International and Comparative Law, 2012, (1) 16.
[391] See also ibidem.

review of potential reasons for refusing enforceability, could not have sufficiently served the rule of law trick whilst better serving procedural expediency and the Internal Market.

2.2.16 Recognition and Enforcement

To recognise foreign judgments is to admit for the territory of the recognising State the authority which they enjoy in the State where they were handed down.[392]

Chapter III of the JR was of course the true starting point of the whole BC and JR system, indeed it was the very raison d'être for what has become a very extensive body of secondary EU law (see more on this in the introductory chapter). As a result of the safeguards granted to the defendant in the original proceedings, Title III of the Regulation is very liberal on the question of recognition and enforcement. As already stated, it seeks to facilitate as far as possible the free movement of judgments, and should be interpreted in this spirit. This liberal approach is evidenced in Title III first by a reduction in the number of grounds which can operate to prevent the recognition and enforcement of judgments and secondly, by the simplification of the enforcement procedure which is common to all Member States.[393]

To some degree Chapter III of the JR, in conjunction with other EU law instruments including the European Small Claims Procedure Regulation,[394] have become near-automatic and indeed notary practice. It is, as noted before, precisely the near-automatic recognition and enforcement procedures which first triggered the wish of the drafters of the BC to include provisions on jurisdiction and which subsequently encouraged the ECJ to emphasise the need for mutual trust and legal certainty in the application of the JR.

Chapter III on recognition and enforcement has three sections: one on recognition; one on 'enforcement'; and finally one with common provisions. The 'enforcement' section has a misleading title,[395] for it does not actually lead to enforcement of the judgments at issue, rather to paving the way to such enforcement in the relevant Member State. Enforcement itself is left to national law — what is meant therefore is 'exequatur'.

The section on recognition firstly ensures the automatic recognition of judgments without any special procedure being needed; a cross-reference to the swift procedure foreseen for exequatur, should one for a particular reason require express recognition of a foreign judgment; and finally a limited number of grounds which may lead to a court refusing recognition. The latter are in turn cross-referred to in the section on exequatur: in other words recognition and exequatur may be refused only on the basis of the same grounds.

Finally, Section 3 'common provisions' concerns formalities, in particular the documentation required to be submitted upon application for either recognition or enforcement.

---

[392] Virgos-Schmit Report sub the Insolvency Regulation, para 143, p.92: the report has not been officially published for reasons explained elsewhere in this volume. It may downloaded from the Archives of European Integration, e.g. via http://aei.pitt.edu/952/. See further below.

[393] Report Jenard, 42.

[394] Regulation 861/2007, OJ [2007] L199/1.

[395] Storme, H., 'Het Europese Recht van het erkennen en uitvoerbaar verklaren van beslissingen en akten', in Erauw, J., *Internationaal Privaatrecht*, Mechelen, Kluwer, 2009, (237) 250.

Article 33

1. A judgment given in a Member State shall be recognised in the other Member States without any special procedure being required.

2. Any interested party who raises the recognition of a judgment as the principal issue in a dispute may, in accordance with the procedures provided for in Sections 2 and 3 of this Chapter, apply for a decision that the judgment be recognised.

3. If the outcome of proceedings in a court of a Member State depends on the determination of an incidental question of recognition that court shall have jurisdiction over that question.

Article 33 includes 3 rules on recognition[396]:

- judgments have to be recognised automatically. Member States must not make recognition per se subject to a special procedure and any party wishing to invoke a judgment against another party, typically as a defence in a proceeding initiated by that other party, can do so without having to make recourse to any prior special procedure. There is a presumption in favour or recognition, and it takes a special procedure to rebut that presumption.
- in the event of a dispute, if recognition is itself the principal issue, the simplified procedure for enforcement provided for in the Regulation may be applied (as opposed to the situation prior to the BC, where complicated national procedures had to be followed);
- if the outcome of proceedings depends on the determination of an incidental question of recognition, the court entertaining those proceedings has jurisdiction on the question of recognition.

Two conditions which are frequently inserted in enforcement treaties are not included in the JR: it is not necessary that the foreign judgment should have become res judicata, and the jurisdiction of the court which gave the original judgment does not have to be verified by the court of the State in which the recognition is sought — lest heading d, below, applies.[397]

2.2.16.1 Recognition

The conditions for recognition are included in Article 33 ff:[398] the judgment [a] must be an adjudication from a court in a Member State; [b] must be given in a civil or commercial matter; [c] must not have been in proceedings instituted after the entry into force of the Regulation; [d] must not be impeachable for jurisdictional error; [e] must not be impeachable for procedural or substantive reasons; and [f] must not be excluded from recognition by a relevant other Treaty.

---

[396] Meaning conferring judgments the authority and effectiveness accorded to them in the State in which they were given: Report Jenard, 43.

[397] Report Jenard, 44.

[398] The format for listing these conditions is taken from Briggs, A., *The Conflict of Laws*, Oxford, OUP, 2008, 121 ff.

2.2.16.1 [a] Must be an Adjudication from a Court in a Member State

Article 32

For the purposes of this Regulation, "judgment" means any judgment given by a court or tribunal of a Member State, whatever the judgment may be called, including a decree, order, decision or writ of execution, as well as the determination of costs or expenses by an officer of the court.

The definition of Article 32 JR[399] clearly excludes judgments from non-Member States, even if they have been held enforceable by a judge in another MS (recognition of whose judgment is subsequently sought). Article 57 extends recognition to authentic acts, such as from notary publics.

Chapter III applies regardless of whether the judgment was issued on the basis of a jurisdictional rule of the Regulation or not – see also below: national public policy must certainly not be invoked to refuse recognition of judgments issued in the basis of exorbitant national rules of jurisdiction vis-à-vis non- EU domiciled defendants.

The very wording of Article 32 shows that the definition of "judgment" given in that provision refers, for the purposes of the application of the various provisions of the Regulation in which the term is used, solely to judicial decisions actually given by a court or tribunal of a Member State. In order to be a "judgment" for the purposes of the Regulation the decision must emanate from a judicial body of a Member State deciding on its own authority on the issues between the parties. That condition is not fulfilled in the case of a settlement, even if it was reached in a court of a Member State and brings legal proceedings to an end. Settlements in court are essentially contractual in that their terms depend first and foremost on the parties' intention.[400] The ECJ in *Solo Kleinmotoren* reached this decision with reference to the discussion in the Report Jenard on the German *Kostenfestsetzungsbeschlug des Urkundsbeamten*, a decision on costs which would seem fairly administrative however of which the Expert Committee justified its inclusion because of the potential for the full court to intervene where parties disagree as to the initial decision by the court clerk.

More generally, the Court has (within the context of the Brussels Convention however transferable to the JR), made the rights of the defence infiltrate into the very definition of a 'judgment' under the Regulation: all the provisions of the JR, both those contained in the Title on jurisdiction and those contained in the Title on recognition and enforcement, express the intention to ensure that, within the scope of the objectives of the Regulation, proceedings leading to the delivery of judicial decisions take place in such a way that the rights of the defence are observed. For such decisions to fall within the scope of the Regulation, it is sufficient (but also required) if they are judicial decisions which, before their recognition and enforcement are sought in a State other than the State of origin, have been, or have been capable of being, the subject in that State of origin and under various procedures, of an inquiry in adversarial proceedings.[401]

How this applies to court recognition or adoption, or any other equivalent terminology used, of *arbitral awards* is unclear. Briggs argues that recognition does not apply to judgments which validate or approve a decision taken by someone who is not a court,

---

[399] In the current review of the JR, all definitional Articles are thankfully regrouped into Article 1.
[400] Case C-414/92 *Solo Kleinmotoren*, [1994] ECR I-237.
[401] Case 125/79 *Denilauler*, [1980] ECR 1553, para 13; Case C-394/07 *Gambazzi*, [2009] ECR I-2563, para 23.

and that this would include enforceability of an arbitration award.[402] However while most definitely one needs to approach the issue cautiously given the very exclusion from the JR of arbitration, I do not think court decisions recognising arbitral awards are excluded from the recognition title merely because they validate a decision made by someone who is not a court within the meaning of the Regulation. Depending both on the extent of review by the court of a Member State, in accordance with that State's national civil procedure rules, and on the actual review carried out by that court, court rulings which validate a ruling by a non-court, may in my view qualify, on an ad hoc basis, as an 'inquiry in adversarial proceedings' per the *Denilauler* and *Gambazzi* formula.[403]

In *Gothaer*[404] Bot AG summarises the Court's case law on what a 'judgment' entails into three criteria: organic, procedural (closely related to organic), and substantive.

> The first criterion is organic. The judgment must emanate from a court or tribunal, that is to say, a body which acted independently of the other institutions of the State and impartially. (...) The second criterion, which cannot be separated from the first, is procedural. It requires that the rights of the defence were observed in the procedure which led up to the adoption of the judgment.(...) The third criterion is substantive. The judgment is characterised by the exercise of a power of assessment by the judicial body from which it emanates. That criterion means that a distinction must be drawn depending on whether the authority has a decision-making role or restricts itself to a more passive function, consisting for example in receiving the intentions of the parties to the proceedings. (...)' (ad 36 ff)

Consequently, in the AG's view, a judgment by a court in a Member State, finding that it does not have jurisdiction because of a choice of forum clause pointing away from the EU (in the case at issue: Iceland), is a 'judgment' within the meaning of Article 32 JR.

2.2.16.1 [b] Must be Given in a Civil or Commercial Matter. The matter at issue does have to come within the scope of application of the JR as it otherwise simply falls outside the scope of the Regulation per se.[405] It follows that Title III cannot be invoked for the recognition and enforcement of judgments given on matters excluded from the scope of the Regulation (status and legal capacity of persons, rules governing rights in property arising out of matrimonial relationship, wills and succession, bankruptcy and other similar proceedings, social security, and arbitration including arbitral awards).[406]

May the recognising court second-guess the decision by the adjudicating court on whether the issue falls within the scope of application of the JR? Scholarship is divided on the issue. It has been argued that especially in those cases where the issue had not really been raised before the court whose judgment needs to be recognised, the court in the latter Member State must consider the issue, while in those cases where the issue has been raised and the adjudicating court has held that the matter is within the scope of the Regulation, discretion by the recognising court is arguably required.[407] Others have argued quite in passing that the scope of the Regulation is and needs to be looked at both at the adjudication stage and at the recognition and enforcement stage, and point to

---

[402] n 398 above.
[403] n 401 above.
[404] Case C-456/11 *Gothaer Allgemeine Versichering et al*, Opinion Bot AG, not yet published in ECR.
[405] Report Jenard para 43.
[406] *Ibid.*
[407] Briggs, A., n 398 above, 123.

the fact that quite a few of the ECJ judgments on the scope of application resulted from preliminary review after the review of jurisdiction by a national court.[408]

2.2.16.1 [c] Must not have been in Proceedings Instituted after the Entry into Force of the Regulation. Article 66 however foresees in an extended application of Title III of the JR in cases of parallel application of the BC/Lugano Convention in both recognising and adjudicating Member Sate; and where the adjudicating court has held its recognition on the basis of rules which conform to the Regulation

2.2.16.1 [d] Must not be Impeachable for Jurisdictional Error

Article 35

1. Moreover, a judgment shall not be recognised if it conflicts with Sections 3, 4 or 6 of Chapter II, or in a case provided for in Article 72.

2. In its examination of the grounds of jurisdiction referred to in the foregoing paragraph, the court or authority applied to shall be bound by the findings of fact on which the court of the Member State of origin based its jurisdiction.

3. Subject to the paragraph 1, the jurisdiction of the court of the Member State of origin may not be reviewed. The test of public policy referred to in point 1 of Article 34 may not be applied to the rules relating to jurisdiction.

Evidently the starting point of both Article 34 and Article 35 is to limit the scope for the courts in the State where recognition is sought, to refuse that recognition. There is a presumption in favour of recognition (which is the exact opposite of all Conventions, bi- and multilateral, prior to the BC) and the limited grounds which may justify a refusal of recognition are listed exhaustively in the JR.

'Jurisdictional error'[409] is included in Article 35, which discusses the room for the courts in the Member State of recognition to review the application of the JR by the courts in the Member State of adjudication. The principle is that *no* second-guessing must take place of the jurisdictional rules once it is clear that the matter is within the scope of the Regulation (see above re 'civil or commercial matters' and whether the view on this by the adjudicating court can be second-guessed), and any alleged wrong application of jurisdiction (other than those listed in Article 35(1)) cannot be categorised as infringing public policy in the Member State of recognition (Article 35(3)).

As noted once or twice already, the exercise by the national courts of their national rules of jurisdiction as per Article 4 JR, is covered by Chapter III. Consequently there is in principle no room for the courts of other Member States to question the application of these rules by their counterparts in other Member States.

The only exceptions are the jurisdictional rules for insurance contracts, consumer contracts (as noted, rather oddly *not* employment contracts) and exclusive jurisdiction on the basis of Article 22. *Not* infringement of exclusive jurisdiction clauses validly made under Article 23. However as a result of The Hague Convention on Choice of Court Agreements Convention, an amendment of the Regulation on this point is quite likely.

---

[408] Fawcett, JJ and Carruthers, JM, n 183 above, 601.

[409] The courts in the State of recognition certainly must not review a foreign judgment as to its substance in law or in fact: see Article 36 JR: 'Under no circumstances may a foreign judgment be reviewed as to its substance.'

2.2.16.1 [e] Must not be Impeachable for Procedural or Substantive Reasons

Article 34

A judgment shall not be recognised:

1. if such recognition is manifestly contrary to public policy in the Member State in which recognition is sought;
2. where it was given in default of appearance, if the defendant was not served with the document which instituted the proceedings or with an equivalent document in sufficient time and in such a way as to enable him to arrange for his defence, unless the defendant failed to commence proceedings to challenge the judgment when it was possible for him to do so;
3. if it is irreconcilable with a judgment given in a dispute between the same parties in the Member State in which recognition is sought;
4. if it is irreconcilable with an earlier judgment given in another Member State or in a third State involving the same cause of action and between the same parties, provided that the earlier judgment fulfils the conditions necessary for its recognition in the Member State addressed.

Here, too, the Regulation is of course very limited: there are only four such reasons and they are exclusively listed in Article 34:

1 Public Policy
The notion of 'public policy' in Article 34 is that of *ordre public international*. The notion may be confusing for the continental lawyers, as civil law tends to employ the same notion (loosely translated as 'public order') for quite a variety of contexts:

- those of contract law, limiting the contractual freedom of parties in the event of interests which serve the public interest as a whole, as opposed to 'mandatory' law which protects the interest of specific categories of individuals only;
- of European law, particularly in the context of the four freedoms and the degree to which a Member State may create obstacles to such freedoms; and
- of private international law, in the context of recognition and enforcement (leading to a refusal of such steps in the event doing so would be contrary to core principles of the legal order where recognition is sought); and finally in the context of applicable law/choice of law: leading to the forum ignoring provisions of the applicable law).

The recognition itself must be 'manifestly' contrary to (national) public policy. 'This means firstly that the court in the State of recognition must not review whether the judgment itself is contrary to its national public policy, but rather, its enforcement'.[410]

'Public policy in the Member State in which recognition is sought', is by its very nature a matter for the courts of that Member State to define, however the ECJ has held that the nature of the JR necessarily implies that the ECJ has to exercise a degree of control. It has held that the clause on public policy may be relied on only in exceptional cases.[411] While the Member States remain free in principle to determine according to

---

[410] Report Jenard, 44.
[411] Case 145/86 *Hoffmann*, [1988] ECR 645, para 21, and Case C-78/95 *Hendrikman*, [1996] ECR I-4943, para 23.

their own conception what public policy requires, the limits of that concept are a matter of interpretation of the JR.[412]

Recourse to the clause on public policy can be envisaged only where recognition or enforcement of the judgment delivered in another Member State would be at variance to an unacceptable degree with the legal order of the State in which enforcement is sought inasmuch as it infringes a fundamental principle. In order for the prohibition of any review of the foreign judgment as to its substance to be observed, the infringement would have to constitute a manifest breach of a rule of law regarded as essential in the legal order of the State in which enforcement is sought or of a right recognised as being fundamental within that legal order.[413]

The possibility that the court of the State of origin erred in applying certain rules of EU law, including free movement of goods and competition law, does not qualify as such — that these rules concern Union[414] as opposed to national law, does not as such have an impact on the application of Article 34;[415] the means to correct errors in applying European competition law are national appeals procedures, judicial review with the ECJ, and, one imagines, direct appeal to the European Commission that in having its courts wrongly apply European competition law, is an infringement of that Member State's duties under the Treaty.

Disregard for rights under the ECHR have famously been upheld as within reach of a national court's option to apply Article 34 JR in *Krombach v Bamberski*.[416] Public policy is certainly not to be invoked as a ground for refusing to recognize a judgment given by a court of a Member State which has based its jurisdiction over a defendant domiciled outside the Union on a provision of its internal law, such as the provisions listed in Annex to the JR (the exorbitant national jurisdictional grounds).[417]

2 Judgments in Default of Appearance

This is the necessary corollary of Article 24 JR, and a matter of factual appreciation. It is typically difficult to apply in the event of *pro forma* service e.g. to the local consul, the last known address, the public prosecutor's office etc.[418] Whether the document which instituted the proceedings was duly served or not, has to be judged in accordance with the internal law of the Member State where the judgment was issued,[419] however the second leg of that exception ('in a way as to enable him to arrange his defence') indicates that the courts in the State of recognition have room to judge the timeliness in particular viz

---

[412] Case C-7/98 *Krombach* [2000] ECR I-1935, para 22.

[413] *Ibid* para 37.

[414] Specifically in the case of competition law, Union law of a very high standing: see Case C-126/07 *Eco Swiss*, [1999] ECR I-3055: Where domestic rules of procedure require a national court to grant an application for annulment of an arbitration award where such an application is founded on failure to observe national rules of public policy, it must also grant such an application where it is founded on failure to comply with the prohibition laid down in Article 85 of the Treaty (now Article 81 EC). That provision constitutes a fundamental provision which is essential for the accomplishment of the tasks entrusted to the Community and, in particular, for the functioning of the internal market. Also, Community law requires that questions concerning the interpretation of the prohibition laid down in Article 85 should be open to examination by national courts when they are asked to determine the validity of an arbitration award and that it should be possible for those questions to be referred, if necessary, to the Court of Justice for a preliminary ruling.

[415] Case C-38/98 *Renault*, [2000] ECR I-2973, para 31 ff.

[416] n 412 above.

[417] Report Jenard, 79.

[418] Briggs, A., n 398 above, 128.

[419] Report Jenard, 44.

the ECHR. The Report Jenard itself indicated that this provision does leave a crucial role for the courts in the State of recognition and hence must not be too restrictively applied.[420]

The observance of the rights of defence of a defendant in default of appearance is effectively ensured by a double review, one each by the Court of origin and the Court which is asked to recognise the judgment.[421] In the original proceedings in the State in which the judgment was given, the combined application of Articles 26(2) JR and Article 19(1) of Regulation 1393/2007,[422] mean that the court hearing the case must stay the proceedings so long as it is not shown that the defendant has been able to receive the document which instituted the proceedings or an equivalent document in sufficient time to enable him to arrange for his defence, or that all necessary steps have been taken to this end. If, during recognition and enforcement proceedings in the State in which enforcement is sought, the defendant commences proceedings against a declaration of enforceability issued in the State in which the judgment was given, the court hearing the action must also examine the proper observance of the rights of the defence.

3 Irreconcilability with Other Judgment of the MS of Forum
This exception applies whether these other judgments are issued sooner or later, however the application of *lis alibi pendens* and related actions ought greatly to reduce the number of irreconcilable judgments. Article 34(3) requires the same parties only, not the same cause of action.

4 Irreconcilability with other Judgment of Other MS (than the Adjudicating MS) or of a Third State
This exception does require the same parties and the same cause of action. Recognition may be refused if the proceedings which gave rise to the judgment whose recognition is sought have already resulted in a judgment which was given in a third State or another Member State and which would be entitled to recognition and enforcement under the law of the State in which recognition is sought.

2.2.16.1 [f] Must not be Excluded from Recognition by a Relevant Other Treaty. See Article 72, which has limited application.

With respect to enforcement, Article 38 ff detail the relevant procedure and documents, and these will be further simplified in amendments to the Brussels I Regulation. The enforcement procedure of the JR constitutes an autonomous and complete system, independent of the legal systems of the Contracting States, including the matter of appeals.[423]

2.2.16.2 Enforcement

Unlike recognition, enforcement (as noted above, this really amounts to 'exequatur') does always require a procedure, albeit a simplified one.

The procedure has two stages: the first one effectively introduces the judgment, enforcement of which will be subsequently sought, into the legal order of the Member

---

[420] *Ibid*, 44 and 45.
[421] Case C-283/05 *ASML*, [2006] ECR I-12041, para 29.
[422] On service of documents in civil or commercial matters, OJ [2007] L324/79. It replaced Regulation 1348/2000.
[423] Case 148/84 *Deutsche Genossenschaftsbank*, [1985] ECR 1981; and, for the JR, Case C-167/08 *Draka NK Cables*, [2009] ECR I-3477.

State in which enforcement is sought. This stage of the procedure (to be introduced with a court identified in Annex) is formal only. The applicant produces the documents and certificates referred to in Article 53 ff JR, following which the court merely ensures that those formalities are complete. The authorities listed in Annex, at this stage of the procedure may not indeed must not carry out any other assessment (in particular, they may not review the conditions for refusal of exequatur, listed in Articles 34 and 35 precited).[424] The result of this formal exercise is a declaration of enforceability, which in accordance with Article 42 is served upon the party against whom enforcement is sought.

Once served, the decision may then be appealed, following which the relevant court (again identified in Annex) reviews the grounds for refusal, which are the same as those listed for the refusal of recognition.

The Court of Justice in *Trade Agency* emphasised the relevance of the potential for review of the grounds for objection, listed in Articles 34 and 35, and in particular the rights of defence, listed in Article 34(2), and the public policy arguments, included in Article 34(1). The certificate produced in accordance with Article 54, which is issued by the Member State of origin and which confirms the enforceability of the judgment in the Member State of origin, does not amount to an irrefutable presumption of the judgment being issued in accordance with the rights of the defence referred to in Article 34(2). The court in the Member State of enforcement therefore, in this second stage of the enforcement procedure, has full authority to review whether in fact the proceedings in the Member State of origin meet with the requirements of the rights of the defence as included in Article 34(2), in particular whether the timing of service of the document initiating the proceedings (the date of which is confirmed by the certificate produced in accordance with Article 54) allowed the defendant in default of appearance enough time to raise their defence.

In *Trade Agency* the Court of Justice also held that the same court moreover, has the right not to grant, under Article 34(1)'s public policy exception, enforcement of a judgment following national proceedings in which an uncontested claim leads to the claim being granted, without the judgment listing legal grounds assessing and confirming the merits of the case. However the court in which exequatur is sought, may only refuse after review of the individual merits of the case: it has to in other words review whether in the case at issue, the defendant knew of the applicant's statement of claim and decided not to defend himself against it.[425] It may not decide that the foreign system as such as contrary to public policy in the state of enforcement.

The exequatur procedure of the Brussels I Regulation has been overhauled in the current review. However it is exactly on issues of the rights of the defence, such as those raised in *Trade Agency*, that a number of Member States continue to insist that exequatur can never be entirely automatic, even among EU Member States.

---

[424] Case C-139/10 *Prism Investments* [2011] ECR I-0000, para 28 ff.

[425] Case C-619/10 *Trade Agency*, not yet published in ECR. The case at issue confirmed England and Wales' procedure for uncontested claims, in which the court merely grants the claim without expressis verbis summarising the merits of the claim. However the UK had pointed out in the proceedings before the Court of Justice, that a judgment given in default of appearance, such as that given by the High Court in the main proceedings, cannot be obtained until, first, the applicant serves the claim form and the particulars of claim, containing a detailed description of the pleas in law and the material facts, to which the judgment itself impliedly refers, and, second, the defendant, although he has been informed of the legal proceedings instituted against him, does not appear or does not express his intention to submit a defence within the period prescribed.

3

The Core of European Private International Law: Applicable Law – Contracts

3.1 SUMMARY

Applicable law or 'Choice of law' for contracts is currently regulated by the so-called 'Rome I' Regulation: Regulation 593/2008.[426] The precursor of the Regulation was the 1980 Rome Convention.[427] . It is noteworthy that as with the BC, for the Rome Convention there is a supplementary means of interpretation with a 'Report', in this case the *Giuliano-Lagarde* report.[428]

Unlike the Brussels Convention on jurisdiction (see above), common law countries joined in with the European harmonisation of choice of law rules from the start, which arguably helped integrate common law elements better into this leg of the exercise than in jurisdiction issues.

Just like the Rome II Regulation (below), Rome I applies in all situations within its scope of application, involving a conflict of laws.[429] In civil and commercial matters, therefore, and as far as the subject-matter has not been excluded from the Regulation by virtue of Article 1, Rome I applies for all civil and commercial contractual matters, whether the court of the Member State has jurisdiction to hear the case on the basis of the JR, or on the basis of its national PIL. The Regulation (and the Convention before it[430]) is a uniform measure of private international law which replaces the PIL law in force.

3.1.1 Principles

The Rome I Regulation runs along three basic principles: the freedom of the parties to choose applicable law; a high degree of predictability, so as to assist with the Internal

---

[426] OJ [2008] L177/6.

[427] 1980 Rome Convention on the law applicable to contractual obligations, consolidated version in [1998] OJ C27/34. As with the Brussels Convention, for the Rome Convention there is a supplementary means of interpretation in the form of a 'Report', the Guiliano-Lagarde Report, OJ [1980] C282/1.

[428] OJ [1980] C282/1.

[429] Readers will remember from the introduction to this volume that the second step of private international law, i.e. where the court which has jurisdiction to rule on the matter, is typically called 'conflict of laws', *stricto sensu*, in common law.

[430] Report Guiliano-Lagarde, 13, and article 2.

Market; and at the same time room for manoeuvre for the forum to correct the default choice in favour of the country with which the contract is 'most closely connected'.

3.1.2 Scope of application

Rome I applies to contracts concluded after 17 December 2009 (Article 28),[431] leaving the Rome Convention in operation for contracts concluded before that date. It applies more specifically to *contractual obligations in civil and commercial matters* (Article 1(1)) hence *not* to torts or other non-contractual obligations, such as unjust enrichment (for which we now have the Rome II Regulation: see below), nor to contracts in non-civil or non-commercial matters (such as public law, tax and customs). Article 1(2) provides for a list of largely self-explanatory exclusions.

The Regulation has a universal scope(see Article 2), meaning that any law specified by the Regulation shall be applied, whether or not it is the law of a Member State.

3.1.3 Basic principle: Freedom of choice

In accordance with Article 3(1), the main principle of the Regulation is the free choice of the parties: *a contract shall be governed by the law chosen by the parties*. The choice — as long as it has been made validly, of course — is absolutely free: the law chosen need not have any connection with the parties or the contract.[432] The choice can be expressly made, or implied, however it at any rate has to be clear:

> The choice shall be made expressly or clearly demonstrated by the terms of the contract or the circumstances of the case (Article 3(1).

'Implied choice' is *inter alia* influenced by any exclusive choice of court clauses which may have been agreed to. Recital 12 of the Regulation mentions these as 'one of the factors' to be taken into account however it is clear in practice that the impact of such choice of court clauses is very strong, in the absence of express choice of law clauses. 'Implied' certainly requires that somehow the parties need to have considered the issue consciously: again choice of court clauses may testify to this, as may the use of clauses which are specific to the laws of a given State.

As is not uncommon in European private international law, the Regulation includes a number of provisions protecting parties perceived to be in a weaker position: consumers, insurance contracts, and individual employment contracts.

3.1.4 Applicable law in the absence of choice

The Rome convention applied the 'closest connection' test in the absence of choice of law by the parties; it included a number of presumptions on the basis of the characteristic performance doctrine (see below) and further employed an escape clause, correcting characteristic performance if in reality the contract was more closely connected to another country than that of the characteristic performance. Especially in continental Europe, the

---

[431] The temporal application of the Regulation has raised a number of issues in practice, which are reviewed below.

[432] The only exceptions being Article 5(2) in the case of carriage of passengers, and Article 7(3) for small insured risks. These allow free choice but among a closed list of options only.

characteristic performance test had become the norm, pushing the more factual 'closest connection' test to the background. The Regulation therefore wanted to correct the uneasy relationship between these two concepts, and kill the two birds of predictability (civil law) with factual appropriateness (common law). The Regulation now requires the court to *characterise* the contract and

[1] assess whether it fits within any of the contracts described in Article 4(1);
[2] in the negative, or if the contract falls within more than one of these categories, the court applies the *characteristic performance* test: Article 4(2);
[3] both [1] and [2] may be corrected if there is a *manifestly closer connection* with another State: that is the escape clause: Article 4(3);

If neither [1] nor [2] can be applied, the law of the State with the closest connection shall apply: Article 4(4).

The whistles and bells associated with each of these are reviewed below. The provisions with the most relevant application in a wider context are Article 4(1)(a) of the Regulation, which provides that – in the absence of choice – *a contract for the sale of goods shall be governed by the law of the country where the seller has his habitual residence*, and Article 6, which deals with consumer contracts and aims to protect the weaker party (i.e. the consumer).

3.2 DETAILED REVIEW OF THE REGULATION

3.2.1 Scope of application

Article 1

Material scope

1. This Regulation shall apply, in situations involving a conflict of laws, to contractual obligations in civil and commercial matters.

It shall not apply, in particular, to revenue, customs or administrative matters.

2. The following shall be excluded from the scope of this Regulation:

(a) questions involving the status or legal capacity of natural persons, without prejudice to Article 13;
(b) obligations arising out of family relationships and relationships deemed by the law applicable to such relationships to have comparable effects, including maintenance obligations;
(c) obligations arising out of matrimonial property regimes, property regimes of relationships deemed by the law applicable to such relationships to have comparable effects to marriage, and wills and succession;
(d) obligations arising under bills of exchange, cheques and promissory notes and other negotiable instruments to the extent that the obligations under such other negotiable instruments arise out of their negotiable character;
(e) arbitration agreements and agreements on the choice of court;
(f) questions governed by the law of companies and other bodies, corporate or unincorporated, such as the creation, by registration or otherwise, legal capacity, internal organisation or

winding-up of companies and other bodies, corporate or unincorporated, and the personal liability of officers and members as such for the obligations of the company or body;

(g) the question whether an agent is able to bind a principal, or an organ to bind a company or other body corporate or unincorporated, in relation to a third party;

(h) the constitution of trusts and the relationship between settlors, trustees and beneficiaries;

(i) obligations arising out of dealings prior to the conclusion of a contract;

(j) insurance contracts arising out of operations carried out by organisations other than undertakings referred to in Article 2 of Directive 2002/83/EC of the European Parliament and of the Council of 5 November 2002 concerning life assurance [14] the object of which is to provide benefits for employed or self-employed persons belonging to an undertaking or group of undertakings, or to a trade or group of trades, in the event of death or survival or of discontinuance or curtailment of activity, or of sickness related to work or accidents at work.

3. This Regulation shall not apply to evidence and procedure, without prejudice to Article 18.

4. In this Regulation, the term "Member State" shall mean Member States to which this Regulation applies. However, in Article 3(4) and Article 7 the term shall mean all the Member States.

The Regulation does not apply to Denmark, however it does to Ireland (from the start) and to the United Kingdom (after some hesitation).

The Regulation first of all only applies 'in situations involving a conflict of laws', this is

> Situations which involve one or more elements foreign to the internal social system of a country (for example, the fact that one or all of the parties to the contract are foreign nationals or persons habitually resident abroad, the fact that the contract was made abroad the fact that one or more of the obligations of the parties are to be performed in a foreign country, etc. thereby giving the legal systems of several countries claims to apply.[433]

Where a State consists of several territorial units each with its own substantive law of contractual obligations, the Regulation also applies to conflicts of laws between those territorial units so as to ensure foreseeability and certainty on the law and the uniform application of European rules to all conflict situations.[434]

The three basic principles of the Regulation are: freedom of the parties to choose applicable law; a high degree of predictability, so as to assist the internal market; and at the same time room for manoeuvre for the court to correct choice in favour of country with which the contract is 'most closely connected'.

Rome I applies to contracts concluded after 17 December 2009 (see Article 28). For contracts concluded before that date, the Rome Convention continues to apply (see below for major differences). This evidently means that the Rome Convention will be of relevance for some time still.

The Regulation applies to 'contractual obligations', but does not define these. In light of the need to apply the Regulation consistently with the JR,[435] it is generally said that a 'contractual obligation' must be understood to mean an 'obligation freely assumed',[436]

---

[433] Giuliano Lagarde report, 10.
[434] Commission proposal, 9. This was also the case under the Convention: see the Giuliano Lagarde report.
[435] See recital 7: 'The substantive scope of the provisions of this Regulation should be consistent with [the JR] and [Rome II].'
[436] Case C-26/91 *Handte*, n 296 above.

however as noted above (when discussing Article 5(1)(a) of the Jurisdiction Regulation), one must be cautious with this assumption.

3.2.2 Exclusions

Culpa in contrahendo is specifically excluded (it is covered by the Rome II Regulation), as provided for in Article 1(2)(i): 'The following shall be excluded from this Regulation' (…) (i) obligations arising out of dealings prior to the conclusion of a contract.'

Among the other exclusions, quite a few are aligned with the exemptions from the JR, although the joint exclusion from both the JR and Rome I (and indeed previously from the Brussels Convention and the Rome Convention: the nature of the exclusions is not dramatically different between the 'old' and the 'new' generation of European PIL instruments) should not be done intuitively: there might be good reason for harmonising jurisdiction in certain areas, but not applicable law, or indeed conversely.

Alignment in exclusions from the JR and Rome I exists for the specific exemption of revenue, customs and administrative matters; arbitration agreements; matrimonial property regimes [where following a Green Paper,[437] the Commission has now taken a separate initiative which will lead to two twin Regulations on jurisdiction, applicable law, recognition and enforcement of decisions and authentic instruments in respectively matters of matrimonial property regimes[438] and registered partnerships.[439]], wills and succession [where the Commission has taken a separate initiative which led to a Regulation on jurisdiction, applicable law, recognition and enforcement of decisions and authentic instruments in matters of succession and the creation of a European Certificate of Succession[440]]; and 'questions involving the status or legal capacity of natural persons, without prejudice to Article 13'. Article 13 as we shall see below, deals with incapacity.

'Obligations arising out of family relationships and relationships deemed by the law applicable to such relationships to have comparable effects, including maintenance obligations' are as far as maintenance is concerned, now covered for all Member States by Regulation 4/2009,[441] and as far as divorce and legal separation are concerned, by Regulation 1259/2010 ('Rome III'),[442] however only for the 14 Member States which are a party to this very first application of the 'Enhanced Co-operation' mechanism. Choice of court agreements are excluded in one breath with arbitration agreements. Issues with respect to their validity are being dealt to some degree with in the review of the JR (see above).

The exclusion for arbitration agreements, just as in the JR, is a result of the deference to pre-existing international agreements, and to the feeling that the matter was very complex and settling it one way or another might even have endangered ratification of the Rome Convention. The parties to the Rome Convention aired the expectation that the issue would be addressed by international law.[443] The New York Convention famously leaves

---

[437] Commission Green Paper of 17 July 2006 on conflict of laws in matters concerning matrimonial property regimes, including the question of jurisdiction and mutual recognition, COM (2006) 400.-

[438] COM(2011) 126/2.

[439] COM(2011) 127/2.

[440] COM(2009) 154. Regulation 650/2012, [2012] L201/107. Note that this Regulation deals with succession only: not with matrimonial property regimes.

[441] n 97 above.

[442] Regulation 1259/2010 implementing enhanced cooperation in the area of the law applicable to divorce and legal separation, OJ [2010] L343/10.

[443] Report Guiliano-Lagarde, 12.

the entire validity question of arbitration clauses to the forum, rendering the statement of the Commission in its proposal for the Rome I Regulation, that arbitration clauses were 'already covered by satisfactory international regulations'[444] a bit puzzling.

Where the arbitration clause forms an integral part of a contract, the exclusion relates only to the clause itself and not to the contract as a whole.[445]

Whether to exclude choice of court agreements from Rome I was subject to lively debate. One might be forgiven for assuming that choice of court agreements are agreements or 'contracts' just like any other. This is indeed the case in some jurisdictions, and ordinary choice of law rules are applied to discover the law applicable to such contract. However as the review of the JR showed, choice of court agreements, even if they are 'contracts', are evidently seen by the Member States as being of a peculiar nature, seeing as the adjudication of jurisdiction is considered an exercise of State authority and public policy,[446] with the JR, the Brussels Convention and national laws alike severely constraining contractual freedom for choice of court. Those in favour of excluding choice of court agreements from the Convention, also pointed to the provisions of the BC, now JR, with respect to choice of court agreements, which, they argued, effectively harmonise at least insofar as Union courts are concerned, the conditions for validity of the clause and form, hence suggesting that the outstanding points, notably those relating to consent, '*do not arise in practice.*'[447] With reference to the review above of the not altogether undisputed application of the relevant provisions of the JR, that statement seemed a bit optimistic.

Also excluded are questions governed by the law of companies etc. The Giuliano Lagarde Report goes into a bit more detail as to what is and is not excluded:

Confirming this exclusion, the Group stated that it affects all the complex acts (contractual administrative, registration) which are necessary to the creation of a company or firm and to the regulation of its internal organization and winding up, i. e. acts which fall within the scope of company law. On the other hand, acts or preliminary contracts whose sole purpose is to create obligations between interested parties (promoters) with a view to forming a company or firm are not covered by the exclusion.

The subject may be a body with or without legal personality, profit-making or non-profit-making. Having regard to the differences which exist, it may be that certain relationships will be regarded as within the scope of company law or might be treated as being governed by that law (for example, societe de droit civil nicht-rechtsfahiger Verein, partnership, Vennootschap onder firma, etc.) in some countries but not in others. The rule has been made flexible in order to take account of the diversity of national laws.

Examples of 'internal organization' are: the calling of meetings, the right to vote, the necessary quorum, the appointment of officers of the company or firm, etc. 'Winding-up' would cover either the termination of the company or firm as provided by its constitution or by operation of law, or its disappearance by merger or other similar process.

---

[444] COM(2005) 650, 3.
[445] Report Guiliano-Lagarde, 12 (para 5 *in fine*).
[446] See also Report Guiliano-Lagarde, 11 (para 5).
[447] Report Guiliano-Lagarde, 11 (para 5).

At the request of the German delegation the Group extended the subparagraph (e) exclusion to the personal liability of members and organs, and also to the legal capacity of companies or firms. On the other hand the Group did not adopt the proposal that mergers and groupings should also be expressly mentioned, most of the delegations being of the opinion that mergers and groupings were already covered by the present wording.

This explanation ought to give a better understanding of the exact scope, however it does not necessarily clarify all. For instance, the Report would seem to suggest that 'mergers and groupings' are covered by the exception, which presumably, given the nature of the remainder of the exception, is limited to the actual final agreement creating the JV or merged company, and not to the complex set of agreements leading up to such creation, such as Memoranda of Understanding (MOUs), or non-disclosure agreements (NDAs).

3.2.3 Universal Application

Article 2 Universal application

Any law specified by this Regulation shall be applied whether or not it is the law of a Member State.

The Regulation has *universal scope*: the application of its rules may well lead to the application of the laws of Ruritania, a non-Member-State. This led to the predictable criticism that the Internal Market credentials of the Regulation are quite questionable. However in view of the Commission's insistence that the main obstacle to the Internal Market in this respect is uncertainty, rather than unfamiliarity, and given the blessing which the EU Member States had already for some time given to a for European PIL (see the introductory chapter in relevant part), this criticism had little impact.[448] Incidentally, the universal application rule applies not just for contracts where the parties have freely chosen the applicable law, but also where the court has to apply the close connection rules in the absence of choice.

In accordance with Article 22(2), the Regulation does *not* apply to intra-Member State conflicts; however a Member State may opt to do so.[449]

3.2.4 Freedom of Choice

Article 3

Freedom of choice

1. A contract shall be governed by the law chosen by the parties. The choice shall be made expressly or clearly demonstrated by the terms of the contract or the circumstances of the case. By their choice the parties can select the law applicable to the whole or to part only of the contract.

2. The parties may at any time agree to subject the contract to a law other than that which previously governed it, whether as a result of an earlier choice made under this Article or of

---

[448] Other than in the United Kingdom, Ireland and Denmark where, as noted, Government has to decide on opting in (or in the case of Denmark on the conclusion of a specific Protocol) for each individual instrument.
[449] E.g. in the United Kingdom.

other provisions of this Regulation. Any change in the law to be applied that is made after the conclusion of the contract shall not prejudice its formal validity under Article 11 or adversely affect the rights of third parties.

3. Where all other elements relevant to the situation at the time of the choice are located in a country other than the country whose law has been chosen, the choice of the parties shall not prejudice the application of provisions of the law of that other country which cannot be derogated from by agreement.

4. Where all other elements relevant to the situation at the time of the choice are located in one or more Member States, the parties' choice of applicable law other than that of a Member State shall not prejudice the application of provisions of Community law, where appropriate as implemented in the Member State of the forum, which cannot be derogated from by agreement.

5. The existence and validity of the consent of the parties as to the choice of the applicable law shall be determined in accordance with the provisions of Articles 10, 11 and 13.

As noted, the choice (referred to in common law as 'the proper law of the contract': the law which the parties intended to govern the contract) is absolutely free: the law chosen need not have any connection with the parties or the contract. There are two exceptions to this rule: Article 5 limits the choice to one of 5 countries[450] in the case of contracts of carriage; and Article 7 has a similar rule for small insured risks.

The choice can be express, or tacit, but at any rate it has to be *clearly demonstrated*:[451] the parties somehow need to have considered the issue consciously. Article 3 requires the courts to ascertain the true tacit will of the parties rather than a purely hypothetical will;[452] in that respect 'clearly demonstrated' and 'tacit' are probably better terminology than 'implicit' or 'inferred', both often used in practice. A 'clearly demonstrated' choice is i.a. influenced by any choice of court clauses (see recital 12 of the Regulation[453]) however this can only be one element to consider (albeit a strong one). The Commission proposal had included a presumption in favour of a choice of law when parties had a choice of court agreement[454] – this presumption was not withheld in the final text.

Including a number of clauses specific to the law of a particular State, is another indication of choice of law,[455] as is the previous course of dealing between the parties under contracts containing an express choice of law, where the choice of law clause has been omitted in circumstances which do not indicate a deliberate change of policy by the parties.[456]

---

[450] Note that Article 22(1) holds that 'Where a State comprises several territorial units, each of which has its own rules of law in respect of contractual obligations, each territorial unit shall be considered as a country for the purposes of identifying the law applicable under this Regulation.'

[451] The Rome Convention language read 'demonstrated with reasonable certainty', however this change was introduced not with a view to changing the standard of proof, or level of intensity, but rather to co-ordinate the various language versions of the text (in particular, to have all language versions co-ordinate with the French version). See Heiss, H., 'Party Autonomy', in Ferrari and Leible (eds.), *Rome I Regulation – The Law Applicable to Contractual Obligations in Europe*, Munich, Sellier, 2009, (1) 1.

[452] See the Commission proposal, COM(2005) 650, page 5.

[453] 'An agreement between the parties to confer on one or more courts or tribunals of a Member State exclusive jurisdiction to determine disputes under the contract should be one of the factors to be taken into account in determining whether a choice of law has been clearly demonstrated.'

[454] 'If the parties have agreed to confer jurisdiction on one or more courts or tribunals of a Member State to hear and determine disputes that have arisen or may arise out of the contract, they shall also be presumed to have chosen the law of that Member State.'

[455] Report Guiliano-Lagarde, p.17, para 3.

[456] *Ibid.*

Can parties opt to make the law of a non-State, e.g. terms and conditions drafted by a non-State body and never adopted by any State, the applicable law to their contract? The understanding in the Rome Convention was that this was not allowed, inter alia given that the Convention referred in Article 1(1) to 'The rules of this Convention shall apply to contractual obligations in any situation involving a choice between the laws of different countries.' Choosing non-State law however was discussed in the run-up to the Regulation, and the Commission proposal was very favourable at this point, having included a specific para in Article 3 to that effect.[457] The form of words used would have authorised the choice of the UNIDROIT principles, the *Principles of European Contract Law* or a possible future optional Community instrument, while excluding the *lex mercatoria*, which was seen as not precise enough, or private codifications not adequately recognised by the international community.[458] Parliament suggested dropping the reference to the DFCR, Council however in the end had the reference to non-State law dropped altogether.[459] According to recital 13, parties are free to 'incorporating by reference into their contract a non-State body of law or an international convention.' It is not exactly clear what is meant 'by reference', and linguistic comparison does not help much.[460] While 'by reference' in ordinary language arguably could mean to include a simple reference to the non-State system, the preparatory works, with their professed scepticism[461] towards such non-State law, suggest that at the very least one would have to include specific clauses of the non-State system in the contract. Especially in a business context, one ought to be safe rather than sorry and hence I would certainly recommend including as much as possible by full integration of terms into the contract.

The use of the word 'any *law*' in Article 3 Rome I is generally understood to underline the conclusion that the choice must be for the laws of a State. However linguistic reference to a number of language versions in my view does not back up that overall conclusion, and even in English surely 'law' can mean law '*sensu latu*', not just 'State law'. Consequently the strongest authority against the choice of law for a non-country, is recital 13 combined with the *travaux préparatoires*.

Recital 14 – 'Should the Community adopt, in an appropriate legal instrument, rules of substantive contract law, including standard terms and conditions, such instrument may provide that the parties may choose to apply those rules' – is a clear reference to the possibility of a future optional instrument of European contract law, most likely linked to the 'Draft Common Frame of Reference'.[462] One such instrument was proposed by

---

[457] 'The parties may also choose as the applicable law the principles and rules of the substantive law of contract recognised internationally or in the Community. However, questions relating to matters governed by such principles or rules which are not expressly settled by them shall be governed by the general principles underlying them or, failing such principles, in accordance with the law applicable in the absence of a choice under this Regulation.' Note that the reference to 'or in the Community' in the first sentence, was a reference to the then 'draft' Draft Common Frame of Reference – which Parliament opined was a bit odd, given that neither the nature nor the text of that draft was at all agreed: 'it is unclear what shape that body of contract terms will take and on what legal basis it will be adopted.': Draft Report by Committee, August 2006, PE374.427.

[458] Explanatory Memorandum to the Commission Proposal, n 452 above.

[459] Compromise package by the Presidency, April 2007, JUSTCIV 73.

[460] English, French, German and Dutch all include 'referring'/'reference'.

[461] See also Symeonides, S, 'Party autonomy in Rome I and II from a comparative perspective', in Boele-Woelki, K., Einhorn, T., Girsberger, D., and Symeonides, S. (eds), *Convergence and Divergence in Private International Law – Liber Amicorum Kurt Siehr*, Munchen, Schulthess, 2010, (513) 540.

[462] See also Zoll, F. 'The Draft Common Frame of Reference as an instrument of the autonomous qualification in the context of the Rome I Regulation', in Ferrari and Leible (eds), n 451 above, (17).

the European Commission in October 2011, for sales.[463] However the exact relationship between this proposal and Rome I is far from clear, especially in relation to mandatory rules of Union law. No doubt discussions in Parliament and Council will help clarify things.

Neither the contract nor the parties need to have any link to the chosen law, in contrast with US conflict of laws. Limitations to the freedom of choice as a result of mandatory law and similar provisions are reviewed below.

The Regulation allows for *dépeçage* or 'severance': parties are free to have different laws regulate different parts of the contract,[464,465] albeit that the choice must be logically consistent, i.e. it must relate to elements in the contract which can be governed by different laws without giving rise to contradictions.[466] For instance, repudiation of the contract for non-performance cannot be subjected to two different laws, one for the vendor and one for the purchaser. If the chosen laws cannot be logically reconciled, applicable law will have to be decided in accordance with Article 4.

Choice of law (and a change thereof) can be made at the start of the contract or throughout the duration of the contract, and is subject to the same rules as the initial choice,[467] albeit that it must not adversely affect the position of third parties. Consequently choice post-initiation or change in the choice of law can also be made tacitly. If the choice of law is made or changed in the course of the proceedings, the limits within which the choice or change can be effective falls within the ambit of national law of procedure.[468]

3.2.5 Protected Categories

Articles 5 through to 8 of Rome I provide for specific provisions for contracts of carriage (goods and passengers), consumers, insurance, and employment contracts — reference is made to the provisions of the Regulation for they speak mostly for themselves.

In the case of consumers and employees, the provisions of the Regulation by and large re-iterate the regime of the Rome Convention. For both categories, the specific conflicts rules have a double aim: protecting the weaker category, as well as ensuring predictability.[469]

---

[463] COM(2011) 635 on a Common European Sales Law. A the time of writing (November 2012) still awaiting Parliament first reading.

[464] See Article 3(1) *in fine*: By their choice the parties can select the law applicable to the whole or to part only of the contract.

[465] This is not as odd as it may seem at first sight, as different laws of the Member States have different attractions to the parties. Especially in complex transactions and complex areas of the law, intellectual property rights, say, or securitisation, one would ideally also have the court with the perceived know-how rule on the case, however, '*dépeçage*' for choice of court is certainly not possible.

[466] Report Guiliano-Lagarde, 17, para 4.

[467] Report Guiliano-Lagarde, 18, para 6.

[468] *Ibid.*

[469] See most recently judgment of 15 December 2011 in Case C-384/10 *Voogsgeerd*, not yet published in ECR, and before that Case C-29/10 *Koelzsch*, not yet published in ECR. These judgments apply the Rome Convention however the provisions have not materially changed.

These two judgments are likely to be very relevant to employment law practice for some time to come.

The judgment in *Koelzsch* ruled 'Article 6(2)(a) of the Convention on the law applicable to contractual obligations [ ] must be interpreted as meaning that, in a situation in which an employee carries out his activities in more than one Contracting State, the country in which the employee habitually carries out his work in performance of the contract, within the meaning of that provision, is that in which or from which, in the light

For insurance contracts, the relevant articles have been lifted from the various Directives on insurance law. Article 7 juncto Article 23 oddly mean that while for insurance law, the Regulation effectively codifies the various insurance law Directives, for all other categories (including those with specific regimes in the Regulation, such as consumer law), the Regulation is *lex generalis* and any sectorial Directives will continue to rule the roost.

Article 23

Relationship with other provisions of Community law

With the exception of Article 7, this Regulation shall not prejudice the application of provisions of Community law which, in relation to particular matters, lay down conflict-of-law rules relating to contractual obligations.

The newly adopted Directive on consumer rights[470] provides specifically that it does not in principle interfere with the applicable law rules laid down by the Rome I Regulation.[471] However it does explicitly qualify as mandatory EU law,[472] as we shall review below.

3.2.6 Applicable Law in the Absence of Choice

Article 4

Applicable law in the absence of choice

1. To the extent that the law applicable to the contract has not been chosen in accordance with Article 3 and without prejudice to Articles 5 to 8, the law governing the contract shall be determined as follows:

---

of all the factors which characterise that activity, the employee performs the greater part of his obligations towards his employer'.

In *Voogsgeerd*, the ECJ held: '1. Article 6(2) of the Rome Convention on the law applicable to contractual obligations [ ] must be interpreted as meaning that the national court seised of the case must first establish whether the employee, in the performance of his contract, habitually carries out his work in the same country, which is the country in which or from which, in the light of all the factors which characterise that activity, the employee performs the main part of his obligations towards his employer. 2. In the case where the national court takes the view that it cannot rule on the dispute before it under Article 6(2)(a) of that convention, Article 6(2) (b) of the Rome Convention must be interpreted as follows: – the concept of 'the place of business through which the employee was engaged' must be understood as referring exclusively to the place of business which engaged the employee and not to that with which the employee is connected by his actual employment; – the possession of legal personality does not constitute a requirement which must be fulfilled by the place of business of the employer within the meaning of that provision; – the place of business of an undertaking other than that which is formally referred to as the employer, with which that undertaking has connections, may be classified as a 'place of business' if there are objective factors enabling an actual situation to be established which differs from that which appears from the terms of the contract, and even though the authority of the employer has not been formally transferred to that other undertaking.

[470] At the time of writing, the Directive had been adopted by Council but had not yet appeared in the Official Journal, neither had it been given a number. The text of the Directive is available via http://register.consilium. europa.eu/pdf/en/11/pe00/pe00026.en11.pdf. Eventually published as Directive 2011/83, [2011] L304/64.

[471] Recital 10: This Directive should be without prejudice to Regulation (EC) No 593/2008 of the European Parliament and of the Council of 17 June 2008 on the law applicable to contractual obligations (Rome I).

[472] Article 25 – Imperative nature of the Directive. If the law applicable to the contract is the law of a Member State, consumers may not waive the rights conferred on them by the national measures transposing this Directive. Any contractual terms which directly or indirectly waive or restrict the rights resulting from this Directive shall not be binding on the consumer.

(a) a contract for the sale of goods shall be governed by the law of the country where the seller has his habitual residence;

(b) a contract for the provision of services shall be governed by the law of the country where the service provider has his habitual residence;

(c) a contract relating to a right in rem in immovable property or to a tenancy of immovable property shall be governed by the law of the country where the property is situated;

(d) notwithstanding point (c), a tenancy of immovable property concluded for temporary private use for a period of no more than six consecutive months shall be governed by the law of the country where the landlord has his habitual residence, provided that the tenant is a natural person and has his habitual residence in the same country;

(e) a franchise contract shall be governed by the law of the country where the franchisee has his habitual residence;

(f) a distribution contract shall be governed by the law of the country where the distributor has his habitual residence;

(g) a contract for the sale of goods by auction shall be governed by the law of the country where the auction takes place, if such a place can be determined;

(h) a contract concluded within a multilateral system which brings together or facilitates the bringing together of multiple third-party buying and selling interests in financial instruments, as defined by Article 4(1), point (17) of Directive 2004/39/EC, in accordance with non-discretionary rules and governed by a single law, shall be governed by that law.

2. Where the contract is not covered by paragraph 1 or where the elements of the contract would be covered by more than one of points (a) to (h) of paragraph 1, the contract shall be governed by the law of the country where the party required to effect the characteristic performance of the contract has his habitual residence.

3. Where it is clear from all the circumstances of the case that the contract is manifestly more closely connected with a country other than that indicated in paragraphs 1 or 2, the law of that other country shall apply.

4. Where the law applicable cannot be determined pursuant to paragraphs 1 or 2, the contract shall be governed by the law of the country with which it is most closely connected.

Both the Convention and now the Regulation opted to define applicable law in the absence of choice in as precisely a way as possible. This, the drafters of the Convention argued, allows parties proper weighing and balancing of the need to make an express choice.

The Rome Convention applied the closest connection test; it then included a number of presumptions on the basis of the characteristic performance doctrine (see below); and it then had an escape clause, correcting characteristic performance if in reality the contract was clearly more closely connected to another country than that of the characteristic performance.[473] Interestingly, the convention text specifically mentioned the possibility of *dépeçage*, also in the absence of choice of law (in such case therefore judge-made rather than expressly intended by the parties). There are strong arguments to hold that the Rome Regulation no longer allows for *dépeçage* in the absence of choice.[474]

The Regulation wanted to correct the uneasy relationship between close connection/ characteristic performance (the latter had become the norm, especially in continental Europe), and marry predictability (typically more the concern of continental Europe, and of course the staple diet of European private international law, rooted within the internal

---

[473] See also Case C-133/08 *Intercontainer*, [2009] ECR I-9687 (re the Rome Convention).

[474] Pro this conclusion (hence against *dépeçage*: Magnus, U., 'Article 4 Rome I Regulation: The Applicable Law in the Absence of Choice', in Ferrari and Leible (eds.), n 451 above, (27) 31.

market) with appropriateness (common law). It now requires the court to characterise the contract and

[1] check as to whether it fits within any of the contracts described in Article 4(1)
[2] in the negative, or if the contract falls within more than one of these categories, the court applies the *characteristic performance* test: Article 4(2)
[3] both [1] and [2] may be corrected if there is a manifestly closer connection with another State: that is the escape clause: Article 4(3)

If neither [1] nor [2] can be applied: the law of the State with the closest connection" will be the applicable law: Article 4(4).
Some more detail on each of these.

Characterisation of the Contract. The court must characterise the contract: Article 18 of the Rome Convention provided that

> In the interpretation and application of the preceding uniform rules, regard shall be had to their international character and to the desirability of achieving uniformity in their interpretation and application.

The Regulation no longer includes such provision, which is not surprising: the Convention lay outside the E(E)(C)(U) framework, the Regulation evidently lies squarely within it. Moreover, the ECJ for a long time had no jurisdiction over the Convention – now evidently it does over the Regulation. Consequently the Court of Justice can be expected to push for an 'autonomous' interpretation of the various concepts – a tall order for some of the terminology used in them.[475]
After the court has characterised the contract, it must

[1] check as to whether it fits within any of the contracts described in Article 4(1).[476] Four of the subdivisions in Article 4(1) are an expression of the *characteristic performance* test: a, b, e, and f. Several of the rules of Article 4(1) apply the connecting factor 'habitual residence' (which is defined in Article 19). Article 19 specifies that for the purposes of determining the habitual residence, the relevant point in time is the time of the conclusion of the contract. This prevents *conflits mobiles* (possibility of changes in the connecting factor).

Habitual Residence. Article 19 defines 'habitual residence' as

> 1. For the purposes of this Regulation, the habitual residence of companies and other bodies, corporate or unincorporated, shall be the place of central administration.

> The habitual residence of a natural person acting in the course of his business activity shall be his principal place of business.

---

[475] This may be contrasted with for instance the term 'employment contract' on which the ECJ has settled case-law through other parts of EU law, although here, too, an argument could always be made that 'employment contract' in other parts of EU law (e.g. non-discrimination, equal pay, social security…) need not necessarily determine the term in the application of the Brussels Regulation. Incidentally, the Regulation does not specify whether the term needs to be determined by lex causae (here: lex contractus) or lex fori. For an example of lex contractus, see *Simpson v Intralinks*, Employment Appeal Tribunal (EAT), UKEAT/0593/11/RN.
[476] For detail on each of them, see inter alia Magnus, U, n 474 above, 34 ff.

2. Where the contract is concluded in the course of the operations of a branch, agency or any other establishment, or if, under the contract, performance is the responsibility of such a branch, agency or establishment, the place where the branch, agency or any other establishment is located shall be treated as the place of habitual residence.

3. For the purposes of determining the habitual residence, the relevant point in time shall be the time of the conclusion of the contract.'

Note that under the Convention, for companies the 'principal place of business' was the place of habitual residence.

The habitual residence for a natural person is only defined when it comes to his acting in the course of his business activity. 'Habitual residence' is a concept which is not used in Brussels I, however it is used in the Brussels II bis Regulation on jurisdiction and the recognition and enforcement of judgments in matrimonial matters and the matter of parental responsibility,[477] where it is left undefined, and in the Rome III Regulation (an instrument of enhanced co-operation and hence not applicable in all Member States) implementing enhanced cooperation in the area of applicable law to divorce and legal separation,[478] where, too, somewhat oddly given its date of adoption (after Rome I and II) it is left undefined.

The Court of Justice has defined 'habitual residence' in *Swaddling* within the context of social security law (entitlement of benefits subject to a residence requirement) as the place

> where the habitual centre of their interests is to be found. In that context, account should be taken in particular of the employed person's family situation; the reasons which have led him to move; the length and continuity of his residence; the fact (where this is the case) that he is in stable employment; and his intention as it appears from all the circumstances.[479]

Undoubtedly the context of the adjudication needs to be taken into account,[480] such as in *Swaddling*, a social security case, in which the seeking of holding of employment is likely to have a much greater relevance for determining habitual residence than in the context of, say, maintenance or parental responsibility (where, for instance, the interest and 'anchorage' of the child is likely to be much more relevant). Moreover, the Court itself has warned that its case-law on habitual residence in one area, cannot be directly transposed in the context of any other.[481] It is obvious however that the 'centre of interest' test which in one way or another finds its way into habitual residence in all relevant EU law, includes a subjective or 'qualitative'[482] element.

Of interest is the difference between the notion of 'habitual residence' as compared to 'domicile' for companies in the Rome I (and Rome II, see below) Regulations and the Jurisdiction Regulation. As noted in the relevant chapter, 'domicile' under the JR is defined using a triple alternative – leading to potential positive jurisdiction conflicts (i.e. more than one court claiming jurisdiction, with all the ensuing lis alibi pendens and related complications as a result). By contrast, in Rome I and Rome II the definition of

---

[477] OJ [2003] L338/1.
[478] OJ [2010] L343/10.
[479] Case C-90/97 *Swaddling v Adjudication Officer*, ECR [1999] I-1075, para 29.
[480] See also House of Lords *M v M*, [2007] EWHC 2047 (Fam).
[481] See Case C-523/07 *A*, [2009] ECR I-2805, para 36. In the case at issue, even for application of the notion to two different parts of the same Regulation, Brussels II Bis.
[482] Clarkson, C., and Hill, J., *The Conflict of Laws*, Oxford, OUP, 2011 (4th ed), 338.

'habitual residence' ought to lead to just one location (and hence just one applicable law). The EU's autonomous concept of habitual leads to a singular 'habitual residence' which is not necessarily the case, for instance, in English law.

Finally, Article 19(2) fixes the habitual residence of a business to a specific branch etc., to such branch etc., where the contract is concluded in the course of the operations of a branch, or where said contract is to be performed by such branch etc.

[2] If the contract does not fit within any of the listed categories, or if it falls within more than one of them, the court applies the *characteristic performance* test: Article 4(2). This in other words is a direct application of the characteristic performance doctrine: Article 4(1) merely contains a number of applications of the doctrine. Note that the doctrine (which has Swiss origin) refers *not* to the law of the State where the characteristic performance needs to be carried out, but rather to the law of the State where the party which has to carry out the characteristic performance, has its habitual residence.

Recital 19 emphasises that for contracts with rights and obligations which belong to a variety of the categories listed in Article 4(1), [and for which hence Art.4(2) prescribes that the characteristic performance needs to be identified], the characteristic performance is determined on the basis of that element of the contract where the gravity of the contract lies. If that is impossible, Article 4(4) needs to be applied.

[3] both [1] and [2] may be corrected (Article 4(3))if there is a manifestly closer connection with another State: that is the escape clause/the appropriateness idea, which underlies relevant common law on the matter.

The Rome Convention had a similar escape clause but without the denoter 'manifestly'. Evidently this will have to be applied restrictively.

If neither [1] nor [2] can be applied, then the court will apply the law of the State with the closest connection": Article 4(4). Note there the absence of 'manifestly'.

3.2.7 Formal Validity, Consent and Capacity

Article 10

Consent and material validity

1. The existence and validity of a contract, or of any term of a contract, shall be determined by the law which would govern it under this Regulation if the contract or term were valid.

2. Nevertheless, a party, in order to establish that he did not consent, may rely upon the law of the country in which he has his habitual residence if it appears from the circumstances that it would not be reasonable to determine the effect of his conduct in accordance with the law specified in paragraph 1.

Article 11

Formal validity

1. A contract concluded between persons who, or whose agents, are in the same country at the time of its conclusion is formally valid if it satisfies the formal requirements of the law which governs it in substance under this Regulation or of the law of the country where it is concluded.

2. A contract concluded between persons who, or whose agents, are in different countries at the time of its conclusion is formally valid if it satisfies the formal requirements of the law which governs it in substance under this Regulation, or of the law of either of the countries where either of the parties or their agent is present at the time of conclusion, or of the law of the country where either of the parties had his habitual residence at that time.

3. A unilateral act intended to have legal effect relating to an existing or contemplated contract is formally valid if it satisfies the formal requirements of the law which governs or would govern the contract in substance under this Regulation, or of the law of the country where the act was done, or of the law of the country where the person by whom it was done had his habitual residence at that time.

4. Paragraphs 1, 2 and 3 of this Article shall not apply to contracts that fall within the scope of Article 6. The form of such contracts shall be governed by the law of the country where the consumer has his habitual residence.

5. Notwithstanding paragraphs 1 to 4, a contract the subject matter of which is a right in rem in immovable property or a tenancy of immovable property shall be subject to the requirements of form of the law of the country where the property is situated if by that law:

(a) those requirements are imposed irrespective of the country where the contract is concluded and irrespective of the law governing the contract; and
(b) those requirements cannot be derogated from by agreement.

Article 13

Incapacity

In a contract concluded between persons who are in the same country, a natural person who would have capacity under the law of that country may invoke his incapacity resulting from the law of another country, only if the other party to the contract was aware of that incapacity at the time of the conclusion of the contract or was not aware thereof as a result of negligence.

Consent and Material Validity, included in Article 10, are textbook examples of what in this introduction was referred to as the '*Vorfrage*'. How does one determine the contractual obligations of parties, if the very validity of this contract, and/or the existence of consent of one of the parties to the contract, is disputed? In conflict of laws terms: what law determines the existence of consent and the (in)validity of a contract? The Giuliano and Lagarde report explains it in terms of circularity: 'the circular argument that where there is a choice of the applicable law no law can be said to be applicable until the contract is found to be valid'.[483] The Convention and now the JR solve the riddle by use of the putative applicable law:[484] the existence and the validity of a contract or any terms of it, is determined by the law which would govern it under the Regulation, if the contract or term were valid. 'In other words, the parties are able to pull themselves up by their own bootstraps':[485] awkward clauses or awkward contracts can be ensured of validity by choosing an applicable law of which one is certain that it approves. Evidently, there are general safeguards to protect against choice of law becoming a simple means to circumvent mandatory law of the forum, which we review below.

---

[483] Report Guiliano Lagarde, 28.
[484] Fawcett, JJ and Carruthers, JM, n 183 above, 744.
[485] *Ibid*, 745.

Article 10 itself however also limits the possibility of the 'bootstrap', by protecting bona fide parties: a party may rely upon the law of the country in which he has his habitual residence, to establish that he did not consent, if it appears from the circumstances that it would not be reasonable to determine the effect of his conduct in accordance with the putative applicable law. 'The circumstances' include the parties' previous practices among themselves, their business relationship, and whether the transaction is a conventional one.[486] The burden of proof evidently lies with the party wanting to establish that it did not consent.

Incapacity. As noted above, in the scope of application of Rome I, the legal capacity of natural persons or of bodies corporate or unincorporate is in principle excluded from the scope of the Convention. This exclusion means that each Member State continues to apply its own system of private international law to contractual capacity. However, in the case of natural persons,[487] the question of capacity is not entirely excluded. Article 13 (and Article 11 of the Rome convention before it) is intended to protect a party who in good faith believed himself to be contracting with a person of full capacity and who, after the contract has been entered into, is confronted by the incapacity of the other contracting party. There is in other words an anxiety to protect a party in good faith against the risk of a contract being held voidable or void on the ground of the other party's incapacity on account of the application of a law other than that of the place where the contract was concluded.[488]

Article 13 subjects the protection of the other party to the contract to very stringent conditions.[489] *First*, the contract must be concluded between persons who are in the same country. The provision does not wish to prejudice the protection of a party under a disability where the contract is concluded at a distance, between persons who are in different countries, even if, under the law governing the contract, the latter is deemed to have been concluded in the country where the party with full capacity is. *Secondly*, Article 13 is only to be applied where there is a conflict of laws. The law which, according to the private international law of the court hearing the case, governs the capacity of the person claiming to be under a disability must be different from the law of the country where the contract was concluded. *Thirdly*, the person claiming to be under a disability must be deemed to have full capacity by the law of the country where the contract was concluded. This is because it is only in this case that the other party may rely on apparent capacity.

In principle these three conditions are sufficient to prevent the incapacitated person from pleading his incapacity against the other contracting party. This will not however be so 'if the other party to the contract was aware of his incapacity at the time of the conclusion of the contract or was not aware thereof as a result of negligence'. This wording implies that the burden of proof lies on the incapacitated party. It is he who must establish that the other party knew of his incapacity or should have known of it.

Article 13 therefore does not have an Article 10(2)-like provision. This is a result of the focus of the two articles being different: Article 10 wishes to protect bona fide parties

---

[486] *Ibid*, and references to case-law.

[487] In the discussions leading to the Regulation, an extension of this provision to legal persons was pondered, however in the end abandoned, mainly due to the differences associated with applying 'incapacity' to legal persons: see Garcimartín Alférez, F., 'The Rome I Regulation: Much ado about nothing?', *The European Legal Forum (E)* 2–2008, (61) 63.

[488] Report Guiliano Lagarde, 30.

[489] *Ibid*. The wording of Article 13 of the Rome I Regulation is identical (only one comma was added) to Article 11 of the Rome Convention.

against mala fide parties who trick them into consent. Article 13 on the other hand aims to protect bona fide parties who rely on the validity of the contract, against mala fide parties who, post factum, claim incapacity.

Formal Validity is determined by the *lex contractus*. Article 11 contains general rules; a rule for unilateral acts intended to have legal effect; and special rules for consumer contracts and contracts in respect of immovable property.[490] The Giuliano and Lagarde report discusses Article 11 (which does not differ dramatically from the provision in the Convention, other than for one more specific alternative connection factor introduced for contracts concluded at a distance) at length. It suggests that it would be unwise to determine too specifically what is meant to be covered by the 'form' of the contract, but does venture

> It is nevertheless permissible to consider 'form', for the purposes of Article [11], as including every external manifestation required on the part of a person expressing the will to be legally bound, and in the absence of which such expression of will would not be regarded as fully effective. This definition does not include the special requirements which have to be fulfilled where there are persons under a disability to be protected, such as the need in French law for the consent of a family council to an act for the benefit of a minor, or where an act is to be valid against third parties, for example the need in English law for a notice of a statutory assignment of a chose in action.

3.2.8 Mandatory Law, and Public Order

There are effectively three cases of application: two for 'mandatory law' [Articles 3(3) and (4); and Article 9], one for 'public order' (Article 21).

Mandatory law: Articles 3(3) and (4)

Article 3

(…)

3. Where all other elements relevant to the situation at the time of the choice are located in a country other than the country whose law has been chosen, the choice of the parties shall not prejudice the application of provisions of the law of that other country which cannot be derogated from by agreement.

4. Where all other elements relevant to the situation at the time of the choice are located in one or more Member States, the parties' choice of applicable law other than that of a Member State shall not prejudice the application of provisions of Community law, where appropriate as implemented in the Member State of the forum, which cannot be derogated from by agreement.

Article 3 of the Regulation defines 'mandatory law' as 'provisions of law which cannot be derogated from by agreement'. There is obviously no *ius commune* on this: other than for EU law (where the ECJ is the final and sole judge) whether national law is mandatory or not is determined by the State which issues the law – often requiring analysis of case-law. The forum is bound to apply this provision in accordance with the law of the State whose 'mandatory' (or not) law is under consideration.

---

[490] Fawcett, JJ and Carruthers, JM, n 183 above, 746.

Both for Article 3(3) and for Article 3(4), *all other elements* relevant to the 'situation'[491] need to be located in a country other than the one whose law has been chosen. Therefore the issue needs to be exclusively linked to that country: a partial link with any other country (other than the choice of law) will break the chain of mandatory law.

Purely Domestic Contracts: Article 3(3). Some Member States (already at the time of the Convention) wanted to ban parties from making a choice of law for another Member State where all elements pointed to one Member State: they were in other words against allowing parties to employ choice of law to 'internationalise' an otherwise purely domestic situation.[492] Notably the United Kingdom however were against such restriction, as it would deny the very essence of freedom of choice, given that many parties bona fide make such choice. Financial services were once again the main sector that Article 3(3) is a compromise. The Regulation does not clarify what 'all relevant elements' (other than choice of law) means. That is hence left to national law to determine, albeit that recital 15 clarifies that choice of court is no factor in this assessment: in other words, 'all other elements' can still be located in a country other than that of the choice of law, even if a choice of court agreement points away from it.

Mandatory EU law: Article 3(4). This is a completely new provision, which was not present at least in the text of the Convention. It had however been held by the ECJ, in particular in *Ingmar GB*.[493]

Examples include the Commercial Agents Directive, Directive 86/653, per *Ingmar GB*, however arguably also quite a few provisions in secondary law with respect to various kinds of distribution, and consumer law. With respect to the latter, the newly adopted consumer rights Directive,[494] provides that

> If the law applicable to the contract is the law of a Member State, consumers may not waive the rights conferred on them by the national measures transposing this Directive. Any contractual terms which directly or indirectly waive or restrict the rights resulting from this Directive shall not be binding on the consumer.

In other words, this Directive unequivocally declares itself to be of a mandatory EU nature. Moreover, the Directive reaffirms the provisions of the consumer contracts title of Article 6 of Rome I, with specific reference for contracts with choice of law in favour of a third country.[495] Recital 58 of the consumer rights Directive provides

---

[491] 'Situation' (already used in the Rome Convention) is used in (i.a.) the English, French and German version of the Regulation, not e.g. the Dutch version. Why none of them use 'contract' is not clear; see also Harris, n 404 above, note 215.

[492] See also Kruger, T., 'Wanneer is een zaak 'internationaal' voor het Europese IPR?', TBH 2006, (941) 946.

[493] Case C-381/98 *Ingmar GB*, [2000] ECR I-9305, para 25: 'It must therefore be held that it is essential for the Community legal order that a principal established in a non-member country, whose commercial agent carries on his activity within the Community, cannot evade those provisions by the simple expedient of a choice-of-law clause. The purpose served by the provisions in question requires that they be applied where the situation is closely connected with the Community, in particular where the commercial agent carries on his activity in the territory of a Member State, irrespective of the law by which the parties intended the contract to be governed.' *(in the case at issue, a choice of law clause had been inserted which made the contract applicable to the laws of California).*

[494] n 470 above.

[495] In particular, Article 6(2): 'Notwithstanding paragraph 1, the parties may choose the law applicable to a contract which fulfils the requirements of paragraph 1, in accordance with Article 3. Such a choice may not, however, have the result of depriving the consumer of the protection afforded to him by provisions that

Where the law applicable to the contract is that of a third country, Regulation (EC) No 593/2008 should apply, in order to determine whether the consumer retains the protection granted by this Directive.

Consumer law in the Member States becoming ever more harmonised, choice of law for one Member State or another in consumer contracts will not make much difference. Together with the (see in relevant chapter, above) extension of some of the special juris-dictional rules of the JR, including the protected categories, to defendants not domiciled in the EU, the consumer rights Directive establishes a wide territorial reach of the EU's consumer laws. However, in the event of choice of law for a third country, this often means that the professional party involved has its domicile in that third country. In such instances, the specific instruction of Article 3(4) [as in Article 3(3), that 'all other ele-ments (…) are located in one or more Member States', would seem to rule out its applica-tion: for the domicile of one of the parties firmly puts at least one such element outside of the EU. This is strikingly different from the *Ingmar* case itself, where the ECJ held that the place of residence of the principal (in the case at issue: California) in the commercial agents relationship was irrelevant. In other words, by virtue of the formulation of Article 3(3) (and 3(4)), *Ingmar* decided today would arguably[496] have a very different outcome.

Insofar as (or indeed as long as[497]) these EU rules require national implementation, the insertion of 'where appropriate as implemented in the Member State of the forum' means that the qualification of 'EU mandatory law' in that instance arguably extends to any more further-going ('gold plated') national implementation measures[498] (only) in the forum. Interestingly, Article 1(4)[499] extends the meaning of 'Member State' to Denmark, for the specific purpose of Article 3(4) and Article 7 (insurance contracts). Failure to have done so in the Rome II Regulation enables choice of law in torts for a third country, in the event the only EU connection is a Danish one, hereby arguably depriving Danish citizens from the protection of a set of mandatory EU rules.[500]

'Overriding' Mandatory Law: Article 9

Article 9

Overriding mandatory provisions

1. Overriding mandatory provisions are provisions the respect for which is regarded as crucial by a country for safeguarding its public interests, such as its political, social or economic

---

cannot be derogated from by agreement by virtue of the law which, in the absence of choice, would have been applicable on the basis of paragraph 1.'

[496] Pro: Harris, n 509 above, 341.

[497] EU consumer law is an area of law where positive harmonisation at the EU level is increasingly taking the form of 'maximum' harmonisation, leaving ever fewer – if any – room for manoeuvre for the Member States to implement legislation offering increased protection for consumers. See Article 4 of the consumer rights Directive: 'Article 4, Level of harmonisation. Member States shall not maintain or introduce, in their national law, provisions diverging from those laid down in this Directive, including more or less stringent provisions to ensure a different level of consumer protection, unless otherwise provided for in this Directive.'

[498] Pro: Heiss, H., n 451 above, 5.

[499] 'In this Regulation, the term 'Member State' shall mean Member States to which this Regulation applies. However, in Article 3(4) and Article 7 the term shall mean all the Member States.'

[500] Heiss, H., n 451 above, 6. I disagree that the clear provisions of Rome II (where they define 'Member State') should really read 'including Denmark' for the purpose of Article 14(3) Rome II. *In claris*, I would argue, *not fit interpretatio*.

organisation, to such an extent that they are applicable to any situation falling within their scope, irrespective of the law otherwise applicable to the contract under this Regulation.

2. Nothing in this Regulation shall restrict the application of the overriding mandatory provisions of the law of the forum.

3. Effect may be given to the overriding mandatory provisions of the law of the country where the obligations arising out of the contract have to be or have been performed, in so far as those overriding mandatory provisions render the performance of the contract unlawful. In considering whether to give effect to those provisions, regard shall be had to their nature and purpose and to the consequences of their application or non-application.

'Overriding mandatory provisions' is what French private international law refers to as *lois de police*,[501] also known as *lois d'application immédiate* or *lois d'application nécessaire*.[502] *Lois de police* is the term used in the French version of the Regulation. '*Lois de police*' effectively are a specific form of application of *ordre public*, namely functioning in an assertive sense,[503] akin to US-style government interest analysis: the close contact between the forum (or indeed other States), the contract and the parties in this analysis justifies the application of a set of provisions of the law of that forum or the other State, over and above the law which would otherwise be applicable.[504]

The definition of 'overriding mandatory provisions' is inspired by the ECJ's *Arblade* decision, which concerned free movement of services and the application of *lois de police* in Belgian legal practice, also known as *lois d'application immédiate*. The ECJ described 'public order legislation' as

national provisions compliance with which has been deemed to be so crucial for the protection of the political, social or economic order in the Member State concerned as to require compliance therewith by all persons present on the national territory of that Member State and all legal relationships within that State.[505]

After the definition (evidently a restricted sub-set of 'mandatory law'), Article 9 draws a sharp distinction between overriding mandatory law of the forum, and mandatory law of the country of performance (which more often than not is *not* the country whose law governs the contract). Article 9(2) imposes no restrictions on the application of overriding mandatory law of the forum. However 'foreign' mandatory law may only be brought into play by the forum if it is the overriding mandatory law of the country where the obligations arising out of the contract have to be or have been performed.[506] The forum *may* apply these, but only if that law makes the acts to be performed in that country unlawful, thus creating protection against the effects of unlawfulness in the country of performance.

---

[501] See for detailed analysis Bonomi, A., 'Overriding Mandatory Provisions in the Rome I Regulation on the Law Applicable to Contracts', *Yearbook of Private International Law*, Volume 10 (2008), 285–300.

[502] See also Rigaux, F., and Fallon, M., *Droit international privé*, Brussels, Larcier, 2nd ed, 1993, para 1342.

[503] Forde, M., 'The '*Ordre Public*' Exception and Adjudicative Jurisdiction Conventions', *ICLQ*, 1980, (259) 260.

[504] See *ibid* for a pre-Regulation example in the Paris Court of Appeal: *Club Mediterranée v Caisse des congés spectacles*, (1976) 54 RCDIP 485.

[505] Joined Cases C-369/96 and C-376/96 *Arblade* and *Leloup*, [1999] ECR I-8453.

[506] Creating an additional layer of complexity in cases where the contract has been performed but not in the place where it was supposed to have been performed.

This is quite a departure from the Rome Convention, where the forum could apply the mandatory provisions (without the qualifier 'overriding') of each country with a close connection to the contract: Article 7 of the Convention read

Article 7 – Mandatory rules

1. When applying under this Convention the law of a country, effect may be given to the mandatory rules of the law of another country with which the situation has a close connection, if and in so far as, under the law of the latter country, those rules must be applied whatever the law applicable to the contract. In considering whether to give effect to these mandatory rules, regard shall be had to their nature and purpose and to the consequences of their application or non-application.

2. Nothing in this Convention shall restrict the application of the rules of the law of the forum in a situation where they are mandatory irrespective of the law otherwise applicable to the contract.

This large room for manoeuvre was not acceptable to many of the Member States, and some of them had opted out of Article 7(1)[507]: including Germany and the United Kingdom. Under the Convention, this was perfectly acceptable as this was a classic instrument of international law. Under the Rome I Regulation, however, such opt-out of course is impossible and hence the provision needed tightening up.

The 'overriding' mandatory law provision is one of those 'just in case' provisions of the Regulation. Even in those Member States which had not made the reservation against the application of the Rome Convention equivalent of this provision, there had been no reported cases of courts applying the mandatory rules of a foreign country.[508] [509] Nevertheless, in the discussions on the Rome I proposal, it was suggested that the very inclusion of a foreign mandatory law rule in the Regulation, regardless of the unlikeliness of its application, might be enough to deter commercial transactions.[510] The discussions on the proposal somewhat stumbled in the dark, as the Member States which were most concerned with the rule, especially because of the potential impact on their financial services sector (UK, Germany, Luxembourg), had expressed a reservation against the Rome Convention's provisions at this point. Contractual certainty was the goal of the relevant Member States vis-a-vis this provision. The United Kingdom's initial position in the negotiations was to seek deletion of the provision altogether – an unfeasible position as the majority of Member States already applied the similar provision of the Conven-

---

[507] Not of Article 7(2). For an application of that provision in the employment law context, see *Simpson v Intralinks*, Employment Appeal Tribunal (EAT), UKEAT/0593/11/RN.

[508] Lando, O., Nielson, P., 'The Rome I Proposal', *Journal of Private International Law*, 2007, (29) 46.

[509] Indeed an often quoted example is a 2000 judgment by the Commercial Court in Mons, Belgium [Tribunal de Commerce de Mons, 2 November 2000, Rev.dr.Com.Belge, 2001, 617. The Belgian court decided not to apply Tunisian mandatory law, in casu competition law, under which exclusive distribution agreements are unlawful. The court seemed to hesitate to apply Tunisian law in particular because it felt that the prohibition of these agreements, so to speak, was exclusive to Tunisia. I would concur [see also Harris, J., 'Mandatory Rules and Public Policy under the Rome I Regulation', in Ferrari, F., and Leible, S., n 451 above, (269) 327] that under the current Regulation, this view would fit uneasily with the Regulation, for the agreement would indeed render performance in the state unlawful (the forum of course is not obliged to apply the rule, however the case would seem to represent a textbook example of circumstances in which application of Article 9 would be suitable).

[510] See *inter alia* Harris, J., *ibid*, 282 ff. Harris (at 288 ff) also points out the inconsistency of the UK's approach of courts' flexibility in the negotiations leading to the Regulation: for applicable law in the absence of choice, it was the UK's insistence which led to the escape clause on the closer connection test; for mandatory law, the same UK insistence led to great suspicion of judges' discretion.

tion without, as noted above, any great upheaval.[511] The current provision is therefore a compromise:

> Effect may be given to the overriding mandatory provisions of the law of the country where the obligations arising out of the contract have to be or have been performed, in so far as those overriding mandatory provisions render the performance of the contract unlawful. In considering whether to give effect to those provisions, regard shall be had to their nature and purpose and to the consequences of their application or non-application.

The compromise moreover already had authority under English law.[512] Denning LJ held in *Foster v Driscoll*[513]

> If two persons agree together on a transaction which to their knowledge is intended to be carried out by means of one or other of them breaking the laws of a friendly country, or procuring or assisting another person in the breach of such laws, then the courts of this country [Author: meaning England] will not lend their aid to the enforcement of the transaction.

Foster v Driscoll[514] prevents enforcement of such contract on the basis that to do so would be contrary to English public policy on grounds of comity of nations.[515] Linking its authority directly to the overriding mandatory law provision, of course begs the question as whether there is in substance any difference between this provision, and the section on public policy (below). Indeed prior to the Rome Convention, English law did not distinguish between 'mandatory law' and 'public policy': both went under the denoter 'public policy'.

There is nothing to suggest that 'overriding mandatory law' may not also include provisions of EU law. However given the difference between Article 3(4) – provisions which cannot be derogated from by agreement – and Article 9 – overriding mandatory provisions, I would argue that there must be a difference between both, including where they are applied to Union law. In other words to safeguard the effet utile of Article 9 as applied to Union law, in Union law, too, there must be a difference between EU law provisions of different stature: those of EU law which cannot be derogated from by agreement, v those which have to be considered overriding mandatory provisions. In my view,[516] therefore, Article 9 cannot be used simply to resurrect provisions of EU law which have fallen by the Article 3(4) wayside (in particular because the 'all other elements test' has not been met, as reported above).

The exact relationship between mandatory and overriding mandatory provisions of EU and national law will hopefully be clarified to some degree by the Court of Justice in *Unamar*.[517] Belgium's stronger protection of the agent, long held by Belgian law to be of

---

[511] United Kingdom Ministry of Justice, 'Rome I – Should the UK opt in?', Consultation Paper CP05/08, 2 April 2008, at 79.

[512] Reported *ibid*.

[513] [1929] 1 K.B. 470.

[514] The rule was confirmed by the Court of Appeal in *inter alia Regazzoni v K.C.Sethia (1944) Ltd* [1956] 3 W.L.R. 79, and see case note Jennings, R.Y., 'Conflict of Laws. Contract Illegal by Foreign Law. Whether Enforceable in England', *The Cambridge Law Journal*, Vol. 14, No. 2 (Nov., 1956), 141–143.

[515] Consultation Paper, n 511 above, 79.

[516] Contra: Harris, n 451 above, 341.

[517] Case C-184/12 *Unamar v Navigation Maritime Bulgare*, pending. The question referred reads 'having regard, not least, to the classification under Belgian law of the provisions at issue in this case (Articles 18, 20 and 21 of the Belgian Law of 13 April 1995 relating to commercial agency contracts) as special mandatory rules of law within the terms of Article 7(2) of the Rome Convention, must Articles 3 and 7(2) of the Rome Convention, 2 read, as appropriate, in conjunction with Council Directive 86/653/EEC of 18 December 1986 on

'special' (in the Rome Convention jargon) mandatory rules calibre, gold plates the regime of the Commercial Agents Directive, Directive 86/653. In *Unamar*, parties have agreed on Bulgarian law being applicable law (as well as incidentally on the case having to go to arbitration in Bulgaria first, circumventing Belgian law which proscribes the use of arbitration for disputes such as those at issue). The question therefore arises as to whether Belgian law, the lex fori, can justifiably trump Bulgarian law of which no suggestion is being made that it does not meet the minimum standard of the precited Directive. Were the case to be decided under the Rome I Regulation, I would argue in view of the effet utile argument made above, that in the absence of a reference to gold plating in Article 9, and its presence in Article 3, that the allowance for national rules of overriding mandatory nature, does not cover gold plating. However in the Rome Convention which is applicable to the case referred, EU law as mandatory law does not figure at all, and the room for overriding rules is much wider than it is in the Rome Regulation.

Public Policy: Article 21

> Article 21
>
> Public policy of the forum
>
> The application of a provision of the law of any country specified by this Regulation may be refused only if such application is manifestly incompatible with the public policy (ordre public) of the forum.

The 'ordre public' at issue can only have an impact on the case if the *application* of the applicable law is *manifestly* incompatible with the ordre public of the forum (and of the forum alone).

It is useful to consider the difference with Articles 3 and 9: these concern a provision of mandatory law which *positively* comes in lieu of the offending provision. By contrast, the application of Article 21 blanks out the offending provision and the alternative appears by default: e.g. a clause giving right to damages in case of non-payment of a dowry (or e.g. non-supply of slaves or offending images; non-supply of counterfeit goods; use of illegal funds to purchase goods; etc.): public order will apply and the clause or more likely the contract as a whole will simply vanish. One could also conceivably have a situation where the overriding mandatory law of the forum conflicts with that of the applicable law: in such case, the forum could arguably call upon *ordre public* to justify setting aside the latter.[518]

There remains considerable uncertainty as to the precise distinction between Article 9(3), and Article 21, which has inter alia led the Commission to order a study to map national case-law in this area.

---

the coordination of the laws of the Member States relating to self-employed commercial agents, be interpreted as meaning that special mandatory rules of law of the forum that offer wider protection than the minimum laid down by Directive 86/653/EEC may be applied to the contract, even if it appears that the law applicable to the contract is the law of another Member State of the European Union in which the minimum protection provided by Directive 86/653/EEC has also been implemented?'

[518] Similarly: Fawcett, JJ and Carruthers, JM, n 183 above, 742.

3.2.9 The Relationship with Other Conventions

By virtue of Article 25, the regulation does not prejudice the application of international Conventions to which one or more Member States are parties at the time when the Regulation was adopted and which lay down conflict rules relating to contractual obligations. The Member States were under a duty to notify these.[519]

---

[519] See Article 26, and the Commission notice, Notifications under Article 26(1) of Regulation (EC) No 593/2008 of the European Parliament and of the Council on the law applicable to contractual obligations (Rome I), OJ [2010] C343/3.

4

The Core of European Private International Law: Applicable Law – Tort

4.1 INTRODUCTION

Regulation 864/2007,[520] the 'Rome II'[521] Regulation, was the first instrument of European private international law to have been created using the co-decision procedure. One had attempted to include torts in the Rome Convention, however that was later abandoned. It took a very long time to agree what has now become the Rome II Regulation.[522,523] This

---

[520] OJ [2007] L199/40.

[521] The Rome II Regulation having been adopted a year earlier than Rome I, its later numbering is a sign of deference to the ancestor of the Rome I Regulation, the 1980 Rome Convention.

[522] Dickinson, A., *The Rome II Regulation*, Oxford, OUP, 2008, 4 ff and 23 ff.

[523] Commission Proposal, COM (2003) 427, 3: The Commission convened two meetings of experts in 1969, at which it was agreed to focus initially on questions having the greatest impact on the operation of the common market the law applicable to tangible and intangible property, contractual and non-contractual obligations and the form of legal documents. On 23 June 1972, the experts presented a first preliminary draft convention on the law applicable to contractual and non-contractual obligations. Following the accession of the United Kingdom, Ireland and Denmark, the group was expanded in 1973, and that slowed progress. In March 1978, the decision was taken to confine attention to contractual obligations so that negotiations could be completed within a reasonable time and to commence negotiations later for a second convention on non-contractual obligations. In June 1980 the Convention on the law applicable to contractual obligations (the "Rome Convention") was opened for signature, and it entered into force on 1 April 1991. As there was no proper legal basis in the EC Treaty at the time of its signing, the convention takes the traditional form of an international treaty. But as it was seen as the indispensable adjunct to the Brussels Convention, the complementarity being referred to expressly in the Preamble, it is treated in the same way as the instruments adopted on the basis of Article 293 (ex-220) and is an integral part of the Community acquis. (…) Article K.1(6) of the Union Treaty in the Maastricht version classified judicial cooperation in civil matters in the areas of common interest to the Member States of the European Union. In its Resolution of 14 October 1996 laying down the priorities for cooperation in the field of justice and home affairs for the period from 1 July 1996 to 30 June 1998, the Council stated that, in pursuing the objectives set by the European Council, it intended to concentrate during the above period on certain priority areas, which included the "launching of discussions on the necessity and possibility of drawing up ... a convention on the law applicable to extra-contractual obligations". In February 1998 the Commission sent the Member States a questionnaire on a draft convention on the law applicable to non-contractual obligations. The Austrian Presidency held four working meetings to examine the replies to the questionnaire. It was established that all the Member States supported the principle of an instrument on the law applicable to non-contractual obligations. At the same time the Commission financed a GROTIUS project presented by the European Private International Law Group (GEDIP) to examine the feasibility of a European Convention on the law applicable to non-contractual obligations, which culminated in a draft text. The Council's ad hoc "Rome II" Working Party continued to meet throughout 1999 under the German and Finnish Presidencies, examining the draft texts presented by the Austrian Presidency and by Gedip. An initial consensus emerged on a number of conflict rules, which this proposal for a Regulation duly reflects. The Amsterdam Treaty, which entered into force on 1 May

evidently is not just the result of the level of complexity of the subject-matter concerned. There are far more complicated areas of EU law, in financial services, say, or in tax or corporate law, international trade, environmental protection, energy etc., where the development of regulation may have been cumbersome but never quite this long in the making.

The particular complexity in the case of conflict rules for tort lies in the intensity with which the proposal and the eventual Regulation have been linked to the efforts to create a European *Ius Commune*. In particular one recital of the Regulation is quite telling in this respect. Recital 6 notes

> The proper functioning of the internal market creates a need, in order to improve the predictability of the outcome of litigation, certainty as to the law applicable and the free movement of judgments, for the conflict-of-law rules in the Member States to designate the same national law irrespective of the country of the court in which an action is brought.

'Improving the predictability of the outcome of litigation' is the higher goal which this recital identifies with specific reference to what was then the core legal basis for European private international law (Internal Market) and presumably, which it therefore sees as the ultimate goal of European private international law full stop. The European Commission formulated it as follows in its proposal:[524]

> The mere fact that there are rules governing the jurisdiction of the courts does not generate reasonable foreseeability as to the outcome of a case being heard on the merits. The Brussels Convention and the 'Brussels I' Regulation that superseded it on 1 March 2002 contain a number of options enabling claimants to prefer this or that court. The risk is that parties will opt for the courts of one Member State rather than another simply because the law applicable in the courts of this state would be more favourable to them. That is why work began on codifying the rules on conflicts of laws in the Community in 1967.

One need not overdramatize, however, the seemingly fairly casual reference in the recitals, and in one of the very opening statements of the Commission proposal, to predictability in outcome of litigation (as opposed to 'simply' predictability in competent court and applicable law) arguably is best served by unity in substantive law itself. If this is indeed the eventual goal of the Institutions, then both the Rome I and II Regulations may well prove to be only a transitional phase. To be superseded in the not too distant feature by some kind of harmonisation of substantive private law in the Member States.[525]

The legal basis of the Regulation as it then stood certainly required necessity within the meaning of then Article 65 EC: 'in so far as necessary for the proper functioning of

---

1999, having moved cooperation in civil matters into the Community context, the Justice and Home Affairs Council on 3 December 1998 adopted the Action Plan of the Council and the Commission on how best to implement the provisions of the Treaty of Amsterdam on an area of freedom, security and justice. It recalls that principles such as certainty in the law and equal access to justice require among other things "clear designation of the applicable law" and states in paragraph 40 that "The following measures should be taken within two years after the entry into force of the Treaty: ... b) drawing up a legal instrument on the law applicable to non-contractual obligations (Rome II)". On 3 May 2002, the Commission launched consultations with interested circles on an initial preliminary draft proposal for a "Rome II" Regulation prepared by the Directorate-General for Justice and Home Affairs. The consultations prompted a very wide response, and the Commission received 80 or so written contributions from the Member States, academics, representatives of industry and consumers' associations. The written consultation procedure was followed by a public hearing in Brussels on 7 January 2003. This proposal duly reflects the comments received. [footnotes omitted]

[524] Commission Proposal, COM (2003) 427, 3.
[525] With the Draft Common Frame of Reference – DCFR as the most obvious vehicle.

the internal market'. I concur with the view that the justification of the Regulation under Article 65 EC was fanciful at best, indeed in my own experience no client has ever hesitated to venture into a Member State market, citing uncertainty as to the applicable law should it ever come to a case of tort. In the view of Sir Peter North,

> (N)o clear and convincing need for this proposed Regulation had been identified by the Commission in terms of the operation of the internal market. It looks rather like harmonisation on the basis of tidiness.[526]

and that, consequently, the Regulation was quite clearly *ultra vires*. There is now less of an urgency in this consideration,[527] as the legal basis for Union action in this field has widened as per the TFEU (and reported elsewhere in this volume). However the fact that the European Institutions overruled the vires arguments (and that notwithstanding muttering, Member States in the end went along with the Regulation), is a telling sign of the tenacity and speed of the development of European private international law.

4.2 GENERAL PRINCIPLES

The Regulation follows a familiar pattern in EU private international law: it defines material and temporal scope; it includes a general rule with one general exception and one escape clause; it has specific choice of law rules for specific kinds of torts; it respects parties' freedom to choose applicable law; it excludes *renvoi*; and it has a number of provisions on mandatory law and public order.

Rome II applies to events giving rise to damage which occur (the events, not the damage) after 11 January 2009 (Article 31 combined with 32). The discussion on the temporal scope of the Regulation was the result of, frankly, a bit of a muddle in the wording of the more traditional end formulas of secondary EU law, which typically deal with 'entry into force' and 'application'. In *Homawoo*,[528] the Court held that

> It is open to the legislature to separate the date for the entry into force from that of the application of the act that it adopts, by delaying the second in relation to the first. Such a procedure may in particular, once the act has entered into force and is therefore part of the legal order of the European Union, enable the Member States or European Union institutions to perform, on the basis of that act, the prior obligations which are necessary for its subsequent full application to all persons concerned (Homawoo, at 24).

In a few language versions of the Rome II Regulation, Article 32 carries the title 'entry into force' (in the equivalent language – English was not one of them) however in their substance effectively deal with application. In the light of the content of the provision which is the same in all of the language versions, the Court held that Article 32 of the Regulation does not set the date for its entry into force but sets the date of its application.

---

[526] House of Lords Report on the Proposed Rome II Regulation, Evidence, cited by Dickinson, A., n 522 above, 44.

[527] Indeed it would have been very difficult to convince the ECJ of *ultra vires* arguments, in the face of the adoption of the Regulation after prolonged discussion.

[528] Case C-412/10 *Homawoo v GMF Assurances*, not yet published in ECR (judgment of 17 November 2011).

It follows that, as there is no specific provision that sets the date for the entry into force of the Regulation, that date must be determined in accordance with the general rule laid down in the third subparagraph of Article 297(1) TFEU. As the Regulation was published in the Official Journal of the European Union on 31 July 2007, it entered into force on 20 August 2007, that is to say the 20th day following that of its publication.[529]

Article 3 confirms the universal character: the Regulation applies regardless of whether it leads to the law of a non-Member State being applicable. That was contested in the run-up to the Regulation (i.a. because it undermines the Internal Market credentials of the Regulation: Chinese law, say, may apply and that would hardly seem to support the Internal Market) however in the end it was upheld because of the fear of fragmentation in an area which could do with more clarity and less sophistication.

4.3 SCOPE OF APPLICATION

Article 1(1)

Scope

This Regulation shall apply, in situations involving a conflict of laws, to non-contractual obligations in civil and commercial matters. It shall not apply, in particular, to revenue, customs or administrative matters or to the liability of the State for acts and omissions in the exercise of State authority (acta iure imperii).

4.3.1 'Situations Involving a Conflict of Laws'

The phrase *situations involving a conflict of laws/comportant un conflit de lois* basically refers to the trigger required of any private international law situations. There has to be some kind of factual foreign connection to the case which makes that the forum has to contemplate at least the possibility of laws other than its own applying. I do not support unnecessary complication of this requirement, and indeed agree with the view[530] that the Commission overcomplicates (but now also confuses) things by stating in its proposal that

The proposed Regulation would apply to all situations involving a conflict of laws, i.e. situations in which there are one or more elements that are alien to the domestic social life of a country that entail applying several systems of law.[531]

for which it would seem to have sought inspiration in the Giuliano Lagarde Report.[532]

---

[529] Para 30 of the judgment.
[530] Dickinson, A., n 522 above, 157.
[531] Commission Proposal, COM (2003) 427, 8.
[532] Para 10.

4.3.2 Only Courts and Tribunals? Application to Arbitration Tribunals

It has been argued that the Regulation applies only to situations where courts and tribunals exercising judicial functions of a Member State, hear the case at issue.[533] On this view, arbitration tribunals sitting in a Member State would be free not to apply the Regulation and determine applicable law in line with the arbitration law of the seat of arbitration, and with the arbitration agreement. This argument is made with particular reference to the need to apply Rome II in conjunction with Brussels I (and Rome I). See in this respect also recital 7:

> The substantive scope and the provisions of this Regulation should be consistent with Council Regulation (EC) No 44/2001 of 22 December 2000 on jurisdiction and the recognition and enforcement of judgments in civil and commercial matters (Brussels I) and the instruments dealing with the law applicable to contractual obligations.

In my view, while arbitration agreements could certainly take great advantage of the freedom of choice included in Article 14 (see further below), a simple exclusion of the applicability of the Regulation to arbitration tribunals, cannot necessarily be derived from the text of the Regulation. Unlike the Rome I Regulation, which excludes arbitration agreements from its scope of application, Rome II does not mention arbitration. It does mention 'courts', and indeed 'courts' only, including in recital 6:

> The proper functioning of the internal market creates a need, in order to improve the predictability of the outcome of litigation, certainty as to the law applicable and the free movement of judgments, for the conflict-of-law rules in the Member States to designate the same national law irrespective of the country of the court in which an action is brought.

'The country of *the court* in which an action is brought': that would indeed seem to point specifically to the 'courts and tribunals', most probably to be understood in the JR sense, only. Notwithstanding the absence of textual reference, however, one can scarcely fathom how the Regulation would apply to such tribunals, given that parties often either identify their own choice of law provisions, or refer to arbitration rules which do (UNCITRAL, ICC, NCIA all do).[534] Unlimited application of the Regulation would utterly ignore these. Of course, the room for circumvention of the Regulation might argue for its applicability to arbitration, which however in turn would undoubtedly make the EU less attractive to locate arbitration tribunals. The proverbial jury is out on this point, the arguments pro and contra quite extensive,[535] and a judgment by the European Court of Justice likely at some point (it would require a court reviewing some or other aspect of an arbitration ruling, to refer to Luxembourg).

4.3.3 'Non-Contractual Obligations'

The scope of the Regulation covers all non-contractual obligations except those in matters listed in paragraph 2 of Article 2. Neither the Regulation nor its recitals refer to any kind of 'positive' definition of non-contractual obligations.

---

[533] Dickinson, A., n 522 above, 159 (at para 3.79 and before).

[534] See also Buys, C. 'The Arbitrators' Duty to Respect the Parties' Choice of Law in Commercial Arbitration', *St John's Law Review,* 2005, 59–96.

[535] See in particular Dickinson, A., n 522 above, 158 ff.

The concept of a non-contractual obligation varies from one Member State to another. Therefore for the purposes of this Regulation non-contractual obligation should be understood as an autonomous concept (recital 11).

An abstract definition of 'non-contractual obligations' was not even attempted in the run-up to the Regulation, as Member States legal traditions simply vary too widely on the concept.[536]

Following the ruling in *Kalfelis*, where the ECJ defined 'tort' as *all actions which seek to establish liability of a defendant and which are not related to a 'contract' within the meaning of Article 5(1)*,[537] and the subsequent judgment in *Handte*[538] and *Engler*,[539] the Commission posits tort, and the Rome II Regulation, as 'residual'[540] in relation to contract cases which it argues, with reference to the pre-cited ECJ case-law, must be defined in strict terms.

However while this is fairly clear for tort (or 'delict'), it was clear that this would be less obvious for what in some jurisdictions is termed "quasi-delict" or "quasi-contract", including in particular unjust enrichment and agency without authority (*'negotiorum gestio'*), which is comparable with a quasi-contract in common law. Moreover, the texts of both the Brussels Convention (upon which the pre-cited case-law is based) and its Regulation successor do not speak of 'non-contractual obligations', but rather of 'tort, delict or quasi-delict'. As far as contracts are concerned, they do not employ the term 'contractual obligations' as Rome I does, but rather 'matters relating to a contract'. Consequently and notwithstanding the link made between the three Regulations, one must not simply lift concepts from either Rome I, II or Brussels I, and mutually apply them without hesitation.

The Regulation tries to pre-empt some of the likely disputes by listing the obligations which are covered by it. Article 2(1) lists as non-contractual obligations:

> For the purposes of this Regulation, damage shall cover any consequence arising out of tort/ delict, unjust enrichment, negotiorum gestio or culpa in contrahendo.

There are considerable possibilities for confusion, including the existence in a number of Member States of concurrent contractual and non-contractual liability arising from one and the same factual situation.[541] The EC alludes to the difficulty in discussing the escape-clause (see below) of manifest closer connection:

> The text states that the pre-existing relationship may consist of a contract that is closely connected with the non-contractual obligations in question. This solution is particularly interesting for Member States whose legal system allows both contractual and non-contractual obligations between the same parties. But the text is flexible enough to allow the court to take account of a contractual relationship that is still only contemplated, as in the case of the breakdown of negotiations or of annulment of a contract, or of a family relationship. By having the same law

---

[536] A complication also experienced by the product liability Directive: Directive 85/374 on the approximation of laws, regulations and administrative provisions of the Member States concerning liability for defective products [1985] OJ L210/29, as amended.

[537] Case 189/87 *Kalfelis*, [1988] ECR 5565, para 18, see also above.

[538] Case C-26/91 *Jakob Handte*, [1992] ECR I-3967, para 15. See also above, the review of the special jurisdictional rule for 'contract' under the Brussels I Regulation.

[539] Case C-27/02 *Engler*, [2005] ECR I-481. See also above, the review of the special jurisdictional rule for 'tort' under the Brussels I Regulation.

[540] Commission Proposal, COM (2003) 427, 8.

[541] See inter alia Dickinson, A., n 522 above, 185 ff and the references to scholarship there.

apply to all their relationships, this solution respects the parties' legitimate expectations and meets the need for sound administration of justice. On a more technical level, it means that the consequences of the fact that one and the same relationship may be covered by the law of contract in one Member State and the law of tort/delict in another can be mitigated, until such time as the Court of Justice comes up with its own autonomous response to the situation.[542]

4.3.4 Excluded Matters

Most of the exclusions[543] listed in Article 1(2) are the usual suspects. The excluded matters to a large degree mirror those of the Rome I Regulation and, with the necessary caution, one may apply the reasons for exclusion there, to the Rome II Regulation, too (including the explanations given in the Giuliano Lagarde Report).

1. This Regulation shall apply, in situations involving a conflict of laws, to non-contractual obligations in civil and commercial matters. It shall not apply, in particular, to revenue, customs or administrative matters or to the liability of the State for acts and omissions in the exercise of State authority (acta iure imperii).

2. The following shall be excluded from the scope of this Regulation:

(a) non-contractual obligations arising out of family relationships and relationships deemed by the law applicable to such relationships to have comparable effects including maintenance obligations;

(b) non-contractual obligations arising out of matrimonial property regimes, property regimes of relationships deemed by the law applicable to such relationships to have comparable effects to marriage, and wills and succession;

(c) non-contractual obligations arising under bills of exchange, cheques and promissory notes and other negotiable instruments to the extent that the obligations under such other negotiable instruments arise out of their negotiable character;

(d) non-contractual obligations arising out of the law of companies and other bodies corporate or unincorporated regarding matters such as the creation, by registration or otherwise, legal capacity, internal organisation or winding-up of companies and other bodies corporate or unincorporated, the personal liability of officers and members as such for the obligations of the company or body and the personal liability of auditors to a company or to its members in the statutory audits of accounting documents;

(e) non-contractual obligations arising out of the relations between the settlors, trustees and beneficiaries of a trust created voluntarily;

(f) non-contractual obligations arising out of nuclear damage;

(g) non-contractual obligations arising out of violations of privacy and rights relating to personality, including defamation.

3. This Regulation shall not apply to evidence and procedure, without prejudice to Articles 21 and 22.

4.3.4.1 Non-Contractual Obligations Arising out of Family or Similar Relationships

The Commission justified their exclusion as follows:

---

[542] Commission Proposal, COM (2003) 427, 12–13.
[543] Obviously national PIL applies to the excluded sectors.

family obligations do not in general arise from a tort or delict. But such obligations can occasionally appear in the family context, as is the case of an action for compensation for damage caused by late payment of a maintenance obligation. Some commentators have suggested including these obligations within the scope of the Regulation on the grounds that they are governed by the exception clause in Article 3(3), which expressly refers to the mechanism of the 'secondary connection' that places them under the same law as the underlying family relationship. Since there are so far no harmonised conflict-of-laws rules in the Community as regards family law, it has been found preferable to exclude non-contractual obligations arising out of such relationships from the scope of the proposed Regulation.[544]

Recital 10 defines 'family relationships' as

> Family relationships should cover parentage, marriage, affinity and collateral relatives. The reference in Article 1(2) to relationships having comparable effects to marriage and other family relationships should be interpreted in accordance with the law of the Member State in which the court is seised.

In the meantime of course the argument that 'there are so far no harmonised conflict-of-laws rules in the Community as regards family law' has been overtaken by legislative developments. Regulation 4/2009 on jurisdiction, applicable law, recognition and decisions and cooperation in matters relating to maintenance obligations,[545] and for the relevant Member States by the Rome III Regulation re applicable law in divorce and legal separation, Regulation 1259/2010.[546] The justification for non-inclusion may be nugatory, however the impact on Rome II of these recent pieces of secondary law is the same: the disputes at issue are not covered by it.

The non-contractual relationship has to 'arise out of' the family relationship. The simple fact that there is a non-contractual relationship between family members clearly is not enough for it to be excluded from the Regulation, in cases where 'simple' tort happens to arise between family members.

4.3.4.2 Non-contractual Obligations Arising out of Matrimonial Property Regimes, Property Regimes of Relationships Deemed by the law Applicable to such Relationships to have Comparable Effects to Marriage, and Wills and Succession

This exclusion follows a similar pattern as the one for family relationships: principal exclusion for the same reason, gradual harmonisation via other routes: in particular, for wills and succession, Regulation 650/2012,[547] and for matrimonial property regimes, a 2011 twin proposal on matrimonial property regimes[548] and registered partnerships.[549]

---

[544] Commission Proposal, COM (2003) 427, 8.

[545] OJ [2009] L7/1.

[546] Regulation 1259/2010 implementing enhanced cooperation in the area of the law applicable to divorce and legal separation, OJ [2010] L343/10.

[547] [2012] L201/107.

[548] COM(2011) 126/2, n 438 above.

[549] COM(2011) 127/2, n 439 above.

4.3.4.3 Non-Contractual Obligations arising under Bills of Exchange, Cheques and Promissory Notes and other Negotiable Instruments to the Extent that the Obligations under such other Negotiable Instruments arise out of their Negotiable Character

This exception is a bit of a mouthful and also somewhat of an anachronism. It mirrors the exclusion under the Rome I Regulation, where the Commission referred to the Giuliano Lagarde Report justification for the exclusion under the Rome Convention:

> In retaining this exclusion, for which provision had already been made in the original preliminary draft, the Group took the view that the provisions of the Convention were not suited to the regulation of obligations of this kind. Their inclusion would have involved rather complicated special rules. Moreover the Geneva Conventions to which several Member States of the Community are parties govern most of these areas. Also, certain Member States of the Community regard these obligations as non-contractual.[550]

The latter element of the Giuliano Lagarde justification, could have conceivably re-opened the debate in the negotiation of the Rome II Regulation, however, many of the others arguments for not including these opaque instruments still stood and, perhaps most importantly, it would have seemed a disproportionate investment of time to regulate the conflict of laws aspects of these instruments which inevitably are of ever smaller importance in commercial markets dominated by electronic money transfer.[551]

4.3.4.4 Non-Contractual Obligations Arising out of the Law of Companies and Other Bodies Corporate or Unincorporated Regarding Matters such as the Creation, by Registration or Otherwise, Legal Capacity, Internal Organisation or Winding-up of Companies and Other Bodies Corporate or Unincorporated, the Personal Liability of Officers and Members as such for the Obligations of the Company or Body and the Personal Liability of Auditors to a Company or to its Members in the Statutory Audits of Accounting Documents

Such non-contractual liability cannot be separated from the law governing companies or firms or other bodies corporate or unincorporate that is applicable to the company or firm or other body corporate or unincorporate in connection with whose management the question of liability arises.[552] The Rome Convention had excluded these matters for the same reason,[553] given the work on positive harmonisation of company law, which was in full swing at the time (and to some degree continues to be).

As also noted above for the 'family relationships' exception, current exception only applies to those non-contractual obligations 'arising out of' the excluded matter. A simple connection with it does not suffice. The Giuliano Lagarde Report goes into a bit more detail as to what is and is not excluded, as discussed above, under the Rome I Regulation.[554] As with all other exceptions, they need to be interpreted strictly,[555] which arguably

---

[550] n 428 above, 11.
[551] Dickinson, n 522 above, 203, with reference to Dalhuisen.
[552] Commission Proposal, COM(2003) 427, 9.
[553] Guiliano-Lagarde Report, OJ [1980] C282/1, n 427 above, 12.
[554] Above, Sub the Rome I Regulation, Scope of application.
[555] As noted before, there is no general principle in EU law to apply exceptions restrictively; rather, exceptions need to be applied in accordance with the context and aim of the EU law concerned. In the case at issue, the need for restrictive application arises out of the express indications in the travaux préparatoires: see in particular the Commission proposal, 9.

indeed means that general directors liability does fall under the Rome II (or indeed as the case may be, Rome I) Regulation.[556]

4.3.4.5 *Violations of Privacy and Rights Relating to Personality, Including Defamation*

These were not included in the scope simply because no agreement could eventually be reached on the connecting factor. The Commission had proposed not to exclude violations of privacy and rights relating to the personality, instead opting to propose a specific conflicts rule:

> 1. The law applicable to a non-contractual obligation arising out of a violation of privacy or rights relating to the personality shall be the law of the forum where the application of the law designated by Article 3 would be contrary to the fundamental principles of the forum as regards freedom of expression and information.
>
> 2. The law applicable to the right of reply or equivalent measures shall be the law of the country in which the broadcaster or publisher has its habitual residence.

[Author note: Article 3 was the general rule in the initial Commission Proposal]

The Commission's justification for this heading referred in particular to the difficulties in deciding on a suitable conflicts rule in particular given the impact of the mass media, and referred to the problems in the application of the *Shevill* rule[557] in the information society. It then noted:

A study of the conflict rules in the Member States shows that there is not only a degree of diversity in the solutions adopted but also considerable uncertainty as to the law. In the absence of codification, court decisions laying down general rules are still lacking in many Member States. The connecting factors in the other Member States vary widely: the publisher's headquarters or the place where the product was published (Germany and Italy, at the victim's option); the place where the product was distributed and brought to the knowledge of third parties (Belgium, France, Luxembourg); the place where the victim enjoys a reputation, presumed to be his habitual residence (Austria). Other Member States follow the principle of favouring the victim, by giving the victim the option (Germany, Italy), or applying the law of the place where the damage is sustained where the *lex loci delicti* does not provide for compensation (Portugal). The UK solution is very different from the solutions applied in other Member States, for it differentiates depending whether the publication is distributed in the UK or elsewhere: in the former case the only law applicable is the law of the place of distribution; in the latter case the court applies both the law of the place of distribution and the *lex fori* ("double actionability rule"). This rule protects the national press, as the English courts cannot give judgment against it if there is no provision for this in English law.

Given the diversity and the uncertainties of the current situation, harmonising the conflict rule in the Community will increase certainty in the law.

The content of the uniform rule must reflect the rules of international jurisdiction in the "Brussels I" Regulation. The effect of the *Mines de Potasse d'Alsace* and *Fiona Shevill* judgments is that the

---

[556] Dickinson, n 522 above, 205 ff, with reference to and discussion of national case-law.

[557] Case C-68/93 *Shevill v Presse Alliance*, [1995] ECR I-415. See *The special jurisdictional rule for tort: Article 5(3) JR – Forum delicti commissi*, under the review of the Brussels I Regulation.

victim may sue for damages either in the courts of the State where the publisher of the defamatory material is established, which have full jurisdiction to compensate for all damage sustained, or in the courts of each State in which the publication was distributed and the victim claims to have suffered a loss of reputation, with jurisdiction to award damages only for damage sustained in their own State. Consequently, if the victim decides to bring the action in a court in a State where the publication is distributed, that court will apply its own law to the damage sustained in that State. But if the victim brings the action in the court for the place where the publisher is headquartered, that court will have jurisdiction to rule on the entire claim for damages: the *lex fori* will then govern the damage sustained in that country and the court will apply the laws involved on a distributive basis if the victim also claims compensation for damage sustained in other States.

In view of the practical difficulties in the distributive application of several laws to a given situation, the Commission proposed, in its draft proposal for a Council Regulation of May 2002 that the law of the victim's habitual residence be applied. But there was extensive criticism of this during the consultations, one of the grounds being that it is not always easy to ascertain the habitual residence of a celebrity and another being that the combination of rules of jurisdiction and conflict rules could produce a situation in which the courts of the State of the publisher's establishment would have to give judgment against the publisher under the law of the victim's habitual residence even though the product was perfectly in conformity with the rules of the publisher's State of establishment and no single copy of the product was distributed in the victim's State of residence. The Commission has taken these criticisms on board and reviewed its proposal. (...)

The EC's view however did not convince and led to a quite extraordinarily wide discussion, one assumes partly because of the very nature of the profession of those most affected (the media), as well as given the close interaction with freedom of expression and privacy issues.

The discussion resulted in the current exclusion altogether. It has been noted first of all that the exclusion itself leads to qualification issues, as there is no EU definition of 'privacy' or 'defamation'.[558] The issue has nevertheless not been dropped. A 'positive sunset clause' or 'review clause' was inserted in the Regulation: the EC was instructed in Article 30(2)[559] to present a study by 31 December 2008. Following the study,[560] all has turned quiet from the part of the Commission. The European Parliament produced a report in June 2010 to follow-up on the study.[561] Parliament's interest is not surprising: it was the EP which made the most effort in trying to broker a compromise in the negotiations which led to the Regulation. Parliament argues in particular that inclusion of

[558] Dickinson, A., 'By royal appointment: No closer to an EU private international law settlement?', conflictoflaws.net, 24 October 2014 (and last consulted by me on that date).

[559] 'Not later than 31 December 2008, the Commission shall submit to the European Parliament, the Council and the European Economic and Social Committee a study on the situation in the field of the law applicable to non-contractual obligations arising out of violations of privacy and rights relating to personality, taking into account rules relating to freedom of the press and freedom of expression in the media, and conflict-of-law issues related to Directive 95/46/EC of the European Parliament and of the Council of 24 October 1995 on the protection of individuals with regard to the processing of personal data and on the free movement of such data.'

[560] The MainStrat Report of February 2009, Comparative study on the situation in the 27 Member States as regards the law applicable to non-contractual obligations arising out of violations of privacy and rights relating to personality. JLS/2007/C4/028. Final Report available via http://ec.europa.eu/justice/doc_centre/civil/studies/doc/study_privacy_en.pdf

[561] Working document of 23 June 2010 on the amendment of the Rome II Regulation, Rapporteur Diana Wallis MEP, PE 443.025, available via http://conflictoflaws.net/News/2010/07/Working-document-Rome-II.doc.

personality rights in the Regulation, would counter the threat of the 'chilling effect' on the press of so-called 'libel tourism',

> a type of forum shopping in which a claimant elects to bring an action for defamation in the jurisdiction which is considered most likely to produce a favourable result – generally that of England and Wales, which is 'regarded as the most claimant-friendly in the world' (…) the high costs of litigating in that jurisdiction and the potentially high level of damages that may be awarded there allegedly have a chilling effect on freedom of expression; (…) where legal costs are high, publishers may be forced to settle even where they consider that they have a good defence.[562]

The 2010 EP Report arguably has not entirely advanced things. Rather than focusing on concrete proposals, the Report provides for a complete round-up of various views and possibilities. Complete as it may be, it does nothing to advance the choice for a specific conflicts rule. Following the *eDate Advertising* judgment,[563] which added an additional jurisdictional rule on the basis of centre of interests,[564] Ms Wallis MEP issued a new Report,[565] which this time round does include specific proposals and calls upon the Commission to issue a proposal for amendment to the Rome II Regulation. On the conflicts rule, Ms Wallis proposes the following specific new rule:

Article 5a – Privacy and rights relating to personality

(1) Without prejudice to Article 4(2) and (3), the law applicable to a non-contractual obligation arising out of violations of privacy and rights relating to personality, including defamation, shall be the law of the country in which the rights of the person seeking compensation for damage are, or are likely to be, directly and substantially affected. However, the law applicable shall be the law of the country in which the person claimed to be liable is habitually resident if he or she could not reasonably have foreseen substantial consequences of his or her act occurring in the country designated by the first sentence.

(2) When the rights of the person seeking compensation for damage are, or are likely to be, affected in more than one country, and that person sues in the court of the domicile of the defendant, the claimant may instead choose to base his or her claim on the law of the court seised.

(3) The law applicable to the right of reply or equivalent measures shall be the law of the country in which the broadcaster or publisher has its habitual residence.

(4) The law applicable under this Article may be derogated from by an agreement pursuant to Article 14.

---

[562] EP Committee on Legal Affairs Draft Report of 2 December 2012 (Diana Wallis MEP), with recommendations to the Commission on the amendment of Regulation 864/2007 on the law applicable to non-contractual obligations (Rome II), 2009/2170 INI, recital C and D.

[563] n 318 above.

[564] 'a person who has suffered an infringement of a personality right by means of the internet may bring an action in one forum in respect of all of the damage caused, depending on the place in which the damage caused in the European Union by that infringement occurred. Given that the impact which material placed online is liable to have on an individual's personality rights might best be assessed by the court of the place where the alleged victim has his centre of interests'. See the discussion of the eDate Advertising case, above, under the Brussels I Regulation.

[565] n 562 above.

This proposal therefore suggests 'direct and substantial impact[566]' as the criterion for determining applicable law. The inspiration which this report therefore takes from the *eDate Advertising* case, does not lie directly in any kind of recycling of the 'centre of interest' criterion of the ECJ, but rather in the Court's view on predictability. This is especially apparent in the correction to the main rule, namely that the law applicable be the law of the country in which the person claimed to be liable is habitually resident if he could not reasonably have foreseen substantial consequences of his act occurring in the country designated by the 'direct and substantial impact' test.

The EC is not obliged to propose any kind of amendment. It is not likely to be tempted soon.

4.3.4.6 Other Exclusions

The exclusion for *voluntary* trusts without a doubt is crucial for UK (and Irish) legal practice, however outside the scope of current volume. *Nuclear damage* is excluded given the extensive body of international law on the issue.

4.3.5 Civil and Commercial Matters

In accordance with Article 1, the Regulation applies to 'non contractual obligations in civil and commercial matters' which evidently ties into the relevant discussion under the Jurisdiction Regulation (see above in this volume).[567] Both the JR and Rome II specifically exclude 'revenue, customs and administrative matters'. Other than in the JR, however, Rome II also specifically excludes 'the liability of the State for acts and omissions in the exercise of State authority (*acta iure imperii*). Recital 7 stipulates that the latter element needs to be applied in symmetry with the Brussels I Regulation.

4.4 APPLICABLE LAW – GENERAL RULE: *LEX LOCI DAMNI*

Article 4(1) includes the general rule for choice of law and instructs to apply the law of the country where the damage occurs (*lex loci damni*). This is a departure from the previously EU-wide held principle of *lex loci delicti commissi*, and was 'simply' intended to lead to less discussions in most cases:

> The principle of the lex loci delicti commissi is the basic solution for non-contractual obligations in virtually all the Member States, but the practical application of the principle where the component factors of the case are spread over several countries varies. This situation engenders uncertainty as to the law applicable. (recital 15)

Indeed the geography of the (physical) damage is generally easier to identify than the 'place of the tort'. Similarly, in Brussels I, Article 5(3) has a specific jurisdiction rule for torts: the place where the damage *occurs* as distinct from the place where it is suffered, or ramifies.

---

[566] For want of a noun for 'affected'.
[567] In particular also the review of the *Lechouritou* case: n 89 above.

Article 4(1) of Rome II specifically instructs to ignore the *lex loci delicti commissi*, as well as the law of the countries where the indirect consequences of the *delict* are felt (a similar rule applies for jurisdiction in Brussels I, i.a. following the *Marinari*[568] ruling).[569]

Lex loci damni most often will lead to the application of the law of the victim, and is indeed seen as not favouring the tortfeasor. This choice is not without its consequences from a tort policy point of view. Combined with the specific rules for product liability and environmental damage (see below), the overall angle of the Regulation approaches tort from the perspective of the sufferer. This

> favours the philosophy that tort law, in particular, should take as its primary objective the distribution of loss among members of society, rather than the regulation of conduct.[570]

And indeed the Regulation would seem to view this as the 'modern' way forward:

> Uniform rules should enhance the foreseeability of court decisions and ensure a reasonable balance between the interests of the person claimed to be liable and the person who has sustained damage. A connection with the country where the direct damage occurred (lex loci damni) strikes a fair balance between the interests of the person claimed to be liable and the person sustaining the damage, and also reflects the modern approach to civil liability and the development of systems of strict liability. (recital 16)

In reality, of course, it could very well be that in cross-border torts, the state of conduct prescribed higher standards of conduct for the tortfeasor than the State of injury, in which case (and subject to the specific categories below), the lex loci damni rule does not in fact protect the victim.[571]

The connecting factor also means that different laws will apply in the case of different places of damages [the so-called 'Mosaic' principle, even if, e.g. by virtue of Article 2 of Brussels I (domicile of the defendant), the case is pending in one court only]. This of course may be remedied in certain cases by virtue of the exception and escape clause in 4(2) and (3) (see below); moreover, in accordance with Article 17, some rules of the *lex loci delicti commissi* must in any even be 'taken into account' (which arguably is not the same as 'applied'[572]), such as general health and safety and Highway code provisions.

'Damage' is defined by Article 2(1) by reference to various types of non-contractual obligations, by listing torts, plus 3 other categories (a clarification included in the 2006 amended proposal, so as to ensure no doubt remains): tort/delict, unjust enrichment, *negotiorum gestio* and *culpa in contrahendo*. It also clarifies that within the scope are both obligations which have arisen *and* those which are likely to arise – that is the same under the JR/Brussels I Regulation.

---

[568] Case C-364/93 *Antonio Marinari v Lloyds Bank et al*, [1995] ECR I-2719.

[569] See also Symeonides, S., 'Rome II and Tort Conflicts: A missed opportunity', *American Journal of Comparative Law*, 2008, 9–16: 'translated into simpler English, Article 4(1) provides that the applicable law is the law of the country in which the *injury* occurs, and more precisely the harmful physical *impact*.'

[570] Dickinson, A., n 522 above, 7.

[571] See Symeonides, S., note 569 above.

[572] See also the Commission proposal, COM(2003) 427, 25: 'The rule in Article [17] is based on the fact that the perpetrator must abide by the rules of safety and conduct in force in the country in which he operates, irrespective of the law applicable to the civil consequences of his action, and that these rules must also be taken into consideration when ascertaining liability. Taking account of foreign law is not the same thing as applying it: the court will apply only the law that is applicable under the conflict rule, but it must take account of another law as a point of fact, for example when assessing the seriousness of the fault or the author's good or bad faith for the purposes of the measure of damages.'

4.5 ONE GENERAL EXCEPTION TO THE GENERAL RULE AND ONE ESCAPE CLAUSE

4.5.1 General Exception: Parties Habitually Resident in the Same Country

Article 4(2) provides that where both parties are habitually resident in the same country when the damage occurs, the law of that country shall apply. This is a 'consequences' based connecting factor.

Note that both the specific provision on product liability and that on collective action (see further below) leave Article 4(2) in place – hence for those two specific categories, Article 4(2) in practice will be the most determinant connection factor.

As is the case in Rome I, Article 23 gives a specific definition of 'habitual residence'; and as is also the case in Rome I, no specific definition is given of the 'normal' habitual residence of a natural person (as opposed to when in the exercise of his professional activities). The remarks on habitual residence made in the course of the analysis of Rome I, apply here, too.

Article 23

Habitual residence

1. For the purposes of this Regulation, the habitual residence of companies and other bodies, corporate or unincorporated, shall be the place of central administration.

Where the event giving rise to the damage occurs, or the damage arises, in the course of operation of a branch, agency or any other establishment, the place where the branch, agency or any other establishment is located shall be treated as the place of habitual residence.

2. For the purposes of this Regulation, the habitual residence of a natural person acting in the course of his or her business activity shall be his or her principal place of business.

4.5.2 Escape Clause: Case Manifestly More Closely Connected with Other Country

Article 4(3) more generally includes an escape clause: when it is clear from the circumstances of the case that it is '*manifestly*' more closely connected with a country other than the one indicated by 4(1) or 4 (2), the law of that country shall apply instead. '*The*' tort has to have that manifestly closer relationship: one of its elements (for instance where only one of the elements is *sub judice*, typically the quantum of the damages following admitted liability by one of the parties) is not enough.[573] Evidently contractual relations between parties prior to the occurrence of the tort may indicate such manifest closer connection – this avoids fabrication of a tort to avoid applicable law under Rome I. The reference to a contract in Article 4(3) is by way of example only. The text is flexible enough to allow the court to take account of a contractual relationship that is still only contemplated, as in the case of the breakdown of negotiations or of annulment of a contract, or of a family relationship.[574] The escape clause also is at least partially an answer to the not too uncommonly occurring co-incidence of contractual and non-contractual liability between parties to a contract.

---

[573] *Dépeçage* therefore, despite the EP's wish, is not accepted. Cf. the Rome I Regulation's article 3(1) *in fine*.

[574] Commission Proposal, COM(2003) 427, 13.

4.6 SPECIFIC CHOICE OF LAW RULES FOR SPECIFIC TORTS – NO SPECIFIC RULES FOR 'PROTECTED CATEGORIES'

The Regulation includes specific rules for specific torts, however it does not have specific provisions for specific categories of victims. Some of the specific torts arguably lead to protection of what may be seen as the weaker victim of the tort, however this is not the case for all of them. The Commission wrote in its proposal

> where the pre-existing relationship consists of a consumer or employment contract and the contract contains a choice-of-law clause in favour of a law other than the law of the consumer's habitual place of residence, the place where the employment contract is habitually performed or, exceptionally, the place where the employee was hired, the secondary connection mechanism cannot have the effect of depriving the weaker party of the protection of the law otherwise applicable. The proposed Regulation does not contain an express rule to this effect since the Commission considers that the solution is already implicit in the protective rules of the Rome Convention: Articles 5 and 6 would be deflected from their objective if the secondary connection validated the choice of the parties as regards non-contractual obligations but their choice was at least partly invalid as regards their contract.[575] (Author note: references now of course having to be made to the Rome I Regulation instead of the Convention).

This may well be implicit in the Rome Regulation – however in my view if this is the course the EC (and Council/EP) wanted to ensure, they really ought to have included it in the text of the Regulation.[576]

Product liability, unfair competition, environmental damage, infringement of Intellectual Property, and industrial action, each have a specific choice of law rule in the Regulation. These all aim at identifying one or more specific connection factors for specific situations, to ensure that the most closely related laws will be applied. Recital 19 justifies the existence of specific rules:

> Specific rules should be laid down for special torts/delicts where the general rule does not allow a reasonable balance to be struck between the interests at stake.

Evidently the danger is (and a sticky point during the negotiations was) how far one goes in describing such specific categories.

4.6.1 Product Liability

Article 5

Product liability

1. Without prejudice to Article 4(2), the law applicable to a non-contractual obligation arising out of damage caused by a product shall be:

(a) the law of the country in which the person sustaining the damage had his or her habitual residence when the damage occurred, if the product was marketed in that country; or, failing that,
(b) the law of the country in which the product was acquired, if the product was marketed in that country; or, failing that,

---

[575] *Ibid.*
[576] See also Dickinson, A., n 522 above, 345–346.

(c) the law of the country in which the damage occurred, if the product was marketed in that country.

However, the law applicable shall be the law of the country in which the person claimed to be liable is habitually resident if he or she could not reasonably foresee the marketing of the product, or a product of the same type, in the country the law of which is applicable under (a), (b) or (c).

2. Where it is clear from all the circumstances of the case that the tort/delict is manifestly more closely connected with a country other than that indicated in paragraph 1, the law of that other country shall apply. A manifestly closer connection with another country might be based in particular on a pre-existing relationship between the parties, such as a contract, that is closely connected with the tort/delict in question.

Recital 20 of the Regulation clarifies:

The conflict-of-law rule in matters of product liability should meet the objectives of fairly spreading the risks inherent in a modern high-technology society, protecting consumers' health, stimulating innovation, securing undistorted competition and facilitating trade. Creation of a cascade system of connecting factors, together with a foreseeability clause, is a balanced solution in regard to these objectives. The first element to be taken into account is the law of the country in which the person sustaining the damage had his or her habitual residence when the damage occurred, if the product was marketed in that country. The other elements of the cascade are triggered if the product was not marketed in that country, without prejudice to Article 4(2) and to the possibility of a manifestly closer connection to another country.

It is noteworthy that by virtue of Article 28[577] (which employs the same mechanism as Article 25 of Rome I), the Hague Products Liability Convention[578] continues to apply between the EU Member States that are also Party to the Hague Convention (similarly for the Hague Convention on Traffic accidents).[579]

The Commission's original proposal on product liability (in its proposal: Article 4), was much more straightforward:

Without prejudice to Article 3(2) and (3), the law applicable to a non-contractual obligation arising out of damage or a risk of damage caused by a defective product shall be that of the country in which the person sustaining the damage is habitually resident, unless the person claimed to be liable can show that the product was marketed in that country without his consent, in which case the applicable law shall be that of the country in which the person claimed to be liable is habitually resident.

---

[577] 'Article 28: Relationship with existing international conventions: 1. This Regulation shall not prejudice the application of international conventions to which one or more Member States are parties at the time when this Regulation is adopted and which lay down conflict-of-law rules relating to non-contractual obligations. 2. However, this Regulation shall, as between Member States, take precedence over conventions concluded exclusively between two or more of them in so far as such conventions concern matters governed by this Regulation.' See Commission notice, Notifications under Article 29(1) of Regulation (EC) No 864/2007 of the European Parliament and of the Council on the law applicable to contractual obligations (Rome I), OJ [2010] C343/7. Notably, Belgium did not notify any such Conventions at all, which arguably has no impact in law however, is somewhat unfortunate.

[578] Convention on the Law Applicable to Products Liability, 11 I.L.M. 1283 (1972).

[579] See also Graziano, T., 'The Rome II Regulation and the Hague Conventions on Traffic Accidents and Product Liability – Interaction, Conflicts and Future Perspectives', *Nederlands Internationaal Privaatrecht*, 2008, 425–429, and Kramer, X., 'The Rome II Regulation on the law applicable to non-contractual obligations: The European private international law tradition continued', *Nederlands Internationaal Privaatrecht*, 2008, 414–424.

It is worthwhile recalling the Commission's justification for the specific rule, for the product liability scenario is likely to arise quite frequently (always bearing in mind the potential existence of international Conventions per Article 28):

'The proposed Regulation acknowledges the specific constraints inherent in the subject-matter in issue but nevertheless proceeds from the need for a rule to avoid being unnecessarily complex.

Under Article 4, the applicable law is basically the law of the place of where the person sustaining damage has his habitual residence. But this solution is conditional on the product having been marketed in that country with the consent of the person claimed to be liable. In the absence of consent, the applicable law is the law of the country in which the person claimed to be liable has his habitual residence. Article 3(2) (common habitual residence) and (3) (general exception clause) also apply.

The fact that this is a simple and predictable rule means that it is particularly suitable in an area where the number of out-of-court settlements is very high, partly because insurers are so often involved. Article 4 strikes a reasonable balance between the interests in issue. Given the requirement that the product be marketed in the country of the victim's habitual residence for his law to be applicable, the solution is foreseeable for the producer, who has control over his sales network. It also reflects the legitimate interests of the person sustaining damage, who will generally have acquired a product that is lawfully marketed in his country of residence. Where the victim acquires the product in a country other than that of his habitual residence, perhaps while travelling, two hypotheses need to be distinguished: the first is where the victim acquired abroad a product also marketed in their country of residence, for instance in order to enjoy a special offer. In this case the producer had already foreseen that his activity might be evaluated by the yardstick of the rules in force in that country, and Article 4 designates the law of that country, since both parties could foresee that it would be applicable.

In the second hypothesis, by contrast, where the victim acquired abroad a product that is not lawfully marketed in their country of habitual residence, none of the parties would have expected that law to be applied. A subsidiary rule is consequently needed. The two connecting factors discussed during the Commission's consultations were the place where the damage is sustained and the habitual residence of the person claimed to be liable. Since the large-scale mobility of consumer goods means that the connection to the place where the damage is sustained no longer meets the need for certainty in the law or for protection of the victim, the Commission has opted for the second solution.

The rule in Article 4 corresponds not only to the parties' expectations but also to the European Union's more general objectives of a high level of protection of consumers' health and the preservation of fair competition on a given market. By ensuring that all competitors on a given market are subject to the same safety standards, producers established in a low protection country could no longer export their low standards to other countries, which will be a general incentive to innovation and scientific and technical development.

The expression "*person claimed to be liable*" does not necessarily mean the manufacturer of a finished product; it might also be the producer of a component or commodity, or even an intermediary or a retailer. Anybody who imports a product into the Community is considered in certain conditions to be responsible for the safety of the products in the same way as the producer.' *(footnotes omitted)*

The rule subsequently became almost mind-bogglingly complex. The Commission in particular was not happy with the cascade system and noted in its position vis-a-vis the Council Common Position

> **Article 5** on product liability departs in its drafting approach considerably from the Commission's proposal (Article 6 of the amended proposal), albeit not in its intention. The common position reflects the need for a specific rule on products liability which strikes an appropriate balance between the interests of the victim and the person liable.
>
> The Commission continues to regret the approach in the common position which provides for a rather complex system of cascade application of connecting factors. It remains persuaded that its original solution offered an equally balanced solution for the interests at stake, while expressed in much simpler drafting.[580] (use of bold in the original)

I am not entirely convinced that the 'foreseeability' rule is 'unduly generous' to the defendant,[581] since certainty as to the law applicable is a general objective of the Regulation, as emphasised by the recitals. However 'foreseeability' obviously is a factual consideration which inevitably leads to discussion in the courtroom — comparative reference (albeit at the level of jurisdiction) may be made to the US 'minimum contacts' rule as applied in product liability cases, in particular and most recently in *McIntyre* (United States Supreme Court, June 2011).[582]

For the definition of product and defective product, the Commission had wanted Articles 2 and 6 of Directive 85/374[583] to apply. However even in the Commission proposal, this was not as such included in the text. In the eventual Regulation, there is no trace whatsoever of any reference to the product liability Directive, not even in the recitals. It is quite extraordinary that notwithstanding the space devoted in negotiation, to the product liability provisions, many core questions remain unanswered. For instance, the text of Article 5 very clearly relates to damage caused *by* a product, not *to* a product (and likewise in other language versions of the Regulation). Just as, incidentally, the product liability Directive itself does not apply to warranty issues of faulty goods, I do not see how the provision of Article 5 can be read in any other way than to mean that it does not apply to damage to the product itself,[584] although it does of course apply to damage caused to other products and to life and property of those other than the purchaser of the product.

'Damage' is not defined either, nor is 'marketed'. The Commission proposal includes some hints as to what 'marketing' might mean (including a reference to a controlled sales network), however given the fog of discussions leading to the final text, and the considerable differences between final text and original proposal, it is not entirely safe to assume that the Court will be using the Commission's suggestions as a yardstick. The element of foreseeability for the producer harbours a strong indication that there needs to have been a degree of activity of the producer vis-à-vis the territory in which the product

---

[580] COM(2006) 66, p.3.

[581] Symeonides, S., 'Rome II and Tort Conflicts: A Missed Opportunity', *American Journal of Comparative Law,* 2008, 206.

[582] *J. McIntyre Mach., Ltd. v Nicastro,* 131 S. Ct. 2780 (2011). See also Morrison, A.B., 'The Impacts of *McIntyre* on Minimum Contacts', *Arguendo,* September 2011.

[583] Directive 85/374 on the approximation of the laws, regulations and administrative provisions of the Member States concerning liability for defective products, OJ [1985] L210/29, as amended.

[584] Pro: Légier, G., 'Le règlement 'Rome II' sur la loi Applicable aux Obligations Non Contractuelles', *La Semaine Juridique,* 21 November 2007, I-207, 15–17. Contra: Dickinson, n 520 above, 367.

ended up causing damage,[585] which is reminiscent of the jurisdictional rules of the JR on consumer contracts (and indeed the specific provisions for consumer contracts in the Rome I Regulation), however one cannot of course draw too much a parallel with those.

The concept at any rate differs from what is understood as 'marketed' or 'placed on the market' in the most general of relevant EU laws, the 'Blue Book'. According to the Guide to the implementation of directives based on the New Approach and the Global Approach (Blue Book),

> "A product is placed on the Community market when it is made available for the first time. This is considered to take place when a product is transferred from the stage of manufacture with the intention of distribution or use on the Community market. Moreover, the concept of placing on the market refers to each individual product, not to a type of product, and whether it was manufactured as an individual unit or in series. The transfer of the product takes place either from the manufacturer, or the manufacturer's authorised representative in the Community, to the importer established in the Community or to the person responsible for distributing the product on the Community market. The transfer may also take place directly from the manufacturer, or authorised representative in the Community, to the final consumer or user.

> The product is considered to be transferred either when the physical hand-over or the transfer of ownership has taken place. This transfer can be for payment or free of charge, and it can be based on any type of legal instrument. Thus, a transfer of a product is considered to have taken place, for instance, in the circumstances of sale, loan, hire, leasing and gift." (footnotes omitted)[586]

4.6.2 Unfair Competition and Acts Restricting Free Competition

Article 6

Unfair competition and acts restricting free competition

1. The law applicable to a non-contractual obligation arising out of an act of unfair competition shall be the law of the country where competitive relations or the collective interests of consumers are, or are likely to be, affected.

2. Where an act of unfair competition affects exclusively the interests of a specific competitor, Article 4 shall apply.

3. (a) The law applicable to a non-contractual obligation arising out of a restriction of competition shall be the law of the country where the market is, or is likely to be, affected.
   (b) When the market is, or is likely to be, affected in more than one country, the person seeking compensation for damage who sues in the court of the domicile of the defendant, may instead choose to base his or her claim on the law of the court seised, provided that the market in that Member State is amongst those directly and substantially affected by

---

[585] Although this would seem less apt to apply in the context of manufacturers of components, who (see the Commission proposal) arguably are also included in this specific provision. Other than for the purposes of dual-use regulation, component manufacturers tend to have no direct interest or control of the product chain downstream.

[586] Section 2.3 in the most recent edition, which is the 2000 version. Sectorial Directives tend to employ a more general concept, and then often refer to the Blue Book in implementing measures. See e.g. Article 2(4) of Directive 2005/32 on ecodesign requirements for energy-using products, OJ 2005 [L191/29: '"Placing on the market" means making an EuP available for the first time on the Community market with a view to its distribution or use within the Community whether for reward or free of charge and irrespective of the selling technique.'

the restriction of competition out of which the non-contractual obligation on which the claim is based arises; where the claimant sues, in accordance with the applicable rules on jurisdiction, more than one defendant in that court, he or she can only choose to base his or her claim on the law of that court if the restriction of competition on which the claim against each of these defendants relies directly and substantially affects also the market in the Member State of that court.

4. The law applicable under this Article may not be derogated from by an agreement pursuant to Article 14.

Quite aside from the difficulty for a number of Member States in recognising the very concept of 'unfair competition',[587] the rules of Article 6 are even more arcane than those of Article 5.

In its justification for an autonomous connection for damage arising out of an act of unfair competition, the Commission refers to the 'three dimensional function' of competition law:

The purpose of the rules against unfair competition is to protect fair competition by obliging all participants to play the game by the same rules. Among other things they outlaw acts calculated to influence demand (misleading advertising, forced sales, etc.), acts that impede competing supplies (disruption of deliveries by competitors, enticing away a competitor's staff, boycotts), and acts that exploit a competitor's value (passing off and the like). The modern competition law seeks to protect not only competitors (horizontal dimension) but also consumers and the public in general (vertical relations). This three-dimensional function of competition law must be reflected in a modern conflict-of-laws instrument.[588]

Its initial proposal was succinct (it was listed as Article 5 in the proposal):

1. The law applicable to a non-contractual obligation arising out of an act of unfair competition shall be the law of the country where competitive relations or the collective interests of consumers are or are likely to be directly and substantially affected.

2. Where an act of unfair competition affects exclusively the interests of a specific competitor, Article 3(2) and (3) shall apply.

The brevity of its proposal however contrasts sharply with the discussion which ensued. The use of 'unfair competition' only in the proposed article (which for those Member States which employ national legislation of similar ilk, puts it firmly within general consumer protection law) as opposed to the inclusion of competition law in the explanatory memorandum, led to discussions as to whether competition law ought to be included at all. The Commission clarified that it had not wanted to include competition law,[589] however the horse by then had bolted and despite attempts by Austria and Germany, as well as the European Parliament, to drop competition law from the Regulation altogether, and by the UK to draft a separate rule for damage caused by Article 101–102 TFEU

---

[587] One can detect a whiff of, if not intended than at the least real, self-fulfilling harmonisation prophecy here. Just as the core concepts of the products liability rule have not been defined, the vagueness of concepts for Article 6, the very absence in a number of Member States of the category whose conflicts rule is being harmonised, and the confusing nature of the eventual rules included in Article 6, undoubtedly will lead to a lot of confusion in practice, need for preliminary review, etc. This in turn may strengthen the hand of advocates of harmonisation of national private law.

[588] Commission proposal, COM(2003) 427, 15.

[589] Outcome of proceedings, Council Committee on Civil Law matters, document 5430/04, 27 January 2004, 2.

infringements, competition law infringements came to exist alongside unfair competition, and the 'affected market' criterion introduced.

The rules are complex, as the Article shows, the concepts employed vague and not exactly leading to much predictability, the link with Commission policy documents on competition policy (e.g. re 'relevant' markets etc.) unclear, and the article as a whole hanging in the balance in view of the Commission initiatives on private enforcement of competition law[590] and on collective proceedings in the same. As for the latter, the EU has developed a growing interest in the Europeanization of the system of class actions. The Commission is pondering policy options for European collective redress in consumer law[591] and tort law,[592] and has flagged whether specific jurisdiction rules are necessary for collective actions.[593]

The Rome II provisions on this topic therefore may very well (hopefully) run out of steam before they have managed to create too much confusion in practice.[594]

4.6.3 Environmental Damage

Article 7

Environmental damage

The law applicable to a non-contractual obligation arising out of environmental damage or damage sustained by persons or property as a result of such damage shall be the law determined pursuant to Article 4(1), unless the person seeking compensation for damage chooses to base his or her claim on the law of the country in which the event giving rise to the damage occurred.

The Commission proposal had not initially specifically distinguished between 'environmental damage'[595] and 'damage sustained by persons or property', although the Commission had clarified that ecological damage was included in what it simply called 'a violation of the environment'. Without specifically mentioning it, the Commission's reference to recent developments which recognise 'ecological damage' as being included, undoubtedly relates to the Environmental Liability Directive ('ELD').[596] The ELD mentions specifically in Article 3(2) that

This Directive shall apply without prejudice to more stringent Community legislation regulating the operation of any of the activities falling within the scope of this Directive and without prejudice to Community legislation containing rules on conflicts of jurisdiction.

The ELD's recitals refer in this respect even more specifically to the Jurisdiction Regulation, not to Rome I or II. The specific reference to 'Community legislation containing

---

[590] White paper on damages actions for breach of the EC antitrust rules, COM(2008) 165.

[591] White Paper, COM(2008)165.

[592] Green Paper, COM(2008)794

[593] Green Paper on the review of the Brussels I Regulation, COM(2009)175.

[594] One particularly savoury question is the degree to which EU competition law may bear relevance in actions for damages sustained in the EU, by behaviour to which EU competition law is in principle not applicable (this is quite distinct from the question of the territorial reach of EU competition law).

[595] Note that the damage has to be 'environmental' (or damage sustained by persons or property as a result of such damage), not the event leading to the damage.

[596] Directive 2004/35, OJ [2004] L143/56.

rules on conflicts of jurisdiction' in my view therefore has to mean[597] that an impact of the ELD on the issue of applicable law, must not be excluded, however in view of the altogether limited scope of the Directive,[598] it must not be exaggerated either.

The Commission had noted that in most countries, the conflicts rule applied the *lex loci damni*. However it argued that the exclusive connection to the place where the damage is sustained would also mean that a victim in a low-protection country would not enjoy the higher level of protection available in neighbouring countries. Considering the Union's more general objectives in environmental matters, the Commission argued that the point of the connection rule must be not only to respect the victim's legitimate interests but also to establish a legislative policy that contributes to raising the general level of environmental protection, especially as the author of the environmental damage, unlike other torts or delicts, generally derives an economic benefit from his harmful activity. Applying exclusively the law of the place where the damage is sustained could give an operator an incentive 'to establish his facilities at the border so as to discharge toxic substances into a river and enjoy the benefit of the neighbouring country's laxer rules', a somewhat clumsy reference by the Commission to the so-called pollution haven theory. This solution, the Commission argued, would be contrary to the underlying philosophy of the European substantive law of the environment and the "polluter pays" principle.[599]

The Commission also argued that sustaining as a starting point the general *loci damni* rule is in conformity with developments in environmental protection policy 'which tends to support strict liability'. This surely is only true for those Member States which do indeed operate strict liability – which despite the ELD is not the case overall and even in those Member States where it is, it is not the case across the board.

Much like with the unfair competition rule, there were plenty of proposals, including from the European Parliament, to delete the specific rule altogether. After discussion to and fro, current text was reached (and Parliament overruled). Recital 24 now specifies

> 'Environmental damage' should be understood as meaning adverse change in a natural resource, such as water, land or air, impairment of a function performed by that resource for the benefit of another natural resource or the public, or impairment of the variability among living organisms.

Recital 25 refers to the full plethora of environmental principles of the Treaty to justify what it calls 'discriminating in favour of the person sustaining the damage'. The question of when the person seeking compensation can make the choice of the law applicable has to be determined in accordance with the law of the Member State in which the court is seised (see recital 25).

The 'conduct and safety rules' provision of Article 17, bears specific relevance in the context of environmental damage,[600] although it is unclear whether this covers the 'permit

---

[597] Pro albeit in the more sophisticated aspect of public authorities' actions to ensure compliance with environmental law: Betlem, G., and Bernasconi, C., 'European Private International law, the Environment, and Obstacles for Public Authorities', *Law Quarterly Review*, 2006, 124 ff. Contra: Dickinson, n 522 above, 431 ff.

[598] See in particular its recital 14: 'This Directive does not apply to cases of personal injury, to damage to private property or to any economic loss and does not affect any right regarding these types of damages.' The original Commission ambition was much more extensive than that.

[599] Commission proposal, COM(2003) 427, 18–19.

[600] The Commission gives the example of 'the consequences of an activity that is authorised and legitimate in State A (where, for example, a certain level of toxic emissions is tolerated) but causes damage to be sustained in State B, where it is not authorised (and where the emissions exceed the tolerated level). Under Article [17], the court must then be able to have regard to the fact that the perpetrator has complied with the rules in force in the country in which he is in business.'

defence' rule which Member States may (but are not obliged to) adopt under the ELD. Under Article 8(4)(a) of the Directive,

> The Member States may allow the operator not to bear the cost of remedial actions taken pursuant to this Directive where he demonstrates that he was not at fault or negligent and that the environmental damage was caused by: (a) an emission or event expressly authorised by, and fully in accordance with the conditions of, an authorisation conferred by or given under applicable national laws and regulations which implement those legislative measures adopted by the Community specified in Annex III, as applied at the date of the emission or event; (...)

I would argue that an environmental permit, as a much more extensive instrument than merely containing 'rules of safety and conduct',[601] is not captured by Article 17, meaning that permits of the *lex loci delicti commissi*[602] will not have any impact if the applicable law is the *lex loci damni*.

Finally, an interesting suggestion has been made[603] that because of the ELD's wide definition of 'operator' responsible for environmental damage, the link with Rome II Regulation opens the possibility of a decision taken at a corporation's headquarters, being considered the 'event giving rise to the damage'. Article 6 and 8 of the Directive establish liability with the 'operator' i.e. (Article 2(6)):

> 'operator' means any natural or legal, private or public person who operates or controls the occupational activity or, where this is provided for in national legislation, *to whom decisive economic power over the technical functioning of such an activity has been delegated*, including the holder of a permit or authorisation for such an activity or the person registering or notifying such an activity; (emphasis added)

4.6.4 Damage Caused by Infringement of Intellectual Property Rights

Article 8

Infringement of intellectual property rights

1. The law applicable to a non-contractual obligation arising from an infringement of an intellectual property right shall be the law of the country for which protection is claimed.

2. In the case of a non-contractual obligation arising from an infringement of a unitary Community intellectual property right, the law applicable shall, for any question that is not governed by the relevant Community instrument, be the law of the country in which the act of infringement was committed.

3. The law applicable under this Article may not be derogated from by an agreement pursuant to Article 14.

Recital 26 clarifies what must be understood by 'intellectual property rights', albeit in a non-exhaustive manner: 'For the purposes of this Regulation, the term 'intellectual

---

[601] In the context of an environmental permit, rules of conduct and safety may potentially be included in the occupational health and safety rules, however not all Member States include these in environmental legislation and the corresponding permits.

[602] EU environmental law may be harmonised to quite a degree, however there is plenty of space for national, regional and even local distinction, hence the exclusion of these permits does matter.

[603] Otero Garcia-Castrillon, C., 'International litigation trends in environmental liability: A European Union – United States comparative perspective', *Journal of Private International Law*, 2011, (551) 571.

property rights' should be interpreted as meaning, for instance, copyright, related rights, the sui generis right for the protection of databases and industrial property rights.'

The treatment of intellectual property was one of the questions that was debated intensely during the Commission's consultations. Many of the contributions to the consultation referred to the universally recognised principle of *lex loci protectionis*, meaning the law of the country in which protection is claimed. This principle underpins e.g. the Berne Convention for the Protection of Literary and Artistic Works of 1886 and the Paris Convention for the Protection of Industrial Property of 1883. This rule, also known as the "territorial principle", enables each country to apply its own law to an infringement of an intellectual property right which is in force in its territory. Counterfeiting an industrial property right is governed by the law of the country in which the patent was issued or the trade mark or model was registered; in copyright cases the courts apply the law of the country where the violation was committed. This solution confirms that the rights held in each country are independent.[604]

The general *lex loci damni* rule does not reflect the overall solution favoured by the international agreements. Consequently two options were open: either to lift infringement of intellectual property rights from the Regulation altogether, or to include a special rule for them in the Regulation. The latter won the day.

The *lex loci protectionis* rule however does not work when the infringement concerns unitary 'Community' (now Union) marks: here, the protection is extended to the Union as a whole – whence the specific rule for them.

4.6.5 Damage Caused by Industrial Action

Article 9

Industrial action

Without prejudice to Article 4(2), the law applicable to a non-contractual obligation in respect of the liability of a person in the capacity of a worker or an employer or the organisations representing their professional interests for damages caused by an industrial action, pending or carried out, shall be the law of the country where the action is to be, or has been, taken.

Article 9 is a direct outcome of the *DFDS Torline* case.[605] The ECJ left open the possibility of (financial, which was the only and the direct) damage having occurred on board the ship withdrawn from service following industrial action, which would make the flag State (Denmark) a potential forum, and, consequently, applicable law Danish law. The Swedish delegation noted[606]

'In case C-18/02 *DFDS Torline*, 5.2.2004, somewhat simplified, a Swedish trade union brought an industrial action in order to achieve an agreement for the crew of a ship trafficking the route Harwich-Gothenburg. In order to avoid the industrial action, which consisted in a noticed blockade against loading and unloading of cargo and against anchoring in the port of Gothenburg, the Danish shipping company decided to replace the ship with another one rented for this purpose. The Danish

---

[604] Commission proposal, COM(2003) 427, 20.
[605] Case C-18/02 *DFDS Torline*, [2004] ECR I-1417, n 329 above.
[606] Document 9009/04 ADD 8 of 18 May 2004, JUSTCIV 71 CODEC 645, 12.

shipping company then brought an action against the Swedish trade union in a Danish court and claimed damages for costs incurred.

In a preliminary ruling on the meaning of "place where the damage occurred" in Article 5(3) of the Brussels Convention, the European Court of Justice stated that it is a task for the national court to judge where the damage occurred and that the flag State only is one circumstance among others to take account of in this assessment.

Since the wording of Article 3 of the proposed Rome II Regulation is very similar, the consequence of this case is that the legality of an industrial action, carried out in order to secure that the working conditions in the state in which the work is to be performed, could be governed by another law.

This runs contrary to the spirit of Directive 96/71/EC of the European Parliament and of the Council of 16 December 1996 concerning the posting of workers in the framework of the provision of services (…). Article 3(1) of the Directive lists the matters to which the terms and conditions of employment of the host state must be applied irrespective of the law applicable to the employment contract. The terms and conditions include such matters as the minimum rates of pay, minimum paid annual holidays and health and safety at work. The terms and conditions can be laid down by law, regulation or administrative provisions. Moreover, they can be based on collective agreements or arbitration awards that have been declared universally applicable.

The unique problem for Sweden is that there are no minimum rates of pay laid down by law and also no system of declaring a collective agreement universally applicable. It is left to the trade unions to bring about the same result, if necessary through industrial action. The Swedish method for bringing about compliance with local employment conditions falls within the scope of both the Brussels I Regulation and the proposed Rome II Regulation whereas other methods used by other countries such as minimum legislation or a system of declaring collective agreements universally applicable do not.

The Swedish delegation had thought that it would not be necessary but after the ruling in *DFDS Torline* Sweden must ask for a particular rule on the law applicable to industrial action. We are quite certain that other delegations will understand this and recognize that the question is of paramount importance to Sweden.' (original emphasis omitted, current emphasis added)

Sweden therefore suggested the insertion of the clause

Article 8a – Industrial action

The law applicable to a non-contractual obligation arising out of a noticed or executed industrial action shall be the law of the country where the action has been taken.

The proposal met with only lukewarm support, however it did in the end win the day, albeit in its current, reworded fashion. The Commission[607] continued not to be enthused, however it did note with satisfaction that 'its scope is now defined more precisely and is, in particular, limited to the issue of liability of employers, workers and/or trade unions in the context of an industrial action. The text is, however, still unclear that it should not extend to relationships vis-à-vis third parties and the Commission regrets this lack of clarity.'

Recitals 27 and 28 of the Regulation do not do much to calm the ensuing nervousness:

---

[607] COM(2006) 566, 4.

(27) The exact concept of industrial action, such as strike action or lock-out, varies from one Member State to another and is governed by each Member State's internal rules. Therefore, this Regulation assumes as a general principle that the law of the country where the industrial action was taken should apply, with the aim of protecting the rights and obligations of workers and employers.

(28) The special rule on industrial action in Article 9 is without prejudice to the conditions relating to the exercise of such action in accordance with national law and without prejudice to the legal status of trade unions or of the representative organisations of workers as provided for in the law of the Member States.

Latvia and Estonia voted against the Common Position specifically because of Article 9. They feared in particular that the Article would serve as a restriction to the free movement of services. The *Viking*[608] and *Lavalle*[609] cases on the free movement of services did not exactly help to quieten their dismay.

4.7 FREEDOM TO CHOOSE APPLICABLE LAW

Article 14

Freedom of choice

1. The parties may agree to submit non-contractual obligations to the law of their choice:

(a) by an agreement entered into after the event giving rise to the damage occurred; or
(b) where all the parties are pursuing a commercial activity, also by an agreement freely negotiated before the event giving rise to the damage occurred.

The choice shall be expressed or demonstrated with reasonable certainty by the circumstances of the case and shall not prejudice the rights of third parties.

2. Where all the elements relevant to the situation at the time when the event giving rise to the damage occurs are located in a country other than the country whose law has been chosen, the choice of the parties shall not prejudice the application of provisions of the law of that other country which cannot be derogated from by agreement.

3. Where all the elements relevant to the situation at the time when the event giving rise to the damage occurs are located in one or more of the Member States, the parties' choice of the law applicable other than that of a Member State shall not prejudice the application of provisions of Community law, where appropriate as implemented in the Member State of the forum, which cannot be derogated from by agreement.

Recital 31 clarifies

To respect the principle of party autonomy and to enhance legal certainty, the parties should be allowed to make a choice as to the law applicable to a non-contractual obligation. This choice should be expressed or demonstrated with reasonable certainty by the circumstances of the case. Where establishing the existence of the agreement, the court has to respect the intentions of the parties. Protection should be given to weaker parties by imposing certain conditions on the choice.

---

[608] Case C-438/05 *International Transport Workers' Federation and Finnish Seamen's Union v Viking Line ABP and OÜ Viking Line Eesti*, [2007] ECR I-10779.
[609] Case C-341/05 *Laval un Partneri Ltd v Svenska Byggnadsarbetareförbundet, Svenska Byggnadsarbetareförbundets avdelning 1, Byggettan and Svenska Elektrikerförbundet*, [2007] ECR I-11767.

In the Jurisdiction Regulation, there continues to be confusion as to the role, if any, of national law on the question of the very existence of consent in the agreement which underlies the forum clause.[610] The current redraft of the Regulation is likely to settle the issue in favour of the law of the State assigned by the forum clause. It is most attractive to follow the same course for prorogation of jurisdiction under the Rome II Regulation, and let the validity of the applicable law clause be decided by the law of the State whose laws are assigned by the applicable law clause. However as Dickinson rightly points out,[611] unlike forum clauses, which are excluded from the Rome I Regulation, agreements on the law applicable to non-contractual obligations, are within the scope of Rome I. That gives a strong hand in favour of making the law applicable to the choice of law clause, the law which under the Rome I Regulation is applicable to the agreement.

Article 14 confirms that parties may agree to submit non-contractual obligations to the law of their choice. Conditions do apply:

- for non-commercial activities only after the dispute has arisen; this protects the weaker party.
- *not* for unfair competition and intellectual property rights: for the former, because of the collective interests involved, and for the latter, because it relies largely still on the principle of territoriality, and it involves public interest.[612]
- *not* for purely domestic cases: to as to avoid circumvention of mandatory law; and finally
- Article 14(3) provides for a similar condition for mandatory Union law (whether or not to be implemented by the Member States) where all the elements relevant to the tort are located in one or more Member State(s).[613]

4.8 SCOPE OF THE LAW APPLICABLE

Article 15 clarifies that the scope of the law applicable is very wide.

Article 15

Scope of the law applicable

The law applicable to non-contractual obligations under this Regulation shall govern in particular:

(a) the basis and extent of liability, including the determination of persons who may be held liable for acts performed by them;
(b) the grounds for exemption from liability, any limitation of liability and any division of liability;
(c) the existence, the nature and the assessment of damage or the remedy claimed;
(d) within the limits of powers conferred on the court by its procedural law, the measures which a court may take to prevent or terminate injury or damage or to ensure the provision of compensation;

---

[610] See the Heading Agreements on Jurisdiction ('choice of forum' or 'prorogation of jurisdiction'): Article 23, above.

[611] Dickinson, A., n 522 above, 550.

[612] These stated reasons are not entirely convincing: e.g. environmental issues also involve public interest yet are not excluded.

[613] Rome I includes similar provisions for contracts.

(e) the question whether a right to claim damages or a remedy may be transferred, including by inheritance;
(f) persons entitled to compensation for damage sustained personally;
(g) liability for the acts of another person;
(h) the manner in which an obligation may be extinguished and rules of prescription and limitation, including rules relating to the commencement, interruption and suspension of a period of prescription or limitation.

The provision is important, because jurisdictions may differ quite substantially as to which parts of the dispute they consider to relate to the substantive matter of 'tort', as opposed to procedural law. Procedural matters are governed by the *lex fori*[614] and continue to be so under the Rome II Regulation: Article 1(3) provides specifically

> This Regulation shall not apply to evidence and procedure, without prejudice to Articles 21 and 22.

Article 15 clearly has a limiting effect on Article 1(3), given that it qualifies a number of issues as being substantive law, even though national law may have considered these to be procedural.

The EC explained that (what became) Article 15, broadly takes over Article 10 of the Rome convention, although in reality the sources which inspired Article 15 would seem to have been more extensive than that. In its proposal,[615] the Commission outlines quite a few of the provisions of Article 15 in more detail (please do note the one or two instances where the Commission proposal does differ from the final text):

'a) "The conditions and extent of liability, including the determination of persons who are liable for acts performed by them"; the expression "conditions ... of liability" refers to intrinsic factors of liability. The following questions are particularly concerned: nature of liability (strict or fault-based); the definition of fault, including the question whether an omission can constitute a fault; the causal link between the event giving rise to the damage and the damage; the persons potentially liable; etc.

"Extent of liability" refers to the limitations laid down by law on liability, including the maximum extent of that liability and the contribution to be made by each of the persons liable for the damage which is to be compensated for. The expression also includes division of liability between joint perpetrators.

b) "The grounds for exemption from liability, any limitation of liability and any division of liability": these are extrinsic factors of liability. The grounds for release from liability include force majeure; necessity; third-party fault and fault by the victim. The concept also includes the inadmissibility of actions between spouses and the exclusion of the perpetrator's liability in relation to certain categories of persons.

---

[614] For instance so far as concerns the assessment of damages, case-law, in particular the decision of the House of Lords in *Harding v Wealands* [2007] 2 AC 1, had established that the assessment of damages is a procedural matter, governed by English law as the *lex fori* – clearly overruled now for those cases covered by the Rome II Regulation..
[615] COM(2003) 427, 24.

c) "The existence and kinds of damage for which compensation may be due": this is to determine the damage for which compensation may be due, such as personal injury, damage to property, moral damage and environmental damage, and financial loss or loss of an opportunity.

d) "the measures which a court has power to take under its procedural law to prevent or terminate damage or to ensure the provision of compensation": this refers to forms of compensation, such as the question whether the damage can be repaired by payment of damages, and ways of preventing or halting the damage, such as an interlocutory injunction, though without actually obliging the court to order measures that are unknown in the procedural law of the forum.

e) "the measure of damages in so far as prescribed by law": if the applicable law provides for rules on the measure of damages, the court must apply them.

f) "the question whether a right to compensation may be assigned or inherited": this is self-explanatory. In succession cases, the designated law governs the question whether an action can be brought by a victim's heir to obtain compensation for damage sustained by the victim. In assignment cases, the designated law governs the question whether a claim is assignable and the relationship between assignor and debtor.

g) The law that is designated will also determine the "persons entitled to compensation for damage sustained personally": this concept particularly refers to the question whether a person other than the "direct victim" can obtain compensation for damage sustained on a "knock-on" basis, following damage sustained by the victim. Such damage might be non-material, as in the pain and suffering caused by a bereavement, or financial, as in the loss sustained by the children or spouse of a deceased person.

h) "liability for the acts of another person": this concept concerns provisions in the law designated for vicarious liability. It covers the liability of parents for their children and of principals for their agents.

i) "the manners in which an obligation may be extinguished and rules of prescription and limitation, including rules relating to the commencement of a period of prescription or limitation and the interruption and suspension of the period"; the law designated governs the loss of a right following failure to exercise it, on the conditions set by the law.'

'Persons' under littera a) arguably needs to be applied both with a view to legal persons and to natural persons. Consequently whether legal persons can be held liable for tort, which is most likely to have been committed ultra vires, is subject to the *lex causae*, even if the *lex incorporationis* were to rule out such corporate liability. Recital 12 has been inserted to underline this, at the instigation of the European Parliament: '(12) The law applicable should also govern the question of the capacity to incur liability in tort/delict.'[616]

Despite the clarification in the Regulation, combined with the EC proposal and with the recitals, difficulties do of course remain. However in particular 'assessment of damage' under Article 15(c) has a very wide scope indeed. For instance the scope of the applicable law arguably includes the determination of whether damages need to be determined 'net', taking into account subsequent history which impacts upon the dependency of the party

---

[616] See also Dickinson, A., n 522 above, 570. Cf. the Rome I Regulation, where legal capacity of natural persons is largely excluded.

that is being compensated, or rather 'gross', at the moment of death.[617] Nevertheless the exact meaning of 'assessment of damage' is unclear, even after review of the various language versions.

4.9 CONTRACT-RELATED TORT CLAIMS

Unjust enrichment, *negotiorum gestio* and *culpa in contrahendo* each have a specific article assigned to them. Article 10(1), 11(1) and 12(1) of Rome II each increase the scope for choice of law for each of the three categories. As noted, the general choice of law rule for Rome II is rather restricted, in particular, for pre-tort scenarios, choice of law is only possible between parties who both pursue a commercial activity. In the three contract-related scenarios, however, the tort piggy-backs on the choice of law under contracts (Rome I).[618]

4.10 'OVERRIDING' MANDATORY LAW AND PUBLIC ORDER

Article 16

Overriding mandatory provisions

Nothing in this Regulation shall restrict the application of the provisions of the law of the forum in a situation where they are mandatory irrespective of the law otherwise applicable to the non-contractual obligation.

Article 26

Public policy of the forum

The application of a provision of the law of any country specified by this Regulation may be refused only if such application is manifestly incompatible with the public policy (ordre public) of the forum.

Recital 32 specifies that these Articles apply in particular where the designated law were to allow for non-compensatory exemplary or punitive damages of an excessive nature:

(32) Considerations of public interest justify giving the courts of the Member States the possibility, in exceptional circumstances, of applying exceptions based on public policy and overriding mandatory provisions. In particular, the application of a provision of the law designated by this

---

[617] In that respect *Cox v Ergo Versicherung*, which was not decided under the Regulation, would not have to be decided differently post the Regulation. In this case, the deceased was a British Army officer killed in a traffic accident in Germany (not related to his active duty). His widow sued Ergo, the insurer of the German driver who was held to be entirely at fault. Mrs Cox sued in the UK, hoping that English law would apply to the net/gross issue (English law being more favourable on this issue). Both the High Court ([2011] EWHC 2806 (QB)] and the Court of Appeal [2012] EWCA Civ 1001] agreed that the net/gross issue was not procedural but rather substantive and hence ruled by the lex causae, which was German law. It was effectively held that the 'Heads of damages' allowed or indeed not taken into account in the claim (future earnings, new partner etc.) are substantive law, not covered by 'quantification' of the damage which under the pre-Rome II Regulation English regime were held to be procedural law. Hence in view of the Court of appeal, heads of damages, including net v gross, are not part of what the regulation now calls 'evidence and procedure' which by virtue of Article 1(3) Rome II continue to be ruled by lex fori.

[618] See also Heiss, H., n 451 above, 8.

Regulation which would have the effect of causing non-compensatory exemplary or punitive damages of an excessive nature to be awarded may, depending on the circumstances of the case and the legal order of the Member State of the court seised, be regarded as being contrary to the public policy (ordre public) of the forum.

5

The Insolvency Regulation

5.1 THE OVERALL NATURE OF AND CORE APPROACHES TO INSOLVENCY AND PRIVATE INTERNATIONAL LAW

This whole volume and many others with it arguably are testimony to private international law's overall intricate nature. Insolvency proceedings however involve additional challenges. The subject of insolvency proceedings by its nature almost always involves a multitude of stakeholders, and the subject-matter of the multitude of claims is much more varied than in the average private international law scenario.[619]

There are two core approaches to insolvency and private international law. *'Universality'* argues that against one particular insolvent person (whether he be a private individual or an undertaking), only one insolvency procedure ought to be opened. This one procedure would then (have to) include all debts and assets, and decisions reached in its course ought to be recognised by all other jurisdictions. In its purest form, universality combines universality of effects, with unity of proceedings. The often used term 'lex concursus' is more or less uniquely[620] attached to the universality doctrine. It refers to the law of the place where insolvency proceedings have been opened (*'concursus'*, as a variety of claims 'concur'), and hints at the standard Gleichlauf[621] between forum and applicable law in insolvency proceedings.

The *territorial approach* to insolvency proceedings focuses on the location of the assets: an insolvency proceeding may/must be opened in each State where the insolvent has assets, and, in its purest form any consequences of such proceeding are limited to the territory concerned: territoriality of effects and plurality of proceedings.

One does not really 'support' one theory or the other. Rather, universality is what one aspires to; territoriality is the interim (potentially ultimate) reality. The universal approach can only work when other States accept the exclusivity of the proceedings in a different State, and are happy to attach consequences to the findings of those proceedings. This

---

[619] For a good illustration see the United Kingdom Supreme Court in *Rubin v Eurofinance SA* [2012] UKSC 46 (not within the scope of the Insolvency Regulation as none of the debtors had their centre of commercial interest in the EU).

[620] Grammatically of course there is no reason why 'lex concursus' could not also apply to the territoriality doctrine, however standard terminology is such as to reserve it for the universality doctrine.

[621] See The 3 processes of PIL, and standard 'connecting factors', above.

requires bi- or multilateral agreements and eventually a global approach to insolvency proceedings.

5.2 GENESIS OF THE INSOLVENCY REGULATION

As noted above in the review of the JR, insolvency was exempt from the Brussels Convention. This was evidently not because it was not deemed to have any relevance to business. Rather it was seen to be of such high relevance to cross-border business, that it required a specific, tailor-made regime. Unlike the majority of issues dealt with in the Brussels Convention (and the subsequent Regulation), the subject of insolvency proceedings by its nature almost always involves a multitude of stakeholders, and the subject-matter of the multitude of claims is much more varied than in the average Rome I or Rome II situation.

There have been plenty of attempts to come to a Convention in the insolvency field.[622] In May 1996 one was very nearly there. The entry into force of the 23 November 1995 Convention on insolvency proceedings[623] was made subject to ratification by all fifteen Member States at the time,[624] within a period of 6 months. This period lapsed on 24 May 1996 without the United Kingdom having ratified (due to strategic quarrels over the institutional position of Gibraltar, and the lingering animosity between the UK and the other Member States over the fall-out of the BSE crisis). Having nearly succeeded, it would of course have been foolish not to somehow recycle the 1995 text. In the meantime, the legal basis for the initiative had changed. Article 65 EC, juncto 67(1) EC, post Amsterdam, no longer kept the issue outside of the EC's legal framework:

> Article 65: 'Measures in the field of judicial cooperation in civil matters having cross-border implications, to be taken in accordance with Article 67 and in so far as necessary for the proper functioning of the internal market, shall include: (...)
>
> Article 67: 1. During a transitional period of five years following the entry into force of the Treaty of Amsterdam, the Council shall act unanimously on a proposal from the Commission or on the initiative of a Member State and after consulting the European Parliament.

The Member States taking the 'initiative' where Germany and Finland under their respective 1999 presidencies of the Union. The 'Insolvency Regulation', Regulation 1346/2000,[625] which is reviewed in this heading, by default has become a global focal point for attempts to reach a multilateral approach to jurisdiction and applicable law in insolvency proceedings. There is no global or truly multilateral equivalent of the Regulation. Especially given the use of some of the core concepts of the Regulation (first and foremost the 'Centre of Main Interest – COMI, as the main jurisdictional driver) in other

---

[622] See the overview in Moss, G., Fletcher, I.F., and Isaacs, S. (eds.), *The EC Regulation on insolvency proceedings*, second edition, Oxford, OUP, 2009, p.2 ff.

[623] It can be downloaded from the Archives of European Integration, e.g. via http://aei.pitt.edu/2840/.

[624] Article 49(3): *'This Convention shall not enter into force until it has been ratified, accepted or approved by all the Member States of the European Union as constituted on the date on which this Convention is closed for signature.'*

[625] OJ [2000] L160/1.

jurisdictions, too, their interpretation by courts of the Member States under the guidance of the European Court of Justice, has become of global interest.[626]

Interestingly, given the collapse of the 1995 Convention at the last moment only, it already had all the trimmings of EC private international law Conventions, including the accompanying 'Report', in this case the Virgos-Schmit Report.[627] The Report never having been formally adopted, one can nevertheless safely assume that it will have some influence in the application of the Insolvency Regulation. The institutional awkwardness is made more poignant by the aforementioned legal basis of the Regulation. In the five-year interim period post Amsterdam, the Commission did not have sole right of initiative. In this case, given the history of the Regulation, Germany and Finland revived the Convention text more or less as it stood, leading to a lack of Commission proposal (and explanatory Memorandum) and, given the streamlined decision-making procedure, neither any extensive Parliament involvement. The Regulation's travaux préparatoires in other words are thin on the ground, making the Virgos-Schmit Report an important (if unofficial and never formally adopted) reference. The eventual Regulation tries to pre-empt some of the perhaps expected controversy by making full albeit not unusual use of recitals.

The Regulation does not apply to Denmark, which has created one or two peculiar difficulties.

5.3 SCOPE OF APPLICATION AND OVERALL AIM

5.3.1 Link with the 'bankruptcy' exception under the Jurisdiction Regulation

The first sentence of the sixth recital in the preamble to Regulation No 1346/2000, clarifies that the Regulation should, in accordance with the principle of proportionality,

> be confined to provisions governing jurisdiction for opening insolvency proceedings and judgments which are delivered directly on the basis of the insolvency proceedings and are closely connected with such proceedings.

Consequently, the scope of application of Regulation No 1346/2000 should not be broadly interpreted.[628] Per *Gourdain*, an action is related to bankruptcy only if it derives directly from the bankruptcy and is closely linked to proceedings for realising the assets or judicial supervision.[629] It is the closeness of the link, in the sense of the case-law resulting from *Gourdain*, between a court action and the insolvency proceedings that is decisive for the purposes of deciding whether the exclusion in Article 1(2)(b) of the JR is applicable.[630] The mere fact that the liquidator is a party to the proceedings is not sufficient

---

[626] See e.g. Ragan, A., 'COMI strikes a discordant note', *Emory Bankruptcy Developments Journal*, 2010, 117–168.

[627] It can be downloaded from the Archives of European Integration, e.g. via http://aei.pitt.edu/952/.

[628] Case C-292/08 *German Graphics*, [2009] ECR I-8421, para 25.

[629] Case 133/78 *Gourdain* [1979] ECR 733, para 4: case-law under the JR is not irrelevant in this respect, as the JR, like the Brussels Convention, excludes 'bankruptcy' from its scope of application.

[630] For instance *not* an action seeking to ensure the reservation of a title clause over goods in possession of the debtor: the answer to that question of law is independent of the opening of insolvency proceedings. See *German Graphics*, note 628 above, para 31. The judgment also clarifies that Article 7 of the Regulation, on

to classify the proceedings as deriving directly from the insolvency and being closely linked to proceedings for realising assets.[631] Relevant case-law is aptly summarised by the United Kingdom Supreme Court in *Rubin v Eurofinance*.[632]

Article 1

Scope

1. This Regulation shall apply to collective insolvency proceedings which entail the partial or total divestment of a debtor and the appointment of a liquidator.

2. This Regulation shall not apply to insolvency proceedings concerning insurance undertakings, credit institutions, investment undertakings which provide services involving the holding of funds or securities for third parties, or to collective investment undertakings.

One has to apply Article 1 jointly with some of the definitions of Article 2:

Article 2

Definitions

For the purposes of this Regulation:

(a) 'insolvency proceedings' shall mean the collective proceedings referred to in Article 1(1). These proceedings are listed in Annex A;

(b) 'liquidator' shall mean any person or body whose function is to administer or liquidate assets of which the debtor has been divested or to supervise the administration of his affairs. Those persons and bodies are listed in Annex C;

(c) 'winding-up proceedings' shall mean insolvency proceedings within the meaning of point (a) involving realising the assets of the debtor, including where the proceedings have been closed by a composition or other measure terminating the insolvency, or closed by reason of the insufficiency of the assets. Those proceedings are listed in Annex B;

(...)

---

reservation of title (see further analysis below), only constitutes a substantive rule intended to protect the seller with respect to assets which are situated outside the Member State of opening of insolvency proceedings: it is not concerned with the delineation between the JR and the Insolvency Regulation. By contrast, per *SCT Industri* , the exception does apply (and hence the insolvency Regulation is applicable) to a judgment of a court of Member State A regarding registration of ownership of shares in a company having its registered office in Member State A, according to which the transfer of those shares was to be regarded as invalid on the ground that the court of Member State A did not recognise the powers of a liquidator from a Member State B in the context of insolvency proceedings conducted and closed in Member State B. The action which gave rise to such a decision derives directly from insolvency proceedings and is closely linked to them. First, the link between the court action and the insolvency proceedings is particularly close since the dispute concerns solely the ownership of the shares which were transferred in insolvency proceedings by a liquidator on the basis of provisions, such as those enacted under the legislation of Member State B on insolvency proceedings, which derogate from the general rules of private law and, in particular, from property law. Thus, the transfer of the shares and the action for restitution of title to which it gave rise are the direct and indissociable consequence of the exercise by the liquidator – an individual who intervenes only after the insolvency proceedings have been opened – of a power which he derives specifically from the provisions of national law governing insolvency proceedings. Second, the content and the scope of the decision declaring the transfer to be invalid are intimately linked to the conduct of the insolvency proceedings since the ground on which the transfer was held invalid relates, specifically and exclusively, to the extent of the powers of that liquidator in insolvency proceedings: Case C-111/08 *SCT Industri v Alpenblume*, [2009] ECR I-5655.

[631] Case 133/78 *Gourdain*, [1979] ECR 733.
[632] *Rubin v Eurofinance SA*, [2012] UKSC 46.

'Insolvency' is not defined by the Regulation. Article 1(1) clarifies that the Regulation at any rate only applies to

- *collective* proceedings, which are
- based on *insolvency*,
- which entail the *partial or total divestment* of a debtor, and
- the appointment of a '*liquidator*'. 'Liquidator' is further defined in Article 2(b).

The combined application of these Articles with the associated Annexes means that the Member States furnish the scope of application of the Regulation by virtue of their including, or not, relevant procedures in Annex.[633] Article 45 provides for a simplified amendment of the Annexes, in particular, allowing the Member States to propose an amendment, rather than leaving the initiative with the EC, and granting the Council the right subsequently to amend the Annexes without having to go via Parliament.[634]

Needless to say, a number of what might seem to be insolvency proceedings existing in the Member States, have not been included in the Annexes, hence the Regulation does not apply to them. This evidently may influence the choice of procedure by creditors in insolvency-relevant national procedures. Where the business involved has cross-border dimensions, the recognition and enforcement leg of the Regulation in particular may well push the creditor into choosing a procedure which is covered by the Regulation.

National insolvency proceedings which meet the requirements of Article 1(1) however which have not been included by the Member State concerned in Annex A, are not covered by the Regulation.[635] It is not sufficient that national proceedings meet the conditions of Article 1 in a generic way.[636] Arguably, proceedings which have been included in that Annex however which do not meet with those same conditions, are not covered by the Regulation either: otherwise the conditions of said Article would be nugatory.

By virtue of Article 1(2), the Regulation does not apply to insolvency proceedings concerning insurance undertakings, credit institutions, investment undertakings which provide services involving the holding of funds or securities for third parties, or to collective investment undertakings. The regulatory environment for these undertakings was considered too specific, and, to some extent, the national supervisory (prudential) authorities have extremely wide-ranging powers of intervention.[637] In the meantime, the EU has put in place tailored insolvency regimes for some[638] of these categories,[639] urged on by the drafters of the Convention (the then 15 Member States). For while they recognised the need for a specific regime for these specific undertakings, they did not want the exclusion to gain a more than temporary character.

---

[633] The 1990 Council of Europe's 'Istanbul' Convention, the 'European Convention on Certain International Aspects of Bankruptcy', employs the same method and to that effect inspired the Regulation.

[634] The most recent such amendment was made by Council Implementing Regulation 583/2011, [2011] OJ L160/52.

[635] Moss, G., Fletcher, I.F., and Isaacs, S. (eds.), note 622 above, p.42.

[636] Virgos-Schmit Report, note 627 above, para 48, p.32.

[637] Recital 9 of the Regulation.

[638] However not for collective investment undertakings, which leaves a considerable gap.

[639] For insurance undertakings: Directive 2001/17, OJ [2001] L110/28; for 'credit institutions': Directive 2001/24, OJ [2001] L125/15.

5.3.2 Four cumulative conditions

The Regulation only applies to *collective* proceedings, which are based on *insolvency*, which entail the *partial or total divestment* of a debtor, and the appointment of a *'liquidator'*.

The debtor need not have a particular status: the Regulation applies equally to all proceedings, whether these involve a natural person or a legal person, a trader or an individual.[640]

The Regulation is not limited to winding-up proceedings (which have their own definition in Article 2(c)),[641] contrary to earlier mooted versions of the Convention: this would have included a fifth condition, that the proceedings may lead to the realisation of the debtor's assets. Such limitation would have had the advantage of simplifying the resulting rules, as the spread of national proceedings involved would have been a lot thinner.[642] However it would also have ruled out application of the Regulation to a considerable amount of 'reorganisation'[643] procedures in the Member States, now more generally referred to as 'restructuring'. A compromise was found to extend the system of the Regulation to insolvency proceedings, the main aim of which was not winding-up but reorganisation. However as part of the compromise, negotiated under the draft Convention, local territorial proceedings opened after the main proceedings may only be winding-up proceedings (see further below). The often unfortunate consequence of this compromise is that when main proceedings have been initiated with a view to restructuring a company with assets in a variety of Member States, the step or threat by some of the creditors of opening up (a) secondary proceeding(s) in another Member State(s) —which, as just noted, have to be winding-up proceedings —may derail the very chances of success of the restructuring.[644]

5.3.2.1 Collective proceedings

Individual action by one creditor only is precluded from cover by the Regulation,[645] lest arguably circumstances are such that there is only one individual creditor, who consequently equals collectivity (in which case at any rate one of the collective proceedings included in Annex A has to be followed).

5.3.2.2 Based on the debtor's insolvency

Procedures based on any other ground are not covered by the Regulation. 'Insolvency' is not defined by the Regulation.

---

[640] Virgos-Schmit Report, para 53, p.39, and recital 9 of the Regulation.

[641] '"winding-up proceedings" shall mean insolvency proceedings within the meaning of point (a) involving realising the assets of the debtor, including where the proceedings have been closed by a composition or other measure terminating the insolvency, or closed by reason of the insufficiency of the assets. Those proceedings are listed in Annex B;'.

[642] Virgos-Schmit Report, para 51, p.35.

[643] Ibidem, p.36.

[644] See also Moss, G., Fletcher, I.F., and Isaacs, S. (eds.), note 635 above, p.51.

[645] Virgos-Schmit Report, para 49, p.32.

'The [Regulation] is based on the idea of financial crisis, but does not provide its own definition of insolvency. It takes this from the national law of the country in which proceedings are opened. There is no test of insolvency other than that demanded by the national legislation of the State in which proceedings are opened. Thus, if a national law is based on the occurrence of an act of bankruptcy listed in the bankruptcy law or on the evidence that the debtor has ceased to pay his debts, it is sufficient for one of these facts to be established in order that insolvency proceedings be opened and the [Regulation] applied.'[646]

5.3.2.3 Which entail the partial or total divestment of a debtor

The requirement of 'divestment' (French: *dessaisissement*; German: *Vermögensbeschlag*), means that the debtor must lose control, partially or totally, of his estate and business:

> that is to say the transfer to another person, the liquidator, of the powers of administration and of disposal over all or part of his assets, or the limitation of these powers through the intervention and control of his actions.[647]

5.3.2.4 Which entail the appointment of a 'liquidator'

This requirement is directly linked to the previous condition: it is the liquidator who gains control over administration and disposal of the debtor's assets. 'Liquidator' is defined in Article 2(b) which again employs the Annex approach: specific legal positions in the Member States are qualified (or not) as 'liquidator'. The definition of Article 2(b) however re-emphasises the aforementioned condition of divestment. The liquidator has to be in control of at least part of the debtor's affairs. Courts may be themselves be 'liquidator' in the sense of Article 2(b), however this needs to be indicated in so many words in Annex C.

5.3.3 Opening by a 'court' or judicial authority?

For insolvency proceedings to be within the scope of the Regulation, they need not be opened by a judicial authority (a great many of the procedures included in Annex A are of this variety, however not all). This was done

- mostly[648] for the same reason as the inclusion of proceedings which may not lead to a winding-up of the debtor (see above). Ordinary non-judicial collective proceedings in particular in the UK and Ireland (especially creditor's voluntary winding-up) represent an important percentage of all corporate insolvency cases. Excluding them would have excluded a sizeable portion of insolvency practice particularly in those countries.
- Further, these proceedings are not of the 'cloak and dagger' variety. They offer sufficient guarantees (including access to the courts, for the legality of the proceedings to

---

[646] Ibidem, p.32–33.
[647] Ibidem, p.34.
[648] Ibidem, para 52, p.37.

be supervised and for any questions which may arise to be settled) in order that they be brought under the Regulation.[649]

- Finally, one of the crucial aims of the Regulation is to safeguard the position of creditors in other Member States, for which it has enough mechanisms to defend the positions of the creditors (the possibility of secondary proceedings, public order exceptions, safeguard of acquired rights, etc.) to enable these proceedings to benefit from the Regulation system.

As shall also be reviewed below, the fact that insolvency proceedings not opened by a judicial authority, are covered by the Regulation to the degree they are included in Annex A and meet with the conditions of Article 1(1), does not mean that they receive all the benefits of the Regulation. In particular, decisions adopted in the course of these proceedings do not enjoy automatic recognition and enforcement.[650] They do however benefit from two core consequences of inclusion in the Regulation:[651]

'1. these proceedings have to be recognized as collective insolvency proceedings pursuant to Article 1. Once proceedings have been opened in a [Member] State in accordance with Article 3, the creditors must seek payment of their debts through these collective proceedings, even if they are not conducted by the courts. Any question relating to the conduct of the proceedings or the decisions taken in the course of those proceedings, should be referred to the courts of that State;

2. the appointment of the liquidator and the powers conferred on him by the law of the State where proceedings were opened must be recognized in other [Member] States. However if the liquidator wishes to exercise his powers in another [Member] State, it is necessary for the [Member] States having proceedings of this type (the United Kingdom and Ireland) to introduce into their national legislation a system of confirmation by the courts of the nature of the proceedings and the appointment of the liquidator. This condition is shown in the list in Annex A which contains the proceedings designated by each country. In both cases these are termed proceedings "with confirmation of or by a court".'

5.3.4 Core aim of the Regulation

High on the list of aims of the Regulation, is the avoidance of forum shopping: 'It is necessary for the proper functioning of the internal market to avoid incentives for the parties to transfer assets or judicial proceedings from one Member State to another, seeking to obtain a more favourable legal position (forum shopping).' (recital 4). Paradoxically, akin to the impact of the Owusu ruling on the popularity of forum non conveniens in Member States outside of the UK, one of the results of the insolvency Regulation may well have been precisely to kindle interest in forum shopping in insolvency proceedings — and

---

[649] In particular, the automatic recognition of the judgment under the Regulation, requires one to be sure that the proceedings included in it, are sound from the point of view of the rule of law.
[650] Virgos-Schmit Report, para 52, p.37.
[651] Ibidem, p.38.

rightly so. The Regulation all too readily dismisses forum shopping as unwarranted in all its forms.[652]

As will be highlighted in the analysis below, the insolvency Regulation does *not* harmonise insolvency law. There are substantial differences in the general approach to insolvency proceedings: what level of protection is given to 'weaker' creditors, such as employees; whether and how there is State intervention in the proceedings; whether courts play a central role or leave creditors (or certain categories of creditors) in the driving seat; etc. These are not at all addressed by the Regulation.

5.4 THE INTERNATIONAL IMPACT OF THE REGULATION

The Regulation applies only to proceedings where the centre of the debtor's main interests is located in the Union,[653] even if the debtor's registered office or place of incorporation or any other concept used by other States to determine corporate 'domicile', is located outside of the EU.[654]

The Regulation does not however regulate the effect of the proceedings vis-à-vis third States. In relation to third States, the Regulation does not impair the freedom of the Member States to adopt the appropriate rules:[655] conflict rules for impact on third States are determined by the private international law of each Member State. They are free to choose whether to copy the Regulation's model for the residual jurisdictional and applicable law rules. Consequently in insolvency proceedings, much more so than under the rules of the Jurisdiction Regulation for standard civil and commercial issues, there is a much wider scope for interaction between conflicting EU and national rules.

When the centre of the debtor's main interests is outside the EU, the Regulation does not apply. In such a case, it is up to the private international law of Member States to decide whether insolvency proceedings may be opened against the debtor and on the rules and conditions to be applied. This holds true regardless of whether the debtor has assets or creditors in other Member States and whether the question of the effects of such proceedings in other Member States is raised.[656]

---

[652] See generally Ringe, W-G., 'Forum shopping under the EU insolvency Regulation', *European Business Organization Law Review*, 2008, 579–620.

[653] Recital 14 of the Regulation; Virgos-Schmit Report, para 11, p.12.

[654] See e.g. *Brac rent-a-car international Inc* (2003) EWHC (Ch) 128, in which there had been a petition for an administration order against the company, which had been incorporated in Delaware however had conducted all its operations in the UK. A creditor had been awarded an arbitration award in Italy and had had this award registered as a judgment in the UK. This creditor opposed the opening of insolvency proceedings in the UK.

[655] Virgos-Schmit Report, para 11, p.12.

[656] Virgos-Schmit Report, para 44, p.29.

5.5 THE JURISDICTIONAL MODEL: UNIVERSAL JURISDICTION BASED ON COMI, ALONGSIDE LIMITED TERRITORIAL PROCEDURES

Draft Convention and Regulation came to the same conclusion: universal jurisdiction and the co-inciding lex concursus as the law of the State of opening of the proceedings, may well be tempting from an organisation point of view, however neither practically achievable nor always warranted. Recital 11 notes in this respect

This Regulation acknowledges the fact that as a result of widely differing substantive laws it is not practical to introduce insolvency proceedings with universal scope in the entire Community. The application without exception of the law of the State of opening of proceedings would, against this background, frequently lead to difficulties. This applies, for example, to the widely differing laws on security interests to be found in the Community. Furthermore, the preferential rights enjoyed by some creditors in the insolvency proceedings are, in some cases, completely different. This Regulation should take account of this in two different ways. On the one hand, provision should be made for special rules on applicable law in the case of particularly significant rights and legal relationships (e.g. rights in rem and contracts of employment). On the other hand, national proceedings covering only assets situated in the State of opening should also be allowed alongside main insolvency proceedings with universal scope.

The result is a combined model of the existing principles of regulation of international bankruptcies (universality or territoriality of effects and unity or plurality of proceedings), a combined model which permits local proceedings to coexist with the main universal proceedings. Insolvency proceedings may be opened in the Member State where the debtor has the 'centre of his main interests'. Insolvency proceedings opened in that State will be main proceedings of universal character:

- "main", because if local proceedings are opened, they will be subject to mandatory rules of coordination and subordination to it, and
- "universal", because, unless local proceedings are opened, all assets of the debtor will be encompassed therein, wherever located.

Single main proceedings are always possible within the Union. However the Regulation does not exclude the opening of local proceedings, controlled and governed by the national law concerned, to protect those local interests. Local proceedings have only territorial scope, limited to the assets located in the State concerned. To open such local proceedings it is necessary that the debtor possess an establishment in the territory of the State of the opening of proceedings. In relation to the main proceedings, local insolvency proceedings can only be "secondary proceedings", since the latter are to be coordinated with and subordinated to the main proceedings.[657]

---

[657] Virgos-Schmit Report, para 13 ff, p.13–14.

5.5.1 Main insolvency proceeding: Centre of Main Interest – COMI

5.5.1.1 'COMI' as (un)defined by the Regulation

COMI is not defined in the Regulation. As the core connecting factor of the Regulation, this is of course unfortunate, however perhaps not all that surprising. It gives the courts and tribunals flexibility in tackling scenarios which arise in practice and which any form of abstract definition or criteria simply cannot catch. There is however one important clarification in the Recitals of the Regulation, which identifies the angle from which COMI needs to be approached. Recital 13 reads[658]

> The "centre of main interests" should correspond to the place where the debtor conducts the administration of his interests on a regular basis and is therefore ascertainable by third parties.

COMI is therefore linked to foreseeability by the (potential) creditors, all the more so because of the principal *Gleichlauf* between forum and applicable law. Those doing business with the undertaking or private individual or thus in a position to calculate the legal risks in the event of an insolvency. The Virgos-Schmit report adds the following clarifications:[659]

- By using the term "interests", the intention was to encompass not only commercial, industrial or professional activities, but also general economic activities, so as to include the activities of private individuals (e.g. consumers).
- The expression "main" serves as a criterion for the cases where these interests include activities of different types which are run from different centres.
- In principle, the centre of main interests will in the case of professionals be the place of their professional domicile and for natural persons in general, the place of their habitual residence. Where companies and legal persons are concerned, the Regulation in Article 3(1) presumes, unless proved to the contrary, that the debtor's centre of main interests is the 'place of the registered office'. The Virgos-Schmit Report adds that this place normally corresponds to the debtor's 'head office', however this is a concept which in itself is open to a great many interpretations. In practice, national courts have been quite happy to set aside the presumption (as Article 3(1) specifically allows them to), given the presumption arguably a lot less weight than perhaps had been assumed by the drafters of the Regulation.[660] The ECJ itself had singled out mailbox companies as not being in a position simply to claim the protection of the State in which they are incorporated:

> in determining the centre of the main interests of a debtor company, the simple presumption laid down by the Community legislature in favour of the registered office of that company can be rebutted only if factors which are both objective and ascertainable by third parties enable it to be established that an actual situation exists which is different from that which locating it at that registered office is deemed to reflect. That could be so in particular in the case of a 'letterbox' company not carrying out any business in the territory of the Member State in which its registered office is situated.[661]

---

[658] In a direct copy from the Virgos Schmit Report, para 75.

[659] Para 75, p.51 ff.

[660] Wautelet, P., 'Some considerations on the center of main interests as jurisdictional test under the European insolvency Regulation', in Affaki, G. (ed), *Cross-border insolvency and conflicts of jurisdictions: A US-EU experience*, Brussels, Bruylant, 2007, (73) 86 ff.

[661] Case C-341/04 *Eurofood IFSC* [2006] ECR I-3813, para 34–35.

5.5.1.2 European and national case-law on COMI

5.5.1.2.1 Need for autonomous interpretation. 'It follows from the need for uniform application of European Union law and from the principle of equality that the terms of a provision of that law which makes no express reference to the law of the Member States for the purpose of determining its meaning and scope must normally be given an autonomous and uniform interpretation throughout the Union, having regard to the context of the provision and the objective pursued by the legislation in question': that is a bit of a mouthful however it is established case-law of the European Court of Justice and gains extra gloss within the context of the application by the Court of European private international law. As highlighted repeatedly throughout this volume, the Court insist on the need for predictability of the application of European PIL Regulations, and the need for autonomous interpretation of core concepts of those regulations.

The concept 'the centre of a debtor's main interests' is peculiar to the Regulation, thus having an autonomous meaning, and must therefore be interpreted in a uniform way, independently of national legislation. [662] The reference in recital 13 in the preamble to the Regulation to the place where the debtor conducts the administration of his interests reflects the European Union legislature's intention to attach greater importance to the place in which the company has its central administration as the criterion for jurisdiction.

5.5.1.2.2 Objective and ascertainable by third parties: *Eurofood, Rastelli, Interedil*. With reference to recital 13, the Court has held that the centre of a debtor's main interests must be identified by reference to criteria that are both objective and ascertainable by third parties, in order to ensure legal certainty and foreseeability concerning the determination of the court with jurisdiction to open the main insolvency proceedings.[663]

The relevance of foreseeability by the potential creditors was emphasised in *Rastelli*, too.[664] The centre of a debtor's main interests must be identified by reference to criteria that are both objective and ascertainable by third parties, in order to ensure legal certainty and foreseeability concerning the determination of the court with jurisdiction to open the main insolvency proceedings. In the case at issue, the property of two companies was intermixed, which led to French courts, under national procedural rules, being able to join the property to the insolvency proceeding. However to characterise such a situation, the French court uses two alternative criteria drawn, respectively, from the existence of intermingled accounts and from abnormal financial relations between the companies, such as the deliberate organisation of transfers of assets without consideration. Neither of these circumstances are easy to ascertain by third parties, rather, they are the subject of accounting hocus pocus which typically is not visible to third parties and hence cannot influence their view on the COMI of the parties concerned. Even if these circumstances were quite transparent, they need not necessarily lead to a singular COMI: such inter-mixing may be organised from two management and supervision centres situated in two different Member States.

Where the bodies responsible for its management and supervision are in the same place as its registered office and the management decisions of the company are taken, in

---

[662] *Eurofood* para 31; and Case C-396/09 *Interedil*, not yet published in ECR, para 43 (judgment of 20 October 2011).

[663] *Eurofood* para 33, and *Interedil* para 49.

[664] Case C-191/10 *Rastelli v Hidoux* (qq liquidator), not yet published in ECR (Judgment of 15 December 2011), para 33 ff.

a manner that is ascertainable by third parties, in that place, the presumption in the second sentence of Article 3(1) of the Regulation is wholly applicable (*Interedil*, paragraph 50). That presumption may be rebutted where, from the viewpoint of third parties, the place in which a company's central administration is located is not the same as that of its registered office. In that event, the simple presumption laid down by the EU legislature in favour of the registered office of that company can be rebutted if factors which are both objective and ascertainable by third parties enable it to be established that an actual situation exists which is different from that which locating it at that registered office is deemed to reflect (*Eurofood IFSC*, paragraph 34, and *Interedil*, paragraph 51).

5.5.1.2.3 Eurofood: individuality of COMI. The Regulation itself contains no specific rules on determining COMI for groups of companies. The 'Convention offers no rule for groups of affiliated companies (parent-subsidiary schemes').[665] Each debtor constituting a distinct legal entity is subject to its own COMI determination.[666] The mere fact that a daughter company's economic choices are or can be controlled by a parent company in another Member State is not enough to rebut the presumption laid down by Article 3(1) of the Regulation.[667]

5.5.1.2.4 'Actual centre of management and supervision and of the management of its interests'. In *Interedil*, the Court emphasises transparency and publicity: the requirement for objectivity and that possibility of ascertainment by third parties may be considered to be met where the material factors taken into account for the purpose of establishing the place in which the debtor company conducts the administration of its interests on a regular basis have been made public or, at the very least, made sufficiently accessible to enable third parties, that is to say in particular the company's creditors, to be aware of them (at para 49). The factors to be taken into account to rebut the presumption of Article 3(1), second sentence, include, in particular, all the places in which the debtor company pursues economic activities and all those in which it holds assets, in so far as those places are ascertainable by third parties (*Interedil*, at para 52).

All relevant considerations tempted the Court into what may be regarded as a definition of 'COMI': in the case of a company at least, the company's actual centre of management and supervision and of the management of its interests, is its COMI. However one must not be tempted to treat this extract as a stand-alone definition of COMI (and one which arguably closely resembles the 'Head Office' approach): throughout the *Interedil* judgment, the Court emphasises the element of transparency and publicity.

5.5.1.2.5 Additional jurisdiction for Member State of COMI for actions 'closely connected' with the insolvency proceedings. In *Seagon*, the Court of Justice employed recital 6 of the Regulation[668] to hold that Article 3(1) must be interpreted as meaning that it

---

[665] Virgos-Schmit Report, para 76, p.52.

[666] See the opposite view, prior to the Eurofood judgment, *In re Collins & Aikman Corp. Group*, [2005] EWHC 1754 (Ch), in which the High Court addressed COMI vis-a-vis Michigan-based company with twenty-four corporations registered in the EU. The group was treated as a single unit.

[667] Case C-341/04 *Eurofood*, [2006] ECR I-3813, para 30 ff.

[668] Which, paradoxically, speaks of the principle of proportionality which in principle functions as a limiting factor on EU competence: '(6) In accordance with the principle of proportionality this Regulation should be confined to provisions governing jurisdiction for opening insolvency proceedings and judgments which are delivered directly on the basis of the insolvency proceedings and are closely connected with such proceedings. In addition, this Regulation should contain provisions regarding the recognition of those judgments and the applicable law which also satisfy that principle.'

also confers international jurisdiction on the courts of the Member State within the territory of which insolvency proceedings were opened to hear an action which derives directly from the initial insolvency proceedings and which is 'closely connected' with them, within the meaning of recital 6 in the preamble to the Regulation.[669] In that judgment the Court of Justice linked its findings directly to the Regulation's aim of discouraging forum shopping. Actions to set a transaction aside by virtue of insolvency, are closely connected to the opening of the proceedings, given that assets transfers in the run-up to insolvency proceedings are probably the oldest trick of the trade to frustrate one's creditors.

A 'close connection' is not present, per *Rastelli*,[670] where a national court seeks to join to the main proceeding, a proceeding concerning a different debtor with COMI in another Member State and no establishment in the former, simply because the debtor concerned possesses property which is intermixed with the debtor in the main proceeding. Joining to the initial proceedings an additional debtor, legally distinct from the debtor concerned by those proceedings, produces with regard to that additional debtor the same effects as the decision to open insolvency proceedings. The latter cannot be done simply on the basis of a procedural mechanism such as a joinder, but rather requires the national court at issue to carry out a de novo assessment of the conditions of the Regulation: either a main proceeding on the basis of COMI, or a territorial procedure on the basis of locally present assets and 'establishment'.

5.5.1.2.6 The relevant date for the purpose of locating the centre of the debtor's main interests, and transfer after lodging of request to open a proceeding. The Regulation does not contain any express provisions concerning the specific case involving the transfer of a debtor's centre of interests. Per *Interedil*, in the light of the general terms in which Article 3(1) of the Regulation is worded, the last place in which that centre was located must therefore be regarded as the relevant place for the purpose of determining the court having jurisdiction to open the main insolvency proceedings.[671] This is also indicated by the use of the present tense: jurisdiction is granted to the courts of the Member State within the territory of which the centre of a debtor's main interest *is* situated.[672]

Where the centre of a debtor's main interests is transferred after the lodging of a request to open insolvency proceedings, but before the proceedings are opened, the courts of the Member State within the territory of which the centre of main interests was situated at the time when the request was lodged retain jurisdiction to rule on those proceedings.[673] However where the COMI has been transferred before a request to open insolvency proceedings is lodged, the centre of the debtor's main interests is therefore presumed, in accordance with the second sentence of Article 3(1) of the Regulation, to be located at the place of the new registered office and, accordingly, it is the courts of the Member State within the territory of which the new registered office is located which, in principle, have jurisdiction to open the main insolvency proceedings, unless the presumption in Article 3(1) of the Regulation is rebutted by evidence that the centre of main interests has not followed the change of registered office.[674]

---

[669] Case C-339/07 *Seagon*, [2009] ECR I-767, para 19 to 21.
[670] n 664 above.
[671] *Interedil*, n 662 above, para 54.
[672] See also Moss, G., Fletcher, I.F., and Isaacs, S. (eds.), note 635 above, p.47.
[673] Case C-1/04 *Staubitz-Schreiber*, [2006] ECR I-701, para 29, with specific reference to the need to avoid forum shopping.
[674] *Interedil*, para 56.

The Court's case-law on the timing of determination of COMI is made all the more relevant given the case-law on the freedom of establishment (see elsewhere in this volume), which has given rise to an increase in corporate mobility in the EU.[675] The resulting room for forum shopping (both in the case of a group of companies, and in the event of a single company seeking to take advantage of advantageous insolvency proceedings) prima facie sits uneasily of course with the Regulation's declared intent of combatting forum shopping, however, as the cases above illustrate, the result of the Court's case-law on COMI is that any change in COMI most certainly cannot be carried out on a whim.[676]

5.5.1.3 Universality of the proceedings opened in the COMI Member State

The main proceedings are always universal. This has a number of important legal consequences:

(a) Assets located outside the State of opening are also included in the proceedings and sequestrated as from the opening of proceedings on a world-wide basis;

(b) All creditors are encompassed;

(c) Proceedings opened in one [Member State] will produce effects throughout the whole territory of the [Member States] (i.e. the [Union]). The recognition of the effects of the proceedings in other [Member States] is automatic, by force of law, without the need for an exequatur, and is independent of publication; However, enforcement of judgments will require prior limited control by the national courts, through an exequatur. If the conditions set out by the [Regulation] are satisfied, the national Courts are obliged to grant it.

(d) The liquidator appointed in the main proceedings has authority to act in all the other [Member States], without the need for an exequatur. He may remove assets from the State in which they are located. In exercising these powers (granted by the State of opening), the liquidator must comply with the laws of the State concerned. This is particularly the case if coercion is necessary to gain control of the assets (he must then request the assistance of the local authorities);

(e) Individual execution is not possible against the assets of a debtor located in any [Member State];

(f) There is a legal duty to surrender to the insolvency proceedings the proceeds recovered by individual execution or obtained from the debtor's voluntary payment out of assets located abroad.[677]

---

[675] Whether the increase reflects a permanent rise and re-occurring phenomenon, is more difficult to ascertain: see also Brattonn, W., McCahery, J., and Vermeulen, E., 'How does corporate mobility affect lawmaking? A comparative analysis', Law Working Paper No. 91 (European Corporate Governance Institute 2008). To be sure, in the immediate aftermath of the *Centros* and related case-law (reviewed below), there was quite a bit of corporate mobility, especially into the United Kingdom. However arguably a lot of that potential has now been 'mopped up', especially in view of the regulatory competition that followed, leading to more inviting corporate requirements in those Member States which saw a lot of corporations disappear. See also Enriques, L., and Gelter, M., 'How the Old World Encountered the New One: Regulatory Competition and Cooperation in European Corporate and Bankruptcy Law', European Corporate Governance Institute (ECGI) – Law Research Paper Series, no. 63/2006.

[676] Incidentally I disagree with the suggestion (Ringe, W-G., n 652 above) that the 'fuzziness' of COMI (a phrase said to be first used by Horst Eidenmüller in 'Free Choice in international company insolvency law in Europe', *European Business Organization Law Review*, 2005, (423) 428) contributes to its alleged incompatibility with the Treaty's freedom of establishment.

[677] Virgos-Schmit Report, Para 19, p.15 ff.

The impact of the main proceedings and the corresponding powers of the liquidator, within the constraints of Article 18 ff, are at their highest for as long as no secondary proceedings have been opened. 'Only the opening of secondary insolvency proceedings is capable of restricting the universal effect of the main insolvency proceedings'.[678]

The impact of this priority, must not be underestimated, especially given the link (detailed below) with applicable law. Because of the universal effect which all main insolvency proceedings must be accorded, main insolvency proceedings encompass all of the debtor's EU assets. The law of the State of opening of the main proceedings determines not only the opening of insolvency proceedings, but also their course and closure. On that basis, that law is required to govern the treatment of assets situated in all Member States and the effects of the insolvency proceedings on the measures to which those assets are liable to be subject — inevitably of course leading to a race to court just as under the JR by virtue of that latter Regulation's lis alibi pendens rule. The insolvency Regulation however does not have a 'guillotine-like'[679] lis alibi pendens rule. Article 16's priority rule, reviewed below, has required flanking measures (in particular the limited scope for refusal of recognition) and the firm hand of European Court of Justice case-law (in particular the emphasis on the principle of mutual trust, see the para just below) to render it relevant in practice.

Given the impact of the opening of the main proceedings: may the jurisdiction assumed by a court of a Member State to open main insolvency proceedings be reviewed by a court of another Member State in which recognition has been applied for? The rule of priority laid down in Article 16(1) of the Regulation, which provides that insolvency proceedings opened in one Member State are to be recognised in all Member States from the time that they produce their effects in the State of the opening of proceedings, is based on the principle of mutual trust. This element of mutual trust is of exactly the same nature as the corresponding provisions and case-law under the Jurisdiction Regulation (per *Gasser*, *Turner* etc.: reviewed elsewhere in this volume). It is inherent in that principle of mutual trust that the court of a Member State hearing an application for the opening of main insolvency proceedings check that it has jurisdiction, i.e. examine whether the centre of the debtor's main interests is situated in that Member State. In return, as the 22nd recital of the Regulation makes clear, the principle of mutual trust requires that the courts of the other Member States recognise the decision opening main insolvency proceedings, without being able to review the assessment made by the first court as to its jurisdiction: any challenge of that view has to be brought in the courts of the Member State which has detected COMI and has upheld jurisdiction.[680]

5.5.1.4 When is an insolvency procedure 'opened' within the meaning of the Regulation?

In particular, given the drastic impact of the opening of (main) proceedings, is there some kind of active review required by the relevant court whether the substantive conditions

---

[678] Case C-444/07 *MG Probud*, [2010] ECR I-417, para 24.
[679] Wautelet, P., n 660 above, 77.
[680] Case C-341/04 *Eurofood*, [2006] EC I-3813, para 38 ff.

for insolvency have been met, or can a near-automatic trigger of the proceedings suffice, in particular following initiative by one of the creditors?

The conditions and formalities required for opening insolvency proceedings are a matter for national law, and vary considerably from one Member State to another. In some Member States, the proceedings are opened very shortly after the submission of the application, the necessary verifications being carried out later. In other Member States, certain essential findings, which may be quite time-consuming, must be made before proceedings are opened. Under the national law of certain Member States, the proceedings may be opened 'provisionally' for several months. it is necessary, in order to ensure the effectiveness of the system established by the Regulation, that the recognition principle laid down in the first subparagraph of Article 16(1) of the Regulation, be capable of being applied as soon as possible in the course of the proceedings. The mechanism providing that only one main set of proceedings may be opened, producing its effects in all the Member States in which the Regulation applies, could be seriously disrupted if the courts of those States, hearing applications based on a debtor's insolvency at the same time, could claim concurrent jurisdiction over an extended period. In those circumstances, a 'decision to open insolvency proceedings' for the purposes of the Regulation must be regarded as including not only a decision which is formally described as an opening decision by the legislation of the Member State of the court that handed it down, but also a decision handed down following an application, based on the debtor's insolvency, seeking the opening of proceedings referred to in Annex A to the Regulation, where that decision involves divestment of the debtor and the appointment of a liquidator referred to in Annex C to the Regulation. Such divestment involves the debtor losing the powers of management which he has over his assets. In such a case, the two characteristic consequences of insolvency proceedings, namely the appointment of a liquidator referred to in Annex C and the divestment of the debtor, have taken effect, and thus all the elements constituting the definition of such proceedings, given in Article 1(1) of the Regulation, are present.[681]

5.5.2 Secondary and territorial insolvency proceedings

Secondary and territorial proceedings may only be opened if the debtor possesses an establishment within the territory of that other Member State, and only vis-a-vis the debtor's assets in that State. Article 2(h) of the Regulation defines 'establishment' as

> any place of operations where the debtor carries out a non-transitory economic activity with human means and goods

which the Court of Justice has specified in less philosophical terms as[682]

> a structure with a minimum level of organisation and a degree of stability for the purpose of pursuing an economic activity

basically a combination of pursuit of an economic activity and the presence of human resources. This has to be determined in the same way as the location of the centre of

---

[681] Case C-341/04 *Eurofood*, [2006] EC I-3813, para 51 ff.
[682] *Interedil*, n 662 above, para 62.

main interests, namely on the basis of objective factors which are ascertainable by third parties.[683]

The opening of secondary or territorial proceedings is subject to different conditions according to whether or not main proceedings have already been opened. In the first situation (main proceedings have already been opened), the proceedings are described as 'secondary proceedings' and are governed by the provisions of Chapter III of the Regulation (mainly designed to ensure proper co-ordination with and in effect subordination to, the main proceedings: for as noted below, the Regulation does encourage collectivity of the proceedings). In the second situation (no main proceeding has been opened), the proceedings are described as 'territorial insolvency proceedings' and the circumstances in which proceedings can be opened are determined by Article 3(4) of the Regulation. If and when the main proceedings have been opened, the 'territorial' procedure becomes 'secondary'.

5.5.2.1 Territorial insolvency proceedings

Article 3(2) ff concerns two situations: first, where it is impossible to open main proceedings because of the conditions laid down by the law of the Member State where the debtor has the centre of its main interests and, secondly, where the opening of territorial proceedings in the Member State within the territory of which the debtor has an establishment is requested by certain creditors having a particular connection with that territory.

Recital 17 to the Regulation hints at restrictive interpretation: '(…) cases where territorial insolvency proceedings are requested before the main insolvency proceedings are intended to be limited to what is absolutely necessary.' This is compounded by the need for co-ordination which is also emphasised in recital 12, in fine: 'Mandatory rules of coordination with the main proceedings satisfy the need for unity in the [Union]'. Such coordination cannot be ensured if main proceedings have not been opened, and hence the Court held in *Zaza Retail* that cases where under Article 3(4)(a) the opening of territorial insolvency proceedings can be requested before that of the main insolvency proceedings are limited to what is absolutely necessary.[684] In particular, the requirement of 'conditions' present in that Article, cannot be extended to conditions excluding particular persons (such as the public prosecutor) from the category of persons empowered to request the opening of such proceedings. Hence they are limited to substantive conditions of insolvency, such as whether one needs to be a trader to be declared insolvent etc. In the case at issue, the Belgian public prosecutor, empowered under Belgian law to request insolvency in the general interest, had wanted to open territorial proceedings in Belgium prior to opening of the main proceedings in The Netherlands, were Zaza had its COMI.

In the same restrictive vain, a party has to have a claim of its own to lodge against the debtor's estate, for it to be a 'creditor' within the meaning of Article 3(4)(b). A claim in the general interest is not enough.[685]

---

[683] Ibidem, para 63.
[684] Case C-112/10 *Zaza Retail*, not yet published in ECR, para 22 (judgment of 17 November 2011).
[685] Ibidem, para 31. Note the contrast with secondary proceedings, where Article 29 allows for a much wider category of persons to request the opening of such.

Local insolvency proceedings opened in accordance with the [Regulation] limit the universal cope of the main proceedings. Assets located in the [Member State] where a court opens local insolvency proceedings are subject only to the local proceedings. However, the universal character of the main proceedings reveals itself through the mandatory rules of coordination of the local proceedings with the main proceedings, which include some specific powers of intervention given by the [Regulation] to the liquidator of the main proceedings (...) and the transfer of any surplus in the local proceedings to the main proceedings.[686]

5.5.2.2 Secondary insolvency proceedings

Here, locus standi is more flexible: see Article 29 of the Regulation.

5.6 APPLICABLE LAW

Article 4

Law applicable

1. Save as otherwise provided in this Regulation, the law applicable to insolvency proceedings and their effects shall be that of the Member State within the territory of which such proceedings are opened, hereafter referred to as the "State of the opening of proceedings".

2. The law of the State of the opening of proceedings shall determine the conditions for the opening of those proceedings, their conduct and their closure. It shall determine in particular:

(a) against which debtors insolvency proceedings may be brought on account of their capacity;
(b) the assets which form part of the estate and the treatment of assets acquired by or devolving on the debtor after the opening of the insolvency proceedings;
(c) the respective powers of the debtor and the liquidator;
(d) the conditions under which set-offs may be invoked;
(e) the effects of insolvency proceedings on current contracts to which the debtor is party;
(f) the effects of the insolvency proceedings on proceedings brought by individual creditors, with the exception of lawsuits pending;
(g) the claims which are to be lodged against the debtor's estate and the treatment of claims arising after the opening of insolvency proceedings;
(h) the rules governing the lodging, verification and admission of claims;
(i) the rules governing the distribution of proceeds from the realisation of assets, the ranking of claims and the rights of creditors who have obtained partial satisfaction after the opening of insolvency proceedings by virtue of a right in rem or through a set-off;
(j) the conditions for and the effects of closure of insolvency proceedings, in particular by composition;
(k) creditors' rights after the closure of insolvency proceedings;
(l) who is to bear the costs and expenses incurred in the insolvency proceedings;

---

[686] Virgos-Schmit Report, para 20, p.17

(m) the rules relating to the voidness, voidability or unenforceability of legal acts detrimental to all the creditors.

Article 28

Applicable law

Save as otherwise provided in this Regulation, the law applicable to secondary proceedings shall be that of the Member State within the territory of which the secondary proceedings are opened.

Article 4 of the Regulation is the general rule: unless otherwise stated by the Regulation, the law of the State of the opening of proceedings is applicable. *Renvoi* is not specifically excluded by the Regulation however it is safe to assume that it is.[687] To avoid doubt, Article 28 reiterates the same conflict rule for secondary proceedings. The Regulation has omitted doing the same for territorial proceedings however the lex concursus rule may be viewed as the general conflicts rule of the Regulation and is hence arguably also valid for territorial proceedings[688] (validly opened).

The list of issues part of the applicable law, included in Article 4, is non-exhaustive. Many of the issues listed are more specifically dealt with or at least additionally referred to in other parts of the Regulation.

5.6.1 Exceptions

The general rule of Article 4 inevitably had to be softened for quite a number of instances. As noted in the introduction, insolvency proceedings involve a wide array of interests. The expediency, efficiency and effectiveness craved inter alia by recital 2 of the Regulation, has led in particular to the automatic extension of all the effects of the application of the lex concursus by the courts in the State of opening of the proceedings. That could not be done without there being exceptions to the general rule:[689]

1. In certain cases, the Regulation excludes some rights over assets located abroad from the effects of the insolvency proceedings (as in Articles 5, 6 and 7).
2. In other cases, it ensures that certain effects of the insolvency proceedings are governed not by the law of the State of the opening, but by the law of another State, defined in the abstract by Articles 8, 9, 10, 11, 14 and 15. In such cases, the effects to be given to the proceedings opened in other States are the same effects attributed to a domestic proceedings of equivalent nature (liquidation, composition, or reorganization proceedings) by the law of the State concerned. Of particular note are Article 5 on third parties' rights in rem, Article 10 on employment contracts, and Article 13 on 'detrimental acts'.

The latter is a good example of the European harmonisation of the *Vorfrage*, alluded to elsewhere in this volume. Within the context of the insolvency Regulation, the *Vorfrage* takes on a specific form in Article 13 on 'detrimental' acts, in conjunction with its Article 4(2)(m) on 'the rules relating to the voidness, voidability or unenforceability of legal acts detrimental to all creditors'.[690]

---

[687] See also Virgos-Schmit Report, para 87, p.63.
[688] Virgos-Schmit Report, para 89, p.64.
[689] Ibidem, para 92, p.68 ff. The Virgos-Schmit report contains detail for each of the exceptions.
[690] Ibidem, para 135 ff, p.87 ff.

The basic rule of the Regulation is that the law of the State of the opening governs, under Article 4, any possible voidness, voidability or unenforceability of acts which may be detrimental to all the creditors' interests. This same law determines the conditions to be met, the manner in which the nullity and voidability function (automatically, by allocating retrospective effects to the proceedings or pursuant to an action taken by the liquidator, etc.) and the legal consequences of nullity and voidability.

Article 13 represents a defence against the application of the law of the State of the opening, which must be pursued by the interested party, who must claim it. It acts as a "veto" against the invalidity of the act decreed by the law of the State of the opening. Article 13 provides that the rules of the law of the State of the opening shall not apply when the person who has benefited from the contested act provides proof that:

1. the act in question (e.g. a contract) is subject to the law of a Contracting State other than the State of the opening of the proceedings; and

2. the law of that other State does not allow for this act to be challenged by any means.

By 'any means it is understood that the act must not be capable of being challenged using either rules on insolvency or general rules of the national law applicable to the act (e.g. to the contract referred to in paragraph (1)). "In the relevant case" means that the act should not be capable of being challenged in fact i.e. after taking into account all the concrete circumstances of the case. It is not sufficient to determine whether it can be challenged in the abstract.

The aim of Article 13 is to uphold legitimate expectations of creditors or third parties of the validity of the act in accordance to the normally applicable national law, against interference from a different "lex concursus". From the perspective of the protection of legitimate expectations, the operation of Article 13 is justified with regard to acts carried out prior to the opening of the insolvency proceedings, and threatened by either the retroactive nature of the insolvency proceedings opened in another country or actions to set aside previous acts of the debtor brought by the liquidator in those proceedings. After the proceedings have been opened in a Member State, the creditor's reliance on the validity of the transaction under the national law applicable in non-insolvency situations is no longer justified. Thenceforth, all unauthorised disposals by the debtor are in principle ineffective by virtue of the divestment of his powers to dispose of the assets and such effect is recognised in all Member States. Article 13 does not protect against such an effect of the insolvency proceedings and it is not applicable to disposals occurring after the opening of the insolvency proceedings.

It is noteworthy that Articles 8–15 do not affect the international workings of the Regulation: as noted, in relation to third States, the Regulation does not impair the freedom of the Member States to adopt the appropriate rules. Consequently, where the relevant applicable law as determined by Articles 8–15 is not that of a Member State, the law of the State of the opening of proceedings does not slot in by default: 'The need to protect legitimate expectations and the certainty of transactions is equally valid in relations with non-[Member] States.'[691] The Regulation is restricted to the intra-EU effect of insolvency

---

[691] Ibidem, para 93, p.69.

proceedings and Member States are therefore free to decide which rules they deem most appropriate in other cases.

The applicable law identified by the Regulation is a national law (as signalled above, typically albeit not always of one of the Member States). The Regulation harmonises jurisdiction and choice of laws rules on insolvency *proceedings*. It does not harmonise insolvency law. One important common principle of insolvency law is however promoted by the Regulation, namely the principle of collective satisfaction. A creditor who, after the opening of proceedings, obtains total or partial satisfaction of his claim individually breaches the principle of collective satisfaction on which the insolvency proceedings are based. Hence, the obligation to return 'what has been obtained'. The liquidator may demand either the return of the assets received or the equivalent in money, as provided for in Article 20:

Article 20

Return and imputation

1. A creditor who, after the opening of the proceedings referred to in Article 3(1) obtains by any means, in particular through enforcement, total or partial satisfaction of his claim on the assets belonging to the debtor situated within the territory of another Member State, shall return what he has obtained to the liquidator, subject to Articles 5 and 7.

2. In order to ensure equal treatment of creditors a creditor who has, in the course of insolvency proceedings, obtained a dividend on his claim shall share in distributions made in other proceedings only where creditors of the same ranking or category have, in those other proceedings, obtained an equivalent dividend.

5.7 RECOGNITION AND ENFORCEMENT OF INSOLVENCY PROCEEDINGS

To recognize foreign judgments is to admit for the territory of the recognising State the authority which they enjoy in the State where they were handed down.[692]

The Regulation accords immediate recognition of judgments concerning the opening, course and closure of insolvency proceedings which come within its scope and of judgments handed down in direct connection with such insolvency proceedings.[693] Within the system of the Regulation, therefore, recognition is automatic. It requires no preliminary decision by a court of the requested State. The automatic recognition however only applies to 'judgments'. Non-judicial proceedings which, as noted above, may be covered by the Regulation, are not subject to its provisions on recognition and enforcement.

---

[692] Ibidem, para 143, p.92.
[693] Ibidem.

5.7.1 Judgments concerning the opening of insolvency proceedings

With respect to the *opening* of the proceedings, the rule is laid down in Article 16, and the effects of the recognition is regulated in Articles 17 to 24.

Article 16

Principle

1. Any judgment opening insolvency proceedings handed down by a court of a Member State which has jurisdiction pursuant to Article 3 shall be recognised in all the other Member States from the time that it becomes effective in the State of the opening of proceedings.

This rule shall also apply where, on account of his capacity, insolvency proceedings cannot be brought against the debtor in other Member States.

2. Recognition of the proceedings referred to in Article 3(1) shall not preclude the opening of the proceedings referred to in Article 3(2) by a court in another Member State. The latter proceedings shall be secondary insolvency proceedings within the meaning of Chapter III.

The automatic recognition of the judgments opening insolvency proceedings has practical impact mostly in that it means an 'occupation of the field', and fixation of applicable law.

The law of the State of the opening of proceedings provides for the relevant trigger: the automatic recognition requires that the judgment opening insolvency proceedings become 'effective' in the State of opening. It is not necessary for it to be 'final': even if it is a provisional opening, e.g. subject to appeal in the State of opening, the judgment still enjoys recognition under Article 16. That insolvency proceedings cannot be brought in the State of recognition on account of the debtor's capacity (one imagines in particular: those Member States which do not have in insolvency procedure for natural persons who are not acting in a professional ('trader') capacity), is specifically ruled out as relevant by the second para of Article 16(1). Article 26 adds moreover specifically that the State requested can in such instance not invoke public policy in its territory to oppose recognition on those grounds.

Article 17 distinguishes between the recognition of main cq territorial proceedings:

Article 17

Effects of recognition

1. The judgment opening the proceedings referred to in Article 3(1) shall, with no further formalities, produce the same effects in any other Member State as under this law of the State of the opening of proceedings, unless this Regulation provides otherwise and as long as no proceedings referred to in Article 3(2) are opened in that other Member State.

2. The effects of the proceedings referred to in Article 3(2) may not be challenged in other Member States. Any restriction of the creditors' rights, in particular a stay or discharge, shall produce effects vis-à-vis assets situated within the territory of another Member State only in the case of those creditors who have given their consent.

The Regulation uses what is known as the 'extension' model: proceedings in another Member State will not, as regard their effects, be simply equated with national proceedings of the State where recognition is sought. Rather, they will be recognised in those States with the same effects attributed to them by the law of the State of opening, and subject to the limitations outlined above under applicable law: insolvency proceedings have both procedural as well as substantive effects and the latter operate within the limits of applicable law (see Articles 5 ff of the Regulation).

The main proceeding cannot produce its effects in respect of the assets and legal situations which come within the jurisdiction of territorial proceedings opened: that is the result of Article 17(2) and it is of course logical given the very existence of those proceedings. These proceedings may generate effects in other Member States, in particular, they may lead to other Member States having to enforce the return of assets which were abroad without authorisation, after the opening of the territorial proceedings. In that respect, the territorial proceedings limit the reach of the main proceedings.

The main proceedings are not however without any relevance at all for the assets included in any territorial proceedings. In particular, the Regulation includes a number of co-ordination and supervision requirements in Articles 31 to 37.

5.7.2 Other judgments in the course of insolvency proceedings

Article 25 of the Insolvency Regulation concerns, in particular, the recognition and enforceability of judgments other than those directly concerning the *opening* of insolvency proceedings.

1. The first subpar of Article 25(1), applies to judgments which concern the 'course and closure' of such proceedings.
2. The second subpar of Article 25(1) applies to 'judgments deriving directly from insolvency proceedings and which are closely linked to them', and
3. The third subpar. applies to judgments relating to preservation measures taken after the request for the opening of the proceedings. Finally
4. Article 25(2) applies to judgments other than all the above, however presumably with some kind of more or less remote link to the insolvency proceeding.

The latter may or may not be covered by the Jurisdiction Regulation. Where they are, the court concerned evidently has to apply the relevant rules of the JR.[694]

Article 25(3) provides that Member States are not obliged to recognise or enforce a judgment covered by Article 25(1) which might result in a limitation of personal freedom or postal secrecy.

5.7.3 Defences against recognition and enforcement

As reviewed above in the analysis of COMI, the Regulation is based on the principle of Union trust and consequently on the general assumption that a foreign judgment is valid. Article 26's provision on public policy therefore is formulated in a restrictive sense:[695]

Article 26

Public policy

Any Member State may refuse to recognise insolvency proceedings opened in another Member State or to enforce a judgment handed down in the context of such proceedings where the effects

---

[694] Case C-292/08 *German Graphics*, [2009] ECR I-8421.
[695] Portugal issued a Declaration to this Article, see OJ [2000] C183/1.

of such recognition or enforcement would be manifestly contrary to that State's public policy, in particular its fundamental principles or the constitutional rights and liberties of the individual.

The only ground for opposing recognition is that the foreign judgment is contrary to the public policy of the requested State. Consequently[696]

---

1. The foreign judgment cannot be the subject of review as regards its substance (*révision au fond*). All questions regarding the substance must be discussed before the courts of the State of the opening of proceedings. In the State where recognition or enforcement is requested, the court may only decide whether the foreign judgment will have effects contrary to its public policy.

2. The [Regulation] contains no provisions as to the verification of the international jurisdiction of the court of the State of origin (the court in the State of the opening of proceedings which has jurisdiction under Article 3 of the [Regulation]). The courts of the requested States may not review the jurisdiction of the court of the State of origin, but only verify that the judgment emanates from a court of a [Member] State which claims jurisdiction under Article 3 of the [Regulation].

5.8 POWERS OF THE LIQUIDATOR

Article 18, too, uses the extension model: the liquidator's powers, their nature and their scope are determined by the law of the State of the opening of the proceedings in respect of which he was appointed. That law also establishes the liquidator's obligations (the exercise of which moreover is influenced by the limitations to the applicable law under Article 5 ff). Articles 31 to 37 confer powers on the liquidator of the main proceedings to coordinate those proceedings and any secondary proceedings (which, by virtue of Article 29, he may himself request in the Member State(s) concerned.

Frustration is aired by many commentators that the supervision, co-operation and co-ordination provisions of the Regulation apply to and between liquidators only, not, at least not formally, to and between courts. While such requirement of co-operation may be assumed to be implied in the Regulation, it would nevertheless have been useful to have had specific instructions to that effect.

5.9 FUTURE AMENDMENT OF THE REGULATION

A report on the functioning of the Regulation was scheduled for June 2012, with the Commission having tendered a study late 2011, collecting information on the practice

---

[696] Virgos-Schmit Report, para 202, p.126.

in the Member States. The Commission has identified a number or changes in the insolvency environment since the adoption of the Regulation: [697]

The number of Member States has increased twice since: in 2004 and 2007, meaning 12 new Member States have entered the arena, some of whom with rather specific insolvency procedures. Generally, Some Member States adopted new legal schemes for restructuring and treatment of insolvency, based on the Uncitral Model Law. Finally, the organisation of business itself has changed: companies are incorporated in international groups (parent company and subsidiaries), they apply corporate governance rules, and have access to capital in the financial markets. Faced with new risks (global economy, relocation of business, unemployment, financial crisis of 2008), European companies have had to adapt continuously to a changing environment.

In most Member States bankruptcy law has been modernised to fit with the new economic context: beside traditional collective insolvency proceedings decided by the court on the basis of the debtor's insolvency, new schemes applicable to a group of main creditors (for example banks, public bodies) at a pre-insolvency stage are regarded as being more efficient for the purposes of business continuation and preservation of jobs. At the same time, new procedures for the treatment of over-indebtedness of natural persons have been put in place in many countries (for example "civil bankruptcy") with a view to guaranteeing a decent life to the poorest debtors (as a principle of social justice).

As a consequence, the EC has flagged difficulties in application which may, or may not, require an amendment to the Regulation, in particular: [698]

1. Scope of the Regulation

— the limitation of the scope of the Regulation to insolvency and winding-up proceedings as defined in Articles 1 and 2 and listed in Annexes A and B thereof and a possible extension to hybrid proceedings (i.e. pre-insolvency compulsory arrangements to prevent the formal insolvency proceedings, for example in the UK; *"pre-pack"*, French *"sauvegarde"*);
— the exclusion from the scope of the institutions referred to in Article 1 (2). The re-organisation of financial undertakings and payment systems and from the Directives should be examined as a possible extension of the scope of the Regulation;
— the limitation of the territorial scope and its effect on insolvency procedures involving debtors with a COMI or assets in Denmark and/or non-EU States; in particular, the effect of Danish decisions in relation to insolvency proceedings opened in other Member States;
— the delineation of the scope with other Union instruments in the area of civil justice, notably the JR.

2. The system of main and secondary proceedings:

— jurisdiction for opening proceedings: the concept of COMI;
— the issue of transfer of seat/shift of COMI to another Member State (Case C-1/04 Staubitz-Schreiber, case C-396/09 Interedil) and the relationship with the principle of freedom of establishment and corporate mobility (Article 49 TFEU, Case C-210/06 Cartesio, conclusions of the Experts' Group on European Company Law 2011) and Directive on the approximation of the laws of the Member States and the safeguarding of employees' rights in the event of transfers of undertakings, businesses or parts of businesses;

---

[697] Open invitation to tender JUST/2011/JCIV/PR/0049/A4.
[698] Ibidem, footnotes omitted.

— the division of powers between main and secondary proceedings;
— pending parallel insolvency proceedings;
— recognition and enforcement of decision opening insolvency proceedings in another Member State;
— the public policy exception;
— recognition and enforcement of other decisions under the Regulation.

3. The insolvency of groups of companies, the application of the Regulation taken by national courts in such situations.

4. Debt adjustment of private individuals ("consumer bankruptcy").

5. Insolvency proceedings and arbitration/ADR: effect of insolvency on arbitration/ADR clauses, effect of arbitration/ADR proceedings in context of Article 15.

6. Applicable law rules: *lex fori* vs *lex situs*, rules on protection of rights *in rem*, set-off, reservation of title.

7. Claims handling and distribution, priority of security.

8. Detrimental acts, avoidance actions.

9. Jurisdiction over actions related to insolvency proceedings, in particular for civil claims to set a transaction aside (*actio pauliana*).

10. Registration and publication of proceedings.

11. Cooperation and communication between liquidators, judicial cooperation between courts, electronic forms in all languages, interconnection of insolvency registers beyond the scope of the project currently carried out in the framework of the European e-Justice Portal.

12. Coherence, synergies and coordination between the Regulation, particularly Articles 3, 10 and Annex A, and the Directive on the protection of employees in case of insolvency of the employer – (including case law where co-operation between the various national guarantee institutions is needed and analysed).

The timing of the review, if any, of the Regulation is as yet unclear. The report issued on the basis of the points of interest, originally due for the summer of 2012, was made public in December 2012. In October 2012, the Insolvency Regulation did feature in the European Commission's second round (list of intended) of proposals to shake up the Single Market, 'Single Market Act II'.[699] A proposal for review was published as COM(2012) 744.

As noted above, there is one very important limit to the Insolvency Regulation in its current form: it does *not* harmonise insolvency law. There are substantial differences in the general approach to insolvency proceedings: what level of protection is given to 'weaker' creditors, such as employees; whether and how there is State intervention in the proceedings; whether courts play a central role or leave creditors (or certain categories of creditors) in the driving seat; etc. These are not at all addressed by the Regulation.

The Commission eventually tabled a proposal with two angles: firstly, what one could call a procedural angle (firmly within the Conflicts area, especially in terms of recognition

---

[699] COM(2012) 573: Communication on the 'Single Market Act II – Together for new growth'.

and enforcement), which would continue the current focus of not harmonising insolvency law (although the last element of these comes close): SIMA II on this angle:

> We thus need to establish conditions for the EU wide recognition of national insolvency and debt-discharge schemes, which enable financially distressed enterprises to become again competitive participants in the economy. We need to ensure simple and efficient insolvency proceedings, whenever there are assets or debts in several Member States. Rules are needed for the insolvency of groups of companies that maximise their chances of survival. To this end, the Commission will table a legislative proposal modernising the European Insolvency Regulation.

Secondly, a more substantial angle which would actually aim to create a (step-up to a) European insolvency law: SIMA II on this angle:

> However, we need to go further. At present, there is in many Member States little tolerance for failure and current rules do not allow honest innovators to fail 'quickly and cheaply'. We need to set up the route towards measures and incentives for Member States to take away the stigma of failure associated with insolvency and to reduce overly long debt discharge periods. We also need to consider how the efficiency of national insolvency laws can be further improved with a view to creating a level playing field for companies, entrepreneurs and private persons within the internal market. To this end, the Commission will table a Communication together with the revision of the European Insolvency Regulation.

The Commission effectively already throws in the towel on trying to convince Member States that some kind of harmonised Insolvency laws (especially with a view to installing a 'right to fail') ought to be agreed: the second leg of the exercise, as the above extract indicates, will probably merely consist of a Communication.

6

Free Movement of Establishment, *Lex Societatis* and Private International Law

In family law, the status and capacity of a natural person is largely determined by a person's nationality, which generally stays with it for life,[700] or, particularly in common law countries, by a person's domicile, which is less fixed but nevertheless assumes strong links with a particularly State.[701]-[702] The corporate equivalent of nationality and domicile is the *lex societatis*. It is the 'personal law' or corporate identity of companies.[703] It often determines 'whether the company had been validly created; what its constitution is; what the powers are of its organs, officers and shareholders; whether it has been merged with another company; and whether it has been dissolved.'[704] These in others words are the corporate equivalents of life and death, capacity, marriage, divorce, adoption etc. However one must not assume too much consensus on what is covered by the *lex societatis*. For instance there is no consensus on corporate governance regulations being part of the *lex societatis*, or shareholder agreements either before or after the creation of the company.

What State determines the *lex societatis*, in other words what State may assign (or deprive) corporate identity to a company, in practice is largely confined to two competing models. Just as in family law nationality does not always sit easily with domicile, so, too, in company law, the 'real seat' theory does not see eye to eye with the 'incorporation' theory. Both theories represent different views on corporate identity; and because corporate identity, as noted, determines a whole range of issues, obtaining and losing one's corporate identity has an immediate private international law impact. In the EU, the extent to which national law links consequences to the (loss of) attachment with a Member State's territory is closely tied in with the application by the Court of Justice of the Treaty's Articles on the free movement of establishment: it is to these cases that current chapter turns its attention.[705]

---

[700] Lest of course the person changes nationality, or loses one through the particulars of the nationality laws of the State concerned.

[701] See also Meeusen, J., Pertegas, M., Straetmans, G., and Swennen, F., (eds.) *International Family Law for the European Union*, Oxford, Intersentia, 2007.

[702] The notion of 'habitual residence' is something of an attempt at reconciling both.

[703] Hartley, T.C., *International Commercial Litigation*, Cambridge, CUP, 2009, 506.

[704] *Ibid.*

[705] See generally and extensively, Borg-Barthet, J., *The governing law of companies in EU law*, Oxford, Hart, 2012.

The real seat theory determines that the *lex societatis* is that of the State where the company has its 'real seat', or effective seat. This will be the case if or from the moment the company concerned carries out a certain level of activity within that Member State. Such activity can be quite diverse and States using the real seat theory operate different types of thresholds to that effect: turnover, presence of staff, presence of head office and/or senior management.[706] The incorporation theory, by contrast, holds that the *lex societatis* is that of the State where the company was incorporated. The factual development of the activities of that company, in this view, has no impact on the determination of the *lex societatis*.[707]

Contrary to intuition, it is the incorporation theory which is generally seen as being favoured by countries with a liberal outlook on economic policy. Proponents of the incorporation theory argue that the country of incorporation not only determines applicable law[708] (for the issues that are covered by the *lex societatis* see the discussion above), but also that other countries need to recognise the corporate nationality of the undertaking thus established. Countries who favour the real seat theory (which at first sight would seem more hospitable to unrestricted freedom of manoeuvre), argue that a State's laws (including tax laws, labour laws, minority shareholder rights etc.) ought to apply to all companies who exceed a certain threshold of activity on their territory. Moreover, some of the real seat countries (indeed arguably the purest form of the theory) insist that such threshold having been met, a company ought to formalise its factual relationship with that country by re-incorporating as a company of that State. Germany's *Bundesgerichtshof* argues that where the connecting factor is taken to be the place of incorporation, the company's founding members are placed at an advantage, since they are able, when choosing the place of incorporation, to choose the legal system which suits them best. Therein, according to the *Bundesgerichtshof*, lies the fundamental weakness of the incorporation principle, which fails to take account of the fact that a company's incorporation and activities also affect the interests of third parties and of the State in which the company has its actual centre of administration, where that is located in a State other than the one in which the company was incorporated. By contrast, where the connecting factor is taken to be the actual centre of administration, that prevents the provisions of company law in the State in which the actual centre of administration is situated, which are intended to protect certain vital interests, notably those of the company's creditors, from being circumvented by incorporating the company abroad.[709]

The latter element of course is where the EU's freedom of establishment comes in: back and forth re-incorporation evidently is not conducive to the Internal Market.[710] Exercising the right of establishment can take two forms: on the one hand, subsidiaries,

---

[706] I appreciate the comparison does not hold, however the fact that the connecting factor for the *lex societatis* is therefore changeable in accordance with factual circumstances of firm character makes this theory akin to the domicile approach for natural persons.

[707] Therefore this approach is more akin to the nationality approach for natural persons.

[708] Although even the most staunch supporters of the incorporation theory will apply a certain form of border regulatory adjustment, applying national law to incoming corporations, to protect a number of interests (e.g. legitimate expectations of third parties).

[709] See the reference to the view of the *Bundesgerichtshof* in Case C-208/00 *Überseering* [2002] ECR I-9919, para 15–16.

[710] Indeed the serious consequences attached to the lack of re-incorporation in the country of destination, may even be regarded as a breach of proprietary rights under the European Convention for the Protection of Human Rights and Fundamental Freedoms – ECHR.

branches or agencies may be set up. That is known as secondary establishment. Establishment may also take the form of the setting-up of a new company or the transfer of the central management and control of the company, often regarded as its real head office. That is called "primary establishment.[711]

Article 49

(ex Article 43 TEC)

Within the framework of the provisions set out below, restrictions on the freedom of establishment of nationals of a Member State in the territory of another Member State shall be prohibited. Such prohibition shall also apply to restrictions on the setting-up of agencies, branches or subsidiaries by nationals of any Member State established in the territory of any Member State.

Freedom of establishment shall include the right to take up and pursue activities as self-employed persons and to set up and manage undertakings, in particular companies or firms within the meaning of the second paragraph of Article 54, under the conditions laid down for its own nationals by the law of the country where such establishment is effected, subject to the provisions of the Chapter relating to capital.

Article 50 TFEU foresees harmonisation to accompany the principal freedom:

Article 50

(ex Article 44 TEC)

1. In order to attain freedom of establishment as regards a particular activity, the European Parliament and the Council, acting in accordance with the ordinary legislative procedure and after consulting the Economic and Social Committee, shall act by means of directives.

2. The European Parliament, the Council and the Commission shall carry out the duties devolving upon them under the preceding provisions, in particular:

(a) by according, as a general rule, priority treatment to activities where freedom of establishment makes a particularly valuable contribution to the development of production and trade;
(b) by ensuring close cooperation between the competent authorities in the Member States in order to ascertain the particular situation within the Union of the various activities concerned;
(c) by abolishing those administrative procedures and practices, whether resulting from national legislation or from agreements previously concluded between Member States, the maintenance of which would form an obstacle to freedom of establishment;
(d) by ensuring that workers of one Member State employed in the territory of another Member State may remain in that territory for the purpose of taking up activities therein as self-employed persons, where they satisfy the conditions which they would be required to satisfy if they were entering that State at the time when they intended to take up such activities;
(e) by enabling a national of one Member State to acquire and use land and buildings situated in the territory of another Member State, in so far as this does not conflict with the principles laid down in Article 39(2);
(f) by effecting the progressive abolition of restrictions on freedom of establishment in every branch of activity under consideration, both as regards the conditions for setting up agencies, branches or subsidiaries in the territory of a Member State and as regards the subsidiaries in the territory of a Member State and as regards the conditions governing the entry of

---

[711] Darmon AG in Case 81/87 *Daily Mail*, [1988] ECR 5483, 4.

personnel belonging to the main establishment into managerial or supervisory posts in such agencies, branches or subsidiaries;

(g) by coordinating to the necessary extent the safeguards which, for the protection of the interests of members and others, are required by Member States of companies or firms within the meaning of the second paragraph of Article 54 with a view to making such safeguards equivalent throughout the Union;

(h) by satisfying themselves that the conditions of establishment are not distorted by aids granted by Member States.

However it is fair to say that the harmonisation envisaged by this Article is very incomplete (the *Societas Europaea Directive*[712] and the Cross-border Merger Directive[713] being the limited successes so far).

Article 293 EC (formerly Article 220 EEC, repealed after Lisbon) provided

Member States shall, so far as is necessary, enter into negotiations with each other with a view to securing for the benefit of their nationals: (…)

— the mutual recognition of companies or firms within the meaning of the second paragraph of Article 48, the retention of legal personality in the event of transfer of their seat from one country to another, and the possibility of mergers between companies or firms governed by the laws of different countries;(…)

This Article however did not constitute a reserve of legislative competence vested in the Member States. Although Article 293 EC gave Member States the opportunity to enter into negotiations with a view, *inter alia*, to facilitating the resolution of problems arising from the discrepancies between the various laws relating to the mutual recognition of companies and the retention of legal personality in the event of the transfer of their seat from one country to another, it does so solely 'so far as is necessary', that is to say if the provisions of the Treaty do not enable its objectives to be attained.[714]

The provisions of the Treaty concerning freedom of establishment apply to measures of the Member State of origin which affect the establishment in another Member State of one of its nationals or of a company incorporated under its legislation,[715] and to measures of the Member State of destination which affect the establishment in that Member State of a nationals or of a company incorporated under the legislation of another Member State.[716]

---

[712] Regulation 2157/2001 on the Statute for a European company (SE), OJ [2001] L294/1, and Directive 2001/86 supplementing the Statute for a European company with regard to the involvement of employees, OJ [2001] L294/22.

[713] Directive 2005/56 on cross-border mergers of limited liability companies, OJ [2005] L310/1.

[714] Case C-208/00 *Überseering*, n 709 above, para 54.

[715] See ex multis Case C-9/02 *deLasteyrie du Saillant* [2004] ECR I-2409, para 42; Case C-418/07 *Papillon* [2008] ECR I-8947, para 16; Case C-247/08 *Gaz de France – Berliner Investissement* [2009] ECR I-9225, para 55; and Case C-311/08 *SGI* [2010] ECR I-487, para 39.

[716] Case C-212/97 *Centros* [1999] ECR I-1459.

6.1 *DAILY MAIL*

In *Daily Mail*,[717] in the words of Darmon AG, company law met tax law. In the United Kingdom, the connecting factors governing the application to a legal person of those branches of law are not necessarily the same. The concept of incorporation, as it is understood in English law, makes it possible to dissociate a company's domicile, expressed through its registered office, and its nationality, on the one hand, from its residence, which largely determines the tax rules applicable to it, on the other. The proceedings pending before the national court arose from the possibility of such a separation. Daily Mail wanted to transfer its central management and control – but continue its incorporation under UK law – purely for tax reasons: it wishes to escape capital gains tax after the sale of a significant part of its non-permanent assets, to use the proceeds of that sale to by its own shares.[718] Under UK company legislation a company such as the defendant, incorporated under that legislation and having its registered office in the UK, may establish its central management and control outside the UK without losing legal personality or ceasing to be a company incorporated in the UK. According to the relevant tax legislation, only companies which are resident for tax purposes in the UK are as a rule liable to UK corporation tax. A company is resident for tax purposes in the place in which its central management and control is located. The Income and Corporation Taxes Act 1970 prohibited companies resident for tax purposes in the UK from ceasing to be so resident without the consent of the Treasury. The Treasury agreed but only on condition of sales of a number of assets: in other words, the Treasury wanted to claw back at least part of the tax this lost. Does this infringe Daily Mail's free movement of establishment?

The ECJ held that freedom of establishment works both ways: it protects both companies entering a Member State and those leaving a Member State. However, in the then state of Community law, there was no harmonisation of the laws of incorporation (even now this is embryonic); corporations exist by virtue of the law, and at that moment, this was national law (and it continues to be so):

> (…) it should be borne in mind that, unlike natural persons, companies are creatures of the law and, in the present state of Community law, creatures of national law. They exist only by virtue of the varying national legislation which determines their incorporation and functioning. (Daily Mail, at para 19).

Any harmonisation which had taken place had not dealt with any of the differences in national law which were at issue in the Daily Mail proceedings, hence the Court held that the scope for a Member State to attach consequences to a corporation leaving its territory, in the absence moreover of Community law imposing a specific connecting factor (real seat or incorporation), is necessarily wide.

It must therefore be held that the Treaty regards the differences in national legislation concerning the required connecting factor and the question whether – and if so how – the registered office

---

[717] Case 81/87 *Daily Mail and General Trust* ('*Daily Mail*') [1988] ECR 5483.

[718] After establishing its central management and control in the Netherlands the applicant would be subject to Netherlands corporation tax, but the transactions envisaged would be taxed only on the basis of any capital gains which accrued after the transfer of its residence for tax purposes.

or real head office of a company incorporated under national law may be transferred from one Member State to another as problems which are not resolved by the rules concerning the right of establishment but must be dealt with by future legislation or conventions. Under those circumstances, Articles 52 and 58 of the Treaty cannot be interpreted as conferring on companies incorporated under the law of a Member State a right to transfer their central management and control and their central administration to another Member State while retaining their status as companies incorporated under the legislation of the first Member State. (Daily Mail, at para 23–24).

The Court therefore did not question the principal right, under the freedom of establishment, for a company to move its registered or real head office, but gave the State or origin a wide margin of manoeuvre in attaching consequences to such move. Incidentally, Darmon AG did opine on what minimum kind of (economic) presence would be required for a company to be able to be enjoy the freedom of establishment: he emphasises that the freedom of establishment requires a genuine economic link, that EU law should provide criteria for national authorities to decide whether such exercise was genuine, and, with reference to *Leclerc*,[719] that Community law offers no assistance where 'objective factors' show that a particular activity was carried out 'in order to circumvent' national legislation:

> In order to determine whether the transfer of the central management and control of a company constitutes establishment within the meaning of the Treaty it is therefore necessary to take into consideration a range of factors . The place at which the management of the company meets is undoubtedly one of the foremost of those factors, as is the place, normally the same, at which general policy decisions are made. However, in certain circumstances those factors may be neither exclusive nor even decisive. It might be necessary to take account of the residence of the principal managers, the place at which general meetings are held, the place at which administrative and accounting documents are kept and the place at which the company's principal financial activities are carried on, in particular, the place at which it operates a bank account. That list cannot be regarded as exhaustive. Moreover, those factors may have to be given different weight according to whether, for example, the company is engaged in production or investment. In the latter case, it may be perfectly legitimate to take account of the market on which the company's commercial or stock exchange transactions are mainly carried out and the scale of those transactions.[720]

Finally, it is worth emphasising that *Daily Mail* only concerns the treatment by the State of origin in the case of identity-preserving outbound corporate immigration.[721]

---

[719] Case 229/83 *Edouard Leclerc*, [1985] ECR 1.

[720] n 711 above, 8.

[721] See also Panayi, C., 'Corporate Mobility in Private International Law and European Community Law: Debunking Some Myths' *Oxford Yearbook of European Law*, 2009, 124–130.

6.2 *CENTROS*

In *Centros*,[722] a private (i.e. non-listed) limited liability company which had never traded in England, its State of incorporation, wishes to establish a branch (not: relocate its seat to) in Denmark however Denmark refuses: it suggested the absence of trading in the UK effectively meant that Centros wanted to really establish its principal establishment in Denmark, rather than a branch. Allowing this, so Denmark suggested, effectively would give Centros an opportunity to circumvent Danish corporate requirements, including minimum capital requirements. In other words: Denmark argued that one had to have a minimum economic activity in the State of origin for one to enjoy the free movement of establishment to another Member State.

The ECJ disagreed: a company formed in accordance with the laws of the home Member State, enjoys free movement of establishment even if that initial incorporation was purely meant subsequently to use the free movement of establishment to move to another Member State. This does not prevent a receiving Member State from taking measures to prevent fraud, however such measures need to be case-specific. Not generic and certainly not aimed at cases such as this:[723] the Treaty articles on the free movement of establishment were designed to enable exactly the kind of corporate movement as attempted by Centros.[724] 'Exercising the right of establishment in the Member State that offered it the most favourable conditions in respect of the paid-up capital requirement, a procedure which is exactly one of the objectives freedom of establishment is designed to achieve. The ability to take advantage of the opportunities offered by different types of company in other countries and differences in the regulations of Member States does not in itself constitute unlawful circumvention of national rules.'[725]

The fact that a national of a Member State who wishes to set up a company chooses to form it in the Member State whose rules of company law seem to him the least restrictive and to set up branches in other Member States was not, in itself, an abuse of the right of establishment. In *Kefalas*, the Court defined 'abuse' as follows: a person abuses the right conferred on him if he exercises it unreasonably to derive, to the detriment of others, an improper advantage, manifestly contrary to the objective' pursued by the legislator in conferring that particular right on the individual.[726]

In other words, in *Centros* the Court employed an extensive interpretation of the concept of freedom of establishment and a narrow interpretation of the concept of abuse. La Pergola AG, incidentally, rejected the attempts at identifying a 'minimum' economic activity which would be enough to trigger protection under the Treaty. Such minimum

---

[722] Case C-212/97 *Centros* [1999] ECR I-1459.

[723] '[A]lthough, in such circumstances, the national courts may, case by case, take account – on the basis of objective evidence – of abuse or fraudulent conduct on the part of the persons concerned in order, where appropriate, to deny them the benefit of the provisions of Community law on which they seek to rely, they must nevertheless assess such conduct in the light of the objectives pursued by those provisions': *Centros*, para 25.

[724] It did not help that the Danish authorities conceded that, had the company concerned had conducted even a tiny bit of business in the United Kingdom, its branch would have been registered in Denmark, even though Danish creditors might have been equally exposed to risk: see *Centros*, para 35.

[725] This is the Commission's view as summarised by La Pergola AG in *Centros*, [1999] ECR I-1461, at 10.

[726] Case C-367/96 *Kefalas* [1998] ECR I-2843, para 28.

economic link is only specifically provided for third countries,[727] while for intra-Union companies, there is no need to inquire into the nature and content of the activities the company is pursuing or intends to pursue: Article 49 very clearly has no provisions whatsoever to that effect.[728]

Daily Mail distinguishes from *Centros*: the former deals with identity-preserving outbound corporate immigration: what is the scope of manoeuvre for the home State? *Centros* deals with inbound corporate immigration: what freedom does the receiving Member State have to restrict this?

6.3 *ÜBERSEERING*

In *Überseering*,[729] a Dutch company, with two sites in Germany which it is having refurbished, had a disagreement over the works with its contractors and wishes to sue in Germany. In the meantime, two German nationals have acquired all the shares in the company. The German court dismisses the action: it holds, in line with established German case-law, that since the claims was initiated, the company has transferred its actual seat of administration and hence should have re-incorporated under German law; its failure to do so meant that it could not sue in Germany. According to the settled case-law of the *Bundesgerichtshof*, a company's legal capacity is determined by reference to the law applicable in the place where its actual centre of administration is established ('*Sitztheorie*' or company seat principle), as opposed to the '*Gründungstheorie*' or incor-poration principle, by virtue of which legal capacity is determined in accordance with the law of the State in which the company was incorporated. That rule also applies where a company has been validly incorporated in another State and has subsequently transferred its actual centre of administration to Germany. This case in other words presented the Court with the distinction between the real seat theory and the incorporation theory in its purest form.

The Court took great care to distinguish *Daily Mail*: in *Daily Mail* the company pur-posely wished to transfer its actual centre of administration from the Member State where it had incorporated, and to retain its legal incorporation there – *Überseering* by contrast concerns the *recognition* by one Member State of a company incorporated under the laws of another Member State. *Überseering* never gave any indication that it intended to transfer its seat to Germany. Its legal existence was never called in question under the law of the State where it was incorporated as a result of all its shares being transferred to persons resident in Germany. In particular, the company was not subject to any winding-up measures under Netherlands law. Under Netherlands law, it did not cease to be validly incorporated. The Court added that even if arguendo the dispute before the national court is seen as concerning a transfer of the actual centre of administration from one country to another, the interpretation of *Daily Mail* put forward by inter alia Germany, was incorrect.

---

[727] The need for 'an effective and continuous link' with the economy of a Member State, solely in a case in which the company has nothing but its registered office within the Union, is required by the General Programme for the abolition of restrictions on freedom to provide services, OJ [1962] 2/32.

[728] La Pergola AG in *Centros*, n 725 above, 1473–74.

[729] Case C-208/00 *Überseering*, n 709 above.

The Court did not rule on the question whether where, as here, a company incorporated under the law of a Member State ('A') is found, under the law of another Member State ('B'), to have moved its actual centre of administration to Member State B, that State is entitled to refuse to recognise the legal personality which the company enjoys under the law of its State of incorporation ('A'). The Court did not intend to recognise a Member State as having the power, *vis-à-vis* companies validly incorporated in other Member States and found by it to have transferred their seat to its territory, to subject those companies' effective exercise in its territory of the freedom of establishment to compliance with its domestic company law.[730]

The refusal to give standing or to recognise the legal capacity of a company validly incorporated in another Member State was a restriction to the freedom of establishment which could not be justified. The requirement of reincorporation of the same company in Germany was tantamount to outright negation of freedom of establishment. Germany argued that the German rules of private international company law enhance legal certainty and creditor protection. It played specifically no the absence of harmonisation and hence the absence of any kind of pre-emption: There is no harmonisation at Union level of the rules for protecting the share capital of limited liability companies and such companies are subject in Member States other than Germany to requirements which are in some respects much less strict. The company seat principle as applied by German law ensures that a company whose principal place of business is in Germany has a fixed minimum share capital, something which is instrumental in protecting parties with whom it enters into contracts and its creditors. That also prevents distortions of competition since all companies whose principal place of business is in Germany are subject to the same legal requirements.[731] Germany also referred to employee protection and tax administration. The Court however dealt with these arguments briefly. It is not inconceivable that overriding requirements relating to the general interest, such as the protection of the interests of creditors, minority shareholders, employees and even the taxation authorities, may, in certain circumstances and subject to certain conditions, justify restrictions on freedom of establishment The sudden death implications of the German rule, are tantamount to an outright negation of the freedom of establishment conferred on companies, for which there can be no justification.[732]

In *Überseering*, the Court was at pains to judge on the specific issue of the change in shareholder structure leading to the company not having any standing at all in Germany.

6.4 *INSPIRE ART*

The facts in *Inspire Art*[733] were similar to *Centros*. Inspire Art Ltd was formed under the law of the United Kingdom, and the dispute concerns principally whether the entry relating to its Netherlands branch in the Netherlands commercial register must be supplemented by the words 'formally foreign company'. The *Dutch Wet op de formeel*

---

[730] *Ibid*, para 72.
[731] *Ibid* para 87.
[732] *Ibid* para 92–93.
[733] Case C-167//01 *Inspire Art* [2003] ECR I-10155.

buitenlandse vennootschappen (Law on formally foreign companies) provides that these supplementary words must appear in the commercial register and must be used in the course of business. There were also other, connected legal obligations which may also restrict freedom of establishment, such as minimum capital requirements, personal joint and several liability of directors and other formal requirements.

All of Inspire Art's activities were carried out in The Netherlands and there was no firm intention to carry out any activity in the UK. The only reason for incorporation in the UK, were the rules on minimum share capital.

The Court firstly took its references to absent harmonisation, in *Daily Mail* and *Centros*, to their logical conclusion: to the degree that provisions of the Dutch Law on formally foreign companies concerned disclosure regulations which had been harmonised by the company Directives, and were compatible with those provisions, they cannot be regarded as constituting any impediment to freedom of establishment. On the other hand, there were a number of disclosure obligations under the Dutch law which were not included in the harmonisation directives. The relevant Directive having been found by the Court to be exhaustive, the ECJ held that any additional disclosure requirements were illegal.

The assessment *vis-a-vis* the freedom of establishment was therefore eventually limited to those obligations which were not disclosure obligations, in particular, the rules relating to the minimum capital required, both at the time of registration and for so long as a formally foreign company exists, and those relating to the penalty attaching to non-compliance with the obligations laid down by the Dutch law namely, the joint and several liability of the directors with the company. The Court again was unimpressed by the reference by the Dutch government to the fact that more and more companies employed the favourable regime in other Member States, to incorporate there, and carry out their activities mainly or even exclusively in The Netherlands ('brass-plate companies: those with no real connection with the State of formation). The reasons for which a company chooses to be formed in a particular Member State are, save in the case of fraud, irrelevant with regard to application of the rules on freedom of establishment.[734]

The ECJ again held that the blank application[735] by the Dutch authorities of their domestic rules was incompatible with the free movement of establishment. It failed to indicate where the boundaries of national room for manoeuvre would lie, were the Member State to apply such restriction *ad hoc*, case-specific, rather than across the board in an absolute manner. In other words: exactly which laws of the State of incorporation travel with it and which the receiving State can impose, remained unclear, as did whether those requirements would then come on top of the rules of the state of incorporation, or would replace them.

---

[734] *Ibid*, para 95.
[735] With a complication for those arguments relating to public interest whose use had been pre-empted by the relevant Directive.

6.5 *CARTESIO* – AND ITS MIRROR IMAGE: *VALE*

In *Cartesio*[736] a company incorporated in Hungary wanted to change its operational headquarters to Italy but keep Hungarian incorporation. Hungarian corporate law does not allow for this: a company can keep its Hungarian incorporation but only if it moves headquarters within Hungary. Otherwise it has to dissolve in Hungary and incorporate elsewhere. Pursuant to Hungarian company law, the seat of a company constituted under Hungarian law is the place where its operational headquarters are situated. In other words, the place where a company has its operational headquarters is supposed to coincide with its place of incorporation. A transfer of the operational headquarters of a company constituted under Hungarian law will normally be entered into the commercial register if the transfer takes place within Hungary. Cartesio seeks to transfer its operational headquarters to Italy. However, instead of reconstituting itself as an Italian company, Cartesio wishes to remain incorporated in Hungary and thus subject to Hungarian company law. The *Cartesio* scenario in other words was the first opportunity for the Court to revisit the very scenario which led to *Daily Mail*: outbound corporate migration, with a question mark on the room for manoeuvre for the home State.

Maduro AG suggested overruling *Daily Mail* on the grounds that case-law has evolved since. In particular: in case-law on the room for manoeuvre for the receiving State, the Court has held, see above, that absolute refusals such as these are *non sequitur*: one may have specific *ad hoc* reasons. The Advocate General argued that the efforts by the ECJ at distinguishing *Daily Mail* were unconvincing and confusing. With reference to a crucial consideration in *Daily Mail*, Maduro AG opined that

> it is impossible, in my view, to argue on the basis of the current state of Community law that Member States enjoy an absolute freedom to determine the 'life and death' of companies constituted under their domestic law, irrespective of the consequences for the freedom of establishment.[737]

In applying the *Centros* et al case-law, the AG suggested that the blank Hungarian refusal fell foul of the freedom of establishment:

> The rules currently under consideration completely deny the possibility for a company constituted under Hungarian law to transfer its operational headquarters to another Member State. Hungarian law, as applied by the commercial court, does not merely set conditions for such a transfer, but instead requires that the company be dissolved. Especially since the Hungarian Government has not put forward any grounds of justification, it is difficult to see how such 'an outright negation of the freedom of establishment' could be necessary for reasons of public interest.[738]

The ECJ disagreed, however, and found the Hungarian rules to be acceptable, citing the crucial considerations of the *Daily Mail* case. The Court insisted that the state of harmonisation of company law was not such as to take away the differences between the Member States in the core issues which are at issue in the facts of the case.[739] The one distinction which the Court made, related to the 'sudden death' sanction in case *Cartesio* were to have sought re-incorporation under Italian law: *Cartesio* itself sought to transfer its seat

---

[736] Case C-210/06 *Cartesio* [2008] ECR I-9641.
[737] Opinion Maduro AG in Case C-210/06 *Cartesio*, [2008] ECR I-9641, at 31.
[738] *Ibid*, at 34 (footnotes omitted).
[739] *Cartesio* para 114.

without re-incorporation; that can be stopped by Hungarian law. However this would be different, were Cartesio to have sought reincorporation under Italian law (assuming Italian law would be happy to let such re-incorporation go ahead): that would also have been denied by Hungarian law, which requires liquidation in Hungary first. That would be unacceptable in the view of the Court.[740]

In Cartesio, therefore, the Court stuck to its perceived dichotomy between in- and outbound migration, despite a plea by Maduro AG to approximate the two. The court then added an obiter in para 112:

> In fact, in that latter case, the power referred to in paragraph 110 above, far from implying that national legislation on the incorporation and winding-up of companies enjoys any form of immunity from the rules of the EC Treaty on freedom of establishment, cannot, in particular, justify the Member State of incorporation, by requiring the winding-up or liquidation of the company, in preventing that company from converting itself into a company governed by the law of the other Member State, to the extent that it is permitted under that law to do so.

[the English version of the text in fact is not the clearest]

That obiter got many excited, and confused: do the final words of para 112 imply that the host Member State can choose whether to accept such re-incorporation, or rather, does Article 49 TFEU imply that the host Member State has no choice but to accept such re-incorporation?

In *Cartesio*, a company incorporated in Hungary wanted to change its operational headquarters to Italy but keep Hungarian incorporation. Hungarian corporate law does not allow for this: a company can keep its Hungarian incorporation but only if it moves headquarters within Hungary. Otherwise it has to dissolve in Hungary and incorporate elsewhere.

Case C-378/10 *Vale*[741], is a mirror image:[742] an Italian company wants to dissolve in Italy and re-incorporate in Hungary, and it wishes its Italian predecessor to be recognised as its legal predecessor, meaning all rights and obligations of the old company transfer to the new. A procedure which is perfectly possible for Hungarian companies, within Hungary: in particular, by changing company form. Vale's application for registration was rejected. The obiter in *Cartesio* led to speculation whether the host Member State is under a duty to co-operate with such conversion (as opposed to *Cartesio*, which sought to establish the limits to obstruction by the home Member State).

The Court in my view/in my reading of the judgment took a perfectly logical approach to the obiter: 'to the extent that it is permitted under that law to do so' refers to the existence of a national conversion procedure. If nationally incorporated companies may convert and transfer all rights and obligations to the new company, any restrictions on foreign companies employing this mechanism come within the reach of Article 49 TFEU.

There may be reasons for the host Member State to restrict this possibility in specific instances (for reasons of e.g. protection of the interests of creditors, minority shareholders and employees, the preservation of the effectiveness of fiscal supervision and the fairness of commercial transactions: see para 39 of *Vale*), however none of these apply here:

---

[740] *Ibid* paras 112–113.
[741] Judgment of 12 July 2012, not yet reported in ECR.
[742] See also Rammeloo, S., 'Companies migrating in Europe', Workshop corporate law Ius Commune Research School, Utrecht November 2011, slide-deck available via http://www.rechten.unimaas.nl/iuscommune/activities/2011/2011–11–24/workshop3_Rammeloo.pdf (last consulted 11 November 2012).

Hungarian law precludes, in a general manner, cross-border conversions, with the result that it prevents such operations from being carried out even if the interests mentioned in paragraph 39 above are not threatened in any event (para 40).

The host Member State must therefore open the possibility of conversion to foreign registered companies, (only) if it has such conversion possibility in its own corporate laws. Any conditions imposed by national law (documentation, proof of actual economic continuity of operations etc.) may also be imposed on these foreign companies, provided this is done in a transparent, non-discriminatory fashion, and in a way which does not jeopardise the actual freedom of establishment.

It is interesting to note that the Court recycled (as it did in Cartesio), the very core Daily Mail quote which explains its hesitation effectively to harmonise corporate law itself, through too drastic an interpretation of Article 49 TFEU:

> companies are creatures of national law and exist only by virtue of the national legislation which determines their incorporation and functioning (Vale, para 27).

No doubt many corporate law implications escape me,[743] and will lead to further cases at the Court.

6.6 *GRID INDUS*

Grid Indus[744] is the most recent development (other than Vale reported above) in this area. National Grid Indus is a limited liability company incorporated under Netherlands law. Until 15 December 2000 its place of effective management was in the Netherlands. The company has since 10 June 1996 had a considerable claim, in Sterling, against National Grid Company plc., a company established in the UK. Following the rise in value of the pound sterling against the Dutch guilder, an unrealised exchange rate gain was generated on that claim. On 15 December 2000 National Grid Indus transferred its place of effective management to the UK. National Grid Indus in principle remained liable to tax indefinitely in the Netherlands, because it was incorporated under Netherlands law. However, by virtue of Article 4(3) of the double taxation Convention between the UK and The Netherlands, National Grid Indus was deemed to be resident in the UK after the transfer of its place of effective management. Since after that transfer it no longer had a permanent establishment within the meaning of the Convention in the Netherlands, only the UK was entitled to tax its profits and capital gains after the transfer, in accordance with the Convention. There had to be a final settlement of the unrealised capital gains at the time of the transfer of the company's place of management. The tax authorities ruled that National Grid Indus should be taxed immediately, inter alia on the exchange rate gain mentioned above.

Can a company incorporated under the law of a Member State which transfers its place of effective management to another Member State and is taxed by the former Member

---

[743] See Biermeyer, T., and Holtrichter, T. 'The missing puzzle in judge-made European law on corporate migration?', *Columbia Journal of European Law*, 2011, online version: http://www.cjel.net/online/18_1-biermeyer/(last consulted 25 October 2012).

[744] Case C-371/10 *National Grid Indus VB*, not yet published in ECR (judgment of 29 November 2011).

State on the occasion of that transfer rely on Article 49 TFEU against that Member State? The UK and The Netherlands referred to *Daily Mail* to argue that Article 49 TFEU leaves untouched the Member States' power to enact legislation, including fiscal rules relating to transfers between Member States of the places of management of undertakings. The Court's interpretation of that article in *Daily Mail and General Trust* and *Cartesio*, they suggested, does not concern solely the conditions of the incorporation and functioning of companies under national company law. They submitted that, if a Member State has power to require a company leaving its territory to be wound up and liquidated, it must also be regarded as having power to impose fiscal requirements if it applies the system – more advantageous from the point of view of the single market – of transferring the place of management while retaining legal personality.

The Court held firstly that neither the judgments in *Daily Mail* and *Cartesio* nor the Treaty itself, negate the possibility for companies such as in the case at issue, to call upon the freedom of establishment to challenge the lawfulness of a tax imposed on it by the former Member State on the occasion of the transfer of the place of effective management.[745] Further, the Court held that a company incorporated under Netherlands law wishing to transfer its place of effective management outside Netherlands territory, in the exercise of its right guaranteed by Article 49 TFEU, is placed at a disadvantage in terms of cash flow compared to a similar company retaining its place of effective management in the Netherlands: the later are not taxed until the gains are actually realised and to the extent that they are realised. That difference of treatment relating to the taxation of capital gains is liable to deter a company incorporated under Netherlands law from transferring its place of management to another Member State.

Can the difference be justified? The Court recognised of course the importance of preserving the allocation of powers of taxation between the Member States. The transfer of the place of effective management of a company of one Member State to another Member State cannot mean that the Member State of origin has to abandon its right to tax a capital gain which arose within the ambit of its powers of taxation before the transfer. Establishing *the amount of tax* at the time of the transfer of a company's place of effective management complies with the principle of proportionality. It is proportionate for that Member State, for the purpose of safeguarding the exercise of its powers of taxation, to determine the tax due on the unrealised capital gains that have arisen in its territory at the time when its power of taxation in respect of the company in question ceases to exist, in the present case the time of the transfer of the company's place of effective management to another Member State.[746]

However, while determination of the tax at that time may be proportionate, *immediate recovery* at the same time, may not. Recovery of the tax debt at the time of the actual realisation in the host Member State of the asset in respect of which a capital gain was established by the authorities of the Member State of origin on the occasion of the transfer of a company's place of effective management to the host Member State may avoid the cash-flow problems which could be produced by the immediate recovery of the tax due on unrealised capital gains. Whether or not the Member State of origin's duty to set in motion an administrative follow-up of the company's assets, so as to allow it to trace when the asset is being realised, in itself may impose on the company a burden of

---

[745] *Grid Indus* para 33.
[746] *Ibid* para 52.

such nature as to also restrict the freedom of establishment, depends on the complexity or not of the company's asset movements. The State of origin may for instance also make recourse to bank guarantees to cover the recovery risk.

Deferred payment of tax does not represent, for the tax authorities of the Member States, an excessive burden in connection with tracing all the assets of a company in respect of which a capital gain had been ascertained at the time of the transfer of the company's place of effective management.[747] The Court held that the existing machinery for mutual assistance between the authorities of the Member States is sufficient to enable the Member State of origin to check the truthfulness of the returns made by companies which have opted for deferred payment of the tax.

Grid Indus does not overrule *Daily Mail* or *Cartesio*, and its ramifications are foremost relevant for the tax administration between the Member States (immediate recovery of the tax at the time the company transfers its place of management is not an option; deferred payment of tax has to be an option given the high opportunities for Member States to co-operate[748]). The Court does emphasise that contrary to the some of the Member States' wildest dreams perhaps, Daily Mail does not imply that the freedom of establishment cannot be invoked in the case of outgoing corporate mobility.

---

[747] *Ibid* para 75.

[748] It is noteworthy that the freedom of establishment (and the relevant case-law of the ECJ) applies to EFTA States, too. Hence Norway for instance has already (had to) adapt its relevant legislation. It has been pointed out ['Norway modifies exit tax rules to comply with ECJ ruling', DLA Piper international tax briefing, 26 June 2012, http://www.dlapiper.com/norway-modifies-exit-tax-rules-to-comply-with-ecj-ruling/(last visited 24 October 2012)] that in the absence of either an EU-wide or set of national definitions of when an unrealised capital gain is actually realised, 'tax planning opportunities' (indefinite forum shopping, effectively) arise so as to defer exit taxation near-indefinitely.

7

Private International Law, Corporate Social Responsibility and Extraterritoriality

7.1 THE ROLE OF PRIVATE INTERNATIONAL LAW IN OPERATIONALIZING CORPORATE SOCIAL RESPONSIBILITY

The EU is seeking ways to impose European law on activities carried out abroad. This is especially the case in the environmental and human rights fields, which are core elements of the so-called 'Corporate Social Responsibility' (CSR) Agenda. The European Commission used to describe CSR as 'a concept whereby companies integrate social and environmental concerns in their business operations and in their interaction with their stakeholders on a voluntary basis'.[749] It has in the meantime changed this to 'the responsibility of enterprises for their impacts on society.'[750] This is undoubtedly an attempt to re-align the EU approach to CSR, with international developments, in particular the *Ruggie* report: indeed the United Nations, too, has optimistically referred to the extraterritorial application of national law as being a key element in operationalizing human rights, labour rights and environmental protection. On the other hand, the very United States case-law on the Alien Torts Statute, often cited as the textbook example of employing national and international law, applied by national courts, to further the international community, has recently been reversed by the same circuit which launched its application. Appeal with the United States Supreme Court is underway.

Extraterritorial application of national law raises specific difficulties in each of the three steps of Private International Law: jurisdiction of national courts to hear the case; the choice of law to apply to the facts at issue; and the foreign recognition and enforcement of any resulting judgments. Adequate national/international private law scenarios are suggested as offering faster and less complex solutions than interstate disputes involving State responsibility and International Public Law issues.[751] Since the path-breaking *Doe v Unocal* litigation in 1997, more than 50 cases have been brought in the United States against companies under the Alien Tort Statute alleging corporate involvement in human

---

[749] COM(2001) 366.
[750] COM(2011) 681.
[751] Birnie, P., Boyle, A., Redgwell, C., *International Law & the Environment*, 3rd ed., Oxford, OUP, 2009; 303.

rights abuse abroad.[752] Amendments to EU Private International Law instruments are being suggested to increase jurisdiction for European courts in cases involving companies without European corporate 'roots', and to expand the application of European law to acts carried out outside of the EU.[753]

Reviewing the suitability of employing private international law as a way forward for what are essentially disputes with a high potential for upsetting inter-State relations, is particularly relevant in light of recent developments in case-law involving the Alien Tort Statute. In *Kiobel v Royal Dutch Petroleum*, the United States Court of Appeals for the Second Circuit held that corporations cannot be sued under the Alien Tort State for violations of customary international law because 'the concept of corporate liability [...] has not achieved universal recognition or acceptance of a norm in the relations of States with each other.'[754] In denying re-hearing, Chief Judge Jacobs argued in February 2011 that

> All the cases of the class affected by this case involve transnational corporations, many of them foreign. Such foreign companies are creatures of other states. They are subject to corporate governance and government regulation at home. They are often engines of their national economies, sustaining employees, pensioners and creditors–and paying taxes. I cannot think that there is some consensus among nations that American courts and lawyers have the power to bring to court transnational corporations of other countries, to inquire into their operations in third countries, to regulate them–and to beggar them by rendering their assets into compensatory damages, punitive damages, and (American) legal fees. Such proceedings have the natural tendency to provoke international rivalry, divisive interests, competition, and grievance–the very opposite of the universal consensus that sustains customary international law.

Judge Jacobs' frank assessment of the respective roles of public and private international law are particularly interesting when one considers the roots of modern private international law.

7.2 THE UNITED STATES: LITIGATION BASED ON THE ALIEN TORT STATUTE[755]

The Alien Tort Statute, a product of the United States' first congress, creates a domestic forum for violations of international law.

It is noteworthy that over and above the ATS controversy which we review below, more classic problems involving in particular recognition and enforcement, have an impact on the CSR debate, too. There is no better illustration than what is informally known as Ecuador v Chevron, which goes back to Chevron's acquisition of Texaco, and the pollution caused by Texaco operations in the area affected, in the 1980s and 90s.

---

[752] Ruggie, J., United Nations Human Rights Council, 22 April 2009, Report of the Special Representative, John Ruggie on the issue of human rights and transnational corporations and other business enterprises, A/HRC/11/13, http://www2.ohchr.org/english/bodies/hrcouncil/docs/11session/A.HRC.11.13.pdf, 26.

[753] Augenstein, D., "Study of the Legal Framework on Human Rights and the Environment Applicable to European Enterprises Operating Outside the European Union" (2010), available via http://ec.europa.eu/enterprise/policies/sustainable-business/files/business-human-rights/101025_ec_study_final_report_en.pdf .

[754] 17 September 2010, 49. See further references below.

[755] This heading co-authored with Charlotte Luks at Hampshire College. Thanks are due to the EuroScholars program for their assistance in enabling the research which led to this heading.

The most recent development in this particular case is the denial of certiorari[756] by the United States Supreme Court in October 2012.[757] The case throws light on the difficulties which may arise in trying to enforce a judgment of a third country in a jurisdiction such as the United States. Chevron essentially argue that rule of law principles have been violated in the Ecuadorian rulings on the liability, consequently barring enforcement in the US. It is interesting to note in this respect, as has been outlined above, that rule of law considerations, in particular rights of the defence, are one of the very few grounds which may lead an EU court to reject enforcement of a judgment of another EU court, under the Brussels I Regulation.

Turning to the subject of current heading: the relevant text of the ATS reads,

> The district courts shall have original jurisdiction of any civil action by an alien for a tort only, committed in violation of the law of nations or a treaty of the United States.[758]

Though there has been some debate over the original intention of Congress in creating the statute, the accepted use of ATS litigation, in its broadest terms, has become one in which aliens may bring suit against other foreign nationals or American citizens for breach of commonly accepted international norms. The statute remained unused in the courts for roughly 200 years after its creation until *Filartiga v Pena-Irala* (1980).[759] The United States Second Circuit Court of Appeals, the court that serves Connecticut, New York and Vermont, upheld the claims of the defendants, Paraguayan nationals, that the rights of their family member, as defined by international law, were violated when another Paraguayan tortured and killed him. Following the success of the trial, ATS litigation has had an increased presence in US courts, though the vast majority of claims do not find the success that *Filartiga* did. The original trial also set a precedent for the use of ATS in cases regarding human rights. A few notable cases have arisen in the last few decades and have helped to further define the goal of ATS litigation, though not to an extent that has made the statute any less controversial.

The ATS case most commonly cited in scholarly attempts to define the statute and its acceptable uses is *Sosa v Alvarez-Machain* (2004).[760] In *Sosa*, a Mexican national claimed violation of his right to be free from arbitrary detention when he was abducted and detained overnight by other Mexican nationals. Though the court determined that one night of detention followed by being turned over to lawful authorities and a prompt arraignment was not a major violation of international norms, the results of the case significantly narrowed the scope of jurisdiction in ATS cases. The court held that in order to qualify for ATS, a plaintiff must provide significant evidence for the violation of well-defined and universally accepted norms of common international law. The *Sosa* court made clear the argument that the Statute was not intended to be read broadly and as such, future courts should be conservative in terms of recognizing new violations of international law. The Court writes, 'The judicial power should be exercised on the

---

[756] Denial of certiorari is quite routine (the USSC being able to cherry pick its cases) and typically signals that the Court sees no new points of law to be settled in the case. Denial has no impact on the merits of the underlying case and reasons for denial of certiorari are never given. This latest development therefore is exactly that: the latest, however by no means the last.

[757] *Chevron corporation v Hugo Gerardo Camacho Naranjo, et al.*

[758] Alien Tort Statute, 28 U.S.C. §1350(2000).

[759] *Filartiga v Pena-Irala*, 630 F.2d 876, 878 (2d Cir. 1980).

[760] *Sosa v Alvarez-Machain*, 124 S. Ct. 2739, 2769 (2004).

understanding that the door is still ajar subject to vigilant doorkeeping, and thus open to a narrow class of international norms today.'[761,762]

Post *Sosa,* plaintiffs are burdened with the task of not only proving that a defendant has violated international law, but that the international law in question is amply defined as well as a universally accepted and documented international norm. In the original text of the 1789 statute, there were three requirements: the plaintiff had to be an alien, allege a tort, and offer evidence towards the defendant's guilt in violation of 'the law of nations'. The specific 'law of nations' was not further defined in the original text of the document but with the 200 year gap in cases using ATS, the language did not become controversial until recent years. After the *Sosa* decision, plaintiffs were saddled with the burden providing evidence for a law's validity by 'consulting the works of jurists, writing professedly on public law; or by the general usage and practice of nations; or by judicial decisions recognizing and enforcing that law.'[763] The plaintiff also had to demonstrate a level of consensus among nations as well as international treaties and statutes to demonstrate the validity of an international norm, however the *Sosa* decision drastically narrowed the scope of documents that may be used to claim common international law.[764] For 200 years the Alien Tort Statute was an ill-defined, unused piece of legislation. Now more commonly used, each case brought before US courts employing ATS litigation further restricts the acceptable use of the statute.

7.2.1 Corporate Liability under ATS

Whether corporations may be held liable for violations of international human rights law has long been a topic of debate in the legal community. The debate extends back to the post-Nazi era and the Nuremberg Trials. At the trials, various German industrialists were convicted of war crimes including the use of slave labour.[765] However, while the Nuremberg Courts were allowed to find organizations guilty of war crimes, they could do so only through the trial of an individual. Essentially, a corporation could be found criminal but could not be tried separately, only through an individual who facilitated the corporation's criminal enterprises.[766] The Nuremberg trials are relevant to American ATS litigation in that their precedents are often consulted by judges in ATS cases. Notably, in a recent case brought before the second circuit, *Kiobel v Royal Dutch Petroleum*[767] (2010), the verdict relied heavily on precedents set by international tribunals, including the Nuremberg trials, in relation to corporate liability for violation of international law.[768]

In recent years, the debate has become more focused to the question of corporate culpability for violations of human rights rather than simply corporate liability. Multina-

---

[761] See *Sosa.*

[762] Caron, D.D., and Buxbaum, R.M. "The Alien Tort Statute: An Overview of Current Issues" (2010) 28:2 *Berkeley Journal of International Law* 514.

[763] Morris, S.M. "The Intersection of Equal and Environmental Protection: A New Direction for Environmental Alien Tort Claims After *Sarei* and *Sosa*" (2010) 41 *Columbia Human Rights Law Review* 281.

[764] *Ibid,* 283.

[765] Cassel, D., "Corporate Aiding and Abetting of Human Rights Violations: Confusion in the Courts" (2008) 6:2 *Northwestern Journal of International Human Rights* 306.

[766] *Ibid,* 315.

[767] *Kiobel v Royal Dutch Petroleum Co.,* 621 F. 3d 111 (2d Cir. Sept. 17, 2010).

[768] Crook, J.R., "Contemporary Practices of the United States Relating to International Law: International Human Rights: Second Circuit Panel Finds Alien Tort Statute Does Not Apply To Corporations" (2011) 105 *American Journal of International Law* 139.

tional corporations are often in the position of violating human rights because they form partnerships with developing countries for their cheap labour, lax governmental regulation and unexploited resources.[769] Though governments themselves can be responsible for these violations of international norms and human rights, bringing suit against governments comes with a variety of obstacles including questions of sovereign immunity, lack of personal jurisdiction and in the event of a successful trial, enforceability.[770] For these reasons plaintiffs often find corporations a more desirable opponent as they do not have sovereign immunity and if the trial is successful, corporations' resources can more readily be used to compensate plaintiffs.

There have been a series of cases tried before various federal courts which have revolved around questions of corporate culpability, particularly to what extent corporations can be held liable before the law. *Kiobel* found that, due to what it perceived as a lack of precedent in international law, corporations cannot be held liable for violations of customary international law in US courts under ATS litigation.[771] However this decision only adds to a growing list of corporate ATS cases with incongruent results. In *Doe I v Unocal Corporation* (2002),[772] the Ninth Circuit Court unanimously decided that corporations can be sued for aiding and abetting foreign human rights violators. Similarly in *Khulamani v Barclay National Bank Limited* (2007),[773] the court agreed that corporations can be held liable for aiding and abetting in violations of international law.[774] This lack of congruency among ATS cases involving corporations is largely due to the fact that most of the cases are presented before the circuit courts rather than the Supreme Court. Any decisions the Supreme Court makes regarding ATS then becomes law for all of the lower courts, but without this guidance, each Circuit Court may continue to operate independently of the other Circuit Courts. Without a singular ruling judicial body to set cohesive standards for ATS litigation, the question of whether or not corporations can be held liable for human rights violations will remain unanswered.

The answer to this question may be decided upon sooner rather than later. The *Kiobel* plaintiffs recently filed a petition to appeal the results of the trial at the United States Supreme Court. The court has accepted the case, which leaves two main concerns that need to be addressed. First, the actions of the Circuit Court would need to be reviewed. None of the lower courts in the trials prior to the last appeal had addressed the issue of corporate liability on a subject matter jurisdictional basis, yet the Circuit Court ruled that corporations cannot face charges under ATS litigation. Therefore it would be up to the Supreme Court to determine if the question of corporate liability is a merits question, as the consensus had been before the case was brought to the Circuit Court, or an issue of subject matter jurisdiction. The second question that would come before the Supreme Court would be the more substantive issue of corporate liability; whether or not corporations can be held responsible for their violations of international law before US Courts

---

[769] Abadie, P., "A New Story of David and Goliath: The Alien Tort Claims Act Gives Victims of Environmental Injustice in the Developing World a Viable Claim against Multinational Corporations" (2010) 34:3 *Environmental Law Journal* 745.

[770] Ainscough, C., "Choice of Law and Accomplice Liability under the Alien Tort Statute" (2010) 28:2 *Berkeley Journal of International Law* 589.

[771] Crook, n 768 above, 139.

[772] *Doe I v Unocal Corp.*, 395 F.3d 932 (9th Cir. 2002), *rehearing en banc granted*, 395 F.3d 978 (9th Cir. 2003), *and vacated and appeal dismissed following settlement*, 403 F. 3d 708 (9th Cir. 2005).

[773] *Khulumani v Barclay Nat'l Bank Ltd.*, 504 F.3d 254 (2d Cir. 2007).

[774] Cassel, n 765 above, 319.

under the Alien Tort Statute.[775] If the USSC upholds the ruling of the Circuit Court, the results would effectively remove an important path to justice for victims of corporate human rights abuse. If the court overturns the ruling, it could perhaps usher in a new era of corporate responsibility.

7.2.2 Standard Operating Procedure or a Lack Thereof

There is currently a noticeable gap, as far as ATS litigation is concerned, in terms of a standard operating procedure. There has been as noted little Supreme Court involvement in ATS litigation and this lack of guidance by the Court has led to immense diversity in how the lower federal courts handle cases. In the one relevant ATS case tried by the Supreme Court, it has set a standard for determining actionable norms, but has offered the lower courts nothing in the way of practical guidance.[776] This case, *Sosa,* addressed jurisdiction but did little to clarify the substantive questions associated with ATS litigation. The few notable cases tried before the Supreme Court have broadly defined the act's jurisdiction but have not dealt with substantive issues such as, 'what constitutes an international norm under the act,' or 'how to assess vicarious liability for corporate actors.'[777] As such, until the Supreme Court or congress step in with clearly defined boundaries of ATS litigation, it is up to the lower courts to establish a body of precedent.

There is not only extreme diversity among the lower courts in terms of judicial procedure but also in determining liability for corporations. As clarified in the previous section, each district court confronted with an ATS case of corporate liability has handled it differently. It is therefore necessary for the Supreme Court, as the singular ruling body of the American judicial system, to step in with unambiguous standards for corporate liability.[778]

7.2.3 International or Domestic Law

There has been some contention in the courts over whether ATS decisions should be based on international or domestic law. Though ATS litigation should, according to the statutory provision, employ only international standards, such a goal is fairly impossible to achieve due to the fact that ATS litigation is so unique and can therefore not mimic international law. The text of the statute creates jurisdiction for violations of international customary law and US treaties, but in terms of how to process relevant complaints, many gaps exist in the text. In previous cases, courts have used international laws and norms to judge alien tort claims and domestic law to determine judicial procedure. However, depending on the reading of the original statute, this could be seen as a violation of the drafters' intent, 'while in practice an American court would be inclined to apply American standards...a court holding true to the ATS's text should resist this impulse and look solely to customary law.'[779] Yet from another perspective, applying domestic procedure to ATS litigation could create a more consistent standard for these cases, leaving only the

---

[775] *Kiobel v Royal Dutch Petroleum Co.*, 621 F. 3d 111 (2d Cir. Sept. 17, 2010) Cert. Filed (U.S. June 6, 2011).

[776] Waugh, R., "Exhaustion of Remedies and the Alien Tort Statute" (2010) 28:2 *Berkeley Journal of International Law* 557.

[777] O'Gara, R.T., "Procedural Dismissals under the Alien Tort Statute" (2010) 52 *Arizona Law Review* 797.

[778] Cassel, n 765 above, 325.

[779] Morris, n 763 above, 297.

judgment of alleged crimes in the realm of international law. This type of consistency in judgment would be beneficial to plaintiffs with no other forum to turn to who are often denied justice due to confusion about source law.

Despite the language in the Statute that calls for the sole use of international law in ATS trials, many circuit courts have relied on domestic law in their proceedings, adding further confusion to the question of source law. In *Bowota v Chevron*[780] (2010) the Ninth Circuit Court determined that California substantive law should be applied to the proceedings, despite claims from the defendants that Nigerian law should be applied. The court found that, 'California's interest in ensuring that its corporations behave in an appropriate manner outweighed Nigeria's regulatory interests.'[781] The decision to do so adds to the inconsistency among lower courts in terms of whether to use international or domestic law to rule on ATS cases.

ATS litigation exists to offer a forum to victims of abuse of international law to present their case where they might not be able to do so in the country where the offense took place. However, in many cases the violations they allege are not considered common international law and their claims are dismissed. This was the case recently in the afore-mentioned *Kiobel* (2010) holding, in which the Second Circuit Court determined that, until it became an international norm to do so, corporations could not be tried for viola-tions of human rights. This is problematic because US courts may well have been the last forum that would hold corporations responsible for their actions, but *Kiobel* effec-tively removed the courts' power to do so.[782] This decision was based on international norms despite the fact that the US justice system allows corporations to be convicted of crimes.[783] In the case of *Kiobel,* the court's reliance on international rather than domestic law narrowed the scope of crimes the courts could try under ATS litigation.

Had *Kiobel* been tried in the ninth circuit, rather than the second, the plaintiffs might have found that the court had a more favourable approach to the question of source law. In this regard there has also been a lack of consistency among the lower courts as a result of minimal guidance from the Supreme Court. In *Doe I v Unocal* (2002), [784] Judge Reinhardt argued that courts should apply domestic common law principles when necessary, to fill in the gaps present in the text of the Statute. He continued to write that without a statutory mandate, courts should use established federal common law rather than the principles of international law.[785]

This approach would allow for corporations to be held liable for their actions in ATS cases as the Statute itself makes no comments on the matter and established federal law allows for corporate liability. The Supreme Court decided that the word 'individual' is synonymous with 'person', a word which has a broader legal definition than common definition, and 'considering that a corporation is a juridical person that has no particular immunity under domestic law and possesses the ability to sue and be sued, and that a cor-poration is generally viewed as a person in other areas of the law, a statutory reference to

---

[780] *Bowota v Chevron*, 621 F.3d 1116 (9th Cir. 2010).
[781] Childless, D.E. III, "The Alien Tort Statute, Federalism and the Next Wave of International Law Litiga-tion" (2011) 9 *Pepperdine University School of Law Legal Studies Research Paper Series* 40.
[782] Crook, n 768 above, 143.
[783] Cassel, n 765 above, 315.
[784] See *Doe I.*
[785] Ainscough, n 770 above, 592.

"individual" or "person" shouldn't exclude corporations'[786]. This inconsistency in terms of how to treat corporations is symptomatic of the larger problem that the future of ATS litigation faces.

7.2.4 Obstacles to Justice

The noticeable lack of clear direction under which Federal courts operate when dealing with the Alien Tort Statute has created an atmosphere in which it is common to dismiss cases on procedural grounds to avoid a more substantive ruling. While the ruling in *Sosa* established a need for defendants to demonstrate a violation of international norms and customary laws, the Court did not establish a standard by which to judge the validity of an international law nor did it mandate the sources from which these laws could be drawn.[787] The vagueness of the instructions handed down from the Court post-*Sosa* has contributed to the common use of procedural dismissals in the early stages of the proceedings on the basis of *forum non conveniens*. Cases can also be dismissed on more political grounds via the doctrine of international comity and the act of state doctrine. These represent significant obstacles to justice for the plaintiffs in ATS cases. Even the defendants suffer from the lack of standard definition as they spend significant money trying to fight claims presented to the courts under a vague statute.

7.2.4.1 Procedural Dismissal

One of the most common reasons for dismissal of an ATS case is the doctrine of *forum non conveniens*. Essentially, courts decide not to try a case, 'if an adequate alternate forum exists and the balance of private and public interest factors weigh strongly in favor of the alternate forum adjudicating the case'.[788]

In deciding whether or not to apply *forum non conveniens* dismissal, courts apply a two-part analysis. First the court must determine whether an alternate forum is available and, should that be the case, whether the alternate forum is adequate.[789] While it is the burden of the defendant to convince the court that another forum would be more appropriate, courts are reluctant to declare foreign courts inadequate and often dismissal results.[790] Even without this political influence, defendants are usually able to build a strong case for use of another forum as, more often than not, the alleged crime has taken place abroad and the cost of bringing in evidence and witnesses is a burden that could be avoided by trying the case in a domestic court rather than within the US.[791] The doctrine has been used in a series of cases that could've been crucial in defining the role of ATS litigation in corporate culpability for violation of international law had the cases not been dismissed on procedural grounds.

---

[786] Christensen, D.D., "Corporate Liability for Overseas Human Rights Abuses: The Alien Tort Statute after *Sosa v Alvarez-Machain*" (2005) 62 *Washington and Lee Law Review* 1238.

[787] O'Gara, n 777 above, 803.

[788] Baldwin, J.E., "International Human Rights Plaintiffs and the Doctrine of *Forum Non Conveniens*" (2007) 40 *Cornell International Law Journal* 750.

[789] Abadie, n 769 above, 768.

[790] O'Gara, n 777 above, 804.

[791] Baldwin, n 788 above, 757.

In the case of *Aguinda v Texaco*[792](2001), Ecuadorian and Peruvian plaintiffs brought suit against the Texaco oil corporation claiming that Texaco had polluted the Ecuadorian Amazon, endangering both the environment and the health and livelihoods of those living in the rainforest.[793] This suit had the potential to be a landmark case in terms of defining the boundaries of ATS litigation; it raised questions concerning the extent to which corporations can be held responsible for the destruction caused by their contractors as well as to what extent environmental damage and resulting health concerns violates customary international law. However the case was dismissed on the grounds of forum non conveniens, a decision that was confirmed upon appeal.

7.2.4.2 Political Dismissal

The Alien Tort Statute is by definition entangled with political issues beyond the scope of the judicial system. This has created tensions between the three branches of the US government, most recently in 2002 when the Bush administration expressed concerns about the Act's potential for creating strain between the US and foreign governments.[794]

These concerns were addressed long before the Bush administration however. For example, the political question doctrine stems from the Supreme Court's 1803 ruling in *Marbury v Madison*.[795] The doctrine essentially asserts that a federal court may decline to hear a dispute if its content would best be addressed by other branches of government,[796] 'under this doctrine, US courts are precluded from adjudicating a case which may require them to take positions on quintessential political questions related to the foreign policy choices of the executive branch'.[797] This is a common concern in ATS litigation because cases presented under the statute are concerned with actions that take place within the jurisdiction of governments outside of the US.

Under this doctrine, courts accept 'statements of interest' from the executive branch; taking into consideration the political implications of trying a case.[798] However the decision of whether or not to allow trial to proceed remains with the courts. The case of *Sarei v Rio Tinto*[799](2000) represented the first time in the history of ATS litigation that a trial proceeded despite a recommendation for dismissal from the Executive branch. In the case, residents of Bougainville Island in Papua New Guinea sued an international mining group for 'destroying their island's environment, harming the health of their people and inciting a ten year civil war.' The government of Papua New Guinea stated its objections and in response the US Department of Justice sent a letter to the district judge in charge of the case 'highly [inviting]' him to consider the possible US-PNG foreign relation implications.[800] Judge W. H. Taft responded, 'It is [the court's] responsibility to determine whether a political question is present, rather than to dismiss on that ground simply because the Executive Branch expresses some hesitancy about a case proceeding.'[801]

---

[792] *Aguinda v Texaco, Inc.*, 303 F.3d 470, 478 (2d Cir. 2002).
[793] Baldwin, n 788 above, 760.
[794] O'Gara, n 777 above, 810.
[795] *Marbury v Madison*, 5 U.S. (1 Cranch) 137 (1803).
[796] O'Gara, n 777 above, 811.
[797] Abadie, n 769 above, 770.
[798] O'Gara, n 777 above, 812.
[799] *Sarei v Rio Tinto PLC*, 221 F.Supp.2d 1116, 1121 (C.D. Cal. 2002).
[800] Abadie, n 769 above, 770.
[801] O'Gara, n 777 above, 812.

The Ninth Circuit asserted its independence in *Sarei* but the political question doctrine remains a valid option for dismissal and a considerable obstacle to justice.

Another doctrine with the potential for political dismissal in ATS cases is that of international comity.[802] The doctrine of international comity considers the jurisdiction of foreign court's as well as the sovereignty of foreign nations in making decisions within their own borders. While not mandated by any means, courts look to international comity as a means of respecting foreign nations when the alleged actions before the court are not as black and white as torture or murder but fall into a grey area, as drilling for oil with potential for health risks to native populations might. Similar to the international comity doctrine, the act of state doctrine, 'bars courts from questioning the validity of foreign nations; sovereign acts that occur within their own jurisdictions.'[803]

This doctrine played a large role in the denial of an en banc claim as requested by the plaintiffs in *Kiobel*.[804] In denying the claim, Chief Judge Dennis Jacobs not only found that the ruling in the original case was sufficient, but that trying corporations in US courts was problematic in terms of the policies of foreign nations. Judge Jacobs argued that foreign corporations operate under the regulations and laws of the country's wherein they reside and that

> [He] cannot think that there is some consensus among nations that American courts and lawyers have the power to bring to court transnational corporations of other countries, to inquire into their operations in third countries, to regulate them–and to beggar them by rendering their assets into compensatory damages, punitive damages, and (American) legal fees.[805]

Despite his opinion, this is precisely the intention of the Alien Tort Statute, to try foreign nationals in US courts for violations of international law. The reasons for the dismissal are decidedly political and fall under the doctrine of international comity. As with any political motive for dismissal, use of international comity or act of state as a reason for declining to hear a case looks suspicious for a body that is supposed to be impartial to political trends.[806]

Early dismissals of ATS cases on both procedural and political grounds create obstacles not only to justice but to further definition of what ATS litigation covers. On a case by case basis, dismissals deny plaintiffs their 'day in court'. On a larger scale, when cases do not reach the ruling stage, the Statute cannot be further defined by increased precedent and its boundaries remain ambiguous, harming future defendants who may be unclear as to what they may be held accountable for. While it is understandable that federal courts would rather dismiss cases early rather than run the risk of interpreting the statute in a way that might harm future proceedings, continual dismissals only keeps the act from reaching its full potential as a means of bringing justice to victims of human rights violations.

---

[802] See excellently Briggs, A., 'The principle of comity in private international law', Recueil des Cours, Hague Academy of International Law, Volume 354, 2012, p.69–182.

[803] Abadie, n 769 above, 770.

[804] See *Kiobel*.

[805] *Kiobel et al v Shell*, 06–4800-cv & 064876-cv (2nd cir. 2011).

[806] O'Gara, n 777 above, 814.

7.2.5 Conclusion on the United States

Alien Tort legislation is seen by many as one of the last great hopes for effective enforcement of human rights violations internationally. While the need for a more extensive list of cases tried is evident, as more cases are tried before US courts the statute's potential decreases significantly. Rather than increasing the understanding of the act, new cases have either narrowed the scope of ATS litigation or left the statute's definition stagnant through procedural dismissals prior to more substantive proceedings. In these cases plaintiffs must navigate a proverbial legal obstacle course to avoid procedural dismissal before the trial can even begin. Should a case make it all the way to trial, there remains debate and confusion in terms of standard operating procedure, legal sources, and whether corporate liability exists in the present forum. ATS may indeed be a bright hope for the eventual goal of corporate culpability for human rights violations, but until the Supreme Court or Congress step in to further define the statute,[807] very little progress will be made.

7.3 THE EUROPEAN UNION

In European Private International Law, as with the ATS, the two main concerns that arise when addressing matters of corporate violation of rights are whether or not EU member state courts have jurisdiction and, if so, what laws, national or international, apply.[808]

7.3.1 Jurisdiction

7.3.1.1 General jurisdictional rule: Article 2 JR

Following the Brussels I Regulation, it is enough for a court in an EU Member State to establish jurisdiction, if the defendant is domiciled in an EU Member State. Consequently truly multinational corporations may in theory at least be quite easily pursued in the courts of an EU Member State, even for actions committed outside of the EU: the principal jurisdictional ground of the defendant's domicile, included in Article 2 of the JR, operates independently of the activities to which the action relates.

A good example of the ease in bringing a case against European holding companies, in the EU, is *Milieudefensie et al v Shell*. Shell's top holding has been hauled before a Dutch court by a Dutch environmental NGO (Milieudefensie), seeking (with a number of Nigerian farmers) to have the mother holding being held liable for environmental pollution caused in Nigeria. The media have been somewhat wrong-footed in reporting on the issue. Establishing jurisdiction in an EU court vis-a-vis a company with seat in the EU, is not exactly rocket science. It is a simple application of the Brussels I Regulation. As readers of this volume will be aware, the ECJ has barred national courts from even pondering rejection of such jurisdiction (*Owusu*: rejection of forum non conveniens considerations). What is interesting, is the fact that Milieudefensie and the individual

---

[807] A decision is expected end 2012 or early 2013. For an update after completion of this book, please refer to the blog: www.gavclaw.com .

[808] Augenstein, n 753 above, 16. See also Van Den Eeckhout, V., "Promoting Human Rights within the Union: The Role of European Private International Law", *European Law Journal*, 2008, (105) 127.

applicants are also pursuing the Nigerian daughter company in The Netherlands. In an interim ruling going back to 2009,[809] the court held that the case against the Nigerian daughter may prima facie at least be bundled with the case against the mother holding. I understand however that the bundling issue will be revisited in the substantive proceedings.

Pursuing a holding company which were to have domicile in the EU, may be possible from the jurisdiction point of view however will be more challenging with respect to applicable law (see below). However corporate reality of course dictates that even though the firms concerned may operate under one global brand, in practice they are organised in separate corporate entities. As a result, one will find that International Business Inc. is actually made up of most probably as many separate corporate entities as the countries in which it operates: this will rule out jurisdiction under the Brussels I Regulation, it may however pave the way for jurisdiction under national rules of the Member States, for instance in those Member States which operate a *forum necessitatis* rule (see also the discussion below, on the *forum necessitatis* rule mooted in the review of the Brussels I Regulation).

7.3.1.2 Special jurisdictional rule: Article 5(5) JR: operations arising out of a branch

As noted in the discussion of the Brussels I Regulation, in the case of corporations, it extends to branches of international companies by virtue of Article 5(5)'s special jurisdictional rule:

> A person domiciled in a Member State may, in another Member State, be sued: (...)
>
> 5. as regards a dispute arising out of the operations of a branch, agency or other establishment, in the courts for the place in which the branch, agency or other establishment is situated; (...)

The use of the words 'arising out of' however indicates the limited potential for this rule in the case of international litigation in a CSR context.

> This concept of operations (...) also comprises (...) actions concerning non-contractual obligations arising from the activities in which the branch, agency or other establishment within the above defined meaning, has engaged at the place in which it is established on behalf of the parent body.[810]

It can hardly be said that the non-contractual obligations of International Business Ruritania Ltd can be allocated to International Business [EU Member State]; they do not 'arise out of' the operation of the EU Member State, and moreover, would require International Business Ruritania Ltd to be domiciled in another EU Member State: Article 5(5) concerns only defendants domiciled in a Member State (Article 5), that is, companies or firms having their seat in one Member State and having a branch, agency or other establishment in another Member State. Companies or firms which have their seat outside the Community but have a branch, etc. in a Member State, are covered by Article 4 JR.

---

[809] BK8616, Rechtbank's-Gravenhage, HA ZA 330891 09-579, *Vereniging Milieudefensie et al v Royal Dutch Shell plc and Shell Petroleum Development Company of Nigeria Ltd.*
[810] Case 33/78 *Somafer*, [1979] ECR 2183, para 13. See also n 242 above and review in the body of the text.

7.3.1.3 Special jurisdictional rule: Article 5(3) JR: Tort

The special jurisdictional rule for tort may potentially be triggered by the *Bier*[811] extension to the locus *delicti commissi*, in cases where plaintiff is able to show that International Business [EU Member State] is behind the actions which led to the tort. One would have to convince a court in an EU Member State that either direct instructions or negligent lack of oversight by International Business [EU Member State] led to the damage at issue.

7.3.1.4 Special jurisdictional rule: Article 5(4) JR

Courts which have jurisdiction in a criminal procedure, also have jurisdiction for the civil leg of the prosecution.

7.3.1.5 Review of the JR – The 'international dimension' of the Regulation

As reported above in the review of the Brussels I Regulation, the proposed introduction of both an assets-based jurisdictional rule and a *forum necessitatis* option would have had an impact on the issue discussed here. However, neither of them made it into the revised Regulation.

7.3.2 Applicable law

Establishing jurisdiction leaves open the question of what law to apply to the fact at issue — as also illustrated by the challenges hitting the application of the ATS. The EU does not operate an ATS-like system, which employs *international* law to advance the case of plaintiffs seeking 'justice' in environmental or human rights cases. The route which must be followed in the EU is one of *Gleichlauf* between having a court in the EU hear the case, and having that court apply the human rights/environmental law of that forum, as a benchmark for deciding the merits of the action.[812]

The most likely route to pursue a corporation in a court in the EU is via an action in tort. As the above review of the Rome II Regulation shows, this generally entails the application of the *lex loci damni*. Given that plaintiffs generally shy away from pursuing the case on the basis of tort law of Ruritania, the general rule of the Rome II Regulation in all likelihood is not the goal of the plaintiffs concerned.

Might any of the exceptions in the Rome II Regulation apply? If both parties are habitually resident in the same country when the damage occurs, the law of that country applies (Article 4(2) Rome II). This may be relevant in exceptional cases, however the more standard CSR scenario is for victims resident in the *locus damni*, outside of the EU, to sue in the EU. Article 4(3) more generally includes an escape clause: when it is clear from the circumstances of the case that it is '*manifestly*' more closely connected with a country other than the one indicated by 4(1) or 4 (2), the law of that country shall apply

---

[811] Case 21/76 *Mines de Potasse d'Alsace*, [1976] ECR 1735. See also n 310 above and review in the body of the text.
[812] Given the high degree of harmonisation of environmental law, as well as (to a slightly lesser degree) of occupational health and safety laws, and of course the impact of the European Convention on Human Rights as well as the EU's Charter of Fundamental Rights, the relevant law of an EU Member State will not differ in great substance.

instead. *'The'* tort has to have that manifestly closer relationship: in particular in the CSR context, this is problematic given the occurrence of the damage abroad.

Finally, Article 7 Rome II, as discussed above, contains a special rule for environmental damage:

Article 7

Environmental damage

The law applicable to a non-contractual obligation arising out of environmental damage or damage sustained by persons or property as a result of such damage shall be the law determined pursuant to Article 4(1), unless the person seeking compensation for damage chooses to base his or her claim on the law of the country in which the event giving rise to the damage occurred.

This Article ties in with one of the options for establishing jurisdiction for an EU court, as highlighted above: one would have to convince a court in an EU Member State that either direct instructions or negligent lack of oversight by International Business [EU Member State] led to the damage at issue and hence constitute 'the event giving rise to the damage'. I have already suggested above that the additional rule on 'rules of safety and conduct' of Article 17 arguably have less of a calling for environmental litigation than may be prima facie assumed.[813]

In summary, therefore, while it is relatively straightforward in the case of acts committed abroad, to sue a corporation in the EU, in the case of that corporation having a corporate bridgehead in the EU, applicable law almost certainly will *not* be European law.[814] There does not at this moment seem much of a constituency in EU Institutions to have this changed.

---

[813] Contra: Van Den Eeckhout, V., 'Corporate Human Rights Violations and Private International Law', working paper July 2011, available via SSRN (last consulted 20 December 2011).

[814] Similarly, see Van Dam, C., 'Tort law and human rights: Brothers in arms. On the role of tort law in the area of business and human rights', *Journal of European Tort Law*, 2011, (221) 231–232.

Annexes

I

(Acts whose publication is obligatory)

COUNCIL REGULATION (EC) No 44/2001

of 22 December 2000

on jurisdiction and the recognition and enforcement of judgments in civil and commercial matters

THE COUNCIL OF THE EUROPEAN UNION,

Having regard to the Treaty establishing the European Community, and in particular Article 61(c) and Article 67(1) thereof,

Having regard to the proposal from the Commission ([1]),

Having regard to the opinion of the European Parliament ([2]),

Having regard to the opinion of the Economic and Social Committee ([3]),

Whereas:

(1) The Community has set itself the objective of maintaining and developing an area of freedom, security and justice, in which the free movement of persons is ensured. In order to establish progressively such an area, the Community should adopt, amongst other things, the measures relating to judicial cooperation in civil matters which are necessary for the sound operation of the internal market.

(2) Certain differences between national rules governing jurisdiction and recognition of judgments hamper the sound operation of the internal market. Provisions to unify the rules of conflict of jurisdiction in civil and commercial matters and to simplify the formalities with a view to rapid and simple recognition and enforcement of judgments from Member States bound by this Regulation are essential.

(3) This area is within the field of judicial cooperation in civil matters within the meaning of Article 65 of the Treaty.

(4) In accordance with the principles of subsidiarity and proportionality as set out in Article 5 of the Treaty, the objectives of this Regulation cannot be sufficiently achieved by the Member States and can therefore be better achieved by the Community. This Regulation confines itself to the minimum required in order to achieve those objectives and does not go beyond what is necessary for that purpose.

(5) On 27 September 1968 the Member States, acting under Article 293, fourth indent, of the Treaty, concluded the Brussels Convention on Jurisdiction and the Enforcement of Judgments in Civil and Commercial Matters, as amended by Conventions on the Accession of the New Member States to that Convention (hereinafter referred to as the 'Brussels Convention') ([4]). On 16 September 1988 Member States and EFTA States concluded the Lugano Convention on Jurisdiction and the Enforcement of Judgments in Civil and Commercial Matters, which is a parallel Convention to the 1968 Brussels Convention. Work has been undertaken for the revision of those Conventions, and the Council has approved the content of the revised texts. Continuity in the results achieved in that revision should be ensured.

(6) In order to attain the objective of free movement of judgments in civil and commercial matters, it is necessary and appropriate that the rules governing jurisdiction and the recognition and enforcement of judgments be governed by a Community legal instrument which is binding and directly applicable.

(7) The scope of this Regulation must cover all the main civil and commercial matters apart from certain well-defined matters.

([1]) OJ C 376, 28.12.1999, p. 1.
([2]) Opinion delivered on 21 September 2000 (not yet published in the Official Journal).
([3]) OJ C 117, 26.4.2000, p. 6.

([4]) OJ L 299, 31.12.1972, p. 32.
OJ L 304, 30.10.1978, p. 1.
OJ L 388, 31.12.1982, p. 1.
OJ L 285, 3.10.1989, p. 1.
OJ C 15, 15.1.1997, p. 1.
For a consolidated text, see OJ C 27, 26.1.1998, p. 1.

(8) There must be a link between proceedings to which this Regulation applies and the territory of the Member States bound by this Regulation. Accordingly common rules on jurisdiction should, in principle, apply when the defendant is domiciled in one of those Member States.

(9) A defendant not domiciled in a Member State is in general subject to national rules of jurisdiction applicable in the territory of the Member State of the court seised, and a defendant domiciled in a Member State not bound by this Regulation must remain subject to the Brussels Convention.

(10) For the purposes of the free movement of judgments, judgments given in a Member State bound by this Regulation should be recognised and enforced in another Member State bound by this Regulation, even if the judgment debtor is domiciled in a third State.

(11) The rules of jurisdiction must be highly predictable and founded on the principle that jurisdiction is generally based on the defendant's domicile and jurisdiction must always be available on this ground save in a few well-defined situations in which the subject-matter of the litigation or the autonomy of the parties warrants a different linking factor. The domicile of a legal person must be defined autonomously so as to make the common rules more transparent and avoid conflicts of jurisdiction.

(12) In addition to the defendant's domicile, there should be alternative grounds of jurisdiction based on a close link between the court and the action or in order to facilitate the sound administration of justice.

(13) In relation to insurance, consumer contracts and employment, the weaker party should be protected by rules of jurisdiction more favourable to his interests than the general rules provide for.

(14) The autonomy of the parties to a contract, other than an insurance, consumer or employment contract, where only limited autonomy to determine the courts having jurisdiction is allowed, must be respected subject to the exclusive grounds of jurisdiction laid down in this Regulation.

(15) In the interests of the harmonious administration of justice it is necessary to minimise the possibility of concurrent proceedings and to ensure that irreconcilable judgments will not be given in two Member States. There must be a clear and effective mechanism for resolving cases of *lis pendens* and related actions and for

obviating problems flowing from national differences as to the determination of the time when a case is regarded as pending. For the purposes of this Regulation that time should be defined autonomously.

(16) Mutual trust in the administration of justice in the Community justifies judgments given in a Member State being recognised automatically without the need for any procedure except in cases of dispute.

(17) By virtue of the same principle of mutual trust, the procedure for making enforceable in one Member State a judgment given in another must be efficient and rapid. To that end, the declaration that a judgment is enforceable should be issued virtually automatically after purely formal checks of the documents supplied, without there being any possibility for the court to raise of its own motion any of the grounds for non-enforcement provided for by this Regulation.

(18) However, respect for the rights of the defence means that the defendant should be able to appeal in an adversarial procedure, against the declaration of enforceability, if he considers one of the grounds for non-enforcement to be present. Redress procedures should also be available to the claimant where his application for a declaration of enforceability has been rejected.

(19) Continuity between the Brussels Convention and this Regulation should be ensured, and transitional provisions should be laid down to that end. The same need for continuity applies as regards the interpretation of the Brussels Convention by the Court of Justice of the European Communities and the 1971 Protocol([1]) should remain applicable also to cases already pending when this Regulation enters into force.

(20) The United Kingdom and Ireland, in accordance with Article 3 of the Protocol on the position of the United Kingdom and Ireland annexed to the Treaty on European Union and to the Treaty establishing the European Community, have given notice of their wish to take part in the adoption and application of this Regulation.

(21) Denmark, in accordance with Articles 1 and 2 of the Protocol on the position of Denmark annexed to the Treaty on European Union and to the Treaty

---

([1]) OJ L 204, 2.8.1975, p. 28.
  OJ L 304, 30.10.1978, p. 1.
  OJ L 388, 31.12.1982, p. 1.
  OJ L 285, 3.10.1989, p. 1.
  OJ C 15, 15.1.1997, p. 1.
  For a consolidated text see OJ C 27, 26.1.1998, p. 28.

establishing the European Community, is not participating in the adoption of this Regulation, and is therefore not bound by it nor subject to its application.

(22) Since the Brussels Convention remains in force in relations between Denmark and the Member States that are bound by this Regulation, both the Convention and the 1971 Protocol continue to apply between Denmark and the Member States bound by this Regulation.

(23) The Brussels Convention also continues to apply to the territories of the Member States which fall within the territorial scope of that Convention and which are excluded from this Regulation pursuant to Article 299 of the Treaty.

(24) Likewise for the sake of consistency, this Regulation should not affect rules governing jurisdiction and the recognition of judgments contained in specific Community instruments.

(25) Respect for international commitments entered into by the Member States means that this Regulation should not affect conventions relating to specific matters to which the Member States are parties.

(26) The necessary flexibility should be provided for in the basic rules of this Regulation in order to take account of the specific procedural rules of certain Member States. Certain provisions of the Protocol annexed to the Brussels Convention should accordingly be incorporated in this Regulation.

(27) In order to allow a harmonious transition in certain areas which were the subject of special provisions in the Protocol annexed to the Brussels Convention, this Regulation lays down, for a transitional period, provisions taking into consideration the specific situation in certain Member States.

(28) No later than five years after entry into force of this Regulation the Commission will present a report on its application and, if need be, submit proposals for adaptations.

(29) The Commission will have to adjust Annexes I to IV on the rules of national jurisdiction, the courts or competent authorities and redress procedures available on the basis of the amendments forwarded by the Member State concerned; amendments made to Annexes V and VI should be adopted in accordance with Council Decision 1999/468/EC of 28 June 1999 laying down the procedures for the exercise of implementing powers conferred on the Commission([1]),

---

([1]) OJ L 184, 17.7.1999, p. 23.

HAS ADOPTED THIS REGULATION:

CHAPTER I

SCOPE

Article 1

1. This Regulation shall apply in civil and commercial matters whatever the nature of the court or tribunal. It shall not extend, in particular, to revenue, customs or administrative matters.

2. The Regulation shall not apply to:

(a) the status or legal capacity of natural persons, rights in property arising out of a matrimonial relationship, wills and succession;

(b) bankruptcy, proceedings relating to the winding-up of insolvent companies or other legal persons, judicial arrangements, compositions and analogous proceedings;

(c) social security;

(d) arbitration.

3. In this Regulation, the term 'Member State' shall mean Member States with the exception of Denmark.

CHAPTER II

JURISDICTION

Section 1

General provisions

Article 2

1. Subject to this Regulation, persons domiciled in a Member State shall, whatever their nationality, be sued in the courts of that Member State.

2. Persons who are not nationals of the Member State in which they are domiciled shall be governed by the rules of jurisdiction applicable to nationals of that State.

Article 3

1.   Persons domiciled in a Member State may be sued in the courts of another Member State only by virtue of the rules set out in Sections 2 to 7 of this Chapter.

2.   In particular the rules of national jurisdiction set out in Annex I shall not be applicable as against them.

Article 4

1.   If the defendant is not domiciled in a Member State, the jurisdiction of the courts of each Member State shall, subject to Articles 22 and 23, be determined by the law of that Member State.

2.   As against such a defendant, any person domiciled in a Member State may, whatever his nationality, avail himself in that State of the rules of jurisdiction there in force, and in particular those specified in Annex I, in the same way as the nationals of that State.

Section 2

Special jurisdiction

Article 5

A person domiciled in a Member State may, in another Member State, be sued:

1.   (a) in matters relating to a contract, in the courts for the place of performance of the obligation in question;

   (b) for the purpose of this provision and unless otherwise agreed, the place of performance of the obligation in question shall be:

   — in the case of the sale of goods, the place in a Member State where, under the contract, the goods were delivered or should have been delivered,

   — in the case of the provision of services, the place in a Member State where, under the contract, the services were provided or should have been provided,

   (c) if subparagraph (b) does not apply then subparagraph (a) applies;

2.   in matters relating to maintenance, in the courts for the place where the maintenance creditor is domiciled or habitually resident or, if the matter is ancillary to proceedings concerning the status of a person, in the court which, according to its own law, has jurisdiction to entertain those proceedings, unless that jurisdiction is based solely on the nationality of one of the parties;

3.   in matters relating to tort, *delict* or *quasi-delict*, in the courts for the place where the harmful event occurred or may occur;

4.   as regards a civil claim for damages or restitution which is based on an act giving rise to criminal proceedings, in the court seised of those proceedings, to the extent that that court has jurisdiction under its own law to entertain civil proceedings;

5.   as regards a dispute arising out of the operations of a branch, agency or other establishment, in the courts for the place in which the branch, agency or other establishment is situated;

6.   as settlor, trustee or beneficiary of a trust created by the operation of a statute, or by a written instrument, or created orally and evidenced in writing, in the courts of the Member State in which the trust is domiciled;

7.   as regards a dispute concerning the payment of remuneration claimed in respect of the salvage of a cargo or freight, in the court under the authority of which the cargo or freight in question:

   (a) has been arrested to secure such payment, or

   (b) could have been so arrested, but bail or other security has been given;

provided that this provision shall apply only if it is claimed that the defendant has an interest in the cargo or freight or had such an interest at the time of salvage.

Article 6

A person domiciled in a Member State may also be sued:

1.   where he is one of a number of defendants, in the courts for the place where any one of them is domiciled,

provided the claims are so closely connected that it is expedient to hear and determine them together to avoid the risk of irreconcilable judgments resulting from separate proceedings;

2. as a third party in an action on a warranty or guarantee or in any other third party proceedings, in the court seised of the original proceedings, unless these were instituted solely with the object of removing him from the jurisdiction of the court which would be competent in his case;

3. on a counter-claim arising from the same contract or facts on which the original claim was based, in the court in which the original claim is pending;

4. in matters relating to a contract, if the action may be combined with an action against the same defendant in matters relating to rights *in rem* in immovable property, in the court of the Member State in which the property is situated.

Article 7

Where by virtue of this Regulation a court of a Member State has jurisdiction in actions relating to liability from the use or operation of a ship, that court, or any other court substituted for this purpose by the internal law of that Member State, shall also have jurisdiction over claims for limitation of such liability.

Section 3

Jurisdiction in matters relating to insurance

Article 8

In matters relating to insurance, jurisdiction shall be determined by this Section, without prejudice to Article 4 and point 5 of Article 5.

Article 9

1. An insurer domiciled in a Member State may be sued:

(a) in the courts of the Member State where he is domiciled, or

(b) in another Member State, in the case of actions brought by the policyholder, the insured or a beneficiary, in the courts for the place where the plaintiff is domiciled,

(c) if he is a co-insurer, in the courts of a Member State in which proceedings are brought against the leading insurer.

2. An insurer who is not domiciled in a Member State but has a branch, agency or other establishment in one of the Member States shall, in disputes arising out of the operations of the branch, agency or establishment, be deemed to be domiciled in that Member State.

Article 10

In respect of liability insurance or insurance of immovable property, the insurer may in addition be sued in the courts for the place where the harmful event occurred. The same applies if movable and immovable property are covered by the same insurance policy and both are adversely affected by the same contingency.

Article 11

1. In respect of liability insurance, the insurer may also, if the law of the court permits it, be joined in proceedings which the injured party has brought against the insured.

2. Articles 8, 9 and 10 shall apply to actions brought by the injured party directly against the insurer, where such direct actions are permitted.

3. If the law governing such direct actions provides that the policyholder or the insured may be joined as a party to the action, the same court shall have jurisdiction over them.

Article 12

1. Without prejudice to Article 11(3), an insurer may bring proceedings only in the courts of the Member State in which the defendant is domiciled, irrespective of whether he is the policyholder, the insured or a beneficiary.

2. The provisions of this Section shall not affect the right to bring a counter-claim in the court in which, in accordance with this Section, the original claim is pending.

Article 13

The provisions of this Section may be departed from only by an agreement:

1. which is entered into after the dispute has arisen, or

2. which allows the policyholder, the insured or a beneficiary to bring proceedings in courts other than those indicated in this Section, or

3. which is concluded between a policyholder and an insurer, both of whom are at the time of conclusion of the contract domiciled or habitually resident in the same Member State, and which has the effect of conferring jurisdiction on the courts of that State even if the harmful event were to occur abroad, provided that such an agreement is not contrary to the law of that State, or

4. which is concluded with a policyholder who is not domiciled in a Member State, except in so far as the insurance is compulsory or relates to immovable property in a Member State, or

5. which relates to a contract of insurance in so far as it covers one or more of the risks set out in Article 14.

Article 14

The following are the risks referred to in Article 13(5):

1. any loss of or damage to:

    (a) seagoing ships, installations situated offshore or on the high seas, or aircraft, arising from perils which relate to their use for commercial purposes;

    (b) goods in transit other than passengers' baggage where the transit consists of or includes carriage by such ships or aircraft;

2. any liability, other than for bodily injury to passengers or loss of or damage to their baggage:

    (a) arising out of the use or operation of ships, installations or aircraft as referred to in point 1(a) in so far as, in respect of the latter, the law of the Member State in which such aircraft are registered does not prohibit agreements on jurisdiction regarding insurance of such risks;

    (b) for loss or damage caused by goods in transit as described in point 1(b);

3. any financial loss connected with the use or operation of ships, installations or aircraft as referred to in point 1(a), in particular loss of freight or charter-hire;

4. any risk or interest connected with any of those referred to in points 1 to 3;

5. notwithstanding points 1 to 4, all 'large risks' as defined in Council Directive 73/239/EEC ([1]), as amended by Council Directives 88/357/EEC ([2]) and 90/618/EEC ([3]), as they may be amended.

Section 4

Jurisdiction over consumer contracts

Article 15

1.   In matters relating to a contract concluded by a person, the consumer, for a purpose which can be regarded as being outside his trade or profession, jurisdiction shall be determined by this Section, without prejudice to Article 4 and point 5 of Article 5, if:

(a) it is a contract for the sale of goods on instalment credit terms; or

(b) it is a contract for a loan repayable by instalments, or for any other form of credit, made to finance the sale of goods; or

(c) in all other cases, the contract has been concluded with a person who pursues commercial or professional activities in the Member State of the consumer's domicile or, by any means, directs such activities to that Member State or to several States including that Member State, and the contract falls within the scope of such activities.

2.   Where a consumer enters into a contract with a party who is not domiciled in the Member State but has a branch, agency or other establishment in one of the Member States, that party shall, in disputes arising out of the operations of the branch, agency or establishment, be deemed to be domiciled in that State.

3.   This Section shall not apply to a contract of transport other than a contract which, for an inclusive price, provides for a combination of travel and accommodation.

([1]) OJ L 228, 16.8.1973, p. 3. Directive as last amended by Directive 2000/26/EC of the European Parliament and of the Council (OJ L 181, 20.7.2000, p. 65).
([2]) OJ L 172, 4.7.1988, p. 1. Directive as last amended by Directive 2000/26/EC.
([3]) OJ L 330, 29.11.1990, p. 44.

Article 16

1. A consumer may bring proceedings against the other party to a contract either in the courts of the Member State in which that party is domiciled or in the courts for the place where the consumer is domiciled.

2. Proceedings may be brought against a consumer by the other party to the contract only in the courts of the Member State in which the consumer is domiciled.

3. This Article shall not affect the right to bring a counter-claim in the court in which, in accordance with this Section, the original claim is pending.

Article 17

The provisions of this Section may be departed from only by an agreement:

1. which is entered into after the dispute has arisen; or

2. which allows the consumer to bring proceedings in courts other than those indicated in this Section; or

3. which is entered into by the consumer and the other party to the contract, both of whom are at the time of conclusion of the contract domiciled or habitually resident in the same Member State, and which confers jurisdiction on the courts of that Member State, provided that such an agreement is not contrary to the law of that Member State.

Section 5

Jurisdiction over individual contracts of employment

Article 18

1. In matters relating to individual contracts of employment, jurisdiction shall be determined by this Section, without prejudice to Article 4 and point 5 of Article 5.

2. Where an employee enters into an individual contract of employment with an employer who is not domiciled in a Member State but has a branch, agency or other establishment in one of the Member States, the employer shall, in disputes arising out of the operations of the branch, agency or establishment, be deemed to be domiciled in that Member State.

Article 19

An employer domiciled in a Member State may be sued:

1. in the courts of the Member State where he is domiciled; or

2. in another Member State:

   (a) in the courts for the place where the employee habitually carries out his work or in the courts for the last place where he did so, or

   (b) if the employee does not or did not habitually carry out his work in any one country, in the courts for the place where the business which engaged the employee is or was situated.

Article 20

1. An employer may bring proceedings only in the courts of the Member State in which the employee is domiciled.

2. The provisions of this Section shall not affect the right to bring a counter-claim in the court in which, in accordance with this Section, the original claim is pending.

Article 21

The provisions of this Section may be departed from only by an agreement on jurisdiction:

1. which is entered into after the dispute has arisen; or

2. which allows the employee to bring proceedings in courts other than those indicated in this Section.

Section 6

Exclusive jurisdiction

Article 22

The following courts shall have exclusive jurisdiction, regardless of domicile:

1. in proceedings which have as their object rights *in rem* in immovable property or tenancies of immovable property, the courts of the Member State in which the property is situated.

However, in proceedings which have as their object tenancies of immovable property concluded for temporary private use for a maximum period of six consecutive months, the courts of the Member State in which the defendant is domiciled shall also have jurisdiction, provided that the tenant is a natural person and that the landlord and the tenant are domiciled in the same Member State;

2. in proceedings which have as their object the validity of the constitution, the nullity or the dissolution of companies or other legal persons or associations of natural or legal persons, or of the validity of the decisions of their organs, the courts of the Member State in which the company, legal person or association has its seat. In order to determine that seat, the court shall apply its rules of private international law;

3. in proceedings which have as their object the validity of entries in public registers, the courts of the Member State in which the register is kept;

4. in proceedings concerned with the registration or validity of patents, trade marks, designs, or other similar rights required to be deposited or registered, the courts of the Member State in which the deposit or registration has been applied for, has taken place or is under the terms of a Community instrument or an international convention deemed to have taken place.

Without prejudice to the jurisdiction of the European Patent Office under the Convention on the Grant of European Patents, signed at Munich on 5 October 1973, the courts of each Member State shall have exclusive jurisdiction, regardless of domicile, in proceedings concerned with the registration or validity of any European patent granted for that State;

5. in proceedings concerned with the enforcement of judgments, the courts of the Member State in which the judgment has been or is to be enforced.

Section 7

Prorogation of jurisdiction

Article 23

1.   If the parties, one or more of whom is domiciled in a Member State, have agreed that a court or the courts of a Member State are to have jurisdiction to settle any disputes which have arisen or which may arise in connection with a particular legal relationship, that court or those courts shall

have jurisdiction. Such jurisdiction shall be exclusive unless the parties have agreed otherwise. Such an agreement conferring jurisdiction shall be either:

(a) in writing or evidenced in writing; or

(b) in a form which accords with practices which the parties have established between themselves; or

(c) in international trade or commerce, in a form which accords with a usage of which the parties are or ought to have been aware and which in such trade or commerce is widely known to, and regularly observed by, parties to contracts of the type involved in the particular trade or commerce concerned.

2.   Any communication by electronic means which provides a durable record of the agreement shall be equivalent to 'writing'.

3.   Where such an agreement is concluded by parties, none of whom is domiciled in a Member State, the courts of other Member States shall have no jurisdiction over their disputes unless the court or courts chosen have declined jurisdiction.

4.   The court or courts of a Member State on which a trust instrument has conferred jurisdiction shall have exclusive jurisdiction in any proceedings brought against a settlor, trustee or beneficiary, if relations between these persons or their rights or obligations under the trust are involved.

5.   Agreements or provisions of a trust instrument conferring jurisdiction shall have no legal force if they are contrary to Articles 13, 17 or 21, or if the courts whose jurisdiction they purport to exclude have exclusive jurisdiction by virtue of Article 22.

Article 24

Apart from jurisdiction derived from other provisions of this Regulation, a court of a Member State before which a defendant enters an appearance shall have jurisdiction. This rule shall not apply where appearance was entered to contest the jurisdiction, or where another court has exclusive jurisdiction by virtue of Article 22.

Section 8

Examination as to jurisdiction and admissibility

Article 25

Where a court of a Member State is seised of a claim which is principally concerned with a matter over which the courts of another Member State have exclusive jurisdiction by virtue of Article 22, it shall declare of its own motion that it has no jurisdiction.

Article 26

1.   Where a defendant domiciled in one Member State is sued in a court of another Member State and does not enter an appearance, the court shall declare of its own motion that it has no jurisdiction unless its jurisdiction is derived from the provisions of this Regulation.

2.   The court shall stay the proceedings so long as it is not shown that the defendant has been able to receive the document instituting the proceedings or an equivalent document in sufficient time to enable him to arrange for his defence, or that all necessary steps have been taken to this end.

3.   Article 19 of Council Regulation (EC) No 1348/2000 of 29 May 2000 on the service in the Member States of judicial and extrajudicial documents in civil or commercial matters (¹) shall apply instead of the provisions of paragraph 2 if the document instituting the proceedings or an equivalent document had to be transmitted from one Member State to another pursuant to this Regulation.

4.   Where the provisions of Regulation (EC) No 1348/2000 are not applicable, Article 15 of the Hague Convention of 15 November 1965 on the Service Abroad of Judicial and Extrajudicial Documents in Civil or Commercial Matters shall apply if the document instituting the proceedings or an equivalent document had to be transmitted pursuant to that Convention.

Section 9

Lis pendens — related actions

Article 27

1.   Where proceedings involving the same cause of action and between the same parties are brought in the courts of

(¹) OJ L 160, 30.6.2000, p. 37.

different Member States, any court other than the court first seised shall of its own motion stay its proceedings until such time as the jurisdiction of the court first seised is established.

2.   Where the jurisdiction of the court first seised is established, any court other than the court first seised shall decline jurisdiction in favour of that court.

Article 28

1.   Where related actions are pending in the courts of different Member States, any court other than the court first seised may stay its proceedings.

2.   Where these actions are pending at first instance, any court other than the court first seised may also, on the application of one of the parties, decline jurisdiction if the court first seised has jurisdiction over the actions in question and its law permits the consolidation thereof.

3.   For the purposes of this Article, actions are deemed to be related where they are so closely connected that it is expedient to hear and determine them together to avoid the risk of irreconcilable judgments resulting from separate proceedings.

Article 29

Where actions come within the exclusive jurisdiction of several courts, any court other than the court first seised shall decline jurisdiction in favour of that court.

Article 30

For the purposes of this Section, a court shall be deemed to be seised:

1. at the time when the document instituting the proceedings or an equivalent document is lodged with the court, provided that the plaintiff has not subsequently failed to take the steps he was required to take to have service effected on the defendant, or

2. if the document has to be served before being lodged with the court, at the time when it is received by the authority responsible for service, provided that the plaintiff has not subsequently failed to take the steps he was required to take to have the document lodged with the court.

Section 10

Provisional, including protective, measures

Article 31

Application may be made to the courts of a Member State for such provisional, including protective, measures as may be available under the law of that State, even if, under this Regulation, the courts of another Member State have jurisdiction as to the substance of the matter.

CHAPTER III

RECOGNITION AND ENFORCEMENT

Article 32

For the purposes of this Regulation, 'judgment' means any judgment given by a court or tribunal of a Member State, whatever the judgment may be called, including a decree, order, decision or writ of execution, as well as the determination of costs or expenses by an officer of the court.

Section 1

Recognition

Article 33

1.   A judgment given in a Member State shall be recognised in the other Member States without any special procedure being required.

2.   Any interested party who raises the recognition of a judgment as the principal issue in a dispute may, in accordance with the procedures provided for in Sections 2 and 3 of this Chapter, apply for a decision that the judgment be recognised.

3.   If the outcome of proceedings in a court of a Member State depends on the determination of an incidental question of recognition that court shall have jurisdiction over that question.

Article 34

A judgment shall not be recognised:

1.   if such recognition is manifestly contrary to public policy in the Member State in which recognition is sought;

2.   where it was given in default of appearance, if the defendant was not served with the document which instituted the proceedings or with an equivalent document in sufficient time and in such a way as to enable him to arrange for his defence, unless the defendant failed to commence proceedings to challenge the judgment when it was possible for him to do so;

3.   if it is irreconcilable with a judgment given in a dispute between the same parties in the Member State in which recognition is sought;

4.   if it is irreconcilable with an earlier judgment given in another Member State or in a third State involving the same cause of action and between the same parties, provided that the earlier judgment fulfils the conditions necessary for its recognition in the Member State addressed.

Article 35

1.   Moreover, a judgment shall not be recognised if it conflicts with Sections 3, 4 or 6 of Chapter II, or in a case provided for in Article 72.

2.   In its examination of the grounds of jurisdiction referred to in the foregoing paragraph, the court or authority applied to shall be bound by the findings of fact on which the court of the Member State of origin based its jurisdiction.

3.   Subject to the paragraph 1, the jurisdiction of the court of the Member State of origin may not be reviewed. The test of public policy referred to in point 1 of Article 34 may not be applied to the rules relating to jurisdiction.

Article 36

Under no circumstances may a foreign judgment be reviewed as to its substance.

Article 37

1.   A court of a Member State in which recognition is sought of a judgment given in another Member State may stay the proceedings if an ordinary appeal against the judgment has been lodged.

2.   A court of a Member State in which recognition is sought of a judgment given in Ireland or the United Kingdom may stay the proceedings if enforcement is suspended in the State of origin, by reason of an appeal.

Section 2

Enforcement

Article 38

1.   A judgment given in a Member State and enforceable in that State shall be enforced in another Member State when, on the application of any interested party, it has been declared enforceable there.

2.   However, in the United Kingdom, such a judgment shall be enforced in England and Wales, in Scotland, or in Northern Ireland when, on the application of any interested party, it has been registered for enforcement in that part of the United Kingdom.

Article 39

1.   The application shall be submitted to the court or competent authority indicated in the list in Annex II.

2.   The local jurisdiction shall be determined by reference to the place of domicile of the party against whom enforcement is sought, or to the place of enforcement.

Article 40

1.   The procedure for making the application shall be governed by the law of the Member State in which enforcement is sought.

2.   The applicant must give an address for service of process within the area of jurisdiction of the court applied to. However, if the law of the Member State in which enforcement is sought does not provide for the furnishing of such an address, the applicant shall appoint a representative *ad litem*.

3.   The documents referred to in Article 53 shall be attached to the application.

Article 41

The judgment shall be declared enforceable immediately on completion of the formalities in Article 53 without any review under Articles 34 and 35. The party against whom enforcement is sought shall not at this stage of the proceedings be entitled to make any submissions on the application.

Article 42

1.   The decision on the application for a declaration of enforceability shall forthwith be brought to the notice of the applicant in accordance with the procedure laid down by the law of the Member State in which enforcement is sought.

2.   The declaration of enforceability shall be served on the party against whom enforcement is sought, accompanied by the judgment, if not already served on that party.

Article 43

1.   The decision on the application for a declaration of enforceability may be appealed against by either party.

2.   The appeal is to be lodged with the court indicated in the list in Annex III.

3.   The appeal shall be dealt with in accordance with the rules governing procedure in contradictory matters.

4.   If the party against whom enforcement is sought fails to appear before the appellate court in proceedings concerning an appeal brought by the applicant, Article 26(2) to (4) shall apply even where the party against whom enforcement is sought is not domiciled in any of the Member States.

5.   An appeal against the declaration of enforceability is to be lodged within one month of service thereof. If the party against whom enforcement is sought is domiciled in a Member State other than that in which the declaration of enforceability was given, the time for appealing shall be two months and shall run from the date of service, either on him in person or at his residence. No extension of time may be granted on account of distance.

Article 44

The judgment given on the appeal may be contested only by the appeal referred to in Annex IV.

Article 45

1.   The court with which an appeal is lodged under Article 43 or Article 44 shall refuse or revoke a declaration of enforceability only on one of the grounds specified in Articles 34 and 35. It shall give its decision without delay.

2.   Under no circumstances may the foreign judgment be reviewed as to its substance.

Article 46

1.   The court with which an appeal is lodged under Article 43 or Article 44 may, on the application of the party against whom enforcement is sought, stay the proceedings if an ordinary appeal has been lodged against the judgment in the Member State of origin or if the time for such an appeal has not yet expired; in the latter case, the court may specify the time within which such an appeal is to be lodged.

2.   Where the judgment was given in Ireland or the United Kingdom, any form of appeal available in the Member State of origin shall be treated as an ordinary appeal for the purposes of paragraph 1.

3. The court may also make enforcement conditional on the provision of such security as it shall determine.

Article 47

1. When a judgment must be recognised in accordance with this Regulation, nothing shall prevent the applicant from availing himself of provisional, including protective, measures in accordance with the law of the Member State requested without a declaration of enforceability under Article 41 being required.

2. The declaration of enforceability shall carry with it the power to proceed to any protective measures.

3. During the time specified for an appeal pursuant to Article 43(5) against the declaration of enforceability and until any such appeal has been determined, no measures of enforcement may be taken other than protective measures against the property of the party against whom enforcement is sought.

Article 48

1. Where a foreign judgment has been given in respect of several matters and the declaration of enforceability cannot be given for all of them, the court or competent authority shall give it for one or more of them.

2. An applicant may request a declaration of enforceability limited to parts of a judgment.

Article 49

A foreign judgment which orders a periodic payment by way of a penalty shall be enforceable in the Member State in which enforcement is sought only if the amount of the payment has been finally determined by the courts of the Member State of origin.

Article 50

An applicant who, in the Member State of origin has benefited from complete or partial legal aid or exemption from costs or expenses, shall be entitled, in the procedure provided for in this Section, to benefit from the most favourable legal aid or the most extensive exemption from costs or expenses provided for by the law of the Member State addressed.

Article 51

No security, bond or deposit, however described, shall be required of a party who in one Member State applies for enforcement of a judgment given in another Member State on the ground that he is a foreign national or that he is not domiciled or resident in the State in which enforcement is sought.

Article 52

In proceedings for the issue of a declaration of enforceability, no charge, duty or fee calculated by reference to the value of the matter at issue may be levied in the Member State in which enforcement is sought.

Section 3

Common provisions

Article 53

1. A party seeking recognition or applying for a declaration of enforceability shall produce a copy of the judgment which satisfies the conditions necessary to establish its authenticity.

2. A party applying for a declaration of enforceability shall also produce the certificate referred to in Article 54, without prejudice to Article 55.

Article 54

The court or competent authority of a Member State where a judgment was given shall issue, at the request of any interested party, a certificate using the standard form in Annex V to this Regulation.

Article 55

1. If the certificate referred to in Article 54 is not produced, the court or competent authority may specify a time for its production or accept an equivalent document or, if it considers that it has sufficient information before it, dispense with its production.

2. If the court or competent authority so requires, a translation of the documents shall be produced. The translation shall be certified by a person qualified to do so in one of the Member States.

Article 56

No legalisation or other similar formality shall be required in respect of the documents referred to in Article 53 or Article 55(2), or in respect of a document appointing a representative *ad litem*.

CHAPTER IV

AUTHENTIC INSTRUMENTS AND COURT SETTLEMENTS

Article 57

1.   A document which has been formally drawn up or registered as an authentic instrument and is enforceable in one Member State shall, in another Member State, be declared enforceable there, on application made in accordance with the procedures provided for in Articles 38, et seq. The court with which an appeal is lodged under Article 43 or Article 44 shall refuse or revoke a declaration of enforceability only if enforcement of the instrument is manifestly contrary to public policy in the Member State addressed.

2.   Arrangements relating to maintenance obligations concluded with administrative authorities or authenticated by them shall also be regarded as authentic instruments within the meaning of paragraph 1.

3.   The instrument produced must satisfy the conditions necessary to establish its authenticity in the Member State of origin.

4.   Section 3 of Chapter III shall apply as appropriate. The competent authority of a Member State where an authentic instrument was drawn up or registered shall issue, at the request of any interested party, a certificate using the standard form in Annex VI to this Regulation.

Article 58

A settlement which has been approved by a court in the course of proceedings and is enforceable in the Member State in which it was concluded shall be enforceable in the State addressed under the same conditions as authentic instruments. The court or competent authority of a Member State where a court settlement was approved shall issue, at the request of any interested party, a certificate using the standard form in Annex V to this Regulation.

CHAPTER V

GENERAL PROVISIONS

Article 59

1.   In order to determine whether a party is domiciled in the Member State whose courts are seised of a matter, the court shall apply its internal law.

2.   If a party is not domiciled in the Member State whose courts are seised of the matter, then, in order to determine whether the party is domiciled in another Member State, the court shall apply the law of that Member State.

Article 60

1.   For the purposes of this Regulation, a company or other legal person or association of natural or legal persons is domiciled at the place where it has its:

(a) statutory seat, or

(b) central administration, or

(c) principal place of business.

2.   For the purposes of the United Kingdom and Ireland 'statutory seat' means the registered office or, where there is no such office anywhere, the place of incorporation or, where there is no such place anywhere, the place under the law of which the formation took place.

3.   In order to determine whether a trust is domiciled in the Member State whose courts are seised of the matter, the court shall apply its rules of private international law.

Article 61

Without prejudice to any more favourable provisions of national laws, persons domiciled in a Member State who are being prosecuted in the criminal courts of another Member State of which they are not nationals for an offence which was not intentionally committed may be defended by persons qualified to do so, even if they do not appear in person. However, the court seised of the matter may order appearance in person; in the case of failure to appear, a judgment given in the civil action without the person concerned having had the opportunity to arrange for his defence need not be recognised or enforced in the other Member States.

Article 62

In Sweden, in summary proceedings concerning orders to pay (*betalningsföreläggande*) and assistance (*handräckning*), the expression 'court' includes the 'Swedish enforcement service' (*kronofogdemyndighet*).

Article 63

1.   A person domiciled in the territory of the Grand Duchy of Luxembourg and sued in the court of another Member State pursuant to Article 5(1) may refuse to submit to the jurisdiction of that court if the final place of delivery of the goods or provision of the services is in Luxembourg.

2.   Where, under paragraph 1, the final place of delivery of the goods or provision of the services is in Luxembourg, any agreement conferring jurisdiction must, in order to be valid, be accepted in writing or evidenced in writing within the meaning of Article 23(1)(a).

3.   The provisions of this Article shall not apply to contracts for the provision of financial services.

4.   The provisions of this Article shall apply for a period of six years from entry into force of this Regulation.

Article 64

1.   In proceedings involving a dispute between the master and a member of the crew of a seagoing ship registered in Greece or in Portugal, concerning remuneration or other conditions of service, a court in a Member State shall establish whether the diplomatic or consular officer responsible for the ship has been notified of the dispute. It may act as soon as that officer has been notified.

2.   The provisions of this Article shall apply for a period of six years from entry into force of this Regulation.

Article 65

1.   The jurisdiction specified in Article 6(2), and Article 11 in actions on a warranty of guarantee or in any other third party proceedings may not be resorted to in Germany and Austria. Any person domiciled in another Member State may be sued in the courts:

(a) of Germany, pursuant to Articles 68 and 72 to 74 of the Code of Civil Procedure (*Zivilprozessordnung*) concerning third-party notices,

(b) of Austria, pursuant to Article 21 of the Code of Civil Procedure (*Zivilprozessordnung*) concerning third-party notices.

2.   Judgments given in other Member States by virtue of Article 6(2), or Article 11 shall be recognised and enforced in Germany and Austria in accordance with Chapter III. Any effects which judgments given in these States may have on third parties by application of the provisions in paragraph 1 shall also be recognised in the other Member States.

CHAPTER VI

TRANSITIONAL PROVISIONS

Article 66

1.   This Regulation shall apply only to legal proceedings instituted and to documents formally drawn up or registered as authentic instruments after the entry into force thereof.

2.   However, if the proceedings in the Member State of origin were instituted before the entry into force of this Regulation, judgments given after that date shall be recognised and enforced in accordance with Chapter III,

(a) if the proceedings in the Member State of origin were instituted after the entry into force of the Brussels or the Lugano Convention both in the Member State or origin and in the Member State addressed;

(b) in all other cases, if jurisdiction was founded upon rules which accorded with those provided for either in Chapter II or in a convention concluded between the Member State of origin and the Member State addressed which was in force when the proceedings were instituted.

CHAPTER VII

RELATIONS WITH OTHER INSTRUMENTS

Article 67

This Regulation shall not prejudice the application of provisions governing jurisdiction and the recognition and enforcement of judgments in specific matters which are contained in Community instruments or in national legislation harmonised pursuant to such instruments.

Article 68

1.   This Regulation shall, as between the Member States, supersede the Brussels Convention, except as regards the territories of the Member States which fall within the territorial scope of that Convention and which are excluded from this Regulation pursuant to Article 299 of the Treaty.

2.   In so far as this Regulation replaces the provisions of the Brussels Convention between Member States, any reference to the Convention shall be understood as a reference to this Regulation.

Article 69

Subject to Article 66(2) and Article 70, this Regulation shall, as between Member States, supersede the following conventions and treaty concluded between two or more of them:

— the Convention between Belgium and France on Jurisdiction and the Validity and Enforcement of Judgments, Arbitration Awards and Authentic Instruments, signed at Paris on 8 July 1899,

— the Convention between Belgium and the Netherlands on Jurisdiction, Bankruptcy, and the Validity and Enforcement of Judgments, Arbitration Awards and Authentic Instruments, signed at Brussels on 28 March 1925,

— the Convention between France and Italy on the Enforcement of Judgments in Civil and Commercial Matters, signed at Rome on 3 June 1930,

— the Convention between Germany and Italy on the Recognition and Enforcement of Judgments in Civil and Commercial Matters, signed at Rome on 9 March 1936,

— the Convention between Belgium and Austria on the Reciprocal Recognition and Enforcement of Judgments and Authentic Instruments relating to Maintenance Obligations, signed at Vienna on 25 October 1957,

— the Convention between Germany and Belgium on the Mutual Recognition and Enforcement of Judgments, Arbitration Awards and Authentic Instruments in Civil and Commercial Matters, signed at Bonn on 30 June 1958,

— the Convention between the Netherlands and Italy on the Recognition and Enforcement of Judgments in Civil and Commercial Matters, signed at Rome on 17 April 1959,

— the Convention between Germany and Austria on the Reciprocal Recognition and Enforcement of Judgments, Settlements and Authentic Instruments in Civil and Commercial Matters, signed at Vienna on 6 June 1959,

— the Convention between Belgium and Austria on the Reciprocal Recognition and Enforcement of Judgments, Arbitral Awards and Authentic Instruments in Civil and Commercial Matters, signed at Vienna on 16 June 1959,

— the Convention between Greece and Germany for the Reciprocal Recognition and Enforcement of Judgments, Settlements and Authentic Instruments in Civil and Commercial Matters, signed in Athens on 4 November 1961,

— the Convention between Belgium and Italy on the Recognition and Enforcement of Judgments and other Enforceable Instruments in Civil and Commercial Matters, signed at Rome on 6 April 1962,

— the Convention between the Netherlands and Germany on the Mutual Recognition and Enforcement of Judgments and Other Enforceable Instruments in Civil and Commercial Matters, signed at The Hague on 30 August 1962,

— the Convention between the Netherlands and Austria on the Reciprocal Recognition and Enforcement of Judgments and Authentic Instruments in Civil and Commercial Matters, signed at The Hague on 6 February 1963,

— the Convention between France and Austria on the Recognition and Enforcement of Judgments and Authentic Instruments in Civil and Commercial Matters, signed at Vienna on 15 July 1966,

— the Convention between Spain and France on the Recognition and Enforcement of Judgment Arbitration Awards in Civil and Commercial Matters, signed at Paris on 28 May 1969,

— the Convention between Luxembourg and Austria on the Recognition and Enforcement of Judgments and Authentic Instruments in Civil and Commercial Matters, signed at Luxembourg on 29 July 1971,

— the Convention between Italy and Austria on the Recognition and Enforcement of Judgments in Civil and Commercial Matters, of Judicial Settlements and of Authentic Instruments, signed at Rome on 16 November 1971,

— the Convention between Spain and Italy regarding Legal Aid and the Recognition and Enforcement of Judgments in Civil and Commercial Matters, signed at Madrid on 22 May 1973,

— the Convention between Finland, Iceland, Norway, Sweden and Denmark on the Recognition and Enforcement of Judgments in Civil Matters, signed at Copenhagen on 11 October 1977,

— the Convention between Austria and Sweden on the Recognition and Enforcement of Judgments in Civil Matters, signed at Stockholm on 16 September 1982,

— the Convention between Spain and the Federal Republic of Germany on the Recognition and Enforcement of Judgments, Settlements and Enforceable Authentic Instruments in Civil and Commercial Matters, signed at Bonn on 14 November 1983,

— the Convention between Austria and Spain on the Recognition and Enforcement of Judgments, Settlements and Enforceable Authentic Instruments in Civil and Commercial Matters, signed at Vienna on 17 February 1984,

— the Convention between Finland and Austria on the Recognition and Enforcement of Judgments in Civil Matters, signed at Vienna on 17 November 1986, and

— the Treaty between Belgium, the Netherlands and Luxembourg in Jurisdiction, Bankruptcy, and the Validity and Enforcement of Judgments, Arbitration Awards and Authentic Instruments, signed at Brussels on 24 November 1961, in so far as it is in force.

Article 70

1. The Treaty and the Conventions referred to in Article 69 shall continue to have effect in relation to matters to which this Regulation does not apply.

2. They shall continue to have effect in respect of judgments given and documents formally drawn up or registered as authentic instruments before the entry into force of this Regulation.

Article 71

1. This Regulation shall not affect any conventions to which the Member States are parties and which in relation to particular matters, govern jurisdiction or the recognition or enforcement of judgments.

2. With a view to its uniform interpretation, paragraph 1 shall be applied in the following manner:

(a) this Regulation shall not prevent a court of a Member State, which is a party to a convention on a particular matter, from assuming jurisdiction in accordance with that convention, even where the defendant is domiciled in another Member State which is not a party to that convention. The court hearing the action shall, in any event, apply Article 26 of this Regulation;

(b) judgments given in a Member State by a court in the exercise of jurisdiction provided for in a convention on a particular matter shall be recognised and enforced in the other Member States in accordance with this Regulation.

Where a convention on a particular matter to which both the Member State of origin and the Member State addressed are parties lays down conditions for the recognition or enforcement of judgments, those conditions shall apply. In any event, the provisions of this Regulation which concern the procedure for recognition and enforcement of judgments may be applied.

Article 72

This Regulation shall not affect agreements by which Member States undertook, prior to the entry into force of this

Regulation pursuant to Article 59 of the Brussels Convention, not to recognise judgments given, in particular in other Contracting States to that Convention, against defendants domiciled or habitually resident in a third country where, in cases provided for in Article 4 of that Convention, the judgment could only be founded on a ground of jurisdiction specified in the second paragraph of Article 3 of that Convention.

CHAPTER VIII

FINAL PROVISIONS

Article 73

No later than five years after the entry into force of this Regulation, the Commission shall present to the European Parliament, the Council and the Economic and Social Committee a report on the application of this Regulation. The report shall be accompanied, if need be, by proposals for adaptations to this Regulation.

Article 74

1. The Member States shall notify the Commission of the texts amending the lists set out in Annexes I to IV. The Commission shall adapt the Annexes concerned accordingly.

2. The updating or technical adjustment of the forms, specimens of which appear in Annexes V and VI, shall be adopted in accordance with the advisory procedure referred to in Article 75(2).

Article 75

1. The Commission shall be assisted by a committee.

2. Where reference is made to this paragraph, Articles 3 and 7 of Decision 1999/468/EC shall apply.

3. The Committee shall adopt its rules of procedure.

Article 76

This Regulation shall enter into force on 1 March 2002.

This Regulation is binding in its entirety and directly applicable in the Member States in accordance with the Treaty establishing the European Community.

Done at Brussels, 22 December 2000.

For the Council
The President
C. PIERRET

_____

ANNEX I

Rules of jurisdiction referred to in Article 3(2) and Article 4(2)

The rules of jurisdiction referred to in Article 3(2) and Article 4(2) are the following:

— in Belgium: Article 15 of the Civil Code (*Code civil/Burgerlijk Wetboek*) and Article 638 of the Judicial Code (*Code judiciaire/Gerechtelijk Wetboek*);

— in Germany: Article 23 of the Code of Civil Procedure (*Zivilprozessordnung*),

— in Greece, Article 40 of the Code of Civil Procedure (*Κώδικας Πολιτικής Δικονομίας*),

— in France: Articles 14 and 15 of the Civil Code (*Code civil*),

— in Ireland: the rules which enable jurisdiction to be founded on the document instituting the proceedings having been served on the defendant during his temporary presence in Ireland,

— in Italy: Articles 3 and 4 of Act 218 of 31 May 1995,

— in Luxembourg: Articles 14 and 15 of the Civil Code (*Code civil*),

— in the Netherlands: Articles 126(3) and 127 of the Code of Civil Procedure (*Wetboek van Burgerlijke Rechtsvordering*),

— in Austria: Article 99 of the Court Jurisdiction Act (*Jurisdiktionsnorm*),

— in Portugal: Articles 65 and 65A of the Code of Civil Procedure (*Código de Processo Civil*) and Article 11 of the Code of Labour Procedure (*Código de Processo de Trabalho*),

— in Finland: the second, third and fourth sentences of the first paragraph of Section 1 of Chapter 10 of the Code of Judicial Procedure (*oikeudenkäymiskaari/rättegångsbalken*),

— in Sweden: the first sentence of the first paragraph of Section 3 of Chapter 10 of the Code of Judicial Procedure (*rättegångsbalken*),

— in the United Kingdom: rules which enable jurisdiction to be founded on:

(a) the document instituting the proceedings having been served on the defendant during his temporary presence in the United Kingdom; or

(b) the presence within the United Kingdom of property belonging to the defendant; or

(c) the seizure by the plaintiff of property situated in the United Kingdom.

———

ANNEX II

The courts or competent authorities to which the application referred to in Article 39 may be submitted are the following:

— in Belgium, the '*tribunal de première instance*' or '*rechtbank van eerste aanleg*' or '*erstinstanzliches Gericht*',

— in Germany, the presiding judge of a chamber of the '*Landgericht*',

— in Greece, the 'Μονομελές Πρωτοδικείο',

— in Spain, the '*Juzgado de Primera Instancia*',

— in France, the presiding judge of the '*tribunal de grande instance*',

— in Ireland, the High Court,

— in Italy, the '*Corte d'appello*',

— in Luxembourg, the presiding judge of the '*tribunal d'arrondissement*',

— in the Netherlands, the presiding judge of the '*arrondissementsrechtbank*';

— in Austria, the '*Bezirksgericht*',

— in Portugal, the '*Tribunal de Comarca*',

— in Finland, the '*käräjäoikeus/tingsrätt*',

— in Sweden, the '*Svea hovrätt*',

— in the United Kingdom:

    (a) in England and Wales, the High Court of Justice, or in the case of a maintenance judgment, the Magistrate's Court on transmission by the Secretary of State;

    (b) in Scotland, the Court of Session, or in the case of a maintenance judgment, the Sheriff Court on transmission by the Secretary of State;

    (c) in Northern Ireland, the High Court of Justice, or in the case of a maintenance judgment, the Magistrate's Court on transmission by the Secretary of State;

    (d) in Gibraltar, the Supreme Court of Gibraltar, or in the case of a maintenance judgment, the Magistrates' Court on transmission by the Attorney General of Gibraltar.

———

ANNEX III

The courts with which appeals referred to in Article 43(2) may be lodged are the following:

— in Belgium,

    (a) as regards appeal by the defendant: the '*tribunal de première instance*' or '*rechtbank van eerste aanleg*' or '*erstinstanzliches Gericht*',

    (b) as regards appeal by the applicant: the '*Cour d'appel*' or '*hof van beroep*',

— in the Federal Republic of Germany, the '*Oberlandesgericht*',

— in Greece, the '*Εφετείο*',

— in Spain, the '*Audiencia Provincial*',

— in France, the '*cour d'appel*',

— in Ireland, the High Court,

— in Italy, the '*corte d'appello*',

— in Luxembourg, the '*Cour supérieure de Justice*' sitting as a court of civil appeal,

— in the Netherlands:

    (a) for the defendant: the '*arrondissementsrechtbank*',

    (b) for the applicant: the '*gerechtshof*',

— in Austria, the '*Bezirksgericht*',

— in Portugal, the '*Tribunal de Relação*',

— in Finland, the '*hovioikeus/hovrätt*',

— in Sweden, the '*Svea hovrätt*',

— in the United Kingdom:

    (a) in England and Wales, the High Court of Justice, or in the case of a maintenance judgment, the Magistrate's Court;

    (b) in Scotland, the Court of Session, or in the case of a maintenance judgment, the Sheriff Court;

    (c) in Northern Ireland, the High Court of Justice, or in the case of a maintenance judgment, the Magistrate's Court;

    (d) in Gibraltar, the Supreme Court of Gibraltar, or in the case of a maintenance judgment, the Magistrates' Court.

———

ANNEX IV

The appeals which may be lodged pursuant to Article 44 are the following

— in Belgium, Greece, Spain, France, Italy, Luxembourg and the Netherlands, an appeal in cassation,

— in Germany, a '*Rechtsbeschwerde*',

— in Ireland, an appeal on a point of law to the Supreme Court,

— in Austria, a '*Revisionsrekurs*',

— in Portugal, an appeal on a point of law,

— in Finland, an appeal to the '*korkein oikeus/högsta domstolen*',

— in Sweden, an appeal to the '*Högsta domstolen*',

— in the United Kingdom, a single further appeal on a point of law.

———

ANNEX V

Certificate referred to in Articles 54 and 58 of the Regulation on judgments and court settlements

(English, inglés, anglais, inglese, ...)

1. Member State of origin

2. Court or competent authority issuing the certificate

    2.1. Name

    2.2. Address

    2.3. Tel./fax/e-mail

3. Court which delivered the judgment/approved the court settlement (*)

    3.1. Type of court

    3.2. Place of court

4. Judgment/court settlement (*)

    4.1. Date

    4.2. Reference number

    4.3. The parties to the judgment/court settlement (*)

        4.3.1. Name(s) of plaintiff(s)

        4.3.2. Name(s) of defendant(s)

        4.3.3. Name(s) of other party(ies), if any

    4.4. Date of service of the document instituting the proceedings where judgment was given in default of appearance

    4.5. Text of the judgment/court settlement (*) as annexed to this certificate

5. Names of parties to whom legal aid has been granted

The judgment/court settlement (*) is enforceable in the Member State of origin (Articles 38 and 58 of the Regulation) against:

Name:

Done at . . . . , date . . . .

Signature and/or stamp . . . .

———

———

(*) Delete as appropriate.

ANNEX VI

Certificate referred to in Article 57(4) of the Regulation on authentic instruments

(English, inglés, anglais, inglese ....)

1. Member State of origin

2. Competent authority issuing the certificate

    2.1. Name

    2.2. Address

    2.3. Tel./fax/e-mail

3. Authority which has given authenticity to the instrument

    3.1. Authority involved in the drawing up of the authentic instrument (if applicable)

       3.1.1. Name and designation of authority

       3.1.2. Place of authority

    3.2. Authority which has registered the authentic instrument (if applicable)

       3.2.1. Type of authority

       3.2.2. Place of authority

4. Authentic instrument

    4.1. Description of the instrument

    4.2. Date

       4.2.1. on which the instrument was drawn up

       4.2.2. if different: on which the instrument was registered

    4.3. Reference number

    4.4. Parties to the instrument

       4.4.1. Name of the creditor

       4.4.2. Name of the debtor

5. Text of the enforceable obligation as annexed to this certificate

The authentic instrument is enforceable against the debtor in the Member State of origin (Article 57(1) of the Regulation)

Done at ...., date ....

Signature and/or stamp ....

I

(Legislative acts)

REGULATIONS

REGULATION (EU) No 1215/2012 OF THE EUROPEAN PARLIAMENT AND OF THE COUNCIL

of 12 December 2012

on jurisdiction and the recognition and enforcement of judgments in civil and commercial matters

(recast)

THE EUROPEAN PARLIAMENT AND THE COUNCIL OF THE EUROPEAN UNION,

Having regard to the Treaty on the Functioning of the European Union, and in particular Article 67(4) and points (a), (c) and (e) of Article 81(2) thereof,

Having regard to the proposal from the European Commission,

After transmission of the draft legislative act to the national parliaments,

Having regard to the opinion of the European Economic and Social Committee [1],

Acting in accordance with the ordinary legislative procedure [2],

Whereas:

(1)　On 21 April 2009, the Commission adopted a report on the application of Council Regulation (EC) No 44/2001 of 22 December 2000 on jurisdiction and the recognition and enforcement of judgments in civil and commercial matters [3]. The report concluded that, in general, the operation of that Regulation is satisfactory, but that it is desirable to improve the application of certain of its provisions, to further facilitate the free circulation of judgments and to further enhance access to justice. Since a number of amendments are to be made to that Regulation it should, in the interests of clarity, be recast.

(2)　At its meeting in Brussels on 10 and 11 December 2009, the European Council adopted a new multiannual programme entitled 'The Stockholm Programme – an open and secure Europe serving and protecting citizens' [4]. In the Stockholm Programme the European Council considered that the process of abolishing all intermediate measures (the exequatur) should be continued during the period covered by that Programme. At the same time the abolition of the exequatur should also be accompanied by a series of safeguards.

(3)　The Union has set itself the objective of maintaining and developing an area of freedom, security and justice, inter alia, by facilitating access to justice, in particular through the principle of mutual recognition of judicial and extrajudicial decisions in civil matters. For the gradual establishment of such an area, the Union is to adopt measures relating to judicial cooperation in civil matters having cross-border implications, particularly when necessary for the proper functioning of the internal market.

(4)　Certain differences between national rules governing jurisdiction and recognition of judgments hamper the sound operation of the internal market. Provisions to unify the rules of conflict of jurisdiction in civil and commercial matters, and to ensure rapid and simple recognition and enforcement of judgments given in a Member State, are essential.

(5)　Such provisions fall within the area of judicial cooperation in civil matters within the meaning of Article 81 of the Treaty on the Functioning of the European Union (TFEU).

[1] OJ C 218, 23.7.2011, p. 78.
[2] Position of the European Parliament of 20 November 2012 (not yet published in the Official Journal) and decision of the Council of 6 December 2012.
[3] OJ L 12, 16.1.2001, p. 1.

[4] OJ C 115, 4.5.2010, p. 1.

(6) In order to attain the objective of free circulation of judgments in civil and commercial matters, it is necessary and appropriate that the rules governing jurisdiction and the recognition and enforcement of judgments be governed by a legal instrument of the Union which is binding and directly applicable.

(7) On 27 September 1968, the then Member States of the European Communities, acting under Article 220, fourth indent, of the Treaty establishing the European Economic Community, concluded the Brussels Convention on Jurisdiction and the Enforcement of Judgments in Civil and Commercial Matters, subsequently amended by conventions on the accession to that Convention of new Member States [1] ('the 1968 Brussels Convention'). On 16 September 1988, the then Member States of the European Communities and certain EFTA States concluded the Lugano Convention on Jurisdiction and the Enforcement of Judgments in Civil and Commercial Matters [2] ('the 1988 Lugano Convention'), which is a parallel convention to the 1968 Brussels Convention. The 1988 Lugano Convention became applicable to Poland on 1 February 2000.

(8) On 22 December 2000, the Council adopted Regulation (EC) No 44/2001, which replaces the 1968 Brussels Convention with regard to the territories of the Member States covered by the TFEU, as between the Member States except Denmark. By Council Decision 2006/325/EC [3], the Community concluded an agreement with Denmark ensuring the application of the provisions of Regulation (EC) No 44/2001 in Denmark. The 1988 Lugano Convention was revised by the Convention on Jurisdiction and the Recognition and Enforcement of Judgments in Civil and Commercial Matters [4], signed at Lugano on 30 October 2007 by the Community, Denmark, Iceland, Norway and Switzerland ('the 2007 Lugano Convention').

(9) The 1968 Brussels Convention continues to apply to the territories of the Member States which fall within the territorial scope of that Convention and which are excluded from this Regulation pursuant to Article 355 of the TFEU.

(10) The scope of this Regulation should cover all the main civil and commercial matters apart from certain well-defined matters, in particular maintenance obligations, which should be excluded from the scope of this Regulation following the adoption of Council Regulation (EC)

No 4/2009 of 18 December 2008 on jurisdiction, applicable law, recognition and enforcement of decisions and cooperation in matters relating to maintenance obligations [5].

(11) For the purposes of this Regulation, courts or tribunals of the Member States should include courts or tribunals common to several Member States, such as the Benelux Court of Justice when it exercises jurisdiction on matters falling within the scope of this Regulation. Therefore, judgments given by such courts should be recognised and enforced in accordance with this Regulation.

(12) This Regulation should not apply to arbitration. Nothing in this Regulation should prevent the courts of a Member State, when seised of an action in a matter in respect of which the parties have entered into an arbitration agreement, from referring the parties to arbitration, from staying or dismissing the proceedings, or from examining whether the arbitration agreement is null and void, inoperative or incapable of being performed, in accordance with their national law.

A ruling given by a court of a Member State as to whether or not an arbitration agreement is null and void, inoperative or incapable of being performed should not be subject to the rules of recognition and enforcement laid down in this Regulation, regardless of whether the court decided on this as a principal issue or as an incidental question.

On the other hand, where a court of a Member State, exercising jurisdiction under this Regulation or under national law, has determined that an arbitration agreement is null and void, inoperative or incapable of being performed, this should not preclude that court's judgment on the substance of the matter from being recognised or, as the case may be, enforced in accordance with this Regulation. This should be without prejudice to the competence of the courts of the Member States to decide on the recognition and enforcement of arbitral awards in accordance with the Convention on the Recognition and Enforcement of Foreign Arbitral Awards, done at New York on 10 June 1958 ('the 1958 New York Convention'), which takes precedence over this Regulation.

This Regulation should not apply to any action or ancillary proceedings relating to, in particular, the establishment of an arbitral tribunal, the powers of arbitrators, the conduct of an arbitration procedure or any other aspects of such a procedure, nor to any action or judgment concerning the annulment, review, appeal, recognition or enforcement of an arbitral award.

---

[1] OJ L 299, 31.12.1972, p. 32, OJ L 304, 30.10.1978, p. 1, OJ L 388, 31.12.1982, p. 1, OJ L 285, 3.10.1989, p. 1, OJ C 15, 15.1.1997, p. 1. For a consolidated text, see OJ C 27, 26.1.1998, p. 1.
[2] OJ L 319, 25.11.1988, p. 9.
[3] OJ L 120, 5.5.2006, p. 22.
[4] OJ L 147, 10.6.2009, p. 5.

---

[5] OJ L 7, 10.1.2009, p. 1.

(13) There must be a connection between proceedings to which this Regulation applies and the territory of the Member States. Accordingly, common rules of jurisdiction should, in principle, apply when the defendant is domiciled in a Member State.

(14) A defendant not domiciled in a Member State should in general be subject to the national rules of jurisdiction applicable in the territory of the Member State of the court seised.

However, in order to ensure the protection of consumers and employees, to safeguard the jurisdiction of the courts of the Member States in situations where they have exclusive jurisdiction and to respect the autonomy of the parties, certain rules of jurisdiction in this Regulation should apply regardless of the defendant's domicile.

(15) The rules of jurisdiction should be highly predictable and founded on the principle that jurisdiction is generally based on the defendant's domicile. Jurisdiction should always be available on this ground save in a few well-defined situations in which the subject-matter of the dispute or the autonomy of the parties warrants a different connecting factor. The domicile of a legal person must be defined autonomously so as to make the common rules more transparent and avoid conflicts of jurisdiction.

(16) In addition to the defendant's domicile, there should be alternative grounds of jurisdiction based on a close connection between the court and the action or in order to facilitate the sound administration of justice. The existence of a close connection should ensure legal certainty and avoid the possibility of the defendant being sued in a court of a Member State which he could not reasonably have foreseen. This is important, particularly in disputes concerning non-contractual obligations arising out of violations of privacy and rights relating to personality, including defamation.

(17) The owner of a cultural object as defined in Article 1(1) of Council Directive 93/7/EEC of 15 March 1993 on the return of cultural objects unlawfully removed from the territory of a Member State (¹) should be able under this Regulation to initiate proceedings as regards a civil claim for the recovery, based on ownership, of such a cultural object in the courts for the place where the cultural object is situated at the time the court is seised. Such proceedings should be without prejudice to proceedings initiated under Directive 93/7/EEC.

(¹) OJ L 74, 27.3.1993, p. 74.

(18) In relation to insurance, consumer and employment contracts, the weaker party should be protected by rules of jurisdiction more favourable to his interests than the general rules.

(19) The autonomy of the parties to a contract, other than an insurance, consumer or employment contract, where only limited autonomy to determine the courts having jurisdiction is allowed, should be respected subject to the exclusive grounds of jurisdiction laid down in this Regulation.

(20) Where a question arises as to whether a choice-of-court agreement in favour of a court or the courts of a Member State is null and void as to its substantive validity, that question should be decided in accordance with the law of the Member State of the court or courts designated in the agreement, including the conflict-of-laws rules of that Member State.

(21) In the interests of the harmonious administration of justice it is necessary to minimise the possibility of concurrent proceedings and to ensure that irreconcilable judgments will not be given in different Member States. There should be a clear and effective mechanism for resolving cases of *lis pendens* and related actions, and for obviating problems flowing from national differences as to the determination of the time when a case is regarded as pending. For the purposes of this Regulation, that time should be defined autonomously.

(22) However, in order to enhance the effectiveness of exclusive choice-of-court agreements and to avoid abusive litigation tactics, it is necessary to provide for an exception to the general *lis pendens* rule in order to deal satisfactorily with a particular situation in which concurrent proceedings may arise. This is the situation where a court not designated in an exclusive choice-of-court agreement has been seised of proceedings and the designated court is seised subsequently of proceedings involving the same cause of action and between the same parties. In such a case, the court first seised should be required to stay its proceedings as soon as the designated court has been seised and until such time as the latter court declares that it has no jurisdiction under the exclusive choice-of-court agreement. This is to ensure that, in such a situation, the designated court has priority to decide on the validity of the agreement and on the extent to which the agreement applies to the dispute pending before it. The designated court should be able to proceed irrespective of whether the non-designated court has already decided on the stay of proceedings.

This exception should not cover situations where the parties have entered into conflicting exclusive choice-of-court agreements or where a court designated in an exclusive choice-of-court agreement has been seised first. In such cases, the general *lis pendens* rule of this Regulation should apply.

(23) This Regulation should provide for a flexible mechanism allowing the courts of the Member States to take into account proceedings pending before the courts of third States, considering in particular whether a judgment of a third State will be capable of recognition and enforcement in the Member State concerned under the law of that Member State and the proper administration of justice.

(24) When taking into account the proper administration of justice, the court of the Member State concerned should assess all the circumstances of the case before it. Such circumstances may include connections between the facts of the case and the parties and the third State concerned, the stage to which the proceedings in the third State have progressed by the time proceedings are initiated in the court of the Member State and whether or not the court of the third State can be expected to give a judgment within a reasonable time.

That assessment may also include consideration of the question whether the court of the third State has exclusive jurisdiction in the particular case in circumstances where a court of a Member State would have exclusive jurisdiction.

(25) The notion of provisional, including protective, measures should include, for example, protective orders aimed at obtaining information or preserving evidence as referred to in Articles 6 and 7 of Directive 2004/48/EC of the European Parliament and of the Council of 29 April 2004 on the enforcement of intellectual property rights (¹). It should not include measures which are not of a protective nature, such as measures ordering the hearing of a witness. This should be without prejudice to the application of Council Regulation (EC) No 1206/2001 of 28 May 2001 on cooperation between the courts of the Member States in the taking of evidence in civil or commercial matters (²).

(26) Mutual trust in the administration of justice in the Union justifies the principle that judgments given in a Member State should be recognised in all Member States without

(¹) OJ L 157, 30.4.2004, p. 45.
(²) OJ L 174, 27.6.2001, p. 1.

the need for any special procedure. In addition, the aim of making cross-border litigation less time-consuming and costly justifies the abolition of the declaration of enforceability prior to enforcement in the Member State addressed. As a result, a judgment given by the courts of a Member State should be treated as if it had been given in the Member State addressed.

(27) For the purposes of the free circulation of judgments, a judgment given in a Member State should be recognised and enforced in another Member State even if it is given against a person not domiciled in a Member State.

(28) Where a judgment contains a measure or order which is not known in the law of the Member State addressed, that measure or order, including any right indicated therein, should, to the extent possible, be adapted to one which, under the law of that Member State, has equivalent effects attached to it and pursues similar aims. How, and by whom, the adaptation is to be carried out should be determined by each Member State.

(29) The direct enforcement in the Member State addressed of a judgment given in another Member State without a declaration of enforceability should not jeopardise respect for the rights of the defence. Therefore, the person against whom enforcement is sought should be able to apply for refusal of the recognition or enforcement of a judgment if he considers one of the grounds for refusal of recognition to be present. This should include the ground that he had not had the opportunity to arrange for his defence where the judgment was given in default of appearance in a civil action linked to criminal proceedings. It should also include the grounds which could be invoked on the basis of an agreement between the Member State addressed and a third State concluded pursuant to Article 59 of the 1968 Brussels Convention.

(30) A party challenging the enforcement of a judgment given in another Member State should, to the extent possible and in accordance with the legal system of the Member State addressed, be able to invoke, in the same procedure, in addition to the grounds for refusal provided for in this Regulation, the grounds for refusal available under national law and within the time-limits laid down in that law.

The recognition of a judgment should, however, be refused only if one or more of the grounds for refusal provided for in this Regulation are present.

(31) Pending a challenge to the enforcement of a judgment, it should be possible for the courts in the Member State addressed, during the entire proceedings relating to such a challenge, including any appeal, to allow the enforcement to proceed subject to a limitation of the enforcement or to the provision of security.

(32) In order to inform the person against whom enforcement is sought of the enforcement of a judgment given in another Member State, the certificate established under this Regulation, if necessary accompanied by the judgment, should be served on that person in reasonable time before the first enforcement measure. In this context, the first enforcement measure should mean the first enforcement measure after such service.

(33) Where provisional, including protective, measures are ordered by a court having jurisdiction as to the substance of the matter, their free circulation should be ensured under this Regulation. However, provisional, including protective, measures which were ordered by such a court without the defendant being summoned to appear should not be recognised and enforced under this Regulation unless the judgment containing the measure is served on the defendant prior to enforcement. This should not preclude the recognition and enforcement of such measures under national law. Where provisional, including protective, measures are ordered by a court of a Member State not having jurisdiction as to the substance of the matter, the effect of such measures should be confined, under this Regulation, to the territory of that Member State.

(34) Continuity between the 1968 Brussels Convention, Regulation (EC) No 44/2001 and this Regulation should be ensured, and transitional provisions should be laid down to that end. The same need for continuity applies as regards the interpretation by the Court of Justice of the European Union of the 1968 Brussels Convention and of the Regulations replacing it.

(35) Respect for international commitments entered into by the Member States means that this Regulation should not affect conventions relating to specific matters to which the Member States are parties.

(36) Without prejudice to the obligations of the Member States under the Treaties, this Regulation should not affect the application of bilateral conventions and agreements between a third State and a Member State concluded before the date of entry into force of Regulation (EC) No 44/2001 which concern matters governed by this Regulation.

(37) In order to ensure that the certificates to be used in connection with the recognition or enforcement of judgments, authentic instruments and court settlements under this Regulation are kept up-to-date, the power to adopt acts in accordance with Article 290 of the TFEU should be delegated to the Commission in respect of amendments to Annexes I and II to this Regulation. It is of particular importance that the Commission carry out appropriate consultations during its preparatory work, including at expert level. The Commission, when preparing and drawing up delegated acts, should ensure a simultaneous, timely and appropriate transmission of relevant documents to the European Parliament and to the Council.

(38) This Regulation respects fundamental rights and observes the principles recognised in the Charter of Fundamental Rights of the European Union, in particular the right to an effective remedy and to a fair trial guaranteed in Article 47 of the Charter.

(39) Since the objective of this Regulation cannot be sufficiently achieved by the Member States and can be better achieved at Union level, the Union may adopt measures in accordance with the principle of subsidiarity as set out in Article 5 of the Treaty on European Union (TEU). In accordance with the principle of proportionality, as set out in that Article, this Regulation does not go beyond what is necessary in order to achieve that objective.

(40) The United Kingdom and Ireland, in accordance with Article 3 of the Protocol on the position of the United Kingdom and Ireland, annexed to the TEU and to the then Treaty establishing the European Community, took part in the adoption and application of Regulation (EC) No 44/2001. In accordance with Article 3 of Protocol No 21 on the position of the United Kingdom and Ireland in respect of the area of freedom, security and justice, annexed to the TEU and to the TFEU, the United Kingdom and Ireland have notified their wish to take part in the adoption and application of this Regulation.

(41) In accordance with Articles 1 and 2 of Protocol No 22 on the position of Denmark annexed to the TEU and to the TFEU, Denmark is not taking part in the adoption of this Regulation and is not bound by it or subject to its application, without prejudice to the possibility for Denmark of applying the amendments to Regulation (EC) No 44/2001 pursuant to Article 3 of the Agreement of 19 October 2005 between the European Community and the Kingdom of Denmark on jurisdiction and the recognition and enforcement of judgments in civil and commercial matters [1],

---

[1] OJ L 299, 16.11.2005, p. 62.

HAVE ADOPTED THIS REGULATION:

CHAPTER I

SCOPE AND DEFINITIONS

Article 1

1. This Regulation shall apply in civil and commercial matters whatever the nature of the court or tribunal. It shall not extend, in particular, to revenue, customs or administrative matters or to the liability of the State for acts and omissions in the exercise of State authority (*acta iure imperii*).

2. This Regulation shall not apply to:

(a) the status or legal capacity of natural persons, rights in property arising out of a matrimonial relationship or out of a relationship deemed by the law applicable to such relationship to have comparable effects to marriage;

(b) bankruptcy, proceedings relating to the winding-up of insolvent companies or other legal persons, judicial arrangements, compositions and analogous proceedings;

(c) social security;

(d) arbitration;

(e) maintenance obligations arising from a family relationship, parentage, marriage or affinity;

(f) wills and succession, including maintenance obligations arising by reason of death.

Article 2

For the purposes of this Regulation:

(a) 'judgment' means any judgment given by a court or tribunal of a Member State, whatever the judgment may be called, including a decree, order, decision or writ of execution, as well as a decision on the determination of costs or expenses by an officer of the court.

For the purposes of Chapter III, 'judgment' includes provisional, including protective, measures ordered by a court or tribunal which by virtue of this Regulation has jurisdiction as to the substance of the matter. It does not include a provisional, including protective, measure which is ordered by such a court or tribunal without the defendant being summoned to appear, unless the judgment containing the measure is served on the defendant prior to enforcement;

(b) 'court settlement' means a settlement which has been approved by a court of a Member State or concluded before a court of a Member State in the course of proceedings;

(c) 'authentic instrument' means a document which has been formally drawn up or registered as an authentic instrument in the Member State of origin and the authenticity of which:

  (i) relates to the signature and the content of the instrument; and

  (ii) has been established by a public authority or other authority empowered for that purpose;

(d) 'Member State of origin' means the Member State in which, as the case may be, the judgment has been given, the court settlement has been approved or concluded, or the authentic instrument has been formally drawn up or registered;

(e) 'Member State addressed' means the Member State in which the recognition of the judgment is invoked or in which the enforcement of the judgment, the court settlement or the authentic instrument is sought;

(f) 'court of origin' means the court which has given the judgment the recognition of which is invoked or the enforcement of which is sought.

Article 3

For the purposes of this Regulation, 'court' includes the following authorities to the extent that they have jurisdiction in matters falling within the scope of this Regulation:

(a) in Hungary, in summary proceedings concerning orders to pay (fizetési meghagyásos eljárás), the notary (közjegyző);

(b) in Sweden, in summary proceedings concerning orders to pay (betalningsföreläggande) and assistance (handräckning), the Enforcement Authority (Kronofogdemyndigheten).

CHAPTER II

JURISDICTION

SECTION 1

General provisions

Article 4

1. Subject to this Regulation, persons domiciled in a Member State shall, whatever their nationality, be sued in the courts of that Member State.

2. Persons who are not nationals of the Member State in which they are domiciled shall be governed by the rules of jurisdiction applicable to nationals of that Member State.

Article 5

1. Persons domiciled in a Member State may be sued in the courts of another Member State only by virtue of the rules set out in Sections 2 to 7 of this Chapter.

2. In particular, the rules of national jurisdiction of which the Member States are to notify the Commission pursuant to point (a) of Article 76(1) shall not be applicable as against the persons referred to in paragraph 1.

Article 6

1. If the defendant is not domiciled in a Member State, the jurisdiction of the courts of each Member State shall, subject to Article 18(1), Article 21(2) and Articles 24 and 25, be determined by the law of that Member State.

2. As against such a defendant, any person domiciled in a Member State may, whatever his nationality, avail himself in that Member State of the rules of jurisdiction there in force, and in particular those of which the Member States are to notify the Commission pursuant to point (a) of Article 76(1), in the same way as nationals of that Member State.

SECTION 2

Special jurisdiction

Article 7

A person domiciled in a Member State may be sued in another Member State:

(1) (a) in matters relating to a contract, in the courts for the place of performance of the obligation in question;

    (b) for the purpose of this provision and unless otherwise agreed, the place of performance of the obligation in question shall be:

— in the case of the sale of goods, the place in a Member State where, under the contract, the goods were delivered or should have been delivered,

— in the case of the provision of services, the place in a Member State where, under the contract, the services were provided or should have been provided;

(c) if point (b) does not apply then point (a) applies;

(2) in matters relating to tort, delict or quasi-delict, in the courts for the place where the harmful event occurred or may occur;

(3) as regards a civil claim for damages or restitution which is based on an act giving rise to criminal proceedings, in the court seised of those proceedings, to the extent that that court has jurisdiction under its own law to entertain civil proceedings;

(4) as regards a civil claim for the recovery, based on ownership, of a cultural object as defined in point 1 of Article 1 of Directive 93/7/EEC initiated by the person claiming the right to recover such an object, in the courts for the place where the cultural object is situated at the time when the court is seised;

(5) as regards a dispute arising out of the operations of a branch, agency or other establishment, in the courts for the place where the branch, agency or other establishment is situated;

(6) as regards a dispute brought against a settlor, trustee or beneficiary of a trust created by the operation of a statute, or by a written instrument, or created orally and evidenced in writing, in the courts of the Member State in which the trust is domiciled;

(7) as regards a dispute concerning the payment of remuneration claimed in respect of the salvage of a cargo or freight, in the court under the authority of which the cargo or freight in question:

(a) has been arrested to secure such payment; or

(b) could have been so arrested, but bail or other security has been given;

provided that this provision shall apply only if it is claimed that the defendant has an interest in the cargo or freight or had such an interest at the time of salvage.

Article 8

A person domiciled in a Member State may also be sued:

(1) where he is one of a number of defendants, in the courts for the place where any one of them is domiciled, provided the claims are so closely connected that it is expedient to hear and determine them together to avoid the risk of irreconcilable judgments resulting from separate proceedings;

(2) as a third party in an action on a warranty or guarantee or in any other third-party proceedings, in the court seised of the original proceedings, unless these were instituted solely with the object of removing him from the jurisdiction of the court which would be competent in his case;

(3) on a counter-claim arising from the same contract or facts on which the original claim was based, in the court in which the original claim is pending;

(4) in matters relating to a contract, if the action may be combined with an action against the same defendant in matters relating to rights *in rem* in immovable property, in the court of the Member State in which the property is situated.

Article 9

Where by virtue of this Regulation a court of a Member State has jurisdiction in actions relating to liability from the use or operation of a ship, that court, or any other court substituted for this purpose by the internal law of that Member State, shall also have jurisdiction over claims for limitation of such liability.

SECTION 3

Jurisdiction in matters relating to insurance

Article 10

In matters relating to insurance, jurisdiction shall be determined by this Section, without prejudice to Article 6 and point 5 of Article 7.

Article 11

1. An insurer domiciled in a Member State may be sued:

(a) in the courts of the Member State in which he is domiciled;

(b) in another Member State, in the case of actions brought by the policyholder, the insured or a beneficiary, in the courts for the place where the claimant is domiciled; or

(c) if he is a co-insurer, in the courts of a Member State in which proceedings are brought against the leading insurer.

2. An insurer who is not domiciled in a Member State but has a branch, agency or other establishment in one of the Member States shall, in disputes arising out of the operations of the branch, agency or establishment, be deemed to be domiciled in that Member State.

Article 12

In respect of liability insurance or insurance of immovable property, the insurer may in addition be sued in the courts for the place where the harmful event occurred. The same applies if movable and immovable property are covered by the same insurance policy and both are adversely affected by the same contingency.

Article 13

1. In respect of liability insurance, the insurer may also, if the law of the court permits it, be joined in proceedings which the injured party has brought against the insured.

2. Articles 10, 11 and 12 shall apply to actions brought by the injured party directly against the insurer, where such direct actions are permitted.

3. If the law governing such direct actions provides that the policyholder or the insured may be joined as a party to the action, the same court shall have jurisdiction over them.

Article 14

1. Without prejudice to Article 13(3), an insurer may bring proceedings only in the courts of the Member State in which the defendant is domiciled, irrespective of whether he is the policyholder, the insured or a beneficiary.

2. The provisions of this Section shall not affect the right to bring a counter-claim in the court in which, in accordance with this Section, the original claim is pending.

Article 15

The provisions of this Section may be departed from only by an agreement:

(1) which is entered into after the dispute has arisen;

(2) which allows the policyholder, the insured or a beneficiary to bring proceedings in courts other than those indicated in this Section;

(3) which is concluded between a policyholder and an insurer, both of whom are at the time of conclusion of the contract domiciled or habitually resident in the same Member State, and which has the effect of conferring jurisdiction on the courts of that Member State even if the harmful event were to occur abroad, provided that such an agreement is not contrary to the law of that Member State;

(4) which is concluded with a policyholder who is not domiciled in a Member State, except in so far as the insurance is compulsory or relates to immovable property in a Member State; or

(5) which relates to a contract of insurance in so far as it covers one or more of the risks set out in Article 16.

Article 16

The following are the risks referred to in point 5 of Article 15:

(1) any loss of or damage to:

    (a) seagoing ships, installations situated offshore or on the high seas, or aircraft, arising from perils which relate to their use for commercial purposes;

    (b) goods in transit other than passengers' baggage where the transit consists of or includes carriage by such ships or aircraft;

(2) any liability, other than for bodily injury to passengers or loss of or damage to their baggage:

    (a) arising out of the use or operation of ships, installations or aircraft as referred to in point 1(a) in so far as, in respect of the latter, the law of the Member State in which such aircraft are registered does not prohibit agreements on jurisdiction regarding insurance of such risks;

    (b) for loss or damage caused by goods in transit as described in point 1(b);

(3) any financial loss connected with the use or operation of ships, installations or aircraft as referred to in point 1(a), in particular loss of freight or charter-hire;

(4) any risk or interest connected with any of those referred to in points 1 to 3;

(5) notwithstanding points 1 to 4, all 'large risks' as defined in Directive 2009/138/EC of the European Parliament and of the Council of 25 November 2009 on the taking-up and pursuit of the business of Insurance and Reinsurance (Solvency II) [1].

---

[1] OJ L 335, 17.12.2009, p. 1.

Jurisdiction over consumer contracts

Article 17

1.   In matters relating to a contract concluded by a person, the consumer, for a purpose which can be regarded as being outside his trade or profession, jurisdiction shall be determined by this Section, without prejudice to Article 6 and point 5 of Article 7, if:

(a) it is a contract for the sale of goods on instalment credit terms;

(b) it is a contract for a loan repayable by instalments, or for any other form of credit, made to finance the sale of goods; or

(c) in all other cases, the contract has been concluded with a person who pursues commercial or professional activities in the Member State of the consumer's domicile or, by any means, directs such activities to that Member State or to several States including that Member State, and the contract falls within the scope of such activities.

2.   Where a consumer enters into a contract with a party who is not domiciled in a Member State but has a branch, agency or other establishment in one of the Member States, that party shall, in disputes arising out of the operations of the branch, agency or establishment, be deemed to be domiciled in that Member State.

3.   This Section shall not apply to a contract of transport other than a contract which, for an inclusive price, provides for a combination of travel and accommodation.

Article 18

1.   A consumer may bring proceedings against the other party to a contract either in the courts of the Member State in which that party is domiciled or, regardless of the domicile of the other party, in the courts for the place where the consumer is domiciled.

2.   Proceedings may be brought against a consumer by the other party to the contract only in the courts of the Member State in which the consumer is domiciled.

3.   This Article shall not affect the right to bring a counter-claim in the court in which, in accordance with this Section, the original claim is pending.

Article 19

The provisions of this Section may be departed from only by an agreement:

(1) which is entered into after the dispute has arisen;

(2) which allows the consumer to bring proceedings in courts other than those indicated in this Section; or

(3) which is entered into by the consumer and the other party to the contract, both of whom are at the time of conclusion of the contract domiciled or habitually resident in the same Member State, and which confers jurisdiction on the courts of that Member State, provided that such an agreement is not contrary to the law of that Member State.

SECTION 5

Jurisdiction over individual contracts of employment

Article 20

1.   In matters relating to individual contracts of employment, jurisdiction shall be determined by this Section, without prejudice to Article 6, point 5 of Article 7 and, in the case of proceedings brought against an employer, point 1 of Article 8.

2.   Where an employee enters into an individual contract of employment with an employer who is not domiciled in a Member State but has a branch, agency or other establishment in one of the Member States, the employer shall, in disputes arising out of the operations of the branch, agency or establishment, be deemed to be domiciled in that Member State.

Article 21

1.   An employer domiciled in a Member State may be sued:

(a) in the courts of the Member State in which he is domiciled; or

(b) in another Member State:

(i) in the courts for the place where or from where the employee habitually carries out his work or in the courts for the last place where he did so; or

(ii) if the employee does not or did not habitually carry out his work in any one country, in the courts for the place where the business which engaged the employee is or was situated.

2.   An employer not domiciled in a Member State may be sued in a court of a Member State in accordance with point (b) of paragraph 1.

Article 22

1.   An employer may bring proceedings only in the courts of the Member State in which the employee is domiciled.

2.   The provisions of this Section shall not affect the right to bring a counter-claim in the court in which, in accordance with this Section, the original claim is pending.

Article 23

The provisions of this Section may be departed from only by an agreement:

(1) which is entered into after the dispute has arisen; or

(2) which allows the employee to bring proceedings in courts other than those indicated in this Section.

SECTION 6

Exclusive jurisdiction

Article 24

The following courts of a Member State shall have exclusive jurisdiction, regardless of the domicile of the parties:

(1) in proceedings which have as their object rights *in rem* in immovable property or tenancies of immovable property, the courts of the Member State in which the property is situated.

However, in proceedings which have as their object tenancies of immovable property concluded for temporary private use for a maximum period of six consecutive months, the courts of the Member State in which the defendant is domiciled shall also have jurisdiction, provided that the tenant is a natural person and that the landlord and the tenant are domiciled in the same Member State;

(2) in proceedings which have as their object the validity of the constitution, the nullity or the dissolution of companies or other legal persons or associations of natural or legal persons, or the validity of the decisions of their organs, the courts of the Member State in which the company, legal person or association has its seat. In order to determine that seat, the court shall apply its rules of private international law;

(3) in proceedings which have as their object the validity of entries in public registers, the courts of the Member State in which the register is kept;

(4) in proceedings concerned with the registration or validity of patents, trade marks, designs, or other similar rights required to be deposited or registered, irrespective of whether the issue is raised by way of an action or as a defence, the courts of the Member State in which the deposit or registration has been applied for, has taken place or is under the terms of an instrument of the Union or an international convention deemed to have taken place.

Without prejudice to the jurisdiction of the European Patent Office under the Convention on the Grant of European Patents, signed at Munich on 5 October 1973, the courts of each Member State shall have exclusive jurisdiction in proceedings concerned with the registration or validity of any European patent granted for that Member State;

(5) in proceedings concerned with the enforcement of judgments, the courts of the Member State in which the judgment has been or is to be enforced.

SECTION 7

Prorogation of jurisdiction

Article 25

1. If the parties, regardless of their domicile, have agreed that a court or the courts of a Member State are to have jurisdiction to settle any disputes which have arisen or which may arise in connection with a particular legal relationship, that court or those courts shall have jurisdiction, unless the agreement is null and void as to its substantive validity under the law of that Member State. Such jurisdiction shall be exclusive unless the parties have agreed otherwise. The agreement conferring jurisdiction shall be either:

(a) in writing or evidenced in writing;

(b) in a form which accords with practices which the parties have established between themselves; or

(c) in international trade or commerce, in a form which accords with a usage of which the parties are or ought to have been aware and which in such trade or commerce is widely known to, and regularly observed by, parties to contracts of the type involved in the particular trade or commerce concerned.

2. Any communication by electronic means which provides a durable record of the agreement shall be equivalent to 'writing'.

3. The court or courts of a Member State on which a trust instrument has conferred jurisdiction shall have exclusive jurisdiction in any proceedings brought against a settlor, trustee or beneficiary, if relations between those persons or their rights or obligations under the trust are involved.

4. Agreements or provisions of a trust instrument conferring jurisdiction shall have no legal force if they are contrary to Articles 15, 19 or 23, or if the courts whose jurisdiction they purport to exclude have exclusive jurisdiction by virtue of Article 24.

5. An agreement conferring jurisdiction which forms part of a contract shall be treated as an agreement independent of the other terms of the contract.

The validity of the agreement conferring jurisdiction cannot be contested solely on the ground that the contract is not valid.

Article 26

1. Apart from jurisdiction derived from other provisions of this Regulation, a court of a Member State before which a defendant enters an appearance shall have jurisdiction. This rule shall not apply where appearance was entered to contest the jurisdiction, or where another court has exclusive jurisdiction by virtue of Article 24.

2. In matters referred to in Sections 3, 4 or 5 where the policyholder, the insured, a beneficiary of the insurance contract, the injured party, the consumer or the employee is the defendant, the court shall, before assuming jurisdiction under paragraph 1, ensure that the defendant is informed of his right to contest the jurisdiction of the court and of the consequences of entering or not entering an appearance.

SECTION 8

Examination as to jurisdiction and admissibility

Article 27

Where a court of a Member State is seised of a claim which is principally concerned with a matter over which the courts of another Member State have exclusive jurisdiction by virtue of Article 24, it shall declare of its own motion that it has no jurisdiction.

Article 28

1. Where a defendant domiciled in one Member State is sued in a court of another Member State and does not enter an appearance, the court shall declare of its own motion that it has no jurisdiction unless its jurisdiction is derived from the provisions of this Regulation.

2. The court shall stay the proceedings so long as it is not shown that the defendant has been able to receive the document instituting the proceedings or an equivalent document in sufficient time to enable him to arrange for his defence, or that all necessary steps have been taken to this end.

3. Article 19 of Regulation (EC) No 1393/2007 of the European Parliament and of the Council of 13 November 2007 on the service in the Member States of judicial and extra-judicial documents in civil or commercial matters (service of documents) (¹) shall apply instead of paragraph 2 of this Article if the document instituting the proceedings or an equivalent document had to be transmitted from one Member State to another pursuant to that Regulation.

4. Where Regulation (EC) No 1393/2007 is not applicable, Article 15 of the Hague Convention of 15 November 1965 on the Service Abroad of Judicial and Extrajudicial Documents in Civil or Commercial Matters shall apply if the document insti-tuting the proceedings or an equivalent document had to be transmitted abroad pursuant to that Convention.

SECTION 9

Lis pendens — related actions

Article 29

1. Without prejudice to Article 31(2), where proceedings involving the same cause of action and between the same parties are brought in the courts of different Member States, any court other than the court first seised shall of its own motion stay its proceedings until such time as the jurisdiction of the court first seised is established.

2. In cases referred to in paragraph 1, upon request by a court seised of the dispute, any other court seised shall without delay inform the former court of the date when it was seised in accordance with Article 32.

3. Where the jurisdiction of the court first seised is estab-lished, any court other than the court first seised shall decline jurisdiction in favour of that court.

Article 30

1. Where related actions are pending in the courts of different Member States, any court other than the court first seised may stay its proceedings.

2. Where the action in the court first seised is pending at first instance, any other court may also, on the application of

---

(¹) OJ L 324, 10.12.2007, p. 79.

one of the parties, decline jurisdiction if the court first seised has jurisdiction over the actions in question and its law permits the consolidation thereof.

3. For the purposes of this Article, actions are deemed to be related where they are so closely connected that it is expedient to hear and determine them together to avoid the risk of irrec-oncilable judgments resulting from separate proceedings.

Article 31

1. Where actions come within the exclusive jurisdiction of several courts, any court other than the court first seised shall decline jurisdiction in favour of that court.

2. Without prejudice to Article 26, where a court of a Member State on which an agreement as referred to in Article 25 confers exclusive jurisdiction is seised, any court of another Member State shall stay the proceedings until such time as the court seised on the basis of the agreement declares that it has no jurisdiction under the agreement.

3. Where the court designated in the agreement has estab-lished jurisdiction in accordance with the agreement, any court of another Member State shall decline jurisdiction in favour of that court.

4. Paragraphs 2 and 3 shall not apply to matters referred to in Sections 3, 4 or 5 where the policyholder, the insured, a beneficiary of the insurance contract, the injured party, the consumer or the employee is the claimant and the agreement is not valid under a provision contained within those Sections.

Article 32

1. For the purposes of this Section, a court shall be deemed to be seised:

(a) at the time when the document instituting the proceedings or an equivalent document is lodged with the court, provided that the claimant has not subsequently failed to take the steps he was required to take to have service effected on the defendant; or

(b) if the document has to be served before being lodged with the court, at the time when it is received by the authority responsible for service, provided that the claimant has not subsequently failed to take the steps he was required to take to have the document lodged with the court.

The authority responsible for service referred to in point (b) shall be the first authority receiving the documents to be served.

2.   The court, or the authority responsible for service, referred to in paragraph 1, shall note, respectively, the date of the lodging of the document instituting the proceedings or the equivalent document, or the date of receipt of the documents to be served.

Article 33

1.   Where jurisdiction is based on Article 4 or on Articles 7, 8 or 9 and proceedings are pending before a court of a third State at the time when a court in a Member State is seised of an action involving the same cause of action and between the same parties as the proceedings in the court of the third State, the court of the Member State may stay the proceedings if:

(a) it is expected that the court of the third State will give a judgment capable of recognition and, where applicable, of enforcement in that Member State; and

(b) the court of the Member State is satisfied that a stay is necessary for the proper administration of justice.

2.   The court of the Member State may continue the proceedings at any time if:

(a) the proceedings in the court of the third State are themselves stayed or discontinued;

(b) it appears to the court of the Member State that the proceedings in the court of the third State are unlikely to be concluded within a reasonable time; or

(c) the continuation of the proceedings is required for the proper administration of justice.

3.   The court of the Member State shall dismiss the proceedings if the proceedings in the court of the third State are concluded and have resulted in a judgment capable of recognition and, where applicable, of enforcement in that Member State.

4.   The court of the Member State shall apply this Article on the application of one of the parties or, where possible under national law, of its own motion.

Article 34

1.   Where jurisdiction is based on Article 4 or on Articles 7, 8 or 9 and an action is pending before a court of a third State at the time when a court in a Member State is seised of an action which is related to the action in the court of the third State, the court of the Member State may stay the proceedings if:

(a) it is expedient to hear and determine the related actions together to avoid the risk of irreconcilable judgments resulting from separate proceedings;

(b) it is expected that the court of the third State will give a judgment capable of recognition and, where applicable, of enforcement in that Member State; and

(c) the court of the Member State is satisfied that a stay is necessary for the proper administration of justice.

2.   The court of the Member State may continue the proceedings at any time if:

(a) it appears to the court of the Member State that there is no longer a risk of irreconcilable judgments;

(b) the proceedings in the court of the third State are themselves stayed or discontinued;

(c) it appears to the court of the Member State that the proceedings in the court of the third State are unlikely to be concluded within a reasonable time; or

(d) the continuation of the proceedings is required for the proper administration of justice.

3.   The court of the Member State may dismiss the proceedings if the proceedings in the court of the third State are concluded and have resulted in a judgment capable of recognition and, where applicable, of enforcement in that Member State.

4.   The court of the Member State shall apply this Article on the application of one of the parties or, where possible under national law, of its own motion.

SECTION 10

Provisional, including protective, measures

Article 35

Application may be made to the courts of a Member State for such provisional, including protective, measures as may be available under the law of that Member State, even if the courts of another Member State have jurisdiction as to the substance of the matter.

CHAPTER III

RECOGNITION AND ENFORCEMENT

SECTION 1

Recognition

Article 36

1. A judgment given in a Member State shall be recognised in the other Member States without any special procedure being required.

2. Any interested party may, in accordance with the procedure provided for in Subsection 2 of Section 3, apply for a decision that there are no grounds for refusal of recognition as referred to in Article 45.

3. If the outcome of proceedings in a court of a Member State depends on the determination of an incidental question of refusal of recognition, that court shall have jurisdiction over that question.

Article 37

1. A party who wishes to invoke in a Member State a judgment given in another Member State shall produce:

(a) a copy of the judgment which satisfies the conditions necessary to establish its authenticity; and

(b) the certificate issued pursuant to Article 53.

2. The court or authority before which a judgment given in another Member State is invoked may, where necessary, require the party invoking it to provide, in accordance with Article 57, a translation or a transliteration of the contents of the certificate referred to in point (b) of paragraph 1. The court or authority may require the party to provide a translation of the judgment instead of a translation of the contents of the certificate if it is unable to proceed without such a translation.

Article 38

The court or authority before which a judgment given in another Member State is invoked may suspend the proceedings, in whole or in part, if:

(a) the judgment is challenged in the Member State of origin; or

(b) an application has been submitted for a decision that there are no grounds for refusal of recognition as referred to in Article 45 or for a decision that the recognition is to be refused on the basis of one of those grounds.

SECTION 2

Enforcement

Article 39

A judgment given in a Member State which is enforceable in that Member State shall be enforceable in the other Member States without any declaration of enforceability being required.

Article 40

An enforceable judgment shall carry with it by operation of law the power to proceed to any protective measures which exist under the law of the Member State addressed.

Article 41

1. Subject to the provisions of this Section, the procedure for the enforcement of judgments given in another Member State shall be governed by the law of the Member State addressed. A judgment given in a Member State which is enforceable in the Member State addressed shall be enforced there under the same conditions as a judgment given in the Member State addressed.

2. Notwithstanding paragraph 1, the grounds for refusal or of suspension of enforcement under the law of the Member State addressed shall apply in so far as they are not incompatible with the grounds referred to in Article 45.

3. The party seeking the enforcement of a judgment given in another Member State shall not be required to have a postal address in the Member State addressed. Nor shall that party be required to have an authorised representative in the Member State addressed unless such a representative is mandatory irrespective of the nationality or the domicile of the parties.

Article 42

1. For the purposes of enforcement in a Member State of a judgment given in another Member State, the applicant shall provide the competent enforcement authority with:

(a) a copy of the judgment which satisfies the conditions necessary to establish its authenticity; and

(b) the certificate issued pursuant to Article 53, certifying that the judgment is enforceable and containing an extract of the judgment as well as, where appropriate, relevant information on the recoverable costs of the proceedings and the calculation of interest.

2. For the purposes of enforcement in a Member State of a judgment given in another Member State ordering a provisional, including a protective, measure, the applicant shall provide the competent enforcement authority with:

(a) a copy of the judgment which satisfies the conditions necessary to establish its authenticity;

(b) the certificate issued pursuant to Article 53, containing a description of the measure and certifying that:

(i) the court has jurisdiction as to the substance of the matter;

(ii) the judgment is enforceable in the Member State of origin; and

(c) where the measure was ordered without the defendant being summoned to appear, proof of service of the judgment.

3. The competent enforcement authority may, where necessary, require the applicant to provide, in accordance with Article 57, a translation or a transliteration of the contents of the certificate.

4. The competent enforcement authority may require the applicant to provide a translation of the judgment only if it is unable to proceed without such a translation.

Article 43

1. Where enforcement is sought of a judgment given in another Member State, the certificate issued pursuant to Article 53 shall be served on the person against whom the enforcement is sought prior to the first enforcement measure. The certificate shall be accompanied by the judgment, if not already served on that person.

2. Where the person against whom enforcement is sought is domiciled in a Member State other than the Member State of origin, he may request a translation of the judgment in order to contest the enforcement if the judgment is not written in or accompanied by a translation into either of the following languages:

(a) a language which he understands; or

(b) the official language of the Member State in which he is domiciled or, where there are several official languages in that Member State, the official language or one of the official languages of the place where he is domiciled.

Where a translation of the judgment is requested under the first subparagraph, no measures of enforcement may be taken other than protective measures until that translation has been provided to the person against whom enforcement is sought.

This paragraph shall not apply if the judgment has already been served on the person against whom enforcement is sought in one of the languages referred to in the first subparagraph or is accompanied by a translation into one of those languages.

3. This Article shall not apply to the enforcement of a protective measure in a judgment or where the person seeking enforcement proceeds to protective measures in accordance with Article 40.

Article 44

1. In the event of an application for refusal of enforcement of a judgment pursuant to Subsection 2 of Section 3, the court in the Member State addressed may, on the application of the person against whom enforcement is sought:

(a) limit the enforcement proceedings to protective measures;

(b) make enforcement conditional on the provision of such security as it shall determine; or

(c) suspend, either wholly or in part, the enforcement proceedings.

2. The competent authority in the Member State addressed shall, on the application of the person against whom enforcement is sought, suspend the enforcement proceedings where the enforceability of the judgment is suspended in the Member State of origin.

SECTION 3

Refusal of recognition and enforcement

Subsection 1

Refusal of recognition

Article 45

1. On the application of any interested party, the recognition of a judgment shall be refused:

(a) if such recognition is manifestly contrary to public policy (ordre public) in the Member State addressed;

(b) where the judgment was given in default of appearance, if the defendant was not served with the document which instituted the proceedings or with an equivalent document in sufficient time and in such a way as to enable him to arrange for his defence, unless the defendant failed to commence proceedings to challenge the judgment when it was possible for him to do so;

(c) if the judgment is irreconcilable with a judgment given between the same parties in the Member State addressed;

(d) if the judgment is irreconcilable with an earlier judgment given in another Member State or in a third State involving the same cause of action and between the same parties, provided that the earlier judgment fulfils the conditions necessary for its recognition in the Member State addressed; or

(e) if the judgment conflicts with:

(i) Sections 3, 4 or 5 of Chapter II where the policyholder, the insured, a beneficiary of the insurance contract, the injured party, the consumer or the employee was the defendant; or

(ii) Section 6 of Chapter II.

2.   In its examination of the grounds of jurisdiction referred to in point (e) of paragraph 1, the court to which the application was submitted shall be bound by the findings of fact on which the court of origin based its jurisdiction.

3.   Without prejudice to point (e) of paragraph 1, the jurisdiction of the court of origin may not be reviewed. The test of public policy referred to in point (a) of paragraph 1 may not be applied to the rules relating to jurisdiction.

4.   The application for refusal of recognition shall be made in accordance with the procedures provided for in Subsection 2 and, where appropriate, Section 4.

Subsection 2

Refusal of enforcement

Article 46

On the application of the person against whom enforcement is sought, the enforcement of a judgment shall be refused where one of the grounds referred to in Article 45 is found to exist.

Article 47

1.   The application for refusal of enforcement shall be submitted to the court which the Member State concerned has communicated to the Commission pursuant to point (a) of Article 75 as the court to which the application is to be submitted.

2.   The procedure for refusal of enforcement shall, in so far as it is not covered by this Regulation, be governed by the law of the Member State addressed.

3.   The applicant shall provide the court with a copy of the judgment and, where necessary, a translation or transliteration of it.

The court may dispense with the production of the documents referred to in the first subparagraph if it already possesses them or if it considers it unreasonable to require the applicant to provide them. In the latter case, the court may require the other party to provide those documents.

4.   The party seeking the refusal of enforcement of a judgment given in another Member State shall not be required to have a postal address in the Member State addressed. Nor shall that party be required to have an authorised representative in the Member State addressed unless such a representative is mandatory irrespective of the nationality or the domicile of the parties.

Article 48

The court shall decide on the application for refusal of enforcement without delay.

Article 49

1.   The decision on the application for refusal of enforcement may be appealed against by either party.

2.   The appeal is to be lodged with the court which the Member State concerned has communicated to the Commission pursuant to point (b) of Article 75 as the court with which such an appeal is to be lodged.

Article 50

The decision given on the appeal may only be contested by an appeal where the courts with which any further appeal is to be lodged have been communicated by the Member State concerned to the Commission pursuant to point (c) of Article 75.

Article 51

1.   The court to which an application for refusal of enforcement is submitted or the court which hears an appeal lodged under Article 49 or Article 50 may stay the proceedings if an ordinary appeal has been lodged against the judgment in the Member State of origin or if the time for such an appeal has not yet expired. In the latter case, the court may specify the time within which such an appeal is to be lodged.

2.   Where the judgment was given in Ireland, Cyprus or the United Kingdom, any form of appeal available in the Member State of origin shall be treated as an ordinary appeal for the purposes of paragraph 1.

SECTION 4

Common provisions

Article 52

Under no circumstances may a judgment given in a Member State be reviewed as to its substance in the Member State addressed.

Article 53

The court of origin shall, at the request of any interested party, issue the certificate using the form set out in Annex I.

Article 54

1. If a judgment contains a measure or an order which is not known in the law of the Member State addressed, that measure or order shall, to the extent possible, be adapted to a measure or an order known in the law of that Member State which has equivalent effects attached to it and which pursues similar aims and interests.

Such adaptation shall not result in effects going beyond those provided for in the law of the Member State of origin.

2. Any party may challenge the adaptation of the measure or order before a court.

3. If necessary, the party invoking the judgment or seeking its enforcement may be required to provide a translation or a transliteration of the judgment.

Article 55

A judgment given in a Member State which orders a payment by way of a penalty shall be enforceable in the Member State addressed only if the amount of the payment has been finally determined by the court of origin.

Article 56

No security, bond or deposit, however described, shall be required of a party who in one Member State applies for the enforcement of a judgment given in another Member State on the ground that he is a foreign national or that he is not domiciled or resident in the Member State addressed.

Article 57

1. When a translation or a transliteration is required under this Regulation, such translation or transliteration shall be into the official language of the Member State concerned or, where there are several official languages in that Member State, into the official language or one of the official languages of court proceedings of the place where a judgment given in another Member State is invoked or an application is made, in accordance with the law of that Member State.

2. For the purposes of the forms referred to in Articles 53 and 60, translations or transliterations may also be into any other official language or languages of the institutions of the Union that the Member State concerned has indicated it can accept.

3. Any translation made under this Regulation shall be done by a person qualified to do translations in one of the Member States.

CHAPTER IV

AUTHENTIC INSTRUMENTS AND COURT SETTLEMENTS

Article 58

1. An authentic instrument which is enforceable in the Member State of origin shall be enforceable in the other Member States without any declaration of enforceability being required. Enforcement of the authentic instrument may be refused only if such enforcement is manifestly contrary to public policy (ordre public) in the Member State addressed.

The provisions of Section 2, Subsection 2 of Section 3, and Section 4 of Chapter III shall apply as appropriate to authentic instruments.

2. The authentic instrument produced must satisfy the conditions necessary to establish its authenticity in the Member State of origin.

Article 59

A court settlement which is enforceable in the Member State of origin shall be enforced in the other Member States under the same conditions as authentic instruments.

Article 60

The competent authority or court of the Member State of origin shall, at the request of any interested party, issue the certificate using the form set out in Annex II containing a summary of the enforceable obligation recorded in the authentic instrument or of the agreement between the parties recorded in the court settlement.

CHAPTER V

GENERAL PROVISIONS

Article 61

No legalisation or other similar formality shall be required for documents issued in a Member State in the context of this Regulation.

Article 62

1.   In order to determine whether a party is domiciled in the Member State whose courts are seised of a matter, the court shall apply its internal law.

2.   If a party is not domiciled in the Member State whose courts are seised of the matter, then, in order to determine whether the party is domiciled in another Member State, the court shall apply the law of that Member State.

Article 63

1.   For the purposes of this Regulation, a company or other legal person or association of natural or legal persons is domiciled at the place where it has its:

(a) statutory seat;

(b) central administration; or

(c) principal place of business.

2.   For the purposes of Ireland, Cyprus and the United Kingdom, 'statutory seat' means the registered office or, where there is no such office anywhere, the place of incorporation or, where there is no such place anywhere, the place under the law of which the formation took place.

3.   In order to determine whether a trust is domiciled in the Member State whose courts are seised of the matter, the court shall apply its rules of private international law.

Article 64

Without prejudice to any more favourable provisions of national laws, persons domiciled in a Member State who are being prosecuted in the criminal courts of another Member State of which they are not nationals for an offence which was not intentionally committed may be defended by persons qualified to do so, even if they do not appear in person. However, the court seised of the matter may order appearance in person; in the case of failure to appear, a judgment given in the civil action without the person concerned having had the opportunity to arrange for his defence need not be recognised or enforced in the other Member States.

Article 65

1.   The jurisdiction specified in point 2 of Article 8 and Article 13 in actions on a warranty or guarantee or in any other third-party proceedings may be resorted to in the Member States included in the list established by the Commission pursuant to point (b) of Article 76(1) and Article 76(2) only in so far as permitted under national law. A person domiciled in another Member State may be invited to join the proceedings before the courts of those Member States pursuant to the rules on third-party notice referred to in that list.

2.   Judgments given in a Member State by virtue of point 2 of Article 8 or Article 13 shall be recognised and enforced in accordance with Chapter III in any other Member State. Any effects which judgments given in the Member States included in the list referred to in paragraph 1 may have, in accordance with the law of those Member States, on third parties by application of paragraph 1 shall be recognised in all Member States.

3.   The Member States included in the list referred to in paragraph 1 shall, within the framework of the European Judicial Network in civil and commercial matters established by Council Decision 2001/470/EC (¹) ('the European Judicial Network') provide information on how to determine, in accordance with their national law, the effects of the judgments referred to in the second sentence of paragraph 2.

CHAPTER VI

TRANSITIONAL PROVISIONS

Article 66

1.   This Regulation shall apply only to legal proceedings insti-tuted, to authentic instruments formally drawn up or registered and to court settlements approved or concluded on or after 10 January 2015.

2.   Notwithstanding Article 80, Regulation (EC) No 44/2001 shall continue to apply to judgments given in legal proceedings instituted, to authentic instruments formally drawn up or registered and to court settlements approved or concluded before 10 January 2015 which fall within the scope of that Regulation.

CHAPTER VII

RELATIONSHIP WITH OTHER INSTRUMENTS

Article 67

This Regulation shall not prejudice the application of provisions governing jurisdiction and the recognition and enforcement of judgments in specific matters which are contained in instruments of the Union or in national legislation harmonised pursuant to such instruments.

(¹) OJ L 174, 27.6.2001, p. 25.

Article 68

1.   This Regulation shall, as between the Member States, supersede the 1968 Brussels Convention, except as regards the territories of the Member States which fall within the territorial scope of that Convention and which are excluded from this Regulation pursuant to Article 355 of the TFEU.

2.   In so far as this Regulation replaces the provisions of the 1968 Brussels Convention between the Member States, any reference to that Convention shall be understood as a reference to this Regulation.

Article 69

Subject to Articles 70 and 71, this Regulation shall, as between the Member States, supersede the conventions that cover the same matters as those to which this Regulation applies. In particular, the conventions included in the list established by the Commission pursuant to point (c) of Article 76(1) and Article 76(2) shall be superseded.

Article 70

1.   The conventions referred to in Article 69 shall continue to have effect in relation to matters to which this Regulation does not apply.

2.   They shall continue to have effect in respect of judgments given, authentic instruments formally drawn up or registered and court settlements approved or concluded before the date of entry into force of Regulation (EC) No 44/2001.

Article 71

1.   This Regulation shall not affect any conventions to which the Member States are parties and which, in relation to particular matters, govern jurisdiction or the recognition or enforcement of judgments.

2.   With a view to its uniform interpretation, paragraph 1 shall be applied in the following manner:

(a) this Regulation shall not prevent a court of a Member State which is party to a convention on a particular matter from assuming jurisdiction in accordance with that convention, even where the defendant is domiciled in another Member State which is not party to that convention. The court hearing the action shall, in any event, apply Article 28 of this Regulation;

(b) judgments given in a Member State by a court in the exercise of jurisdiction provided for in a convention on a particular matter shall be recognised and enforced in the other Member States in accordance with this Regulation.

Where a convention on a particular matter to which both the Member State of origin and the Member State addressed are parties lays down conditions for the recognition or enforcement of judgments, those conditions shall apply. In any event, the provisions of this Regulation on recognition and enforcement of judgments may be applied.

Article 72

This Regulation shall not affect agreements by which Member States, prior to the entry into force of Regulation (EC) No 44/2001, undertook pursuant to Article 59 of the 1968 Brussels Convention not to recognise judgments given, in particular in other Contracting States to that Convention, against defendants domiciled or habitually resident in a third State where, in cases provided for in Article 4 of that Convention, the judgment could only be founded on a ground of jurisdiction specified in the second paragraph of Article 3 of that Convention.

Article 73

1.   This Regulation shall not affect the application of the 2007 Lugano Convention.

2.   This Regulation shall not affect the application of the 1958 New York Convention.

3.   This Regulation shall not affect the application of bilateral conventions and agreements between a third State and a Member State concluded before the date of entry into force of Regulation (EC) No 44/2001 which concern matters governed by this Regulation.

CHAPTER VIII

FINAL PROVISIONS

Article 74

The Member States shall provide, within the framework of the European Judicial Network and with a view to making the information available to the public, a description of national rules and procedures concerning enforcement, including authorities competent for enforcement, and information on any limitations on enforcement, in particular debtor protection rules and limitation or prescription periods.

The Member States shall keep this information permanently updated.

Article 75

By 10 January 2014, the Member States shall communicate to the Commission:

(a) the courts to which the application for refusal of enforcement is to be submitted pursuant to Article 47(1);

(b) the courts with which an appeal against the decision on the application for refusal of enforcement is to be lodged pursuant to Article 49(2);

(c) the courts with which any further appeal is to be lodged pursuant to Article 50; and

(d) the languages accepted for translations of the forms as referred to in Article 57(2).

The Commission shall make the information publicly available through any appropriate means, in particular through the European Judicial Network.

Article 76

1. The Member States shall notify the Commission of:

(a) the rules of jurisdiction referred to in Articles 5(2) and 6(2);

(b) the rules on third-party notice referred to in Article 65; and

(c) the conventions referred to in Article 69.

2. The Commission shall, on the basis of the notifications by the Member States referred to in paragraph 1, establish the corresponding lists.

3. The Member States shall notify the Commission of any subsequent amendments required to be made to those lists. The Commission shall amend those lists accordingly.

4. The Commission shall publish the lists and any subsequent amendments made to them in the *Official Journal of the European Union*.

5. The Commission shall make all information notified pursuant to paragraphs 1 and 3 publicly available through any other appropriate means, in particular through the European Judicial Network.

Article 77

The Commission shall be empowered to adopt delegated acts in accordance with Article 78 concerning the amendment of Annexes I and II.

Article 78

1. The power to adopt delegated acts is conferred on the Commission subject to the conditions laid down in this Article.

2. The power to adopt delegated acts referred to in Article 77 shall be conferred on the Commission for an indeterminate period of time from 9 January 2013.

3. The delegation of power referred to in Article 77 may be revoked at any time by the European Parliament or by the Council. A decision to revoke shall put an end to the delegation of the power specified in that decision. It shall take effect the day following the publication of the decision in the *Official Journal of the European Union* or at a later date specified therein. It shall not affect the validity of any delegated acts already in force.

4. As soon as it adopts a delegated act, the Commission shall notify it simultaneously to the European Parliament and to the Council.

5. A delegated act adopted pursuant to Article 77 shall enter into force only if no objection has been expressed either by the European Parliament or the Council within a period of two months of notification of that act to the European Parliament and the Council or if, before the expiry of that period, the European Parliament and the Council have both informed the Commission that they will not object. That period shall be extended by two months at the initiative of the European Parliament or of the Council.

Article 79

By 11 January 2022 the Commission shall present a report to the European Parliament, to the Council and to the European Economic and Social Committee on the application of this Regulation. That report shall include an evaluation of the possible need for a further extension of the rules on jurisdiction to defendants not domiciled in a Member State, taking into account the operation of this Regulation and possible developments at international level. Where appropriate, the report shall be accompanied by a proposal for amendment of this Regulation.

Article 80

This Regulation shall repeal Regulation (EC) No 44/2001. References to the repealed Regulation shall be construed as references to this Regulation and shall be read in accordance with the correlation table set out in Annex III.

Article 81

This Regulation shall enter into force on the twentieth day following that of its publication in the *Official Journal of the European Union*.

It shall apply from 10 January 2015, with the exception of Articles 75 and 76, which shall apply from 10 January 2014.

This Regulation shall be binding in its entirety and directly applicable in the Member States in accordance with the Treaties.

Done at Strasbourg, 12 December 2012.

For the European Parliament	*For the Council*
The President	*The President*
M. SCHULZ	A. D. MAVROYIANNIS

———

ANNEX I

CERTIFICATE CONCERNING A JUDGMENT IN CIVIL AND COMMERCIAL MATTERS

Article 53 of Regulation (EU) No 1215/2012 of the European Parliament and of the Council on jurisdiction and the recognition and enforcement of judgments in civil and commercial matters

1.   COURT OF ORIGIN

1.1.   Name:

1.2.   Address:

1.2.1.   Street and number/PO box:

1.2.2.   Place and postal code:

1.2.3.   Member State:

    AT ☐ BE ☐ BG ☐ CY ☐ CZ ☐ DE ☐ EE ☐ EL ☐ ES ☐ FI ☐ FR ☐ HU ☐ IE ☐ IT ☐ LT ☐LU ☐ LV ☐ MT ☐ NL ☐ PL ☐ PT ☐ RO ☐ SE ☐ SI ☐ SK ☐ UK ☐

1.3.   Telephone:

1.4.   Fax

1.5.   E-mail (if available):

2.   CLAIMANT(S) (^{1})

2.1.   Surname and given name(s)/name of company or organisation:

2.2.   Identification number (if applicable and if available):

2.3.   Date (dd/mm/yyyy) and place of birth or, if legal person, of incorporation/formation/registration (if relevant and if available):

2.4.   Address:

2.4.1.   Street and number/PO box:

2.4.2.   Place and postal code:

2.4.3.   Country:

    AT ☐ BE ☐ BG ☐ CY ☐ CZ ☐ DE ☐ EE ☐ EL ☐ ES ☐ FI ☐ FR ☐ HU ☐ IE ☐ IT ☐ LT ☐ LU ☐ LV ☐ MT ☐ NL ☐ PL ☐ PT ☐ RO ☐ SE ☐ SI ☐ SK ☐ UK ☐ Other (please specify (ISO-code)) ☐

2.5.   E-mail (if available):

3.   DEFENDANT(S) (^{2})

3.1.   Surname and given name(s)/name of company or organisation:

3.2.   Identification number (if applicable and if available):

3.3.   Date (dd/mm/yyyy) and place of birth or, if legal person, of incorporation/formation/registration (if relevant and if available):

3.4.   Address:

3.4.1.   Street and number/PO box:

3.4.2.   Place and postal code:

3.4.3.   Country:

    AT ☐ BE ☐ BG ☐ CY ☐ CZ ☐ DE ☐ EE ☐ EL ☐ ES ☐ FI ☐ FR ☐ HU ☐ IE ☐ IT ☐ LT ☐ LU ☐ LV ☐ MT ☐ NL ☐ PL ☐ PT ☐ RO ☐ SE ☐ SI ☐ SK ☐ UK ☐ Other (please specify (ISO-code)) ☐

3.5.   E-mail (if available):

4.   THE JUDGMENT

4.1.   Date (dd/mm/yyyy) of the judgment:

4.2.   Reference number of the judgment:

4.3.   The judgment was given in default of appearance:

4.3.1.   ☐ No

4.3.2.   ☐ Yes (please indicate the date (dd/mm/yyyy) on which the document instituting the proceedings or an equivalent document was served on the defendant):

4.4.   The judgment is enforceable in the Member State of origin without any further conditions having to be met:

4.4.1.   ☐ Yes (please indicate the date (dd/mm/yyyy) on which the judgment was declared enforceable, if applicable):

4.4.2.   ☐ Yes, but only against the following person(s) (please specify):

4.4.3.   ☐ Yes, but limited to part(s) of the judgment (please specify):

4.4.4.   ☐ The judgment does not contain an enforceable obligation

4.5.   As of the date of issue of the certificate, the judgment has been served on the defendant(s):

4.5.1.   ☐ Yes (please indicate the date of service (dd/mm/yyyy) if known):

4.5.1.1.   The judgment was served in the following language(s):
            BG ☐ ES ☐ CS ☐ DE ☐ ET ☐ EL ☐ EN ☐ FR ☐ GA ☐ IT ☐ LV ☐ LT ☐ HU ☐ MT ☐ NL ☐ PL ☐ PT ☐ RO ☐ SK ☐ SL ☐ FI ☐ SV ☐ Other (please specify (ISO-code)) ☐

4.5.2.   ☐ Not to the knowledge of the court

4.6.   Terms of the judgment and interest:

4.6.1.   Judgment on a monetary claim ([3])

4.6.1.1.   Short description of the subject-matter of the case:

4.6.1.2.   The court has ordered
            .... (surname and given name(s)/name of company or organisation) ([4])
            to make a payment to:
            .... (surname and given name(s)/name of company or organisation)

4.6.1.2.1. If more than one person has been held liable for one and the same claim, the whole amount may be collected from any one of them:

4.6.1.2.1.1. ☐ Yes

4.6.1.2.1.2. ☐ No

4.6.1.3.   Currency:
            ☐ euro (EUR) ☐ Bulgarian lev (BGN) ☐ Czech koruna (CZK) ☐ Hungarian forint (HUF) ☐ Lithuanian litas (LTL) ☐ Latvian lats (LVL) ☐ Polish zloty (PLN) ☐ Pound Sterling (GBP) ☐ Romanian leu (RON) ☐ Swedish krona (SEK) ☐ Other (please specify (ISO code)):

4.6.1.4.   Principal amount:

4.6.1.4.1. ☐ Amount to be paid in one sum

4.6.1.4.2. ☐ Amount to be paid in instalments (⁵)

Due date (dd/mm/yyyy)	Amount

4.6.1.4.3. ☐ Amount to be paid regularly

4.6.1.4.3.1. ☐ per day

4.6.1.4.3.2. ☐ per week

4.6.1.4.3.3. ☐ other (state frequency):

4.6.1.4.3.4. From date (dd/mm/yyyy) or event:

4.6.1.4.3.5. If applicable, until (date (dd/mm/yyyy) or event):

4.6.1.5. Interest, if applicable:

4.6.1.5.1. Interest:

4.6.1.5.1.1. ☐ Not specified in the judgment

4.6.1.5.1.2. ☐ Yes, specified in the judgment as follows:

4.6.1.5.1.2.1. Amount:

or:

4.6.1.5.1.2.2. Rate ... %

4.6.1.5.1.2.3. Interest due from .... (date (dd/mm/yyyy) or event) to .... (date (dd/mm/yyyy) or event) (⁶)

4.6.1.5.2. ☐ Statutory interest (if applicable) to be calculated in accordance with (please specify relevant statute):

4.6.1.5.2.1. Interest due from .... (date (dd/mm/yyyy) or event) to .... (date (dd/mm/yyyy) or event) (⁶)

4.6.1.5.3. ☐ Capitalisation of interest (if applicable, please specify):

4.6.2. Judgment ordering a provisional, including a protective, measure:

4.6.2.1. Short description of the subject-matter of the case and the measure ordered:

4.6.2.2. The measure was ordered by a court having jurisdiction as to the substance of the matter

4.6.2.2.1. ☐ Yes

4.6.3. Other type of judgment:

4.6.3.1. Short description of the subject-matter of the case and the ruling by the court:

4.7. Costs (⁷):

4.7.1. Currency:

☐ euro (EUR) ☐ Bulgarian lev (BGN) ☐ Czech koruna (CZK) ☐ Hungarian forint (HUF) ☐ Lithuanian litas (LTL) ☐ Latvian lats (LVL) ☐ Polish zloty (PLN) ☐ Pound Sterling (GBP) ☐ Romanian leu (RON) ☐ Swedish krona (SEK) ☐ Other (please specify (ISO code)):

4.7.2. The following person(s) against whom enforcement is sought has/have been ordered to bear the costs:

4.7.2.1. Surname and given name(s)/name of company or organisation: (⁸)

4.7.2.2. If more than one person has been ordered to bear the costs, the whole amount may be collected from any one of them:

4.7.2.2.1.   □ Yes

4.7.2.2.2.   □ No

4.7.3.   The costs of which recovery is sought are as follows: (^{9})

4.7.3.1.   □ The costs have been fixed in the judgment by way of a total amount (please specify amount):

4.7.3.2.   □ The costs have been fixed in the judgment by way of a percentage of total costs (please specify percentage of total):

4.7.3.3.   □ Liability for the costs has been determined in the judgment and the exact amounts are as follows:

4.7.3.3.1.   □ Court fees:

4.7.3.3.2.   □ Lawyers' fees:

4.7.3.3.3.   □ Cost of service of documents:

4.7.3.3.4.   □ Other:

4.7.3.4.   □ Other (please specify):

4.7.4.   Interest on costs:

4.7.4.1.   □ Not applicable

4.7.4.2.   □ Interest specified in the judgment

4.7.4.2.1.   □ Amount:
                  or

4.7.4.2.2.   □ Rate … %

4.7.4.2.2.1.   Interest due from .... (date (dd/mm/yyyy) or event) to .... (date (dd/mm/yyyy) or event) (^{6})

4.7.4.3.   □ Statutory interest (if applicable) to be calculated in accordance with (please specify relevant statute):

4.7.4.3.1.   Interest due from .... (date (dd/mm/yyyy) or event) to .... (date (dd/mm/yyyy) or event) (^{6})

4.7.4.4.   □ Capitalisation of interest (if applicable, please specify):

Done at: …

Signature and/or stamp of the court of origin:

(^{1}) Insert information for all claimants if the judgment concerns more than one.
(^{2}) Insert information for all defendants if the judgment concerns more than one.
(^{3}) If the judgment only concerns costs relating to a claim which has been decided in an earlier judgment, leave point 4.6.1 blank and go to point 4.7.
(^{4}) If more than one person has been ordered to make a payment, insert information for all persons.
(^{5}) Insert information for each instalment.
(^{6}) Insert information for all periods if more than one.
(^{7}) This point also covers situations where the costs are awarded in a separate judgment.
(^{8}) Insert information for all persons if more than one.
(^{9}) In the event that the costs may be recovered from several persons, insert the breakdown for each person separately.

———

CERTIFICATE CONCERNING AN AUTHENTIC INSTRUMENT/COURT SETTLEMENT (^{1}) IN CIVIL AND COMMERCIAL MATTERS

Article 60 of Regulation (EU) No 1215/2012 of the European Parliament and of the Council on jurisdiction and the recognition and enforcement of judgments in civil and commercial matters

1. COURT OR COMPETENT AUTHORITY ISSUING THE CERTIFICATE

1.1. Name:

1.2. Address:

1.2.1. Street and number/PO box:

1.2.2. Place and postal code:

1.2.3. Member State:

 AT ☐ BE ☐ BG ☐ CY ☐ CZ ☐ DE ☐ EE ☐ EL ☐ ES ☐ FI ☐ FR ☐ HU ☐ IE ☐ IT ☐ LT ☐ LU ☐ LV ☐ MT ☐ NL ☐ PL ☐ PT ☐ RO ☐ SE ☐ SI ☐ SK ☐ UK ☐

1.3. Telephone:

1.4. Fax

1.5. E-mail (if available):

2. AUTHENTIC INSTRUMENT

2.1. Authority which has drawn up the authentic instrument (if different from the authority issuing the certificate)

2.1.1. Name and designation of authority:

2.1.2. Address:

2.2. Date (dd/mm/yyyy) on which the authentic instrument was drawn up by the authority referred to in point 2.1:

2.3. Reference number of the authentic instrument (if applicable):

2.4. Date (dd/mm/yyyy) on which the authentic instrument was registered in the Member State of origin (to be filled in only if the date of registration determines the legal effect of the instrument and this date is different from the date indicated in point 2.2):

2.4.1. Reference number in the register (if applicable):

3. COURT SETTLEMENT

3.1. Court which approved the court settlement or before which the court settlement was concluded (if different from the court issuing the certificate)

3.1.1. Name of court:

3.1.2. Address:

3.2. Date (dd/mm/yyyy) of the court settlement:

3.3. Reference number of the court settlement:

4. PARTIES TO THE AUTHENTIC INSTRUMENT/COURT SETTLEMENT:

4.1. Name(s) of creditor(s) (surname and given name(s)/name of company or organisation) (^{2}):

4.1.1. Identification number (if applicable and if available):

4.1.2. Date (dd/mm/yyyy) and place of birth or, if legal person, of incorporation/formation/registration (if relevant and if available):

4.2. Name(s) of debtor(s) (surname and given name(s)/name of company or organisation) (^{3}):

4.2.1. Identification number (if applicable and if available):

4.2.2. Date (dd/mm/yyyy) and place of birth or, if legal person, of incorporation/formation/registration (if relevant and if available):

4.3. Name of other parties, if any (surname and given name(s)/name of company or organisation) (^{4})

4.3.1.   Identification number (if applicable and if available):

4.3.2.   Date (dd/mm/yyyy) and place of birth or, if legal person, of incorporation/formation/registration (if relevant and if available):

5.   ENFORCEABILITY OF THE AUTHENTIC INSTRUMENT/COURT SETTLEMENT IN THE MEMBER STATE OF ORIGIN

5.1.   The authentic instrument/court settlement is enforceable in the Member State of origin

5.1.1.   ☐ Yes

5.2.   Terms of the authentic instrument/court settlement and interest

5.2.1   Authentic instrument/court settlement relating to a monetary claim

5.2.1.1.   Short description of the subject matter:

5.2.1.2.   Under the authentic instrument/court settlement

              .... (surname and given name(s)/name of company or organisation) (5)

              has to make a payment to:

              .... (surname and given name(s)/name of company or organisation)

5.2.1.2.1.   If more than one person has been held liable for one and the same claim, the whole amount may be collected from any one of them:

5.2.1.2.1.1. ☐ Yes

5.2.1.2.1.2. ☐ No

5.2.1.3.   Currency:

              ☐ euro (EUR) ☐ Bulgarian lev (BGN) ☐ Czech koruna (CZK) ☐ Hungarian forint (HUF) ☐ Lithuanian litas (LTL) ☐ Latvian lats (LVL) ☐ Polish zloty (PLN) ☐ Pound Sterling (GBP) ☐ Romanian leu (RON) ☐ Swedish krona (SEK) ☐ Other (please specify (ISO code)):

5.2.1.4.   Principal amount:

5.2.1.4.1.   ☐ Amount to be paid in one sum

5.2.1.4.2.   ☐ Amount to be paid in instalments (6)

Due date (dd/mm/yyyy)	Amount

5.2.1.4.3.   ☐ Amount to be paid regularly

5.2.1.4.3.1. ☐ per day

5.2.1.4.3.2. ☐ per week

5.2.1.4.3.3. ☐ other (state frequency):

5.2.1.4.3.4. From date (dd/mm/yyyy) or event:

5.2.1.4.3.5. If applicable, until .... (date (dd/mm/yyyy) or event)

5.2.1.5.   Interest, if applicable

5.2.1.5.1.   Interest:

5.2.1.5.1.1. ☐ Not specified in the authentic instrument/court settlement

5.2.1.5.1.2. ☐ Yes, specified in the authentic instrument/court settlement as follows:

5.2.1.5.1.2.1. Amount:

or

5.2.1.5.1.2.2. Rate ... %

5.2.1.5.1.2.3. Interest due from .... (date (dd/mm/yyyy) or event) to .... (date (dd/mm/yyyy) or event) [7]

5.2.1.5.2. ☐ Statutory interest (if applicable) to be calculated in accordance with (please specify relevant statute):

5.2.1.5.2.1. Interest due from .... (date (dd/mm/yyyy) or event) to .... (date (dd/mm/yyyy) or event) [7]

5.2.1.5.3. ☐ Capitalisation of interest (if applicable, please specify):

5.2.2. Authentic instrument/court settlement relating to a non-monetary enforceable obligation:

5.2.2.1. Short description of the enforceable obligation

5.2.2.2. The obligation referred to in point 5.2.2.1 is enforceable against the following person(s) [8] (surname and given name(s)/name of company or organisation):

Done at: ...

Signature and/or stamp of the court or competent authority issuing the certificate:

---

[1] Delete as appropriate throughout the certificate.
[2] Insert information for all creditors if more than one.
[3] Insert information for all debtors if more than one.
[4] Insert information for other parties (if any).
[5] If more than one person has been ordered to make a payment, insert information for all persons.
[6] Insert information for each instalment.
[7] Insert information for all periods if more than one.
[8] Insert information for all persons if more than one.

ANNEX III

CORRELATION TABLE

Regulation (EC) No 44/2001	This Regulation
Article 1(1)	Article 1(1)
Article 1(2), introductory words	Article 1(2), introductory words
Article 1(2) point (a)	Article 1(2), points (a) and (f)
Article 1(2), points (b) to (d)	Article 1(2), points (b) to (d)
—	Article 1(2), point (e)
Article 1(3)	—
—	Article 2
Article 2	Article 4
Article 3	Article 5
Article 4	Article 6
Article 5, introductory words	Article 7, introductory words
Article 5, point (1)	Article 7, point (1)
Article 5, point (2)	—
Article 5, points (3) and (4)	Article 7, points (2) and (3)
—	Article 7, point (4)
Article 5, points (5) to (7)	Article 7, points (5) to (7)
Article 6	Article 8
Article 7	Article 9
Article 8	Article 10
Article 9	Article 11
Article 10	Article 12
Article 11	Article 13
Article 12	Article 14
Article 13	Article 15
Article 14	Article 16
Article 15	Article 17
Article 16	Article 18
Article 17	Article 19
Article 18	Article 20
Article 19, points (1) and (2)	Article 21(1)
—	Article 21(2)
Article 20	Article 22
Article 21	Article 23
Article 22	Article 24
Article 23(1) and (2)	Article 25(1) and (2)

Regulation (EC) No 44/2001	This Regulation
Article 23(3)	—
Article 23(4) and (5)	Article 25(3) and (4)
—	Article 25(5)
Article 24	Article 26(1)
—	Article 26(2)
Article 25	Article 27
Article 26	Article 28
Article 27(1)	Article 29(1)
—	Article 29(2)
Article 27(2)	Article 29(3)
Article 28	Article 30
Article 29	Article 31(1)
—	Article 31(2)
—	Article 31(3)
—	Article 31(4)
Article 30	Article 32(1), points (a) and (b)
—	Article 32(1), second subparagraph
—	Article 32(2)
—	Article 33
—	Article 34
Article 31	Article 35
Article 32	Article 2, point (a)
Article 33	Article 36
—	Article 37
—	Article 39
—	Article 40
—	Article 41
—	Article 42
—	Article 43
—	Article 44
Article 34	Article 45(1), points (a) to (d)
Article 35(1)	Article 45(1), point (e)
Article 35(2)	Article 45(2)
Article 35(3)	Article 45(3)
—	Article 45(4)
Article 36	Article 52
Article 37(1)	Article 38, point (a)
Article 38	—

Regulation (EC) No 44/2001	This Regulation
Article 39	—
Article 40	—
Article 41	—
Article 42	—
Article 43	—
Article 44	—
Article 45	—
Article 46	—
Article 47	—
Article 48	—
—	Article 46
—	Article 47
—	Article 48
—	Article 49
—	Article 50
—	Article 51
—	Article 54
Article 49	Article 55
Article 50	—
Article 51	Article 56
Article 52	—
Article 53	—
Article 54	Article 53
Article 55(1)	—
Article 55(2)	Article 37(2), Article 47(3) and Article 57
Article 56	Article 61
Article 57(1)	Article 58(1)
Article 57(2)	—
Article 57(3)	Article 58(2)
Article 57(4)	Article 60
Article 58	Article 59 and Article 60
Article 59	Article 62
Article 60	Article 63
Article 61	Article 64
Article 62	Article 3
Article 63	—
Article 64	—
Article 65	Article 65(1) and (2)

Regulation (EC) No 44/2001	This Regulation
—	Article 65(3)
Article 66	Article 66
Article 67	Article 67
Article 68	Article 68
Article 69	Article 69
Article 70	Article 70
Article 71	Article 71
Article 72	Article 72
—	Article 73
Article 73	Article 79
Article 74(1)	Article 75, first paragraph, points (a), (b) and (c), and Article 76(1), point (a)
Article 74(2)	Article 77
—	Article 78
—	Article 80
Article 75	—
Article 76	Article 81
Annex I	Article 76(1), point (a)
Annex II	Article 75, point (a)
Annex III	Article 75, point (b)
Annex IV	Article 75, point (c)
Annex V	Annex I and Annex II
Annex VI	Annex II
—	Annex III

REGULATION (EC) No 593/2008 OF THE EUROPEAN PARLIAMENT AND OF THE COUNCIL

of 17 June 2008

on the law applicable to contractual obligations (Rome I)

THE EUROPEAN PARLIAMENT AND THE COUNCIL OF THE EUROPEAN UNION,

Having regard to the Treaty establishing the European Community, and in particular Article 61(c) and the second indent of Article 67(5) thereof,

Having regard to the proposal from the Commission,

Having regard to the opinion of the European Economic and Social Committee (¹),

Acting in accordance with the procedure laid down in Article 251 of the Treaty (²),

Whereas:

(1) The Community has set itself the objective of maintaining and developing an area of freedom, security and justice. For the progressive establishment of such an area, the Community is to adopt measures relating to judicial cooperation in civil matters with a cross-border impact to the extent necessary for the proper functioning of the internal market.

(2) According to Article 65, point (b) of the Treaty, these measures are to include those promoting the compatibility of the rules applicable in the Member States concerning the conflict of laws and of jurisdiction.

(3) The European Council meeting in Tampere on 15 and 16 October 1999 endorsed the principle of mutual recognition of judgments and other decisions of judicial authorities as the cornerstone of judicial cooperation in civil matters and invited the Council and the Commission to adopt a programme of measures to implement that principle.

(4) On 30 November 2000 the Council adopted a joint Commission and Council programme of measures for implementation of the principle of mutual recognition of decisions in civil and commercial matters (³). The programme identifies measures relating to the harmonisation of conflict-of-law rules as those facilitating the mutual recognition of judgments.

(5) The Hague Programme (⁴), adopted by the European Council on 5 November 2004, called for work to be pursued actively on the conflict-of-law rules regarding contractual obligations (Rome I).

(6) The proper functioning of the internal market creates a need, in order to improve the predictability of the outcome of litigation, certainty as to the law applicable and the free movement of judgments, for the conflict-of-law rules in the Member States to designate the same national law irrespective of the country of the court in which an action is brought.

(7) The substantive scope and the provisions of this Regulation should be consistent with Council Regulation (EC) No 44/2001 of 22 December 2000 on jurisdiction and the recognition and enforcement of judgments in civil and commercial matters (⁵) (Brussels I) and Regulation (EC) No 864/2007 of the European Parliament and of the Council of 11 July 2007 on the law applicable to non-contractual obligations (Rome II) (⁶).

(8) Family relationships should cover parentage, marriage, affinity and collateral relatives. The reference in Article 1(2) to relationships having comparable effects to marriage and other family relationships should be interpreted in accordance with the law of the Member State in which the court is seised.

(9) Obligations under bills of exchange, cheques and promissory notes and other negotiable instruments should also cover bills of lading to the extent that the obligations under the bill of lading arise out of its negotiable character.

(10) Obligations arising out of dealings prior to the conclusion of the contract are covered by Article 12 of Regulation (EC) No 864/2007. Such obligations should therefore be excluded from the scope of this Regulation.

(11) The parties' freedom to choose the applicable law should be one of the cornerstones of the system of conflict-of-law rules in matters of contractual obligations.

(12) An agreement between the parties to confer on one or more courts or tribunals of a Member State exclusive jurisdiction to determine disputes under the contract should be one of the factors to be taken into account in determining whether a choice of law has been clearly demonstrated.

(13) This Regulation does not preclude parties from incorporating by reference into their contract a non-State body of law or an international convention.

(¹) OJ C 318, 23.12.2006, p. 56.
(²) Opinion of the European Parliament of 29 November 2007 (not yet published in the Official Journal) and Council Decision of 5 June 2008.
(³) OJ C 12, 15.1.2001, p. 1.
(⁴) OJ C 53, 3.3.2005, p. 1.

(⁵) OJ L 12, 16.1.2001, p. 1. Regulation as last amended by Regulation (EC) No 1791/2006 (OJ L 363, 20.12.2006, p. 1).
(⁶) OJ L 199, 31.7.2007, p. 40.

(14) Should the Community adopt, in an appropriate legal instrument, rules of substantive contract law, including standard terms and conditions, such instrument may provide that the parties may choose to apply those rules.

(15) Where a choice of law is made and all other elements relevant to the situation are located in a country other than the country whose law has been chosen, the choice of law should not prejudice the application of provisions of the law of that country which cannot be derogated from by agreement. This rule should apply whether or not the choice of law was accompanied by a choice of court or tribunal. Whereas no substantial change is intended as compared with Article 3(3) of the 1980 Convention on the Law Applicable to Contractual Obligations (¹) (the Rome Convention), the wording of this Regulation is aligned as far as possible with Article 14 of Regulation (EC) No 864/2007.

(16) To contribute to the general objective of this Regulation, legal certainty in the European judicial area, the conflict-of-law rules should be highly foreseeable. The courts should, however, retain a degree of discretion to determine the law that is most closely connected to the situation.

(17) As far as the applicable law in the absence of choice is concerned, the concept of 'provision of services' and 'sale of goods' should be interpreted in the same way as when applying Article 5 of Regulation (EC) No 44/2001 in so far as sale of goods and provision of services are covered by that Regulation. Although franchise and distribution contracts are contracts for services, they are the subject of specific rules.

(18) As far as the applicable law in the absence of choice is concerned, multilateral systems should be those in which trading is conducted, such as regulated markets and multilateral trading facilities as referred to in Article 4 of Directive 2004/39/EC of the European Parliament and of the Council of 21 April 2004 on markets in financial instruments (²), regardless of whether or not they rely on a central counterparty.

(19) Where there has been no choice of law, the applicable law should be determined in accordance with the rule specified for the particular type of contract. Where the contract cannot be categorised as being one of the specified types or where its elements fall within more than one of the specified types, it should be governed by the law of the country where the party required to effect the characteristic performance of the contract has his habitual residence. In the case of a contract consisting of a bundle of rights and obligations capable of being categorised as falling within more than one of the specified types of contract, the characteristic performance of the contract should be determined having regard to its centre of gravity.

(20) Where the contract is manifestly more closely connected with a country other than that indicated in Article 4(1) or (2), an escape clause should provide that the law of that other country is to apply. In order to determine that country, account should be taken, *inter alia*, of whether the contract in question has a very close relationship with another contract or contracts.

(21) In the absence of choice, where the applicable law cannot be determined either on the basis of the fact that the contract can be categorised as one of the specified types or as being the law of the country of habitual residence of the party required to effect the characteristic performance of the contract, the contract should be governed by the law of the country with which it is most closely connected. In order to determine that country, account should be taken, *inter alia*, of whether the contract in question has a very close relationship with another contract or contracts.

(22) As regards the interpretation of contracts for the carriage of goods, no change in substance is intended with respect to Article 4(4), third sentence, of the Rome Convention. Consequently, single-voyage charter parties and other contracts the main purpose of which is the carriage of goods should be treated as contracts for the carriage of goods. For the purposes of this Regulation, the term 'consignor' should refer to any person who enters into a contract of carriage with the carrier and the term 'the carrier' should refer to the party to the contract who undertakes to carry the goods, whether or not he performs the carriage himself.

(23) As regards contracts concluded with parties regarded as being weaker, those parties should be protected by conflict-of-law rules that are more favourable to their interests than the general rules.

(24) With more specific reference to consumer contracts, the conflict-of-law rule should make it possible to cut the cost of settling disputes concerning what are commonly relatively small claims and to take account of the development of distance-selling techniques. Consistency with Regulation (EC) No 44/2001 requires both that there be a reference to the concept of directed activity as a condition for applying the consumer protection rule and that the concept be interpreted harmoniously in Regulation (EC) No 44/2001 and this Regulation, bearing in mind that a joint declaration by the Council and the Commission on Article 15 of Regulation (EC) No 44/2001 states that 'for Article 15(1)(c) to be applicable it is not sufficient for an undertaking to target its activities at the Member State of the consumer's residence, or at a number of Member States including that Member State; a contract must also be concluded within the framework of its activities'. The declaration also states that 'the mere fact that an Internet site is accessible is not sufficient for Article 15 to be applicable, although a factor will be that this Internet site solicits the conclusion of distance contracts and that a contract has actually been concluded at a distance, by

(¹) OJ C 334, 30.12.2005, p. 1.
(²) OJ L 145, 30.4.2004, p. 1. Directive as last amended by Directive 2008/10/EC (OJ L 76, 19.3.2008, p. 33).

whatever means. In this respect, the language or currency which a website uses does not constitute a relevant factor.'.

(25) Consumers should be protected by such rules of the country of their habitual residence that cannot be derogated from by agreement, provided that the consumer contract has been concluded as a result of the professional pursuing his commercial or professional activities in that particular country. The same protection should be guaranteed if the professional, while not pursuing his commercial or professional activities in the country where the consumer has his habitual residence, directs his activities by any means to that country or to several countries, including that country, and the contract is concluded as a result of such activities.

(26) For the purposes of this Regulation, financial services such as investment services and activities and ancillary services provided by a professional to a consumer, as referred to in sections A and B of Annex I to Directive 2004/39/EC, and contracts for the sale of units in collective investment undertakings, whether or not covered by Council Directive 85/611/EEC of 20 December 1985 on the coordination of laws, regulations and administrative provisions relating to undertakings for collective investment in transferable securities (UCITS) (¹), should be subject to Article 6 of this Regulation. Consequently, when a reference is made to terms and conditions governing the issuance or offer to the public of transferable securities or to the subscription and redemption of units in collective investment undertakings, that reference should include all aspects binding the issuer or the offeror to the consumer, but should not include those aspects involving the provision of financial services.

(27) Various exceptions should be made to the general conflict-of-law rule for consumer contracts. Under one such exception the general rule should not apply to contracts relating to rights *in rem* in immovable property or tenancies of such property unless the contract relates to the right to use immovable property on a timeshare basis within the meaning of Directive 94/47/EC of the European Parliament and of the Council of 26 October 1994 on the protection of purchasers in respect of certain aspects of contracts relating to the purchase of the right to use immovable properties on a timeshare basis (²).

(28) It is important to ensure that rights and obligations which constitute a financial instrument are not covered by the general rule applicable to consumer contracts, as that could lead to different laws being applicable to each of the instruments issued, therefore changing their nature and preventing their fungible trading and offering. Likewise, whenever such instruments are issued or offered, the contractual relationship established between the issuer or the offeror and the consumer should not necessarily be

subject to the mandatory application of the law of the country of habitual residence of the consumer, as there is a need to ensure uniformity in the terms and conditions of an issuance or an offer. The same rationale should apply with regard to the multilateral systems covered by Article 4(1)(h), in respect of which it should be ensured that the law of the country of habitual residence of the consumer will not interfere with the rules applicable to contracts concluded within those systems or with the operator of such systems.

(29) For the purposes of this Regulation, references to rights and obligations constituting the terms and conditions governing the issuance, offers to the public or public take-over bids of transferable securities and references to the subscription and redemption of units in collective investment undertakings should include the terms governing, *inter alia*, the allocation of securities or units, rights in the event of over-subscription, withdrawal rights and similar matters in the context of the offer as well as those matters referred to in Articles 10, 11, 12 and 13, thus ensuring that all relevant contractual aspects of an offer binding the issuer or the offeror to the consumer are governed by a single law.

(30) For the purposes of this Regulation, financial instruments and transferable securities are those instruments referred to in Article 4 of Directive 2004/39/EC.

(31) Nothing in this Regulation should prejudice the operation of a formal arrangement designated as a system under Article 2(a) of Directive 98/26/EC of the European Parliament and of the Council of 19 May 1998 on settlement finality in payment and securities settlement systems (³).

(32) Owing to the particular nature of contracts of carriage and insurance contracts, specific provisions should ensure an adequate level of protection of passengers and policy holders. Therefore, Article 6 should not apply in the context of those particular contracts.

(33) Where an insurance contract not covering a large risk covers more than one risk, at least one of which is situated in a Member State and at least one of which is situated in a third country, the special rules on insurance contracts in this Regulation should apply only to the risk or risks situated in the relevant Member State or Member States.

(34) The rule on individual employment contracts should not prejudice the application of the overriding mandatory provisions of the country to which a worker is posted in accordance with Directive 96/71/EC of the European Parliament and of the Council of 16 December 1996 concerning the posting of workers in the framework of the provision of services (⁴).

(¹) OJ L 375, 31.12.1985, p. 3. Directive as last amended by Directive 2008/18/EC of the European Parliament and of the Council (OJ L 76, 19.3.2008, p. 42).
(²) OJ L 280, 29.10.1994, p. 83.

(³) OJ L 166, 11.6.1998, p. 45.
(⁴) OJ L 18, 21.1.1997, p. 1.

(35) Employees should not be deprived of the protection afforded to them by provisions which cannot be derogated from by agreement or which can only be derogated from to their benefit.

(36) As regards individual employment contracts, work carried out in another country should be regarded as temporary if the employee is expected to resume working in the country of origin after carrying out his tasks abroad. The conclusion of a new contract of employment with the original employer or an employer belonging to the same group of companies as the original employer should not preclude the employee from being regarded as carrying out his work in another country temporarily.

(37) Considerations of public interest justify giving the courts of the Member States the possibility, in exceptional circumstances, of applying exceptions based on public policy and overriding mandatory provisions. The concept of 'overriding mandatory provisions' should be distinguished from the expression 'provisions which cannot be derogated from by agreement' and should be construed more restrictively.

(38) In the context of voluntary assignment, the term 'relationship' should make it clear that Article 14(1) also applies to the property aspects of an assignment, as between assignor and assignee, in legal orders where such aspects are treated separately from the aspects under the law of obligations. However, the term 'relationship' should not be understood as relating to any relationship that may exist between assignor and assignee. In particular, it should not cover preliminary questions as regards a voluntary assignment or a contractual subrogation. The term should be strictly limited to the aspects which are directly relevant to the voluntary assignment or contractual subrogation in question.

(39) For the sake of legal certainty there should be a clear definition of habitual residence, in particular for companies and other bodies, corporate or unincorporated. Unlike Article 60(1) of Regulation (EC) No 44/2001, which establishes three criteria, the conflict-of-law rule should proceed on the basis of a single criterion; otherwise, the parties would be unable to foresee the law applicable to their situation.

(40) A situation where conflict-of-law rules are dispersed among several instruments and where there are differences between those rules should be avoided. This Regulation, however, should not exclude the possibility of inclusion of conflict-of-law rules relating to contractual obligations in provisions of Community law with regard to particular matters.

This Regulation should not prejudice the application of other instruments laying down provisions designed to contribute to the proper functioning of the internal market in so far as they cannot be applied in conjunction with the law designated by the rules of this Regulation. The application of provisions of the applicable law designated by the rules of this Regulation should not restrict the free movement of goods and services as regulated by Community instruments, such as Directive 2000/31/EC of the European Parliament and of the Council of 8 June 2000 on certain legal aspects of information society services, in particular electronic commerce, in the Internal Market (Directive on electronic commerce) (¹).

(41) Respect for international commitments entered into by the Member States means that this Regulation should not affect international conventions to which one or more Member States are parties at the time when this Regulation is adopted. To make the rules more accessible, the Commission should publish the list of the relevant conventions in the *Official Journal of the European Union* on the basis of information supplied by the Member States.

(42) The Commission will make a proposal to the European Parliament and to the Council concerning the procedures and conditions according to which Member States would be entitled to negotiate and conclude, on their own behalf, agreements with third countries in individual and exceptional cases, concerning sectoral matters and containing provisions on the law applicable to contractual obligations.

(43) Since the objective of this Regulation cannot be sufficiently achieved by the Member States and can therefore, by reason of the scale and effects of this Regulation, be better achieved at Community level, the Community may adopt measures, in accordance with the principle of subsidiarity as set out in Article 5 of the Treaty. In accordance with the principle of proportionality, as set out in that Article, this Regulation does not go beyond what is necessary to attain its objective.

(44) In accordance with Article 3 of the Protocol on the position of the United Kingdom and Ireland, annexed to the Treaty on European Union and to the Treaty establishing the European Community, Ireland has notified its wish to take part in the adoption and application of the present Regulation.

(45) In accordance with Articles 1 and 2 of the Protocol on the position of the United Kingdom and Ireland, annexed to the Treaty on European Union and to the Treaty establishing the European Community, and without prejudice to Article 4 of the said Protocol, the United Kingdom is not taking part in the adoption of this Regulation and is not bound by it or subject to its application.

(46) In accordance with Articles 1 and 2 of the Protocol on the position of Denmark, annexed to the Treaty on European Union and to the Treaty establishing the European Community, Denmark is not taking part in the adoption of this Regulation and is not bound by it or subject to its application,

---

(¹) OJ L 178, 17.7.2000, p. 1.

HAVE ADOPTED THIS REGULATION:

CHAPTER I

SCOPE

Article 1

Material scope

1.   This Regulation shall apply, in situations involving a conflict of laws, to contractual obligations in civil and commercial matters.

It shall not apply, in particular, to revenue, customs or administrative matters.

2.   The following shall be excluded from the scope of this Regulation:

(a)   questions involving the status or legal capacity of natural persons, without prejudice to Article 13;

(b)   obligations arising out of family relationships and relationships deemed by the law applicable to such relationships to have comparable effects, including maintenance obligations;

(c)   obligations arising out of matrimonial property regimes, property regimes of relationships deemed by the law applicable to such relationships to have comparable effects to marriage, and wills and succession;

(d)   obligations arising under bills of exchange, cheques and promissory notes and other negotiable instruments to the extent that the obligations under such other negotiable instruments arise out of their negotiable character;

(e)   arbitration agreements and agreements on the choice of court;

(f)   questions governed by the law of companies and other bodies, corporate or unincorporated, such as the creation, by registration or otherwise, legal capacity, internal organisation or winding-up of companies and other bodies, corporate or unincorporated, and the personal liability of officers and members as such for the obligations of the company or body;

(g)   the question whether an agent is able to bind a principal, or an organ to bind a company or other body corporate or unincorporated, in relation to a third party;

(h)   the constitution of trusts and the relationship between settlors, trustees and beneficiaries;

(i)   obligations arising out of dealings prior to the conclusion of a contract;

(j)   insurance contracts arising out of operations carried out by organisations other than undertakings referred to in Article 2 of Directive 2002/83/EC of the European Parliament and of the Council of 5 November 2002 concerning life assurance ([1]) the object of which is to provide benefits for employed or self-employed persons belonging to an undertaking or group of undertakings, or to a trade or group of trades, in the event of death or survival or of discontinuance or curtailment of activity, or of sickness related to work or accidents at work.

3.   This Regulation shall not apply to evidence and procedure, without prejudice to Article 18.

4.   In this Regulation, the term 'Member State' shall mean Member States to which this Regulation applies. However, in Article 3(4) and Article 7 the term shall mean all the Member States.

Article 2

Universal application

Any law specified by this Regulation shall be applied whether or not it is the law of a Member State.

CHAPTER II

UNIFORM RULES

Article 3

Freedom of choice

1.   A contract shall be governed by the law chosen by the parties. The choice shall be made expressly or clearly demonstrated by the terms of the contract or the circumstances of the case. By their choice the parties can select the law applicable to the whole or to part only of the contract.

2.   The parties may at any time agree to subject the contract to a law other than that which previously governed it, whether as a result of an earlier choice made under this Article or of other provisions of this Regulation. Any change in the law to be applied that is made after the conclusion of the contract shall not prejudice its formal validity under Article 11 or adversely affect the rights of third parties.

3.   Where all other elements relevant to the situation at the time of the choice are located in a country other than the country whose law has been chosen, the choice of the parties shall not prejudice the application of provisions of the law of that other country which cannot be derogated from by agreement.

4.   Where all other elements relevant to the situation at the time of the choice are located in one or more Member States, the

---
([1])   OJ L 345, 19.12.2002, p. 1. Directive as last amended by Directive 2008/19/EC (OJ L 76, 19.3.2008, p. 44).

parties' choice of applicable law other than that of a Member State shall not prejudice the application of provisions of Community law, where appropriate as implemented in the Member State of the forum, which cannot be derogated from by agreement.

5. The existence and validity of the consent of the parties as to the choice of the applicable law shall be determined in accordance with the provisions of Articles 10, 11 and 13.

Article 4

Applicable law in the absence of choice

1. To the extent that the law applicable to the contract has not been chosen in accordance with Article 3 and without prejudice to Articles 5 to 8, the law governing the contract shall be determined as follows:

(a) a contract for the sale of goods shall be governed by the law of the country where the seller has his habitual residence;

(b) a contract for the provision of services shall be governed by the law of the country where the service provider has his habitual residence;

(c) a contract relating to a right *in rem* in immovable property or to a tenancy of immovable property shall be governed by the law of the country where the property is situated;

(d) notwithstanding point (c), a tenancy of immovable property concluded for temporary private use for a period of no more than six consecutive months shall be governed by the law of the country where the landlord has his habitual residence, provided that the tenant is a natural person and has his habitual residence in the same country;

(e) a franchise contract shall be governed by the law of the country where the franchisee has his habitual residence;

(f) a distribution contract shall be governed by the law of the country where the distributor has his habitual residence;

(g) a contract for the sale of goods by auction shall be governed by the law of the country where the auction takes place, if such a place can be determined;

(h) a contract concluded within a multilateral system which brings together or facilitates the bringing together of multiple third-party buying and selling interests in financial instruments, as defined by Article 4(1), point (17) of Directive 2004/39/EC, in accordance with non-discretionary rules and governed by a single law, shall be governed by that law.

2. Where the contract is not covered by paragraph 1 or where the elements of the contract would be covered by more than one of points (a) to (h) of paragraph 1, the contract shall be governed by the law of the country where the party required to effect the characteristic performance of the contract has his habitual residence.

3. Where it is clear from all the circumstances of the case that the contract is manifestly more closely connected with a country other than that indicated in paragraphs 1 or 2, the law of that other country shall apply.

4. Where the law applicable cannot be determined pursuant to paragraphs 1 or 2, the contract shall be governed by the law of the country with which it is most closely connected.

Article 5

Contracts of carriage

1. To the extent that the law applicable to a contract for the carriage of goods has not been chosen in accordance with Article 3, the law applicable shall be the law of the country of habitual residence of the carrier, provided that the place of receipt or the place of delivery or the habitual residence of the consignor is also situated in that country. If those requirements are not met, the law of the country where the place of delivery as agreed by the parties is situated shall apply.

2. To the extent that the law applicable to a contract for the carriage of passengers has not been chosen by the parties in accordance with the second subparagraph, the law applicable shall be the law of the country where the passenger has his habitual residence, provided that either the place of departure or the place of destination is situated in that country. If these requirements are not met, the law of the country where the carrier has his habitual residence shall apply.

The parties may choose as the law applicable to a contract for the carriage of passengers in accordance with Article 3 only the law of the country where:

(a) the passenger has his habitual residence; or

(b) the carrier has his habitual residence; or

(c) the carrier has his place of central administration; or

(d) the place of departure is situated; or

(e) the place of destination is situated.

3. Where it is clear from all the circumstances of the case that the contract, in the absence of a choice of law, is manifestly more closely connected with a country other than that indicated in paragraphs 1 or 2, the law of that other country shall apply.

Article 6

Consumer contracts

1. Without prejudice to Articles 5 and 7, a contract concluded by a natural person for a purpose which can be regarded as being outside his trade or profession (the consumer) with another

person acting in the exercise of his trade or profession (the professional) shall be governed by the law of the country where the consumer has his habitual residence, provided that the professional:

(a)   pursues his commercial or professional activities in the country where the consumer has his habitual residence, or

(b)   by any means, directs such activities to that country or to several countries including that country,

and the contract falls within the scope of such activities.

2.   Notwithstanding paragraph 1, the parties may choose the law applicable to a contract which fulfils the requirements of paragraph 1, in accordance with Article 3. Such a choice may not, however, have the result of depriving the consumer of the protection afforded to him by provisions that cannot be derogated from by agreement by virtue of the law which, in the absence of choice, would have been applicable on the basis of paragraph 1.

3.   If the requirements in points (a) or (b) of paragraph 1 are not fulfilled, the law applicable to a contract between a consumer and a professional shall be determined pursuant to Articles 3 and 4.

4.   Paragraphs 1 and 2 shall not apply to:

(a)   a contract for the supply of services where the services are to be supplied to the consumer exclusively in a country other than that in which he has his habitual residence;

(b)   a contract of carriage other than a contract relating to package travel within the meaning of Council Directive 90/314/EEC of 13 June 1990 on package travel, package holidays and package tours (¹);

(c)   a contract relating to a right *in rem* in immovable property or a tenancy of immovable property other than a contract relating to the right to use immovable properties on a timeshare basis within the meaning of Directive 94/47/EC;

(d)   rights and obligations which constitute a financial instrument and rights and obligations constituting the terms and conditions governing the issuance or offer to the public and public take-over bids of transferable securities, and the subscription and redemption of units in collective investment undertakings in so far as these activities do not constitute provision of a financial service;

(e)   a contract concluded within the type of system falling within the scope of Article 4(1)(h).

_____
(¹)   OJ L 158, 23.6.1990, p. 59.

Article 7

Insurance contracts

1.   This Article shall apply to contracts referred to in paragraph 2, whether or not the risk covered is situated in a Member State, and to all other insurance contracts covering risks situated inside the territory of the Member States. It shall not apply to reinsurance contracts.

2.   An insurance contract covering a large risk as defined in Article 5(d) of the First Council Directive 73/239/EEC of 24 July 1973 on the coordination of laws, regulations and administrative provisions relating to the taking-up and pursuit of the business of direct insurance other than life assurance (²) shall be governed by the law chosen by the parties in accordance with Article 3 of this Regulation.

To the extent that the applicable law has not been chosen by the parties, the insurance contract shall be governed by the law of the country where the insurer has his habitual residence. Where it is clear from all the circumstances of the case that the contract is manifestly more closely connected with another country, the law of that other country shall apply.

3.   In the case of an insurance contract other than a contract falling within paragraph 2, only the following laws may be chosen by the parties in accordance with Article 3:

(a)   the law of any Member State where the risk is situated at the time of conclusion of the contract;

(b)   the law of the country where the policy holder has his habitual residence;

(c)   in the case of life assurance, the law of the Member State of which the policy holder is a national;

(d)   for insurance contracts covering risks limited to events occurring in one Member State other than the Member State where the risk is situated, the law of that Member State;

(e)   where the policy holder of a contract falling under this paragraph pursues a commercial or industrial activity or a liberal profession and the insurance contract covers two or more risks which relate to those activities and are situated in different Member States, the law of any of the Member States concerned or the law of the country of habitual residence of the policy holder.

Where, in the cases set out in points (a), (b) or (e), the Member States referred to grant greater freedom of choice of the law applicable to the insurance contract, the parties may take advantage of that freedom.

_____
(²)   OJ L 228, 16.8.1973, p. 3. Directive as last amended by Directive 2005/68/EC of the European Parliament and of the Council (OJ L 323, 9.12.2005, p. 1).

To the extent that the law applicable has not been chosen by the parties in accordance with this paragraph, such a contract shall be governed by the law of the Member State in which the risk is situated at the time of conclusion of the contract.

4. The following additional rules shall apply to insurance contracts covering risks for which a Member State imposes an obligation to take out insurance:

(a) the insurance contract shall not satisfy the obligation to take out insurance unless it complies with the specific provisions relating to that insurance laid down by the Member State that imposes the obligation. Where the law of the Member State in which the risk is situated and the law of the Member State imposing the obligation to take out insurance contradict each other, the latter shall prevail;

(b) by way of derogation from paragraphs 2 and 3, a Member State may lay down that the insurance contract shall be governed by the law of the Member State that imposes the obligation to take out insurance.

5. For the purposes of paragraph 3, third subparagraph, and paragraph 4, where the contract covers risks situated in more than one Member State, the contract shall be considered as constituting several contracts each relating to only one Member State.

6. For the purposes of this Article, the country in which the risk is situated shall be determined in accordance with Article 2(d) of the Second Council Directive 88/357/EEC of 22 June 1988 on the coordination of laws, regulations and administrative provisions relating to direct insurance other than life assurance and laying down provisions to facilitate the effective exercise of freedom to provide services (¹) and, in the case of life assurance, the country in which the risk is situated shall be the country of the commitment within the meaning of Article 1(1) (g) of Directive 2002/83/EC.

Article 8

Individual employment contracts

1. An individual employment contract shall be governed by the law chosen by the parties in accordance with Article 3. Such a choice of law may not, however, have the result of depriving the employee of the protection afforded to him by provisions that cannot be derogated from by agreement under the law that, in the absence of choice, would have been applicable pursuant to paragraphs 2, 3 and 4 of this Article.

2. To the extent that the law applicable to the individual employment contract has not been chosen by the parties, the contract shall be governed by the law of the country in which or, failing that, from which the employee habitually carries out his work in performance of the contract. The country where the

___

(¹) OJ L 172, 4.7.1988, p. 1. Directive as last amended by Directive 2005/14/EC of the European Parliament and of the Council (OJ L 149, 11.6.2005, p. 14).

work is habitually carried out shall not be deemed to have changed if he is temporarily employed in another country.

3. Where the law applicable cannot be determined pursuant to paragraph 2, the contract shall be governed by the law of the country where the place of business through which the employee was engaged is situated.

4. Where it appears from the circumstances as a whole that the contract is more closely connected with a country other than that indicated in paragraphs 2 or 3, the law of that other country shall apply.

Article 9

Overriding mandatory provisions

1. Overriding mandatory provisions are provisions the respect for which is regarded as crucial by a country for safeguarding its public interests, such as its political, social or economic organisation, to such an extent that they are applicable to any situation falling within their scope, irrespective of the law otherwise applicable to the contract under this Regulation.

2. Nothing in this Regulation shall restrict the application of the overriding mandatory provisions of the law of the forum.

3. Effect may be given to the overriding mandatory provisions of the law of the country where the obligations arising out of the contract have to be or have been performed, in so far as those overriding mandatory provisions render the performance of the contract unlawful. In considering whether to give effect to those provisions, regard shall be had to their nature and purpose and to the consequences of their application or non-application.

Article 10

Consent and material validity

1. The existence and validity of a contract, or of any term of a contract, shall be determined by the law which would govern it under this Regulation if the contract or term were valid.

2. Nevertheless, a party, in order to establish that he did not consent, may rely upon the law of the country in which he has his habitual residence if it appears from the circumstances that it would not be reasonable to determine the effect of his conduct in accordance with the law specified in paragraph 1.

Article 11

Formal validity

1. A contract concluded between persons who, or whose agents, are in the same country at the time of its conclusion is

formally valid if it satisfies the formal requirements of the law which governs it in substance under this Regulation or of the law of the country where it is concluded.

2. A contract concluded between persons who, or whose agents, are in different countries at the time of its conclusion is formally valid if it satisfies the formal requirements of the law which governs it in substance under this Regulation, or of the law of either of the countries where either of the parties or their agent is present at the time of conclusion, or of the law of the country where either of the parties had his habitual residence at that time.

3. A unilateral act intended to have legal effect relating to an existing or contemplated contract is formally valid if it satisfies the formal requirements of the law which governs or would govern the contract in substance under this Regulation, or of the law of the country where the act was done, or of the law of the country where the person by whom it was done had his habitual residence at that time.

4. Paragraphs 1, 2 and 3 of this Article shall not apply to contracts that fall within the scope of Article 6. The form of such contracts shall be governed by the law of the country where the consumer has his habitual residence.

5. Notwithstanding paragraphs 1 to 4, a contract the subject matter of which is a right *in rem* in immovable property or a tenancy of immovable property shall be subject to the requirements of form of the law of the country where the property is situated if by that law:

(a) those requirements are imposed irrespective of the country where the contract is concluded and irrespective of the law governing the contract; and

(b) those requirements cannot be derogated from by agreement.

Article 12

Scope of the law applicable

1. The law applicable to a contract by virtue of this Regulation shall govern in particular:

(a) interpretation;

(b) performance;

(c) within the limits of the powers conferred on the court by its procedural law, the consequences of a total or partial breach of obligations, including the assessment of damages in so far as it is governed by rules of law;

(d) the various ways of extinguishing obligations, and prescription and limitation of actions;

(e) the consequences of nullity of the contract.

2. In relation to the manner of performance and the steps to be taken in the event of defective performance, regard shall be had to the law of the country in which performance takes place.

Article 13

Incapacity

In a contract concluded between persons who are in the same country, a natural person who would have capacity under the law of that country may invoke his incapacity resulting from the law of another country, only if the other party to the contract was aware of that incapacity at the time of the conclusion of the contract or was not aware thereof as a result of negligence.

Article 14

Voluntary assignment and contractual subrogation

1. The relationship between assignor and assignee under a voluntary assignment or contractual subrogation of a claim against another person (the debtor) shall be governed by the law that applies to the contract between the assignor and assignee under this Regulation.

2. The law governing the assigned or subrogated claim shall determine its assignability, the relationship between the assignee and the debtor, the conditions under which the assignment or subrogation can be invoked against the debtor and whether the debtor's obligations have been discharged.

3. The concept of assignment in this Article includes outright transfers of claims, transfers of claims by way of security and pledges or other security rights over claims.

Article 15

Legal subrogation

Where a person (the creditor) has a contractual claim against another (the debtor) and a third person has a duty to satisfy the creditor, or has in fact satisfied the creditor in discharge of that duty, the law which governs the third person's duty to satisfy the creditor shall determine whether and to what extent the third person is entitled to exercise against the debtor the rights which the creditor had against the debtor under the law governing their relationship.

Article 16

Multiple liability

If a creditor has a claim against several debtors who are liable for the same claim, and one of the debtors has already satisfied the claim in whole or in part, the law governing the debtor's obligation towards the creditor also governs the debtor's right to claim recourse from the other debtors. The other debtors may rely on the defences they had against the creditor to the extent allowed by the law governing their obligations towards the creditor.

Article 17

Set-off

Where the right to set-off is not agreed by the parties, set-off shall be governed by the law applicable to the claim against which the right to set-off is asserted.

Article 18

Burden of proof

1. The law governing a contractual obligation under this Regulation shall apply to the extent that, in matters of contractual obligations, it contains rules which raise presumptions of law or determine the burden of proof.

2. A contract or an act intended to have legal effect may be proved by any mode of proof recognised by the law of the forum or by any of the laws referred to in Article 11 under which that contract or act is formally valid, provided that such mode of proof can be administered by the forum.

CHAPTER III

OTHER PROVISIONS

Article 19

Habitual residence

1. For the purposes of this Regulation, the habitual residence of companies and other bodies, corporate or unincorporated, shall be the place of central administration.

The habitual residence of a natural person acting in the course of his business activity shall be his principal place of business.

2. Where the contract is concluded in the course of the operations of a branch, agency or any other establishment, or if, under the contract, performance is the responsibility of such a branch, agency or establishment, the place where the branch, agency or any other establishment is located shall be treated as the place of habitual residence.

3. For the purposes of determining the habitual residence, the relevant point in time shall be the time of the conclusion of the contract.

Article 20

Exclusion of *renvoi*

The application of the law of any country specified by this Regulation means the application of the rules of law in force in that country other than its rules of private international law, unless provided otherwise in this Regulation.

Article 21

Public policy of the forum

The application of a provision of the law of any country specified by this Regulation may be refused only if such application is manifestly incompatible with the public policy (*ordre public*) of the forum.

Article 22

States with more than one legal system

1. Where a State comprises several territorial units, each of which has its own rules of law in respect of contractual obligations, each territorial unit shall be considered as a country for the purposes of identifying the law applicable under this Regulation.

2. A Member State where different territorial units have their own rules of law in respect of contractual obligations shall not be required to apply this Regulation to conflicts solely between the laws of such units.

Article 23

Relationship with other provisions of Community law

With the exception of Article 7, this Regulation shall not prejudice the application of provisions of Community law which, in relation to particular matters, lay down conflict-of-law rules relating to contractual obligations.

Article 24

Relationship with the Rome Convention

1. This Regulation shall replace the Rome Convention in the Member States, except as regards the territories of the Member States which fall within the territorial scope of that Convention and to which this Regulation does not apply pursuant to Article 299 of the Treaty.

2. In so far as this Regulation replaces the provisions of the Rome Convention, any reference to that Convention shall be understood as a reference to this Regulation.

Article 25

Relationship with existing international conventions

1. This Regulation shall not prejudice the application of international conventions to which one or more Member States are parties at the time when this Regulation is adopted and which lay down conflict-of-law rules relating to contractual obligations.

2.   However, this Regulation shall, as between Member States, take precedence over conventions concluded exclusively between two or more of them in so far as such conventions concern matters governed by this Regulation.

Article 26

List of Conventions

1.   By 17 June 2009, Member States shall notify the Commission of the conventions referred to in Article 25(1). After that date, Member States shall notify the Commission of all denunciations of such conventions.

2.   Within six months of receipt of the notifications referred to in paragraph 1, the Commission shall publish in the *Official Journal of the European Union*:

(a)   a list of the conventions referred to in paragraph 1;

(b)   the denunciations referred to in paragraph 1.

Article 27

Review clause

1.   By 17 June 2013, the Commission shall submit to the European Parliament, the Council and the European Economic and Social Committee a report on the application of this Regulation. If appropriate, the report shall be accompanied by proposals to amend this Regulation. The report shall include:

(a)   a study on the law applicable to insurance contracts and an assessment of the impact of the provisions to be introduced, if any; and

(b)   an evaluation on the application of Article 6, in particular as regards the coherence of Community law in the field of consumer protection.

2.   By 17 June 2010, the Commission shall submit to the European Parliament, the Council and the European Economic and Social Committee a report on the question of the effectiveness of an assignment or subrogation of a claim against third parties and the priority of the assigned or subrogated claim over a right of another person. The report shall be accompanied, if appropriate, by a proposal to amend this Regulation and an assessment of the impact of the provisions to be introduced.

Article 28

Application in time

This Regulation shall apply to contracts concluded after 17 December 2009.

CHAPTER IV

FINAL PROVISIONS

Article 29

Entry into force and application

This Regulation shall enter into force on the 20th day following its publication in the *Official Journal of the European Union*.

It shall apply from 17 December 2009 except for Article 26 which shall apply from 17 June 2009.

This Regulation shall be binding in its entirety and directly applicable in the Member States in accordance with the Treaty establishing the European Community.

Done at Strasbourg, 17 June 2008.

For the European Parliament	*For the Council*
The President	*The President*
H.-G. PÖTTERING	J. LENARČIČ

REGULATION (EC) No 864/2007 OF THE EUROPEAN PARLIAMENT AND OF THE COUNCIL

of 11 July 2007

on the law applicable to non-contractual obligations (Rome II)

THE EUROPEAN PARLIAMENT AND THE COUNCIL OF THE EURO-PEAN UNION,

Having regard to the Treaty establishing the European Community, and in particular Articles 61(c) and 67 thereof,

Having regard to the proposal from the Commission,

Having regard to the opinion of the European Economic and Social Committee (¹),

Acting in accordance with the procedure laid down in Article 251 of the Treaty in the light of the joint text approved by the Conciliation Committee on 25 June 2007 (²),

Whereas:

(1) The Community has set itself the objective of maintaining and developing an area of freedom, security and justice. For the progressive establishment of such an area, the Community is to adopt measures relating to judicial cooperation in civil matters with a cross-border impact to the extent necessary for the proper functioning of the internal market.

(2) According to Article 65(b) of the Treaty, these measures are to include those promoting the compatibility of the rules applicable in the Member States concerning the conflict of laws and of jurisdiction.

(3) The European Council meeting in Tampere on 15 and 16 October 1999 endorsed the principle of mutual recognition of judgments and other decisions of judicial authorities as the cornerstone of judicial cooperation in civil matters and invited the Council and the Commission to adopt a programme of measures to implement the principle of mutual recognition.

(4) On 30 November 2000, the Council adopted a joint Commission and Council programme of measures for implementation of the principle of mutual recognition of decisions in civil and commercial matters (³). The programme identifies measures relating to the harmonisation of conflict-of-law rules as those facilitating the mutual recognition of judgments.

(5) The Hague Programme (⁴), adopted by the European Council on 5 November 2004, called for work to be pursued actively on the rules of conflict of laws regarding non-contractual obligations (Rome II).

(6) The proper functioning of the internal market creates a need, in order to improve the predictability of the outcome of litigation, certainty as to the law applicable and the free movement of judgments, for the conflict-of-law rules in the Member States to designate the same national law irrespective of the country of the court in which an action is brought.

(7) The substantive scope and the provisions of this Regulation should be consistent with Council Regulation (EC) No 44/2001 of 22 December 2000 on jurisdiction and the recognition and enforcement of judgments in civil and commercial matters (⁵) (Brussels I) and the instruments dealing with the law applicable to contractual obligations.

(8) This Regulation should apply irrespective of the nature of the court or tribunal seised.

(9) Claims arising out of *acta iure imperii* should include claims against officials who act on behalf of the State and liability for acts of public authorities, including liability of publicly appointed office-holders. Therefore, these matters should be excluded from the scope of this Regulation.

(10) Family relationships should cover parentage, marriage, affinity and collateral relatives. The reference in Article 1(2) to relationships having comparable effects to marriage and other family relationships should be interpreted in accordance with the law of the Member State in which the court is seised.

(11) The concept of a non-contractual obligation varies from one Member State to another. Therefore for the purposes of this Regulation non-contractual obligation should be understood as an autonomous concept. The conflict-of-law rules set out in this Regulation should also cover non-contractual obligations arising out of strict liability.

(12) The law applicable should also govern the question of the capacity to incur liability in tort/delict.

(¹) OJ C 241, 28.9.2004, p. 1.
(²) Opinion of the European Parliament of 6 July 2005 (OJ C 157 E, 6.7.2006, p. 371), Council Common Position of 25 September 2006 (OJ C 289 E, 28.11.2006, p. 68) and Position of the European Parliament of 18 January 2007 (not yet published in the Official Journal). European Parliament Legislative Resolution of 10 July 2007 and Council Decision of 28 June 2007.
(³) OJ C 12, 15.1.2001, p. 1.

(⁴) OJ C 53, 3.3.2005, p. 1.
(⁵) OJ L 12, 16.1.2001, p. 1. Regulation as last amended by Regulation (EC) No 1791/2006 (OJ L 363, 20.12.2006, p. 1).

(13) Uniform rules applied irrespective of the law they designate may avert the risk of distortions of competition between Community litigants.

(14) The requirement of legal certainty and the need to do justice in individual cases are essential elements of an area of justice. This Regulation provides for the connecting factors which are the most appropriate to achieve these objectives. Therefore, this Regulation provides for a general rule but also for specific rules and, in certain provisions, for an 'escape clause' which allows a departure from these rules where it is clear from all the circumstances of the case that the tort/delict is manifestly more closely connected with another country. This set of rules thus creates a flexible framework of conflict-of-law rules. Equally, it enables the court seised to treat individual cases in an appropriate manner.

(15) The principle of the *lex loci delicti commissi* is the basic solution for non-contractual obligations in virtually all the Member States, but the practical application of the principle where the component factors of the case are spread over several countries varies. This situation engenders uncertainty as to the law applicable.

(16) Uniform rules should enhance the foreseeability of court decisions and ensure a reasonable balance between the interests of the person claimed to be liable and the person who has sustained damage. A connection with the country where the direct damage occurred (*lex loci damni*) strikes a fair balance between the interests of the person claimed to be liable and the person sustaining the damage, and also reflects the modern approach to civil liability and the development of systems of strict liability.

(17) The law applicable should be determined on the basis of where the damage occurs, regardless of the country or countries in which the indirect consequences could occur. Accordingly, in cases of personal injury or damage to property, the country in which the damage occurs should be the country where the injury was sustained or the property was damaged respectively.

(18) The general rule in this Regulation should be the *lex loci damni* provided for in Article 4(1). Article 4(2) should be seen as an exception to this general principle, creating a special connection where the parties have their habitual residence in the same country. Article 4(3) should be understood as an 'escape clause' from Article 4(1) and (2), where it is clear from all the circumstances of the case that the tort/delict is manifestly more closely connected with another country.

(19) Specific rules should be laid down for special torts/delicts where the general rule does not allow a reasonable balance to be struck between the interests at stake.

(20) The conflict-of-law rule in matters of product liability should meet the objectives of fairly spreading the risks inherent in a modern high-technology society, protecting consumers' health, stimulating innovation, securing undistorted competition and facilitating trade. Creation of a cascade system of connecting factors, together with a foreseeability clause, is a balanced solution in regard to these objectives. The first element to be taken into account is the law of the country in which the person sustaining the damage had his or her habitual residence when the damage occurred, if the product was marketed in that country. The other elements of the cascade are triggered if the product was not marketed in that country, without prejudice to Article 4(2) and to the possibility of a manifestly closer connection to another country.

(21) The special rule in Article 6 is not an exception to the general rule in Article 4(1) but rather a clarification of it. In matters of unfair competition, the conflict-of-law rule should protect competitors, consumers and the general public and ensure that the market economy functions properly. The connection to the law of the country where competitive relations or the collective interests of consumers are, or are likely to be, affected generally satisfies these objectives.

(22) The non-contractual obligations arising out of restrictions of competition in Article 6(3) should cover infringements of both national and Community competition law. The law applicable to such non-contractual obligations should be the law of the country where the market is, or is likely to be, affected. In cases where the market is, or is likely to be, affected in more than one country, the claimant should be able in certain circumstances to choose to base his or her claim on the law of the court seised.

(23) For the purposes of this Regulation, the concept of restriction of competition should cover prohibitions on agreements between undertakings, decisions by associations of undertakings and concerted practices which have as their object or effect the prevention, restriction or distortion of competition within a Member State or within the internal market, as well as prohibitions on the abuse of a dominant position within a Member State or within the internal market, where such agreements, decisions, concerted practices or abuses are prohibited by Articles 81 and 82 of the Treaty or by the law of a Member State.

(24) 'Environmental damage' should be understood as meaning adverse change in a natural resource, such as water, land or air, impairment of a function performed by that resource for the benefit of another natural resource or the public, or impairment of the variability among living organisms.

(25) Regarding environmental damage, Article 174 of the Treaty, which provides that there should be a high level of protection based on the precautionary principle and the principle that preventive action should be taken, the principle of priority for corrective action at source and the principle that the polluter pays, fully justifies the use of the principle of discriminating in favour of the person sustaining the damage. The question of when the person seeking compensation can make the choice of the law applicable should be determined in accordance with the law of the Member State in which the court is seised.

(26) Regarding infringements of intellectual property rights, the universally acknowledged principle of the *lex loci protectionis* should be preserved. For the purposes of this Regulation, the term 'intellectual property rights' should be interpreted as meaning, for instance, copyright, related rights, the *sui generis* right for the protection of databases and industrial property rights.

(27) The exact concept of industrial action, such as strike action or lock-out, varies from one Member State to another and is governed by each Member State's internal rules. Therefore, this Regulation assumes as a general principle that the law of the country where the industrial action was taken should apply, with the aim of protecting the rights and obligations of workers and employers.

(28) The special rule on industrial action in Article 9 is without prejudice to the conditions relating to the exercise of such action in accordance with national law and without prejudice to the legal status of trade unions or of the representative organisations of workers as provided for in the law of the Member States.

(29) Provision should be made for special rules where damage is caused by an act other than a tort/delict, such as unjust enrichment, *negotiorum gestio* and *culpa in contrahendo*.

(30) *Culpa in contrahendo* for the purposes of this Regulation is an autonomous concept and should not necessarily be interpreted within the meaning of national law. It should include the violation of the duty of disclosure and the breakdown of contractual negotiations. Article 12 covers only non-contractual obligations presenting a direct link with the dealings prior to the conclusion of a contract. This means that if, while a contract is being negotiated, a person suffers personal injury, Article 4 or other relevant provisions of this Regulation should apply.

(31) To respect the principle of party autonomy and to enhance legal certainty, the parties should be allowed to make a choice as to the law applicable to a non-contractual obligation. This choice should be expressed or demonstrated with reasonable certainty by the circumstances of the case.

Where establishing the existence of the agreement, the court has to respect the intentions of the parties. Protection should be given to weaker parties by imposing certain conditions on the choice.

(32) Considerations of public interest justify giving the courts of the Member States the possibility, in exceptional circumstances, of applying exceptions based on public policy and overriding mandatory provisions. In particular, the application of a provision of the law designated by this Regulation which would have the effect of causing non-compensatory exemplary or punitive damages of an excessive nature to be awarded may, depending on the circumstances of the case and the legal order of the Member State of the court seised, be regarded as being contrary to the public policy (*ordre public*) of the forum.

(33) According to the current national rules on compensation awarded to victims of road traffic accidents, when quantifying damages for personal injury in cases in which the accident takes place in a State other than that of the habitual residence of the victim, the court seised should take into account all the relevant actual circumstances of the specific victim, including in particular the actual losses and costs of after-care and medical attention.

(34) In order to strike a reasonable balance between the parties, account must be taken, in so far as appropriate, of the rules of safety and conduct in operation in the country in which the harmful act was committed, even where the non-contractual obligation is governed by the law of another country. The term 'rules of safety and conduct' should be interpreted as referring to all regulations having any relation to safety and conduct, including, for example, road safety rules in the case of an accident.

(35) A situation where conflict-of-law rules are dispersed among several instruments and where there are differences between those rules should be avoided. This Regulation, however, does not exclude the possibility of inclusion of conflict-of-law rules relating to non-contractual obligations in provisions of Community law with regard to particular matters.

This Regulation should not prejudice the application of other instruments laying down provisions designed to contribute to the proper functioning of the internal market in so far as they cannot be applied in conjunction with the law designated by the rules of this Regulation. The application of provisions of the applicable law designated by the rules of this Regulation should not restrict the free movement of goods and services as regulated by Community instruments, such as Directive 2000/31/EC of the European Parliament and of the Council of 8 June 2000 on certain legal aspects of information society services, in particular electronic commerce, in the Internal Market (Directive on electronic commerce) (¹).

(¹) OJ L 178, 17.7.2000, p. 1.

(36) Respect for international commitments entered into by the Member States means that this Regulation should not affect international conventions to which one or more Member States are parties at the time this Regulation is adopted. To make the rules more accessible, the Commission should publish the list of the relevant conventions in the *Official Journal of the European Union* on the basis of information supplied by the Member States.

(37) The Commission will make a proposal to the European Parliament and the Council concerning the procedures and conditions according to which Member States would be entitled to negotiate and conclude on their own behalf agreements with third countries in individual and exceptional cases, concerning sectoral matters, containing provisions on the law applicable to non-contractual obligations.

(38) Since the objective of this Regulation cannot be sufficiently achieved by the Member States, and can therefore, by reason of the scale and effects of this Regulation, be better achieved at Community level, the Community may adopt measures, in accordance with the principle of subsidiarity set out in Article 5 of the Treaty. In accordance with the principle of proportionality set out in that Article, this Regulation does not go beyond what is necessary to attain that objective.

(39) In accordance with Article 3 of the Protocol on the position of the United Kingdom and Ireland annexed to the Treaty on European Union and to the Treaty establishing the European Community, the United Kingdom and Ireland are taking part in the adoption and application of this Regulation.

(40) In accordance with Articles 1 and 2 of the Protocol on the position of Denmark, annexed to the Treaty on European Union and to the Treaty establishing the European Community, Denmark does not take part in the adoption of this Regulation, and is not bound by it or subject to its application,

HAVE ADOPTED THIS REGULATION:

CHAPTER I

SCOPE

Article 1

Scope

1.   This Regulation shall apply, in situations involving a conflict of laws, to non-contractual obligations in civil and commercial matters. It shall not apply, in particular, to revenue, customs or administrative matters or to the liability of the State for acts and omissions in the exercise of State authority (*acta iure imperii*).

2.   The following shall be excluded from the scope of this Regulation:

(a) non-contractual obligations arising out of family relationships and relationships deemed by the law applicable to such relationships to have comparable effects including maintenance obligations;

(b) non-contractual obligations arising out of matrimonial property regimes, property regimes of relationships deemed by the law applicable to such relationships to have comparable effects to marriage, and wills and succession;

(c) non-contractual obligations arising under bills of exchange, cheques and promissory notes and other negotiable instruments to the extent that the obligations under such other negotiable instruments arise out of their negotiable character;

(d) non-contractual obligations arising out of the law of companies and other bodies corporate or unincorporated regarding matters such as the creation, by registration or otherwise, legal capacity, internal organisation or winding-up of companies and other bodies corporate or unincorporated, the personal liability of officers and members as such for the obligations of the company or body and the personal liability of auditors to a company or to its members in the statutory audits of accounting documents;

(e) non-contractual obligations arising out of the relations between the settlors, trustees and beneficiaries of a trust created voluntarily;

(f) non-contractual obligations arising out of nuclear damage;

(g) non-contractual obligations arising out of violations of privacy and rights relating to personality, including defamation.

3.   This Regulation shall not apply to evidence and procedure, without prejudice to Articles 21 and 22.

4.   For the purposes of this Regulation, 'Member State' shall mean any Member State other than Denmark.

Article 2

Non-contractual obligations

1.   For the purposes of this Regulation, damage shall cover any consequence arising out of tort/delict, unjust enrichment, *negotiorum gestio* or *culpa in contrahendo*.

2.   This Regulation shall apply also to non-contractual obligations that are likely to arise.

3. Any reference in this Regulation to:

(a) an event giving rise to damage shall include events giving rise to damage that are likely to occur; and

(b) damage shall include damage that is likely to occur.

Article 3

Universal application

Any law specified by this Regulation shall be applied whether or not it is the law of a Member State.

CHAPTER II

TORTS/DELICTS

Article 4

General rule

1. Unless otherwise provided for in this Regulation, the law applicable to a non-contractual obligation arising out of a tort/delict shall be the law of the country in which the damage occurs irrespective of the country in which the event giving rise to the damage occurred and irrespective of the country or countries in which the indirect consequences of that event occur.

2. However, where the person claimed to be liable and the person sustaining damage both have their habitual residence in the same country at the time when the damage occurs, the law of that country shall apply.

3. Where it is clear from all the circumstances of the case that the tort/delict is manifestly more closely connected with a country other than that indicated in paragraphs 1 or 2, the law of that other country shall apply. A manifestly closer connection with another country might be based in particular on a pre-existing relationship between the parties, such as a contract, that is closely connected with the tort/delict in question.

Article 5

Product liability

1. Without prejudice to Article 4(2), the law applicable to a non-contractual obligation arising out of damage caused by a product shall be:

(a) the law of the country in which the person sustaining the damage had his or her habitual residence when the damage occurred, if the product was marketed in that country; or, failing that,

(b) the law of the country in which the product was acquired, if the product was marketed in that country; or, failing that,

(c) the law of the country in which the damage occurred, if the product was marketed in that country.

However, the law applicable shall be the law of the country in which the person claimed to be liable is habitually resident if he or she could not reasonably foresee the marketing of the product, or a product of the same type, in the country the law of which is applicable under (a), (b) or (c).

2. Where it is clear from all the circumstances of the case that the tort/delict is manifestly more closely connected with a country other than that indicated in paragraph 1, the law of that other country shall apply. A manifestly closer connection with another country might be based in particular on a pre-existing relationship between the parties, such as a contract, that is closely connected with the tort/delict in question.

Article 6

Unfair competition and acts restricting free competition

1. The law applicable to a non-contractual obligation arising out of an act of unfair competition shall be the law of the country where competitive relations or the collective interests of consumers are, or are likely to be, affected.

2. Where an act of unfair competition affects exclusively the interests of a specific competitor, Article 4 shall apply.

3. (a) The law applicable to a non-contractual obligation arising out of a restriction of competition shall be the law of the country where the market is, or is likely to be, affected.

(b) When the market is, or is likely to be, affected in more than one country, the person seeking compensation for damage who sues in the court of the domicile of the defendant, may instead choose to base his or her claim on the law of the court seised, provided that the market in that Member State is amongst those directly and substantially affected by the restriction of competition out of which the non-contractual obligation on which the claim is based arises; where the claimant sues, in accordance with the applicable rules on jurisdiction, more than one defendant in that court, he or she can only choose to base his or her claim on the law of that court if the restriction of competition on which the claim against each of these defendants relies directly and substantially affects also the market in the Member State of that court.

4. The law applicable under this Article may not be derogated from by an agreement pursuant to Article 14.

Article 7

Environmental damage

The law applicable to a non-contractual obligation arising out of environmental damage or damage sustained by persons or property as a result of such damage shall be the law determined pursuant to Article 4(1), unless the person seeking compensation for damage chooses to base his or her claim on the law of the country in which the event giving rise to the damage occurred.

Article 8

Infringement of intellectual property rights

1. The law applicable to a non-contractual obligation arising from an infringement of an intellectual property right shall be the law of the country for which protection is claimed.

2. In the case of a non-contractual obligation arising from an infringement of a unitary Community intellectual property right, the law applicable shall, for any question that is not governed by the relevant Community instrument, be the law of the country in which the act of infringement was committed.

3. The law applicable under this Article may not be derogated from by an agreement pursuant to Article 14.

Article 9

Industrial action

Without prejudice to Article 4(2), the law applicable to a non-contractual obligation in respect of the liability of a person in the capacity of a worker or an employer or the organisations representing their professional interests for damages caused by an industrial action, pending or carried out, shall be the law of the country where the action is to be, or has been, taken.

CHAPTER III

UNJUST ENRICHMENT, *NEGOTIORUM GESTIO* AND *CULPA IN CONTRAHENDO*

Article 10

Unjust enrichment

1. If a non-contractual obligation arising out of unjust enrichment, including payment of amounts wrongly received, concerns a relationship existing between the parties, such as one arising out of a contract or a tort/delict, that is closely connected with that unjust enrichment, it shall be governed by the law that governs that relationship.

2. Where the law applicable cannot be determined on the basis of paragraph 1 and the parties have their habitual residence in the same country when the event giving rise to unjust enrichment occurs, the law of that country shall apply.

3. Where the law applicable cannot be determined on the basis of paragraphs 1 or 2, it shall be the law of the country in which the unjust enrichment took place.

4. Where it is clear from all the circumstances of the case that the non-contractual obligation arising out of unjust enrichment is manifestly more closely connected with a country other than that indicated in paragraphs 1, 2 and 3, the law of that other country shall apply.

Article 11

Negotiorum gestio

1. If a non-contractual obligation arising out of an act performed without due authority in connection with the affairs of another person concerns a relationship existing between the parties, such as one arising out of a contract or a tort/delict, that is closely connected with that non-contractual obligation, it shall be governed by the law that governs that relationship.

2. Where the law applicable cannot be determined on the basis of paragraph 1, and the parties have their habitual residence in the same country when the event giving rise to the damage occurs, the law of that country shall apply.

3. Where the law applicable cannot be determined on the basis of paragraphs 1 or 2, it shall be the law of the country in which the act was performed.

4. Where it is clear from all the circumstances of the case that the non-contractual obligation arising out of an act performed without due authority in connection with the affairs of another person is manifestly more closely connected with a country other than that indicated in paragraphs 1, 2 and 3, the law of that other country shall apply.

Article 12

Culpa in contrahendo

1. The law applicable to a non-contractual obligation arising out of dealings prior to the conclusion of a contract, regardless of whether the contract was actually concluded or not, shall be the law that applies to the contract or that would have been applicable to it had it been entered into.

2. Where the law applicable cannot be determined on the basis of paragraph 1, it shall be:

(a) the law of the country in which the damage occurs, irrespective of the country in which the event giving rise to the damage occurred and irrespective of the country or countries in which the indirect consequences of that event occurred; or

(b) where the parties have their habitual residence in the same country at the time when the event giving rise to the damage occurs, the law of that country; or

(c) where it is clear from all the circumstances of the case that the non-contractual obligation arising out of dealings prior to the conclusion of a contract is manifestly more closely connected with a country other than that indicated in points (a) and (b), the law of that other country.

Article 13

Applicability of Article 8

For the purposes of this Chapter, Article 8 shall apply to non-contractual obligations arising from an infringement of an intellectual property right.

CHAPTER IV

FREEDOM OF CHOICE

Article 14

Freedom of choice

1.   The parties may agree to submit non-contractual obligations to the law of their choice:

(a) by an agreement entered into after the event giving rise to the damage occurred;

or

(b) where all the parties are pursuing a commercial activity, also by an agreement freely negotiated before the event giving rise to the damage occurred.

The choice shall be expressed or demonstrated with reasonable certainty by the circumstances of the case and shall not prejudice the rights of third parties.

2.   Where all the elements relevant to the situation at the time when the event giving rise to the damage occurs are located in a country other than the country whose law has been chosen, the choice of the parties shall not prejudice the application of provisions of the law of that other country which cannot be derogated from by agreement.

3.   Where all the elements relevant to the situation at the time when the event giving rise to the damage occurs are located in one or more of the Member States, the parties' choice of the law applicable other than that of a Member State shall not prejudice the application of provisions of Community law, where appropriate as implemented in the Member State of the forum, which cannot be derogated from by agreement.

CHAPTER V

COMMON RULES

Article 15

Scope of the law applicable

The law applicable to non-contractual obligations under this Regulation shall govern in particular:

(a) the basis and extent of liability, including the determination of persons who may be held liable for acts performed by them;

(b) the grounds for exemption from liability, any limitation of liability and any division of liability;

(c) the existence, the nature and the assessment of damage or the remedy claimed;

(d) within the limits of powers conferred on the court by its procedural law, the measures which a court may take to prevent or terminate injury or damage or to ensure the provision of compensation;

(e) the question whether a right to claim damages or a remedy may be transferred, including by inheritance;

(f) persons entitled to compensation for damage sustained personally;

(g) liability for the acts of another person;

(h) the manner in which an obligation may be extinguished and rules of prescription and limitation, including rules relating to the commencement, interruption and suspension of a period of prescription or limitation.

Article 16

Overriding mandatory provisions

Nothing in this Regulation shall restrict the application of the provisions of the law of the forum in a situation where they are mandatory irrespective of the law otherwise applicable to the non-contractual obligation.

Article 17

Rules of safety and conduct

In assessing the conduct of the person claimed to be liable, account shall be taken, as a matter of fact and in so far as is appropriate, of the rules of safety and conduct which were in force at the place and time of the event giving rise to the liability.

Article 18

Direct action against the insurer of the person liable

The person having suffered damage may bring his or her claim directly against the insurer of the person liable to provide compensation if the law applicable to the non-contractual obligation or the law applicable to the insurance contract so provides.

Article 19

Subrogation

Where a person (the creditor) has a non-contractual claim upon another (the debtor), and a third person has a duty to satisfy the creditor, or has in fact satisfied the creditor in discharge of that duty, the law which governs the third person's duty to satisfy the creditor shall determine whether, and the extent to which, the third person is entitled to exercise against the debtor the rights which the creditor had against the debtor under the law governing their relationship.

Article 20

Multiple liability

If a creditor has a claim against several debtors who are liable for the same claim, and one of the debtors has already satisfied the claim in whole or in part, the question of that debtor's right to demand compensation from the other debtors shall be governed by the law applicable to that debtor's non-contractual obligation towards the creditor.

Article 21

Formal validity

A unilateral act intended to have legal effect and relating to a non-contractual obligation shall be formally valid if it satisfies the formal requirements of the law governing the non-contractual obligation in question or the law of the country in which the act is performed.

Article 22

Burden of proof

1.   The law governing a non-contractual obligation under this Regulation shall apply to the extent that, in matters of non-contractual obligations, it contains rules which raise presumptions of law or determine the burden of proof.

2.   Acts intended to have legal effect may be proved by any mode of proof recognised by the law of the forum or by any of the laws referred to in Article 21 under which that act is formally valid, provided that such mode of proof can be administered by the forum.

CHAPTER VI

OTHER PROVISIONS

Article 23

Habitual residence

1.   For the purposes of this Regulation, the habitual residence of companies and other bodies, corporate or unincorporated, shall be the place of central administration.

Where the event giving rise to the damage occurs, or the damage arises, in the course of operation of a branch, agency or any other establishment, the place where the branch, agency or any other establishment is located shall be treated as the place of habitual residence.

2.   For the purposes of this Regulation, the habitual residence of a natural person acting in the course of his or her business activity shall be his or her principal place of business.

Article 24

Exclusion of renvoi

The application of the law of any country specified by this Regulation means the application of the rules of law in force in that country other than its rules of private international law.

Article 25

States with more than one legal system

1.   Where a State comprises several territorial units, each of which has its own rules of law in respect of non-contractual obligations, each territorial unit shall be considered as a country for the purposes of identifying the law applicable under this Regulation.

2.   A Member State within which different territorial units have their own rules of law in respect of non-contractual obligations shall not be required to apply this Regulation to conflicts solely between the laws of such units.

Article 26

Public policy of the forum

The application of a provision of the law of any country specified by this Regulation may be refused only if such application is manifestly incompatible with the public policy (*ordre public*) of the forum.

Article 27

Relationship with other provisions of Community law

This Regulation shall not prejudice the application of provisions of Community law which, in relation to particular matters, lay down conflict-of-law rules relating to non-contractual obligations.

Article 28

Relationship with existing international conventions

1.   This Regulation shall not prejudice the application of international conventions to which one or more Member States are parties at the time when this Regulation is adopted and which lay down conflict-of-law rules relating to non-contractual obligations.

2.   However, this Regulation shall, as between Member States, take precedence over conventions concluded exclusively between two or more of them in so far as such conventions concern matters governed by this Regulation.

CHAPTER VII

FINAL PROVISIONS

Article 29

List of conventions

1. By 11 July 2008, Member States shall notify the Commission of the conventions referred to in Article 28(1). After that date, Member States shall notify the Commission of all denunciations of such conventions.

2. The Commission shall publish in the *Official Journal of the European Union* within six months of receipt:

(i) a list of the conventions referred to in paragraph 1;

(ii) the denunciations referred to in paragraph 1.

Article 30

Review clause

1. Not later than 20 August 2011, the Commission shall submit to the European Parliament, the Council and the European Economic and Social Committee a report on the application of this Regulation. If necessary, the report shall be accompanied by proposals to adapt this Regulation. The report shall include:

(i) a study on the effects of the way in which foreign law is treated in the different jurisdictions and on the extent to which courts in the Member States apply foreign law in practice pursuant to this Regulation;

(ii) a study on the effects of Article 28 of this Regulation with respect to the Hague Convention of 4 May 1971 on the law applicable to traffic accidents.

2. Not later than 31 December 2008, the Commission shall submit to the European Parliament, the Council and the European Economic and Social Committee a study on the situation in the field of the law applicable to non-contractual obligations arising out of violations of privacy and rights relating to personality, taking into account rules relating to freedom of the press and freedom of expression in the media, and conflict-of-law issues related to Directive 95/46/EC of the European Parliament and of the Council of 24 October 1995 on the protection of individuals with regard to the processing of personal data and on the free movement of such data ([1]).

Article 31

Application in time

This Regulation shall apply to events giving rise to damage which occur after its entry into force.

Article 32

Date of application

This Regulation shall apply from 11 January 2009, except for Article 29, which shall apply from 11 July 2008.

This Regulation shall be binding in its entirety and directly applicable in the Member States in accordance with the Treaty establishing the European Community.

Done at Strasbourg, 11 July 2007.

For the European Parliament	*For the Council*
The President	*The President*
H.-G. PÖTTERING	M. LOBO ANTUNES

([1]) OJ L 281, 23.11.1995, p. 31.

Commission Statement on the review clause (Article 30)

The Commission, following the invitation by the European Parliament and the Council in the frame of Article 30 of the 'Rome II' Regulation, will submit, not later than December 2008, a study on the situation in the field of the law applicable to non-contractual obligations arising out of violations of privacy and rights relating to personality. The Commission will take into consideration all aspects of the situation and take appropriate measures if necessary.

Commission Statement on road accidents

The Commission, being aware of the different practices followed in the Member States as regards the level of compensation awarded to victims of road traffic accidents, is prepared to examine the specific problems resulting for EU residents involved in road traffic accidents in a Member State other than the Member State of their habitual residence. To that end the Commission will make available to the European Parliament and to the Council, before the end of 2008, a study on all options, including insurance aspects, for improving the position of cross-border victims, which would pave the way for a Green Paper.

Commission Statement on the treatment of foreign law

The Commission, being aware of the different practices followed in the Member States as regards the treatment of foreign law, will publish at the latest four years after the entry into force of the 'Rome II' Regulation and in any event as soon as it is available a horizontal study on the application of foreign law in civil and commercial matters by the courts of the Member States, having regard to the aims of the Hague Programme. It is also prepared to take appropriate measures if necessary.

I

(Acts whose publication is obligatory)

COUNCIL REGULATION (EC) No 1346/2000

of 29 May 2000

on insolvency proceedings

THE COUNCIL OF THE EUROPEAN UNION,

Having regard to the Treaty establishing the European Community, and in particular Articles 61(c) and 67(1) thereof,

Having regard to the initiative of the Federal Republic of Germany and the Republic of Finland,

Having regard to the opinion of the European Parliament [1],

Having regard to the opinion of the Economic and Social Committee [2],

Whereas:

(1) The European Union has set out the aim of establishing an area of freedom, security and justice.

(2) The proper functioning of the internal market requires that cross-border insolvency proceedings should operate efficiently and effectively and this Regulation needs to be adopted in order to achieve this objective which comes within the scope of judicial cooperation in civil matters within the meaning of Article 65 of the Treaty.

(3) The activities of undertakings have more and more cross-border effects and are therefore increasingly being regulated by Community law. While the insolvency of such undertakings also affects the proper functioning of the internal market, there is a need for a Community act requiring coordination of the measures to be taken regarding an insolvent debtor's assets.

(4) It is necessary for the proper functioning of the internal market to avoid incentives for the parties to transfer assets or judicial proceedings from one Member State to another, seeking to obtain a more favourable legal position (forum shopping).

(5) These objectives cannot be achieved to a sufficient degree at national level and action at Community level is therefore justified.

(6) In accordance with the principle of proportionality this Regulation should be confined to provisions governing jurisdiction for opening insolvency proceedings and judgments which are delivered directly on the basis of the insolvency proceedings and are closely connected with such proceedings. In addition, this Regulation should contain provisions regarding the recognition of those judgments and the applicable law which also satisfy that principle.

(7) Insolvency proceedings relating to the winding-up of insolvent companies or other legal persons, judicial arrangements, compositions and analogous proceedings are excluded from the scope of the 1968 Brussels Convention on Jurisdiction and the Enforcement of Judgments in Civil and Commercial Matters [3], as amended by the Conventions on Accession to this Convention [4].

(8) In order to achieve the aim of improving the efficiency and effectiveness of insolvency proceedings having cross-border effects, it is necessary, and appropriate, that the provisions on jurisdiction, recognition and applicable law in this area should be contained in a Community law measure which is binding and directly applicable in Member States.

---

[1] Opinion delivered on 2 March 2000 (not yet published in the Official Journal).
[2] Opinion delivered on 26 January 2000 (not yet published in the Official Journal).

[3] OJ L 299, 31.12.1972, p. 32.
[4] OJ L 204, 2.8.1975, p. 28; OJ L 304, 30.10.1978, p. 1; OJ L 388, 31.12.1982, p. 1; OJ L 285, 3.10.1989, p. 1; OJ C 15, 15.1.1997, p. 1.

(9) This Regulation should apply to insolvency proceedings, whether the debtor is a natural person or a legal person, a trader or an individual. The insolvency proceedings to which this Regulation applies are listed in the Annexes. Insolvency proceedings concerning insurance undertakings, credit institutions, investment undertakings holding funds or securities for third parties and collective investment undertakings should be excluded from the scope of this Regulation. Such undertakings should not be covered by this Regulation since they are subject to special arrangements and, to some extent, the national supervisory authorities have extremely wide-ranging powers of intervention.

(10) Insolvency proceedings do not necessarily involve the intervention of a judicial authority; the expression 'court' in this Regulation should be given a broad meaning and include a person or body empowered by national law to open insolvency proceedings. In order for this Regulation to apply, proceedings (comprising acts and formalities set down in law) should not only have to comply with the provisions of this Regulation, but they should also be officially recognised and legally effective in the Member State in which the insolvency proceedings are opened and should be collective insolvency proceedings which entail the partial or total divestment of the debtor and the appointment of a liquidator.

(11) This Regulation acknowledges the fact that as a result of widely differing substantive laws it is not practical to introduce insolvency proceedings with universal scope in the entire Community. The application without exception of the law of the State of opening of proceedings would, against this background, frequently lead to difficulties. This applies, for example, to the widely differing laws on security interests to be found in the Community. Furthermore, the preferential rights enjoyed by some creditors in the insolvency proceedings are, in some cases, completely different. This Regulation should take account of this in two different ways. On the one hand, provision should be made for special rules on applicable law in the case of particularly significant rights and legal relationships (e.g. rights in rem and contracts of employment). On the other hand, national proceedings covering only assets situated in the State of opening should also be allowed alongside main insolvency proceedings with universal scope.

(12) This Regulation enables the main insolvency proceedings to be opened in the Member State where the debtor has the centre of his main interests. These proceedings have universal scope and aim at encompassing all the debtor's assets. To protect the diversity of interests, this Regulation permits secondary proceedings to be opened to run in parallel with the main proceedings. Secondary proceedings may be opened in the Member State where the

debtor has an establishment. The effects of secondary proceedings are limited to the assets located in that State. Mandatory rules of coordination with the main proceedings satisfy the need for unity in the Community.

(13) The 'centre of main interests' should correspond to the place where the debtor conducts the administration of his interests on a regular basis and is therefore ascertainable by third parties.

(14) This Regulation applies only to proceedings where the centre of the debtor's main interests is located in the Community.

(15) The rules of jurisdiction set out in this Regulation establish only international jurisdiction, that is to say, they designate the Member State the courts of which may open insolvency proceedings. Territorial jurisdiction within that Member State must be established by the national law of the Member State concerned.

(16) The court having jurisdiction to open the main insolvency proceedings should be enabled to order provisional and protective measures from the time of the request to open proceedings. Preservation measures both prior to and after the commencement of the insolvency proceedings are very important to guarantee the effectiveness of the insolvency proceedings. In that connection this Regulation should afford different possibilities. On the one hand, the court competent for the main insolvency proceedings should be able also to order provisional protective measures covering assets situated in the territory of other Member States. On the other hand, a liquidator temporarily appointed prior to the opening of the main insolvency proceedings should be able, in the Member States in which an establishment belonging to the debtor is to be found, to apply for the preservation measures which are possible under the law of those States.

(17) Prior to the opening of the main insolvency proceedings, the right to request the opening of insolvency proceedings in the Member State where the debtor has an establishment should be limited to local creditors and creditors of the local establishment or to cases where main proceedings cannot be opened under the law of the Member State where the debtor has the centre of his main interest. The reason for this restriction is that cases where territorial insolvency proceedings are requested before the main insolvency proceedings are intended to be limited to what is absolutely necessary. If the main insolvency proceedings are opened, the territorial proceedings become secondary.

(18) Following the opening of the main insolvency proceedings, the right to request the opening of insolvency proceedings in a Member State where the debtor has an establishment is not restricted by this Regulation. The liquidator in the main proceedings or any other person empowered under the national law of that Member State may request the opening of secondary insolvency proceedings.

(19) Secondary insolvency proceedings may serve different purposes, besides the protection of local interests. Cases may arise where the estate of the debtor is too complex to administer as a unit or where differences in the legal systems concerned are so great that difficulties may arise from the extension of effects deriving from the law of the State of the opening to the other States where the assets are located. For this reason the liquidator in the main proceedings may request the opening of secondary proceedings when the efficient administration of the estate so requires.

(20) Main insolvency proceedings and secondary proceedings can, however, contribute to the effective realisation of the total assets only if all the concurrent proceedings pending are coordinated. The main condition here is that the various liquidators must cooperate closely, in particular by exchanging a sufficient amount of information. In order to ensure the dominant role of the main insolvency proceedings, the liquidator in such proceedings should be given several possibilities for intervening in secondary insolvency proceedings which are pending at the same time. For example, he should be able to propose a restructuring plan or composition or apply for realisation of the assets in the secondary insolvency proceedings to be suspended.

(21) Every creditor, who has his habitual residence, domicile or registered office in the Community, should have the right to lodge his claims in each of the insolvency proceedings pending in the Community relating to the debtor's assets. This should also apply to tax authorities and social insurance institutions. However, in order to ensure equal treatment of creditors, the distribution of proceeds must be coordinated. Every creditor should be able to keep what he has received in the course of insolvency proceedings but should be entitled only to participate in the distribution of total assets in other proceedings if creditors with the same standing have obtained the same proportion of their claims.

(22) This Regulation should provide for immediate recognition of judgments concerning the opening, conduct and closure of insolvency proceedings which come within its scope and of judgments handed down in direct connection with such insolvency proceedings. Automatic recognition should therefore mean that the effects attributed to the proceedings by the law of the State in which the proceedings were opened extend to all other Member States. Recognition of judgments delivered by the courts of the Member States should be based on the principle of mutual trust. To that end, grounds for non-recognition should be reduced to the minimum necessary. This is also the basis on which any dispute should be resolved where the courts of two Member States both claim competence to open the main insolvency proceedings. The decision of the first court to open proceedings should be recognised in the other Member States without those Member States having the power to scrutinise the court's decision.

(23) This Regulation should set out, for the matters covered by it, uniform rules on conflict of laws which replace, within their scope of application, national rules of private international law. Unless otherwise stated, the law of the Member State of the opening of the proceedings should be applicable (*lex concursus*). This rule on conflict of laws should be valid both for the main proceedings and for local proceedings; the *lex concursus* determines all the effects of the insolvency proceedings, both procedural and substantive, on the persons and legal relations concerned. It governs all the conditions for the opening, conduct and closure of the insolvency proceedings.

(24) Automatic recognition of insolvency proceedings to which the law of the opening State normally applies may interfere with the rules under which transactions are carried out in other Member States. To protect legitimate expectations and the certainty of transactions in Member States other than that in which proceedings are opened, provisions should be made for a number of exceptions to the general rule.

(25) There is a particular need for a special reference diverging from the law of the opening State in the case of rights in rem, since these are of considerable importance for the granting of credit. The basis, validity and extent of such a right in rem should therefore normally be determined according to the *lex situs* and not be affected by the opening of insolvency proceedings. The proprietor of the right in rem should therefore be able to continue to assert his right to segregation or separate settlement of the collateral security. Where assets are subject to rights in rem under the *lex situs* in one Member State but the main proceedings are being carried out in another Member State, the liquidator in the main proceedings should be able to request the opening of secondary proceedings in the jurisdiction where the rights in rem arise if the debtor has an establishment there. If a secondary proceeding is not opened, the surplus on sale of the asset covered by rights in rem must be paid to the liquidator in the main proceedings.

(26) If a set-off is not permitted under the law of the opening State, a creditor should nevertheless be entitled to the set-off if it is possible under the law applicable to the claim of the insolvent debtor. In this way, set-off will acquire a kind of guarantee function based on legal provisions on which the creditor concerned can rely at the time when the claim arises.

(27) There is also a need for special protection in the case of payment systems and financial markets. This applies for example to the position-closing agreements and netting agreements to be found in such systems as well as to the sale of securities and to the guarantees provided for such transactions as governed in particular by Directive 98/26/EC of the European Parliament and of the Council of 19 May 1998 on settlement finality in payment and securities settlement systems(¹). For such transactions, the only law which is material should thus be that applicable to the system or market concerned. This provision is intended to prevent the possibility of mechanisms for the payment and settlement of transactions provided for in the payment and set-off systems or on the regulated financial markets of the Member States being altered in the case of insolvency of a business partner. Directive 98/26/EC contains special provisions which should take precedence over the general rules in this Regulation.

(28) In order to protect employees and jobs, the effects of insolvency proceedings on the continuation or termination of employment and on the rights and obligations of all parties to such employment must be determined by the law applicable to the agreement in accordance with the general rules on conflict of law. Any other insolvency-law questions, such as whether the employees' claims are protected by preferential rights and what status such preferential rights may have, should be determined by the law of the opening State.

(29) For business considerations, the main content of the decision opening the proceedings should be published in the other Member States at the request of the liquidator. If there is an establishment in the Member State concerned, there may be a requirement that publication is compulsory. In neither case, however, should publication be a prior condition for recognition of the foreign proceedings.

(30) It may be the case that some of the persons concerned are not in fact aware that proceedings have been opened

and act in good faith in a way that conflicts with the new situation. In order to protect such persons who make a payment to the debtor because they are unaware that foreign proceedings have been opened when they should in fact have made the payment to the foreign liquidator, it should be provided that such a payment is to have a debt-discharging effect.

(31) This Regulation should include Annexes relating to the organisation of insolvency proceedings. As these Annexes relate exclusively to the legislation of Member States, there are specific and substantiated reasons for the Council to reserve the right to amend these Annexes in order to take account of any amendments to the domestic law of the Member States.

(32) The United Kingdom and Ireland, in accordance with Article 3 of the Protocol on the position of the United Kingdom and Ireland annexed to the Treaty on European Union and the Treaty establishing the European Community, have given notice of their wish to take part in the adoption and application of this Regulation.

(33) Denmark, in accordance with Articles 1 and 2 of the Protocol on the position of Denmark annexed to the Treaty on European Union and the Treaty establishing the European Community, is not participating in the adoption of this Regulation, and is therefore not bound by it nor subject to its application,

HAS ADOPTED THIS REGULATION:

CHAPTER I

GENERAL PROVISIONS

Article 1

Scope

1.   This Regulation shall apply to collective insolvency proceedings which entail the partial or total divestment of a debtor and the appointment of a liquidator.

2.   This Regulation shall not apply to insolvency proceedings concerning insurance undertakings, credit institutions, investment undertakings which provide services involving the holding of funds or securities for third parties, or to collective investment undertakings.

_____

(¹) OJ L 166, 11.6.1998, p. 45.

Article 2

Definitions

For the purposes of this Regulation:

(a) 'insolvency proceedings' shall mean the collective proceedings referred to in Article 1(1). These proceedings are listed in Annex A;

(b) 'liquidator' shall mean any person or body whose function is to administer or liquidate assets of which the debtor has been divested or to supervise the administration of his affairs. Those persons and bodies are listed in Annex C;

(c) 'winding-up proceedings' shall mean insolvency proceedings within the meaning of point (a) involving realising the assets of the debtor, including where the proceedings have been closed by a composition or other measure terminating the insolvency, or closed by reason of the insufficiency of the assets. Those proceedings are listed in Annex B;

(d) 'court' shall mean the judicial body or any other competent body of a Member State empowered to open insolvency proceedings or to take decisions in the course of such proceedings;

(e) 'judgment' in relation to the opening of insolvency proceedings or the appointment of a liquidator shall include the decision of any court empowered to open such proceedings or to appoint a liquidator;

(f) 'the time of the opening of proceedings' shall mean the time at which the judgment opening proceedings becomes effective, whether it is a final judgment or not;

(g) 'the Member State in which assets are situated' shall mean, in the case of:

— tangible property, the Member State within the territory of which the property is situated,

— property and rights ownership of or entitlement to which must be entered in a public register, the Member State under the authority of which the register is kept,

— claims, the Member State within the territory of which the third party required to meet them has the centre of his main interests, as determined in Article 3(1);

(h) 'establishment' shall mean any place of operations where the debtor carries out a non-transitory economic activity with human means and goods.

Article 3

International jurisdiction

1. The courts of the Member State within the territory of which the centre of a debtor's main interests is situated shall have jurisdiction to open insolvency proceedings. In the case of a company or legal person, the place of the registered office shall be presumed to be the centre of its main interests in the absence of proof to the contrary.

2. Where the centre of a debtor's main interests is situated within the territory of a Member State, the courts of another Member State shall have jurisdiction to open insolvency proceedings against that debtor only if he possesses an establishment within the territory of that other Member State. The effects of those proceedings shall be restricted to the assets of the debtor situated in the territory of the latter Member State.

3. Where insolvency proceedings have been opened under paragraph 1, any proceedings opened subsequently under paragraph 2 shall be secondary proceedings. These latter proceedings must be winding-up proceedings.

4. Territorial insolvency proceedings referred to in paragraph 2 may be opened prior to the opening of main insolvency proceedings in accordance with paragraph 1 only:

(a) where insolvency proceedings under paragraph 1 cannot be opened because of the conditions laid down by the law of the Member State within the territory of which the centre of the debtor's main interests is situated; or

(b) where the opening of territorial insolvency proceedings is requested by a creditor who has his domicile, habitual residence or registered office in the Member State within the territory of which the establishment is situated, or whose claim arises from the operation of that establishment.

Article 4

Law applicable

1. Save as otherwise provided in this Regulation, the law applicable to insolvency proceedings and their effects shall be that of the Member State within the territory of which such proceedings are opened, hereafter referred to as the 'State of the opening of proceedings'.

2. The law of the State of the opening of proceedings shall determine the conditions for the opening of those proceedings, their conduct and their closure. It shall determine in particular:

(a) against which debtors insolvency proceedings may be brought on account of their capacity;

(b) the assets which form part of the estate and the treatment of assets acquired by or devolving on the debtor after the opening of the insolvency proceedings;

(c) the respective powers of the debtor and the liquidator;

(d) the conditions under which set-offs may be invoked;

(e) the effects of insolvency proceedings on current contracts to which the debtor is party;

(f) the effects of the insolvency proceedings on proceedings brought by individual creditors, with the exception of lawsuits pending;

(g) the claims which are to be lodged against the debtor's estate and the treatment of claims arising after the opening of insolvency proceedings;

(h) the rules governing the lodging, verification and admission of claims;

(i) the rules governing the distribution of proceeds from the realisation of assets, the ranking of claims and the rights of creditors who have obtained partial satisfaction after the opening of insolvency proceedings by virtue of a right in rem or through a set-off;

(j) the conditions for and the effects of closure of insolvency proceedings, in particular by composition;

(k) creditors' rights after the closure of insolvency proceedings;

(l) who is to bear the costs and expenses incurred in the insolvency proceedings;

(m) the rules relating to the voidness, voidability or unenforceability of legal acts detrimental to all the creditors.

Article 5

Third parties' rights in rem

1. The opening of insolvency proceedings shall not affect the rights in rem of creditors or third parties in respect of tangible or intangible, moveable or immoveable assets — both specific assets and collections of indefinite assets as a whole which change from time to time — belonging to the debtor which are situated within the territory of another Member State at the time of the opening of proceedings.

2. The rights referred to in paragraph 1 shall in particular mean:

(a) the right to dispose of assets or have them disposed of and to obtain satisfaction from the proceeds of or income from those assets, in particular by virtue of a lien or a mortgage;

(b) the exclusive right to have a claim met, in particular a right guaranteed by a lien in respect of the claim or by assignment of the claim by way of a guarantee;

(c) the right to demand the assets from, and/or to require restitution by, anyone having possession or use of them contrary to the wishes of the party so entitled;

(d) a right in rem to the beneficial use of assets.

3. The right, recorded in a public register and enforceable against third parties, under which a right in rem within the meaning of paragraph 1 may be obtained, shall be considered a right in rem.

4. Paragraph 1 shall not preclude actions for voidness, voidability or unenforceability as referred to in Article 4(2)(m).

Article 6

Set-off

1. The opening of insolvency proceedings shall not affect the right of creditors to demand the set-off of their claims against the claims of the debtor, where such a set-off is permitted by the law applicable to the insolvent debtor's claim.

2. Paragraph 1 shall not preclude actions for voidness, voidability or unenforceability as referred to in Article 4(2)(m).

Article 7

Reservation of title

1. The opening of insolvency proceedings against the purchaser of an asset shall not affect the seller's rights based on a reservation of title where at the time of the opening of proceedings the asset is situated within the territory of a Member State other than the State of opening of proceedings.

2. The opening of insolvency proceedings against the seller of an asset, after delivery of the asset, shall not constitute grounds for rescinding or terminating the sale and shall not prevent the purchaser from acquiring title where at the time of the opening of proceedings the asset sold is situated within the territory of a Member State other than the State of the opening of proceedings.

3. Paragraphs 1 and 2 shall not preclude actions for voidness, voidability or unenforceability as referred to in Article 4(2)(m).

Article 8

Contracts relating to immoveable property

The effects of insolvency proceedings on a contract conferring the right to acquire or make use of immoveable property shall be governed solely by the law of the Member State within the territory of which the immoveable property is situated.

Article 9

Payment systems and financial markets

1. Without prejudice to Article 5, the effects of insolvency proceedings on the rights and obligations of the parties to a payment or settlement system or to a financial market shall be governed solely by the law of the Member State applicable to that system or market.

2. Paragraph 1 shall not preclude any action for voidness, voidability or unenforceability which may be taken to set aside payments or transactions under the law applicable to the relevant payment system or financial market.

Article 10

Contracts of employment

The effects of insolvency proceedings on employment contracts and relationships shall be governed solely by the law of the Member State applicable to the contract of employment.

Article 11

Effects on rights subject to registration

The effects of insolvency proceedings on the rights of the debtor in immoveable property, a ship or an aircraft subject to registration in a public register shall be determined by the law of the Member State under the authority of which the register is kept.

Article 12

Community patents and trade marks

For the purposes of this Regulation, a Community patent, a Community trade mark or any other similar right established by Community law may be included only in the proceedings referred to in Article 3(1).

Article 13

Detrimental acts

Article 4(2)(m) shall not apply where the person who benefited from an act detrimental to all the creditors provides proof that:

— the said act is subject to the law of a Member State other than that of the State of the opening of proceedings, and

— that law does not allow any means of challenging that act in the relevant case.

Article 14

Protection of third-party purchasers

Where, by an act concluded after the opening of insolvency proceedings, the debtor disposes, for consideration, of:

— an immoveable asset, or

— a ship or an aircraft subject to registration in a public register, or

— securities whose existence presupposes registration in a register laid down by law,

the validity of that act shall be governed by the law of the State within the territory of which the immoveable asset is situated or under the authority of which the register is kept.

Article 15

Effects of insolvency proceedings on lawsuits pending

The effects of insolvency proceedings on a lawsuit pending concerning an asset or a right of which the debtor has been divested shall be governed solely by the law of the Member State in which that lawsuit is pending.

CHAPTER II

RECOGNITION OF INSOLVENCY PROCEEDINGS

Article 16

Principle

1. Any judgment opening insolvency proceedings handed down by a court of a Member State which has jurisdiction pursuant to Article 3 shall be recognised in all the other Member States from the time that it becomes effective in the State of the opening of proceedings.

This rule shall also apply where, on account of his capacity, insolvency proceedings cannot be brought against the debtor in other Member States.

2.   Recognition of the proceedings referred to in Article 3(1) shall not preclude the opening of the proceedings referred to in Article 3(2) by a court in another Member State. The latter proceedings shall be secondary insolvency proceedings within the meaning of Chapter III.

Article 17

Effects of recognition

1.   The judgment opening the proceedings referred to in Article 3(1) shall, with no further formalities, produce the same effects in any other Member State as under this law of the State of the opening of proceedings, unless this Regulation provides otherwise and as long as no proceedings referred to in Article 3(2) are opened in that other Member State.

2.   The effects of the proceedings referred to in Article 3(2) may not be challenged in other Member States. Any restriction of the creditors' rights, in particular a stay or discharge, shall produce effects vis-à-vis assets situated within the territory of another Member State only in the case of those creditors who have given their consent.

Article 18

Powers of the liquidator

1.   The liquidator appointed by a court which has jurisdiction pursuant to Article 3(1) may exercise all the powers conferred on him by the law of the State of the opening of proceedings in another Member State, as long as no other insolvency proceedings have been opened there nor any preservation measure to the contrary has been taken there further to a request for the opening of insolvency proceedings in that State. He may in particular remove the debtor's assets from the territory of the Member State in which they are situated, subject to Articles 5 and 7.

2.   The liquidator appointed by a court which has jurisdiction pursuant to Article 3(2) may in any other Member State claim through the courts or out of court that moveable property was removed from the territory of the State of the opening of proceedings to the territory of that other Member State after the opening of the insolvency proceedings. He may also bring any action to set aside which is in the interests of the creditors.

3.   In exercising his powers, the liquidator shall comply with the law of the Member State within the territory of which he intends to take action, in particular with regard to procedures for the realisation of assets. Those powers may not include coercive measures or the right to rule on legal proceedings or disputes.

Article 19

Proof of the liquidator's appointment

The liquidator's appointment shall be evidenced by a certified copy of the original decision appointing him or by any other certificate issued by the court which has jurisdiction.

A translation into the official language or one of the official languages of the Member State within the territory of which he intends to act may be required. No legalisation or other similar formality shall be required.

Article 20

Return and imputation

1.   A creditor who, after the opening of the proceedings referred to in Article 3(1) obtains by any means, in particular through enforcement, total or partial satisfaction of his claim on the assets belonging to the debtor situated within the territory of another Member State, shall return what he has obtained to the liquidator, subject to Articles 5 and 7.

2.   In order to ensure equal treatment of creditors a creditor who has, in the course of insolvency proceedings, obtained a dividend on his claim shall share in distributions made in other proceedings only where creditors of the same ranking or category have, in those other proceedings, obtained an equivalent dividend.

Article 21

Publication

1.   The liquidator may request that notice of the judgment opening insolvency proceedings and, where appropriate, the decision appointing him, be published in any other Member State in accordance with the publication procedures provided for in that State. Such publication shall also specify the liquidator appointed and whether the jurisdiction rule applied is that pursuant to Article 3(1) or Article 3(2).

2. However, any Member State within the territory of which the debtor has an establishment may require mandatory publication. In such cases, the liquidator or any authority empowered to that effect in the Member State where the proceedings referred to in Article 3(1) are opened shall take all necessary measures to ensure such publication.

Article 22

Registration in a public register

1. The liquidator may request that the judgment opening the proceedings referred to in Article 3(1) be registered in the land register, the trade register and any other public register kept in the other Member States.

2. However, any Member State may require mandatory registration. In such cases, the liquidator or any authority empowered to that effect in the Member State where the proceedings referred to in Article 3(1) have been opened shall take all necessary measures to ensure such registration.

Article 23

Costs

The costs of the publication and registration provided for in Articles 21 and 22 shall be regarded as costs and expenses incurred in the proceedings.

Article 24

Honouring of an obligation to a debtor

1. Where an obligation has been honoured in a Member State for the benefit of a debtor who is subject to insolvency proceedings opened in another Member State, when it should have been honoured for the benefit of the liquidator in those proceedings, the person honouring the obligation shall be deemed to have discharged it if he was unaware of the opening of proceedings.

2. Where such an obligation is honoured before the publication provided for in Article 21 has been effected, the person honouring the obligation shall be presumed, in the absence of proof to the contrary, to have been unaware of the opening of insolvency proceedings; where the obligation is honoured after such publication has been effected, the person honouring the obligation shall be presumed, in the absence of proof to the contrary, to have been aware of the opening of proceedings.

Article 25

Recognition and enforceability of other judgments

1. Judgments handed down by a court whose judgment concerning the opening of proceedings is recognised in accordance with Article 16 and which concern the course and closure of insolvency proceedings, and compositions approved by that court shall also be recognised with no further formalities. Such judgments shall be enforced in accordance with Articles 31 to 51, with the exception of Article 34(2), of the Brussels Convention on Jurisdiction and the Enforcement of Judgments in Civil and Commercial Matters, as amended by the Conventions of Accession to this Convention.

The first subparagraph shall also apply to judgments deriving directly from the insolvency proceedings and which are closely linked with them, even if they were handed down by another court.

The first subparagraph shall also apply to judgments relating to preservation measures taken after the request for the opening of insolvency proceedings.

2. The recognition and enforcement of judgments other than those referred to in paragraph 1 shall be governed by the Convention referred to in paragraph 1, provided that that Convention is applicable.

3. The Member States shall not be obliged to recognise or enforce a judgment referred to in paragraph 1 which might result in a limitation of personal freedom or postal secrecy.

Article 26 (¹)

Public policy

Any Member State may refuse to recognise insolvency proceedings opened in another Member State or to enforce a judgment handed down in the context of such proceedings where the effects of such recognition or enforcement would be manifestly contrary to that State's public policy, in particular its fundamental principles or the constitutional rights and liberties of the individual.

CHAPTER III

SECONDARY INSOLVENCY PROCEEDINGS

Article 27

Opening of proceedings

The opening of the proceedings referred to in Article 3(1) by a court of a Member State and which is recognised in another Member State (main proceedings) shall permit the opening in that other Member State, a court of which has jurisdiction pursuant to Article 3(2), of secondary insolvency proceedings without the debtor's insolvency being examined in that other State. These latter proceedings must be among the proceedings listed in Annex B. Their effects shall be restricted to the assets of the debtor situated within the territory of that other Member State.

(¹) Note the Declaration by Portugal concerning the application of Articles 26 and 37 (OJ C 183, 30.6.2000, p. 1).

Article 28

Applicable law

Save as otherwise provided in this Regulation, the law applicable to secondary proceedings shall be that of the Member State within the territory of which the secondary proceedings are opened.

Article 29

Right to request the opening of proceedings

The opening of secondary proceedings may be requested by:

(a) the liquidator in the main proceedings;

(b) any other person or authority empowered to request the opening of insolvency proceedings under the law of the Member State within the territory of which the opening of secondary proceedings is requested.

Article 30

Advance payment of costs and expenses

Where the law of the Member State in which the opening of secondary proceedings is requested requires that the debtor's assets be sufficient to cover in whole or in part the costs and expenses of the proceedings, the court may, when it receives such a request, require the applicant to make an advance payment of costs or to provide appropriate security.

Article 31

Duty to cooperate and communicate information

1.   Subject to the rules restricting the communication of information, the liquidator in the main proceedings and the liquidators in the secondary proceedings shall be duty bound to communicate information to each other. They shall immediately communicate any information which may be relevant to the other proceedings, in particular the progress made in lodging and verifying claims and all measures aimed at terminating the proceedings.

2.   Subject to the rules applicable to each of the proceedings, the liquidator in the main proceedings and the liquidators in the secondary proceedings shall be duty bound to cooperate with each other.

3.   The liquidator in the secondary proceedings shall give the liquidator in the main proceedings an early opportunity of submitting proposals on the liquidation or use of the assets in the secondary proceedings.

Article 32

Exercise of creditors' rights

1.   Any creditor may lodge his claim in the main proceedings and in any secondary proceedings.

2.   The liquidators in the main and any secondary proceedings shall lodge in other proceedings claims which have already been lodged in the proceedings for which they were appointed, provided that the interests of creditors in the latter proceedings are served thereby, subject to the right of creditors to oppose that or to withdraw the lodgement of their claims where the law applicable so provides.

3.   The liquidator in the main or secondary proceedings shall be empowered to participate in other proceedings on the same basis as a creditor, in particular by attending creditors' meetings.

Article 33

Stay of liquidation

1.   The court, which opened the secondary proceedings, shall stay the process of liquidation in whole or in part on receipt of a request from the liquidator in the main proceedings, provided that in that event it may require the liquidator in the main proceedings to take any suitable measure to guarantee the interests of the creditors in the secondary proceedings and of individual classes of creditors. Such a request from the liquidator may be rejected only if it is manifestly of no interest to the creditors in the main proceedings. Such a stay of the process of liquidation may be ordered for up to three months. It may be continued or renewed for similar periods.

2.   The court referred to in paragraph 1 shall terminate the stay of the process of liquidation:

— at the request of the liquidator in the main proceedings,

— of its own motion, at the request of a creditor or at the request of the liquidator in the secondary proceedings if that measure no longer appears justified, in particular, by the interests of creditors in the main proceedings or in the secondary proceedings.

Article 34

Measures ending secondary insolvency proceedings

1. Where the law applicable to secondary proceedings allows for such proceedings to be closed without liquidation by a rescue plan, a composition or a comparable measure, the liquidator in the main proceedings shall be empowered to propose such a measure himself.

Closure of the secondary proceedings by a measure referred to in the first subparagraph shall not become final without the consent of the liquidator in the main proceedings; failing his agreement, however, it may become final if the financial interests of the creditors in the main proceedings are not affected by the measure proposed.

2. Any restriction of creditors' rights arising from a measure referred to in paragraph 1 which is proposed in secondary proceedings, such as a stay of payment or discharge of debt, may not have effect in respect of the debtor's assets not covered by those proceedings without the consent of all the creditors having an interest.

3. During a stay of the process of liquidation ordered pursuant to Article 33, only the liquidator in the main proceedings or the debtor, with the former's consent, may propose measures laid down in paragraph 1 of this Article in the secondary proceedings; no other proposal for such a measure shall be put to the vote or approved.

Article 35

Assets remaining in the secondary proceedings

If by the liquidation of assets in the secondary proceedings it is possible to meet all claims allowed under those proceedings, the liquidator appointed in those proceedings shall immediately transfer any assets remaining to the liquidator in the main proceedings.

Article 36

Subsequent opening of the main proceedings

Where the proceedings referred to in Article 3(1) are opened following the opening of the proceedings referred to in Article 3(2) in another Member State, Articles 31 to 35 shall apply to those opened first, in so far as the progress of those proceedings so permits.

Article 37 (¹)

Conversion of earlier proceedings

The liquidator in the main proceedings may request that proceedings listed in Annex A previously opened in another Member State be converted into winding-up proceedings if this proves to be in the interests of the creditors in the main proceedings.

The court with jurisdiction under Article 3(2) shall order conversion into one of the proceedings listed in Annex B.

Article 38

Preservation measures

Where the court of a Member State which has jurisdiction pursuant to Article 3(1) appoints a temporary administrator in order to ensure the preservation of the debtor's assets, that temporary administrator shall be empowered to request any measures to secure and preserve any of the debtor's assets situated in another Member State, provided for under the law of that State, for the period between the request for the opening of insolvency proceedings and the judgment opening the proceedings.

CHAPTER IV

PROVISION OF INFORMATION FOR CREDITORS AND LODGEMENT OF THEIR CLAIMS

Article 39

Right to lodge claims

Any creditor who has his habitual residence, domicile or registered office in a Member State other than the State of the opening of proceedings, including the tax authorities and social security authorities of Member States, shall have the right to lodge claims in the insolvency proceedings in writing.

Article 40

Duty to inform creditors

1. As soon as insolvency proceedings are opened in a Member State, the court of that State having jurisdiction or the liquidator appointed by it shall immediately inform known creditors who have their habitual residences, domiciles or registered offices in the other Member States.

(¹) Note the Declaration by Portugal concerning the application of Articles 26 and 37 (OJ C 183, 30.6.2000, p. 1).

2.   That information, provided by an individual notice, shall in particular include time limits, the penalties laid down in regard to those time limits, the body or authority empowered to accept the lodgement of claims and the other measures laid down. Such notice shall also indicate whether creditors whose claims are preferential or secured in rem need lodge their claims.

Article 41

Content of the lodgement of a claim

A creditor shall send copies of supporting documents, if any, and shall indicate the nature of the claim, the date on which it arose and its amount, as well as whether he alleges preference, security in rem or a reservation of title in respect of the claim and what assets are covered by the guarantee he is invoking.

Article 42

Languages

1.   The information provided for in Article 40 shall be provided in the official language or one of the official languages of the State of the opening of proceedings. For that purpose a form shall be used bearing the heading 'Invitation to lodge a claim. Time limits to be observed' in all the official languages of the institutions of the European Union.

2.   Any creditor who has his habitual residence, domicile or registered office in a Member State other than the State of the opening of proceedings may lodge his claim in the official language or one of the official languages of that other State. In that event, however, the lodgement of his claim shall bear the heading 'Lodgement of claim' in the official language or one of the official languages of the State of the opening of proceedings. In addition, he may be required to provide a translation into the official language or one of the official languages of the State of the opening of proceedings.

CHAPTER V

TRANSITIONAL AND FINAL PROVISIONS

Article 43

Applicability in time

The provisions of this Regulation shall apply only to insolvency proceedings opened after its entry into force. Acts done by a debtor before the entry into force of this Regulation shall continue to be governed by the law which was applicable to them at the time they were done.

Article 44

Relationship to Conventions

1.   After its entry into force, this Regulation replaces, in respect of the matters referred to therein, in the relations between Member States, the Conventions concluded between two or more Member States, in particular:

(a) the Convention between Belgium and France on Jurisdiction and the Validity and Enforcement of Judgments, Arbitration Awards and Authentic Instruments, signed at Paris on 8 July 1899;

(b) the Convention between Belgium and Austria on Bankruptcy, Winding-up, Arrangements, Compositions and Suspension of Payments (with Additional Protocol of 13 June 1973), signed at Brussels on 16 July 1969;

(c) the Convention between Belgium and the Netherlands on Territorial Jurisdiction, Bankruptcy and the Validity and Enforcement of Judgments, Arbitration Awards and Authentic Instruments, signed at Brussels on 28 March 1925;

(d) the Treaty between Germany and Austria on Bankruptcy, Winding-up, Arrangements and Compositions, signed at Vienna on 25 May 1979;

(e) the Convention between France and Austria on Jurisdiction, Recognition and Enforcement of Judgments on Bankruptcy, signed at Vienna on 27 February 1979;

(f) the Convention between France and Italy on the Enforcement of Judgments in Civil and Commercial Matters, signed at Rome on 3 June 1930;

(g) the Convention between Italy and Austria on Bankruptcy, Winding-up, Arrangements and Compositions, signed at Rome on 12 July 1977;

(h) the Convention between the Kingdom of the Netherlands and the Federal Republic of Germany on the Mutual Recognition and Enforcement of Judgments and other Enforceable Instruments in Civil and Commercial Matters, signed at The Hague on 30 August 1962;

(i) the Convention between the United Kingdom and the Kingdom of Belgium providing for the Reciprocal Enforcement of Judgments in Civil and Commercial Matters, with Protocol, signed at Brussels on 2 May 1934;

(j) the Convention between Denmark, Finland, Norway, Sweden and Iceland on Bankruptcy, signed at Copenhagen on 7 November 1933;

(k) the European Convention on Certain International Aspects of Bankruptcy, signed at Istanbul on 5 June 1990.

2.   The Conventions referred to in paragraph 1 shall continue to have effect with regard to proceedings opened before the entry into force of this Regulation.

3. This Regulation shall not apply:

(a) in any Member State, to the extent that it is irreconcilable with the obligations arising in relation to bankruptcy from a convention concluded by that State with one or more third countries before the entry into force of this Regulation;

(b) in the United Kingdom of Great Britain and Northern Ireland, to the extent that is irreconcilable with the obligations arising in relation to bankruptcy and the winding-up of insolvent companies from any arrangements with the Commonwealth existing at the time this Regulation enters into force.

Article 45

Amendment of the Annexes

The Council, acting by qualified majority on the initiative of one of its members or on a proposal from the Commission, may amend the Annexes.

Article 46

Reports

No later than 1 June 2012, and every five years thereafter, the Commission shall present to the European Parliament, the Council and the Economic and Social Committee a report on the application of this Regulation. The report shall be accompanied if need be by a proposal for adaptation of this Regulation.

Article 47

Entry into force

This Regulation shall enter into force on 31 May 2002.

This Regulation shall be binding in its entirety and directly applicable in the Member States in accordance with the Treaty establishing the European Community.

Done at Brussels, 29 May 2000.

For the Council

The President

A. COSTA

———

ANNEX A

Insolvency proceedings referred to in Article 2(a)

BELGIË—BELGIQUE

— Het faillissement/La faillite

— Het gerechtelijk akkoord/Le concordat judiciaire

— De collectieve schuldenregeling/Le règlement collectif de dettes

DEUTSCHLAND

— Das Konkursverfahren

— Das gerichtliche Vergleichsverfahren

— Das Gesamtvollstreckungsverfahren

— Das Insolvenzverfahren

ΕΛΛΑΣ

— Πτώχευση

— Η ειδική εκκαθάριση

— Η προσωρινή διαχείριση εταιρίας. Η διοίκηση και η διαχείριση των πιστωτών

— Η υπαγωγή επιχείρησης υπό επίτροπο με σκοπό τη σύναψη συμβιβασμού με τους πιστωτές

ESPAÑA

— Concurso de acreedores

— Quiebra

— Suspensión de pagos

FRANCE

— Liquidation judiciaire

— Redressement judiciaire avec nomination d'un administrateur

IRELAND

— Compulsory winding up by the court

— Bankruptcy

— The administration in bankruptcy of the estate of persons dying insolvent

— Winding-up in bankruptcy of partnerships

— Creditors' voluntary winding up (with confirmation of a Court)

— Arrangements under the control of the court which involve the vesting of all or part of the property of the debtor in the Official Assignee for realisation and distribution

— Company examinership

ITALIA

— Fallimento

— Concordato preventivo

— Liquidazione coatta amministrativa

— Amministrazione straordinaria

— Amministrazione controllata

LUXEMBOURG

— Faillite

— Gestion contrôlée

— Concordat préventif de faillite (par abandon d'actif)

— Régime spécial de liquidation du notariat

NEDERLAND

— Het faillissement

— De surséance van betaling

— De schuldsaneringsregeling natuurlijke personen

ÖSTERREICH

— Das Konkursverfahren

— Das Ausgleichsverfahren

PORTUGAL

— O processo de falência

— Os processos especiais de recuperação de empresa, ou seja:

— A concordata

— A reconstituição empresarial

— A reestruturação financeira

— A gestão controlada

SUOMI—FINLAND

— Konkurssi/konkurs

— Yrityssaneeraus/företagssanering

SVERIGE

— Konkurs

— Företagsrekonstruktion

UNITED KINGDOM

— Winding up by or subject to the supervision of the court

— Creditors' voluntary winding up (with confirmation by the court)

— Administration

— Voluntary arrangements under insolvency legislation

— Bankruptcy or sequestration

———

ANNEX B

Winding up proceedings referred to in Article 2(c)

BELGIË—BELGIQUE

— Het faillissement/La faillite

DEUTSCHLAND

— Das Konkursverfahren

— Das Gesamtvollstreckungsverfahren

— Das Insolvenzverfahren

ΕΛΛΑΣ

— Πτώχευση

— Η ειδική εκκαθάριση

ESPAÑA

— Concurso de acreedores

— Quiebra

— Suspensión de pagos basada en la insolvencia definitiva

FRANCE

— Liquidation judiciaire

IRELAND

— Compulsory winding up

— Bankruptcy

— The administration in bankruptcy of the estate of persons dying insolvent

— Winding-up in bankruptcy of partnerships

— Creditors' voluntary winding up (with confirmation of a court)

— Arrangements under the control of the court which involve the vesting of all or part of the property of the debtor in the Official Assignee for realisation and distribution

ITALIA

— Fallimento

— Liquidazione coatta amministrativa

LUXEMBOURG

— Faillite

— Régime spécial de liquidation du notariat

NEDERLAND

— Het faillissement

— De schuldsaneringsregeling natuurlijke personen

ÖSTERREICH

— Das Konkursverfahren

PORTUGAL

— O processo de falência

SUOMI—FINLAND

— Konkurssi/konkurs

SVERIGE

— Konkurs

UNITED KINGDOM

— Winding up by or subject to the supervision of the court

— Creditors' voluntary winding up (with confirmation by the court)

— Bankruptcy or sequestration

———

ANNEX C

Liquidators referred to in Article 2(b)

BELGIË—BELGIQUE

— De curator/Le curateur

— De commissaris inzake opschorting/Le commissaire au sursis

— De schuldbemiddelaar/Le médiateur de dettes

DEUTSCHLAND

— Konkursverwalter

— Vergleichsverwalter

— Sachwalter (nach der Vergleichsordnung)

— Verwalter

— Insolvenzverwalter

— Sachwalter (nach der Insolvenzordnung)

— Treuhänder

— Vorläufiger Insolvenzverwalter

ΕΛΛΑΣ

— Ο σύνδικο

— Ο προσωρινός διαχειριστής. Η διοικούσα επιτροπή των πιστωτών

— Ο ειδικός εκκαθαριστής

— Ο επίτροπος

ESPAÑA

— Depositario-administrador

— Interventor o Interventores

— Síndicos

— Comisario

FRANCE

— Représentant des créanciers

— Mandataire liquidateur

— Administrateur judiciaire

— Commissaire à l'exécution de plan

IRELAND

— Liquidator

— Official Assignee

— Trustee in bankruptcy

— Provisional Liquidator

— Examiner

ITALIA

— Curatore

— Commissario

LUXEMBOURG

— Le curateur

— Le commissaire

— Le liquidateur

— Le conseil de gérance de la section d'assainissement du notariat

NEDERLAND

— De curator in het faillissement

— De bewindvoerder in de surséance van betaling

— De bewindvoerder in de schuldsaneringsregeling natuurlijke personen

ÖSTERREICH

— Masseverwalter

— Ausgleichsverwalter

— Sachwalter

— Treuhänder

— Besondere Verwalter

— Vorläufiger Verwalter

— Konkursgericht

PORTUGAL

— Gestor judicial

— Liquidatário judicial

— Comissão de credores

SUOMI—FINLAND

— Pesänhoitaja/boförvaltare

— Selvittäjä/utredare

SVERIGE

— Förvaltare

— God man

— Rekonstruktör

UNITED KINGDOM

— Liquidator

— Supervisor of a voluntary arrangement

— Administrator

— Official Receiver

— Trustee

— Judicial factor

Index

access to justice, 15, 17
Alien Tort Statute (US), 228–37
  corporate liability, 230–2
  enforcement of human rights, 237
  international of domestic law, 232–4
  obstacles to justice, 234–6
  political dismissal, 235–6
  procedural dismissal, 234–5
  Sosa v Alvarez-Machain, 229–30
  standard operating procedure, 232
anti-suit injunctions, 34–8, 105
applicable law, 4–5
  characterisation of the legal question, 5
  contract law, 14
    absence of choice, 126–7, 135–9
    characterisation of the contract, 137
    choice, 126–7
    consent, 139
    exclusions, 129–31
    freedom of choice, 126
    habitual residence, 137–9
    introduction, 125
    mandatory law, 142–8
    principles, 125–6
    public policy, 148
    Rome I Regulation, 125–49
    scope of application, 126, 127–9
    universal application, 131–5
    validity, 138–42
  corporate social responsibility, 239–40
  freedom of choice, 126, 177–8
  general rule, 163–5
    escape clause, 165
    exception, 165
  lex causae, 5
  lex loci damni, 163–5
  linking factors, 5
  Rome 1 Regulation, 7
    absence of choice, 137–9
    applicable law in contracts, 14, 125–49
    choice, 126–7, 135–9
    consent, 139
    exclusions, 129–31
    freedom of choice, 126
    mandatory law, 142–8
    principles, 125–6
    public policy, 148
    relationship with other Conventions, 149

  scope of application, 126, 127–9
  universal application, 131–5
  validity, 138–42
  tort law, 151–4
    application to Arbitration Tribunals, 155
    conflict of laws, 154
    contract-related claims, 181
    defamation, 160–3
    exclusions, 157–63
    freedom of choice, 177–8
    mandatory law, 181–2
    non-contractual obligations, 155–6
    public policy, 181–2
    rights of privacy, 160–3
    Rome II Regulation, 151–82
    scope of application, 154–82
arbitration agreements, 35–40
  exclusion of, 129, 155

bankruptcy:
  Brussels I Regulation, 185–7
  Insolvency Regulation, 189, 208–9
Brussels I Regulation on jurisdiction and the
    recognition and enforcement of judgments
    in civil and commercial matters, 19–21
  appearance, jurisdiction by, 60–1
  arbitration agreements, 129
  bankruptcy, 185–7
  contracts, 61–77
  domicile, 49
    domicile for natural persons, 41–3
    domicile of a legal person, 43–4
    domicile of defendant, 41–2
  employment contracts, 50, 61, 74–6
  enforcement, 46
    proceedings concerned with the
      enforcement of judgments, 59
  exclusions, 32–41
    arbitration, 33, 34, 35–8, 40–1
    bankruptcy, 32–3
    irrelevance to international business, 32–3
    provisional measures, 33–4
  forum, choice of, 77–85
  Hess, Pfeiffer and Schlosser Report, 22(n),
    38, 38(n)
  holiday lets, 54–5
  immovables, 51–3, 55
    enforcement, 59

insurance, 76–7
  multipartite litigation, 100, 104
in rem rights, 51, 52–3, 55
  multipartite litigation, 100, 104
insurance contracts, 76–7
intellectual property rights:
  establishing jurisdiction, 92
  exclusive jurisdiction, 51, 59
  infringement in the internet age, 94–7
international impact
  weaknesses, 45–50
irreconcilable judgments, 99–103, 105, 111,
    122
Jenard Report, 25, 53, 56–62, 122
jurisdictional rules, 23–4, 46–9, 51
  appearance, jurisdiction by, 60–1
  arbitration, 38–9
  domicile conditions, 49–50
  exclusive jurisdiction, 51–9
  protected categories, 61–2
lis alibi pendens, 20–1, 50, 112, 122
  application of the rule, 34–5
  forum non conveniens and, 107
  forum, choice of, 80, 84–5
  loss of jurisdiction, 105–7
  residual jurisdiction, 104
lis pendens, 48, 104
Lugano Convention, 20–1, 52, 75,
mutual trust, 24–5, 34–5
place of incorporation, 22, 41
place of performance of the obligation, 21,
    87–91
place where harmful event occurred, 75–7,
    92–4, 97–9
provisional and protective measures, 112–15
ratione personae, 22–3, 41–4
recognition and enforcement, 46
scope of application:
  civil and commercial matters, 27–32
  exclusions, 32–41
  ratione personae, 22–3, 41–4
  subject matter, 21–2, 25–7
  torts, delict or quasi-delict, 92–9

characterisation of the legal question, 5
  legal categories, 5–6
  renvoi, 7–8
  vorfrage / 'incidental' issue, 6–7
choice of law:
  absence of choice, 126–7, 135–9
  application of choice of law, 126–7
  contract law, 71, 73, 87, 90
  implied choice, 126
  immovables, 53
  protected categories, 166
  pubic policy, 120
  Rome II Regulation, 92

specific torts, 166
  environmental damage, 172–4
  industrial action, 175–7
  infringement of intellectual property rights,
    174–5
  product liability, 166–7
  restriction of free competition, 170–2
  unfair competition, 170–2
  see also applicable law
civil and commercial matters, 28–31
  Brussels I Regulation, 19, 27
  excluded matters
    non-contractual obligations, 157, 163
  jurisdiction, 19
    conflict of jurisdiction, 36–7
  non-contractual obligations, 157, 163
  recognition and enforcement, 96
  Rome I Regulation, 125
    scope of application, 126, 127
  Rome II Regulation
    scope of application, 154, 127
  subject-matter, 125
  Treaty of Amsterdam, 10
companies, 211
  free movement of establishment, 211
    case law, 215–25
    determination, 211–12
    harmonisation, 213–14
    incorporation theory, 212
    real seat theory, 212
    right of establishment, 213–14
company law, 55–6
  case law, 215–25
  domicile, 211
  non-contractual obligations, 159
competition, 14–15
  free movement of goods, 121
  tort, 97, 166
  unfair competition, 92, 170–2
consumer contracts:
  Brussels I Regulation, 62–73
  jurisdiction, 62–73
  protected categories, 61–2
contracts:
  absence of choice, 126–7, 135–9
  characterisation of the contract, 137
  choice, 126–7
  consumer contracts, 61–73
  employment contracts, 61–2, 74–6
  freedom of choice, 126
  habitual residence, 137–9
  insurance contracts, 61–2, 76–7
  Rome I Regulation, 125–49
  validity, 138–42
contractual obligations:
  claims related to a contract, 87–9
  place of incorporation, 22, 41

place of performance of the obligation, 21,
    87–91
place where harmful event occurred, 75–7,
    92–4, 97–9
provisional and protective measures, 112–15
convergence in civil law, 16, 18
corporate social responsibility:
    Alien Tort Statute (US), 228–37
        corporate liability, 230–2
        enforcement of human rights, 237
        international of domestic law, 232–4
        obstacles to justice, 234–6
        political dismissal, 235–6
        procedural dismissal, 234–5
        Sosa v Alvarez-Machain, 229–30
        standard operating procedure, 232
    European Union:
        applicable law, 239–40
        environmental damage, 240
        jurisdiction, 238–9
    role of private international law, 227–8
    United States, 228–37
        Alien Tort Statute (US), 228–37

damage:
    environmental damage, 172–4
    industrial action, caused by, 175–7
    infringement of intellectual property rights,
        caused by, 174–5
declarations of enforceability, 122–3

employment contracts:
    jurisdiction, 74–6
    protected categories, 61–2
enforcement:
    Brussels I Regulation, 46
    jurisdiction, 115–66
environmental damage, 172–4
    corporate social responsibility, 240
European law:
    evolution of legal basis for European Private
        international law:
    Maastrict Treaty, 10
        Treaty establishing the European
            (Economic) Community, 9
        Treaty of Amsterdam, 10–12
        Treaty on the functioning of the EU,
            12–13
    impact on private international law of member
        states, 9–13

forum, choice of, 77–85
    agreement between parties, 82
    ambiguity of jurisdiction clauses, 81
    courts' jurisdiction, 79–80
    international trade or commence, 82–5
    recognition and enforcement, 79

    standard terms and conditions, 81–2
forum non conveniens, 8–9
    loss of jurisdiction and, 107–11
forum shopping, 8
free movement of establishment, 211, 215–25
    determination, 211–12
    harmonisation, 213–14
    incorporation theory, 212
    introduction, 211
    real seat theory, 212
    right of establishment, 213–14

harmonisation:
    company law, 18
    contract law, 7
    family law, 18
    protected categories, 61–2
    Rome II Regulation, 14
    tort law, 7
    vorfrage, 14
Hess, Pfeiffer and Schlosser Report, 22(n), 38,
    38(n)
holiday lets, 54–5

immovables, 51–5
    enforcement, 59
    insurance, 76–7
    multipartite litigation, 100, 104
insolvency law:
    approaches to, 183–4
insolvency proceedings:
    centre of main interest (COMI), 193–9
    course and closure, 206
    limitation of personal freedom, 206
    opening, 189–90
        recognition, 205–6
    preservation measures, 206
    recognition and enforcement, 206, 207–10
        future amendment of the regulation, 207–8
        powers of the liquidator, 207
    rule, 205
    secondary insolvency proceedings:
        applicable law, 201–2
        exceptions, 202–4
    territorial insolvency proceedings, 200–1
Insolvency Regulation 1346/2000, 7
    bankruptcy and, 185–7, 189, 208–9
    centre of main interest:
        case-law, 194–7
        defined by, 193
        universality of proceedings, 197–8
    collective proceedings, 188
    debtors' insolvency, 188–9
        appointment of liquidator, 189
        divestment of debtor, 189
    defences against recognition and enforcement,
        206–10

forum shopping, 190–1
future amendment, 209–10
genesis, 184–5
harmonisation, 209–10
international impact, 191
jurisdiction, 192
limitations, 209
proceedings:
  centre of main interest (COMI), 193–9
  general, 199
  opening, 189–90
  secondary insolvency proceedings, 201–4,
    208–9
  territorial insolvency proceedings, 200–1
scope of application, 185–7, 208
  bankruptcy exception, link with, 185
  principle of proportionality, 185
vorfrage:
  detrimental acts, 7
insurance contracts:
  jurisdiction, 76–7
  protected categories, 61–2
intellectual property, 57–8
  establishing jurisdiction, 92
  exclusive jurisdiction, 51, 59
  infringement in the internet age, 94–7
  infringement of rights, 174–5
internet, 23–4, 65–71, 94–7
  infringement of intellectual property rights,
    94–7
irreconcilable judgments:
  Brussels I Regulation, 99–102, 111, 122

jurisdiction:
  appearance, jurisdiction by, 60–1
  Brussels I Regulation, 19–21
    exclusive jurisdiction, 51–9
    scope, 21–3
  claims relating to contract, 87–8
    consolidation claims, 99–104
  corporate social responsibility
    European Union, 237–9
  enforcement, 115–16
  exclusive jurisdiction
    incorporation of companies, 55–7
    intellectual property, 51, 59
    introduction, 51–2
    proceedings concerned with the
      enforcement of judgments, 59
    rights in rem and tenancies of, immovable
      property, 52–5
    validity of entries in public registers, 57
    validity of patents, trademarks or designs,
      57–9
  forum, choice of, 77–85
  forum contractus, 86–7
  general jurisdiction, 85–6

intellectual property, 51, 57–9, 92
lis alibi pendens, 104–11
loss of jurisdiction, 105
  identity of cause of action, 107
  identity of object or subject-matter, 107
  identity of parties, 106
  lis alibi pendens, 105–6
  lis alibi pendens and the *forum non
    conveniens* doctrine, 107–11
  related actions, 111–12
multipartite litigation and consolidated claims,
  99–104
recognition, 115–23
residual jurisdiction, 104
special jurisdiction, 86
tort law, 92–9
jurisdiction regulation:
  see Brussels I Regulation

legal categories, 5–6
  protected categories, 61–2
    Rome I Regulation, 134–5
lex societatis, 211
  case law, 215–25
  determination, 211–12
  harmonisation, 213–14
  incorporation theory, 212
  real seat theory, 212
  right of establishment, 213–14
lis alibi pendens, 105–6, 20–1, 50, 112, 122
  application of the rule, 34–5
  Brussels I Regulation, 104–11
  forum non conveniens doctrine and, 107–11
  forum, choice of, 80, 84–5
  loss of jurisdiction, 105–7
  residual jurisdiction, 104
lis pendens, 48, 104

Lugano Convention, 20–1, 52, 74–5, 80

multipartite litigation 99–100
  counterclaims, 103
  multiple defendants, 100–3
  rights in rem in immovable property, 104
  third party proceedings, 103
mutual recognition of judicial decisions, 15–16,
  17–18

negligent misstatements, 92
non-contractual obligations:
  see Rome II Regulation

patents:
  exclusive jurisdiction, 57–9
  multiple defendants, 101–3
place of incorporation, 22, 41
place of performance of the obligation, 21, 87–91

place where harmful event occurred, 75–7, 92–4,
  97–9
policy:
  development of European private international
    law policy 13–18
  jurisdiction
    law of contracts, 13
    law of torts, 13–14
    legal basis for harmonisation of choice of
      law, 13–14
private international law:
  application of the law, 4
  characterisation, 5–8
  concept, 2
  convergence, 2
  domestic law and,
    harmonisation, 2
    introduction, 1–2
  forum non conveniens, 8–9
  forum shopping, 8
  nature, 1
  processes
    applicable law, 1, 3
    application of the law
    introduction, 1–2
    jurisdiction, 1, 3
    procedural issues, 3–4
    recognition and enforcement, 1, 3
  renvoi, 7–8
  sources, 3
  Von Savigny, C F, 4
  vorfage, 6–7
procedural issues:
  conditional fees, 3
  legal aid, 3
  obtaining evidence, 4
  recovery of costs, 3
  statutes of limitation, 4
  whether trial by jury, 4
  who pays fees, 3–4
processes, 1, 3
product liability:
  applicable law, tort, 166–70
  lex loci damni, 163–5
  specific choice of law rule, 166–70
protective measures:
  applications for, 112–15
provisional measures:
  applications for, 112–15

real property:
  enforcement of judgments, 59
  matrimonial property, 32, 118, 127
  rights *in rem*, 104
  Rome I Regulation, 127
    exclusions, 129–30
  see also holiday lets; immovables

recognition and enforcement:
  Brussels I Regulation, 46
  defences, 206–10
  forum, choice of, 79
  Insolvency Regulation, 206–10
  jurisdiction:
    conditions for recognition, 116–23
    general, 115–16
  process, 1, 3
renvoi, 7–8
  arguments against, 8
  conflict of laws, 7
  exclusion of, 8, 202
  jurisdiction, 85
rights *in rem* and tenancies of, immovable
    property:
  exclusive jurisdiction:
    contractual action in combination with
      action in rem, 55
    extension to tenancies, 53–4
    short-term holiday lets, 54–5
  multipartite litigation, 104
Rome 1 Regulation on the law applicable to
    contractual obligations, 7
  absence of choice
    characterisation of the contract, 137
    habitual residence, 137–9
  applicable law in contracts, 14, 125–49
  arbitration agreements, 129, 155
  choice, 126–7
    absence of choice, 135–9
  consent, 139
  exclusions, 129–31
  freedom of choice, 126
  mandatory law, 142–8
    domestic contracts, 143
    mandatory EU law, 143–4
    overriding mandatory law, 144–6
    rules, 146–8
  principles, 125–6
  public policy, 148
  relationship with other Conventions, 149
  scope of application, 126, 127–9
  universal application:
    freedom of choice, 131–4
    protected categories, 134–5
  validity:
    capacity, 140–2
    formal validity, 138–9, 142
    material validity, 139
Rome II Regulation on the law applicable to non-
    contractual obligations, 151–3
  application to Arbitration Tribunals, 155
  application to non-contractual obligations, 14
  conflict of laws, 154
  contract-related claims, 181
  defamation, 160–3

determining location of damage, 98–9
exclusions, 157
   civil and commercial matters, 163
   defamation, 160–3
   family relationships, 158
   law of companies, 159–60
   matrimonial property regimes, 158
   non-contractual obligations, 157–60
   registered partnerships, 158
   violations of privacy, 160–3
   wills and succession, 158
freedom of choice, 177–8
general principles, 153–4
introduction, 151–3
mandatory law, 181–2
non-contractual obligations, 155–6
principles, 153–4
public policy, 181–2
rights of privacy, 160–3
scope of application, 154–82

secondary insolvency proceedings:
applicable law, 201–2
exceptions:
   jurisdiction, 202–3
   opening proceedings, 202–4
   recognition and enforcement, 204–6
   return and imputation, 204
   rights over assets, 202, 206
   vorfrage, 202
Stockholm programme, 17–18
abolition of the exequatur, 17

tort law, 92–7
application to Arbitration Tribunals, 155
conflict of laws, 154
contract-related claims, 181
defamation, 160–3
determining location of damage, 98–9
exclusions, 157–63
freedom of choice, 177–8
introduction, 151–3
mandatory law, 181–2
non-contractual obligations, 155–6
principles, 153–4
public policy, 181–2
rights of privacy, 160–3
Rome II Regulation, 151–82
scope of application, 154–82
trademarks:
exclusive jurisdiction, 57–8

United States:
Alien Tort Statute (US), 228–37
   corporate liability, 230–2
   enforcement of human rights, 237
   international of domestic law, 232–4

obstacles to justice, 234–6
political dismissal, 235–6
procedural dismissal, 234–5
Sosa v Alvarez-Machain, 229–30
standard operating procedure, 232
unjust enrichment
contract related tort claims, 181
lex loci damni, 164
non-contractual obligations, 156

Von Savigny, C F
approach to private international law, 4
characterisation, 6
vorfrage, 6–7
consent and material validity, 140
exceptions, 203
harmonisation, 14